EXIT UTOPIA

Architectural Provocations 1956–76

A Sane Revolution

If you make a revolution, make it for fun,
don't make it in ghastly seriousness,
don't do it in deadly earnest,
do it for fun.

Don't do it because you hate people,
do it just to spit in their eye.

Don't do it for the money,
do it and be damned to the money.

Don't do it for equality,
do it because we've got too much equality
and it would be fun to upset the apple-cart
and see which way the apples would go a-rolling.

Don't do it for the working classes.
Do it so that we can all of us be little aristocracies on our own
and kick our heels like jolly escaped asses.

Don't do it, anyhow, for international Labour.
Labour is one thing a man has had too much of.

Let's abolish labour, let's have done with labouring!
Work can be fun, and men can enjoy it; then it's not labour.
Let's have it so! Let's make a revolution for fun!

D. H. Lawrence

EXIT UTOPIA
Architectural Provocations 1956–76

Edited by Martin van Schaik and Otakar Máčel

IHAAU–TU DELFT

PRESTEL MUNICH · BERLIN · LONDON · NEW YORK

CONTENTS

Foreword: Sixties Revisited
Franziska Bollerey

"L'imagination au pouvoir", "Soyez réaliste, demandez l'impossible" or "Sous les pavés la plage" are core slogans of the student revolts in the 1960s. The title of the present book edited by Martin van Schaik and Otakar Máčel refers to events that took place between 1956 and 1976. The activities of the sixties, however, began in the late fifties and went on well into the seventies: not quite 20 years, but in terms of experience an extended decade, perhaps analogous to what historians call the "long Nineteenth Century".

In 1958, Hannah Arendt's philosophical study *The Human Condition* appeared. Here – like Paul Virilio who speaks of "voluntary blindness" (*Unknown Quantity,* 2002) – Arendt expresses her fear that the modern age may end "in the most deadly and sterile passivity history has ever known".

But who can speak of passivity in the 1960s? New attitudes and protests shake the very foundations of the newly arrived middle classes. Among the changes are the provocations which this book recounts. From 1957 on, anti-nuclear protests grow into a well-organized movement: what begins as the Easter marches culminates in a broad spectrum of extra-parliamentary opposition. Widespread and diverse as they are, the protest movements both result from and instigate structural transformations. In the eyes of their protagonists, critique of repressive social conditions is neither a *recherche du temps perdu* nor an idealization of Rousseau's Noble Savage. Nonetheless, Jean-Jacques Rousseau appeals to many as the man who two centuries earlier called for a "rebellion of the heart".

Protest in the 1960s is about laying bare the abuses in established systems of power. In order to abolish reactionary power structures, one first needs to become conscious of them and how they work. The quest for alternatives involves analysis and critical awareness, but the distinction between feasible plans and visionary ideas remains vague. The quest is imbedded in a glance at once backward and forward.

If today we seem to confine our expectations to a narrow horizon, we find no such limited vision among the rebels of the 1960s. "Be realistic: demand the impossible!" mirrors the utopian vigour of those who looked beyond the horizon. Martin van Schaik and his fellow students in the late 1990s encounter the *hic-et-nunc* attitude (which Arendt so lamented) in the dull emptiness of architectural training in Delft. In their search for an alternative, they turn to history. They come across *New Babylon*, a project Constant Nieuwenhuys embarked upon when he was still an active member of the Situationist International. Here they find what they have missed in the Delft curriculum: true passion driven by the will to change the world. They are, quite simply, fed up with the attitude of *behaving* in the face of the privatization of human activities: they are keen on *acting*, both in actual movement and in reflection.

Some of the students found their intellectual home among the historians in the Faculty of Architecture at Delft University of Technology, historians who today comprise the Institute for the History of Art, Architecture and Urbanism – IHAAU. Architectural historian Otakar Máčel – co-editor of this book – and art historians Jan van Geest and Gerrit Oorthuys proved themselves alert observers of the contemporary architectural scene in 1975. Their seminar *Conceptuele kunst en architectuur* analyzed projects by Yona Friedman, Archigram, Superstudio, Archizoom, Haus Rucker, Coop Himmelb(l)au, Salz der Erde, and the young architects Hans Hollein and Rem Koolhaas. Koolhaas, Adolfo Natalini and Cristiano Toraldo di Francia spoke in the lecture series *Capita selecta*. The cultural climate of the day could hardly contrast more strikingly with the attitudes prevalent today: university "leaders" bent on conforming to a given standard, on following trends rather than setting them, on *behaving* rather than *acting*.

In light of the current lack of vision, *Exit Utopia* is a timely book. It compiles a multitude of documents, many of them previously unknown and others never before published in their current form. It throws a critical and reflective light on all of them. Of central importance is the work of Constant Nieuwenhuys. Martin van Schaik's "Psychogeogram – An Artist's Utopia" serves as an Ariadne's thread in a garden that contains seven more exotic plants.

The catalyst for the protest movements of the 1960s and 1970s was the Vietnam War. The rhythm of "Ho-ho-ho-chi-min" resounded as the battle cry when like-minded friends visited each other. The catalyst for alternative visions for architecture and urban planning was the hegemony of functionalism, which had produced, in the words of Aldo van Eyck, "the boredom of hygiene" and "just mile upon mile of organized nowhere". As exemplary pieces in this book demonstrate, criticism of the time falls into one of two categories: concrete-constructive or critical-analytical. To the latter category belong concepts of the Situationist International, a wedding of Asger Jorn's International Movement for an Imaginary Bauhaus and the Lettrist International founded by Guy Ernest Debord.

Schooled by surrealism and Fourierism, Debord's thinking also shaped Constant's *autre ville pour une autre vie,* giving to the turbulent Paris of May 1968 a poetic and playful air. *Sous les pavés la plage* – "under the cobblestones, the beach" – captures the surreal spirit of the day. *L'imagination au pouvoir* – "let the imagination reign" – on the other hand originates in the early nineteenth century in Charles Fourier's *Le nouveau monde amoureux.* At the peak of the student revolts in 1968, people rediscover André Breton's 1924 *Surrealist Manifesto.* "Liberation of the mind" was Breton's goal; and in order to achieve it, he would have us plumb the depths of our inner selves. Breton cautioned us to be wary of such apparent polarities as rationality and irrationality, of reason and stupidity, of reflection and impulse. They only serve to break up the inherent wholeness of all reality. Liberation from an artificially divided reality would give equal rights to other forms of cognition such as imagination and dreams. And was it not Freud who, in *The Interpretation of Dreams*, mentioned free association, feelings, and even intoxication? Debord, Breton and Fourier blamed Cartesian rationality and logic for alienating man from both his inner and his outer world. Shortly after the end of World War II and the first nuclear bomb, Breton writes his *Ode à Charles Fourier*:

Like you Fourier
You erect among the great visionaries
Who thought to have overcome routine and misery …
God of progression forgive me we're still burdened with the same furniture
We're no better provided for in the way of the countermoulds …
Fourier they've scoffed but one day they'll have to try your remedy whether they like it or not

Apathetic complicity, life reduced to routine, the wings of fantasy clipped, a curriculum misformed by bookkeepers: these were the conditions which goaded Martin van Schaik and his fellow students into resistance. In history's medicine chest they found the visions and concepts of the 1960s, hoping they might be the remedy for a world which had sold its vision and, in fact, sold out.

When people come to externalize being, to impoverish their own psychology and emotions; when they try to ignore ethical and moral questions; when they no longer trust what Hannah Arendt calls the "supreme human capacity", then it is time for a dosage of utopian vision. The conditions all about us invite us to delve into records which may give us renewed hope and direction. And that is exactly what this book does.

Introduction
Martin van Schaik

The nineties of the last century were an uncanny interlude.

In the wake of the fall of the Iron Curtain and the end of the first Gulf War, Europe and the United States were lulled into a comatose sleep: in most countries of the West the economy was booming, confidence was high, and in the closing years of the decade endless material growth was boldly proclaimed. Fukuyama's neo-Hegelian promise of the triumph of economic liberalism (and yes, democracy for all), announced at the beginning of the decade, was finally about to become reality. With so much manifestly going wrong accross the Globe, this eschatological optimism was a rude paradox.

During the 1990s *Wirtschaftswunder* experienced in the Netherlands, architects had a ball. This was the age of Superdutch Supermodernism, which, like the country it sprang from, was snug and complacent: playful but vacuous. In Delft, the situation at the Faculty of Architecture reflected the mentality of the country at large, whilst other vagaries were slowly seeping into the curriculum: notions of *research* (deliciously attacked by Elia Zenghelis in this book), *theory* (Anglo-Saxon-style: de-politicized poststructuralist philosophy) and *critique* (with very faint and trendy echoes of Marxism). Professional skill was overtly being abandoned in favour of the myth of tautological managerial efficiency and sales waffle (called *discourse*). This was neither politics nor architecture. True passion had gone, and something mushy and nondescript – something vaguely *in between* – was taking its place.

Is this description over-dramatic? No: it portrays quite accurately the play we found ourselves in; and that play gave birth to this book. We were a small group of students of architecture and we were decidedly angry. When we stumbled across Constant's "New Babylon" in late 1998 in Rotterdam, it focused our frustration: the project was to become the heart of the effort we baptized *New Babylon Manifestatie*. Though we were admittedly ignorant and uninformed about the precise *how* and *why* of Constant's work, it was intuitively clear to us that, given the way the project was now commonly presented and discussed, late-1990s Zeitgeist had rubbed off on it as well. In the Dutch media, New Babylon – now warmly embraced by an American academic elite – suddenly popped up everywhere. Given its *formally* inspirational effect on much of the best of Superdutch architecture being poured into concrete, New Babylon was considered perfectly buildable: a travesty that was delightfully illustrated when the *Rijksplanologische Dienst* (the national planning authority) called us to ask for Constant's phone number. They wanted to design and develop New Babylon with him. The proposal was certainly courageous.

Though we loved the project, it would be wrong to think we approached New Babylon in awe: its implications heavily divided us and became a recurring focal point for fierce, emotional debates. We decided to organize a conference in the spirit of this discussion, one that might also help release New Babylon from its Post-Modernist shackles and reinstate it as a utopian and political project for a post-political world. We centred our discussion on the notion of *utopia* – in and of itself as hazy as all the terms I rejected above – because we felt that it best summarized where architecture and the political *truly* overlap: they are *essentially* driven by a will to change the world and shape it according to one's dreams. Reality – sadly and happily – curbs these absolutist desires. In our appreciation of the utopian genre, Françoise Choay's ideas – reflected in her article in this volume – proved to be vital. Conveniently, the symposium was to coincide with the utopian frenzy at the end of the last Millennium: exhibitions and books about ideal worlds and utopias fairly flooded the intellectual market.

This book is thus an extension of the symposium *New Babylon: the Value of Dreaming the City of Tomorrow*, held in Delft in January 2000. It brought together for the first time a number of key figures of what can superficially be labelled "visionary" architecture from the late 1950s to early 1970s – and Constant. Though this publication was originally intended to be a mere conference report, the book grew to demand a life of its own. Five years later, the time is now ripe for its publication.

Like the conference, the book aims to take a close look at a tight selection of canonical architectural projects – presenting them in detail – and to juxtapose them with New Babylon, which is discussed in two lengthy essays. By taking the magnifying-glass approach, more may be revealed about what actually drove the protagonists. Superficial formal similarities can be swept aside to disclose what separates New Babylon from or connects it to its architectural contemporaries. By looking at seven paper architectural masterpieces – some of the "greatest hits" of the era – up close, it is also possible to outline and to assess the course that "radical", "neo-avant-garde" architecture took through the 1960s and on into the 1970s.

Starting with the playful but practically inspired futurological scheme of Yona Friedman's *Paris Spatial*, we move through the early Archigram revolution – *Plug-in City*, infusing the "fun and flexibility" of *stuff* and gadgetry into dreary post-war modernism – towards the seminal works of Italian *Architettura Radicale*. We look closely at *No-Stop City* and *The Continuous Monument*, discovering that, however similar their media tactics, Archizoom and Superstudio were in many ways polar phenomena: the poetry and rampant nostalgia of Adolfo Natalini and his group distinctly contrast with the sensuous cool and cerebral investigations of Archizoom. In both cases, nightmare and dream are nearly indistinguishable: behind the horror lurks freedom, and vice versa. After the great clean-up act, the overcoming of Architecture in the *Fundamental Acts* (lyrical autobiography as architecture), we truly enter the age of post-modernism: the final end to utopian speculation in the metaphorical *Exodus* and the return to the "traditional city" in Krier's *La Villette*. A belated upsurge of modernist reformism, steeped in Corbusian nostalgia, Krier's project embodies the wish to heal the world and make it beautiful: a child's dream that – gratefully – refuses to die. Several scholarly articles by architectural historians complete the presentation of the individual projects and the written comments provided by the architects themselves.

In this line-up, New Babylon is the yardstick – the utopian conscience paying a visit to architecture's paper playground. New Babylon challenges architectural wayfarers to reveal their true colours. The book illustrates how, after shadowing architecture for some time, New Babylon heads off into a different direction altogether. With the end of heroic modernism in architecture – experiencing its climax and crisis in the megastructure – New Babylon loses its dialectical opposite. Zeitgeist is inescapably a determinant factor, and at a certain point, it turns its ghostly back on Constant's project. Ironically, as the architectural elite withdraws into disciplinary order and autonomy, again surprising parallels emerge: *architecture for architecture's sake* and pure painting both are distinct but similar realms of freedom offering consolation and hope for people ill at ease with the humdrum world.

Naturally, as in all historical assessments, multiple comparisons can be drawn with the present. The past invariably mirrors our own times.

Each of the projects presented is a provocation in its own right: a statement of intent, however clear, however vague. Some architectural projects border on Utopianism, whilst others merely *toy* with the idea of a better society. How to interpret New Babylon – what Constant might have *meant* – is a debate that will continually surface throughout the book.

It is of course impossible to relive past times and to enter the minds of others – to understand what they longed for and how they acted in response to their calling. But perhaps this book can force a tiny opening in their worlds and cast some light into still largely cobwebbed corners.

HP: New Babylon, your design for a future city and a future society, has received quite a lot of attention lately. Your project won a prize at the Biennale in Venice and the Provos are making play with your theories. Don't you feel that your ideas are being hijacked?

Constant: New Babylon cannot be hijacked, because it belongs to everybody. It isn't just a personal expression of mine now, is it? It is a proposition available to everybody. I was delighted when the Provos suggested turning Amsterdam into the first sector of New Babylon. That is more than I ever dared hope for.

HP: Why this sudden interest?

Constant: I once wrote an article, "The Rise and Decline of the Avant-Garde", that ended with the phrase: "As long as mankind is denied the possibility to be creative, this creativity will express itself through aggression." Take, for instance, phenomena like the *nozems, blousons noirs, Halbstarken*, the beatniks, and the *stiljagy* in Russia: young people with their protest songs and aggressive behaviour, caught in the confines of existing social relationships. All this can really be seen as a kind of revolt of the frustrated creative human being. And this revolt will persist until the conditions for the complete unfolding of creativity have finally been realized.

HP: So on this issue you and the Provos see eye to eye. There may be a lot of frustrated creativity around, but does society really prevent anybody from being creative?

Constant: Creativity has always been frustrated – in all people, bar some exceptions – because the struggle for survival has always forced people into useful occupations, utilitarian activities: the fight against nature, the need to provide for food, drink and clothing.

HP: Their creature comforts.

Constant: To put it in your words, yes. In the past there was hunting, then agriculture and now there is the industrial proletariat. People spend all day trying to make a living; they go through life with no other aim but to stay alive.

HP: Suppose everybody had loads of time to spare, would that cause a surge in creativity?

Constant: Every human being is creative, to a greater or lesser degree. That is one of our old Cobra positions. Children playing in the kindergarten play drama, draw. In every manner they express themselves in an amazingly inventive way. But the whole educational system is geared at turning these children into useful, hardworking citizens – people who will grow up to fulfil their productive duties, to assume their role as production units. That doesn't mean that every industrial worker blossoms into an artist the moment he becomes unemployed. This would require a very special process of transformation. It is a question of upbringing, of mentality. And I do not believe the mentality of a person above the age of twenty can still be changed much.

HP: So we have quite a long way to go yet?

Constant: Yes, but I do believe that when people are liberated, *en masse,* from their duties and obligations, a type of society will be born in which man will play with his life, rather than partition it according to the demands of the struggle for existence.

HP: That is clearly the essence of New Babylon. But the question remains whether every inhabitant of New Babylon will want, or in fact be able, to play.

Constant: In any case a lot of energy will be set free. It is becoming clear that in the era of automation all the work that, until now, was done by human labour can be taken over by inanimate machines. For a while people still believed that man was essential to operate the machinery, but even that appears to be a misconception. Automation stands for the operation of machines by other machines. That is cybernetics. So man will become irrevocably redundant.

HP: So you expect this to occur in the short term?

Constant: Yes, in industrialized nations this could become a reality within the next few years. Norbert Wiener writes in *The Human Use of Human Beings* that this would be the scenario with the outbreak of a new world war, as men are drained from the labour force. In The Netherlands, for example, automation received a great boost only a few years ago through substantial pay increases. When investments in automated production facilities become more economical than wages, investments in human productive forces that is, this will again give a new boost. Every pay rise, therefore, is really a positive step on the road to total automation.

HP: But won't there always be a leftover group of people that cannot be replaced by robots?

Constant: Until recently it was indeed a commonly held belief that there is a tertiary sector, which comprises all that is non-agricultural and non-industrial: art, even religion, education and health care, the whole service sector. It is a category without any apparent cohesion. The odd thing is that, more and more, this view is losing ground. In the field of education and scientific research particularly, automation is perfectly feasible. The only thing that cannot be automated is the single, 'unique' act, the creative act. It is through automation that these forces, especially, are unleashed; powers are stimulated that aren't 'useful', but which can be used for the creative, transformational interventions in one's existence. The entire work ethic has been completely undermined. Man the producer is no longer needed.

HP: And yet, in The Netherlands, we are importing Spaniards, Turks, Italians, Greek, Moroccans, and Portuguese.

Constant: Yes, to take over the menial chores that the Dutch refuse to touch. But in America every week 35,000 people lose their jobs as a result of automation.

HP: So you see New Babylon becoming more relevant by the day. In your plans, have you also taken into account any new kind of creativity?

Constant: Yes, yes. Painting, poetry, the novel, the musical composition, as expressions of the exceptional individual, are typical products of the times when the single human being found himself in an exceptional position. Under the wings of an idle upper crust, like the aristocracy in the middle ages or the wealthy merchant classes later in the Renaissance, a few individuals have been given the opportunity to withdraw from the general rule of usefulness, which goes something like: 'in the sweat of thy face shalt thou eat bread'. In New Babylon there will be room for collective creativity.

HP: Can you name an example of this collective creativity? This is something we are rather curious about.

Constant: Yes, well, so am I, hah hah. If I were to design this now, it wouldn't amount to much more than a representation. It is meant to be a spontaneous interaction among different individuals, in which the actions of one person trigger the reaction of the other. To begin with, this presupposes total freedom of expression among people. And this is not the case now. Even a simple happening at the *Lieverdje* meets with immense resistance. The police show up and say: you are obstructing the traffic. As if people are there for the sake of traffic instead of the other way round. In New Babylon one's entire life will have become a happening, and the happening itself redundant.

HP: Even in your society, will there not always be outsiders?

Constant: No, no outsiders. There will of course always be various gradations, intelligent people and less intelligent people, creative and less creative people, but there are hardly any people who are absolutely uncreative. Even a mentally handicapped person has some intelligence in comparison with a dog. He can talk, and react. You cannot claim that the artist is a creative genius, and the cleaning lady uncreative. In traditional folk art one can observe that even a very retarded individual often plays an active role in dances, music or the flamenco.

No daily routine

HP: We still find it pretty hard to picture all this. Could you describe a day in the life of the average New Babylonian?

Constant: Of course I have thought about this quite a lot, but it is incredibly tricky to describe something like that before it actually exists. In fact, you can only really talk about it in a negative sense, about what New Babylon is not. You are talking about a day, but in New Babylon our ordered daily routine will no longer exist. Our present routine of getting up in the morning, going to bed in the evening, having meals at regular times: that whole order is based on the utility of the production unit.

HP: And all that will be different in New Babylon.

Constant: Yes. The climatic conditions are no longer the determinants. And in the enormous sectors of New Babylon I have eliminated daylight altogether, because people are breaking free more and more anyhow, especially from the rhythms of nature. Man wants to follow his own rhythm. Because usefulness has less of a grip on life, the whole rhythm of day and night will disappear.

HP: What novelties does this new human rhythm have in store for us?

Constant: I can outline a few points that clearly differ from how things are now. First: today we all live in one single place, we all live in Amsterdam, because we have to stay close to our work; you have to go to the *Haagse Post* every day, I am dependent on my assignments. As soon as people are no longer required to stay near their work, in the weekends, during holidays, they jump into their cars and get the hell out.

"So what then is New Babylon? Is it a social Utopia? An urban design? An artistic vision? A cultural revolution? Technological conquest? Or a solution to practical problems of the industrial age? Each of these questions touches on one aspect of New Babylon," writes C o n s t a n t   N i e u w e n h u y s , 46 years old and recent winner of the Cardazzo prize, in Randstad no. 2.

This prize, 3000, – Guilders, is the crowning of years of work on this ambitious visionary project, captured partly in drawings and fascinating models ("All my work has in fact been produced in my living room"), and in the New Babylon manuscript, written in German. In German – because our neighbours, especially, show keen interest in Constant's lectures, which are routinely enlivened with colourful slides. Where Constant now regards his New Babylon as his lifetime achievement, and hopes to be able to spend most of his time and energy on the project, in the '50s the picture was a different one.

As the *Auctor intellectualis* of the Dutch Cobra group, he wrote numerous manifestos, and made paintings that rank amongst the finest that the Cobra genre has produced, fetching high prices on the international art market. He has lost touch with his colleagues from those days. Constant: "We've grown apart. We speak the same words, but mean something entirely different. For me, experiment was essential to Cobra. For the others it has become a style, and those are incompatible notions. I feel more kinship with the young."

This inspired the idealist Constant to put his name on an unelectable spot on the Provo ballot list. Says the artist who lives off the income from his numerous assignments: "Out of sympathy, of course. I really don't have any time."

Proud owner of a Citroen 2CV, the thinker Constant spends the greater part of his days in his gigantic studio in the Wittenburg quarter of Amsterdam, assisted by a diligently welding N o l   K n e u l m a n and in the company of robust shepherd dog H e r t h a . At this moment a huge model (scale 1:100) is taking shape there, with which Constant wants to make a film – the ideal way, he believes, to approximate the reality of New Babylon.

The enthusiastic, dark-haired, beer-drinking erudite lives on the Henri Polaklaan, in a ground-floor apartment which he shares with wife N e l and daughter E v a . Other eye-catching flatmates: a big woolly monkey, 'sadly turned lethally dangerous', a couple of parrots and three cats. In his spare time this cheerful bon vivant likes to play the harp, violin, dulcimer, balalaika and especially the guitar. So, naturally, a TV set is nowhere to be found.

As the Marx-quoting son of a civil servant, graduate of a Jesuit secondary school, points out: "In this society we are continuously lied at and cheated on. Like during the war, only then the lies were so obvious that nobody bought them. It is a reality that constricts people; that is why there are so many mind-expanding substances around. In New Babylon all that won't be necessary – it is a kind of paradise."

HP: So the New Babylonian will be some kind of nomad?

Constant: Yes, his radius of action will expand; he will no longer stay in one place. He frees himself from the rhythm of day and night. What you then get is an adventurous way of life, in which you never know in advance what you will run into, where you never know beforehand what will happen. This is the principle of the happening, really.

HP: So these nomads won't all be needing their own little flat. But we can imagine that if you are free to go anywhere, soon enough travelling isn't much of a challenge anymore; especially if all differences in nature are progressively erased. Doesn't travel then become so pointless that no one would really bother to get up?

Constant: Climate regulation doesn't mean that you get a kind of ideal climate everywhere. On the contrary, different climatic conditions are created everywhere: it isn't nice and sunny wherever you go, there is also the occasional thunderstorm. You yourself have a share in the creation of the climate.

HP: Doesn't that require too much energy, all these choices?

Constant: Yes, it will cost a lot of energy, but then creativity simply requires a lot of energy, energy that today is wasted on vacuum cleaning, standing at a workbench, making machine parts, typing wage sheets. All kinds of dumb work that can be performed by a machine. This energy needs to find a new outlet, otherwise it will only build up. New Babylon will be the *décor* for that new creativity, that new culture.

HP: And this cannot take place in cities as we now know them?

Constant: You are bound to come into conflict with the authorities. Take traffic, for instance. The Police on the *Spui* square say: keep moving, you're disturbing the traffic. The Provos say: ban all the traffic from the city centre, the centre is a living space and not a parking lot, and right they are. It is an outrage that people should have to make way for the storage of a few pieces of metal. The type of city that is based on the four functions of traffic, work, dwelling and recreation will be obsolete in the era of automation; especially if you consider that the whole notion of dwelling becomes rather dubious if you are no longer required to stay on the same spot for your job, traffic is only a means of getting from one place to another, work no longer exists with automation,

as does recreation, because that is nothing more than taking a rest after work, relaxation. The whole functional city, all the plans that architects draw up, including the Pampus plan of Van den Broek and Bakema, are all based on the condition of work.

HP: How do you imagine government in New Babylon?

Constant: As the motto for my book on New Babylon I used a statement by a gypsy, who calls himself the chairman of the World Community of Gypsies. This man said: "We have a useful task in this world, because we are the symbols of a free world, a world without borders, in which you can travel freely, from the plains of South Africa to the forests of Finland, from the Atlantic coasts to the Siberian steppes!" So the notion of "state" has withered away, because the state is a product of the struggle for survival, of the competition between one group and another, of the protection of property. When the world economy comes into being, and that will inevitably occur, the state will automatically be eliminated.
The war in Vietnam, the tensions between Russia and China or America and China: all these are battles to control the world markets, a struggle of countries that are more industrialized and more productive, with the aim of suppressing the others so that these remain customers. When the client starts producing, the producer loses his privileged position, but

that battle will invariably end with the industrialization of the whole world – and this means that huge abundance will be created.

HP: And then the time has come for New Babylon … when that moment has arrived, will it cover the entire surface of the earth?

Constant: Yes, it will indeed. A network of sectors will span the globe. I have abandoned the idea of the city as a kind of node, this round shape marked on the map like a red blot. I am thinking about a very open structure, entirely coherent, so that you can travel through it, and with all the fragments of the landscape integrated within.

HP: Like a football in a net.

Constant: Yes, like a net draped over the globe. And in the meshes of this net life will unfold. A life for everybody, especially for the workers; at last they will get their chance. Never have they had any share in a culture of any sorts, and therefore they will not blindly follow existing cultural traditions. This is obvious – they are looking for the new.

HP: We thank you for this conversation.

Originally published in Dutch in *Haagse Post*, August 6, 1966

Constant with Betty van Garrel and Rem Koolhaas

PROGRAMME FOR MOBILE CITY PLANNING: AN UPDATE

by Yona Friedman, Architect

Three billion people inhabit the earth today. This population, increasing unremittingly over time, represents an average density of 80 inhabitants per km of inhabited area, equal to the average density of mainland France. To count up to three billion day and night would take 45 years. To build a car for each of these three billion individuals would take the combined global automobile industry 300 years. If a car is a luxury, however, housing is a necessity: how long would it take to build a shelter for each one of these three billion individuals?

To control the climate of the world's inhabited zones (approximately 50% of the surface of the globe) would appear to be the only feasible option, even though today this seems more in the realm of science fiction than of reality.

A habitat for a population of three billion souls can only be created through the use of nuclear or solar energy. Regulating batteries placed every 100 km would be capable of controlling fluctuations in air pressure and thus keep inhabited and agricultural areas free of any harmful atmospheric phenomena.

Considering the current pace of scientific progress, it should not take in excess of 20 years to set up such an installation on Earth. No prefabricated or industrialized construction could ever attain such prodigious speeds. Moreover, since atmospheric condi-

tioning eliminates the overriding need for shelter from the weather, the solution is as imperative as it is economic, through the advantages that it would bring to everyday life as well as to agriculture.

All this is only a technical hypothesis, which may or may not come to pass. Tomorrow's scientists will find solutions that will further simplify the existence of humankind in the time ahead. Yet, whatever these solutions may be, it is clear that the architect will gradually be phased out, to the point where he will no longer have any place in the town planning of the future.

At the present time, the sole task left open to architecture consists in developing temporary techniques of construction that will bridge the gap between traditional construction (i.e. static buildings that leave a "footprint") and future systems inclining towards the pure sciences.

This is the raison d'être of Mobile Architecture, whose programme we will now try to define.

★

Contemporary society is subject to three kinds of transformation that lie entirely outside our control:

1) — TRANSFORMATIONS IN COLLECTIVE PSY-CHOLOGY, which result from continuous conditioning taking place to some extent "below the surface." These transformations are manifest in the fields of public recreation and entertainment, as well as in the organization of the family (as a consequence of public education). These transformations have prompted the emergence of two opposing tendencies: a fondness for solitude vs. a preference for living in the heart of the crowd. But which of these two will prevail? Which lifestyle will be most popular, and by what percentage will it beat the opposing trend? At the present time, it is simply impossible to answer such questions.

2) — PHYSIOLOGICAL TRANSFORMATIONS are, in themselves, negligible. On the other hand, the biological conditions have changed considerably. New physical factors have surfaced whose importance has not yet been evaluated: disorders caused by radiation or electricity, or reactions to industrially polluted air. Another significant factor is that of time, which, having effectively been extended by artificial lighting, leads people to benefit from longer days. As with transformations in collective psychology, it is impossible to determine the final consequences of the influence of these new factors.

3) — TECHNICAL TRANSFORMATIONS are the most dependent on mankind (since they are conditioned by collective psychology), but technology only enables us to extend the list of possibilities, and is of little help when it comes to choosing sides: contemporary technology can lead as much to the dispersion as to the concentration of individuals. Mechanized organization, the electronic brain, and automation, for instance, all allow for dispersion, further facilitated by telecommunications.

This state of affairs has two possible outcomes:

A) — *A CITY FOR ISOLATED INDIVIDUALS* covering vast areas with low-density population (dispersion), or
B) — *A CITY DEDICATED TO PUBLIC LIFE* with collective amenities (concentration).

Presently, no conceivable compromise seems to exist between these two extreme solutions. The recluse and the sociable, two species of humanity, can never come to terms – hence the current crisis: city planning obliges these two contrary forces to cohabit, contemporary urban planning methods making no allowance for a free choice between dispersion and concentration.

The result is a need for INDETERMINATE TOWN PLAN-NING, a solution that can be achieved through a reorganization of the methodology of town planning – whereby it is a question more of finding new applications for existing technologies than of inventing entirely new techniques.

Indeterminate city planning is made possible in two ways:

1) — Through the convertibility of the forms and use of constructions: most appropriate here are constructions that can be reused after removal, temporary, collapsible constructions, or any structure that can be written off in a short period of time; or else

2) — Through the convertibility of the land by means of a system of ownership of space (instead of the ownership of the surface terrain), and by means of a network of roadways, power supply, and sewerage, similarly adaptable and removable.

N. B. — Above all, the problems in most urgent need of solution are those arising from the concentration of housing, since they are more complicated than the ones posed by dispersion. In fact the problems arising from "dispersed cities" are not currently soluble by city-planning or building techniques alone. Only new physicochemical technologies can fulfil the requirements of dispersion: non-material housing, autonomous services running on photoelectric batteries that eliminate the need for wiring, transport by air or on air cushions eliminating the problem of highways, etc …

Indeterminate city planning (a necessity that follows on from these changes) could be facilitated by:

a) — Applying climate control to any conurbation, either by a material, structural roof (qv. studies by Buckminster Fuller, Frei Otto, etc.) or by an immaterial roof, as proposed by W. Ruhnau; or

b) — Regulating the climate of an entire region, country or continent, a system made feasible by the stationing of nuclear relays.

All these solutions plead in favour of an urbanism of dispersion but this is precluded by the expected increases in the human population. Present growth trends see a global population of six billion by the year 2000. Such a figure forces us to set aside the entire surface of the earth for agriculture and does not permit the huge waste of land that would inevitably be caused by urbanization based on dispersion or low-density occupation (family cottages, villas, even tents). The exploitation of the face of the earth alone no longer suffices.

Concentration, on the other hand, requires the use of multi-level surfaces, i.e. superposition. The essential problem seems to be how to arrive at a technique of multi-layering that allows inhabitants to associate freely or to re-use their dwellings, while damaging the terrestrial surface as little as possible.

The technologies best answering this need are those of superposition – particularly the system of "Spatial quarters".

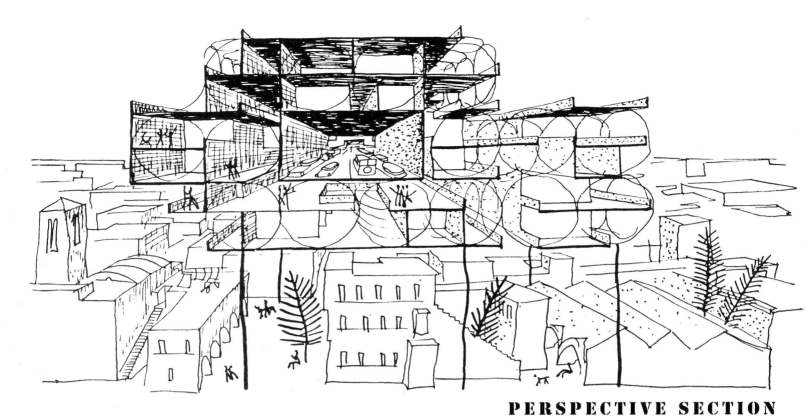

PERSPECTIVE SECTION

Perspective section of a business centre straddling an old quarter (technique of superposition).

The core of the construction (neutral axis) is used as a high-speed thoroughfare. The structures, four to six levels in height, are situated 12 meters above ground level, spanning the existing buildings on pylons set at 20 to 24 metre intervals. The four-lane, 12 metre wide express road on the inside of the structure serves as a connection between quarters; it is surrounded by public and commercial a spaces (terraces, sports facilities, promenades, boutiques, offices, etc.)

Access to the superstructure is provided by mechanical as well as traditional means (elevators, escalators, stairs) from the level of the old quarter and the underlying parking spaces.
The pylons are positioned in such a way, that demolition of existing buildings can be avoided as much as possible.
The steel framework is three-dimensional, combining compression rings and tension rods. The structure requires no more than 45 kg of steel per m^2 of usable surface. It is hyperstatic to the 27th degree and highly resistant to seismic activity.

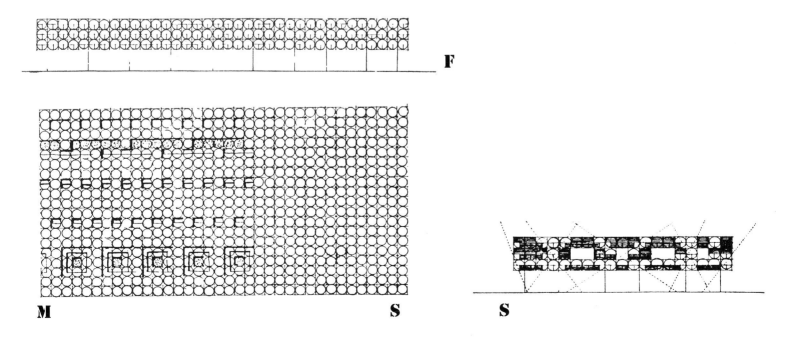

Facade, plan of the framework and section of the same centre. The section also indicates how sunlight reaches the old quarter below the structure.

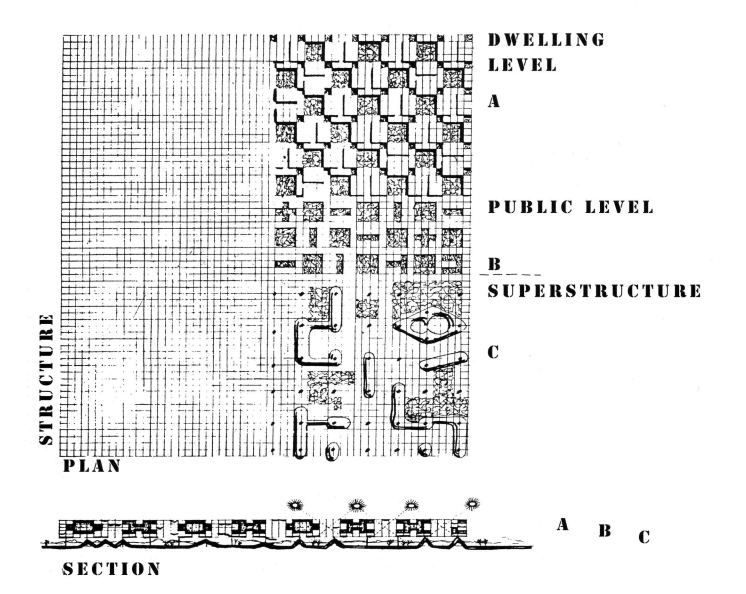

DWELLING LEVEL

A

PUBLIC LEVEL

B _ _ _ _

SUPERSTRUCTURE

C

STRUCTURE

PLAN

SECTION

A   **B**   **C**

This technique can be realized through a system of three-dimensional frameworks, the voids of which provide usable space. Their utilization (bedrooms, offices, housing, courtyards, etc…) is readily interchangeable by erecting (or dismantling) lightweight, prefabricated floors and partitions which are easily rearranged. Climate control of the region or district would reduce the need for such partitions, their principal remaining task being in optical and auditory separation.

★

N. B. — This system introduces a new legal concept of the ownership of a "limited space" or volume, in marked contrast to property based on the Roman law existing to this day that envisages only ownership of a surface, without definition of vertical boundaries.

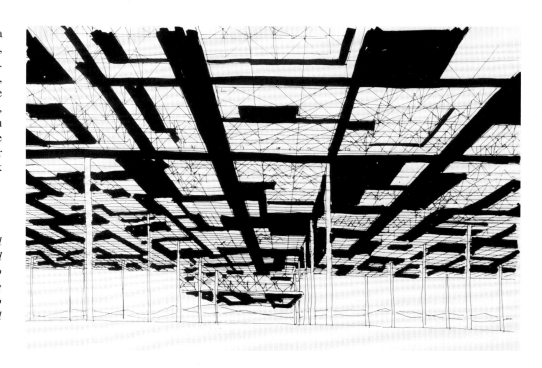

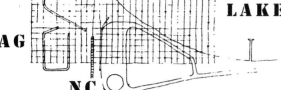

DW

SUPERSTRUCTURE

GROUND LEVEL

SECTION

LAKE

AG

NC

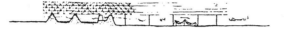

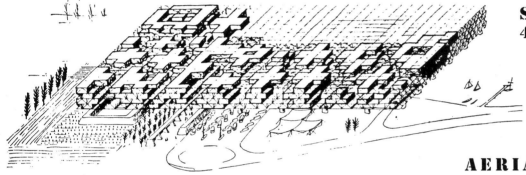

**SPATIAL QUARTER
4000 INHAB.**

AERIAL VIEW

Above: Spatial quarter with a capacity of 4,000 inhabitants.

Opposite: Diagram of a spatial quarter of 350 x 300 meters, with a capacity of 11,000 inhabitants (1,000 inhabitants per hectare, on the basis of 20 m² of living space per person).
The drawing shows (merely as an example) the positioning of dwellings on the different levels.
The section demonstrates that sunlight is able to reach all levels, including the surface of the earth (hence possibilities for agriculture).

In conclusion, the programme required for indeterminate city planning is as follows:
a) — total climate control,
b) — three-dimensional superimposed structures, within which the empty spaces are freely usable,
c) — ground level is reserved for essential production only (agriculture, industry, and, partially, transport).

An example of indeterminate city planning is outlined in the figures above. The housing districts represented show a density of 1,000 inhabitants per hectare, counting 20 m² of viable surface area per capita. (The population density in Paris is 400 inhabitants per hectare.)

The structure applied in this example is based on a system of spheroid trihedrals (hyperstatic system to the 27th degree). The structure calls for the use of annular elements to resist compression forces and struts to counter traction. Since the elements lie parallel or perpendicular at the point of contact, avoiding any other angle between the elements, the joints required by the system are extremely simple.

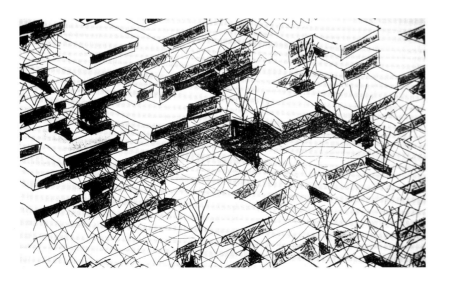

PARIS SPATIAL: A SUGGESTION

Yona Friedman, 1960

The problems of modern-day Paris are well-known and analogous to those met with in all major Western cities.

The present situation is characterized by growth. This growth is not unhealthy in itself. It becomes the cause of "ailments" because planning and the provision of amenities have not kept pace. As children grow, they need bigger clothes …

Features of this annual growth include:

Number of inhabitants	10 %
Number of private cars	8 %
Volume of supplies and provisions	15 %
Temporary occupation (tourism)	20 %
Population density	1 %
Road network density	1 %

In this way, the number of inhabitants will double in ten years, as will the number of automobiles, while the supply of goods required will triple. Temporary occupation will swell these figures still further. At the same time, housing and road network capacity will increase by no more than 10%. Hence, the city will spread out even more …

1. — The radio-concentric city

The present plan for Paris embraces the consequences of this situation: radio-concentric development. This plan is the least economical imaginable: housing numbers are naturally based on demographic data identical for each proposal; but costs for the local community, both direct (road network, public transport, etc.) and indirect (working time wasted, doubling of public services, etc.) are excessive. In consequence: either costs will be too high, or else vital amenities will have to be neglected for economic reasons only.

3. — Paris Parallèle

The Paris Parallèle proposal is to create a new centre equivalent to the Paris of today but at some distance from the city.

Through numerous experiences, we know that is impossible to set up equivalent twin cities due to factors of psychological preference; it is simply not feasible to influence the way people choose a particular place in which to live. It will therefore be impossible to create a centre near Paris that will prove sufficiently attractive to prevent the population from moving, or from wanting to move, to Paris. In this sense, Paris Parallèle can only become a "dormitory town", a suburban outpost in the countryside. The Paris Parallèle of the 18th century was called Versailles …

4. — The Herbé-Preveral project

This project proposes the rational organization of traffic in the built-up areas of Paris. A "multi-parallel" traffic network would permit the rational development of a 48 km square whereby traffic need not pass directly through the city centre. Consequently, radio-concentric expansion can be avoided. Moreover, the plan envisages an increase in housing density in the conurbation ten times higher than the current density.

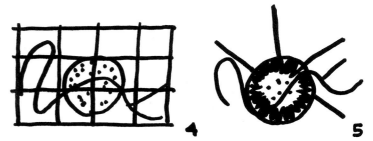

2. — Le Corbusier plan for Paris

This scheme was already obsolete by the time it was drawn up. It envisaged the reorganization of the centre of Paris alone, whereas the problem today extends to the whole city. In fact at the present time the centre is almost the least affected, similarly the first ring road and routes leaving the city centre. At that time Le Corbusier started from the hypothesis that the city centre was congested while the outskirts possessed surplus traffic capacity (which was indeed the case). Moreover, to apply his method to Paris as a whole would entail almost the complete demolition of the present-day city.

5. — The Paris Spatial project

This project proposes tripling the housing density of the city centre itself. In view of the fact that the present-day city will always remain the focus of attraction, it has to be provided with the largest possible number of dwellings. By applying the technique of superposition, new housing, industry, and agriculture will be added, all the while conserving as much of today's city as possible.

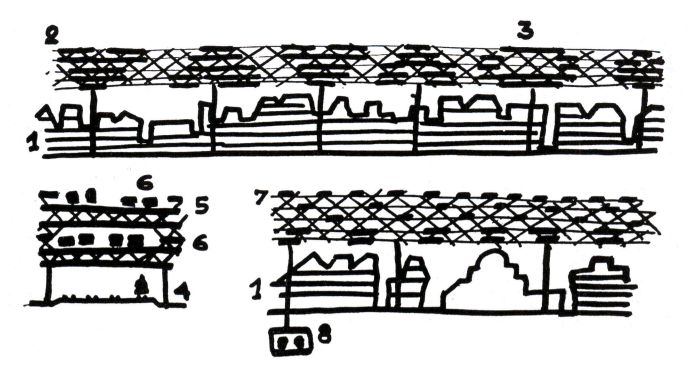

1. Existing city – 2. Superimposed dwellings or offices – 3. Superimposed traffic artery – 4. Existing railway line – 5. Offices or shops – 6. Main thouroughfare/ Spatial trafic artery – 7. Spatial agriculture – 8. Existing métro line.

Below: Proposed construction over the Champs-Élysées. Following pages: the photomontages illustrate the aesthetic experience of the various spatial constructions that might be erected on top of various quarters of the city.

The plan consists essentially in the construction of new districts above the existing city, in such a manner that large-scale demolition of the city is avoided, and whereby the city and its various quarters will preserve their present-day character.

These constructions are to be erected above areas located between the rings of the inner and outer boulevards and over certain parts of the inner city (Quartier des Halles, boulevard Sébastopol, etc.). Hence, the historic city will remain intact.

The space between these two rings represents approximately two-thirds of the city's surface area. Postulating a complementary housing density of 800 inhabitants per hectare, the average housing density of the city will increase from 326 inhabitants per hectare to 850 per hectare ($800 \times 0.66 + 326 = 850$).

The structures utilized to this end are of the same type as those in spatial districts and spatial conurbations. These superimposed structures are characterized above all by a scale far exceeding that of buildings constructed today. Their scale is more like that of an urban district.

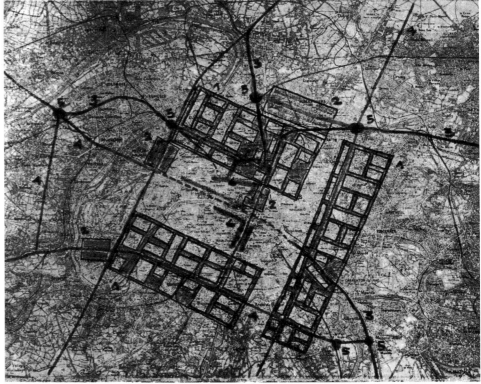

1. Spatial living quarters – 2. Spatial quarters for administration & business – 3. Motorway constructed above railroad tracks – 4. Spatial motorway – 5. Vertical transfer node for goods (between lorries and trains) – 6. Existing centres of attraction (recreational).

The spatial quarter consists of a three-dimensional modular grid. The empty spaces in this grid (a construction based on the trihedral) will incorporate cells measuring 25–30 metres of usable surface area. These cells serve as the basic element for housing and offices.

The arrangement and positioning of used and unused empty spaces depend on the position of existing constructions underneath the superstructures: the voids are arranged in such way that lighting and ventilation in dwellings in the existing constructions are not disrupted. The optimum proportion between filled-in and empty voids would appear to be approximately 50 to 60%.

The logical outcome of the study of superimposed spatial structures is the spatial agglomeration. Much larger than spatial quarters, this would also include: housing, public spaces, traffic zones, and areas set aside for agriculture and industry, while allowing for the free exchange and reconfiguration of these components.

The framework used is to be identical for all these elements (housing, public areas, agricultural and industrial zones). This consistency of construction and structural continuity lie at the basis of the interchangeability mentioned above.

Spatial constructions straddling existing urban quarters along the *grands boulevards* (this page), Les Halles and the Beauborg plateau (opposite). Life underneath continues virtually undisturbed.

Functional differentiation of the elements is ensured by altering the relative position of the floor units within the used spaces in the construction. This interrelation between floor units will conform to the specific conditions (e.g. sunlight, ventilation, traffic, dimensioning, etc.) stipulated by the various functions. By rearranging the floor panels at will, the fabric of the city can be modified so as to accommodate different uses.

The appearance of a spatial quarter or agglomeration recalls a huge openwork slab or lattice with dimensions ranging from 300 to 1,200 metres. Supported on pylons, this slab or lattice overlays the existing city. The apertures are distributed in such a way that the viability of constructions underneath the new structures is not affected.

Spatial cities also make for a great leap forward in terms of the industrial organization of agriculture. The fact that the agrarian zones are located inside a high-density city (1,000 inhabitants per hectare) forestalls habitual but perilous isolation of the farming community by ensuring for it living conditions that are the norm among the urban population.

Moreover, on the administrative level, the incorporation of agricultural zones in the spatial agglomeration easily and economically resolves the problem of food supply. The usual difficulties connected with the provisioning of large cities (road transport, central markets, intermediaries, etc…) disappear. The distribution of food throughout the city becomes easy by using the underground system, which

Spatial quarters can be used to span infrastructural arteries (motorways, railways). Agricultural zones can be integrated in spatial residential quarters: rooftops become veritable hanging gardens producing food for the population.

doubles as a goods-rail network at those hours of the day when passenger trains are not operational.

To illustrate the aesthetic appearance of the constructions proposed, the figures above show photomontages of various spatial constructions that might be erected on top of various quarters of the city.

The Paris Spatial proposal may also bring with it significant improvements in traffic flow within the city and at its exits. Spatial constructions leave the choice whether to:

a) leave the total causeway of the principal arteries free for car use by ensuring pedestrian transit on dedicated levels in the Spatial constructions;

b) or provide high-speed thoroughfares in the statically neutral core of these constructions, leaving the existing streets available for pedestrian use;

c) add new exit roads to the city above four-track railways (Dijon, Orléans, Creil, Rouen, Versailles, Chagny lines) to ensure high-speed routes similar to highways in all directions up to 60–100 km from the city.

Summary

Once developed in this way the city will have the capacity to house and sustain a population increased by 150%, the predicted figure 15 to 20 years hence. The increase in housing density and the density of the road infrastructure will rise from 1% to 10% per annum, thus on a par with demographic growth.

Presently, a synthesis between the Herbé-Preveral and Paris Spatial projects is being examined.

A model of a spatial construction spanning an old quarter, in accordance with the plan by the author of this article, will be presented at the French Exposition in Moscow.

Texts on pp. 13–17 and pp. 19–29 originally published in *Revue technique du bâtiment*, November 1960 and June 1961, respectively.

In the Air
Interview with Yona Friedman — 28 October, 2001

Martin van Schaik: One could say that the beginnings of L'Architecture Mobile were the CIAM conference in Dubrovnik, which you attended in 1956. This is the meeting at which the members of Team X came to the fore, but the work that you did was still relatively isolated. How would you describe what was happening in those early days?

Yona Friedman: Let me go back one step. At the beginning of the 1950s, in Haifa, I started teaching and doing some projects, assignments mostly for social housing. As a student, the years before, I was always involved with one question: why should architects decide for the people who live in their buildings? This was my point of departure: I felt that people should decide for themselves. But then I realized that people cannot express their decision. This is extremely difficult. Even an architect cannot properly explain his intention, so how should the layman? But they know it, instinctively, like dogs *(patting his dog, Balkis, on the head)*, so they find their arrangement. Ideally, if you look at the different floors of any apartment building, you will find that the same flat is completely differently organized on each floor. So I thought: why not? Why shouldn't the partitions indoors – and that means all the architectural elements – be changeable? And then I decided – well it's a very old answer – that only the skeleton should be fixed. So this was one side.

The other side was sociological. I made a diagram, which was published in '57 in *Bauwelt*, that showed that leisure time was increasing and becoming more important. People started to spend more time in the field of leisure, which meant that the proportion of leisure time vis-à-vis the working time was changing. For that reason I was beginning to see that the *raison d' être* of cities had really more to do with leisure than working all day.

MvS: So, in your ideas did you link up the sociological aspect of the steady increase in leisure time with the architectural ambition that people should have the possibility to continually transform their own homes?

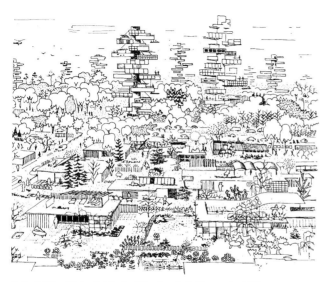

1. Frei Otto, "Adaptable Architecture", in *Bauwelt*, 1958

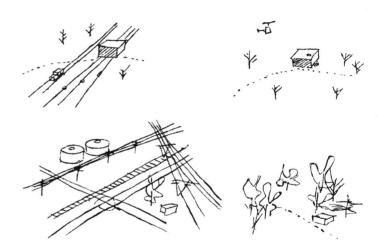

2. Yona Friedman in *Bauwelt*, 1957. Dematerialized architecture/inhabitable nature: "Scheme today: expensive and inflexible. Proposal for the future: cheap and mobile"

YF: Yes. If given more time, they would have more attention for these things. That means that it is a question of intensity. It is a way of self-expression. And I was trying to say: this is not only something that happens in the dwelling, but at every level of the city. So when I started spanning towns with structures this was done with the intention that you can manipulate the collective part as much as the private. It would be as mobile as the individual houses. You cannot separate the two. They have the same properties.

To link it to what I'm doing today: I am more and more involved with the phenomenon of erraticity, unpredictability. But back then, also, I was starting out with the unpredictability – with the fact that I cannot tell how a city will develop. And nowadays I find it as a general principle everywhere: in physics, mathematics. Things are necessarily unpredictable and erratic.

MvS: To what extent is this erraticity something that you tried to foster, but also *control* or *predict*, within the infrastructures that you developed, with a tool like the "Flatwriter" or investigations like "Urban mechanisms"?

YF: There is only the unpredictable. So if things are unpredictable, let the thing decide for itself. It is a question of the point of view: it is unpredictable to *me*. I cannot tell why that person in the street is going this or that way, but he or she knows very well why. I find that mathematics is erratic, but I'm not sure if it is really erratic for the elements making out the mathematics. You know, you can construct any number, any mathematical operation by adding one to one to one and making certain operations. The rule for building up numbers is the simplest thing – it is idiotically simple. But you have absolutely no idea what you build up. You have no idea what the property is of that specific number of so many digits. The only thing you know is that it doesn't share any property with its direct neighbours.

As for the Urban Mechanisms, I will explain: it is exactly the same. In the Urban Mechanisms I look at statistical properties to equilibrate the erraticity using statistics. That means something done now, if you want, might be the same tomorrow and so on. But this is statistical, this is no certitude. It's assumed. And with the Urban Mechanisms my departure is: I have no idea what people are doing in the streets and how and why. I have only statistical data. In trying to build up this system at the level of urban behaviour I described three kinds of views. The first I called God's eye view. God knows everything. Okay, well, let's put that aside immediately. Then the second I referred to as King's eyes' view, in which there is a secret policeman who follows everybody around, and this secret policeman – or a satellite, it doesn't really matter – gives a description of all the movements. But we still don't have any idea why I do certain things. We don't have any idea where I will stop or turn a corner, only after I did it. Then I took the statistical view, which is what underlies the Urban Mechanisms: I don't know why and how people go about their ways, but I can know that at this corner, over a period of 24 hours there are so many people. That's all. And I operate with this rough, absolutely rough, inexact statistical data. Because of the erratic nature of reality I am operating with statistics.

MvS: Let's go back to the late fifties. GEAM was founded about two years after Dubrovnik. In Holland, you had Jan Trapman as a collaborator, for instance.

YF: Trapman I met because his wife was a friend of my girlfriend. You know how things go. I was looking for people who could be involved with the ideas. So I met a few people: Otto and Günschel in Berlin, Trapman in the Netherlands. My point of departure was: they can have their own ideas as much as they want, but they should somehow essentially be converging. What we had to find was a way to leave the urban reorganization as free and changeable as possible. And originally I tried to write the 'Architecture Mobile' as a sort of a manifesto that was left sufficiently open, so that many people could adhere to the basic principles, not making any, if you want, aesthetic or emotional constraints in advance.

MvS: So how did you get in touch with Constant?

YF: That must have been in '61, I think. Maybe it was Schulze-Fielitz who told me about him, and we got in touch somehow. And then I met him in '61 or '62 and, okay, it was more or less the same thing as .... you see, we were friends with the predecessor of Constant. I am thinking of Nicolas Schöffer, because he was doing these things before Constant. This was all a very long time ago, but Constant and I had a very good relationship. We got old … I was thinking to call on him the last time that I was in Holland but I wasn't in Amsterdam at the time, everything was too complicated, you know, with the dog … If you see Constant, don't forget to give him my greetings.

MvS: You both participated at the GEAM conference in 1962 at Knoll International in Amsterdam.

YF: Yes, '62, this was an incredibly busy year. You know, the period when everything started was between '57 and '59, but after that a lot of people joined, which was very good. Many people got involved who had some influence, and Constant, well, yes, when there was that Amsterdam thing, organized by Knoll International, evidently he was there. There was another person I hadn't met but whom I was told about in '62, and that was John Habraken. And so I invited John Habraken to the conference too. Very different characters indeed, the two of them, but both Constant and Habraken agreed with the basic tenets of L'Architecture Mobile. Constant had the artist's view, and Habraken the technical approach. But both are right.

3. Nicolas Schöffer, Spatiodynamic tower for La Défense, Paris, 1970

MvS: In the discussion that is held at the conference, it is Constant and you – rather than he and Habraken – who take the two extreme positions.

YF: The difference between Constant and me was that I started out with the idea that people do things their own way – I set no rules. It is not play in the same sense as with Constant, but it is play in another sense. You know, all communication happens that way. If you communicate something to somebody, the person receiving the message completes it. The message is *necessarily* incomplete. A person completes it according to his own imagination. And this completion is in another way 'play', but not in the sense of Constant. You know, it's a very old principle. I'm very much interested in religion, not because I am religious – I don't care, I really don't care – but as it contains certain traces, historical

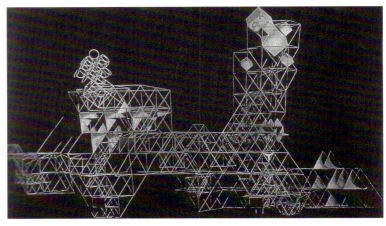

4. Eckhard Schulze-Fielitz, *Raumstadt* (Space city), 1959

5. Friedman and Constant at the exhibition and conference on **L'Architecture Mobile, Amsterdam, May 1962**

traces which are amongst the oldest ones. It gives us an idea about the collective mentality of mankind. And it is very funny that every mythology and religion begins with an act of creation. It can be the Sioux Indians or any African tribe. And one of the interesting things is that the creation by the divine entity is tacitly considered incomplete. And it is always the role of humans to complete it. It is an archetypal fixed idea, you see – and this goes for everything. The fundamental social idea is co-creation: an art-work is created by the public, by the spectators. And you could call that play, but again nothing is even possible without it. It really is part of the mental mechanism of understanding.

MvS: In the book *L'Architecture Mobile*, you mention Johan Huizinga.

YF: Yes, I read Huizinga, and I was very much impressed by him. But the play concept of Huizinga is surely nearer to me than the play concept of Constant. It's not the same. The play of Constant includes a director, a *chef d' orchestre*. There is a leadership. You only need to look at the project, how his models are: in departure they are fixed. That's his personality. He doesn't want it, but the director is there. I know that he has the intention to do otherwise, but still .... But I like him. You have to take people as they are.

I on the other hand was trying to look at the minimum departure, trying to leave the page as blank as possible. You know, in 1961 I made a diagram showing in the first picture the city as it now is. Then, in the second image, l'architecture mobile. And for the next step: nothing at all, no architecture. I called it later: *la nature habitabilisée*, nature made inhabitable.

MvS: Wasn't Werner Ruhnau, who was also a founding member of GEAM, extremely interested in climatization?

YF: Well, that was somewhat different. Ruhnau in a way was a bit like Constant, he was involved with theatre – again there is a director, a *metteur en scène*. I was more driven by the image of, say, people in a field or at the beach, wherever you want. And there are some rules which are tacit, never formulated, but no more than that: that means I'm not sitting on the head of the chap next to me. And it's funny, because I was once asked about the year 2000: what do you think of the architecture of the next millennium? And I told them: architecture will disappear.

MvS: These ideas were put forward by others too, throughout that decade....

YF: Yes, but it's logical. All these ideas … we were not inventing ideas, but completing them. Ideas come from very far away. Again, even religions show this. In the ideas of religions of the golden age, past or coming, nothing is there. Everything is as it is. The idea is not that this is purely realistic: it simply is in the back of your mind, it is a built-in archetype. Today I can explain it in a wider context, but in '57 that was one of the ambitions: architecture has to get rid of all the networks, the street network, electricity network. And today we are there! *(Friedman grabs his cell phone).* That doesn't mean they no longer exist, it means that the networks are dematerialized – that is the exact word. You can have a virtual environment.

MvS: Is your elaborately decorated apartment not proof of the fact that people cling to objects, built things?

8–12. (Opposite:) Ville Spatiale / Architecture Mobile: in Monaco, straddling Les Halles, in New York, and descending on the Centre Pompidou. Bottom right: one of the first cardboard models, 1959

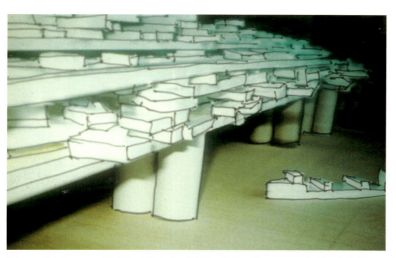

6. **Yona Friedman and Eckhard Schulze-Fielitz: Bridge Town over the English Channel, 1963 (model)**   7. **Railway viaduct, Paris, July 2003**

YF: This doesn't mean that there are no tangible parts of it. But it's not absolute; you can have an environment that is more tangible, or less tangible. You know, in India kings had no palaces – they lived in their gardens. That's very interesting. In Fatehpur Sikri, for instance, there is no building, there are no walls, only platforms. In Indonesia people have a porch, rich people too, and they receive you in their porch, and that's the way they live. In India – I know the country well – people sleep in front of their houses. So they have their house, but the house is not primarily for living in: it's a kind of storage.

MvS: Did you ever think about the possibility of applying climate control to, say, Paris?

YF: No, and that is the difference with Ruhnau. What happens today – and this is one of the trends I believe in – is that people go to the South. The majority of people, 80% of humanity, live in warm climates, or reasonably warm climates. The rich people go there for their own reasons, but the poor live there because you cannot have a shantytown in Murmansk. So shantytowns are in the hot regions; there we don't really need the climatization. In India, all that you need is a roof against the rain. Sadly, shantytowns have a pejorative meaning in our language, so I think it is better to replace the term by squatting. You need minimal protection against the weather. The shantytowns are poor, but really it is the urban poverty that produces it.

MvS: Again, at the same time, roughly, there were other architects who were toying with concepts of radically dematerializing architecture – I'm thinking of Archigram's later projects, for instance, or the work of the Italian Radicals. Even if people weren't aware of each other's projects – you said, for example, that you didn't know Habraken before '61–'62 – it seems they were often coming to the same conclusions.

YF: There was a very funny thing. I don't know whether you know about Kenneth Larson. He was doing structures like my "Space Chains" and I was accused – by others, not by him – of copying things from publications 3 or 4 years earlier. And I'm sure I didn't copy him. But I know that he didn't know what I was doing. You see, sometimes these were small magazines, and so it didn't get around so much. And Larson said to me: yes, but the thing was in the air. And I like this expression: things were in the air. That not only happens in architecture, but also in science: it's a change of paradigm.

13. Yona Friedman in his studio on Boulevard Pasteur, 1963

MvS: One can observe that during the past 25 years architecture has largely returned to matters of form and aesthetics. Is that something you regret, or was this an inevitable shift, do you think?

YF: I don't see anything bad in it except the things I see. Why not? I find the aesthetics very boring. You see, I believe that even rational things are emotional. To come back to what we were talking about before, it is a matter of completing things. What I dislike perhaps about architectural aestheticism today is simply its lack of imagination. It is a platitude. Take one of the people I find sympathetic: Frank Gehry. He did an ordinary building with whipped cream on it. It is decoration. Okay, so it's not my thing; no reason that it shouldn't be there, but it is just so unimaginative, that's what I don't like. And the imagination, I think, cannot be only formal. It must be formal – and something else.

MvS: If we look at the architects that reacted to certain conceptual developments in the '60s: these people, you could say, felt that architecture was trying very hard to be everything except architecture, or what they considered to be architecture. By the late 1960s, it had little to do with aesthetics anymore, but with politics, sociology, event, linguistics, technology, standardization …

YF: You know, personally I think that the terrible thing with architects is that they are only architects. They have no other background. I am very much interested in other things than architecture. In fact I am really not interested in architecture. It's too dull, I'm sorry. I'm interested in processes, in processes in general, I am interested in how we build our view of the world, how we see other people. And architecture is just an aspect, a part of that. My goodness, people who make shoes never have shoemaker's conferences! But, my goodness, a shoe is nearer to me than the building! Only you can more easily change shoes. But shoemakers do not pretend to make something for eternity. And I was once asked: what are the ten best buildings in your view? … And I didn't arrive to ten. Now cities, and this is really again my point, cities are always beautiful. Architecture is not. Because a city is a living thing, with the variety and so on. A city has no façade, no elevation. You have only an inside. There is nearly no object that is preponderant. CIAM, for instance, never had anything with cities. They were talking about cities, but there were no plans for them. Le Corbusier in Chandigarh made a monument to himself, but the city is not there. The city is the shantytown. Same thing in Brasilia – in Brasilia the shantytown is the actual city. There are some beautiful cities in the world. I love Sana'a. I arrived in Sana'a after a night flight, but I just couldn't go to sleep, I had to see all of it. There are living cities, which have a quality, which is not given by the architects nor by the town planner. Do you know what one of the most beautiful buildings in Paris is? *(Walks to the open French window.)* This one out here. *(Points at the iron railway viaduct running along the centre of the Boulevard.)* And the space under it, it is used for parking! When it is empty in August, and there are no cars parked, it could be something very lively, you know. A market, a promenade, a place to live. It would be wonderful!

MvS: Now in 'Paris Spatial', you said that the superimposed structures would have nearly no effect on what went underneath. That would seem a bit unlikely though, wouldn't it?

YF: You know, the system in Paris at the time was that they were demolishing whole neighbourhoods, making a wasteland, and

14. Yona Friedman, *Ville Spatiale*. Drawing from the early 1980s

then building. My point was: leave the things, build above them, and then perhaps you demolish them, or not: the neighbourhood will change, gradually. But it will not become a wasteland, transformation will not be so brutal. I believe in changes taking their time, not the 'tabula rasa'. When I met Le Corbusier for the first time – it was also the first time in my life that I came to France from Israel, and of course he was this huge personality – and I was talking to him about what buildings of his I could best visit, I was a bit naïve and asked: Pessac, perhaps? Oh no, Corbusier exclaimed, you wouldn't want to go there! And I understand him in a way. It was done, he had left his mark – and the people ran away with it *(Friedman beams)*. I installed a decoration here *(waves his arms around, pointing at the walls of his flat)*, and it seems to be mobile, because I have changed it an x number of times. The former decoration is still stowed away because it was going to Rotterdam for the exhibition, and I didn't unpack. But I don't mind: tomorrow I am already doing other things. I like the things that I do, but I am used to the fact that they are slowly crumbling away, crumbling away quite nicely. That's okay. I don't care.

MvS: You make your own things, Mr Friedman. Your flat is the living proof of the satisfaction that people can get from making things. Is that not an underlying idea in all your work: that you would like to encourage people to be more self-sufficient – practically, and in a creative way? Is it not, in many different ways, an encouragement for people to be less passive, less dependent on what industry provides them with and marketing forces down their throats?

YF: Well, it's an equilibration. Once I was invited to a designers' conference in Helsinki. I was trying to tell them that the designer has but very small input. The thing is what people will do with it. A chair is for sitting in. But I have to step up onto the chair if I want to change a light bulb. I can sit down on the floor and use it as a table. You create an object, okay, but you have no idea how people will use it. These wrappings, for example, they are an industrial product. *(Points at a piece of decorative bricolage)*. I use them in my own way. I wouldn't look at the question of industrialization too dogmatically.

MvS: Yes, but the essence still is that you appropriate it, you make it your own by using it and transforming it. Is that perhaps not also the essence of what you would then call 'home', which is essentially a question of creative appropriation – not through ownership, but by making something your own by transforming it, creatively?

YF: Yes. And she will tell you the same thing *(patting Balkis)*. But they do it completely unconsciously. Hmm, this whole idea of human superiority … Humans are necessary to complete the world. But why not simply to live in it?

Psychogeogram: An Artist's Utopia
Martin van Schaik

I think that we should not pretend that we understand what Constant was thinking. If that's the issue then anyway you can ask him – and of course in the one hundred years since Freud you don't trust him, whatever he says.
Mark Wigley, Delft, January 2000

My understanding of Rembrandt would not become more complete if I knew what kind of shirts he wore. (…) Not without reason does an artist express himself indirectly. He is very vulnerable, because he reveals himself in his work.
Constant in an interview with Fanny Kelk, 1974

1. Looking for the totally new: praxis and prefiguration of a *poésie faite par tous*

Sterft, gij oude vormen en gedachten,
Slaafgeborenen, ontwaakt, ontwaakt,
De wereld drijft op nieuwe krachten,
Begeerte heeft ons aangeraakt[1]

1. Constant, *De rode vuist*, 1952

Buried deep in the archives of Constant Nieuwenhuys in The Hague is an explosive letter from fellow painter Asger Jorn. The date, scribbled in pencil at the top of the page, is 1953.[2]

"Your letter has amused me a lot", writes Jorn. "I see you are continuously evolving. But let me give you an advice." In a fatherly tone, he goes on to warn his friend and junior by six years to take care not to trash his own past. On the whole, the epistle is amiable, but Jorn is clearly and quite seriously worried. He acknowledges

that Constant has the tendency to "zigzag" and change direction often – considers it one of his great qualities – but tries to rub it in that one should never reject one's own past outright, something that Constant appears to be doing: "*You are denying yourself, and that is the end of an artist, and the beginning of an epigone.*" Almost desperately, Jorn urges Constant not to sell his soul.

What on earth is going on? The letter testifies that Constant was tearing away from his previous work, cutting the umbilical cord that tied him to his one-time mentor and fellow traveller Jorn. But more is at stake: the underlying issue would continue to divide them in years to come, and like the proverbial sword it would hang over all of their future collaborations. Unwittingly or not, in this letter Jorn lays his finger on what constitutes the core of Constant's concerns that in the following years would give birth to his friend's undisputed masterpiece: "New Babylon", the world of Homo Ludens.

Break-up

Constant's radical reorientation takes place in the course of roughly a year, 1952–53. This shift in his work, encompassing the gradual but decisive transition from figuration to abstraction, the rejection of painting and the move towards investigations into space, colour (and later into construction, applied art and ultimately architecture and urbanism) has often been talked about: it is an integral part of Constant's official biography.[3] Still, this radical move warrants a closer inspection. One can safely say that Jorn saw his friend gradually but surely turning into the antithesis of the painter he had known in the years of their collaboration. A "cold" abstractionist was suddenly rearing his head. Constant was deserting into the enemy camp.

How shocking this change of course must have been to Jorn becomes clear when one considers not only his own, less capricious artistic development, but the position that the members of Cobra held vis-à-vis all things abstract, constructivist and neo-plasticist: the ferocious opposition to the Apollonian strain of modern art was not only a matter of policy but, to most, of the essence of the movement. The contrast between Cobra – of mainly surrealist/expressionist pedigree – and the direction in which Constant was going – in line with Constructivism at best, De Stijl and the Bauhaus at worst – could not have been starker.

Cobra (acronym for Copenhagen, Brussels, Amsterdam – and ferocious serpentine predator) was the name of the journal that marked the collaboration and *de facto* fusion of the Høst group of painters from Denmark, a dissident faction of the 'Revolutionary Surrealist' group from Belgium (writers and poets predominantly) and the Dutch *Experimentele Groep* (instigated by Constant and with the painters Karel Appel and Corneille as the other two main protagonists).[4] The movement lasted a mere three years: 1948–51. Though the members operated mainly from their native countries, it had its cradle in Paris, where the three key members had run into each other at certain moments in time: Asger Jorn, Constant, and the Belgian poet-writer and Marxist militant Christian Dotremont. It was also on the banks of the Seine that the founding document was signed.

Emerging from the cataclysm of World War II – after the *Stunde Null* of Auschwitz and Hiroshima – and countering all 'reactionary' tendencies to rebuild the old world, Cobra brought together birds of a very different feather, but with the declared goal to break the stalemate, to explode the anxious stuffiness of the post-war years, and to move forward into the uncharted territories of truly egalitarian and free artistic creation. The ambition was – through international collaboration and collective experimentation – to bypass the incapacity of the pre-war avant-gardes that had failed to renew their cultural offensive. Most notably: surrealism, to which the Cobra movement owed much of its theoretical background, but which had lost its political edge and had been largely absorbed by the establishment on both sides of the Atlantic. Other forces to be opposed were the politically benign and aesthetically pleasing Ecole de Paris (Paris-based "official" contemporary art) and the trap of Soviet-fostered Socialist realism (Communism gone wrong). *L'union fait la force*, and so the artists from three small European countries teamed up to make a fist, and most importantly: to *create*. Indeed Cobra generated a momentum that in the relative isolation in their home countries these artists would otherwise simply not have had.

Within the Cobra constellation, the three founding fathers Jorn, Dotremont and Constant were the cardinal points. Along with Dotremont – the writer-poet and *secrétaire general* of the group – Constant had soon emerged as the most important "theorist": his "Manifesto", first published in the journal of the Dutch Experimental Group, is still the most lucid expression to date of the ambitions and aims of the movement as a whole.[5] Jorn, who must be credited for bringing the Dutch, the Danes and the Belgians together in the first place, was the prime liaison officer and actual glue of the group. Where for Jorn and his Danish fellow travellers Cobra was in a sense a continuation (but internationalization) of their efforts with *Helhesten* and *Høst*, the formation of the Dutch Experimental Group in 1948 – and Cobra a year later – was a radical move: this was the first wave of original artistic (and certainly avant-garde) activity to lap at Holland's shore in a long time. Clearly, to the Dutch the Høst group was a major influence and inspiration from the very moment that Constant and Jorn became friends, following their 1946 chance meeting in Paris. More so than for the members from other countries, Cobra was the giant leap that helped the Dutch out of their provincial seclusion.

The movement shunned theoretical top-heaviness, and insisted on the primordial role of artistic experimentation to further the cause of the revolution: antidotes to the ivory tower squabbling and theorizing that the young left-wing Surrealists had got themselves into.[6] And though the artists of Cobra, in their artistic output, built heavily on the instinctual and subversive undercurrent of surrealism, they insisted on spontaneous and direct expression in every medium they touched, on an explosion of academic convention, celebrating the fundamental, universal force of life: the creative urge in every human being. Radically anti-elitist, in its painterly output Cobra rejected the *achevé* aesthetics of the surrealism of the likes of Max Ernst, Salvador Dalí, or René Magritte (to pick a few of the "greats") and worked in a direct, uninhibited and intentionally child-like, primitive idiom. What emerged from the paint on their canvases or the flotsam that made up their sculptures was a world of fantasy animals, magical figures, faces, objects, rendered in vibrant colours and charged lines. If anyone, from children to madmen, could imitate or even outdo them at their art, it was proof that they were heading in the right direction. Cobra thus struggled to spell *liberation*, in order to pave the way for a passionate, provocative and therefore communicative art for the people and, most importantly, *by* the people.

Indeed their paintings, murals, sculptures, poetry and writings testify of their frantic search for this authentic life force – far beneath the layers of the decrepit varnish of what they were convinced was a bourgeois culture in its terminal phase: their art thus went straight for the jugular of good taste and mores. Needless to say, their first great exhibition, held at the Stedelijk Museum in Amsterdam in 1949 deeply shocked the burghers of Holland. The impact was seismic, and put the movement in the history books. Not unexpectedly, then, a pet target of Cobra's attacks was the perceived sterility and rationality of the neo-plasticism of De Stijl – Holland's only true avant-garde movement to date – and the art of Mondrian in particular. In Constant's roaring words:

But we who have nothing to lose but our chains, can very well take the risk. We risk nothing in this adventure but a sterile virginity – that of the abstracts. Let us fill in Mondrian's virgin canvas, even if only with our misfortunes.[7]

2. Asger Jorn, *Komposition med Fabeldyr*, 1950

In their revolt against the old world, Cobra at first stood united, but very quickly – too soon – the first cracks appeared: personal but also inherently ideological incompatibilities crept in from which the movement as a whole was never to recover. Not only did the relationship between Constant and Jorn turn sour overnight when the latter eloped with the former's wife in the summer of 1949 (i.e. even before the notorious exhibition in the Stedelijk that cast Cobra into the limelight and from which Jorn was conspicuously absent),[8] but rifts also began to appear in the Dutch front. Personal tragedy and careerism had entered the group and were splitting it up. And though Cobra had spawned collaborations between poets and painters, the creation of numerous collective artworks, graffiti and murals plus two major exhibits (and the magazine *Cobra* itself), the call for collaboration and collective creation began to ring increasingly hollow. The lack of intellectual rigour and the failure of the collective in the face of the painterly egos was something Constant would repeatedly lament.

By the time Jorn and Dotremont fell ill with tuberculosis and were interned in a sanatorium in Jorn's hometown of Silkeborg, Cobra had expanded to include over 50 members from ten different countries, but the spirit of the original movement was in tatters. On the occasion of the second exhibit in Liège in 1951, Cobra was declared officially dead.

The making of the purist[9]

The time of destruction is at an end. A new age is dawning: the age of construction.
De Stijl, Manifesto V, 1923.

Many accounts of Constant's life mention a crucial stay in London during the first half of 1953 as the watershed in his career.[10] The painter, on a grant from the British Arts Council in Paris, walks the streets of the devastated city, drifting through wasteland and construction sites, absorbing and learning. The London experience is seen as the moment when the overriding importance of spatial construction (call it *architecture*) begins to dawn on Constant, and when the promise of the *terrain vague* starts to enthral him.

The period that marks the painter's change of course is slightly tricky to reconstruct. Constant spent a total of two and a half years in Paris (1950–52) before heading for London. At first, the prevailing "abstract" artistic climate in Paris, however cosmopolitan, alienates him profoundly.[11] During his stay, however, Constant becomes close friends with fellow artist Stephen Gilbert, an Englishman and former Cobra member. It is safe to say that this relationship has a crucial influence on Constant during the following years: the artistic development of the two men runs remarkably parallel as both begin to search for ways to move beyond the limits imposed by painting – relic of bourgeois culture

3. The founding members of the Experimentele groep. Top to bottom: Appel, Corneille, and Constant in Appel's attic studio in Amsterdam, ca. 1949.

– and the emotionally tainted Cobra legacy. Very rapidly Constant's work begins to turn into the very direction he so manifestly despised. On his canvases large planes of strong, serene and pure colour slowly begin to take the place of the direct, frenzied "materialism" characteristic of the Cobra period. *De rode vuist* (fig. 1) from 1952 is a good example. The paintings explore the compositional and emotional impact of pure colour and shapes, and with these increasingly *formal* investigations, Constant was not only cleaning the slate, but also learning a new language at an astounding pace.[12] When he comes to collaborate with Aldo van Eyck in the exhibition *Mens en Huis* – which opens at the Stedelijk Museum in November of 1952, shortly before the departure to London – the two men pick a recent painting by Constant to use in their installation: it bears only the slightest trace of figuration or motifs. But it is the composition of the double-cube space *as a whole* – in fully exploring the space-defining quality and capacity of colour – that will have a lasting impact. The fruit of Van Eyck's and Constant's common effort – minimalist, abstract, and artificial – proves to be an exceptionally *moving* experience. Thus with colour, enter *space*.

In the early thirties Paris had become the place of exile for many of the key figures working in an abstract/constructivist idiom in modern art: Naum Gabo and his brother Antoine Pevsner flocked there, as did many former teachers of the Bauhaus and the artists of De Stijl.[13] Much of the work that had centred on the group *Abstraction-Création* was then continued after the war, though many of the masters had either passed away or dispersed; the majority had moved to the United States to flee German occupation. In the post-war years the most important focal point for the revival of the constructivist strain was the gallery of Denise René, the *Salon des Réalités Nouvelles* (an annual art show first held in 1946 with the intent of promoting "abstract, concrete, constructivist and non-figurative art") and the Groupe Espace (founded in 1951 by André Bloc, sculptor-editor-critic and one of the crucial figures in post-war French architecture and art). The developments in Paris were echoed in other countries, and often these were instigated by the original innovators. Laszlo Moholy-Nagy, for instance, in exile in the U.S. like many of his former Bauhaus colleagues, continued throughout World War II with the groundbreaking research he had conducted in Dessau.[14] In Switzerland, another safe haven in wartime, Max Bill and Richard Paul Lohse, amongst others, carried on the torch.[15] In England, finally, artists like Barbara Hepworth and Ben Nicholson, who had been closely involved with the continental constructivist avant-garde, saw their efforts continued after the war by the Constructionists, a group of young artists that included Adrian Heath, Anthony Hill, Victor Pasmore and (on the fringes) Roger Hilton.[16]

In hindsight, Constant's trip to London bears many traits of a pilgrimage.[17] The list of people the artist visited during his stay in England looks like a *Who's Who* of British constructivist art. Not only did he call on Nicholson and Hepworth (as well as the sculptor Henry Moore) in their St. Ives studios, but he also quickly became friends with Anthony Hill and Victor Pasmore, with whom he had lengthy discussions about his budding ideas about space, colour and construction. These encounters, and the invigorating sight of buildings going up all over town – the inebriating ethos of (re)construction – clearly made Constant realize that it was time to think about a new medium. In pursuing this goal, the essential task he had set himself as an artist a few years earlier, his outlook, remained unchanged. Art would be "a weapon of the human spirit, as a tool for the construction, the transformation of the world, and the artist as a diligent worker who subordinates all his abilities, all his activities to the common effort and who does not seek to be great but to be useful."[18] And in the face of the rapid and ubiquitous changes taking place outside the confines of the profession, painting pictures to hang on walls clearly was not going to do the trick. The new art would be spatial and all-encompassing, or not be at all.[19]

Constant returns to Amsterdam in the early summer of 1953, his mind made up. One of his first undertakings is to make a series of lithographs of the installation at the *Mens en Huis* show, accompanied by a text that takes the form of a manifesto, "Voor een spatiaal colorisme",[20] synthesizing his ideas about colour-space synergy. Meanwhile he borrows books on construction from Aldo van Eyck, and immerses himself in the ripping prose of concrete manuals and steel dimension tables.[21] Also he starts to accompany his friend Van Eyck to meetings of the Amsterdam/Rotterdam-based modernist groups De 8 and Opbouw, the Dutch tributaries of CIAM. And with Stephen Gilbert, who still lives in Paris, he begins to elaborate a theoretical framework for their common efforts towards the new art of space, colour and construction. In the three and a half years following his return from London, he and Gilbert effectively form a duo, and both will become members of the *Salon des Réalités Nouvelles*.[22] Not surprisingly, their journey of discovery begins with Piet Mondrian and De Stijl.

There are aspects of Neo-Plasticism that would, at the time, have appealed to Constant instantly. To begin with, De Stijl is not for the faint-hearted. The project put forward by Van Doesburg,

Mondrian, Van Eesteren, et al., in their various manifestoes and writings is nothing less than a call for a totally new beginning, a *tabula rasa* that gives birth to a world of pure form and three-dimensional construction. It proposes an *elementarist*, and therefore intrinsically tectonic, architectural art. Even in its painterly output, it is fundamentally spatial – a point that Constant would repeatedly make with regard to Mondrian.[23] The esoteric, idealist and theosophical overtones would clearly have been shunned by Constant, but the holistic call for a universal and, most importantly, *non-individualistic* art, that transcends style to form an "objective" plastic figuration, would have been music to his ears.[24] In its rejection of the old world, and its attempt to create a universal art, De Stijl, perversely, echoed what to Constant was essential in Cobra. In fact the painting of Cobra – however well-intentioned as an egalitarian people's art – by comparison would seem suspect, too much part of the old idealist culture of the Ego. De Stijl's legendary call for "the development of a universal means of creation for all arts" and "an end to the division between art and life" in its "Creative Demands" of 1922, as well as its insistence that "painting separated from the architectonic construction (i.e. the picture) has no right to exist" struck a chord with Constant: in the creation of this new spatial art, solid teamwork between architects and artists (with the perspective of their synthesis annex dissolution in a spatial meta-art) would be paramount. Finally, the inherent anti-technological undertone of Cobra with its celebration of the primitive and "barbaric"[25] and the difficulties of linking artistic praxis with the reality of the machine age – quite unlike "objective" and "rational" Neo-Plasticism – became glaringly obvious. For the Marxist Constant, ignoring the technological *Unterbau* was little short of a cardinal sin.

The laborious trajectory through the arguments on which line to take vis-à-vis De Stijl and other predecessors, like the Russian Constructivists and Suprematism, is charted in various letters during the course of 1953 and in a little notebook that Gilbert filled with his ideas – still to be found in Constant's archive today, with the Dutchman's comments and "corrections" jotted down in pencil in the margins. From the correspondence it becomes clear that Constant, given his contacts with the Dutch CIAM members, was the first to abandon painting completely, soon to be followed by Gilbert.[26] With his friend, Constant – now completely focussed on furthering the cause of a total spatial art as prophesized and pioneered by De Stijl – would undertake various attempts to issue a magazine and form a movement.

One of the ongoing initiatives in the first two years of their long-distance collaboration (Gilbert still lives in Paris, with a short stay in London in 1954) – is to publish a magazine under the header "Art & Habitat",[27] which shows that Constant's contacts with De 8 and Opbouw were bringing notions into play that were adopted from contemporary architectural discourse.

When the artist joins in with the biweekly meetings in 1953, he finds himself in the middle of the deliberations surrounding the ninth CIAM conference in Aix-en-Provence. It is at this meeting that tensions visibly begin to develop between the older generation – signers of the Athens Charter – and the younger batch, the most radical of whom were to form Team X. The central theme that would dominate discussions throughout the 1950s was "Habitat",

4. Constant and Aldo van Eyck, *Ruimte in kleur* at the *Mens en Huis* exhibition, Stedelijk Museum, Amsterdam, 1952

a notion introduced to broaden the understanding of the city, and to help move beyond the strict functionalist categories of the Athens charter. In many ways "Habitat" was the header under which the older generation hoped to modernize CIAM and avoid an outright rupture between themselves and the young dissidents. Though the notion of Habitat remained somewhat open for interpretation – perhaps surprising as the 1953 conference was originally meant to produce a *Charte de L'Habitat* to complement the Athens Charter – it clearly tried to reconnect to the original CIAM calling: to provide "an environment able to satisfy the material and emotional needs of man and to stimulate his spiritual development." It is this phrase that Constant would quote time and again in his discussions with artists and architects alike.

In the shifting of the balance within CIAM there was not only a new emphasis, for instance, on the core of the city – the main theme of the eighth conference in Hoddeston, 1951 – but also an increasing call for the involvement of artists in the creation of the human environment. In fact the grand old men of CIAM, Le Corbusier – himself a painter – and theorist/historian Siegfried Giedion were the ones who advocated more interdisciplinary collaboration. The theme of the "Synthesis of the Arts" would be the single most important leitmotif of the 1950s, which would inspire modernist architects, painters and sculptors to engage in some form of collaboration: usually (and sadly) quite compromised. That architects were inviting artists to come play with them,

5. Constant, colour scheme for the *Woonsuggestie* designed in collaboration with Gerrit Rietveld, Bijenkorf department store, Amsterdam, 1954

however, was a calling Constant and Gilbert were eager to answer. As Constant put it: "The whole development from two sides means it is time for the painter to abandon his ivory tower of personal expression, to enter space, and with it, engage in society."[28]

In the Netherlands both generations of CIAM were represented in De 8 and Opbouw. Among its members were pre-war greats such as Cornelis van Eesteren, Gerrit Rietveld, and Mart Stam (the first two, of course, with a vital role in De Stijl) but also the eager adepts of Team X: Constant's friend Van Eyck and Jaap Bakema. The intense discussions about the tenets of CIAM urbanism and the collaboration with the arts – all set against the background of the flight that modernist architecture was taking in the years of post-war reconstruction – positively exhilarated Constant. Proximity to the people who were by and large optimistically and zealously committed to modernization, and who were (most importantly) shaping the world along these lines, made him feel he was in a position in which he might actually be *useful*. With De 8 and Opbouw, Constant pays visits to some canonical modernist buildings: a trip to Brinkman en Van der Vlugt's 1929 Van Nelle factory in Rotterdam reportedly brings him to unknown

heights of ecstasy.[29] Not unimportantly, these outings would add to his understanding of the formal idiom of Modernist architecture. His presence at the meetings leads to yet another collaboration with an architect, and this time round it is none other than Gerrit Rietveld. In early 1954 they collaborate on a model interior in the Bijenkorf department store in Amsterdam, and again, as in the "Mens en Huis" exhibit with Van Eyck, Constant is responsible for the colour scheme. In the Bijenkorf, what he produces is truly *applied* art.

If this now appears as rather a pejorative term, one must bear in mind that "application" (i.e. integration into life) was exactly what Constant was happy to engage in and battle for. To him, creating good, modern form was clearly a task that morally and intellectually justified itself: aiding the emergence of the "new art" was intrinsically *political*. Still, with collaboration as the first task at hand in the making of "habitat" and complete teamwork and plastic unity as the final goal, it is also evident that Constant, at first, did not intend actually to *take over* the task of the architect. He repeatedly stresses that in the shaping of the new art, annex human "habitat", *teamwork* is an absolute prerequisite. However, he makes it perfectly clear that the role of the "artist-plastician" (as he comes to coin the phrase) is essential in remedying the failures and limitations of the architect proper. Constant argues that for too long modernism has considered it adequate to look exclusively at functional and economic considerations and material needs, all but neglecting the "psychic and emotional function" of architecture. Colour and plastic quality (i.e. aesthetic, sensorial impact) should therefore become the speciality of the artist-plastician, crucially complementing the task of the architect, who naturally retains his role of engineer-planner.[30] Given the taboo on form in so much of early CIAM rhetoric – and the acute identity crisis modern architecture now found itself in – who could possibly blame the artist for making his case along these lines?

An exchange of letters between Constant and Gerrit Rietveld, shortly after their collaboration in the Bijenkorf, gives us some clues as to how many architects, some of whom certainly not opposed to collaboration *per se*, instinctively reacted to the artist's more radical integrationist "teamwork" views.[31] It is clear that Rietveld is rather sceptical. He considers it irresponsible that the artist should want to give up his autonomy, which enables him to experiment, free from the constraints of an external brief and practical considerations – enabling him thus to discover and prefigure what is *not yet there*. Moreover, in insisting that the décor should not overly impinge on life, Rietveld clearly implies that notions of a "total" interior – as in his own Schröder house – can be entertained in a one-off experiment at best, but certainly not in thinking about the world at large.[32] Finally, though this remains unsaid, Rietveld clearly doubts the usefulness of aesthetic-plastic specialization by the artist, feeling that Constant is moving onto his own turf. This fundamental resistance to interdisciplinary collaboration – architects' egos no more modest than those of painters – would gradually dawn on Constant.[33] More importantly, though, he soon began to see that most architects were quite content with restoring the old world and its social structures with the means of the new.

If we try to understand the art that Constant would like to see developed – intimations of which one can see in the sculptures and constructions he produces at the time – it is clear that regarding the delicate issue of *form* – ergo: *style* – a break with the modernist idiom is the last thing on his mind. Indeed the language of modern architecture is a harbinger of things to come. Constant is clearly thinking in terms of the geometric and the mechanical first and foremost: modern, pure and lyrical. Echoing many a pre-war modernist, he exalts: "in this culture that is in the process of being built, most artists do not partake, whereas an army of constructors, technicians and scientists are unconsciously contributing to the emergence of the world of forms in which the people of tomorrow shall live. A world of forms of a totally new and different beauty…"[34] Constant hence signals an inevitable aesthetic and stylistic convergence between the architectural-artistic on the one hand and the rational imperative of industry and science on the other – the result of increasing mutual cross-fertilization. The aesthetic no longer is out of touch with the "objective", as the emphasis, so he argues, in both domains necessarily shifts from individual genius and arbitrary discovery to teamwork and collective research. Hence emerges an art with a distinct idiom that, if developed to its full potential, can be at once moving and satisfying to the human eye and spirit and fully in tune with the machine age.[35] In the footsteps of Van Doesburg, we see Constant advocating and predicting the emergence of a total spatial art and a new, universal *order* which shall positively penetrate all domains of human habitat and which reflects the much-welcomed "de-subjectivation" of mankind at large.[36] Modern form is embraced in all its sensory delight: not as individualistic expression, but as an objective meta-art. And lest it not be obvious, this art is, of course, anathema to all decoration or ornamentation.[37]

It is with this radical agenda that the difference with most architects – as well as some unexpected similarities with Constant's *Cobra* ideology – begins to emerge. For Constant, the popular rallying call for the synthesis of the arts has a decidedly more far-reaching significance: the artistic perspective explicitly mirrors a social one. In both cases, *de-subjectivation*[38] is the key. In form and in content Constant sees a new, harmonious existence in the making, in which the dialectic of the culture of conflict and strife – outlined in various Cobra texts – come to a definite halt, arriving at an "order that lies at the end of the way".[39] The "decomposition

6. Constant, *Constructie met doorzichtige vlakken*, 1954

of the individual arts"[40] announces a coming social convergence in which oppositions truly fuse in a total, emphatically non-subjective synthesis. The idea of artistic teamwork and the notion of *Habitat* have a distinctly social and *utopian* connotation.

There is an additional observation that should be made. In Constant's various letters and manuscripts of this period there is in fact little discussion about the role the people inhabiting the purportedly emerging world should play: only about the greater historic flow of things. It is striking, in view of Constant's previous (and later) concerns, that his interest in the mid-'50s is primarily in planning and devising a spatial idiom *for* the new world. In this sense, Constant clearly echoes the attitude of many a modernist architectural reformer of his day: the artist-benefactor places himself formally at the service of humanity, and acts on its behalf. As yet, infusing *la poésie* – so desperately lacking – may be a prime concern to Constant, but the imperative *faite par tous* appears to extend mainly to the army of professionals in the field, be they artists, architects, planners or scientists. Judged by the written evidence, the radically egalitarian and participatory ideas of Cobra are either temporarily out of the picture, or simply projected into a faraway, "enlightened" future. So far, the word *play* has not entered Constant's vocabulary, nor has the notion of universal *collective creation*.

Ulitimately, Constant and Gilbert's plans to issue their *Art et Habitat* magazine fail to materialize.

Though Constant manages to get a number of his new 'constructionist' friends in England involved – Hill and Pasmore especially – and compiles an impressive shortlist of his new contacts in De 8 and Opbouw,[41] by the spring of 1954 the two men have to give up due to lack of funding. Nonetheless, during the following two years Constant and Gilbert persist in their attempts to form a movement, albeit in a different constellation. Their partner in the follow-up undertaking, *Néovision* (the name

7. Exhibition Liga Nieuw Beelden, Stedelijk Museum, 1955.
Two of Constant's constructions can be spotted in the background.

strongly reminiscent of the work of Laszlo Moholy-Nagy's 1930 book *The New Vision*), is the Hungarian-born Frenchman Nicolas Schöffer. Though the two years of collaboration are a chapter in their own right, in essence Constant's outlook and goals remain the same.[42] Thus when Holland sees the formation of a group with neoplasticist affinities, the *Liga Nieuw Beelden* (i.e. League of New Plasticism[43]), Constant immediately gets involved. The group, which advocated close interdisciplinary collaboration and equally responded to the new developments within CIAM, included sculptors, painters, graphic designers, and – of course – architects. Its call on artists to abandon their ivory tower, shed their "regressive" fears of the industrial condition, and "forge an alliance between the positive forces in the artistic, technical, pedagogic, scientific and commercial domain"[44] was in many ways directly up Constant's alley. Indeed for several years Constant showed his work at the *Liga* exhibitions in the Stedelijk Museum, and some smaller and larger assignments for outdoor sculptures would come his way, testing his abilities as a spatial "plastician".

The fact remains, however, that the *Liga* was a hotchpotch of rather well-mannered boys, and when the *Néovision* movement, in its turn, implodes in early 1956, the close relationship with Stephen Gilbert also comes to an end. Though Constant is now comfortably cruising in the right direction, his activities so far satisfy him only partly: for here we have a man who embraces progress wholeheartedly, but who feels that what is being produced in the real world invariably fails to live up to the promise of the exhilaratingly new, which he is convinced is within reach. His wish to form a movement radical enough to satisfy his burning desire to create the ultimate, truly ennobling and stimulating human habitat has not become reality.

Constant indeed seems "very far from Cobra"[45] when in the first half of 1956 correspondence with Asger Jorn suddenly intensifies: the Dane quickly takes over from Gilbert as Constant's main intellectual sparring partner. The invitation to the *Primo congresso degli Artisti Liberi*, to be held in Alba that same year, is soon to follow. And with this, things take a turn.

8. The clash of the avant-gardes, with Constant awkwardly in the middle: *Festival d'Art d'Avant-Garde*, Marseille, 1956. The photo shows a performance on the roof of Le Corbusier's Unité d'Habitation by Maurice Béjart's ballet company – featuring *Cysp I* (1956) by Constant's and Gilbert's *Néovision* partner Nicolas Schöffer. The meeting, organized by André Bloc c.s., was furiously attacked and ridiculed by the Paris Lettrists in their *Potlatch* journal.

Fiesta Gitana

Asger Jorn – invariably restless – had moved to Italy together with his new wife in 1954, after a prolonged period of recovery in sanatoria in Silkeborg and in Switzerland. Having acquired a taste for ceramics, he decided to settle in the little town of Albisola in the Piedmont region to work on pottery with the "nuclearist" painter Enrico Baj, whom he had met in Switzerland. From that moment on, Italy would become Jorn's third home (after Denmark and Paris); and though he did not join the *Movimento Nucleare* of which Baj was the leading figure, Jorn quickly got involved in the Italian art scene of the day, centred on nearby Milan. Here he would also become acquainted with Lucio Fontana (the master of *pittura Spaziale* and author of the infamous *White Manifesto*), ex-surrealist Roberto Matta, as well as with Giuseppe Pinot Gallizio, a chemical biologist who had turned to painting at a late age.

In Switzerland another meeting had taken place – with the "constructivist" and ex-Bauhaus-tutor Max Bill – that sparked off a polemic that would call on Jorn to form a movement of his own. Bill, like Laszlo Moholy-Nagy with his Chicago Institute for Design, had taken the initiative to form a "new" Bauhaus in Ulm, West Germany. Walter Gropius himself had given Bill his warmest support and the permission to use the old name for the new school.[46] At first Jorn was enthusiastic and promptly offered to come to teach, but Bill declined, arguing there was no place for painters at his institution. Given the fact that a number of important artists, most notably Kandinsky and Klee (the latter a personal hero of Jorn) had played a vital role at the original Bauhaus, Jorn's bitter disappointment and his subsequent, vicious attack on Bill were understandable. Opposition was promptly mounted under the banner of an "International Movement for an Imaginist Bauhaus, against an Imaginary Bauhaus", or MIBI in short. Insisting that "imagination precedes all creation", Jorn fought what he perceived as the essentially "reactionary" purism and functionalist doctrine that Bill was intent on introducing at the new Bauhaus – to the detriment of the fundamentally progressive and experimental attitude and openness to *imagination* that the old school, for all its justifiable Calvinist iconclasm, in view of the timeframe, had stood for. Jorn was adamant that censoring imagination – introducing a *Bilderverbot* by banning all free and pictoral prefiguration and exclusively focussing on practical development and implementation in the field of industrial design and architecture – was the greatest possible betrayal of the very "artistic inspiration" that had made the first Bauhaus a success. Ironically, many of the arguments Bill and Jorn exchanged in their correspondence mirror the contemporary debates Rietveld and Constant were having regarding "free" versus "applied" art.

The alternatives to Ulm that were – rather spontaneously and intuitively – developed in the ranks of the MIBI did not enjoy Constant's sympathy. On the contrary: Jorn clearly advocated a lyrical and overtly subjective experimental architecture that had little in common with Constant's "objective" spatial ideals, which the Dane considered sterile and retrograde. About which kind of architecture should be developed instead, Jorn was extremely vague.[47] Moreover, in his polemic against Bill, Jorn quickly got many of his painter colleagues on board (including, in the early phase of the MIBI, former Cobra members Appel and Pierre Alechinsky). It is clear that Constant, if pressed to choose, would have sided with Bill in matters of *painting*. In fact

9. Gallizio (wearing a hat) with gypsies in Alba, 1956

– to add an historical footnote – in the spring of 1956 Constant tried to get a teaching assignment in Ulm.[48] What brought Jorn and Constant back together – united in opposition to Bill – was the issue of a purely functionalist architecture.[49]

Jorn had engaged in various isolated polemics on the subject, off and on, ever since his work on a mural in Le Corbusier's *Pavillon des Temps nouveaux* at the Paris Exhibition of 1937, during an apprenticeship with the painter Fernand Léger. Even during the Cobra years, it had been Jorn who had briefly raised the issue of architecture by attacking dire functionalism and making a case for a sculptural and "symbolic" form of building.[50] In the years of the MIBI's polemic leading up to the Alba conference, he had published numerous texts criticizing functionalism for not acknowledging the emotional and aesthetic impact of architecture as a function in itself – for ignoring beauty as an essentially useful complement to strength and utility. Here were manifest parallels to Constant's aesthetic demands. Also, through the campaign against Bill, Jorn was back in an "architectural" frame of mind, and eager to talk about the subject – though only temporarily, as it would turn out. Perhaps surprisingly, it is then Constant who proposes to Jorn that they should further discuss their differences and possibly collaborate, though Constant insists he has not revised his position vis-à-vis the necessity of a total spatial art to replace painting.[51] Indeed Constant remains highly critical of what the MIBI had achieved so far: instead of producing a powerful and inherently architectural counter-proposal, or an all-encompassing strategy to balance the Ulm doctrine, all that Jorn had produced with his painter colleagues at the MIBI were expressionist ceramics.[52] When the avant-garde descends on Alba in September 1956, many disagreements between the "purist" Constant and the "painter" Jorn remain unresolved.[53]

The subsequent story is nearly legendary, as the *Primo Congresso degli Artisti Liberi* is the first major step in the foundation of the Situationist International. Though a tiny affair, from the perspective of Constant it was crucial. Jorn – ever the network person – had intended the conference to be a get-together of the most "advanced" practitioners in the field of art, with the aim of distilling a radical movement or network that incorporated many different, experimental approaches. Again Jorn was convinced

that an exchange of seemingly incompatible views, rather than dogmatic exclusion, was the way forward. On the invitation list one could therefore find Christian Dotremont on behalf of Cobra (who did not show up: Constant – however sceptical of the defunct group – officially took his place), a representative from the Chicago Institute of Design (did not appear, though Constant, ideologically speaking, may just as well have replaced him too) and Gil Wolman, representing a notorious but rather obscure little group from Paris that called itself the Lettrist International. Hosting the show were Jorn, now living in Albisola, a few miles down the road, Piero Simondo and Guiseppe Pinot Gallizio – the three on behalf of the MIBI. It is the confrontation with the ideas of the Lettrists, mainly, that would finally draw Constant back into the radical-surrealist post-Cobra network of Jorn and his friends after a four-year sabbatical in the constructivist desert.

Jorn had got to know Guy Ernest Debord, who headed the Lettrist International (LI), and Gil Wolman in Paris as early as 1954. A little network had soon developed comprising Jorn and his MIBI, the LI, and the radical heirs to the surrealist legacy in Belgium (including Cobra members such as Dotremont), who issued the magazine *Les lèvres nues*. The Lettrists were of the same pedigree, though younger; and, as the name of the movement discloses, they were not painters but mostly writers. Isidore Isou, a neo-Dadaist poet, had started the movement in the late 1940s, only to be bypassed as leader and then sent packing by Guy Debord, a young, leftist filmmaker and writer who had caused many a stir with his cinematic performances that went to great lengths alternately to alienate, to bore or to shock the audience out of their wits – sheer poetic terrorism. With his characteristic modesty, Debord added the suffix "International" to the name of the movement, to indicate the scope of its art and actions, and to make clear that nothing short of the complete overturning of the old world through a new revolutionary praxis was its first and final goal.

It is in the streets of Paris that the Lettrists developed the 'art' that would gain them a place in the history books. While painters such as Constant were shivering in their basements, and Sartre and his groupies were marking their black-sweatered presence in St. Germain-des-Prés, young *clochards* and drunk bohemians were playfully roaming the streets. Amongst these were Debord and his friends. What initially were inebriated wanderings from one bar to the next and getting lost along the way, soon developed into a well-defined activity known as the *dérive*, or "drift". The very word encapsulates the unstable, unplanned, and erratic course the Lettrists would follow through the dense Parisian urban jungle: they were driven wherever their whims and fancy took them. It is during these wanderings that the principles of "psychogeography" were developed, the Lettrist "science" of interpreting and mapping the city in terms of its capacity to stimulate *dérive* and to draw people to certain areas with characteristic, unique *ambiances*. Some areas would be more or less passionately "attractive" at certain moments; some would be more conducive to certain actions and modes of conduct than others. Parts of the city would form distinct "psychogeographic" units, areas of a certain unified *ambiance*. Through their playful spatial automatism – passion unleashed in constructed space rather than on a canvas or paper – the Lettrists discovered the crucial importance of décor, of the *mood* of architecture and of the city on the desires and actions of the drifting players. The two were fundamentally interrelated, so they found, and this insight was to form the basic premise of the artistic revolutionary practice they hoped to develop.

The next step from relatively passive interpretation of the existing urban scenery would be the creation of such unities of décor and act – the planning of even more powerful fragments of a living urban theatre. It is here, finally, that the notions of "Unitary Urbanism" and the constructed "Situation" come into play. If Unitary Urbanism can be seen as the dynamic décor that supports and triggers the unified artistic praxis, the Situation would be the final result: "a moment of life concretely and deliberately constructed by the collective organization of a unitary ambiance and a game of events".[54] Situations would thus be the basic building blocks of a continuous, integrated practice uniting décor and act, architecture and behaviour: a playful, passionate life-art.

Not surprisingly perhaps, the Lettrist dream strikes a chord with Constant, and it is this radical legacy – outlined here in condensed form – which he quickly begins to lap up and digest. A few months after the conference, he returns to the Piedmont town (having had a good time there, and now bringing along his flamenco guitar, and his new wife and children) to work in the "Experimental laboratory" of the MIBI with Pinot Gallizio and Piero Simondo. In December of 1956 Constant finally meets Guy Debord, who is on a little detour from his mother's home in Cannes. They hit it off immediately.

But Alba would leave yet another indelible mark on the artist. During his stay, he is confronted with the harsh conditions under which the local gypsy community tries to subsist. Chased from the town centre where they were used to put up camp, the gypsies had been offered a plot of land bordering the river by Pinot Gallizio. On his first visit to the site, Constant is overwhelmed by the people (their song and dance and *savoir-vivre*) but is shocked to see they live in total squalor. He then promptly decides to make a plan for a "permanent encampment". The model of this scheme – a stunningly beautiful piece made from an old table-top, segments of plexiglass and whirling steel strips and wires – is regarded as the symbolic beginning of New Babylon. Not only is this a plan for a permanent structure for a nomadic people, but it is also the first time that Constant works as a self-appointed planner according to a self-defined architectural brief. The seeming paradox of the programme and the inherently architectural working method would later be repeated and dramatically enhanced in the creation of his New Babylonian world.

Like a thoroughbred architect, Constant sends his plans for the gypsy encampment to the mayor of Alba, and though he receives little more than a polite thank-you[55], "il architetto Constant" comes into his own.

Signing the pact

Constant returns to Holland in early 1957, and does not take part in the founding conference of the Situationist International (SI) at Cosio d' Arroscia in September of that same year. With the foundation of the SI, Jorn's MIBI and Debord's Lettrist International officially fuse.[56]

If Constant's reluctance to get on board may at first seem unexpected, from written evidence it is clear that he was hesitant to join a movement that counted mostly painters amongst its members – it could therefore easily appear a *straightforward* continuation of Cobra, despite Jorn's pre-Alba promises that spatial construction and architecture would now be prime concerns.[57] One must bear in mind that this is the period in which Jorn's career begins to skyrocket, allowing him, after years of financial hardship, to follow Karel Appel down the road of public acclaim.[58] Indeed, by the time that Constant begins to consider joining the SI, the abstract expressionist strain of painting is the artistic standard in the West: the accepted style of the free world taking on the eastern block's socialist realist doctrine. With Pop art still in its infancy, Jackson Pollock, Mark Rothko, Willem de Kooning and others reign supreme in the United States, and Cobra's most glamorous painters – first the explosive Appel and now Jorn – are raised onto their pedestal by the art world. In Holland, Appel becomes a household name (the nation emerging from World War II-devastation now has its own pet Picasso) as the once so venomous Cobra is domesticated and snugly embedded in the nation's reconstruction myth. Jorn's sudden but overwhelming success largely coincides with an extremely fertile and productive phase in his painting, which may partly explain why he – more an initiator than a dogmatic ringleader by nature – leaves the day-to-day business and ideological nitpicking mostly to others, as he had done with Cobra many years before. With Jorn's full support – financial as much as moral – Guy Debord thus takes the reins of the movement and, crucially, is responsible for most of its

10/11. Lettrists in the streets, 1953. Scenes from the photo novella *Love on the Left Bank* by Ed van der Elsken

12. Constant, *Ontwerp voor een Zigeunerkamp*, 1957; 13. Constant, *Nébulose Méchanique*, 1958

publications, including the review *Internationale Situationniste*. Though Jorn's role remains vital, Paris rather than Alba is running the show: hopeful signs that Constant had been waiting for.

Whilst Jorn's star could be seen rising in official circles, Constant had clearly been invigorated and inspired by his stay in Italy. His work in 1957–58 illustrates that after the "purist" period of learning the words and then the language of spatial construction, a poetic and lyrical freedom resolutely sets in – the very poetry that Constant had himself announced and advocated in his contribution to the Alba conference.[59] His formal imagination is now positively running wild, as ovals and ellipses – sheer baroque *acceleration* – take over from the orthogonal framework as the constituent elements of the spatial construction. Though they are still static sculpture rather than architecture, the constructions are highly suggestive: pure energy and dynamism captured in a constructivist-expressionist idiom, revealing some parallels with the work of Tatlin and the Gabo-Pevsner brothers. However, where the constructivist sculptures of the latter two are "clean" and mechanical, Constant's latest constructions – like the gypsy

camp model – now bear all the marks of the intensity of the creative process: the scratched and scarred surfaces generate an intentionally unfinished look, whereas the doubling, tripling, quadrupling of the lines shows that the sculpture is really a chance freezing of motion rather than perfected form, for all its ingenious spatial complexity. The creative act and movement – both powerful and unfinished – are not only suggested through matter but also recorded in space, in every sense of the word. Indeed, references to the cosmic as well as to the ludic abound,[50] indicating that Constant is now not only connecting directly with the Lettrist's notions of play but is equally captivated by the ethos of the emerging space age. Again, these constructions are symbolic gestures that announce a totally modern spatio-dynamic world (to use Schöffer's phrase), in which, however, the glamour of the atomic era meets the raw energy of creation: the outlines of the great new Babylonian synthesis are taking shape. By 1958, not only Sputnik is in orbit: fuelled by years of formal research, Constant has now lifted off as well.

The inevitable pile of correspondence soon builds up between Constant and his new Parisian pen friend Guy Debord. From the start, the SI's *chef d'orchestre* is clearly intent on getting Constant involved in his new movement. His promises are tempting. In one of his first letters, shortly after their meeting, Debord makes a solemn pledge: "This movement must effectively be founded on the questions of psychogeography, the construction of ambiances, behaviour and architecture. Otherwise, there would only be empty waffle about painting or literature – all too well known."[61] Similarly, the infamous "red booklet" that Debord writes for the SI founding conference, the *Rapport sur la construction des situations*, ends on a high note: "We must put forward the slogans of unitary urbanism, experimental behaviour, hyper-political propaganda, and the construction of ambiances. The passions have been sufficiently interpreted; the point now is to discover new ones."[62] The last sentence, boldly echoing Marx' eleventh thesis on Feuerbach, cannot fail to strike a chord – nor can the dramatic call for collective action and a totally new artistic praxis in the paragraphs preceding it In fact, in its outline of the decomposition of bourgeois society and culture and especially in its *tone*, the text is strongly reminiscent of Constant's own 1948

14. Naum Gabo: untitled sculpture, Rotterdam, 1957

Manifesto of the *Experimentele Groep*. But better still, where the Manifesto was still largely concerned with painting, the *Rapport* advocates the search for the unknown total art.

Constant's enthusiasm, however, is heavily compromised. Published at about the same time is the *Rapport*'s counterpart: Jorn's *Critique de la politique économique*.[63] The arguments expanded in this booklet, which would be reiterated in *Pour la Forme*,[64] are by now familiar to Constant, and hark back to the discussion between Jorn and Max Bill. Again, in the critique and the alternatives suggested, Constant detects a fundamental hostility to the industrial condition. To him, the pamphlet only shows that Jorn remains, fundamentally, an Arts-and-Crafts technophobe who embraces perfidious individualist art. Clearly the days of the *rapprochement* between the old Cobra colleagues in early 1956 are now a transitory phase at best. Besides arguing that Jorn's book should be binned, Constant is quick to point out to Debord that the overall strategy presented as a programme for the SI in the *Rapport* is too unfocussed, making it clear that only a commitment to place all emphasis on the discovery of the *new* – as opposed to the techniques of purely artistic *détournement* or other forms of Situationist cultural guerrilla – might convince him to join the club.

Indeed it is the Dutchman's dogged insistence on the primacy of the illusive Unitary Urbanism that in November 1958 leads to the "Déclaration d'Amsterdam", a *de facto* contract with Debord that will bring Constant into the ranks of the SI – and keep him there, temporarily. The "Declaration" – along with the composite tripartite text entitled "On our means and our perspectives", also published in December 1958 in *IS* no. 2 – is the first tangible result of Constant's attempts to steer the SI in his direction.[65] After nearly a year and a half of playing hard to get, he enters the group, guns firing.[66]

In addition to Jorn's questionable architectural predilections and all-embracing temperament – not too consistent with the avant-garde rigour that Constant hopes to find under the wings of Debord – there is much that makes Constant deeply unhappy:

time and again the issue revolves around the question of which artistic praxis is appropriate to the most avant-garde of movements. Both Jorn and Pinot Gallizio, but also other SI members such as Maurice Wyckaert from Belgium, were avidly painting and not feeling too bad about it. Though Constant himself produced the occasional picture, it was clear to him that the interest in architecture amongst the SI's painterly faction – "the right wing", as Debord was to call it, much to Constant's delight – was either fleeting or non-existent: instead, other purportedly situationist practices were cultivated. Gallizio, for instance – together with his son Giors Melanotte – had developed and perfected the art of what he called "industrial painting", which consisted in producing near-endless strips of action brushwork which were then sold by the metre, the idea being that experimental painting could be made with minimal effort and sold to everyone at even lower cost: a Pollock for a pittance. The operation was theoretically legitimized as an effort to devalue individualist painting and, with its economic logic, undermine the art establishment from within. Jorn, with his *défigurations* and *modifications* – rather bland, realist or romantic paintings bought and then artistically 'enhanced', often to very comic effect – operated with the same basic logic. The results of this disciplinary *détournement* were charming and witty and had a pleasing shock effect, but they were bound to be quickly absorbed by the art establishment. Indeed, it does not take long before Gallizio's rolls of painting are bought in bulk (the *Laboratorio Sperimentale* finds it hard to keep up with demand) and Jorn's acts of painterly vandalism fetch astronomical prices. The joke wears thin.

Constant voices his grievances, attacking not only Jorn's less than embracing attitude vis-à-vis the industrial condition but again making it clear that painting, literature (Debord's former home turf), or anything else reeking of individualist art should have no place in the SI. Cultivating or toying with the remnants of them is, in Constant's view, simply too compromising: pointless necrophilia. "Let us leave to the official gravediggers the sad task of burying the corpses of pictorial and literary expression. The devalorization of what no longer serves us is not our affair; let others take care of it."[67]

15/16. At Pinot Gallizio's *Laboratorio Sperimentale*, Alba, 1958: endless rolls of *Pittura Industriale*. **Left: Gallizio, Jorn (centre, with hat) and Sandberg (right) admiring the merchandise**

17. Maurice Wyckaert, *Paysage au grand ciel*, 1961

The abovementioned "Amsterdam Declaration", which marks and cements the in-principle understanding between Debord and Constant, is a short eleven-point text holding the middle between a manifesto and a summary draft programme.[68] By writing six points of the document Constant not only sets the tone but also lays down his minimal demands: in his original points, the emphasis clearly lies on the necessarily progressive and state-of-the-art character of Unitary Urbanism.[69] More interestingly, however, Constant has begun to blend his ideas about interdisciplinary collaboration and teamwork with the ludic concepts of the Lettrists: the absolutely crucial notion of *collective creation*, which will bring forth unitary urbanism, is introduced. Debord then does some editing, adds five points of his own and reshuffles the whole document for publication.[70] Where Constant insists on the importance of science and progress, Debord harps on the realm of behaviour: in accordance with the ideas of psychogeography, he sees "new modes of behaviour" as essential to the new environmental art,[71] stressing the necessity to revolutionize everyday life. And where Constant emphasizes his novel concept of *collective creation*, Debord in his final points underlines the essential role of the construction of situations.

In fact, not a trace of the notion of "situation" had appeared in Constant's lines. Within the same document, though seemingly overlapping, "collective creation" and "situation" battle it out, their juxtaposition foreshadowing other differences of approach between the two men. For the time being, however, an agreement has been reached that appears to make Unitary Urbanism the SI's top priority, creating a formal basis to direct the emphasis away from the SI's painterly faction. With the contract signed, for the two-man "left wing" of the movement, Unitary Urbanism is now officially the way to go. Invigorated, Constant now immediately sets off to further the cause of the new art to come.

The Bureau and the model maker

Despite the budding behind-the-scenes intrigues through divisions into imaginary left and right wings (and an implicit middle ground), the group in early 1959 seems a jolly gang: certainly personal relationships remain quite good. The boisterous and charming Pinot Gallizio sends happy postcards to "architetto Constant Casanova", as does Maurice Wyckaert from Brussels, the city that again functions as a stopover between Paris and Amsterdam for Constant, Debord and the ever mobile Asger Jorn.

Encouraged by Debord and regarded with a certain admiration by the other SI members, Constant begins work on the first designs for a truly new situationist architecture, visualizing and making concrete the idea of Unitary Urbanism on a world scale: a city designed for endless *dérive* and situationist play. What Constant originally refers to as his "covered city" or "Dériville" is New Babylon taking shape, the final title eventually suggested to him by Debord.[72] In 1958, almost immediately after joining the SI, Constant builds the first of his *maquettes* – constructions halfway between an architectural model and a fanciful piece of spatial sculpture, but decidedly meant to be the first – each of which represents a "sector" (i.e. quarter) of the new city. Effectively, he spatially elaborates the schematic "Guide psycho-géographique de Paris" and "The Naked city" maps by Debord, turning an abstract ideogram into something almost buildable. As during his work on the gypsy camp, Constant plays the architect, now resolutely uniting the role of "artist-plastician" and planner, and harnessing all his talents and acquired experience. Within the space of barely a year an impressive number of sector models and various other scale constructions – visualizing sector interiors or the linking of the individual sectors – as well as numerous maps and plans are produced. The creative output is simply stunning. Not surprisingly, Debord is enthusiastic about the fruits of Constant's solo work.[73] As early as 1959, Constant's constructions and models are put on display at the Stedelijk Museum in Amsterdam – Constant's first one-man exhibition there – and Debord is more than happy to legitimize them ideologically.[74]

However, despite his creative burst. Constant is not intent on remaining the exotic loner: teamwork is what he joined the movement for, and given the lack of potential collaborators amongst the existing members of the SI, he is quick to suggest to Debord that they set up a "Research Bureau for Unitary Urbanism"[75] as a practical spearhead of the SI, and attract architects and other planning experts to staff it.[76] But here Debord is a little sceptical. Though claiming not to be unsympathetic to any practical development of unitary urbanism (tied as he is to the tenets of the Declaration), he fears that Constant, in his enthusiasm to remove himself from all that reeks of painting, may be rushing into the arms of other enemies:

But what speaks for itself is that we can hardly place any trust in "specialized collaborators" who do not share the Situationists' experimental positions. Otherwise we will have to learn the hard way that architects, sociologists, urbanists etc. are as narrow-minded as painters in their defence of the typical preconceptions of their specific disciplines (disciplines equally rendered obsolete, as much as the individual arts, by the necessity of a total praxis).[77]

Debord leaves the decision of whether such a Bureau is premature to Constant. The latter instantly starts recruiting, and the obvious place to start is the Liga Nieuw Beelden.

By the spring of 1959, Constant has found three collaborators. But where the notion of a 'bureau' (to architects at least) invokes images of organized, occasionally frenetic collective activity in testosterone-laden rooms with telephones ringing, this is hardly how one would describe Constant's newfangled organization. Though its individual members were quite exceptional characters, they did not make much of a team. First to join were the duo Har Oudejans and Ton Alberts, both architects. Oudejans was an active member of the Liga – in fact one of the first architects to join – and he and Alberts had started an office together. Of the three recruits of the *Bureau*, Oudejans was clearly the most dedicated and most involved in SI activity.[78] The most remarkable new member, however, was the poet-painter-journalist-musician Armando, one of the most interesting figures in post-war Dutch art. His involvement with the Bureau is quite puzzling, as the work he produced was clearly of an entirely different order than that of any member of the SI. Though he participated in the Liga, and was thus engaged in "integrationist" discussions and in the staging of collective exhibits, the position he took was often diametrically opposed to Constant's. Moreover, Armando was a member of the *Hollandse Informele Groep* and would soon emerge as one of the leading figures of the *Nulbeweging* – the Dutch equivalent of the Zero movement. Indeed Constant and Armando made strange bedfellows: for Armando the brief membership of the *Bureau* was nothing but a quirky intermezzo of rather little importance. He would soon lose interest.

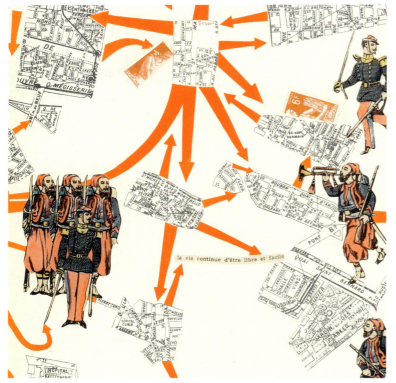

18. Miniature Lettrist universe: collage by Guy Debord, probably from early 1958 and made for Constant, playing with the urban fragments (*plaques tournantes*) and arrows of desire of the ideogrammatic *Guide Psychogéographique de Paris*. In its irony, this tiny gem oozes communard nostalgia.

All in all, Constant's Bureau, however militantly announced and promoted, was mostly bluff – much head but little body, and simply not a sufficiently unified force to be able to take a stand (let alone to develop a "collective" alternative) against the painterly "right wing" – in spite of Oudejans' genuine enthusiasm for the SI's cause. Still, with much aplomb, it is formally founded, and three of its four members – Constant, Oudejans and Armando – head off to Munich for yet another conference, only to find themselves socializing with a zealous gang of young, local painters: Asger Jorn's new recruits.

Men who love only once

The third conference of the SI is planned for the end of April 1959, to coincide with an exhibition of industrial painting by Pinot Gallizio in the gallery of Otto van de Loo, one of Jorn's most important art dealers. The context is not much to Constant's liking. Debord reassures Constant that the overlap between the conference and the Gallizio show is merely a practical coincidence; but to make matters worse, Munich is chosen as the venue so that the *ancien cadre* of the SI can become acquainted with the movement's new "German section": the SPUR group of painters who have recently been drawn into the SI family with the help of its Danish founding father, and with the tacit consent of Debord.

The actual meeting in the back room of a Bavarian hotel is opened by Constant, who makes a plea for the collective practical development of Unitary Urbanism.[79] Furthermore, during one of the sessions the Amsterdam Declaration is discussed, slightly modified (*opened up*, in fact, revealing the hand of Jorn) and adopted as a resolution by all the SI members, keeping Constant moderately happy. Meanwhile the Spur Group – Zimmer, Prem, Stadler and others – do little to conceal their admiration for the organization's semi-suppressed forebear, Cobra: what rings through is plain nostalgia and regret that they were not around ten years earlier. Oudejans – equipped with a camera and feeling like a kid in a candy shop – takes numerous snapshots of the participants, and the evidence shows that a fair amount of time was spent exploring the local beer halls. The conference is topped off by a merry get-together at Otto van de Loo's home, and the following day a Räte-Republik-style flyer – "Ein kultureller Putsch…während ihr schlaft!"– is distributed all over town to give the Bavarian bourgeoisie a pleasant little *frisson*. Despite all the apparent and underlying tensions between the now reinforced right and left wing, the conference is one of the high points in the history of the SI, bringing together all the early members of the movement in what appears an intense but happy little social gathering: Munich was simply great fun.[80]

Henceforth, sadly, it is a downward spiral. In the 14 months following the Munich conference, at regular intervals, tension will mount and rows erupt between Debord and Constant over the former's alleged lack of rigour with regard to the activities of Jorn and the painters. Though Debord was paying lip service to Unitary Urbanism and attacking the "ridiculous *Spuristes*" and the "reactionary buffoonery"[81] of Gallizio in his letters to Constant, he did little to curb effectively the painters' overall influence – and certainly not Jorn's. A manifesto published by the SPUR group co-signed by their Danish mentor (a document, fiercely anti-technological and individualistic to the extreme, ending with a

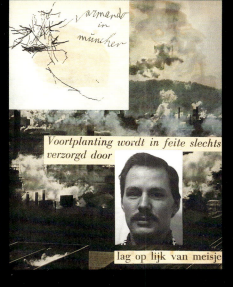

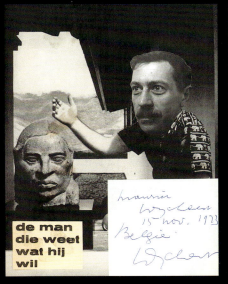

19–25. Collages by Har Oudejans, 1959. "Men who love only once: let them tackle your problem". Some of the main protagonists of the Munich conference. Top row: Constant ("working in the void"), Debord ("influences human behaviour"), and Armando ("reproduction is mainly provided by/lay on young girl's corpse"). In the middle: Helmut Sturm of the SPUR group ("Looking for something better?"), Maurice Wyckaert ("the man who knows what he wants") and Hans Peter Zimmer ("erratic").

clamorous "we are the painters of the future!")[82] is no less than a slap in the face for Constant. Debord does nothing against it, and the Dutchman feels increasingly betrayed. But Debord, too, has reason to complain. The weaknesses of Constant's Bureau become more than apparent as the next phase in the saga unravels: the preparation of the first official SI exhibition, to be held (again) at the Stedelijk Museum in Amsterdam. The overall responsibility for the organization is summarily handed down to Constant and his Bureau. It becomes a test case – but not only for the Bureau, but for the SI as a whole.

Several events pave the way for the tragic denouement. The first – described as the main "catalyst"[83] – is the "church incident" in the August 1959 issue of the Dutch architectural magazine *Forum*. Indeed the issue is symptomatic. The Liga Nieuw Beelden had been invited to guest-edit the issue, which provided an opportunity to promote the organization's annual exhibition.[84] The four Bureau members had seized the opportunity to take their seat on the editorial committee installed by the Liga for the occasion, hoping to turn the issue into a piece of propaganda for the SI. Debord is delighted with the potential PR and helps in the preparation by sending texts. The mission is a partial success, as the published issue of the magazine – dedicated to the Liga's habitual theme of artistic synthesis – culminates in the prophesy of the total fusion of art and life in a praxis of Unitary Urbanism. Oudejans and Alberts are responsible for a great deal of the lay-out,[85] making collages showing feats of technology and engineering – "Good form", to use Max Bill's terminology – with catchy newspaper clippings and Situationist quotes strewn about. However, Debord's initial euphoria is short-lived: he receives the *Forum* issue and discovers that amongst the pretty pictures – bang next to a piece of text on Unitary Urbanism – is a photograph of a model of a church, designed by Oudejans and his partner Alberts. At first Debord is slightly at a loss, wondering whether the church is a bad joke, a piece of *détournement* sadly gone wrong.[86] In fact it turns out to be the first major commission the two young architects received,

26. Constant, Gallizio and Jorn in Munich, 1959; 27. *The Cavern of Anti-matter* at Galerie Drouin, Paris, 1959

and not without pride they had decided to include it.[87] Admittedly, the combination of working for the Roman Catholic Church and being a member of the self-professed, "most advanced" avant-garde around is a bit tricky, so Debord makes it quite clear that should they even for a moment entertain the idea of building their design, they will be instantly excommunicated from the ranks of the SI. And with a warning to Constant and his gang that they should keep track of what is published in their name, the issue seems settled. Still, though the preparation of the Stedelijk exhibition is resumed as if little had happened, the incident clearly adds to Debord's irritation with Constant: in matters of intellectual avant-garde rigour, there seems to be an acute case of the pot calling the kettle black. More importantly, the intended and long-awaited resurrection of *Potlatch* – the "internal" stencilled bulletin of the SI, which Constant had agreed to take charge of as editor-in-chief – completely fails: only one issue makes it to the presses in the summer of 1959. Not only is it the last edition of the former Lettrist publication ever to appear, but the failure to revamp it and turn it into an organ of the SI's "left wing" is also an opportunity missed. Smaller and greater misunderstandings and aggravations pile up on both sides.[88]

The circus surrounding the SI exhibition in the Stedelijk has all the traits of a soap opera. Originally, Willem Sandberg had invited Pinot Gallizio to his museum to stage a solo exhibition of his industrial painting in the form of an installation.[89] Gallizio had done similar, smaller exhibits, for example at the gallery of René Drouin in Paris and at Van de Loo's in Munich. With his painted canvas strips he covered walls, ceilings and even attractive women who paraded through the rooms filled with music and perfume: behold Gallizio's fruity *Cavern of Anti-Matter*. Asger Jorn, however, manages to convince Sandberg that the exhibit should be expanded to become a general SI manifestation, which is then scheduled to open at the end of May 1960.[90] As the show is intended to include not only Gallizio's *tachist* wallpaper grottoes but also some enigmatic contraptions devised by painter Maurice Wyckaert – "detourned fences", all integrated in a labyrinthine configuration featuring lights, sounds, smells and smoke guns – some essential co-ordination and planning are required.

Whereas the installation is meant to approximate the effect of a *micro-ambiance* in Unitary Urbanism, Constant's models, set up in an adjacent "documentation" room, would give the public an

idea of how the condensed ambiance fits into the larger scheme for a totally 'situationist' city. To approximate the future activities on the scale of the city, the idea is floated to complement the extravaganza in the rooms of the museum with a high-tech *dérive* in the streets and alleys of the centre of Amsterdam: situationists equipped with walkie-talkies are to be set free in the urban décor, with Constant as the overall director of operations in a control room charting their course. The various fragments combined – the atmospheric interior labyrinth, Constant's models and the ludic behaviour outside the museum gates – would enable the public to sample what Unitary Urbanism and the construction of situations might actually look like one day.[91]

For a long time, very little happens on the exhibition front. Half a year has passed when an impatient Debord writes to Constant and his Bureau colleagues, asking them how many members of the Dutch section are actually involved and whether they intend to go through with the exhibition given the minimal activity so far.[92] Though plans for the museum installation are then promptly drawn up by Oudejans, Constant for a long time plainly refuses to include most of the painters in the preparations – for reasons well known, and with the initial consent of Debord – resulting in irritation for Jorn and the Spur Group. Financial problems raise their head. Fire-safety requirements are not met. With a great deal of noise, a few weeks before the planned opening, the show is cancelled. The official SI explanation puts the blame on museum director Sandberg for imposing impossible practical limitations, forcing the SI to withdraw entirely so as not to sell out their avant-garde principles.[93] Countering the official version, it has been argued that it is Jorn – the man who had talked Sandberg into hosting the exhibition in the first place – who finally pulls the plug from the crippled manifestation, fed up as he is with the lack

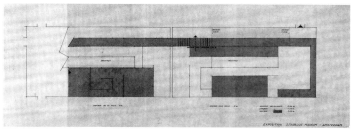

28. Plan for SI exhibition at the Stedelijk Museum, 1960

of goodwill and co-operation amongst the bickering factions.[94] Pinot Gallizio, solo, steps in to fill the gap in the Stedelijk's calendar, as if the SI exhibit had never existed. One can hardly avoid concluding that a public and artistic display of unity in the SI, let alone a timid demonstration of its revolutionary new artistic praxis, was never meant to be.

On our means and our perspectives II

The new architecture shall undertake its first practical exercises with the détournement of once well-defined affective blocks of ambiance (the castle, for example). The use of détournement, in architecture as in the constructing of situations, signifies the re-investment of products abstracted from the ends contemporary socio-economic organization gives them, and a break with the formalist wish to abstractly create the unknown. This means liberating existing desires at once, and deploying them within the new dimensions of an unknown actualization.

Guy Debord, 17 May 1960.[95]

Though it is reasonably clear that Constant and Jorn were on an entirely different wavelength regarding what action merited the label 'situationist' (though it was generally agreed that all undertakings of the SI were at best proto-situationist, an intimation of a superior future practice), the dividing line between Constant and Debord is more difficult to draw. With the signing of the *Amsterdam Declaration*, Constant had hoped that the shift would occur in his favour, by either isolating Jorn (which would have meant causing a break between Jorn and Debord) or converting the Dane to the just cause. One may speculate whether Constant gambled that Debord would perform an encore of his *coup d'état* on the founding fathers of the Lettrist movement, when the "left wing" mercilessly booted out the "right wing". But any of these scenarios would seem rather unrealistic. Not only was Jorn, as he had been in Cobra, the bridge-builder who had brought the LI and MIBI together (though admittedly on the basis of Debord's draft programme in the "Rapport"), but he was also Debord's close friend and ally in a number of satisfying collaborations: Debord's *Mémoires* and *Fin de Copenhague* are but two concrete examples. Last but not least, Jorn had both influence and cash: without him, it is questionable whether the IS journal would have appeared at all.[96] In the Jorn-Debord-Constant triad, the Dutchman was the newcomer. In many ways, Debord and Jorn saw eye to eye. It is here also that the divisive but inevitable overlap of style, attitude and outlook becomes apparent.

The first, most obvious issue – regarding means – is of course the use of the technique of *détournement*, the central concept in Debord's thinking. As long as it was turned against itself, painting, writing, film, any art form or cultural convention could be used in the battle: "by all means, even artistic". The anti-art tactic of intentional alienation was one of Debord's pets, and Constant's rejection of one of the crucial techniques of the SI brought him not only into conflict with the merrily *detourning* painters but ultimately with Debord himself. Though it never was an overt issue between the two men, Constant's insistence on developing and prefiguring a new collective art largely *ex ovo* clearly bothered Debord, as can be inferred from the quote above. In Constant's thinking, *il fallait être absolument moderne* and the old could and should be ignored. To Debord, on the other hand, the old – attacked and reconfigured – was instrumental. Even the very

notion of Situation – Debord's Holy Grail and both *means* and cultural *perspective* – is unthinkable without it: in situations, *normality* is always implicit and history a given. Constant's emphasis, on the other hand, lies exclusively on Unitary Urbanism (or at least on his conception of it): the holistic, radically new spatial art of the permanently extra-ordinary. Though again an overlap seems at hand, one side has Dadaist overtones, whilst the other has a constructivist baseline.

The pedigree and avant-garde predilections of the two men remain telling: where the *Rapport* discusses at length the achievements and failures of Futurism, Dada and Surrealism, nothing is said about the constructivist strain of modern art, let alone De Stijl – Constant's adopted intellectual forebears. The division also becomes apparent in Constant's early attacks on matters near-sacred to Debord, when he rejects not only Gilles Ivain's seminal 1953 essay "Formulary for a new urbanism"[97] – still one of the key texts of Lettrist Unitary Urbanism – but also the *Palais Idéal* by the industrious postman Cheval. Needless to say that Louis II of Bavaria, the mad sovereign with his film-set fairy-tale kitsch (Disney 'camp' *avant la lettre* that aspired to the status of *Gesamtkunstwerk*) and the dramatic sunset *vedutes* of Claude Lorrain[98] were not Constant's cup of tea. In each case, the inherent nostalgia, near-vulgarity and lack of *newness* would have been criticized.[99] And though Constant, in the early phase of their collaboration, goes to great lengths to 'educate' Debord and convince him of

29. Ton Alberts and Har Oudejans: Mariakerk in Volendam, 1957–62

the merits – formal and political – of the De Stijl-Suprematist-Constructivist legacy, to the Frenchman this 'purist', seemingly formalistic modernism remains profoundly alien.[100]

Though style tends to be at the core of most human conflicts, these ancestral rifts – which put Debord in one camp with Jorn, and at a distance from Constant – would not have been an insurmountable obstacle for collaboration on Unitary Urbanism. The tragedy in the short but intense relationship between Debord and Constant is that where the latter remained unwavering in his belief that a *practical* development of Unitary Urbanism was the SI's only way forward, Debord was gradually but unmistakably losing faith. Increasingly doubtful, he began to distance himself from his early promises to Constant that the SI would be a movement that marked the shift from "utopian revolutionary art to a experimental revolutionary art".[101] The very fact that he refused to eliminate the painterly "right wing" is not only an act of tactical scheming – playing one side against the other, merely asserting that it takes two wings to fly – or loyalty to Jorn; it also shows that Debord felt, deep down, that all prefiguration of a future artistic praxis was not only potentially compromised but also a manifest impossibility: a matter, therefore, to be avoided.

As we have seen, from the very beginning Debord expresses his doubts about Constant's ideas for a Bureau for Unitary Urbanism, fearing it may be "premature". Though for a while at least, Debord manages to push his reservations aside, he refuses to put all his eggs in one basket: the Bureau will have to prove itself worthy, before any measures against the painters are undertaken.[102] It is this wait-and-see attitude – the refusal to take a leap of faith – that Constant begins to find increasingly irritating. Both, in fact, had a point: working on the (preferably) full-scale realization of first trials of Unitary Urbanism meant the risk of failure in the limelight. Here Debord's typically avant-gardist fear of being pinned down and "overtaken" (dépassé) becomes apparent. Constant, inversely, would argue that continuing to operate inside gallery land – or worse still: planting bombs and staging coups in splendid theoretical isolation – was not going to advance their declared prime perspective very much either: it necessarily implied getting one's hands dirty. The issue reflects a fundamental difference in outlook regarding the immediate task at hand.

Constant did not fail to insist that a new culture and a new society would emerge – and was *bound* to emerge – by itself or not at all, and that the best that a creative artist could possibly do is to aid in the construction of the world of new forms and new thoughts through practical experiment. To Debord this attitude bordered on reformism.[103] The Frenchman, on the other hand, clearly began to cultivate the idea that an artistic avant-garde had the task to aid in bringing about a *political* revolutionary breakthrough, for which he considered the conditions suitable.[104] Constant, no less politically astute, would in turn dismiss this as revolutionary romanticism and pre-war avant-garde nostalgia: as "utopian" in the pejorative sense of the word.[105] It is clear that though Constant believed that artists should be aware of history's relentless drive, he believed as well that they should move beyond the immediately *political* and focus on preparing for the coming world. Artistically, not politically, they should lead the way. For Debord history (and the moment of its revolutions) must be made; for Constant, history drives itself.

30. Guy Debord, Michèle Bernstein and Asger Jorn in Paris, 1960

Debord's arguments in the correspondence with Constant indeed announce the SI's gradual change of course, away from art and towards the political realm, a movement which will be accelerated when Constant leaves the SI. The field of prefiguration of a future *artistic* praxis – now regarded a "formalist wish abstractly to create the unknown" – would soon be abandoned in favour of a strictly political activism based on a *critique* of the present. As was stated shortly after Constant's departure from the group, "our conception of urbanism is a critique of urbanism" – an echo of Engels' famous dictum from *Die Wohnungsfrage*.[106] Looking beyond the horizon became a taboo. Critique and politics, agitation and causing a stir for its own sake become the preoccupation. Ultimately, the seemingly unshakable optimism that drove Constant – the faith in the *new* that announced the dawning of a new age – was not shared by Debord: though time and again described as being in the ultimate stages of decomposition, the many-headed monster of the spectacle society would not just roll over and die. The old world was all too present and resilient, despite its festering wounds. The attack would have to be intensified. As nothing could ever meet the high and absolute expectations of either the Situation or Unitary Urbanism, the revolution itself became the more immediate concern. The time for a new art had not yet arrived, and it was pointless to look for it. From *détournement* to revolution is but a small linguistic step: the Lettrist dream of Unitary Urbanism is abandoned. A constructive attitude is eclipsed by an activist defeatism.

The importance of the exhibition at the Stedelijk for both men now also becomes clear. Expectations were quite different: for Debord, this was to be a scandal, a media event to rock the world and place his revolutionary avant-garde on the map. Constant hoped it might be a first step, however tentative, in the promotion of Unitary Urbanism, despite the risk that the exhibit might be a compromised show staged by a heavily divided group of people. Neither was to happen. In any case, the setback in the summer of 1960 in the development of an artistic praxis made it clear to Constant that he remained an outsider within the IS: not only were perspectives divergent, but also all superficial consensus on the means had evaporated.

Break-up II

After the Stedelijk exhibition is cancelled things begin to move quickly. Though Debord summarily excludes Pinot Gallizio from the collective for rising to the occasion and doing his solo show in the museum, the SI's presses print a monograph of his work.[107] Meanwhile, Constant's Bureau colleagues Oudejans and Alberts are formally excluded because they have agreed to build their church. Constant is furious. In an acrimonious letter to Debord he attacks the painters and the continuing support for them. Directly criticizing the front man's lack of direction, Constant puts Debord on the spot, and asks him whether he is prepared to honour their original agreement and collaborate with him on the basis of the Amsterdam Declaration. Debord's answer remains evasive: "I'm not contesting that one could, in many respects, find a multitude of weaknesses in our position, but do you really think that anyone would ever seriously hold that against us? Passion is blinding you." The very same day, Constant replies with a telegram: "If passion is blinding me, indecision has made you lose your way."[108] A better summary cannot be provided.

So at the end of June 1960 – after less than two rather tumultuous years as a member – Constant, the last Unitary Urbanist, resigns from the SI. "Unitary Urbanism will historically belong to those who have made something of it" he warns Debord.[109] Turning his back on compromised collective action, Constant decides to continue on his own. The stage is now set for the grand synthesis of the work and experiences of the previous dozen years: poetry made by all. Enter New Babylon.

Notes

1 "Die, ye old forms and thoughts / slave-born, awake! / new forces are now driving this world / Desire has touched us": 5th–9th lines of the Dutch version of the *International*, with which Constant opens his anthology *Opstand van de Homo Ludens. Een bundel voordrachten en artikelen* (Bussum: Paul Brand, 1969).

2 Undated document marked '1953' in Constant's handwriting, File "Correspondentie 1953", Constant archive, Rijksbureau voor Kunsthistorische Documentatie, The Hague (henceforth: RKD). All English translations of RKD correspondence and documents are by the author, unless otherwise mentioned. Jorn's passing remark that he "is currently doing some ceramics" is consistent with his taking up pottery in Silkeborg at the time. See Guy Atkins, *Asger Jorn. The crucial years 1954–1964. A study of Asger Jorn's artistic development from 1954 to 1964 and a catalogue of his oil paintings from the period* (London: Lund Humphries, 1977), pp. 17–18.

3 See for instance H. van Haaren, *Constant* (Amsterdam: Meulenhoff, 1966), F. de Vree, *Constant* (Schelderode: Kunstforum, 1981; Kunstpocket Serie 2 / N. 10), Jean-Clarence Lambert, *Constant: les trois espaces* (Paris: Cercle d'art, 1992), Mark Wigley, *Constant's New Babylon: The Hyper-Architecture of Desire*, exhibition catalogue (Rotterdam: 010 Publishers and Witte de With, Center for contemporary art, 1998), Marcel Hummelink, *Après nous la liberté. Constant en de artistieke avant-garde in de jaren 1946–1960* (Amsterdam: no publisher, 2002). This last book – a PhD thesis by Constant's 'biographer' – is the most detailed chronological account to date of the years leading up to the solo New Babylon work.

4 This is a very summary rendering of Cobra's pre-history. For more facts on the origins and development of Cobra see: Willemijn Stokvis, *Cobra: geschiedenis, voorspel en betekenis van een beweging in de kunst van na de tweede wereldoorlog* (Amsterdam: De Bezige Bij, 1974), updated edition published under the title *Cobra: de weg naar spontaniteit* (Blaricum: V+K Publishing, 2001), French edition *COBRA* (Paris: Gallimard, 2001); Willemijn Stokvis, *Cobra: de Internationale van experimentele kunstenaars* (Amsterdam: Meulenhoff / Landshoff, 1988), English translation *Cobra: An international movement in art after the Second World War* (New York: Rizzoli, 1988); Jean-Clarence Lambert, *Cobra: un art libre* (Paris: Editions du chène, 1983), English translation: *Cobra* (London: Sotheby, 1983).

5 See *Reflex, Orgaan van de Experimentele Groep in Holland* nr. 1, reprinted in Gérard Berreby, *Documents Relatifs à la fondation de l'Internationale Situationniste* (Paris: Editions Allia, 1985), pp. 20–29. This opinion is voiced by Willemijn Stokvis: *Cobra: de weg naar spontaniteit*, p. 186. Though there are numerous polemical writings by Jorn and Dotremont especially, none have the militant drive and sheer evocative power – let alone *focus* – of Constant's roaring text.

6 During my first visit with Gertjan Nijhoff to the artist's studio in the summer of 1999, Constant remarked that the founding members of Cobra shared the view that endless theoretical talk within the ranks of the Surrealists was just not enough: "We wanted to *make* things." According to Constant, Cobra's prime objective lay in the search for a truly authentic artistic praxis.

7 Constant Nieuwenhuys, "C'est notre désir qui fait la revolution", *Cobra. Organe du front international des artistes experimentaux d'avant-garde*, nr. 4. English quote taken from *Figurative Art since 1945* (London: Thames and Hudson, 1971), p.151.

8 This rather sad episode is described in Stokvis, op. cit., p. 261 (see also page 246 regarding the Stedelijk) and Atkins, op. cit., pp. 15–16.

9 The term is used by Jorn in his 1953 letter to Constant (note 2): "As long as it amuses you, feel free to follow this line of action, and I know you will stop and switch over to other things when it no longer intrigues you, and all this is fine: only do not deny yourself ABSOLUTELY by losing all perspective on the past. (…) You have to be generous to be an artist, and you are far too generous to become a purist."

10 The earliest description of the 'London experience' that most historians base their account on can be found in Van Haaren, op. cit., p. 8.

11 "Nearly all that you see here is the same empty, impersonal abstraction, and the reaction of the painter necessarily is one of two: either to give in and sacrifice his personality to the Parisian "Art life", or to turn away more and more from abstract art. Trökes told me yesterday: the longer I am in Paris, the more I feel the urge to paint a portrait. I have never done anything else, I answered, but I feel the same disgust for all these abstract fashionable goings-on. I need something concrete, something clear, something direct." Constant in a letter to Aldo van Eyck, who quoted from it during a speech held at the opening of the solo exhibition *Constant* at Galerie Le Canard, Amsterdam, on February 16, 1951. Aldo van Eyck, *Constant en de abstracten* undated stencilled document in unmarked file, RKD. Cf. Francis Strauven, *Aldo van Eyck: The Shape of Relativity* (Amsterdam: Architectura & Natura, 1998), p. 656.

12 For a detailed account and more about the 1952 paintings see Hummelink, op. cit., pp. 138–146.

13 For pre-war developments in Paris see for instance H.H. Arnason, *A History of Modern Art* (London: Thames and Hudson, 1977: second, revised edition. First edition 1969), pp. 410–417.

14 See Laszlo Moholy-Nagy, *Vision in Motion* (Chicago: Theobald, 1946).

15 It is in Zurich too that Aldo van Eyck, whilst studying architecture, came in touch with members of the exiled avant-garde – knowledge which he would later tap from in his collaborations with the Cobra artists and Constant in particular. See Strauven, op. cit., pp. 73–99 and pp. 123 ff.

16 For an excellent overview of developments in Europe – on which this passage of my text is largely based – see the chapter by Jonneke Fritz-Jobse and Mariette Niermeyer, "Oriëntatie op het buitenland", in Jonneke Fritz-Jobse et al. (ed.), *Een nieuwe synthese, geometrisch-abstracte kunst in Nederland 1945–1960* (Den Haag: SdU, 1988), pp. 73 ff. See also Arnason, op. cit., pp. 588–602. As for the post-war French scene, an interesting cross-section is provided in *Hommage à Denise René – Cinquante ans d'art construit* (Strasbourg: Ronald Hirle, 1996).

17 For details on Constant's stay in England see Fritz-Jobse et al. (ed.), op. cit., pp. 97–99.

18 Constant Nieuwenhuys, "Høsterport", *Cobra*, no. 1. Reprinted in Gérard Berreby, *Documents rélatifs à la fondation de l'Internationale Situationniste* (Paris: Allia, 1985), p. 64. Translation by author.

19 See Constant's intro to *Art & Habitat*, 1955, which makes this point lucidly. Hand-written manuscript, file "Néovision Spatiodynamisme (Constant, Nic. Schöffer, S. Gilbert 1953–56)" (hereafter: file *Neovision*), RKD.

20 English translation by Robyn de Jong-Dalziel, "Spatial Colorism", in Wigley, op. cit., p. 74.

21 See Wigley, op. cit., p. 20.

22 Constant's membership cards of 1953–55 can be found in the archive in The Hague (file *Neovision*).

23 See correspondence between Constant and Gilbert in the *Neovision* and the 1952 and 1953 "Correspondentie" files: the point is repeatedly made there and reiterated in Fanny Kelk's "A talk with Constant", *Constant: schilderijen 1969–77*, exhibition catalogue (Amsterdam: Stedelijk Museum, 1978).

24 See for instance the First Manifesto of *De Stijl*, 1918, reprinted in Ulrich Conrads, *Programmes and manifestoes on 20th-century architecture* (London: Lund Humphries, 1970), pp. 39–40.

25 It was Karel Appel who, especially, embraced the term "barbaric". In later interviews with Christian Dotremont the hostility to the all-pervasive logic of industry and technology is also striking.

26 "You started a discussion about painting…. In the end I think that it will take a while still before I abandon painting, but I would sympathise with your going through with it". Gilbert to Constant, 24 May 1953, file "Correspondentie 1953", RKD.

27 Correspondence shows that it took Constant and Gilbert considerable time to come up with a title: see letters from Gilbert to Constant, 14 September 1953 and 26 October 1953, file "Correspondentie 1953", RKD.

28 Letter from Constant to Gerrit Rietveld, 9 February 1954, file *Neovision*, RKD.

29 For more about Constant's euphoric reaction to the Van Nelle factory see Hummelink, op. cit., p. 150.

30 See for instance the handwritten manuscript titled "Preface", undated (*Neovision* file, RKD): "When one considers the problems that need to be tackled, the almost complete absence of an urban aesthetic is striking, as is the lack of correspondence between the technical and sculptural aspects in general. One can predict that the artist-plastician shall have to play a vital role in the team of constructors, once the point has been reached that the aesthetic function is acknowledged to be essential." This text was evidently written for the first issue of the *Art et Habitat* review (even before it had its name) – a hunch confirmed by a written reaction from Stephen Gilbert: "(In short:) your preface I think is excellent and vigorous, and your criticism of architects justified, just as much as their predictable reservations vis-à-vis what we are proposing to them." Letter from Gilbert to Constant, 30 August 1953, file "Correspondentie 1953", RKD.

31 Letter from Constant to Rietveld, 9 February 1954.

32 See letter from Rietveld to Constant, 7 February 1954, file 'Correspondentie 1953', RKD.

33 Van Eyck, too, could not follow Constant in this matter. His written response, a few years later, to the 'integrationist' ideas of the *Liga Nieuw Beelden* would be quite clear: "Integration=impotence". *Forum* no. 6 (August), 1959, p. 176.

34 Constant: untitled, handwritten document in Dutch. File *Neovision*, RKD.

35 Constant handwritten manuscript "Esthétique et fonction", undated, *Neovision* file, RKD. It is also interesting to note that Constant emphasizes the social objectives of not only the Russian constructivists but also of De Stijl in the pursuit of a new aesthetic.

36 A summary of many of these arguments and Constant's position at the time in general can be found in the article "Van samenwerking naar absolute eenheid van de plastische kunsten" in *Forum* no. 6 (July–August), 1955, p. 207. English translation "From Collaboration to Absolute Unity among the Plastic Arts" in Wigley, op. cit., p. 75.

37 In a direct reference to *De Stijl* Constant points out: "The neo-plasticist conception has done away with decoration once and for all and replaces it by new aesthetic laws that can be applied to all plastic creation, to the point that the borders between architecture, sculpture and painting are effaced." Manuscript "Art et Habitat", *Neovision* file, RKD. Note the word *laws*.

38 "It is a pity that in a society that is working its way up from a collection of individuals to a higher, more organized unity, it is the artists who at this moment form the last bulwark of hyper-individualism and a misunderstood personality cult." Undated, handwritten document, *Neovision* file, RKD.

39 The phrase is from his letter to Gerrit Rietveld, 9 February 1954: "This task of the painter only emerged with the rise of individualism, and it is tied to the rapid, jerky development of our individualistic culture. But with the end of this culture and the birth of a new, more static form of society now in sight, we have to take into consideration that the revolutionary task of the 'free' artist (a revealing term!) is not a permanent one, even though his revolutionary and social activities function side by side for the time being. This gradual end to the revolutionizing function of the artist must, however, not be regarded as an impoverishment, for the many stages on the road from chaos to order are not the goal of art. The goal of art is the order that lies at the end of the way."

40 The phrase comes from the "Amsterdam Declaration", point 3.

41 See letters from Hill to Constant, 9 February 1954, and from Bakema to Constant, 18 February 1954, file "Correspondentie 1953", RKD.

42 For a very terse summary of their activities see Wigley, op.cit., pp. 22–26. A more complete dissection of the arguments between Schoeffer, Constant and Gilbert is provided in Hummelink, op.cit., pp. 187–199.

43 To translate the name as 'League of new *representation*' (Wigley, op.cit., p. 22 and Careri, *New Babylon: una città nomade*, p. 23) is to miss the point entirely.

44 Founding document of the *Liga Nieuw Beelden*.

45 The phrase is from Jorn's 1953 letter, note 2.

46 The school would eventually be known as the 'Hochschule für Gestaltung'

47 Jorn rambles: "I believe that the evolution of modern architecture begins with Ruskin and Morris and I will study them, their motivations and failures, and after that the Style nouveau with *Gaudi* and *Mendelsohn* and then functionalism with *Gropius*, Le Corbusier etc (…) There you have three stages that have been passed but between which one must find a synthesis, but there is also that what is most important, the future. *The architectural Science Fiction.*" Undated letter from Jorn to Constant, probably summer 1956, file "Correspondentie 1956", RKD.

48 See telegram from Hans Gugelot of the Hochschule für Gestaltung to Constant, 29 March 1956, file "Correspondentie 1956", RKD. Jorn was in fact delighted: he saw Constant's guest lectureship as an opportunity to infiltrate in the enemy camp.

49 See for instance Constant's letter to Jorn, 31 July 1956, file "COBRA 1949–1951 Correspondentie", RKD.

50 In 1949 an article by Jorn (translated by Constant) was published in the Dutch journal *Forum*: "Levend ornament". The first issue of *Cobra*, which was prepared by the Danish members of the movement, featured an article on "Symbolic Architecture" by a rather mysterious figure called Michel Colle; the drawings accompanying the article are oddly Jorn-like (resembling his 'automatic' drawings of the period).

51 Constant goes so far as to insist that the final goal ("aboutissement") of the spirit of Cobra should be in architecture. Jorn, in his enthusiasm, readily agrees: letter Jorn to Constant, undated 1956, note 47.

52 "I am realistic enough not to combat functionalist architecture without confronting it with a conception of the same order. (…) I received *Eristica* and had to conclude that all sense of construction is absent from it. One cannot oppose functional architecture as it is taught in Ulm (…) with ceramics like the ones reproduced in *Eristica*. Such an attack lacks clout. (…)" Letter from Constant to Jorn, 31 July 1956.

53 For more on the Constant-Jorn *rapprochement* preceding Alba – and their continuing differences – see Roberto Ohrt, *Phantom Avantgarde: eine Geschichte der Situationistischen Internationale und der modernen Kunst* (Hamburg: Nautilus, 1997; first edition 1990), chapters "Kampf zweier Linien" and "Auf der Landstraße zum Weltkongreß", pp. 99–160.

54 "Définitions", *Internationale Situationniste* no. 1 (June 1958), translation by Ken Knabb.

55 See letter from the mayor of Alba to Constant, 8 March 1957, file "Correspondentie 1957", RKD.

56 Officially there was a third party involved: Ralph Rumney's tiny *London Psychogeographic society*.

57 See for instance letter from Debord to Constant, 26 June 1958, in which he reacts to Constant's doubts and reassures him that "the most advanced tendency in the SI" will prevail. File "Internationale Situationniste Correspondence Constant-Debord" (henceforth: file C–D), RKD.

58 See Atkins, op.cit., for more on Jorn's work and development in these years.

59 Constant, "Demain la poésie logera la vie", translated as "Tomorrow life will reside in poetry" in Wigley, op.cit., p. 78. The text, again, is mainly about the formal impact of technology – not play or collective creativity.

60 Works are entitled, for instance, *Ruimtevaart* (space travel), *Cosmisch landschap* (cosmic landscape) or *Structuren in de ruimte* (structures in space) – three abstract paintings from 1957 – or *Ruimtecircus* (Space Circus), *Abfahrt im Raum* (Departure in Space) – two constructions from 1958.

61 Letter from Debord to Constant, 19 January 1957, file C–D, RKD.

62 G.E. Debord, *Rapport sur la construction des situations et sur les conditions de l'organisation et de l'action de la tendance situationniste internationale* (Paris: Internationale Situationniste, 1957).

63 Full title: *Critique de la politique économique suivie de la Lutte Finale* (Paris: Internationale Situationniste, 1958). The publication was presented as "the second in the series of reports presented to the Situationist International".

64 Asger Jorn, *Pour la forme. Ébauche d'une méthodologie des arts* (Paris: 1958).

65 As *IS* 2 mentions, this tripartite text is based on two letters from Constant to Debord (part 1 and 3) and one from Paris to Amsterdam, see file C–D, RKD. Originally, it had been Constant's intention to write a completely new text for the second issue of *Internationale Situationniste* for his attack on Jorn, an ambition that never materialized. See letters from Debord to Constant 3 October 1958, and 12 October 1958: "I am very happy to have received your final response in the discussion. From these positions the SI can move forward despite the hesitations of its 'right wing'."

66 Constant insisted on getting the green light to attack Jorn's position in the *IS* journal before considering any formal membership of the movement: Debord, after consulting with fellow founding father Jorn, agrees. See letter from Debord to Constant, 25 September 1958, file C–D, RKD.

67 Constant: "On Our Means and Our Perspectives", *Internationale Situationniste*, no. 2 (December 1958).

68 Constant, Guy Debord, "The Amsterdam Declaration" (officially signed Amsterdam, 10 November 1958), *Internationale Situationniste* no. 2 (December 1958).

69 Interestingly, Constant's last point might have been plucked straight from his *Art et Habitat* essay: "The possibility of unitary and collective creativity is already announced in the decomposition of the individual arts and the convergence of the sciences and imagination". Debord edits out the last part of the sentence.

70 See handwritten, undated manuscript in Constant's handwriting with draft version of 6 points of Amsterdam Declaration; file C–D, RKD. Debord answers: "Thank you for your letter and the six points on urbanism" (Undated postcard: collage on Modigliani reproduction). "Here are the proofs of the declaration. Your propositions numbered 1 to 5 are now 5 to 9. The sixth has become our third. I framed all this by five other propositions". (Undated postcard with Lucas Cranach reproduction marked "Lundi" (Monday)). On the second card Debord also mentions trouble with the "experimental" cover of the new IS issue (no. 2, with flaking aluminium laminate), which corroborates that the cards were sent in November 1958. The fact that Debord refers to Constant's text as "points on *urbanism*" – rather than "points for the SI's programme", for instance, is interesting. The letter and postcards indicate that the Declaration was never formally "signed" in Amsterdam (Debord being far too busy preparing the issue) but came into existence through correspondence: its publication in *IS* 2 marked its de facto signing. Mark Wigley's assertion in *Constant's New Babylon*, pp. 30/31 that Constant wrote nine of the eleven points is incorrect.

71 See point 4 in the finally published version.

72 It is still called "ville couverte" (covered city) in *IS* 3, pp. 38 and 39 (see image captions for "Une autre ville pour une autre vie"). Constant acknowledged that Debord suggested the name "New Babylon" in his 1974 interviews with Fanny Kelk. See "Constant, een illustratie van vrijheid" in F. Kelk, *Constant; interview en kritieken*. (Den Haag: Galerie Nouvelles Images, 1980).

73 See for instance his euphoria in a letter to Constant, 28 December 1958 (file C–D, RKD), probably written as a reaction to a photo of one of Constant's first sector constructions.

74 Commenting on the show at the Stedelijk, Debord writes: "These initial experiments by Constant do no more than state the problem of unitary urbanism. Nevertheless, this exhibition could mark the turning point, in the modern world of art production, between self-sufficient merchandise-objects, meant solely to be looked at, and project-objects, whose more complex appreciation calls for some sort of action, an action on a higher level having to do with the totality of life." See "Premières Maquettes pour l'Urbanisme Nouveau", in *Potlatch* no. 30/ no.1 new series (15 July 1959).

75 In French: "Bureau de Recherches pour un Urbanisme Unitaire".

76 Letter from Constant to Debord, 26 February 1959, file C–D, RKD.

77 Undated letter from Debord to Constant, file C–D, RKD. The letter is, however, a direct response to Constant's letter of 26 February 1959.

78 Ton Alberts would later, with his new partner Max van Huut, become the most important protagonist of anthroposophist architecture in the Netherlands.

79 Constant, "Rapport inaugural de la conférence de Munich" – opening speech of the third SI conference, 17–20 April 1959 – published in *Internationale Situationniste* no. 3 (December 1959), pp. 25–27.

80 Armando publishes a witty account of the proceedings – as well as of Gallizio's show at Galerie Van de Loo – in *Haagse Post*, 2 May 1959, pp. 13–14, which shows that his reasons for going to Munich were journalistic mainly. The SI's rendition of the conference can be found in *Internationale Situationnniste* no. 3, pp. 19–22; for a more critical discussion of the Munich conference see for instance Ohrt, op.cit., pp. 199–203.

81 Letter from Debord to Constant, 20 May 1959, file C–D, RKD.

Notes continued on p. 123

Dear Mr Máčel, Dear Mr van Schaik,

You have asked me to bring back to mind thoughts that I and others, sometimes separately, sometimes together, entertained – many, many years ago, forty-five years ago, almost half a century ago now. Nowadays, my memory is no longer as "scientific" as it might have been; it has become a little vague. Over the years those old thoughts have been ousted by new ones, thoughts that try to keep pace with events, thoughts that are perhaps also more complex.

At that time, I was still under the influence of a master, a painter by the name of Luigi Spazzapan, who taught me a great deal about painting. Though I attended architecture school, I was perhaps also very interested in the problems of painting. Why, I don't know.

I remember that when I was about twenty I went off to Paris to see the Grande Exposition, at which I saw the Cubists, Guernica, Matisse and so on. I saw Calder's fountain which, because it was in the Spanish pavilion, did not spout water but mercury. But I also visited Alvar Aalto's pavilion and other exhibits, by Le Corbusier, Gropius and all the rest. I continued to mix up thoughts about art and thoughts about architecture, and in this manner I went on – and go on to this day – mixing up thoughts about art, about architecture, about poetry, about engineering, about finance. Thoughts about everything I happen to come across.

As time passed, I began to see that one has to be very careful about mixing up thoughts about art and those about architecture, and that instead it was a question of trying not to mix them up. If by art we understand the artwork one can see in galleries, that is to say, painting and sculpture, or today, photography as well, then art is an "audience" event, one that is to be looked at: physically, it stands outside us. In this sense architecture isn't art.

Architecture is a "lived-in" event. Architecture is a continuous relationship built up between the inhabitant and colours, lights, temperatures, humidity, dryness agoraphobia and claustrophobia and noise, weight, lightness, fragility. Thus, architecture is an event in which we take part with the whole body, with all senses. Architecture is an event that is "used" with the whole body.

Generally speaking, artists don't like architects because in their work architects use techniques that are very different from those of the artist. Architects, for their part, don't like engineers too much because they employ techniques in their work that are different from the ones architects use. I suspect that surgeons don't much care for GPs either, and that genetic engineering researchers have scant regard for dentists.

At this juncture, I think I can say that the question whether architecture is art or not is tautological, outdated and pointless. Anyhow, if someone took it into their head to ask me if architecture is or isn't art, I'd reply: "architecture is art only when it is architecture".

When I was a student I didn't have much trouble making architecture into an art, but I kept running into the fundamental problem of understanding what on earth architecture itself could possibly be. The dilemma facing me was how to fit

Conference in the *Consiglio Communale*. Seated around the table, left to right: unknown, Gil Wolman, Asger Jorn, Constant, Elena Verrone, Guiseppe Pinot Gallizio, Ettore Sottsass, Jacques Calonne.

thoughts about architecture into a vast and complicated intellectual and emotional space, one that was considerably more mysterious than the space that the great revolutionary architects of the turn of the century believed they had at their disposal. As a student I was just beginning to ponder "how" one might extend the concept of "functionality" and in which direction to carry it. I wondered for example what type of functionality could be designed if one started to imagine and to give importance to the presence of light, temperature, weight, silence, colour and so on …

Thus, in those far-off years when I was really young, I was known as someone trying to formulate and to experiment with defining and using a concept of functionality quite different from that prevailing at the beginning of the century; so one day Enrico Baj came round and asked me: "Ettore, do you feel like joining a theoretical movement we were thinking of calling: 'For an Imaginist Bauhaus'?" And I said: "Yes, sure." Baj then introduced me to Asger Jorn who in those days (we are talking about 1956) often went to Albisola to do ceramics.

Albisola is on the sea, not far from the city of Alba, and the mayor of Alba, Giuseppe Gallizio, was a pharmacist and a painter to boot, a kind of romantic Pollock who painted on long strips of burlap, which he then cut into strips. Jorn and the mayor of Alba with Enrico Baj and an art critic, Piero Simondo, had become friends and founded the movement "For an Imaginist Bauhaus"; they had also organized a convention to air the problem and proclaim that it was high time to get away from the ideas of Gropius and his ilk. They – Jorn, Baj and Gallizio – were all painters. In Bra there was an important chocolate manufacturer called "Ferrero," and the mayor of Bra had managed to get a little cash from the chocolate factory. In his role as mayor he had also made available the hall of the Consiglio Comunale as the venue for the conference.

I had only just returned from the United States. The journey had had a great impact on me because for the first time I had to come to terms with the existence of an "industrial culture". It could be said that in those days "industrial culture" was not yet widespread in Italy. The only industries were heavy ones, military industries, transport industries, etc. Industry had not yet entered the phase of production for private consumption, the phase we call consumerism. In the United States, by 1956 the art scene was host to a homegrown avant-garde that has since been dubbed "Pop culture", an all-American culture in which artists confronted the phenomenon of industrial production, of all-pervasive consumerism, and also of the political uncertainties that the situation heralded.

As soon as I returned from the United States my wife was operated on for a tumour in the intestine – thankfully benign. When my painter friends told me they were organizing the convention, and that I would have to say something because I was an architect, that night in the hospital corridor I wrote a text, which I then read at the convention. When I arrived in the hall of the Consiglio Comunale, there were no more than fifteen people in attendence, including the Mayor, Baj, Asger Jorn, two young theoreticians of the movement, and a French Situationist theorist, Christian Dotremont. It was pretty amusing because the French theorist did not know any Italian and the Italians did not speak any French. Anyway, the symposium went very well, and we were all very pleased; invited by Mr Ferrero, the owner of the chocolate factory, we then went off to eat.

When we arrived at the entrance to the firm's vast reception hall, Mr Ferrero, our sponsor – as we would say today – received us dressed in black and with a black necktie – just as one should present oneself at an international convention. There were only fifteen of us, somewhat despairing and perplexed, and Mr Ferrero asked: "Are you all here?" "Yes," we said, "we're all here." Mr Ferrero opened the door of the great hall, and there in front of us – perfectly laid out and decked with flowers for a group of at least forty people – was a table more than twenty metres long.

We all hovered there, speechless and a bit embarrassed.

I went back to the hospital and from that day on I never saw Baj, Asger Jorn, or any of the others again. And that was my contribution to "For an Imaginist Bauhaus against an imaginary Bauhaus".

Ettore Sottsass

Left to right: Pinot Gallizio with gypsies on the marketplace of Alba; Asger Jorn printing the poster for the *Primo Congresso degli Artisti Liberi*; exhibition of paintings ("all canvases are guaranteed 'pure cotton'") during the conference.

New Babylon versus Plug-in City

Simon Sadler

1 Sparring partners

"Fuck," Peter Cook recalls saying to Michael Webb, "this is good."[1] Cook and Webb had gone to hear Constant present his New Babylon project to the Institute of Contemporary Arts (ICA) in London in November 1963. Webb and Cook, as members of the London-based architecture collective Archigram, were used to the idea that their architecture was the most radical around. Webb had acquired notoriety with his widely published Furniture Manufacturers project of 1958 and with his ongoing Sin Centre project, started in 1959 and looking itself a little like a New Babylonian sector. Now Webb and Cook were faced with slides from the exotic Dutchman.

Two avant-garde strains were coming into brief contact.[2] New Babylon was published in *Archigram* no. 5 in November of 1964, one picture of it printed on the same page as Cook's new Plug-in City, in a feature on the joys of living 'Within the Big Structure'.[3] Yet it was not to be a close relationship. Contact details for "Constant – Rotterdam. Painter, 'Situationist'" were soon mislaid and were being sought again by *Archigram* no. 6 in 1965; New Babylon was conspicuous by its absence from Peter Cook's *Experimental Architecture*, published in 1970. "We can do better," Cook mused as soon as he had got over the initial impact of New Babylon.[4] Though the Plug-in project might be seen as Archigram's snappy answer to New Babylon, it had gestated through several years of study on standardized building units, achieving its definitive form when it was published in the *Sunday Times Colour Magazine* in September 1964.

Three findings, at once obvious and inescapable, emerge from the 'stand-off' between New Babylon and Plug-in City. One is that, in the broad sweep of architecture, New Babylon and Plug-in City were 'sparring partners'. They responded to much the same influences, emerged as utopian schemes at about the same time, defied the decay of Modernism and the avant-garde, and reprieved the promise of collective living from a widespread pessimism about 'urbanism'. Both answered with megastructures devoted to continual circulation, their functions scrambled, their boundaries blurred, but unified by continuous architecture.

With this commonality accepted, a second finding becomes clear: Cook and Constant designed, and drew, in markedly different ways, and the sorts of spatial experiences that the two schemes might have provided if built would have been dissimilar. This provides evidence for a third and final point, that the projects were 'going the distance' using different strategies – Plug-in's was pragmatic and market-based, New Babylon's was of airy, high-ideal non-market conviction. Plug-in was an 'empiricist' response to the 'existentialist' nature of New Babylon and the continental avant-garde. What makes this comparison all the more involved is that it occurs at just the moment when the future of the avant-garde generally had to be decided. The two contenders for the future of world urbanism represented equally brilliant and problematic alternatives, and would both be swept away from architectural discourse within a decade by a reaction against massive visionary architecture and Modernism.

In 1964 New Babylon and Plug-in City were addressing a common problem. Modernist architectural reconstruction had promised a radical agenda, yet felt and looked distinctly conservative in the post-War decades, from the Rotterdam of Jacob Bakema (sometime associate of Constant)[5] to the Harlow of Frederick Gibberd (sometime employer of Archigram's Dennis Crompton). Official sanction of Modernism deprived it of its inherent avant-garde quality. By the 1950s Modernism was instead foregrounding an image of tidy and fair cultural order that stretched back through 1920s De Stijl and Bauhaus work to the socialist reformers of the nineteenth century. Meanwhile, Le Corbusier provided startlingly innovative buildings even for that most conservative of patrons, the Church (the Pilgrimage Church of Ronchamp, 1954, and the Monastery of La Tourette, 1956). Constant and Cook, however, still believed that architecture could change the world. That belief was epitomized in Constant's stormy collaboration, from 1956 to 1960, with the revolutionary Situationist International (which indirectly informed Plug-in City as well).

Such was the fighting spirit of Constant and Cook in 1963–64 that they wanted to exceed the legacy of their immediate 'avant-garde' precursors in architecture, grouped around Team 10. Constant worked in the wake of Team 10 member Aldo van Eyck, whom he first met in 1947 and with whom he collaborated in the mid-'50s on a series of small commissions.[6] Cook worked in the wake of Team 10 members Alison and Peter Smithson, under whom he had completed his thesis studies at the Architectural Association in London. For architects reared on thirty years of received wisdom that Modernist design was dedicated to clarity and rationality, Team 10's call for a pragmatic, multifarious order was impossibly complex. But it delighted Constant and the early Archigram, New Babylon and Plug-in City being their treatises upon the spatial organization of community, the idiosyncrasies of city texture and culture, and the relation of the micro to the macro.

Constant and Cook were truly unrepentant Modernists, of Futurist strain – convinced that the qualities of the everyday could be

1. Archigram news flyer sent to Constant in 1964

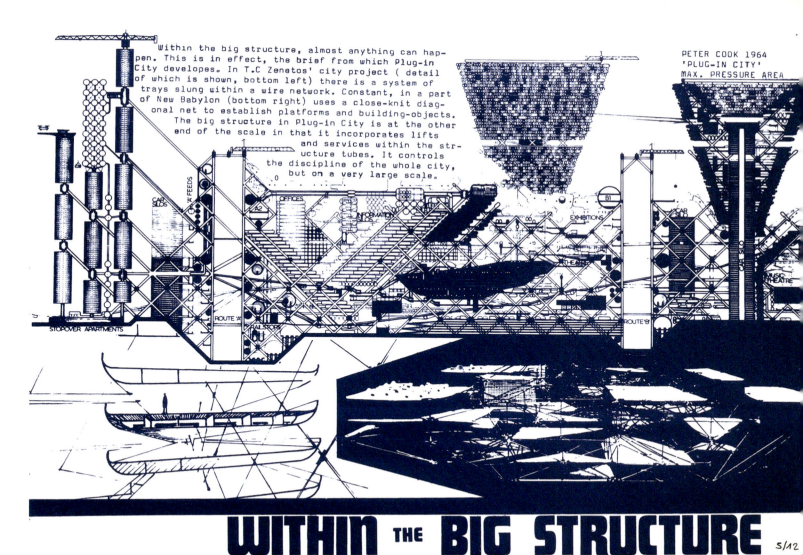

Within the big structure, almost anything can happen. This is in effect, the brief from which Plug-in City developes. In T.C Zenetos' city project (detail of which is shown, bottom left) there is a system of trays slung within a wire network. Constant, in a part of New Babylon (bottom right) uses a close-knit diagonal net to establish platforms and building-objects. The big structure in Plug-in City is at the other end of the scale in that it incorporates lifts and services within the structure tubes. It controls the discipline of the whole city, but on a very large scale.

PETER COOK 1964 'PLUG-IN CITY' MAX. PRESSURE AREA

WITHIN THE BIG STRUCTURE

5/12

2. Page from *Archigram* 5 ("Metropolis"): New Babylon and P.I.C.

enhanced by design, and that technology could lift the passions of humanity from the quagmire of the street into the city of the sky. This helps us to understand a paradox in the way that Constant and Cook saw 'the city'. The Situationist International and Team 10 alike had implied that the seeds for the city of the future lay latent in the city of the now, and perhaps still more so in the city of the past: that, underneath cities suppressed by the rubric of capitalist-rationalist planning, lay cities of magical cultural diversity and latent architectural promise. Constant, however, proposed superimposing an entirely new city over the old one. Likewise, Archigram celebrated London's natural mess in its 1963 exhibition, Living City, at the ICA, then immediately proposed mega-structural developments that would supplant it, like Plug-in City, and the Fulham project for Taylor Woodrow Construction, 1963–64 (a redevelopment of a West London suburb). The Situationist International and Team 10 tended to be a little archaeological in their urban studies, but Constant and Archigram were more interested in outlining the future than in excavating the patterns of the past. They saw their projects as the means to upset the old orders of community and social difference, not reinstate them.

This imposed a distance between Constant and Van Eyck's circle, and between Archigram and the Smithsons' circle; eventually it would distance Constant from the Parisian Situationists too. While Archigram regarded the Smithsons as their heroes for spearheading the break with mainstream Modernism, they made the decision not to become direct followers. Archigram members Warren Chalk, Ron Herron and Dennis Crompton went 'beyond' Brutalism (the architectural idiom of the 1950s–60s which did most to convert the Team 10 mood into built form) by endowing their otherwise Brutalist South Bank Centre in London (1960–62) with more walkways and control towers than was strictly necessary, thereby slipping into Futurist revivalism.

Archigram was so sufficiently confident of superceding Team 10 that it produced a map of 'Networks around the Channel', boldly superimposing the new Archigram nexus of radical architects on top of "the architectural network of Team 10", one embracing Van Eyck and Bakema, the other co-opting the likes of Constant.[7] The *Archigram* magazine was taking the contact-building form of an architectural *samizdat* – ephemeral, subcultural, and dependent upon 'underground' links between marginal practices. It was a network to which one might 'plug-in', a voluntary association, superficially as non-partisan as possible, from which to organize the new architectural 'situation'. For his part, Constant belonged to a stream of organizations working to activate the environment and everyday space including, from

1962, a significant involvement with GEAM (Groupe d'Etude d'Architecture Mobile, founded in 1958 by Yona Friedman).

Forging ahead with the building of the future, New Babylon and Plug-in City reworked two slightly repressed motifs found in Modernism: those of the megastructure and the 'building-in-becoming'.[8] They had been tried in theory in Le Corbusier's Algiers project (1931) and in the Soviet linear city projects of the 1920s; megastructures existed in built form in Karl Ehn's Karl-Marx-Hof in Vienna (1927) and Le Corbusier's Unité d'Habitation (1947–53). New Babylon and Plug-in City combined elements of all of these precedents – the principle of collectivity, of inter-changeable apartment units and the incorporation of rapid transport links. New Babylon even floated upon Corbusier-derived *pilotis*. In this there was a disarming reasonableness about the New Babylon and Plug-in proposals, with their attempt to keep cities viable in an era of rapid change; they were expressions of solidarity with other megastructures being projected as the urban future for the 1950s–60s, particularly the Philadelphia City Tower project created around about 1954 by Louis Kahn and Anne Tyng. The aesthetic of incompleteness, apparent throughout the New Babylon and Plug-in schemes, was partly a product of the building boom following the economic reconstruction of Europe. Constant returned from his visit to London in 1952 obsessed with space, and fascinated by "people building, demolishing, removing … the traffic increased, man disappeared … mechanized technological environments emerged."[9] This modernization was accelerating in Archigram's property boom-fuelled London of the 1960s, as the service cores of office blocks rose above the city prior to the addition of floor slabs and curtain walls. The aesthetic had good ancestry; Erich Mendelsohn had photographed buildings in construction in the 1920s, coining the phrase 'X-ray view' in his Modernist picture books *Amerika* (1926) and *Russland, Europa, Amerika* (1929).[10]

Yet neither New Babylon nor Plug-in City could be mistaken for any one precedent. There was an intoxicated sense of chaos in them unshared by precedents so sensibly bracketed by frames, good taste, economy and spatial evenness. Plug-in heaped up in cliffs of architecture; New Babylon was riven by crumpled spaces. With New Babylon and Plug-in, we are at the outer edge of the early sixties avant-garde, primarily motivated not by making architecture better behaved, but by making architecture change life and alter spatial experience. In 1963 Constant and Archigram shared an enthusiasm for an undiluted 'Pop' or 'science-fiction' architecture, coinciding with the revival in the reputation of the Futurists and other avant-gardes (recovered by Reyner Banham's landmark *Theory and Design in the First Machine Age*, 1960, and in Ulrich Conrads and Hans Gunther Sperlich's *Phantastische Architektur*, 1960, soon afterwards translated into English).[11] The 'Zoom' edition of *Archigram* (no. 4, 1964), celebrated as the issue that brought the Archigram message to wide attention with its science-fiction comic strip action, would not have appeared so extraordinary to Constant. Constant and his colleagues from the Situationist Bureau of Unitary Urbanism dominated the editorial committee of the August 1958 issue of *Forum*, filling it with collages featuring crowds, Brigitte Bardot, jets, highways, telephone book entries and such futuristic exemplars as Konrad Wachsmann's space structures and Eero Saarinen's TWA Terminal.[12] Archigram attempted something similar in its *Living City* show. Through image, text, sound and light, this "assault on the senses"[13] that physically enveloped visitors tried to convey

3. Aldo van Eyck: Orphanage in Amsterdam, 1955–60

the essential property of the city as being its state of continual becoming, and to enshrine physical and cultural pluralism as an key quality of urbanism.

If Archigram's 'Zoom' spirit was not entirely a surprise to Constant, nor was his 'Situationism' totally new to Archigram. At Living City the attraction to Situationism, though never cited explicitly, was made clear by the exhibition's culmination in a section on 'Situation': "all of us in varying degrees, according to our perceptiveness, find Living City in Situation."[14] The notion of 'situation' (originally a Sartrian term, used to describe the complex of living conditions which, moment to moment, the individual must negotiate), was redeployed by Archigram to revel in the *frisson* that was rendering London's old social and architectural orders defunct. "In this second half of the twentieth century, the old idols are crumbling, the old precepts strangely irrelevant, the old dogmas no longer valid," Archigram's assessment of 'Situation' claimed.[15] It was assumed that the encounter between the citizen and the urban environment would accelerate the development of consciousness, society and freedom. The cities heralded by New Babylon and the Living City were the terrains upon which the adventures of life and human progress could be more fully played out.[16]

4. *Sin Centre* by Michael Webb, 1959–62, model

 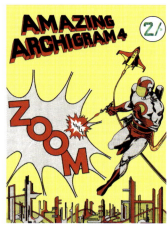

5. Living city exhibition logo; 6. Cover of fourth issue of the *Archigram* magazine

New Babylon and Plug-in City were thus devised to prompt circulation and accelerate the city-in-flux. The clean, zonal, hierarchical separation of rationalist urban planning gave way to Situationist 'unitary urbanism' in New Babylon and to 'come-go' in Plug-in City. Urban experience would consequently be more indeterminate, physically and mentally. The city would now be less an object of vision – a 'spectacle', to adopt Situationist terminology – than a plaything, a toy, a puzzle. If city planning had traditionally encouraged contemplation of the fixed and ideal architectural object, Plug-in and New Babylonian planning promoted architecture as an event and situation which could only be realized by the active involvement of its inhabitants. It was a supposition that would be generally accepted by avant-gardes in the 1960s working in the wake of New Babylon and Archigram: Coop Himmelblau, Haus-Rucker-Co and Utopie. But how could architecture that sustained and stimulated ceaseless movement and change be devised?

Rhetoric about an architecture of movement and change had been briefly focussed around Team 10. But the brevity of the collaboration between Constant and Aldo van Eyck suggested an incompatibility between Team 10's ambition to reinstate the deep structures of human association, and Constant's refusal to subscribe to any pre-existing mode of behaviour or environmental structuring. Yona Friedman felt similarly: he attended the Team 10 co-ordinated CIAM conference at Aix-en-Provence in 1953 but, frustrated by the vagaries of Team 10's ideas about 'mobility', 'development', and 'growth and change', yearned for the truly physically mobile architecture that would be imagined by his GEAM colleagues. New Babylon related specifically to the idea of 'spatial urbanism' (*urbanisme spatial*) developed by Friedman, who began his Ville Spatiale project around the same time that Constant started work on New Babylon (1958).

Archigram too dared to turn the logic of Team 10 and the associated New Brutalism in upon itself: if the Brutalists wanted a frank exposure of process, of circulation, of response, and of technology, Archigram would carry on meting it out. "At that time," Cook recalled, "… the Smithsons had … returned to a classicist interpretation of architecture reminiscent of their early work. When, eventually, our own Archigram group began to articulate our homage to their work … they were frankly embarrassed."[17] The departure point visible in *Archigram* no. 1 was a 'topology'

(to use a word in vogue in the fifties) gone mad: an obsessive interest in circulation; in a separation and expression of services; even in a compositional formlessness derived from Abstract Expressionism and Art Brut. One might, if following the lead of Team 10 or Louis Kahn, legitimately expose the services, but an architecture like Plug-in City that was apparently nothing but services, stacked crazily in a frame, lacked decorum.

The plug-in principle had established a hold in Cook's work by the time of the Nottingham Shopping Centre project of 1962, hatched with his Archigram colleague David Greene, in which the centre of Nottingham was to be stacked from a combination of standardized inverted-U shaped units and geodesics. They were inched into place by all-surveying cranes on a circular rail above, which also fed the supplies down feeding tubes to the shops. With the invention of the Europa/Kent Businesstown scheme of 1963–64, Cook was verging on a full plug-in urbanism. It still deployed the cranes and standard units, and now emphasised the twin design features of vertical silos of units bridged by lateral feeding tubes, a manner probably borrowed from the City Interchange scheme of 1963, by Archigram colleagues Ron Herron and Warren Chalk (derived in turn from science-fiction comics and the conveyance bridges of Brinkman and Van der Vlugt's Van Nelle Factory, Rotterdam, 1925–31). To complete the total Plug-in City effect in 1964, Cook first regularized much of the tubular 'plumbing' as a diamond-shaped lattice that also acted as a structural support for units and more random elements like inflatables; second, he proposed depositing the whole package along lines of communication.

2 Defending different corners

However great this expanse of common interest, the two designers, Cook and Constant, were concentrating on different orders of architectural experience.

First, Cook and Archigram were becoming receptive to the Japanese avant-garde. This was in contrast to the way Japanese visitors to Team 10 meetings had found themselves, in Cook's summation, "sometimes … treated with very harsh criticism by the European élite."[18] One visitor, Kenzo Tange, had embarked upon mega-structural schemes of such ambition, culminating in the Tokyo Bay project of 1960, that Plug-in City, at least in the small portions as illustrated, seemed moderate. The Japanese were also publicizing at that time the message of Metabolism – the design of long-term structures to support short-term components.[19] This was the principle transferred to the heart of Plug-in City. Cook annotated the diagrams of Plug-in City with indications of the lifetime of the various components – 40 years for the tubular structure of the city, 25 for, say, a hotel 'core', three years for the hotel rooms plugged into it.

The proposal was a great deal less conjectural than the Ville Spatiale structures being proposed by Friedman and Constant, which were frequently little more than ideograms; Friedman would show an empty frame with various permutations of partition slotted within, while Constant's structural detailing looked like improvisatory local assemblies of frames and labyrinths. Assuming that his small-scale spatial organization was based upon a 'kit-of-parts' principle, Constant was not, in the last resort, terribly interested in how such details worked. New Babylon was configured as a chain of spatial warehouses, and the details of the structure were not the most pressing issue. More pressing was how to justify such buildings in the first place. Plug-in City on the other hand, demonstrably a giant 'kit-of-parts', had to be judged on whether it showed the world a better way of building. In this it occupied a position between several stools. The Metabolists claimed that theirs was the only solution to building a Japanese economy in rapid development. Plug-in was justified in similar terms, but it was not merely economically pragmatic. Inspired by Futurism and coming from the same intellectual stable that produced Living City, Plug-in wanted to make the life of the modern city more legible and dynamic. The interchangeable 'kit-of-parts' was essential if Plug-in City was to become visibly kinetic.

perfected by the ABS plastic stud-and-tube technology of Lego. Archigram avoided the most fetishistic interests (particularly the universal joint) of architectural engineers like Wachsmann, but Plug-in nonetheless had about it a step-by-step manner that was alien to the inventive, chaotic sprawl of New Babylon.

No more than Constant did Cook show us the smallest structural details in Plug-in City. Some of these were to be left to his colleague Warren Chalk in his Capsule Homes study of 1964, and the sort of detailing of joints that would be necessary to join a capsule to a frame would be relished by High-Tech progenies of the 1970s. What Cook did need to show was that the frame-and-unit method would one day aggregate into urbanism of the quality of that which it would supplant. It was this that was striking

7/8. Metabolism: Japanese Plug-in. Kiyonoru Kikutake's *Ocean City*, **1962. Arata Isozaki,** *Clusters in the Air*, **1963**

For some reason an attention to structural detail was, Cook and his colleagues felt, the trump card that Archigram held over other avant-garde architects like Constant.[20] A typical British boy of Archigram's generation, growing up in the 1940s, was apt to play with Meccano,[21] and we might credit to the rivet-and-connector set the same influence upon the formative Archigram architect as has been ascribed to the Froebel blocks at the disposal of Frank Lloyd Wright in kindergarten. Plug-in City deployed a very Meccano-like iconography. Nobel laureate chemist Professor Sir Harry Kroto – of the same generation as Archigram's members and sharing their passion for graphic design and Buckminster Fuller Geodetics – has drawn a correlation between the decline in British engineering and the decline in Meccano, arguing that Lego, which supplanted Meccano as a toy, produces less didactic structures.[22] But then in one of the most 'conjectural' and 'abstract' models that Archigram produced – that of Plug-in City, Paddington version, 1966[23] – pieces of Lego were inserted into the metal frame: whatever the joys of its Meccano-like frame, Plug-in City implied an equally Lego-like convenience and instantaneous colourful gratification. Archigram pursued the dream of the straight, clean, plug-in plug-out joint that had been

about the big drawings of the Plug-in 'skyline' that became so widely known: the units did indeed stack into profiles which, far from being repetitive, bordered upon the picturesque. Plug-in City convincingly turned architecture inside-out to make its interior life anterior, expendable apartments slung happily down the outside of the giant A-frame substructures, rearranged by the cranes sliding back and forth above. Cook may not have perfected the system in its entirety, but he had achieved a picture of systematic gaiety. To sense the difference in effect we can picture the two visions, New Babylon and Plug-in, in our mind's eye. Plug-in City would be something like an inland port, goods arriving by monorail and transferring by gantry, weather barrage balloons bobbing above, sounds of delight drifting through the open framework from the colourful leisure sectors within. By comparison New Babylon, from the exterior, would have a mausoleum quality. It is viewed in its drawings and collages across wasteland, virtually windowless, monolithic, motionless, muffled sirens and shrieks emanating from the activities taking place within. Only the occasional patrol of an aircraft animates the scene but, as at an airport, the aircraft cannot enliven the terminus buildings themselves.

Approaches to plan and elevation in the two projects are as variant as the treatment of structural detail. Why are there are dozens of plans of New Babylon, and none of Plug-in?[24] And why did Constant draw very few sections of New Babylon, whereas the widely-published image of Plug-in City was its section? Plug-in City was to extend across Britain and across the Channel to the Continent, but pure lateral extension was not Cook's principal interest with Plug-in; stacking was just as important. Constant, too, was interested in stacking, but he primarily thought of New Babylon as a new geography which would be "a sort of extension of the Earth's surface, a new skin that covers the earth and multiplies its living space".[25] Constant's overlapping spaces and functions tended to spread horizontally, Cook's vertically. In the early sixties Archigram felt that much good investigative work had already been carried out on lateral extension – after all, New Babylon's plan was only an enlargement of existing ideas from Team 10 from the previous decade. Plug-in now concentrated upon conjoining events not just along the horizontal axis, nor even just around the orthogonal, but the oblique, and the Plug-in section was able to show this diagrammatically. Furthermore connections could be made and disconnected at will. With due acknowledgement of the work carried out already by the Metabolists, Cook noted how "my own Plug-In City (for example) is a discussion between the possibility of a carrying system which is partly made up of movement tubes and the total transferability of the pieces which are plugged in."[26] New Babylon too depended upon flexibility, though that is probably the crucial difference in emphasis: it was an internal flexibility that contained and layered space, sandwiched within the New Babylon sector and then spread thin and flat across Europe. Not so Plug-in City, aggregating like coral or tumbling down the megastructural cliffs like troglodytes, packaging space into small capsules rather than letting it ooze through, as Constant preferred to do.

What might the experience of space have been in the two schemes? A New Babylon sector might be compared to a verse within an epic poem; Plug-in City, by contrast, was like an endless syntax which largely failed to swell into perceptible chunks – this despite Cook's interest in the 'Max Pressure Area' of the city, the equivalent of a city centre. The Plug-in effect was one of intensive cell-like privatization, whereas New Babylon was of vast public forums. It was insistently nomadic, rivers of space carrying their human cargo *en masse*, much like those spaces of modern airports which Constant celebrated in his address 'On Travelling' to mark the opening of the new Schipol Airport buildings in 1966.[27] As in an airport, New Babylonians might encounter flows of people travelling the other way but screened by glass, or ascending to another level, or negotiating obstacle

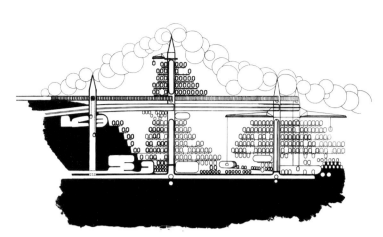

10. Early Plug-in City study, 1962. Drawing by Peter Cook

courses, the equivalents of shopping kiosks and check-in desks. New Babylonians were on a journey not to any particular place, but to a joint destiny, as the super-race *homo ludens*, 'man the player'. Plug-in however seemed to work on the movement of the micro, of one person at a time, of singular units summoned, circulating round something akin to the filaments of a neural network, generating dynamic shifts in scale between the compact and the dispersed. The Plug-in citizen awaking in her or his little apartment-capsule in the morning might have encountered a view from the window much like those greeting occupants of the new Terrassenhäuser schemes (like Patrick Hodgkinson and Leslie Martin's Brunswick Centre, London, 1962–73). Their journey to work – almost certainly a white-collar occupation – might be very short, along weatherproof tubes. The workplace was likely to be handily piled against shops or an entertainments centre, generating the multi-activity crossovers identified by the Living City. Longer journeys to other centres could be taken by car, stacked within local silos, though as Plug-in City was strung out in clusters across linear communications routes it would make sense to hop on the fast monorail. The journey may be unnecessary, since buildings serving the entire region and propelled by the newly-invented hovercraft principle could call by the cluster.

Cook's vision brought the feverish bustle of mid-town Manhattan to all places willing to plug-in to the network, and put the action under remote control – there would be a ghost in the machine. This was the impression conveyed in the Computer City diagram (1964) drawn by Archigram's Dennis Crompton, which abstracted the sorts of monitoring systems – borrowed from radio-controlled taxis, ambulance services and airports – that permitted Plug-in City to work.[28] Archigram remained preoccupied with traffic and flow, as Computer City regulated the feed and return of traffic into the metropolitan pressure area (a version of Plug-in City's 'Maximum Pressure Area'). A 'print-out' running alongside Computer City in *Archigram* no. 5 showed the enormous range of functions being monitored to prevent the urban machine overheating or starving: temperature; transport; goods supply; craneways; levels of self-sufficiency; population; infrastructure ("ADD CORNER SHOP TP8C FLOOR LEVEL L OVER X POINT 37 CAP 112" – clearly connecting it to the plug-in concept); birth rate/death rate; food supply; consumption; recreation, and power supply, amongst others.[29] New Babylon was similarly laden with control technologies although, Constant explained, it was "not primarily a town planning project"[30] and functionality was frankly not its primary aim. There was indeed a deliberate dys-

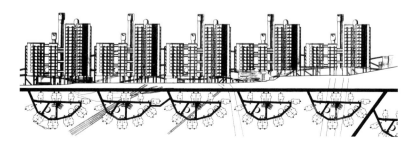

9. Peter Cook, Metal Cabin Housing, 1961. Plan and Elevation

functionality in New Babylon – the reified spaces of functional city planning were after all the conditions that Constant hoped to escape. As fast as Plug-in City facilitated the utility and flow revealed in its sections, New Babylon created the obstacles and labyrinths visible in its plans. The living experience of Plug-in City would be one of busyness, perhaps a more intense business-as-usual, whereas New Babylon was the backdrop to continuous psychodrama and sequences of 'happenings' (at the time the latest idea in the art world). The Babylonian experience was so odd that Constant wrote tracts trying to describe how he imagined it would be.

New Babylon was primarily an exercise in the creation of new social space, which in Plug-in City was more a fortuitous by-product of an organizational system. Plug-in City trusted that qualities of social space would be generated mainly through the collisions of flows around its network and competing uses of latticed space. It was a philosophy articulated in the Living City exhibition:

Cities should generate, reflect, and activate life, their environment organized to precipitate life and movement. Situation, the happenings within spaces in the city, the transient throw-away objects, the passing presence of cars and people are as important as – possibly more important than – the built demarcation of space. Situation can be caused by a single individual, by groups or a crowd, their particular purpose, occupation, movement or direction. Situation can be traffic, its speed, direction, classification.[31]

Constant's Situationist-derived idea of 'situation' embraced a similar set of qualities, but depended much more upon spatial conditioning than upon a myriad of nodal points. It generated a quality of architectural ambience. New Babylonians would for example cross "cool and dark spaces, hot, noisy, chequered, wet [spaces]" and, occasionally, "windy spaces under the bare sky".[32] In its radiograph, diagrammatic form meanwhile, Plug-in City/Computer City looked placeless. It was not immediately apparent how the strips of perpetually regenerating modular units that built Plug-in City would sow the seeds of the classic city 'quarter' celebrated by Archigram's own Living City. New Babylon's sectors hailed the city quarter more directly; however disorienting the nomadic lives of its citizens may be, they would nonetheless take place within variegated spatial and atmospheric conditions.

Those conditions were however extremely difficult to represent. As the project advanced the mass of models and illustrations of New Babylon became more expansive rather than more detailed, struggling to convey a world in motion, of ambience, of spatial emotion. New Babylon, looking like a cross between Constructivism and Abstract Expressionism, was "not intended as a work of art in the traditional sense nor as an example of architectonic structure … [but as] a creative game with an imaginary environment,"[33] Constant wrote, and one wishes to talk about the three-dimensional renderings of New Babylon as *maquettes*, as sculptures, rather than as models – great wrestlings with materials like Plexiglas and copper rod that were chosen for their artistic properties rather than their ability to realistically simulate full-scale architecture. Rough-hewn wood, splattered ink, and various metals are sandwiched by the scored Plexiglas of the *Rode sector* (Red Sector) of 1959. Were we using the language of criticism, we would describe the surfaces as palimpsests and traces. A

11. Constant, *Groep Sectoren*, model, 1959: New Babylon's horizontal sprawl

sense of ongoing, 'existential' struggle was continually apparent in Constant's work – in its violent style of drawing, in its models, bruised by some sort of skirmish between the artist and his materials, caught in the frustrated limbo between his studio and another, better world.

"If Peter could draw it, I could build it" Dennis Crompton has said of the models he created to show Plug-in and other Archigram projects: they were transcriptions, as precise as could be achieved, of drawings which were already exacting. New Babylon maquettes were transcriptions, too – but of crayon drawings, flamboyant ink sketches, and lithographs, not of painstaking, Archigram-detailed rapidograph works on tracing paper. Constant's drawings became daringly loose, and the point of view established for the viewer appeared to rove. Constant and Cook had different ways of persuading the viewer of the plausibility of their cities. New Babylon's paper expression went on and on,[34] in editions of lithographs, sketches, collages, even prose, that created New Babylon through suggestions to the imagination. By contrast to this expansive bulk, Plug-in 'zoomed in' (to coin the lingo), giving us enchanting detail in just a handful of oft-published drawings. Cook made staggering use of the axonometric, showing the maximum amount of detail that the architectural drawing could reveal. Even Zippotone, deployed as flat colouration for Plug-in City, was used expressively by Constant in New Babylon.

3 Going the distance

These variant outcomes of the design process gain more consequence when they are related to the differing architectural ideologies of Constant and Cook. That the affair between Archigram and the Situationists remained unconsummated says something about the Archigram project: opportunist, empiricist and 'English', while the Parisian-centred group pursued the theoretically-elaborate 'strategy'. Plug-in offered a sharply detailed, ready-to-build illusion; New

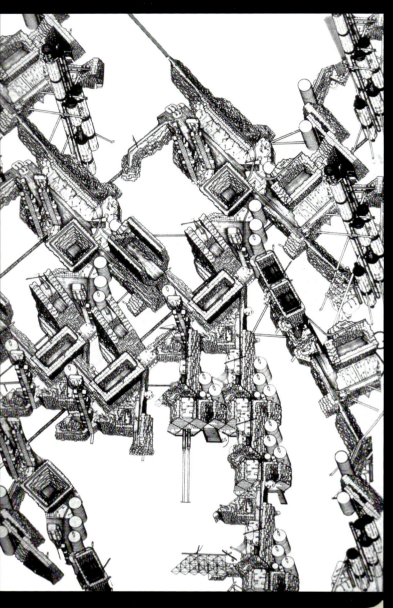

12. Plug-in City, overhead axonometric
13. Late '60s Archigram: *Instant City*, 1968–70. Drawing by Peter Cook

Babylon was a chimera. "With these slides I only want to give you a suggestion like the painter or the poet used to suggest a world different from the utilitarian world he used to escape from," Constant announced to Cook, Webb and other members of the ICA audience in 1963. "I certainly don't want to predict how the world of the future will look like in any detail, for that would be impossible."[35] New Babylon looked into the far-distance, Plug-in to the near distance.

Plug-in and New Babylon would facilitate perpetual change, but with slightly different intent. Constant's architecture was one made sufficiently elastic to accommodate the spontaneous popular will of *homo ludens*. It promised to recover a Ruskinian intimacy with the environment and with society. New Babylon would one day be a vast realm of 'constructed situations' overcomimg the separations imposed by capitalism between people, consciousness and the world. Significantly, though, the Gallic subtleties of neo-Marxist existentialist politics were lost in translation into Archigram's own Pop vernacular. Outright social revolution was not Archigram's bag, certainly not overtly. If these differences between British and Continental approaches were not explicit in 1963, by the end of the decade Archigram had become acutely aware of them, defiantly celebrating a supposed freedom from dogma. "Since we are English, we are most attracted to the characteristically Anglo-Saxon tactic of infiltration as contrasted with the characteristically Latin emotion which demands confrontation," announced *Archigram* no. 9 in 1970. "We are disposed to argue a series of logical propositions that WILL ACTUALLY LEAD TO CHANGE."[36]

Archigram's official line was that whatever political differences existed between its members were left at the studio door; the group existed simply to present design possibilities for the public's consideration. "The consumer today is more a participant than a target," Archigram claimed in 1966.[37] Democracy – more precisely, consumer democracy – would be the final arbiter. Bowing to the 'democratic' pressures of consumption had become regarded as the ethical corrective to all those post-War years of strict planning and austerity. In *The Long Revolution* (1961), cultural critic Raymond Williams noted that "the deep revulsion against general planning, which makes sense again and again in many details of our economic activity … is itself in part a consequence of one aspect of the democratic revolution – the determination not to be regimented."[38] So it was this general, liberal-democratic instinct that informed the flexibility of Plug-in City, not the anarchist tendency that motivated New Babylon. For Situationists like Constant, freedom was the highest ideal, only attainable beyond the fiscal economy and tested by intense socialization.

Notably though, Plug-in and New Babylon shared the 1960s fantasy that looked forward to the end of labour through automation – this much was made clear by Constant's ICA lecture and Archigram's preoccupation with the theme of leisure. Both designs assumed that mechanization was reaching a saturation point at which hard labour would vanish: there are no factories in New Babylon or Plug-in City, no matter that Constant's critics denounced New Babylon as looking like "models of factories",[39] or that Plug-in City was likely inspired in part by oil refineries. "The only activity that will remain beyond automation is the unique act of imagination, by which a human being is distinguished," argued Constant as Cook and Webb listened.[40] "If man

14. *Instant City*, collage by Peter Cook, 1969

is no longer bound to production-labour," Constant went on, "he will also no longer be forced to stick to a fixed place."[41] So both New Babylon and Plug-in City unfixed place (regardless of Constant and Cook's desire to provide a variety of urban experience), thereby permitting *homo ludens* to roam. The physical unsticking of place is evident in the drawings and models of stretched space and demountable elements. As well as this, both schemes unstick social space, through the disestablishment of social order: "the unsatisfaction of the average welfare-state citizen of today has more to do with the world he lives in than with his own capacities"[42] claimed Constant, much as Archigram berated the culture of the British New Towns and the sort of planning procedures that were noted by Raymond Williams. Instead, "all is to happen"[43] (Constant); "the mood of cities is frantic. It is all happening – all the time"[44] (Cook). A world of perpetual revolution was being conjured up.

In both Plug-in City and New Babylon, then, the working class has disappeared, to be absorbed into one vast leisure class for Archigram, into *homo ludens* for Constant. Leisure was a theme which permeated quickly during the 1960s: Archigram's friend Cedric Price had designed an institution for its housing, the Fun Palace project of 1964, and the 1964 Milan Triennale took 'Tempo Libero' as its theme, the Italian Pavilion in particular seemingly designed to create a sense of situation.[45] Constant's prediction of expanded leisure time was a neo-Marxist variant; Archigram sensed that leisure was part of a social and political process, yet they wanted fun to remain apolitical, innocent, hobbyist, teenage, consumerist, as *Archigram* no. 8 put it: "Water/underwater as sport/fun/English 'playing about in boats'. Choice of wardrobe. Switch-on fun. In the brain fun. Hobbies. Airplanes. Moon probe. Personality. Oddballs. Simulated individualism.

Pastiche styling as fun."[46] (The love of innocent fun was partly autobiographical – two members of Archigram, Peter Cook and Dennis Crompton, had grown up in seaside towns; a third, Michael Webb, grew up in the home of the boating regatta, Henley-on-Thames.)

The destiny of the avant-garde hinged upon these differing interpretations of mass leisure and mechanization. Constant had an exceptionally clear vision of the fate of the avant-garde, preempting the well-known arguments that were to be forwarded by Peter Bürger in 1974.[47] Like Bürger, Constant dated the 'true' avant-garde to around 1916–29, that is from Dadaism to the Wall Street Crash,[48] and this 'historical' avant-garde was, Constant felt, "the end of a cultural era, a time the last individualists helplessly tried to resist what in their view signalled the end of individualism: mechanization."[49] The future of culture lay with the social collective brought back to life thanks to the free time liberated by mechanization, Constant argued. New Babylon was the great collective game of art that came after the avant-garde. But Archigram, animated by the emergence of Swinging London, felt that a socially-integrated vanguard position within the existing economy was viable, and that its result might be something looking like Plug-in City. With the ascendancy of Harold Wilson's technocratic socialism in Britain, technocracy had become a vanguard phenomenon, acceptable both to sections of the Right for its promotion of industrial development and to sections of the Left for its promise of a universal improvement in standards of living and social mobility. Political play was generally made of those innovations – the computer, monorail and hovercraft – that were parts of the Plug-in iconography. Technocracy deferred decision-making to 'experts', of the sort that might be trained in the 'brain silos' of Cook's Plug-in University Node, a project of

15. Constant, *Gezicht op Sectoren*, photomontage, 1971

1965 that coincided with the rapid expansion of the British university system.[50] Plug-in was not a curio in the manner of the equally iconic Walking City project of 1964 by Archigram colleague Ron Herron; it was a sincere proposal for a way of building. But, Constant warned, "the pseudo-neo-avant-garde is essentially a conservative movement. A socially integrated avant-garde is an absurdity, as social recognition cannot be reconciled with the militant concept of 'avant-garde' itself."[51] Perhaps it was consciously then that Archigram avoided using the label 'avant-garde', substituting terms like 'experimental'.

"It will often be part of the architect's brief … to exploit the maximum profit from a piece of land" wrote Cook in 1967. "In the past this would have been considered an immoral use of the talents of an artist. It is now simply part of the sophistication of the whole environmental and building process in which finance can be made a creative element in design."[52] The frank admission was a far call from New Babylon's utopian non-commodity socialism, though Constant's work smacked of a similar desire to confine scarcity and suffering to oblivion. "New Babylon is

the product of the non-utilitarian, creative technocracy," Constant confessed.[53] Plug-in and New Babylon alike tackled the interconnected problems of population growth, land use, traffic and its incursion upon common social space, and the erosion by urban sprawl of architectural variegation.[54] New Babylon and Plug-in City were similarly inspired by the systems approach, a universal technology directing "a hundred or a thousand different things, all happening at once."[55] Yet the design and conceptual overlaps of New Babylon and Plug-in City did not grant them the same critical reception during the rest of the decade, and this was probably due to the markedly differing ideologies that underwrote them. New Babylon was adopted as a metaphor for the architectural empowerment of the people, especially for radicals like the Dutch Provos, whereas by the 1970s the maulings received by Archigram had left the group a little bruised and suspect of 'radicals'. Radicals began to worry that architecture *per se* was not a means to empowerment after all, but only ever an expression of power, and in the 1970s Renzo Piano and Richard Rogers's Plug-in-inspired Pompidou Centre, complete with tubular structure and diagonal movement, provided an ideal focal point for bitter acrimony. Intended as a plug-in free-flowing forum for spontaneous culture, the Centre unavoidably functioned as a monument to the state and its beneficence.

Plug-in and New Babylon had been programmed to have rather different effects upon the cultural landscape. Constant projected a landscape of mass movement, of the artificial environment as the final artistic medium, overcoming individualism through collectivity and mechanization. The capillaries and nervous system of Cook's project looked more toward the micro-movements of individuals, goods and information. And if New Babylon was ultimately about social space, Plug-in City was ultimately about pragmatism. "To what extent can we freely build the framework of a social life in which we can be guided by our aspirations and not by our instincts?" reads a lofty quotation in a catalogue for

16. Plug into global networks: Sony advertisement reproduced in *Archigram* 9, 1970

New Babylon.[56] *Archigram* no. 4 enthused rather less poetically about "moving buildings with city functions such as business deals and government going on inside".[57]

In retrospect Archigram's David Greene regretted that his group did not cultivate closer contacts with the Situationists,[58] and of its own volition Archigram moved away from functionality and toward the poetic. In fact Archigram quite rapidly withdrew from the 'hardware' megastructural solution epitomized by Plug-in City, so that its openly-stated project by 1966 was to move 'beyond architecture' into a world of 'software' – pure servicing, information, networking, transience. The project to 'molecularise' space, started in Plug-in, was transferred to an imaginary world of freely-roving, fully-equipped individuals. By comparison New Babylon's ongoing super-hardware and social hangars began to look moribund, and from 1968–74, co-inciding exactly with the gloom of the intelligentsia following the failure of the Paris *Événements*, depictions of New Babylon became panic stricken, and the entire project was terminated.

In the longer term, both the Situationist and Archigram projects have resonated with a new generation fighting 'the system'. The former project inspires festivity, non-commodity direct action and collective social space; the latter suggests uses of information, consumer stealth and molecular space. David Greene has been fond of drawing the comparison between the mobile telephone and architecture: where there is a telephone, there is an office.[59] He might add that information networks also provide the space to coordinate insurrection, as the rioters of London and Seattle demonstrated in 1999, and the text-messaging revolutionaries of the Philippines enacted in January 2001.[60]

Notes

1 Peter Cook, 'Archigram', lecture at the New Babylon conference, Faculty of Architecture, Delft University of Technology, 26/1/00.
2 See letter from Peter Cook to Constant, 20 July 1964, in the Constant archive, Rijksbureau voor Kunsthistorische Documentatie, The Hague.
3 From Anon, 'Within the Big Structure', *Archigram* no. 5, 1964, n.p.
4 Peter Cook, 'Archigram', lecture at the New Babylon conference, Faculty of Architecture, Delft University of Technology, 26/1/00.
5 For an instance of collaboration between Constant and Bakema, see Bakema's commission of Constant's Monument for Reconstruction, 1955, for the Rotterdam E55 exhibition. Details on Constant's contacts with architects and artists are provided in Mark Wigley, *Constant's New Babylon, The Hyper-Architecture of Desire*, Rotterdam: 010 Publishers, 1998.
6 See for instance the collaborations on the *Mens en huis* display at the Stedelijk museum, 1953, the 'Idea for Living' furniture exhibition at the De Bijenkorf department store in 1954, and on the new Amsterdam playgrounds.
7 Anon., 'Networks around the Channel', *Archigram* no. 7, 1966, n.p.
8 The outstanding source on megastructures remains Reyner Banham's *Megastructure*, London: Thames and Hudson, 1976.
9 Cited in Hein van Haaren, *Constant*, Amsterdam: Meulenhoff, 1966, trans. Max Schuchart, p. 8.
10 My thanks to Tim Benton for drawing my attention to Mendelsohn.
11 Ulrich Conrads and Hans Gunther Sperlich, *Fantastic Architecture*, trans. Christine Crasemann Collins & George R. Collins (New York, 1962, and London: Architectural Press, 1963).
12 The *Forum* edition is discussed in Wigley, op.cit., pp. 31–32.
13 Robert Maxwell, 'The 'Living City' exhibition at the ICA', in Theo Crosby and John Bodley, eds., *Living Arts* no. 3, London: Institute of Contemporary Arts and Tillotsons, 1964, pp. 98–100, p. 99.
14 Anon., 'Situation', in Theo Crosby and John Bodley, eds., *Living Arts* no. 2, London: Institute of Contemporary Arts and Tillotsons, 1963, p. 112.
15 Anon., 'Situation', in Crosby and Bodley, eds., *Living Arts* no. 2, p. 112.
16 See Sadie Plant, *The Most Radical Gesture: the Situationist International in a Postmodern Age*, London: Routledge, 1992, p. 21 and *passim*.
17 Peter Cook, 'The Electric Decade: An Atmosphere at the AA School 1963–73', in Gowan, ed., *A Continuing Experiment: Learning and Teaching at the Architectural Association*, London: The Architectural Press, 1975, pp. 137–146, p. 138.
18 Peter Cook, *Experimental Architecture*, London: Studio Vista, 1970, p. 77.
19 See Kiyonori Kikutake, Kisho Kurokawa, Fumihiko Maki and Masato Otaka, 'Metabolism 1960 – A Proposal for New Urbanism' (1958), manifesto delivered to the 1960 World Design Conference, reprinted in Kisho Kurokawa, *Metabolism in Architecture*, London: Studio Vista, 1977, p. 27.
20 This was a point reiterated by Peter Cook, 'Archigram', lecture at the New Babylon conference, Faculty of Architecture, Delft University of Technology, 26/1/00.
21 My thanks to Barry Curtis for first drawing my attention to this.
22 Harry Kroto, 'Desert Island Discs', BBC Radio 4, 24/6/01. Kroto was born 1939; Cook in 1936. Meccano was patented by Frank Hornby in 1901; the current LEGO stud-and-tube coupling system was patented in 1958.
23 Published in *Archigram* no. 7, 1966, n.p., reprinted in Cook, *Experimental Architecture*, p. 106.
24 Unless we count Dennis Crompton's 'meta-plan' of the Plug-in City National Network project, 1964.
25 Cited in Hein van Haaren, op.cit., p. 8
26 Cook, *Experimental Architecture*, p. 101.
27 Constant, 'Over het reizen', read to the BNA (Society of Dutch Architects) on the occasion of the realization of the new Schipol Airport buildings, April 1966, and published in *Opstand van de Homo Ludens*, Bussum: Paul Brand, 1969; trans. 'On Traveling', in Wigley, op.cit., pp. 200–201.
28 Dennis Crompton and Peter Cook, in lectures at the Archigram symposium, Cornerhouse, Manchester, 9/2/98, implied that Computer City and Plug-in City were directly linked.
29 Dennis Crompton, 'Computer City', *Archigram* no. 5, 1965, n.p.
30 Constant, 'New Babylon' (1960), in *Constant – Amsterdam*, cat. Städtische Kunstgalerie Bochum, 1961, trans. in Ulrich Conrads, *Programmes and Manifestoes on Twentieth Century Architecture*, London: Lund Humphries, 1970, pp. 177–178.
31 Ibid.
32 Cited in Van Haaren, pp. 12–13.
33 Constant, 'New Babylon' (1960), trans. Conrads, op.cit., pp. 177–178.
34 Wigley, op.cit., p. 31, counts nearly a hundred New Babylon drawings, and (p. 23 *passim*) notes their slide from 'mechanical' to 'expressive' modes.
35 Constant, Lecture given at the Institute of Contemporary Arts, London, November 7, 1963, reprinted in Mark Wigley, ed., *Drawing Papers 3, Another City for Another Life: Constant's New Babylon*, New York: The Drawing Centre, 1999, pp. a9–a13, p. a13.
36 Anon, 'In this Archigram', *Archigram* no. 9, 1970, n.p.
37 Archigram, dir., *Archigram*, BBC Productions, 1966.
38 Raymond Williams, *The Long Revolution*, London: Chatto & Windus, 1961, p. 321.
39 Guy-Ernest Debord, Attila Kotányi, and Jorgen Nash, 'Critique de l'urbanisme', *Internationale situationniste*, no. 6, Paris, August 1961, pp. 5–11, in Ken Knabb, ed. and trans., *Situationist International Anthology*, Berkeley: Bureau of Public Secrets, 1981, op.cit., note 113, p. 373.
40 Constant, Lecture given at the Institute of Contemporary Arts, in Wigley, ed., *Drawing Papers 3, Another City for Another Life: Constant's New Babylon*, p. a10.
41 Ibid., p. a11.
42 Ibid.
43 Ibid., p. a12.
44 Peter Cook, 'Come-Go', in Crosby and Bodley, eds., *Living Arts* no. 2, p. 80.
45 My thanks to Dr. Pauline Madge for drawing my attention to this.
46 Anon., 'Emancipation', *Archigram* no. 8, 1968, n.p.
47 See Peter Bürger, *Theorie der Avantgarde*, 1974, trans. Michael Shaw, *Theory of the Avant-Garde*, Minneapolis: University of Minnesota Press, 1984.
48 Constant, 'Opkomst en ondergang van de avant-garde', *Randstad*, 1964, trans. 'The Rise and Decline of the Avant-Garde', in Wigley, ed., *Drawing Papers 3, Another City for Another Life: Constant's New Babylon*, pp. a14–a28, p. a14.
49 Ibid., p. a15.
50 See Peter Cook, 'Plug-in University node', *Archigram* no. 6, 1965, n.p.
51 Constant, 'The Rise and Decline of the Avant-Garde', in Wigley, ed., Drawing Papers 3, *Another City for Another Life: Constant's New Babylon*, p. a15.
52 Peter Cook, *Architecture: Action and Plan*, London: Studio Vista/Reinhold, 1967, cited in Kenneth Frampton, *Modern Architecture, A Critical History*, London: Thames and Hudson, 1985, p. 282.
53 Cited in Van Haaren, p. 11.
54 Constant, Lecture given at the Institute of Contemporary Arts, in Wigley, ed., Drawing Papers 3, *Another City for Another Life: Constant's New Babylon*, p. a11.
55 Archigram, dir., *Archigram*, BBC Productions, 1966.
56 In Anon., *Constant*, Paris: Bibliothèque d'Alexandrie, 1959, n.p. The quotation is taken from Paul-Henri Chombart de Lauwe.
57 Anon., 'Plug-in City', *Archigram* no. 4, 1964.
58 Conversation with David Greene, London 24/4/97.
59 See for instance David Greene, 'A Prologue', in Dennis Crompton, ed., *Concerning Archigram*, London: Archigram Archives, 1998, p. 1.
60 For more on networks, see Mark Freestone, 'Crypto-Rhizomes': The Dialectic of Enigmatography, unpublished paper, University of Nottingham Sociology Department seminar, March 2001.

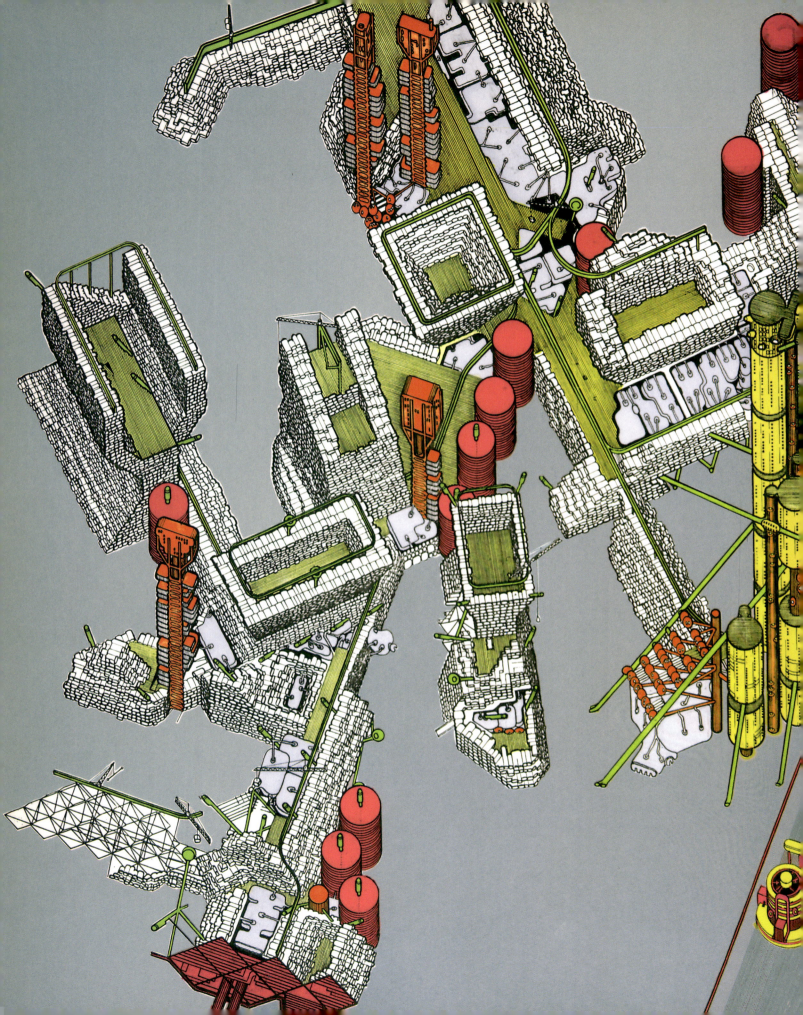

Design for Living
by Priscilla Chapman

THE PLUG-IN CITY

Since the first reaction to most plans for coping with the population explosion is a wild hope that all those people will never show up, an idea with a name like Plug-In City is not going to be popular at first glance. One established and long-disillusioned designer looked at it and said simply: "It's a very good idea. You would need a dictatorship to do it."

To put it in its baldest, least prepossessing terms, Plug-In City is a linear city housed in a high, narrow grid system which would start near London, grow in one direction towards Liverpool and in another, across the Channel, past Paris and on into Europe. It would not knock down London, Liverpool or Paris or any city we're fond of. Its path will lie tangential to them. (Talking to Plug-In City's designers the tense slips from the conditional into the simple future and, from here on, I shall leave it at that).

Along the top of the grid will run the all-important monorail which, besides carrying passengers, will also carry cranes which can in turn carry sections of the grid, so that the city can continually build and re-build itself, tear itself down, change its direction or go off in little spurs like those in the diagram on the left – all with less trouble than digging up a road today. The spaces formed by the grid (next page) is where you would plug yourself in, or more accurately, where the crane plugs in everything that makes up a city, from living rooms to parking lots.

All this sounds soul-destroying, cold and highly unlikely. It has a touch of science fiction: Plug-In City was, in fact, first published in the ZOOM issue of *Archigram*, a fringe architectural magazine put out by its designers,

2

renamed *Amazing Archigram* and done like a space comic for the occasion. *Amazing Archigram* had Superman zooming along over the aerial view reproduced on the left. Superman (puzzled, thinks): "It seems I have been over this city for very many miles." Superman (thinks again): "Yes, indeed ... for it stretches over the Channel and beyond ... into Europe In this part you can see the habitations plugged into the giant network-structure that is 12 stories high ..."

But the three young men who are evolving Plug-In City – Warren Chalk and Dennis Crompton, who also work for Taylor Woodrow, and Peter Cook, who teaches at the Architectural Association – say it could be started right now and in 20 years be well on its way.

On a technical level it is set apart from other plans by its purchase on life as it will be in the

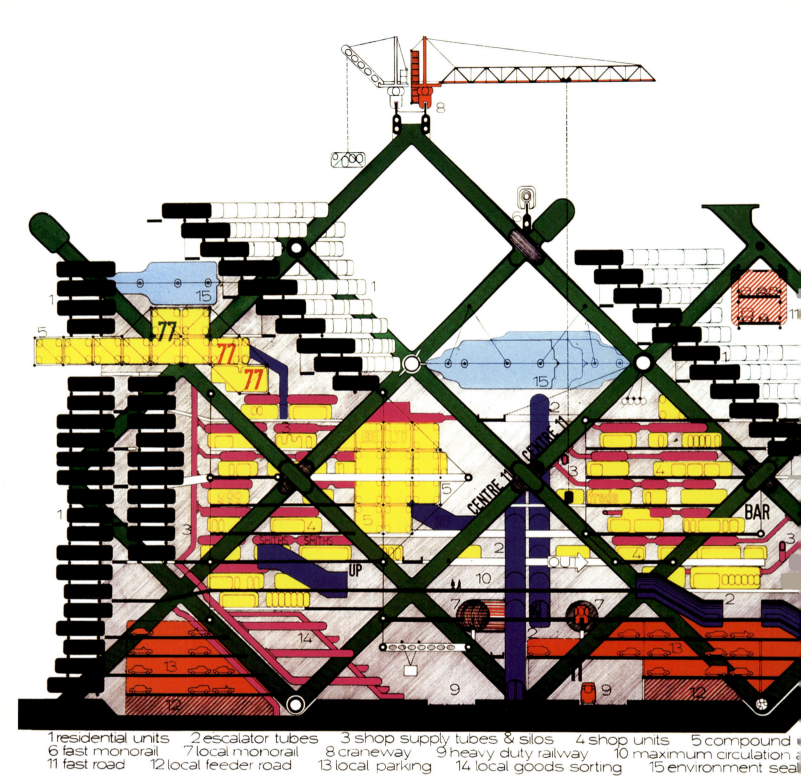

1 residential units   2 escalator tubes   3 shop supply tubes & silos   4 shop units   5 compound
6 fast monorail   7 local monorail   8 craneway   9 heavy duty railway   10 maximum circulation a
11 fast road   12 local feeder road   13 local parking   14 local goods sorting   15 environment sea

So far there isn't a drawing to show what it would be like to walk around Plug-in City, but this cross-section gives an idea and it's reassuring that life will still be recognizable. Note Fred's, a kayf just right of centre, and, left of centre, Big Ltd., which could be a department store. At Christmas or during the sales Big's proprietors could plug in more rooms to absorb the rush. The diagram is best read by the colour key: all yellow sections are shops. All the magenta is a shop-feed system, because there won't be any goods deliveries by lorry to clutter up the roads. Instead, food shops will be like giant cigarette machines with just a refrigerated display. You will be able to get obscure dishes, for which you now have to go to Soho, in any neighbourhood: the proprietor will dial a central depot and they will come through pneumatic tubes or along conveyor belts. The diagonal framework (green) would be the longest-lasting element in the city, and everything plugs into it. It would be self-building and self-destroying, thanks

to the crane (top of diagram) on the monorail, which is shown about to plug in a room but would also carry the big tubular sections of the grid. The grid is adaptable enough to be valid for perhaps 50 years: after that time, the designers feel a whole new system would have begun to replace it. There are lifts and escalators in the grid sections so people can step out of their doors on to a bridge or street, depending on where they live, and get on the escalator to their office. Or they could take an escalator to the local monorail (7 at the bottom of the diagram) and take that either to their stop or to the nearest station on the fast monorail, which being faster moving and quicker to respond to technological change is higher up in the framework at 6. This cross-section is the best diagram for seeing what the designers call "the hierarchy of speed and change". Generally the oldest, slowest-moving and slowest-to-change elements are near the bottom of the grid, the fastest near the top. At ground level are trains future. It grasps the rate at which people and things will change and, in effect, acknowledges throw-away architecture.

But what is going to matter to people now is that this plan is so much less traumatic than others: so much so, in fact, that anyone – anyone, that is, who is totally opposed to the future – could almost welcome the predicted millions and the opportunity to plug in with them. On an even cursory examination of the diagrams on these four pages, Plug-In City turns out not to be as heartless as it sounds. The name is more fuzzy than frightening and the plan itself is humane, benign, even cosy – the work of well-intentioned young men who say the whole point is to have lively neighbourhoods. Chalk, Cook, Crompton and Co. find it hard to say exactly what it will be like to step out of your front door in Plug-In City, but it sounds as though it will be a mixture of a theatre (balconies, aisles and stairs) and Montmartre (passages and stairs connecting different levels): in any event, there will be lots of well-travelled, busy catwalks and streets honeycombing the grid system, all connected by the lifts and escalators. They reckon on a density of 400 people to the acre to ensure the lively neighbourhood feeling (like Mayfair's today), and while the L.C.C. do not generally allow a density of more than 135, these days advanced city planners who want to get away form the New Towns that stretch too far and too dispiritedly, are already thinking in terms of 400.

Plug-In City has two enormous advantages over cities as we know them. The first is that it is a straight line rather than a circle. What this means sinks in when you consider that London has a radius of 20 miles, that under proposals like the South-East Plan it would soon be several times that and week-end cottages wouldn't be anywhere you could get to at a weekend. Its designers see Plug-In City as a magnetic field across Europe, collecting like iron filings all the hopeless little piecemeal building that is smothering the countryside.

The second advantage is that being a self-destroying, self-building system it is easily pushed into the shape people want it to be – rather than its pushing people into shape. What this means sinks in when you remember the traffic jam a building site causes

(for as long as they last), local monorails and local roads. At the top are the fast monorail and the fast road (11 at right), which is suspended from the grid so that it can be easily changed to whatever is needed when cars go out. In the long run everything can be plugged out and replaced without too much fuss, although obviously some things will change slower than others. The black colouring is housing, nine-tenths of which would be on the outside of the grid.
Right: a tower which could be part of Plug-in City includes both parking (the green colouring) and plug-in housing. Basically it's a core with the ubiquitous crane on top to plug in the rooms, which are like super de luxe caravans (see diagrams above and next page). People could hitch up their rooms pretty much as they liked as is suggested by the colouring which indicates each family's plug-ins. As it's drawn here, the tower is only a section of what it could be, it could be much higher, repeating parking and housing at other levels.

1

2

© 1964
PETER
COOK

10ps

on

3

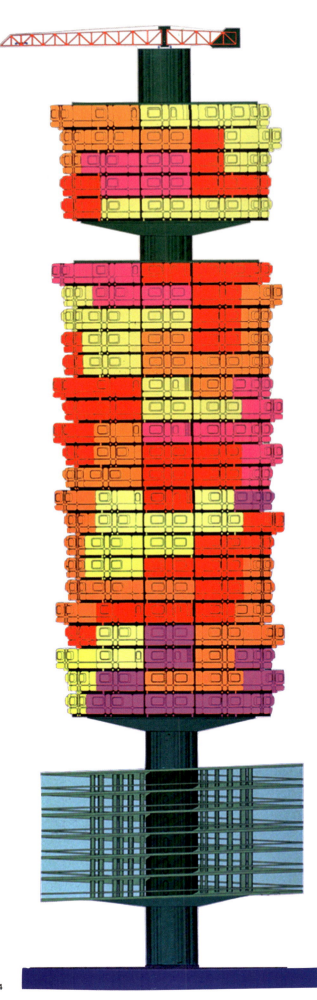

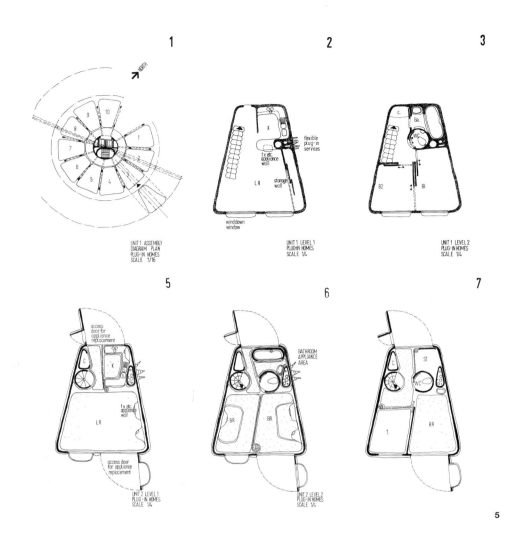

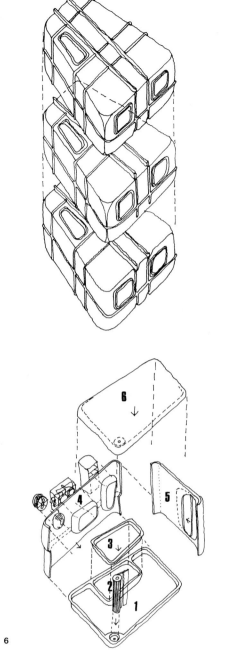

for months on end, or just the mess of having central heating put in. Because the trouble with concrete and brick is that they take a long time to put up, a long time to knock down, and when they are down, all your have is a pile of rubble to shift.

In Plug-In City, when cars become extinct – and they are moving that way as surely as the dinosaurs ever did – you plug out the roads and parking space designed for them, and plug in whatever you need for the new kind of transport – all of it neatly manufactured in sections at a factory.

And while today the job of providing enough houses is appalling, in Plug-In days, according to Warren Chalk, plastic and metal rooms will be mass-produced, cheap and expendable. "You might choose a Ford bathroom and Vauxhall kitchen, and as you rise in the world you can trade in your Hillman living room for a Bentley." Living in the unit he's working on now will be like living in a super de luxe cara-van. Parts of it, like clip-on appliance wall and bathroom/kitchen capsule (see diagrams on pages 72/73) will be designed for future

replacement. The floor will be like a tray. "When someone brings out a great new, heated, car-peted, roll-around-on tray, you hire the crane to slide out your old one and slide in the new one."

This isn't the Georgian house-dweller's dream, nor just the way the bungalow-and-garden lover sees his retirement. But there are two points to assuage any horrors. The first is that you don't have to live in Plug-In City. Retired people probably won't. London and Paris will still be there because, says Peter Cook, Plug-In City will not only leave them standing, it will see that they don't get their life-blood cut off and wither away. Quite early in its develop-ment it will mesh in with one side of each city so there will be a steady commerce among them all.

And then Plug-In City is designed to leave the countryside and sea coast much as it is. Bognor Regis will still be there too. People can always escape, and Chalk, Crompton and Cook all reckon that by the time Plug-In City happens, they will have second flats or houses in "leisure areas", with grass and what-not, and

that for most people the working week will be three days.

They don't think it would take a dictatorship to get Plug-In City started. They think people are a lot nearer being psychologically ready for big changes than we realize and that buying houses off-the-peg isn't going to be such a big step. "We have to skate between people's inhibitions. People like to fee safe and they like to see predictable things around them. New Towns weren't such a shock because they could see a corner pub and washing hanging out on the line. But there is a difference be-tween what's human, and it's important to let people know that something new can be human too."

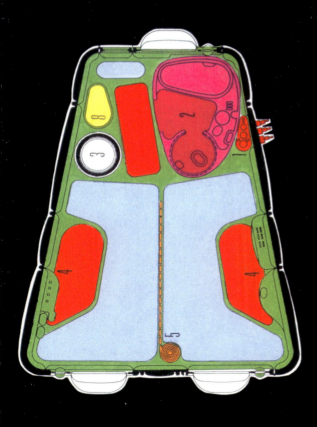

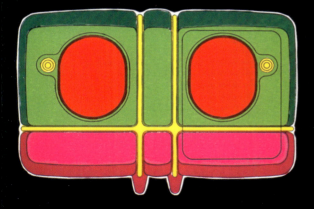

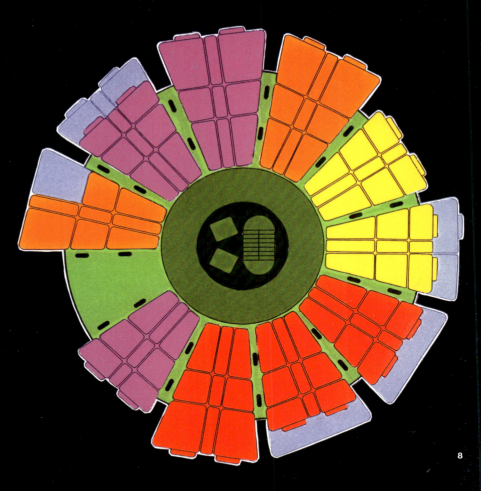

Warren Chalk's floor-plan for the house units (this page, top left) which plug into the tower pursues the hierarchy of change down to the fastest-changing things of all – the appliances. The units themselves could be changed whenever a new, improved one came out, but since new, improved appliances are bound to develop even faster, there is a clip-on appliance wall (4 on the diagram) which can be snapped out and replaced with one fitted with more advanced food mixers, vibro massagers and machines like the American one which makes plastic mixing bowls meant to be thrown away after using. Kitchens and bathrooms are the next areas to become obsolete, so they are contained in a pop-out capsule (2) situated near a wide service door opening into the tower's core. The key to the diagram is: (1) Services duct; (2) Kitchen-bathroom capsule; (3) Pneumatic lift instead of a staircase; (4) Clip-on appliance wall; (5) Spring-loaded space divider; (6) Wide door for removing capsules and walls; (7) Services connection; (8) Storage unit. The dark area is soft flooring for sitting and lying on.

Peter Cook doesn't think it will take long. "After all, my wife wears clothes which will be an embarrassment in two years. Hospitals have paper sheets. Soon it won't be so shocking to throw away a building we have been using."

"Our basic message," says one issue of *Archigram*, "is that the home, the whole city and the frozen pea pack are all the same". (And on the same page of the same issue is the line: "The idea of an expendable environment is still somehow regarded as akin to anarchy … as if in order to make it work would bulldoze Westminster Abbey …")

At the same time they feel designers cannot hang back worrying about politics. "We know people may not accept – but architects are always saying people won't accept something and they have no way of knowing for the plain reason that they have never gone far enough to give people a

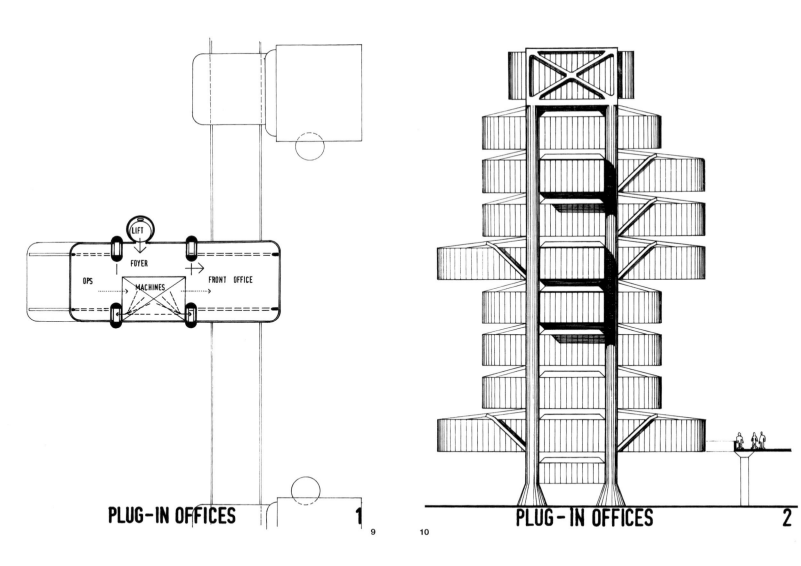

PLUG-IN OFFICES 1

9

10

PLUG-IN OFFICES 2

real choice. We think it would be a good idea to take just one block in a twilight zone, maybe Paddington, and start a Plug-In system just to see how it works, and if it wouldn't be a better choice than another low-density Stevenage.

"But the terrible thing in England is that architects are so over-intellectualized and self-critical that they are afraid of taking a step for fear it won't be right." What worries Peter Cook, who teaches, is that it is even happening to the students. "They are all beginning to think like civil servants. You can just hear them saying 'I am instructed to make this room 20ft. long and 10ft. high' without thinking for themselves." His dearest wish it to get people to lecture to his students in fields which are going to be increasingly related to the architecture of the future – a car designer, an inventor or someone like Jacques Cousteau.

People are always asking Chalk, Crompton and Cook where they plan to keep the baby in Plug-In City or how the groceries will be delivered, and then they go back in fill in details. They try to avoid falling into Superman-at-home-on-the-satellite attitudes and work comparatively soberly, developing solutions for which they know the technical knowledge already exists.

They have noticed a hierarchy of speed and change, which they didn't plan but which seems to be the natural evolution of a rapidly changing city (see diagram on page 70). According to it the small, light, high-speed elements tend to develop faster and to be near the top of the city. The slower, heavier, less responsive elements are near the ground. This is why they thought of the clip-on appliance wall. Dennis Crompton is carrying it further and working out an hotel in which the newest, most up-to-date rooms will be fed in at the top by the crane, while older ones gradually work their way down to the bottom.

They realize that the roads at different levels would inevitably be rushing past people's bedroom windows and, in the tower on page 71, actually linking up with the parking levels. This raises the question of noise and while they cannot foresee the exact answers, Plug-In City will be a lot quieter than cities are now. The plastics the plug-in units are made of will be soundproof and cars are on the way out.

They have given a lot of thought to commuters. In Plug-In City people could take local monorails to work, but they hope that residential and business districts will be so mixed up that most people will just take the escalator down a level or two.

The new means of transport and the shape of the city are linked. One of the reasons they feel that cities of the future will have to be linear is simply that the speed of monorails and hovercraft require it. "A radial city is fine for walking around in or for light, slow traffic, but monorails have to get up high speeds in order to operate economically." It's a point already proven by Manhattan, which is virtually a linear city; its subway system runs express trains at a speed impossible in London's Underground.

"There are all kinds of things which we haven't tackled properly yet and which we are going to

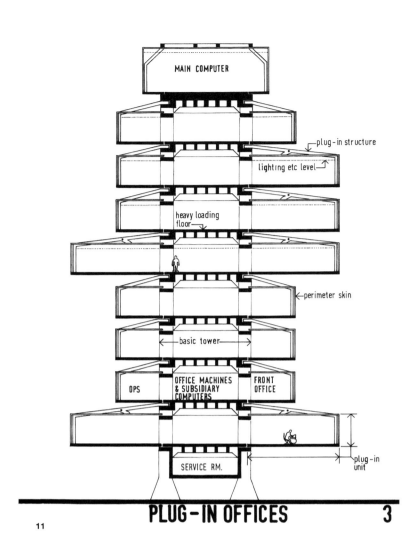

plug-in structure

lighting etc level

heavy loading floor

perimeter skin

basic tower

| OPS | OFFICE MACHINES & SUBSIDIARY COMPUTERS | FRONT OFFICE |

MAIN COMPUTER

plug-in unit

SERVICE RM.

PLUG-IN OFFICES 3

11

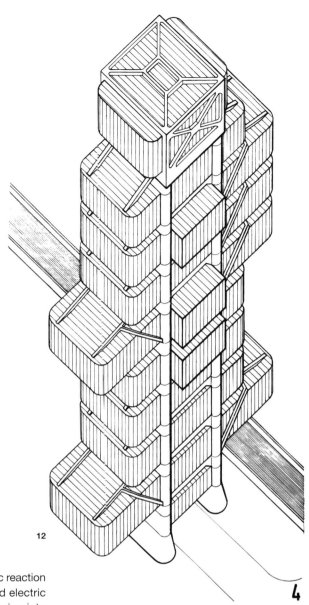

12

4

have to," says Peter Cook, and not the least of them is leisure. People will have more free time and perhaps less reason for going out. If, for instance, groceries are delivered by conveyor belt, a woman won't have to go shopping and will miss the casual socializing that comes with it. Chalk, Crompton and Cook have thought of it and think the answer will be that everything will be geared up, communications will be faster and going out won't be the effort it is now. They also feel that leisure just isn't going to be the way it is these days. "We all separate leisure from life. We 'go out' for a big night and 'save up' for a big-bust holiday once a year. But leisure will be closer to home and more woven with everyday life. We are thinking in terms of plug-on balconies which could be added to the house units. They wouldn't be little 3ft.-wide affairs, but 20ft. outdoor rooms."

Work and leisure and travel will be closely bound up. There will be, says Warren Chalk, giant hovercraft zipping across Europe with a conference going on inside. Businessmen, having started the day with a deal in Berlin, will get off the deal in Moscow.

And they have not forgotten the public reaction to the skyline. (Talk about pylons and electric cables.) The sight of Plug-In City hoving into sight over the downs isn't going to please everyone, but the designers think that it will be on such a grand scale that it will be "great" and also liberate more countryside anyhow.

Do they think Plug-In City has a chance of getting off the ground? Maybe not the way it is now. It changes constantly. Peter Cook says the diagrams on these pages "are like cartoons for a painting. It was important to make the initial leap to a different kind of city because nothing else will make a dent on the problem. And while we hope something will develop from it, we don't say Plug-In City is the only way. It happens to be the best one we have seen and the best one we can thing of at the moment. It certainly doesn't preclude better ones coming along. Like Ron Herron, who worked with us on it – he's got a city that walks."

The Sunday Times,
25 September 1964

13

14

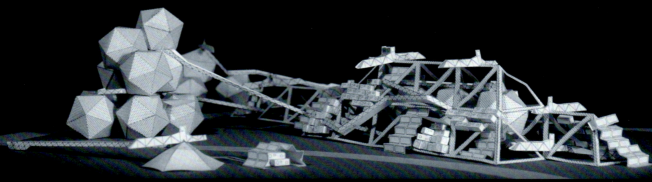

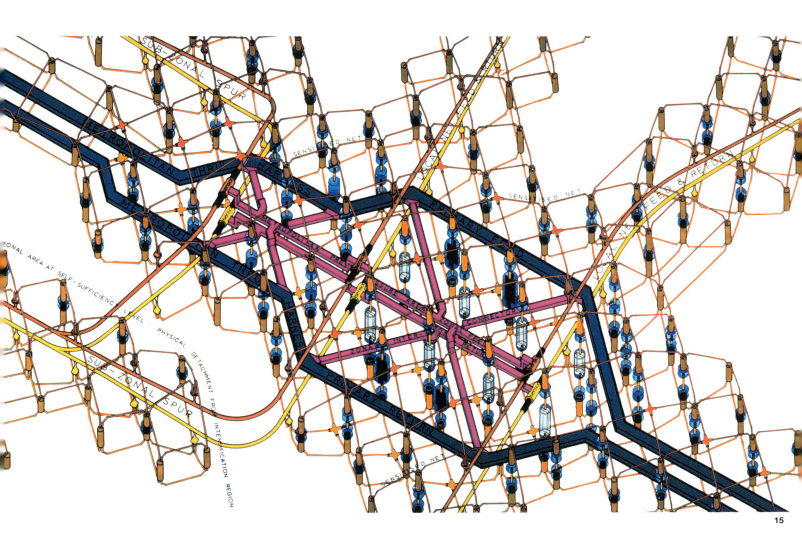

Plug-in City Peter Cook

The Plug-in City as a total project was the combination of a series of ideas that were worked upon between 1962 and 1964. The metal cabin housing was a prototype in the sense that it placed removable house elements into a 'megastructure' of concrete. The discussions of *Archigram* 2 and 3 built up a pressure of argument in favour of expendable buildings: and it was then inevitable that we should investigate what happens if the whole urban environment can be programmed and structured for change.

The 'Living City' exhibition paralleled these material notions with the equally explosive ones regarding the quality of city life: its symbolism, its dynamic, its gregariousness, its dependence upon situation as much as established form. As a final preliminary, the Montreal Tower was useful as a model for the structuring of a large 'plug-in' conglomeration, with its large, regular structure and its movement-tubes (which were to be combined in the 'city' megastructure), and its proof that such a conglomeration does not need to have the dreariness that is normally associated with regularized systems.

It is difficult to state which phase of the work on Plug-in City forms the definitive project. During the whole period 1962–66 elements were being looked at, and notions amended or extended as necessary: so the drawings inevitably contain many inconsistencies. The term 'city' is used as a collective, the project being a portmanteau for several ideas, and does not necessarily imply a replacement of known cities.

The axonometric (1, page 68 / 69) is usually assumed to be the definitive image, for obviously classical reasons. It is 'heroic', apparently an alternative to the known city form, containing 'futurist' but recognizable hierarchies and elements. Craggy but directional, mechanistic but scaleable, it was based upon a drawn plan (21), which placed a structural grid on a square plan at 45 degrees to a monorail route that was to connect existing cities. Alongside ran a giant routeway for hovercraft (the ultimate in mobile buildings), the notion being that some major functions of the several linked parts could travel between them. The essential physical operations are stressed: the craneways and the bad weather balloons, and the lift overruns are deliberately exaggerated. But overriding all this was the deliberate varietousness of each major building outcrop: whatever

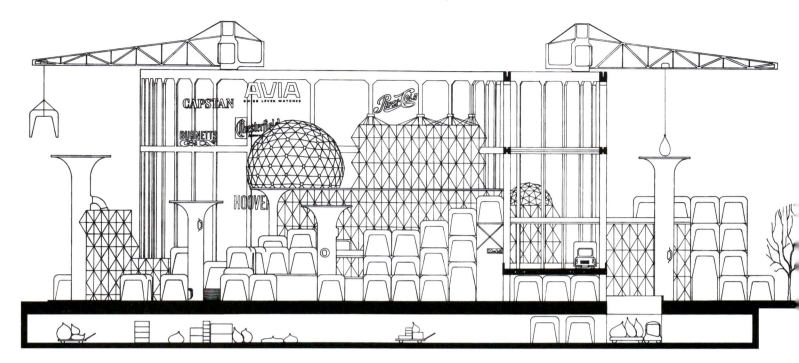

16

else it was to be, this city was not going to be a deadly piece of built mathematics.

In the various studies that built up the total project, one can trace the succession of priorities that are gradually overlaid, and one can see how the sections evolved. The Nottingham project (16) was a proposal for shopping, but the problems of frequent servicing and the breakdown of normal 'department store' or 'lockup' boundaries triggered a notion of a viaduct-like structure against which the shops could lean. The goods servicing and the unit replacement were complementary: and already a major part of the Plug-in proposition existed. With the craneway running along the viaduct and a service tunnel system, it is only a short step to the incorporation of housing elements. In a diagram drawn for the Living City exhibition (18) the business of replacement and transportation are dominant.

We then turned towards a specific application of 'Plug-in' thinking: the rentable office floor. The axonometric (12) shows a pylon that contains lifts and services with a 'tray' hanging off each side. One tray is the 'front' office, the other the 'backroom' office. Each part would be exchangeable. Various ideas about automated shopping and diagonalized movement combine with the Plug-in Office tower

17

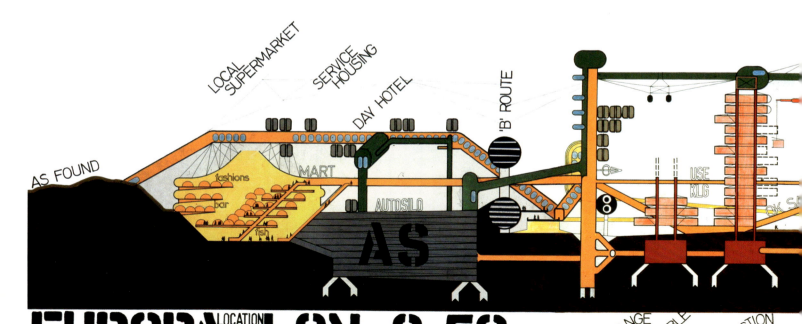

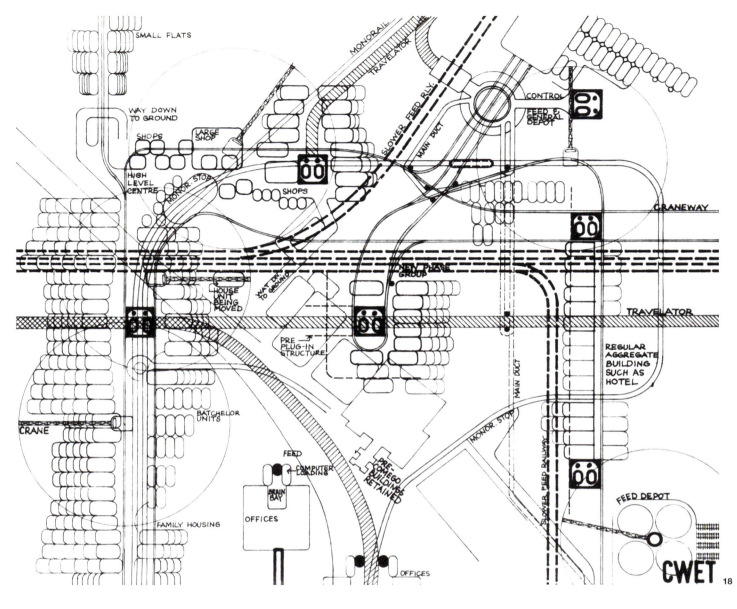

SMALL FLATS

WAY DOWN TO GROUND

SHOPS

LARGE SHOP

HIGH LEVEL CENTRE

MONOR. STOP

SHOPS

MONORAIL TRAVELATOR

SLOWER FEED RLY.

CONTROL

FEED & GENERAL DEPOT

MAIN DUCT

CRANEWAY

NEW PHASE GROUP

WAY ON TO GROUND

HOUSE UNIT BEING MOVED

PRE-PLUG-IN STRUCTURE

TRAVELATOR

REGULAR AGGREGATE BUILDING SUCH AS HOTEL

MAIN DUCT

MONOR. STOP

BATCHELOR UNITS

CRANE

FEED

COMPUTER LOADING

PRE-COMEGO BUILDINGS RETAINED

BRAIN BAY

OFFICES

FAMILY HOUSING

SLOWER FEED RAILWAY

FEED DEPOT

OFFICES

CWET

18

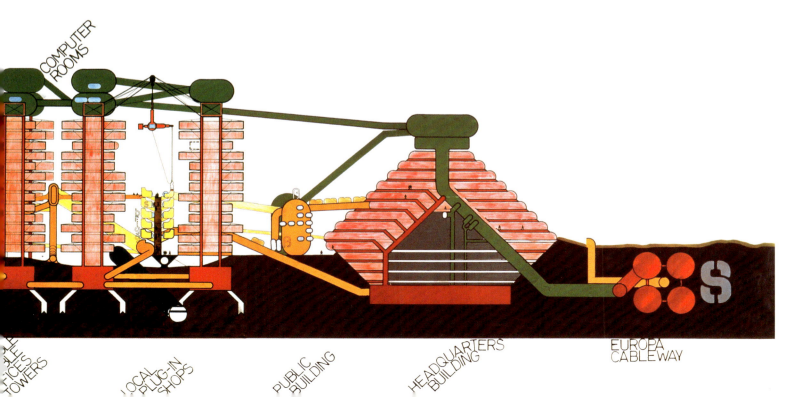

COMPUTER ROOMS

OFFICES TOWERS

LOCAL PLUG-IN SHOPS

PUBLIC BUILDING

HEADQUARTERS BUILDING

EUROPA CABLEWAY

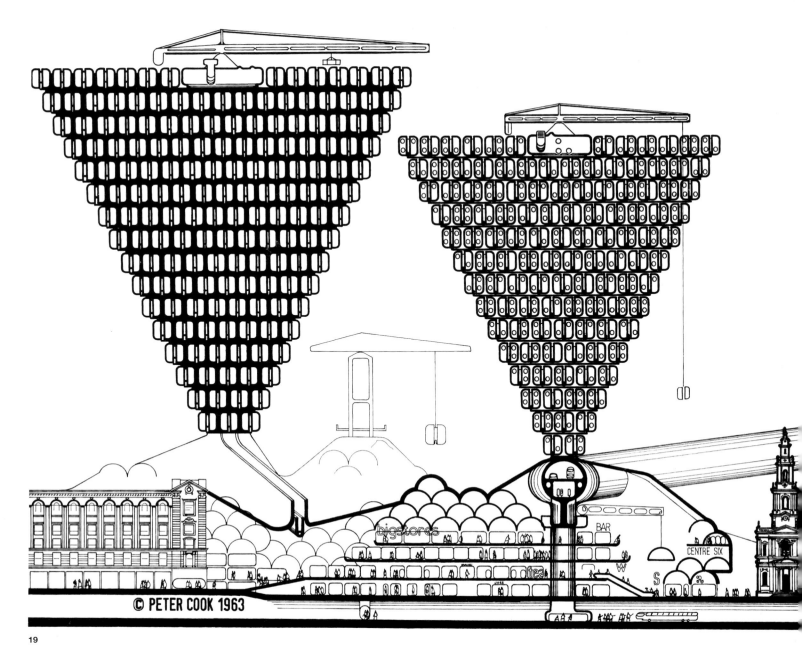

© PETER COOK 1963

19

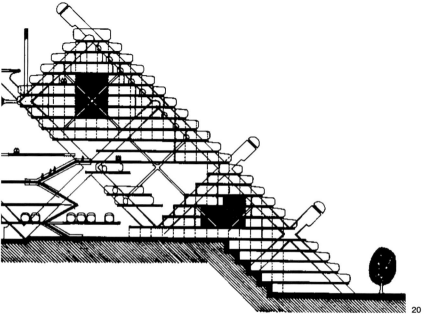

20

Key to illustrations pp. 76–85:

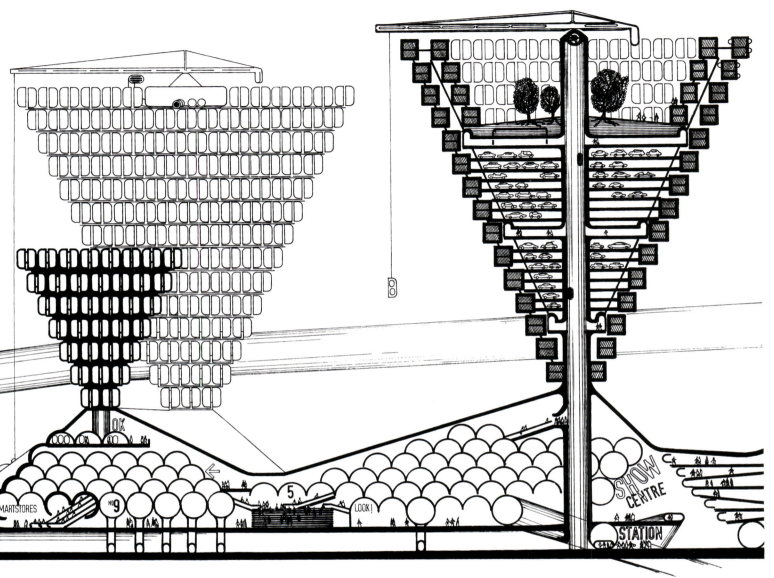

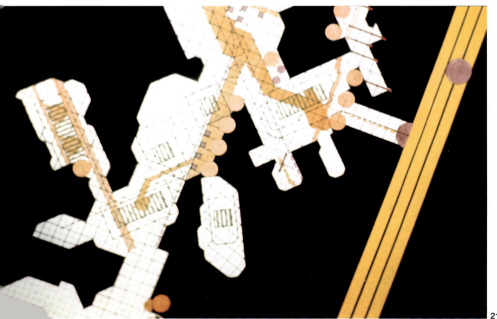

in (17) a hypothetical 'businesstown' along an international route.

In (19) (a preliminary for the Maximum Pressure Section (27)) and (20) housing is the primary element. The problems being worked over were remarkably normal to any high density housing proposal, namely, stacking, access and illumination. In fact (20) is very much of its period: the 'classic' 'A' frame, with community space in the centre. It is transitional in its architecturalness and neatness: the floors are very regularly infilled, the secondary (suspension) structure neatly indicated with dotted lines, the housing units regularly stacked and identical. That the central implication of the Plug-in City is its open-endedness is at this stage belied. If any occurrence can overlay any other, and the boundaries of taste and use are to be eliminated by individual wishes, then any section must not

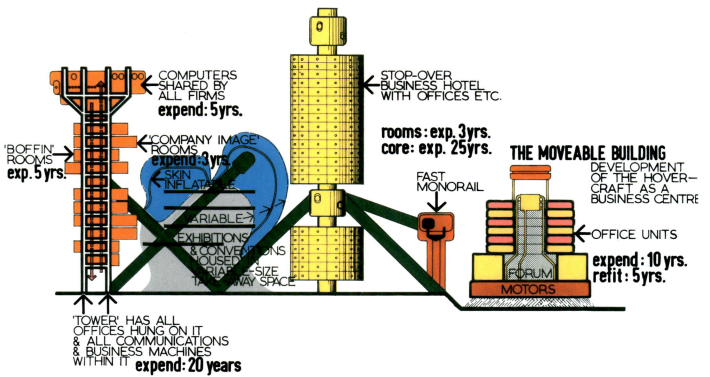

BUSINESS COMPONENTS PLUG-IN CITY SIMPLIFIED GUIDE-SECTION **1**

22

only be capable of extreme limits of absorption, but should try to illustrate them.

This, then, is the real development marked by (3). Its basic functions are illustrated by the two 'cartoon' sections (22), (23). In later work, the majority of these components 'melt': the offices diagonalize in the high intensity areas, the one-storey housing elements become looser 'areas' and the electric city car replaces the monorail. But already the proposition as it stood was throwing back at us confirmation of our hunch – that urban, or architectural, or mechanical or human mechanisms thrive on being stirred together.

Definition: The Plug-in City is set up by applying a large-scale network-structure, containing access ways and essential services, to any terrain. Into this network are placed units which cater for all needs. These units are planned for obsolescence. The units are served and manoeuvred by means of cranes operating from a railway at the apex of the structure. The interior contains several electronic and machine installations intended to replace present-day work operations. Typical permanence ratings would be:

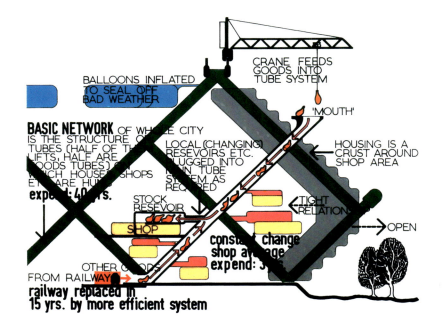

SUSTENANCE COMPONENTS PLUG-IN CITY SIMPLIFIED GUIDE-SECTION **2**

23

– Bathroom, kitchen, living room floor: 3-year obsolescence

– Living rooms, bedrooms: 5–8-year obsolescence

– Location of house unit: 15 years' duration

– Immediate-use sales space in shop: 6 months

– Shopping location: 3–6 years

– Workplaces, computers, etc.: 4 years

– Car silos and roads: 20 years

– Main megastructure: 40 years

In addition to the main craneway there are smaller craneways and mechanized slipways as well as telescopic handling elements.

The maps (24) (25) illustrate the effect of a large infiltration of Plug-in City network upon

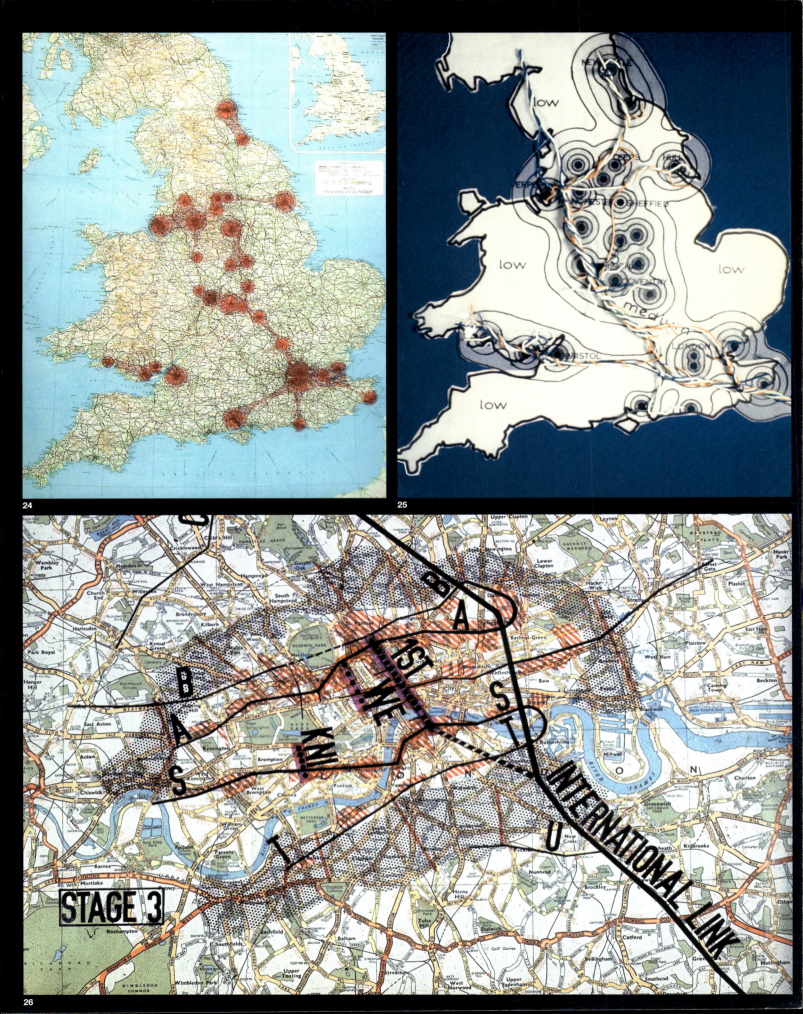

24

25

26

STAGE 3

INTERNATIONAL LINK

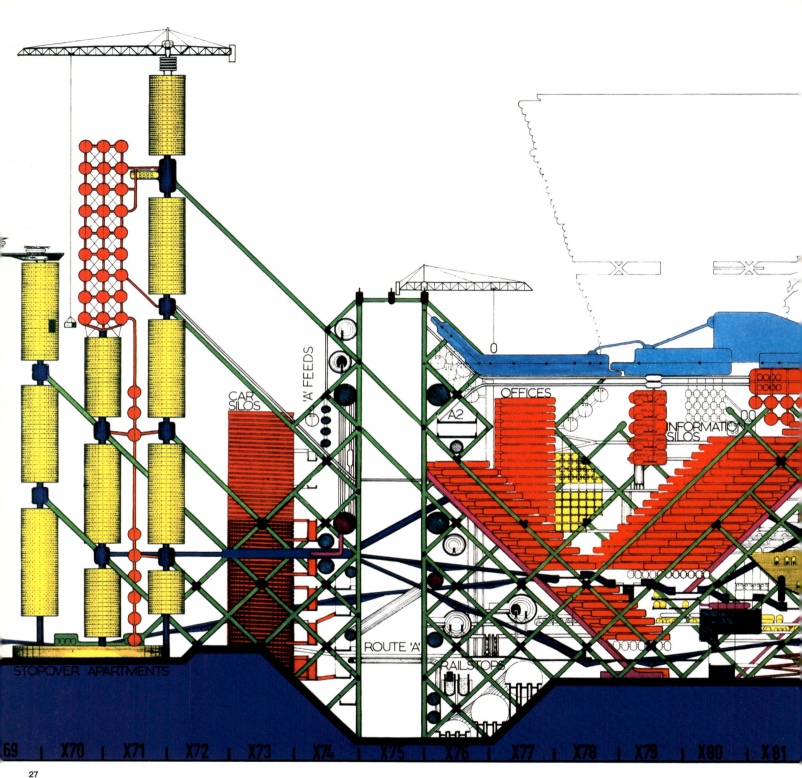

STOPOVER APARTMENTS

CAR SILOS

'A' FEEDS

A2

OFFICES

INFORMATION SILOS

ROUTE 'A'

RAILSTOPS

69   X70   X71   X72   X73   X74   X75   X76   X77   X78   X79   X80   X81

27

the field force of Great Britain, linking the existing centres of population and effecting, eventually, a total city of them all.

The High Intensity area of the Plug-in City is seen as a typical condition of the overlaying of the system upon London (map (26)). Key routeways run East / West through the old 'twilight' zones. They are tangential to a continuing route running from Central Europe to Scotland. In the Section of the High Intensity area (27) the routes 'A' and 'B' form main cleavages in the structure which provide a complete drop for the cranes. Craneways are multiplied along these

routes. Main feeder roads and feeder service-ways are located either side of the routes. Pedestrian ways tend to run at right angles to the routes. They take the form of travelators if spanning from key level to key level, and escalators or stairs in lower key conditions. The section demonstrates several standard features of Plug-in City: the diagonal framework of 9-foot diameter tubes, intersecting at 144-foot intervals in an eight-way joint. One in four of the tubes contains a high-speed lift. One in four contains a slower, local lift. One in four contains an escape tube, and the remaining tube is for goods and servicing. Floor levels are created as necessary

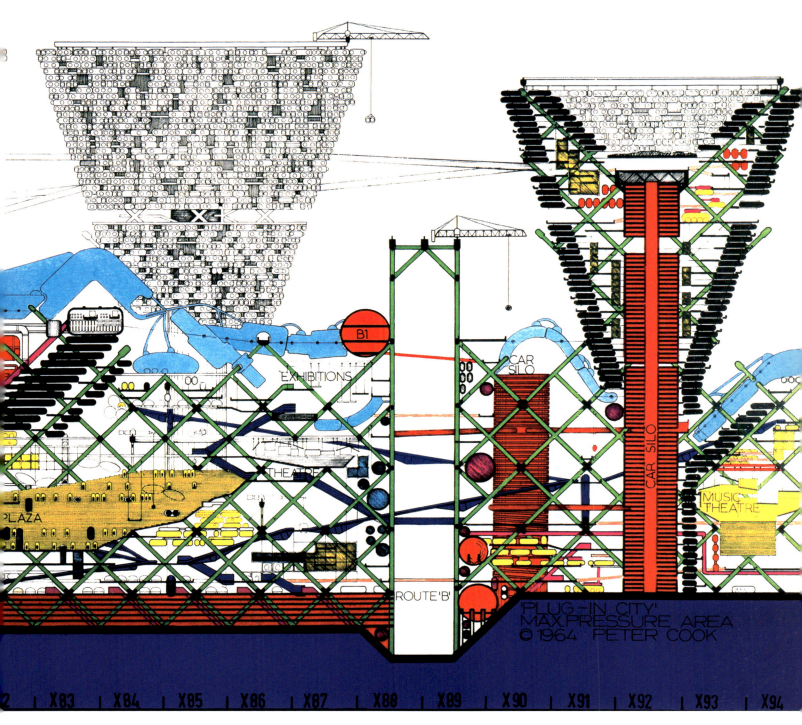

'PLUG-IN CITY'
MAX.PRESSURE AREA
© 1964 PETER COOK

B1

EXHIBITIONS

CAR SILO

CAR SILO

THEATRE

PLAZA

ROUTE 'B'

MUSIC THEATRE

X83 | X84 | X85 | X86 | X87 | X88 | X89 | X90 | X91 | X92 | X93 | X94

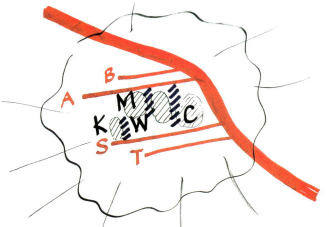

A
B
M
K W C
W
S
T

within the system, and are usually suspended from a subsidiary structure.

There is a hierarchy of relative permanence (page 82), but there is also an inherent relationship between this scale and those of weight and position related to the general cross-section.

This seems to relate to the speed of operation of elements as well. The longest-lasting elements tend to be at the base of the section. The shortest-lasting elements tend to be towards the top (or the

28

PLUG-IN CITY
APPLICATION TO CENTRAL LONDON
KEY
PLUG-IN NET
PARKING SILOS
COMMUNICATION ROUTE
N-S FEED

29

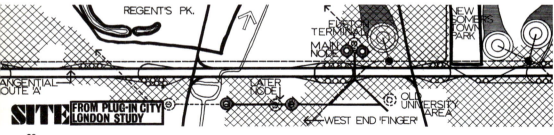

SITE FROM PLUG-IN CITY LONDON STUDY

30

Above: Map of PIC over central London: compare with early map (26) and diagram (28). New mega-structures (yellow) aggregate along new cross-centre routes A, B, S and T (in red), intersecting existing railway lines (bright orange). Max. Pressure Area section (27) cuts across routes A and B. Paddington station with PIC outcrops is on the very left of the plan: see (31) and (33) for detail.

Left: close-up of 'Route A' along Regent's Park with University nodes (32) inserted in PIC nets.

periphery). Hence the heavy railway is at the base, and the environmental seal balloons are at the top. Faster roads and monorails are at the top, parking roads at the base. The lower middle region tends to contain the busy areas of walkabout space. It is here that the plaza is located. It is here also that the main lifts disgorge.

The later application of the project, to the Paddington area of London, incorporates a system of electric city cars, and begins to include a vertical 'cage' structure for dwellings (page 91). It was the last part of the project, though many of the ideas are continued – with totally different interpretation in the 'Control and Choice' project of 1967.

The Computer City Project (15) is a parallel study to Plug-in City. It suggests a system of continual sensing of requirements throughout the city and, using the electronic summoning potential, makes the whole thing responsive on the day-to-day scale as well as on the year-to-year scale of the city structure.

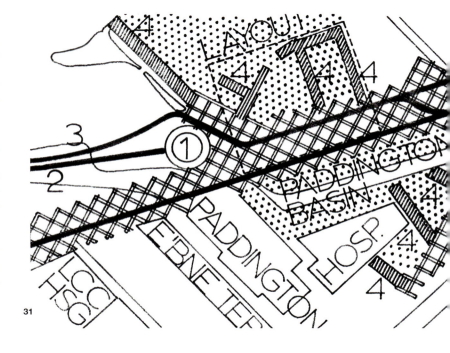

31

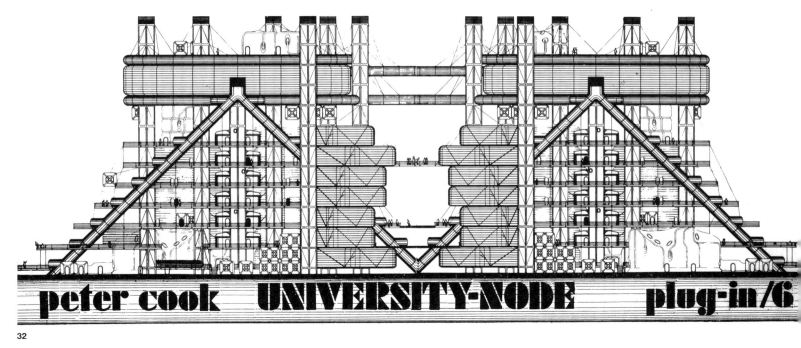

peter cook **UNIVERSITY-NODE** plug-in/6

32

The University Node (above) was an exercise to discover what happened to the various notions of gradual infill, replacement and regeneration of parts on to a Plug-in City megastructure: but with a specific kind of activity. The main enclosures are simply tensioned skins slung on trays which collectively create the 'node'. Each student can have a standard metal box and can choose to have it located anywhere on the decking. In a sense, this anticipates the 'nomad' nature of subsequent projects. The nature of Plug-in City – involving the replacement of one function by another (though occupying the same location) – could be demonstrated and a more intense glimpse of the likely detail of rooms, lift tubes, skins and even handrails be disclosed.

33

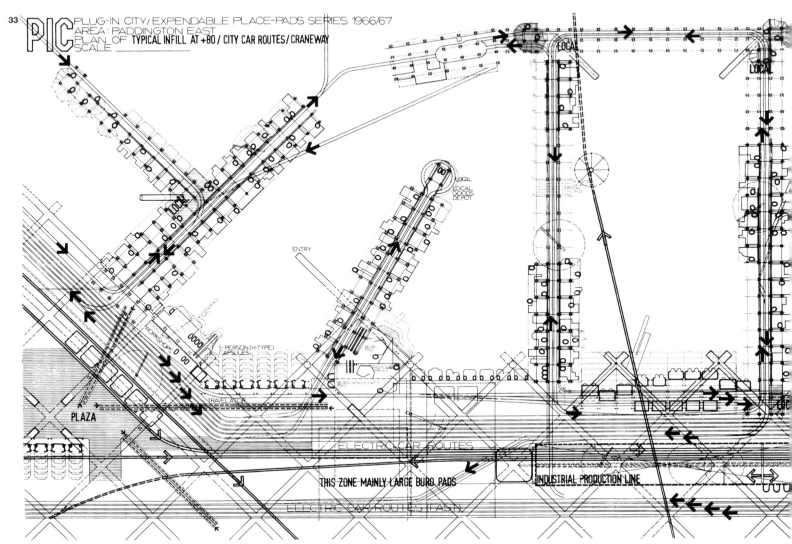

PIC PLUG-IN CITY/EXPENDABLE PLACE-PADS SERIES 1966/67
AREA: PADDINGTON EAST
PLAN OF TYPICAL INFILL AT +80 / CITY CAR ROUTES / CRANEWAY
SCALE

Archigram: At Work
Dennis Crompton

A question we are frequently asked – after "how did we get together" in the first place? – is "how did we work together?" As a group, there was only a brief period of something like two years between 1962 and 1964, slightly longer perhaps, when we were all actually together in the same place. Archigram issues three and four were produced during this time, as were the main parts of the Plug-in City, Walking City and the Living City Exhibition. After that Mike and David went off to teach and live in the United States. Peter started teaching fifth year at the Architectural Association. Ron, Warren and I went to work for other firms of architects before also teaching at the AA. Not only were we no longer all together in the same place but two of us were not even in the same country and by the mid-sixties Ron and Warren had left to live in Los Angeles, teaching at UCLA, whilst Mike and David were on the other side of America.

So how did we work together?

Were there intense, long-range discussions about architectural principles or anything like that?

The quick answer is *No*.

We worked together through the exchange of projects, through the exchange of the ideas which these projects represented through their drawings. This form of communication had started before we had even met each other. Ron, Warren and I, working together for the London County Council, had seen Peter's Gas House and Metal House projects, David's Mosque and Mike's Furniture Factory, whilst they had seen earlier competitions by Ron and Warren and our entries for Lillington Street and Lincoln Civic Centre as well as the beginnings of the designs for South Bank.

In order to try to illustrate this exchange of ideas I am going to look at a few Archigram drawings and models from the period of Plug-In City up to the 1990 House of 1967.

The two source drawings are Peter Cook and David Greene's project for the Nottingham Shopping Viaduct and Peter's Europa City. These were both drawn in the months before we did the Living City exhibition.

THE PASSING PRESENCE

3

Round about the same time, I'd made a model to try to describe my concept of the city. (One of the secondary subjects I'd studied as a student was town planning and urban design.) All those exciting things about a city, the things that make any city a *real* place where it's great to be. The activities, the people and the events they create, flashing signs, the things that you cannot anticipate but happen anyway. It's not the buildings – as we said with the exhibition – it's the events, the passing presence.

So, I made this model, where the actual city was represented by its wild top part but down below there was an armature that was supplying and regulating things to a programme and there were representations of various services. This became part of the Living City Exhibition and the set of drawings for Plug-In City.

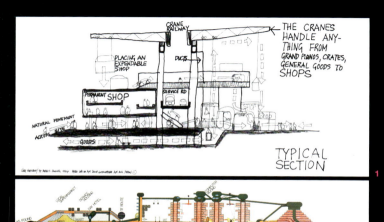

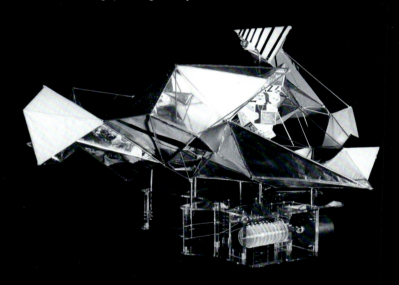

This was the early 1960s, about 1963, a time of great social and cultural change. We were concerned about the way that cities were being developed in the United Kingdom. The population of London (and the southeast of the United Kingdom) was predicted to expand at a tremendous rate for a variety of reasons. The response was to build a series of new and expanded towns around London, which were to absorb most of the increased population.

This is Peter's drawing taking the same sort of concept. The International Link is the same detail as on my drawing of the city as it infiltrates into a part of north London.

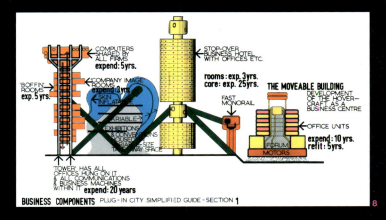

My alternative proposal, not in collusion with Peter but simultaneously with him, was a form of linear city connecting the existing main centres of urban activity and then maybe shooting off across the Channel into Europe. Not an expansion by radial imposition of small cities, dormitory towns, but the generation of an urban intensification that went along a route which responded to the dynamic flow of energy between these centres.

The small detail section through this, again by Peter, showed the way that the city was built up and had the facilities attached to make an urban structure. There is a series of propositions about the relative life spans of different components, like domestic units, shops, office spaces, the sort of things that make up a city but which are constantly changing, at different frequencies.

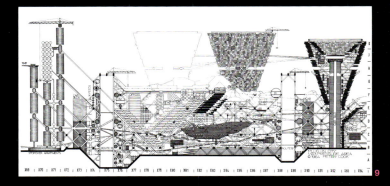

The area of the city that Peter is detailing in his Max Pressure Area drawing was a section going through the northern part of central London. You will see that he actually located the two routes A and B on the plan of London as it existed at that time. My interest in the city was not the fabric of it but how you made it responsive. How you could get a city to work effectively, efficiently and, most importantly, synchronously in response to the way that people were living in it.

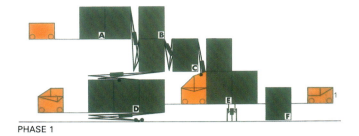

PHASE 1

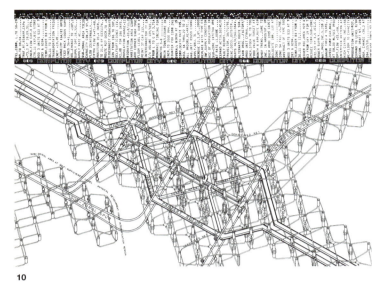

10

This is what the Computer City was all about. Peter's route A and Peter's route B coincide with the two Primary Returns on my drawing. Mine is an electronic network. It is not physical, it's a system for sensing, monitoring and creating response to the activity in the city as suggested by the annotation.

Meanwhile, Warren Chalk was developing the idea of the capsule home. He was exploring how the home itself might be made up of components that could be assembled and reassembled and changed according to the way people were living at the time.

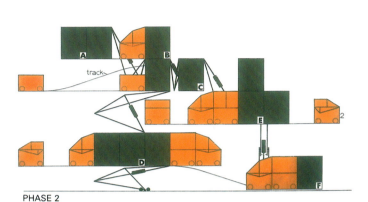

PHASE 2

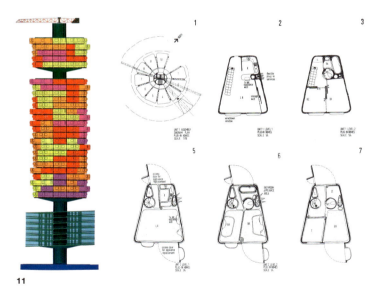

11

That's an overhead view and a tower … but you would have noticed that that tower, or one very similar, appeared in Peter's drawing a little while ago, and these same units are part of the components of Peter's drawing.

Michael Webb took an interest in the way that the city vehicle might be something other than a car that drove up and down the streets and just did car-like things. He saw the vehicle as a potential source of energy, a potential source of servicing. This is a project of Mike's, Drive-in Housing, where the car is the orange-coloured things, and the grey are the static storage cells. The proposal is that as the car joins on to the storage cells – or a number of cars join on – the structure responds by expanding in order to accommodate the increase in population. People arrive by car and the car starts to transform the environment by being reused within it.

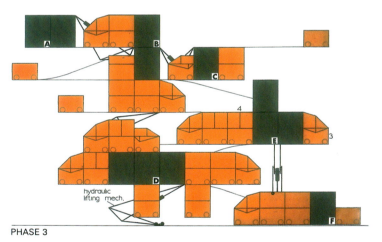

PHASE 3

12

Peter meanwhile was looking at another area of Plug-In City, slightly west along the north side of the West End, an area called Paddington. Here, he is looking at routes, circulation routes, not just pedestrian but also vehicle circulation routes. The influences here are not just Michael and his Drive-in Housing and Auto Environment. At this time some of us were in a research group at Hornsey College of Art in north London. Two other people in the group were Brian Richards, studying urban movement systems, and Richard Fletcher, who was developing an electric car as an alternative city vehicle. These things were happening simultaneously and being absorbed into our projects.

This is a study of part of that structure in Paddington, and you can see electric city cars and the routes, north route and south route and so on, being woven into the Plug-In City. These routes are shown in the model of Paddington as the blue and the red layers integrated with the structure and accommodation.

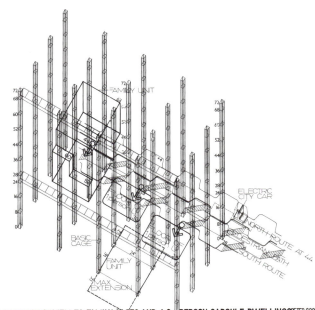

VEHICLE AS SERVICE SYSTEM TO FAMILY CAGES AND 1-2 PERSON CAPSULE DWELLINGS PETER COOK HC/AAS

14

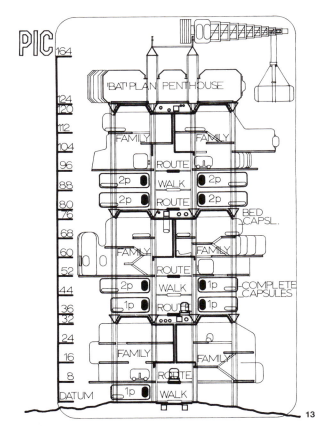

13

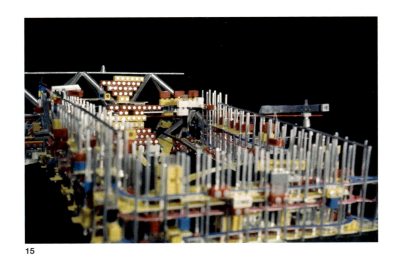

15

17

16

An early drawing from Mike Webb's Drive-in Housing anticipated this arrangement and a later model showed its development in relation to the dwelling.

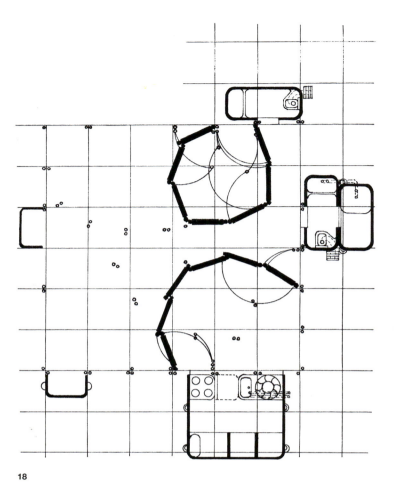

18

During this conversation through drawings, the capsule as dwelling had dissolved. Some eighteen months or so after Warren's Capsule Homes project, the capsule as an idea had become truly restrictive in its application. There are other projects by members of the group looking at the alternatives, the way that the fabric of the domestic accommodation might be changed more easily and more immediately. The domestic divisions respond and flex to accept change such as the inclusion of the city vehicle as service/power module.

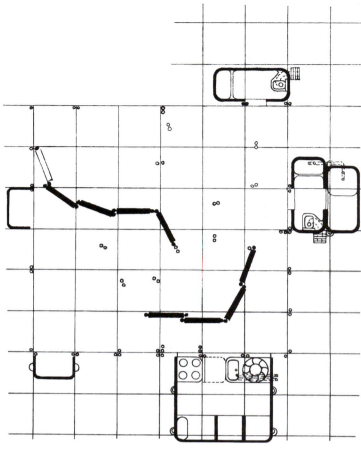

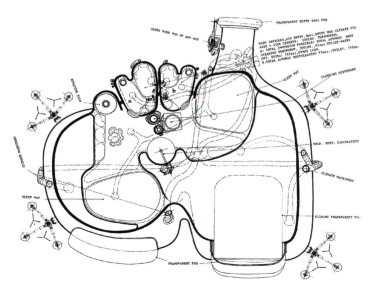

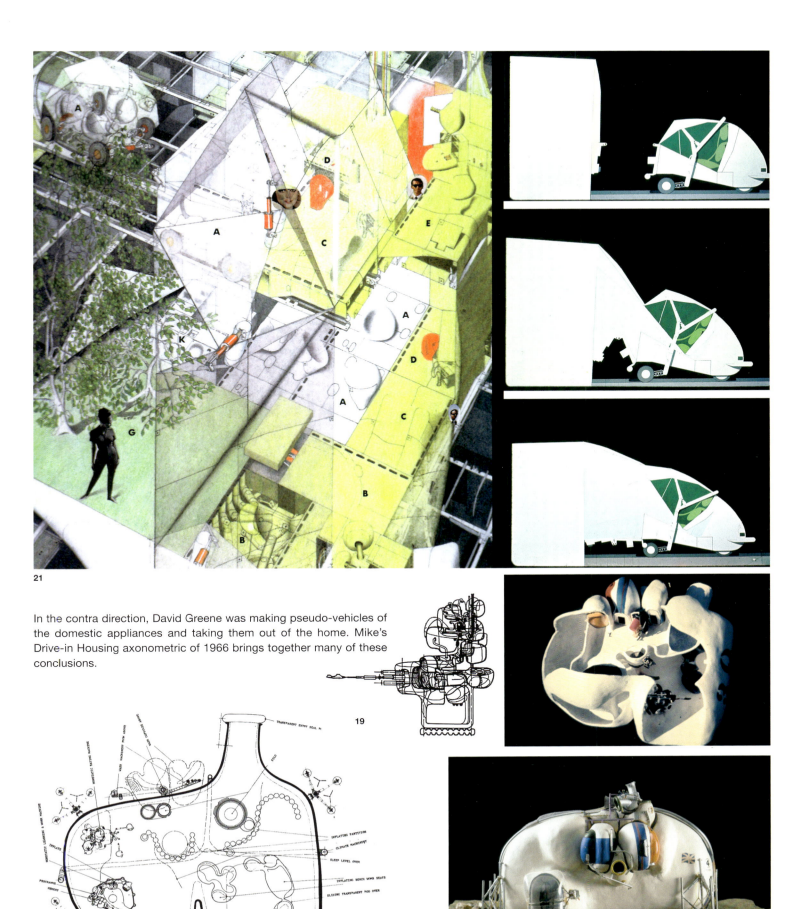

21

In the contra direction, David Greene was making pseudo-vehicles of the domestic appliances and taking them out of the home. Mike's Drive-in Housing axonometric of 1966 brings together many of these conclusions.

19

20

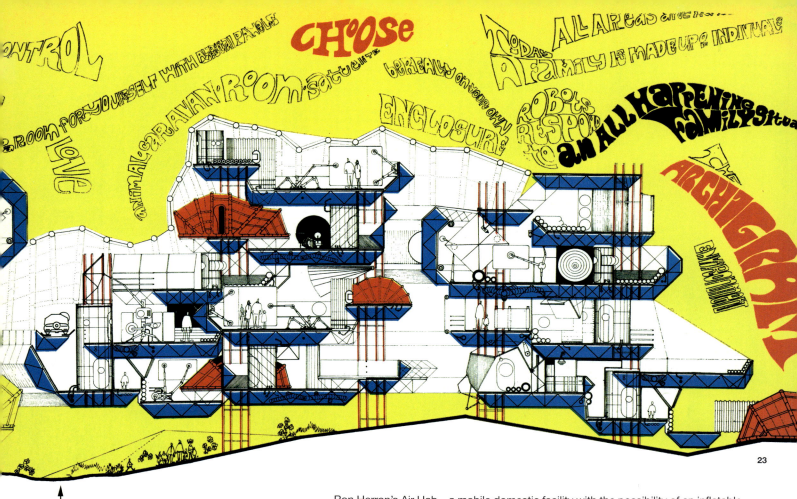

City Car

23

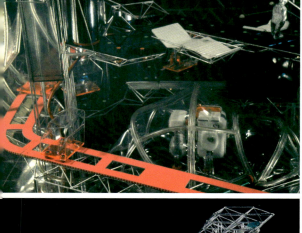

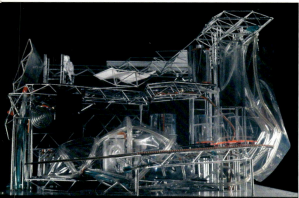

22

Ron Herron's Air Hab – a mobile domestic facility with the possibility of an inflatable enclosure – found itself nestling in the Control and Choice model. The drawing by Ron and Warren from this project incorporated all the different elements with Peter's Metamorphosis collage providing the animation and commentary on the functions.

Lastly, there is the exhibition 1990 House, produced in 1966 for publication and display in 1967. All of the members of the group who were in London at the time worked on this exhibition. Peter's preliminary sketch incorporated the elements of flexible walls and the vehicle. Warren put a time scale to the daily cycle of domestic activity. Ron brought in the robots and I programmed the actual action.

24

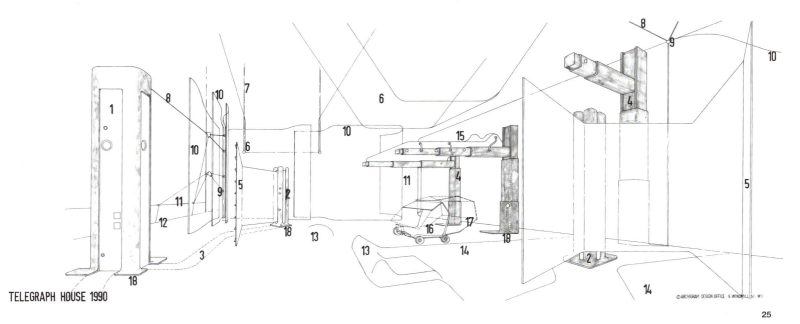

TELEGRAPH HOUSE 1990

© ARCHIGRAM DESIGN OFFICE · 8 WINDMILL ST. W1

25

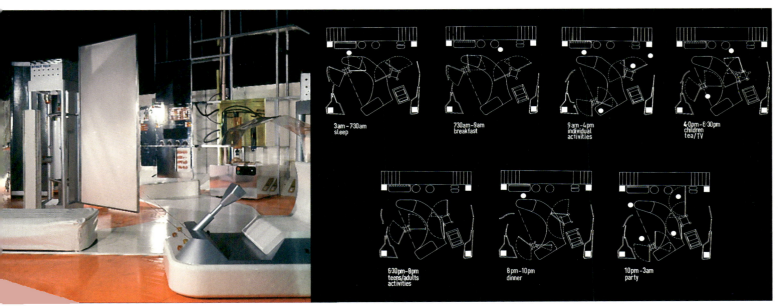

3am–730am
sleep

730am–9am
breakfast

9am–4pm
individual
activities

4·0pm–6·30pm
children
tea/TV

6·30pm–8pm
teens/adults
activities

8pm–10pm
dinner

10pm–3am
party

26

This is just a small part of a much more complex story that extends into the group's writing and teaching – a small indication of the way that the group worked together. Different conversations by different members of the group were absorbed and commented back on by the others in order to produce whatever the next project might be.

I would like to end with a quote from Ron made some years later:

"Plug-In City was produced in 1964 and came out of a lot of conversations amongst the group. I felt that if you were going to take apart this idea of change and mobility and interchangeability, why not interchange and mobility of place? So the idea emerged for a city of the world, something like the United Nations, that would be based in the city but was nowhere and everywhere. A Moving City."

1 Nottingham Shopping Viaduct, Elevation and sketch section, 1962, Peter Cook & David Greene
2 Europa City, 1963–64, Peter Cook
3 The Passing Presence, collage by Warren Chalk, 1963
4 City Synthesis, 1963, 2 model photographs, model and photos Dennis Crompton
5 Living City, Exhibition photo: photo Dennis Crompton
6 Plug-In City, UK Planning study, 1963–65, Dennis Crompton
7 Plug-In City, North-east London plan, Peter Cook, 1963–1965
8 Business Components: Plug-In City, simplified guide section 1, 1964, Peter Cook
9 Plug-In City, Max Pressure Area Section, 1964, Peter Cook
10 Computer City, axonometric and side panel, 1964, Dennis Crompton
11 Capsule Home sketches etc, 1964, Warren Chalk
12 Drive-in Housing, 1964, Michael Webb, sequence of three diagrams
13 Plug-In City, Paddington, section, 1966, Peter Cook
14 Plug-In City, Paddington, axonometric of structure and routes, 1966, Peter Cook
15 Plug-In City, Paddington, model, 1966, Peter Cook, photo Dennis Crompton
16 Drive-in Housing, line axonometric, 1964–66, Michael Webb
17 Drive-in Housing, model 1964–65, Michael Webb, photo Dennis Crompton
18 Plan diagrams from the Auto-Environment, 1964, Michael Webb
19 Living Pod, Plan and Food Machine (kitchen!) section, 1965, David Green
20 Living Pod, model
21 Drive-in Housing, colour axonometric and detail, 1966, Michael Webb
22 Control and Choice model, 1967, Peter Cook, Dennis Crompton, Ron Herron; photo D.C.
23 Control and Choice, detail of section, 1967, Warren Chalk, Ron Herron
24 Control and Choice, Metamorphosis collage, 1967, Peter Cook
25 1990 House, early perspective, 1967, Peter Cook
26 1990 House, photo of installation (by D.C.), 1967 and Typical day sequence, 1967, Warren Chalk

Utopia and the Anthropological Status of Built Space
Françoise Choay

Utopia, a proper noun coined by Thomas More and launched by him into the universe of the printed word in 1516, met with an immediate and extraordinary popularity. Before the end of the sixteenth century, the proper noun had passed into common usage and had come to designate a specific literary genre, its paradigm provided by More's book.

For close to half a millennium, the word has had a strange career, during which (thanks to associations and rough analogies) its conceptual clarity has become dulled by rather woolly social, futuristic and oneiric connotations. The term has even been extended to include reflexive categories alien to More. Karl Mannheim at least had the grace to define precisely the thinking that induced him to contrast the word with 'ideology', while on the basis of the same distinction an American political analyst ventures to assert that "a Utopia is a realizable objective," and that the writings of More reveal "neither a political faith nor a Utopia."

Yet such semantic drift and the aleatory life of languages cannot by themselves account either for the vitality of the term Utopia or the periodic revivals of Utopian literature at certain critical junctures in western history such as the transition from the eighteenth to the nineteenth centuries and the mid-nineteenth century. Nor indeed does it account for the renewed interest the notion of Utopia aroused in the year 2000, with a celebratory exhibition at the Bibliothèque Nationale in Paris among many others.

Taking More's seminal text as my starting point and highlighting the enduring structure of the literary genre it gave rise to, I shall show here that Utopia is a matter of concern to us today more than ever, in particular in the role it accords to space and in the logic underlying it – two inseparable dimensions that I shall try to place within the framework of a general anthropology.

When More talks of his book in his letters, he calls it 'my Utopia', and as editions and translations came and went, the lengthy initial title[1] shrank to just the name of the island. This name, derived from the Greek topos ("place"), is qualified by the prefix U-, understood by More as a contraction of the negating ou- ("non-place") and of the adjective eu- ("good-" or "right-(place)"). Thus from the outset, space is designated as the subject of the book, if in an antinomic way. And this succinct title becomes emblematic since, as we shall see, the framework set up as a spatial device and the antinomy as a logical device are what establish the dynamic of More's text.

More and built space

Before proceeding, let us for the record briefly review the work's form and themes. In a circumstantial narrative, More describes his diplomatic mission to Flanders, his encounter with an unknown traveller, Raphael Hythlodaeus, and his long exchange with the latter concerning politics and English society, in the company of the humanist Peter Giles. It is in the course of this allegedly factual account, with its arsenal of semantic and formal devices, that More describes the island of Utopia and the model society inhabiting it.

Yet this model society, as Raphael has discovered and describes it, does not come out of nowhere: on the one hand, it does not appertain to an arbitrary and unbridled imagination, but is meticulously and systematically constructed on the basis of a radical and uncompromising critique of an existing society – in this case contemporary England, stigmatized in the first part of the exchange – of which it constitutes the antithesis; on the other hand, the functioning of its institutions depends on the establishment of a model built space. In other words, an existing society under criticism, a model society, and a model space are the three interdependent terms that constitute the utopian genre. If a critical approach generates the social conception of Utopia, built space is the instrument of its realization, and of the transformation of a vicious society into a virtuous one. The spatial model (which, as we discover around the middle of the description of the island, was long ago conceived by a certain Utopus) is presented to the reader from the start, before the institutions it served to establish and stabilize. Raphael describes "in order, the terrain, the rivers, the cities, the inhabitants, the traditions, the customs, the laws."[2]

The priority given to this spatial configuration emphasizes the importance More assigns it in the functioning of human societies. Of course Plato, in Laws and Critias, had already attributed to constructed space the stabilizing role of pharmakon[3] in the foundation of colonies and of new societies. But given its discredited status with regard to the ontological truth of the world of ideas, Plato evokes the spatial configuration only as a complementary means, after the institutions it might support. Thomas More, on the contrary and for the first time, proclaims the efficiency and real value of a model built space, that of the cities of Utopia, such space becoming the very pivot of his essay.

Yet the status of this space is less simple than it appears. In the traveller's eyes, its uniformity and its standardization contrast from the first with the particularity and the diversity of the island's natural space, the original form of which – the rugged and craggy coastal perimeter, as well as the hilly terrain – permits the reader to recognize it as a version of England. In contrast, the cities of Utopia, uniformly 24 miles apart, are identical in layout and limited size, as well as in the standardized configuration of their streets, markets, temples, and houses. "The person who knows one of the cities will know them all."[4] This urban configuration permits no extraordinary or whimsical feature. Rationalized and subject to geometry, its function is to ensure the equality of all, to compel each citizen to occupy his own place and to play his part within the community, assuring and reminding everyone at all times of the operation of those domestic, economic and religious institutions that establish social coherence.

At first sight there is no relation between Utopia's physical geography and the space its inhabitants have constructed under the direction of Utopus. Constructed space is superimposed upon natural space, negating the latter's differences and extending the isotropic arrangement of its surface: a grid that offers a certain prefiguration of today's technological networks which blanket territories with an absolute disregard for cultural, natural and local features. We will see later on what to think of this parallel.

A closer reading of Raphael's description shows that there is, occasionally, a surreptitious link, only faintly suggested and immediately occulted, which seems to contradict the absolute autonomy of the two kinds of space: the plan of the capital, Amaurotum, is not a perfect square but "almost perfect"; its surrounding wall is not continuous, because of its geographical position, and certain sophisticated hydraulic devices have been required by the characteristics of the terrain.

More and time

In More's Utopia, the role of built space counterpoises that of time. As it happens, the perfection of model space eliminates temporality in favour of a quasi-eternity. Spatial configuration not only ensures the identical reproduction of institutional functioning; it consecrates the permanent presence of utopian society through the ubiquitous imposition of a panoptic principle – one that can be traced from the syphogrant's table through the winding streets to the temple's interior. Constant maintenance and repair also guarantee the permanence of the spatial grid, safeguarding it from any alteration.

But this non-history, the constant instantaneity of this motionless society is not given from the start. It is the consequence of a radical transformation achieved only in the course of time, within a certain history. The *deus ex machina* to which it must be imputed, according to the archives of Utopia, is the heroic statesman and builder who gave his name to the island: Utopus. It was he who, as a result of an unprecedented project and of enormous labour, separated the territory from the mainland of which it was once a part, and on this island achieved the model plan of Utopia.

The time of creation under Utopus cannot be separated from technological progress, entirely absent from the island according to Hythlodaeus' descriptions of it. Just as the invention of the compass and the perfection of the caravel enabled Raphael to cross the seas and discover an unknown world and society, and just as the invention of the printing press allows him to communicate his discovery to the known world, so it was Utopus' mastery of technology that permitted him to create an artificial island and to equip it with complex hydraulic works.

Evidently space and time are deployed in More's text according to homologous and interrelated modalities. The two superimposed, autonomous, and unconnected spaces correspond to two antinomic relations with time: on the one hand, immersion in a mundane and historical time and, on the other hand, a break with time, the historical epoch in which Utopus performed his labours, having no more relation to utopian eternity than Utopia's natural landscape has with its isotropic urban configuration.

Similarly, just as the island still harbours some isolated remains of non-standardized constructions, so one still discovers the aleatory and unavowed traces of an organic time and of history: confident of his plan, his isotropic grid, Utopus has left to his successors the task – to him, inessential – of decorating cities and houses, and the

1. Title page of first German edition of More's *Utopia*, 1612

memory lingers of the huts that preceded the present-day comfortable dwellings.

Utopia as mythic form

The foregoing analysis attests to the founding role More attributed to built space in the institutionalization of human societies. Since antiquity, in a tradition extending from Lucretius and Ovid to Vitruvius, etiological narratives had traced the origins of architecture and of the built environment to those of society, until Alberti splendidly inverted their relationship and proposed building as the origin and cause of the state of society.[5] Thomas More, however, is less concerned by the etiology of built space than by its corrective or orthopaedic power. Yet, contrary to Plato (to the degree that these authors can be compared at all), More does not conceive this power as restoring an ancient and lost social order, but rather as establishing an unprecedented new one.

At the same time, it becomes apparent that the theme of the spatial model is inscribed in a text that is marked by the antinomy articulated in the title. In his text – through the opposition of its two parts (which the dimensions of this article do not allow

THIS IS THE PICTURE OF THE OLD HOUSE BY THE THAMES TO WHICH THE PEOPLE OF THIS STORY WENT HEREAFTER FOLLOWS THE BOOK IT. SELF WHICH IS CALLED NEWS FROM NOWHERE OR AN EPOCH OF REST & IS WRITTEN BY WILLIAM MORRIS.

2. Frontispiece of William Morris' *News From Nowhere*, 1890

In order to understand why and how Thomas More came to elaborate this analogon of myth, we must restore his enterprise to the destabilized and destabilizing context of his epoch, when the institutions of medieval society are everywhere jeopardized by the opening-up of the natural world, the birth of the physical sciences, the discovery of the relativity of cultures, and the extension of individual liberty. At the same time, technical prowess and effectiveness grow to yet unheard-of levels, due in large part to the development of instruments with an immediate impact on natural space. Utopus' plan allows More to function simultaneously within the range of the future and of the past, to acknowledge the advent of a new world experienced with all its attendant fascination and scandal, and still to preserve social solidarity and the institutional reproduction of tradition. With his plan, Utopus incarnates the freedom and technological possibilities of the developing modern world whilst suspending its unpredictability.

But, always assuming it is by the subject Thomas More, Utopus's solution remains symbolic, confined within the mythical realm of the imaginary. At the very most, one might interpret the surreptitious anomalies noted previously in the description of the model space and the eternity of Utopia as so many botched actions: they indicate a fleeting, repressed desire for a transition to action that would have allowed to bring about an effective link between the concrete world and the model world, between the time of tradition and the time of innovation, between individual liberty and the law.

For all that, does the book-bound nature of More's *Utopia* and its propositions deprive them of any value, or any political and social effectiveness? That it did was the view of Louis Marin.[8] And before him, G.K. Chesterton went even further in asserting that if "More was the founder of all utopias, he nonetheless uses Utopia for what it is – a playground" since "his Utopia was a joke."[9]

For my part, I prefer to treat Utopia in particular and utopias in general as fundamentally serious, the point of which is to fathom, record and spell out insoluble or unformulatable societal problems. Doesn't this in fact make Utopia a kind of reflexive preliminary to all political commitment? Before basically analyzing the status that utopias accord to space, it is moreover reasonable to think that in the particular case of Utopia, the spatial scheme conceived by Utopus takes the place of a lost referent. In other words, far from being the instrument of a manipulative policing "power" as Michel Foucault suggests, this spatial scheme delineates and exposes its obliteration by symbolically assuming the transcendent power of the law.

Fertility and avatars of Utopia

Just as, from generation to generation, from individual, one-off statement to new/novel statement, myth is taken up, transformed and sometimes mutilated by oral transmission, so the 'mythicizing' literary genre created by More has been taken up, transformed and often altered or falsified by successive generations of writers whom the history of western societies confronted with similar contradictory situations and questions that are just as outrageous and apparently insoluble.

me to analyze) as well as within each of them – More posits and multiplies antinomies: life within time and life outside of time, individual freedom and conformity to the norm, innovation and tradition, inauguration and replication. More does not attempt to transcend these antinomies by seeking middle terms: he resolves them by intervention of the hero Utopus and of his quasi-magical plan, which simultaneously establishes a radical change and radically blocks its further development.

The text of Utopia operates in the same way and performs the same function as myth according to Claude Lévi-Strauss' definition[6]: it is a means of symbolically resolving antinomies, contradictions, or unthinkable and unmanageable conflicts by enclosing them in the foliated structure of a narrative. In this instance, such a structure is most apparent in the grand *mise-en-scène* of Raphael's description of Utopia, but it also underlies this description, though in a masked fashion, in a kind of counterpoint.[7]

However, unlike an authentic myth, always transmitted orally in the form of an anonymous narrative, this utopia is inscribed in the very material confines of a book, assumed in the first person by More himself, who signs it with his own name. It is a pseudo-mythic form, then: one that, by a further contradiction, refuses to speak its name.

Thus true utopias have gone on being written in the course of history, adopting at the same time the foliated approach and three structural constituents of More's paradigm, i.e. 1) criticized society, 2) model space, and 3) model society. And it is no surprise that the genre should have flourished especially in the context of two cultural revolutions that determined Western civilization's modern identity: we find utopias first multiplying in More's wake during the revolution of the Renaissance, and subsequently in the eighteenth century, in the slipstream of the industrial revolution.

But in the course of the nineteenth century, the new destitution of cities, the progressive alteration of ancestral environments, technological progress as well as the ideal of efficiency and "economism" promoted by the industrial project, produce a hypertrophy of the spatial model and, for the first time, its projection into reality. Robert Owen's "New Harmony" and Fourier's "Phalanstery" are destined to be constructed and replicated many times over, but by the same token, both fiction and the richness of antinomies disappear from these texts. By an irony of fate, when Marx condemns, in the name of revolutionary realism, those utopian socialists aiming to construct the spatial model of the new society, it is he who remains faithful to the logic of utopia, as Raymond Williams has demonstrated.[10]

In fact, with the major exception of William Morris's *News from Nowhere* (1891), the late nineteenth century and first half of the twentieth witness the decline of utopias in the strict sense. Their remains are appropriated by two new literary genres, both focusing on the built environment and its technical aspects, i.e. theoretical urbanism and the science fiction narrative. Among the urbanistic theories, Ebenezer Howard's garden city is virtually the only one to preserve the societal concept of Utopia, even if in a poor, reduced version that nonetheless retains both the critique and a developed spatial model. Subsequently, 'progressive' urbanistic theory focuses on developing spatial models, which, once turned into reality, proceed in totalitarian fashion to impose a technical order on things. The complexity of the ethical and political project is thereby reduced to a mere social functionalism coupled with a theory of basic human needs. The writings of Le Corbusier indicate the scale of the reduction involved, while betraying an aberrant affinity with Utopia in certain formal characteristics, notably the use of the present tense in descriptive passages.[11]

On the other hand, science fiction – as the name indicates – maintains a book-bound status freed of any axiological aspects of Utopia. It is unreservedly open to a technology-fired imagination that has spawned the specific genres of technotopias and dystopias. Technotopias embrace propositions established under the umbrella of futurology by a number of experts, architects and engineers fascinated by the opportunities for formal innovation that technology offers. Dystopias cover the ferociously critical visions of societies conditioned for the worse by the advances of technology. The genre has given us writers and filmmakers such as Fritz Lang, Aldous Huxley and Ray Bradbury, without any more positive counterparts.

In analyzing this evolution of the utopian tradition and its erratic course, the remarkable nature of the authentic Utopia written by John Ruskin's Marxian disciple William Morris becomes all the more striking. All the ingredients of Utopia co-exist in this work –

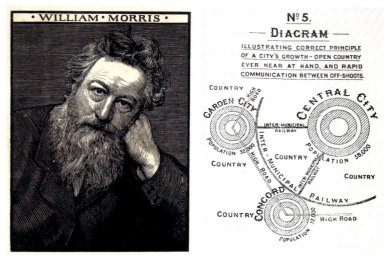

3. Portrait of William Morris by R. Bryden, 1901M; 4. Ebenezer Howard: Diagram of Garden City

1) the formal framework of fiction, 2) the descriptions of the model society and model space needed for its institutions to function, and 3) the antinomies to be resolved. (In effect, the latter amount to the opposition between the mechanization of social practices implicit in the historical development of technology and the organic approach required by an anthropogenic scheme.) And yet the model space conceived by Morris is the antithesis of More's standardized establishment. In fact, the capital of Nowhere with its buildings linked among themselves and to their natural surroundings so as to encourage all possible differences and do away with all standardization seems to be a replica of the old pre-industrial-revolution London. This anomaly is most frequently interpreted as a mark of head-in-the-sand nostalgia or, more positively, a pre-figuration of urbanistic theories opposed to the reductive functionalism of CIAM, whose members I have called culturalists.[12] That is where we need the perspective of the twenty-first century to fully appreciate the significance of the difference. I shall return to the point later.

The end of the twentieth century and the disappearance of utopia

So has the third cultural revolution in Western societies, this transition to an era of electronics and telematics – innovations in the field of which have revolutionized the entirety of Western mental practice and behaviour since the 1950s – again injected utopia with renewed vitality?

It would appear that in the second half of the twentieth century, the fate of utopia as a textual genre was sealed: a demise to be related to the weakening of political thought and the decline of the notion of the State in advanced industrial societies, where the market economy and its rationalizations have laid siege to and indeed conquered the site of a reflexive foundation reduced to the snares of sociologism. Furthermore, the "technotopias", those false utopias which still flourished between 1950 and 1970, have subsequently vanished. Texts and images like those of Nicolas Schöffer, Yona Friedman and Iannis Xenakis are nowadays tinged with archaism without ever having had an impact on the process of urbanization. Not surprisingly: since then, technology has reigned supreme, and its progress has been so accelerated as to outdistance specialists and users alike, to the extent that no measure of anticipation can hope to compete.

Yet the new technological mastery over the natural and human environment has also constituted, in the spirit of 1968, the theme of a literature that loudly and clearly claims affiliation to utopia: these texts offer a militant social dimension in which the built environment represents an essential element. They proceed, in the main, from the Situationist International (with its marked social concerns) and from the British Archigram group and its sympathizers (with their marked spatial concerns). The title of a long article that appeared in the weekly *New Society* in 1969, signed by Reyner Banham, Paul Barker, Peter Hall, and Cedric Price, sets the tone of the controversy: "Non plan, an experiment in freedom."[13]

For these authors, such "planning" as Utopus proposed and as urbanists have continued to understand it, has now become obsolete: all it could offer would be an environment, ill-adapted to human needs, activities, and desires, one that would be rendered chronically anachronistic by the speed of socio-cultural change and the staggering freedoms of the "cybernetic revolution."[14] Under such conditions, the real problem facing the developers is how to enable the individual to determine the establishment that will best safeguard his liberties as well as his freedom within a generalized transformation and mobility.

That such an article and others in the same vein could have been understood to be utopian is readily accounted for by their subversive style, their uncompromising critique of advanced industrial society, and their virulent opposition to urbanism, a discipline whose supposedly scientific knowledge was undisputed at the time. Nonetheless, these were veritable anti-utopias. As a matter of fact, the *New Society* article denies constructed space any founding vocation: far from being in the service of a lasting transformation of society-as-subject, such space becomes an instrument serving to promote the freedom of the individual-as-subject. The antinomies that establish the utopian dynamics have no currency in the *New Society* article or in other related texts. "Non plan", for all its conflictual complexity, unreservedly and without compunction welcomes the real world, both cultural and natural, to which More's Utopia was related only by means of its social critique. When the authors of "Non plan" describe the society they advocate and anticipate, they might be describing our own, which they could foresee in the forms of an unchanged life context.

In fact, the authors of "Non plan", like those of the Archigram group's Instant City, support a situation without precedent: the advent of a

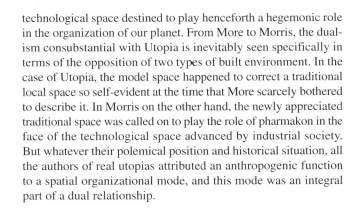

internationale situationniste

3

5. Cover of *IS* no. 3

technological space destined to play henceforth a hegemonic role in the organization of our planet. From More to Morris, the dualism consubstantial with Utopia is inevitably seen specifically in terms of the opposition of two types of built environment. In the case of Utopia, the model space happened to correct a traditional local space so self-evident at the time that More scarcely bothered to describe it. In Morris on the other hand, the newly appreciated traditional space was called on to play the role of pharmakon in the face of the technological space advanced by industrial society. But whatever their polemical position and historical situation, all the authors of real utopias attributed an anthropogenic function to a spatial organizational mode, and this mode was an integral part of a dual relationship.

The disappearance of Utopia at the end of the twentieth century can be explained by the underlying obliteration of this dualism in favour of a mono-space. The same outcome also prompts us to ponder on the nature of this mono-space and the implications of its spread worldwide.

The question of built space in an era of globalization

Since the 1960s, the great standard networks of technological infrastructure (transmission of fluids, energy networks, high-speed transport of people and things, telecommunications, etc. transmitted by all kinds of electronic means) have transformed our ancestral relationship with natural and with man-made space, weaving together regions into territories and continents to form an isotropic mesh on a planetary scale. Henceforth, planning for human settlement is no longer constrained by the need to insert, integrate and accommodate it within local, natural or cultural contexts. All it needs is to plug into the system of networks. A plug-in logic which enables all human establishments, singular or collective, to locate themselves at will on the planet is replacing the traditional logic of articulation. By the same token, individual buildings are no longer regulated by architecture – which is in the process of disappearing despite the permanence of its designation – and instead acquire the status of autonomous technical objects.

As I indicated at the beginning of my analysis, one might be tempted to compare the current global space with More's model space, which it would simply be a refinement of. In a certain respect, the networked space which nowadays unifies all points and all populations on the globe does indeed represent the outcome and fulfilment of the technological process started in More's day, which Utopus would resort to. And standardization by technicization and the instrumentalization of space effectively constitutes the lowest common denominator in both cases. But their affinity stops there. Any other resemblance is an illusion.

What is in fact Utopus's objective when he conceives his plan? To develop a spatial instrument allowing him to submit a social community to the authority of a transcendent institutional scheme. The conditioning power of the model space is at the service of the law. In the case of a global society, what is expected of the networks? Emancipation from a corpus of spatio-temporal constraints in favour of an individual liberty previously unknown – emancipation from all local determining factors imposed by physical geography, vegetation and the accretions of urban and rural history.

Inconceivable in More's day, and even a few decades ago, the power of the networks carries us into a utopia in the negative sense of non-place, nowhere (ou-topos): thanks to (the mediation of) their 'prosthetic' adjuncts, we are delivered from place. On the one hand, standardization or the conditioning of human beings is effected immanently and not for the benefit of a transcendent purpose. The *quid pro quo* for the prosthetic efficacy of networks with the unprecedented liberties they procure for individuals is their globalization, i.e. their integration in the hegemonic civilization of the urban context, or even the obliteration, likewise without precedent, of their differences and societal identities.

On the other hand, the current processes of delocalizing human societies and dematerializing social bonds are interdependent, thanks to the panoply of data communications networks, as Melvin Webber was one of the first to note.[15] In his view, this was a proof of progress, which could be summed up as a ubiquity of multiple unlimited communal affiliations. And that is indeed the line adopted by partisans of cyberspace, who attribute to it the potential for all members of the global society to establish direct, immediate relationships, thereby making cyberspace the living source of an authentic virtual democracy. Would this then mean that these relationships are comparable to the intuitive knowledge of one another that the Utopians had with their panoptic system? Or again, that they are akin to the emotional bonds uniting the members of the small social communities – which could do without physical dwellings – that Fénelon and Rousseau conceived of?

To answer "yes" would mean overlooking that the Utopians are specifically bound up in the actual presence of a communal life. It would mean overlooking that in the Bétique of Fénelon's Adventures of Telemachus and the Clarens of Rousseau's Nouvelle Héloïse, the purpose of not having any buildings is to get rid of all visual barriers that might come between people. Not only do cybernauts share just the immanent communality of their personal interests, but in the guise of immediate contact in 'real time', their relationships are also reduced to instrumental connections, quasi-disembodied and filtered through the prosthetic adjuncts of the medium, while the immediacy (read instantaneity) of these contacts eliminates the very substance of time: duration.

This conclusion requires us to ponder upon the status of developed (landscaped, agricultural, rural, urban) local space, i.e. space with a context. Should we not attribute its development and use to an anthropological skill? Is it not a universal cultural value, demanding that we make our vocation as human animals reality by subjecting ourselves to the land, to the world of living creatures and the company of other people, whose bodies cannot be kept in the cupboard or put aside without denaturalizing them? In other words, we may justly wonder whether attachment to a local horizon is not one of the most essential means through which we define ourselves as human beings. Or whether the networks of cyberspace – in according their users a freedom no longer informed nor transformed by the dual presence of the natural and the man-made world – do not alter this anthropogenetic status and its role in establishing our societal identities.

To go back to Utopia, it should be appreciated that, when he dreamed up his model city, More was not denying for a moment that people, and Utopians in particular, essentially belonged to a specific double (natural and man-made) spatiality. The goal he set himself (at the price of the antinomies that the work of fiction was intended to resolve) was to correct and transform, via a technological space, the faulty functioning of a society. It should nevertheless be reiterated: neither More nor any of his successors down to the second half of the nineteenth century sought to question the status of local space, the existence and importance of which was self-evident to them.

The nature of the bond that ties people to places was suggested at the time by the implicit, attested evidence of the ancient Tuscan language. For three centuries, from the 14th to the 16th century, the word for 'city' was taken from *terra*, highlighting the fact that the institution of society was rooted in the soil, that the talking animal's membership of the world of nature and life stemmed from that. And it was no mere chance that, in his treatise *On the Family*[16] written in Tuscan, Alberti often used the word terra in the sense of 'city'. Today, the mono-space that is the offshoot of globalization demands us to question fundamentally the nature and status of local space.

The lesson of Morris and Ruskin

William Morris's *Nowhere* offers the perfect starting point for an enquiry into what this local space is. In subjecting More's spatial scheme to a Copernican inversion, Morris was the first to raise the issue of local space within the framework of societal dynamics. (In fact, Morris and his mentor John Ruskin were the first to discuss the concept of local space theoretically.) I shall mention here just the chapter on the 'lamp of memory' in the *Seven Lamps of Architecture*. In this, Ruskin describes not only the memorial and anthropogenetic function of architecture and all local installations that, through the agency of our bodies and living memories,[17] integrate us in the creative chain of human endeavour. He also underlines the role devolved on our entire bodies in the constitution and practice of man-made space, and the dangers of ephemeral construction and the dematerialization of everyday things.[18] In this brief but seminal essay, Ruskin also demonstrates the role of place in affirming identity and human identities, anticipating the notion of sustainable development.[19]

But to anticipate the altogether more pressing questions we are confronted with today, Morris (like Ruskin) likewise faced antinomies that he was not capable of resolving and which prompted him to opt for the utopian genre. These included 'divided' industrial labour vs. the organic labour of traditional crafts, revolution vs. tradition, and above all the historical course of progress vs. swimming against the current of the age (a dilemma that could not be resolved through a progress that implied stepping out of time, like in More's *Utopia*). The latter problem was a contradiction rendered all the more obsessive by Morris's awareness as a historian and his political commitment.

But, you will say, had not Ruskin and Morris already begun to exit Utopia? They joined forces specifically to preserve the architectural, rural and urban heritage of England and the European continent. And they brought about an outcome whose effectiveness seems amply proven by the breadth and popularity that campaigns for preserving natural milieus and safeguarding historical and traditional built environments would henceforth enjoy throughout the world. But we should beware. Do not practices of this kind amount in reality to creating museums on a mass scale? Are they not part of a planetary process of standardization, tools of the cultural industry, fostered by global banks and other international institutions that dream only of planetary development and think of space only in terms of prosthetic adjuncts, economy, standards and statistics? We face at best a static, ossified heritage lacking an evolutionary horizon. Since Ruskin's and Morris's day, analysis of the social and societal role played by the local built environment has certainly progressed in favour of a multi-disciplinary investigation, of which Maurice Le Lannou[20] was a key figure, and it no longer demands recourse to utopian fiction. But for all that it does not seem any easier to put this knowledge into practice and move beyond both the gloomy lucidity and cynicism à la Koolhaas.

Despite everything, the last few years have seen a number of attempts at re-localization, in other words endeavours to re-appropriate local development scales. Rare and problematic they may be, but they are specific and remarkable, e. g. in Brazil[21] or even Europe, in countries where the imprint of traditional socio-spatial organizations has remained meaningful despite globalization and in reaction against it. By the same token, a new metamorphosis of Utopia seems to be unfolding. As evidence, I shall take an experiment that its supporters themselves call 'a concrete Utopia',[22] adapting a phrase used by Ernst Bloch.

A new face of Utopia on the Italian scene

Launched in the late 1980s, this experiment has been implemented in key metropolitan regions[23] throughout northern and southern Italy by a team of multidisciplinary university laboratories coordinated by Professor Alberto Magnaghi.[24]

The entire undertaking is based on the in-depth, unstinting, critical assessment of damages to the region brought about by globalization, in other words, by the (successful) integration of the regions in question into a free global economy and into the planetary technical networks, and reveals the universal impact of globalization. It is not so much a matter of denouncing specific ecological disasters (the gradual destruction of the famous hydraulic network of the Po Valley as a consequence of the automobile industry, for example) as of showing how de-territorialization tends toward the complete eradication of the national historic heritage through the long process of anthropization (rural and urban sites as social and practical activities) and exposing the new poverty specific to the late twentieth century.

Whence, according to the project's initiators and their chief theoretician, Magnaghi, the necessity of a radical reversal of the situation. There is no question of defensive ecology or of heritage conservation; nor is there an equilibrium sought between the global and the local ("the glocal"), which would subordinate the latter to the imperatives of the former. Local development and re-territorialization are necessary as "a strategic alternative to global development."

The great innovation of this initiative is the assertion that the natural heritage and the local cultural one (included together in the concept of "territorial heritage") cannot be conceived in static terms – that is, as property to be protected as such – but as indissociable from a totality of activities and behaviours that give them meaning: there can be no preservation of the local natural and built heritage without the social practices that support it and correspond to its scale and its differences – without a local economy associating micro-agriculture and artisanal micro-industry, autonomous labour, and various services coupled with non-mercantile activities.

But such an inversion or subversion of the worldwide process of development does not thereby signify archaism or nostalgia. There is no question of the inhabitants turning their backs on reality and on history and taking up a position outside of or apart from the technological networks. The effectiveness of the latter is fully acknowledged; only their hegemony is contested. In other words, their prosthetic function is put into perspective and subordinated to the creation of another space and a different society. Magnaghi sums this up in a formula, "globalization from below": instead of the local values being destroyed or conditioned by the imperatives of a worldwide market society and of competition subject to decisions and powers from elsewhere, it is starting from an endogenous project, consisting of local forces, attached to external networks, subordinating them to local needs.

The subversive effectiveness of such a project implies that all key local actors be involved in it, regardless of origin, without privileging previous and traditional local roots: it mobilizes "new farmers, producers and consumers, on behalf of a 'creole' society consisting of ethnic and émigré groups that do not necessarily identify themselves with the local residents." Hence, while rejecting exogenous planning, the Italian initiative demystifies the anti-utopia of "Non plan" and substitutes for the splintering of its individual projects a common project, one that reinstates the social bond and "revives the social image-repertoire."

Such a regional integration of metropolitan areas and rural spaces suggests the possibility of an Ecopolis[25], consisting of a constellation of communities restructured, assembled, and redefined within their own spatial limits and yet closely united by means of the most efficient instruments of technology.

For the purposes of my present discussion, this summary of the richness and complexity of Magnaghi's and his associates' work is schematic at best and constitutes only the minimum necessary for continuing my arguments. Still, the reader will, at least, have understood the distance maintained from the utopian project by this experiment, which has freed itself from mythologizing fiction and is inscribed in temporality.

Yet in the very first lines of the article we have quoted, Magnaghi refers to utopia and claims an affiliation with it. Utopian traces are evident in the deployment of 'utopian image-repertoire' above all in the strategic scenario bolstering an experiment "not constructed for purposes of its immediate application by current decision-makers, but to serve potential actors."[26] That is why the analysis of these elements in Magnaghi's enterprise which still bear the structural mark (explicitly or otherwise) of the Morean genre helps us understand better the fate of utopia, its limits, but also its share of immortality.

The truth of Utopia

Let us return to the ternary structure of utopia.

Unlike other penetrating critics of globalization (Riccardo Petrella, for example),[27] the initiators of Ecopolis have preserved the dynamic function and the anthropogenetic aims of the Morean critique. This radical social auto-critique institutes a process of auto-creation, rooted today as yesterday in Western modernity, whether in the Europe of the early sixteenth century, proclaiming for the first time its vocation to master and to transform the world, or on the worldwide stage of the late twentieth century, proclaiming globalization.

In other words, as we have seen, rational analysis seems capable, to some degree at least, of short-circuiting the symbolic function of utopia, whence the syntagm of "concrete utopia." The inventors of Ecopolis assume, in effect, the weight and determinations of the totality of a given local space, as well as the creative dimension of time. Hence their project is based on an inventory of the territorial heritage represented and analyzed in its historical dynamic by means of unprecedented methods and technologies,[28] and it unifies heterogeneous actors animated by conflictual tensions. Loyalty to the long duration of the past and the openness to the unforeseeable are simultaneously affirmed, a coexistence that, in Magnaghi's text, acquires the name "sustainable ecological and human auto-development."

The function of the utopian symbolic resolution is thus transferred to regulatory notions which, by an interplay of extrapolations, integrate the imaginary with the real, binding the projected to the given, the local to the global, the latent to the dominant. The concepts of local society ("an idea to be lent strength and not a heritage to preserve"), of local identity, of new municipal power, the kinds of schemes on the frontiers of the conceivable and the feasible, lead to a "culture of the limit" that strongly resembles a new avatar of utopia.

There remains the role attributed by More to built space in the dynamics of Utopia. Today the notion of model space is undoubtedly obsolete. In the wake of William Morris, Magnaghi has replaced it with that of local development, thus substituting a process for a reified plan. The fact remains nevertheless that More, like no one before him, first highlighted the role played by built space in anthropogenesis, and more precisely in the installation and intentional transformation (or re-installation) of the societal institution. By the same token, he implicitly introduced the dual status of this space, whose polarity it fell to Morris to reverse.

Furthermore, when he condemns the dispersion of structures and circumscribes the cities of Utopia within precise and reduced limits, More symbolically launches a hypothesis as to the dimensions of the political; a hypothesis that remains open and urgent at the hour of globalization and which Magnaghi, as a good utopian, has used for his own purposes.

As our societies enter a world in which the West's prosthetic vocation seems pledged to one-dimensionality, Utopia still remains a living entity. It still beckons us to the subversion of a radical social critique and to the revalorization of an anthropogenetic space. And finally it reminds us of the antinomic condition of human beings, obliging us to explore that condition further in its ineluctable depths.

Notes

1 *Libellus vere aureus nec minus salutaris quam festivus de optimo reip(ublicae) statu, de(que) nova Insula Utopia.*
2 Thomas More, *Utopia*, ed. Edward Surtz (Yale University Press, New Haven/Conn. and London 1964), p. 56, italics mine. All quotations are from this edition.
3 See Jacques Derrida, "La pharmacie de Platon" in his *La Dissemination* (Le Seuil, Paris 1972), and my discussion of Utopia in *La Règle et le modèle* (Paris: Le Seuil, 1980, revised edition 1996), pp. 171–213.
4 *Utopia*, p. 63.
5 Leon Battista Alberti, *De re aedificatoria*, trans. and ed. Giovanni Orlandi as *L'architettura* (Milan: Il Polifilo, 1966), Prologue, p. 9. Alberti's work was first published in 1485 (Nicolò di Lorenzo Alemano, Florence).
6 Claude Lévi-Strauss, *Anthropologie structurale*, vols. I and II (Paris: Plon, 1958, 1973) as well as *Le Cru et le cuit* (Paris: Plon, 1964).
7 *La Règle et le modèle*, Chapter II, pp. 192ff.
8 *Utopiques, Jeux d'espaces* (Paris: Editions de Minuit, 1973).
9 Quoted in E.E. Reynolds, *Thomas More and Erasmus* (London: Burns & Oates, 1965), p. 120.
10 Raymond Williams, *The Country and the City* (New York: Oxford University Press, 1973; London: Chatto and Windus, 1973).
11 *La Règle et le modèle*, Chapter II, pp. 323–26.
12 Cf. *L'urbanisme, utopies et réalités* (Paris: Le Seuil, 1965), pp. 41ff. and 259–93.
13 *New Society*, March 20, 1969.
14 "The cybernetic revolution makes our traditional planning technologically and intellectually obsolete … the word planning itself should be scrapped." Ibid.
15 "The Urban Place and the Non Place Urban Realm" in *Explorations into Urban Structure* (Philadelphia: University of Pennsylvania Press, 1964).
16 *I libri della famiglia*, new edition by F. Furlan (Turin: Einaudi, 1994).
17 John Ruskin, *The Seven Lamps of Architecture* (London, 1849), quoted from the edition by J.M. Dent and sons, 1956, §§2–3, p. 182.
18 §3, p. 184.
19 pp. lx, 189.
20 Maurice Le Lannou, *Le Déménagement du territoire, rêveries d'un géographe* (Paris: Le Seuil, 1967).
21 See L. Kroll, "Curutiba" in *A+*, 1999.
22 Alberto Magnaghi, "Per una costellazione di città solidali", *Ecopolis, Rivista critica di ecologia territoriale* (October–December 1998), p. 26.
23 Milan, Florence, Venice, Turin, Bologna, Rome, Bari and Palermo.
24 He is in charge of territorial planning of the Department of Architecture at the University of Florence and national co-ordinator of the "Per uno sviluppo locale autosostenibile: teorie, metodi e esperienze" project, launched by the Italian Ministry of Universities and Scientific and Technological Studies (MURST). For a synthesis of Magnaghi's ideas, see his latest work *Il progetto locale*, Bollati-Boringhieri, Turin 2000.
25 See Magnaghi, "Per una costellazione". This article includes a valuable bibliography.
26 Ibid, p. 27.
27 Riccardo Petrella, *Le Bien commun, éloge de la solidarité* (Brussels: Labord, 1996).
28 See the Atlases presented in the fascicles of *Rappresentare i luoghi* (Alinea, Florence).

Psychogeogram: An Artist's Utopia
Martin van Schaik

2. The Dream of Homo Ludens

Do you think you are alive? You are not. To live is to be creative, and life does not come after death. Thomas More wanted to bring heaven to this earth, but his only ideal was to make a better man. That is why it has remained a utopia. Now a different situation is emerging: the triumph of mankind over nature, the end of the struggle for existence. Recently I read an account of a laboratory test in which one was able, through electrical impulses, to make a cat become friends with a mouse. It reminded me of the story of the lion and the lamb. At this moment we have realized a small part of that. Should we continue to adapt ourselves to the present? Or has the time come for an "imaginary" project that reveals true possibilities?[110]

The period following Constant's resignation from the SI, which is often considered and even referred to as the "The Afterlife",[111] is in fact the central phase in the New Babylon project.

In the years leading up to 1966, the "Year of Constant", as the Dutch press dubbed it, the artist doggedly continues where he had left off when parting with the Situationists. But the idea of praxis, key phrase in the SI days, is radically altered: now officially operating solo, Constant will focus entirely on the theoretical elaboration and dissemination of his project and thoughts. Prophecy and provocation, rather than experimentation, become the prime tools to engage in reality; propaganda becomes the means. In a continuous series of lectures, exhibitions and publications of articles, Constant tells his audience – architects and planners mainly – about the coming age and the need to prepare for it. The direct and practical aim remains: to convince as many

Amongst Constant's many colourful and stunningly beautiful attempts to make the vision tangible to himself and to others – the many models, drawings, slide shows, lectures and texts that have been repeatedly extolled by historians over the years – one rather obscured but important effort stands out. We shall take this as a starting point to explore Constant's imaginary universe, his world of Homo Ludens. It is the manuscript of the book of New Babylon. For all its inconsistencies and stylistic flaws, this book forms the heart of the artist's Utopia. Like the world it so insistently tries to describe, it is a psychogeogram of the painter Constant.

The importance of the manuscript, written in German and entitled *New-Babylon – Skizze zu einer Kultur* (New Babylon – Outline of a Culture), might well be overlooked, as it never made it to the printing presses and only one copy of it remains.[112] Still, its significance is not only attested by Constant's recurring reference

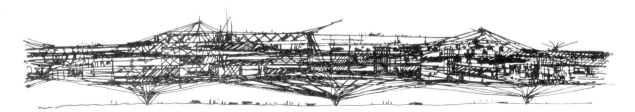

Coupe transversale de la ville couverte

as possible that a better city *could* and indeed urgently *needed* to be planned, to generate a momentum amongst practitioners that might actually usher in radical change. But practical planning in view of the many rapid developments – technological, social, and demographic – that were occurring everywhere by the early 1960s is but one side of the coin: as the artist repeatedly insisted, he was not primarily planning another city for some unforeseeable, fickle future. He was planning another life.

Behind Constant the architect-planner stands Constant the visionary. Both are intertwined in the social and artistic unity that is New Babylon. During the five years after the SI debacle Constant makes the Situationists' rather tentative rendering of a life-to-be entirely his, by synthesizing his ideas from the Cobra days and the subsequent era. With the dawning of a new decade, the overt negativity of Debord and his entourage are left behind, and Constant sets out to imagine, visualize and describe *his* dream of the Golden Age to come.

to it in interviews at the time, but also in many letters that proclaim it as the crucial, all-revealing work. Moreover, it is interesting to note that by the end of 1960 Constant enters a new phase in his artistic production: he stops making models and concentrates on drawing – from technical, exact, architectural plans and constructive schemes, via maps to suggestive sketches of spaces and life in New Babylon. Oddly, the connection with the publication has never been made.[113] By no means incidentally is Constant thinking on paper: his entire production is visibly geared to making a book.

The Vendor of Cities and the Writer of Books

The new episode in Constant's life and oeuvre quietly overlaps the old, in early 1960. In the spring of that year, with SI squabbling in the background, Constant exhibits the first models of his New Babylon in the city of Essen in the Ruhr area of Germany, at the branch of the Munich-based Van de Loo gallery. The showroom is run by Carlheinz Caspari, a theatre director and playwright. It is he who, in a matter of months, will take the place of Debord as Constant's main sparring partner. But this new relationship is a different one: rather than a vociferous critic, Caspari is a faithful supporter, a crucial figure operating largely behind the scenes. The phase of intense collaboration, mutual inspiration and kinship between the two men will last for about six years.

Caspari (who would use the name Christof in his correspondence with Constant) had met young Otto van de Loo – "a kid with a lot of money" – during his years of teaching in drama school.[114] The original Munich gallery which Otto and his wife set up in 1957 was an overnight success; the decision to become one of Asger Jorn's very first art dealers was a stroke of genius: it immediately brought Van de Loo in touch with Jorn's many painter friends and made his gallery one of the hottest and most profitable in Europe. The idea soon emerged to open a second branch up north, motivated, according to Van de Loo, by the conservative and stifling artistic climate in the Bavarian capital. The location would be somewhere in the Ruhr area, which was not only perceived to be a dynamic, up-and-coming region of West Germany but also Van de Loo's original home turf.[115] Carlheinz Caspari, who had curated a number of exhibitions for Van de Loo in Munich, was picked to run it. Many years later Van de Loo observed that Caspari was chiefly a man of letters, "a man who thought in words, not images". So he took something of a risk. Inevitably, therefore, this gallery would become quite distinct.

After the first few exhibits of a more traditional nature, Constant's models were put on display. The meeting of the two men was an instant *coup de foudre*, and to Caspari, especially, it was a turning point that fired up his imagination:

We both felt that Art was over. We would not concern ourselves with art, and instead we would use society and the city as our medium, urbanism. Of course, Constant had experience in this field, I on the other hand had had nothing to do with urban planning before. So I said: right, as a gallerist I will sell cities. Like Le Corbusier. Or Oscar Niemeyer.[116]

Caspari swiftly transformed the branch in the Ruhr not only to be a showroom of the urbanistic vanguard of the day, but also a *Labyratoire* – a "labyratory" in which novel urban concepts would be developed, built and tested. If the commercial benefits of the idea were somewhat doubtful, the thought made perfect sense in view of the gallery's location in Germany's former coal and steel-producing centre. After having been devastated in

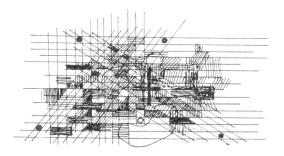

31/32. Constant, *Section and plan of a Covered City, IS* 3, 1959
33. (Opposite, top), Constant and Carlheinz Caspari, Berlin 1963

World War II, by 1960 the region was still desperately in need of large-scale reconstruction: the seemingly far-fetched concept thus definitely answered a need, and up until 1961, when the gallery closed, Caspari would try repeatedly to get things actually built. In Essen, therefore, Constant encountered an altogether different cultural climate and outlook: that he soon felt more at home here than in Situationist pan-European trench warfare should come as little surprise.

With his enthusiasm, the charming and sociable Caspari was soon to establish an impressive local network of sympathizers in the architectural community. He forged links to schools of architecture in the region, which, soon enough, extended to embrace Yona Friedman's multi-national *Groupe d'Etude d'Architecture Mobile* (GEAM). Some members of this group came from the area; amongst them was Eckhard Schulze-Fielitz

34. Architecture Mobile conference at Knoll International, Amsterdam 1962. Left to right: Constant, Habraken, Hartsuyker, Trapman, Cammelbeeck

who exhibited at Caspari's gallery in December 1960. These connections would provide an important part of Constant's new audience, and they vitally extended his network of contacts beyond established ties in the Netherlands, England, Denmark and France.

Constant had entertained the idea of elaborating the concept of Unitary Urbanism in the form of a major publication – thus not only in *immediate* practice – whilst still bickering with Debord. In letters going back as far as early 1959, Constant had repeatedly stressed the need for some kind of large publication or propagandist effort that would attract the right people to collaborate in the development of the future Situationist practice: engineers, architects, *real* scientists (meaning not of Pinot Gallizio's brand).[117] By 1960 a few texts outlining Constant's ideas had indeed been published in *Internationale Situationniste*, but of course the journal was not a medium that had much impact beyond the cultural fringe. Any attempt to engage with the mainstream and propagate the concept of Unitary Urbanism was invariably met with scorn or niftily sabotaged by the SI's

35. "And let's pay him a bonus for the paint that has dripped", cartoon by Enrico. The illustrations on the following pages – all from Constant's archive – were almost certainly intended to be used for the *Skizze* book.

wavering front man. Caspari, however, had none of these sectarian reservations.

According to most sources to date, the manuscript of the book was written during a period of well over five years, from 1960 to 1965.[118] Indeed one can reconstruct that work on the book only started, piecemeal, after Caspari had closed the Essen gallery in 1961 and had secured a job as a theatre director at the *Theater am Dom*, in nearby Cologne. Evidence further suggests that the bulk of the work on the manuscript was done between the end of 1963 and early 1965, when Caspari started work for the NDR broadcasting company in Hamburg.[119]

Constant described his collaboration with Caspari as follows: when they started out, both men were single, and he would drive over to Cologne on weekends with another fresh piece of his manuscript, which he would then discuss and translate with his friend.[120] According to Caspari, these sessions were intense and laborious, and each sentence and argument was rigorously scrutinized and dissected.[121] That Caspari had some influence in terms of content is not surprising: an outspoken and colourful character, he was at the time developing parallel ideas of his own under the header of *Labyr* (short for "Labyrinth"), exploring philosophical concepts – "a mental attitude" – which actually predate and foreshadow the conceptions of non-hierarchical, non-linear thought launched many years later by Gilles Deleuze and Felix Guattari. But despite the fact that Caspari provided vital intellectual backing,[122] the book and its contents are the work of Constant alone.

Sizeable parts of *Skizze zu einer Kultur* overlap with lectures and shorter texts that were written during this period. As a consequence, it is quite difficult to reconstruct what came first: part of the book, in German, or a particular essay or lecture, often in a different language. The divergences between the published texts and the manuscript are usually telltale. Most importantly, however, the manuscript amalgamates Constant's theoretical insights about art, culture, morality, society, and urban planning – all set within a historical-materialist framework – on the one hand and the description of the life in and formal characteristics of New Babylon on the other. The two categories are inseparable: the text thus reaches a theoretical density unparalleled by any other writing the artist produced previously or subsequently.

The book, 160 typed pages in all, is in effect a collection of 74 short numbered chapters grouped into three distinct parts. The first section consists of three seemingly separate essays – "A sociology of the Artist", "The song of Labour" and "The Functional Zion"[123] – and is presented as introduction to New Babylon itself, the subject of the second part. A third, final section completes the tome. Referred to as the "Atlas", it is an illustrated coda: a presentation of maps and illustrations of the project. Though the text often moves capriciously from argument to argument and from chapter to chapter, the underlying structure of the book is exceptionally clear: Part One is a radical cultural and social critique dealing with the past and the present. Part Two and Part Three are its counterpoint, the 'outline' of the culture to come; they describe and tentatively depict the new society and the built form that will foster and sustain it.

Constant sets the contrast between the old and the coming world at the very beginning of the book, even before the text proper begins. In four "definitions" he introduces the terms he will be using repeatedly: "Utilitarian society", "Homo Ludens", "Play", and "Social space".[124] The first term describes the world marked by the primordial struggle for survival – the only one, according to Constant, that man has known so far. The three others, which define marginalized and intrinsically *exceptional* phenomena in the world of want and scarcity, belong to the realm of New Babylon. Moreover, in his description of the "utilitarian society" of Homo Faber, Constant establishes essential connections that underlie every argument in the book: between the material-economic basis of society, the position of creativity and art within it and the morals of that society, on the one hand, and the cities it builds for itself, on the other. It is this Marxist stance that will fundamentally motivate Constant's outline of New Babylonian culture.

Between two worlds

To begin with, it is necessary to bear in mind that the making of *culture* – which according to Constant is produced by being creative in *play* – is indeed the alpha and omega of New Babylon. Constant defines *play* as the freedom to manifest one's existence through creation, as a celebration of life by way of the free, transformational act. *Vitality* is the apt term that Constant had used in the late 1940s, and it is what he celebrates in New Babylon as well. Constant therefore makes it quite clear in his introductory "definitions" that when talking of play he is not thinking in terms of a game with fixed rules of conduct: playing chess is not a creative act. Invention – a continuous search for the new that is ultimately *sui generis* – and freedom from all external constraints are absolute prerequisites. Play is an imaginative, expressive and interventionist activity with its own drive and internal logic. By presenting it as a basic expression of life that can accept no rules other than the ones it generates itself, Constant reiterates the egalitarian tenet of Cobra: the capacity to play and to create is a universal human quality: "*en chaque homme il y a un créateur qui sommeille*".[125] This essential creative instinct needs only to be awakened and liberated.

The term *Homo Ludens* (man at play) that Constant – like the Lettrists – adopted from cultural historian Johan Huizinga must be understood in this connection.[126] In his book of the same title, Huizinga defines play as a universal human impulse that is essentially the basis of all culture. As Constant exalts, "it remains Huizinga's great achievement that he was able to remove the ideological ballast from the notion of culture and bring it back to its original meaning, that is to say to the manifestation of the creative human being."[127] But where each person has the natural ability to play, play itself, according to Huizinga, has its restrictions: he defines it as a temporary suspension of the everyday, a demarcated realm outside of seriousness. The *illusion* of play is therefore limited in time and in space: play creates a magic circle that can at any time be broken by the intrusion of reality or the end of the game. To illustrate his point, Huizinga refers to parties or country fairs. Here, temporarily, Homo Ludens comes to the fore. In its opposition to play, seriousness ultimately takes the upper hand. Constant therefore needs to change the dialectic in a crucial way: the criterion that defines play is not so much its contrast with the earnestness of *reality*, but its moral and practical opposition to *usefulness* or *utility*.

The central idea Huizinga and Constant both embrace is that all cultural production is the result of play in *freedom*. This premise is important, for it is here that the question of creation becomes a political issue. In the course of history, Constant argues, to create in liberty has been the privilege of the few, of those fortunate enough to be relieved of the burden of production labour or the need to keep themselves alive. In a condition of material scarcity, in a battle with nature for survival – which has been near permanent so far – it is only through the exploitation of the majority that a minority has been able to produce culture. Invariably tied to the ruling class, historic cultural elites are by nature parasitic: art is a luxury by and for the few, effectively created on the backs of the many. Though it would appear that Constant voices the guilty conscience of the artist, he nonetheless defends the position as a sad inevitability: without this functional inequality, there would simply never have been any art. This view also forms the basis of his critique of utopias: they invariably aim for social justice through imposed equality and celebrate man as a frugal production animal – as a Homo Faber: "utopias are in their essence hostile to art".[128]

Many of the arguments that Constant elaborates on his trip through history in "A sociology of the Artist" return in his 1964 article "Opkomst en ondergang van de avant-garde";[129] in the book, too, he ends his historical interpretation with a vicious attack on the "pseudo avant-garde" and the neo-Cobra painter: "In this comedy of errors, the painter, especially, plays a comic role. He is the quasi-barbarian in the era of the atom, the caveman in the space age. (…) The artist no longer exists, only his caricature."[130] Of course this immediately brings back memories of his polemic with the SI. If, in Constant's view, the artist's fate had been effectively sealed with industrialization, the prospect of the full automation of production labour – through cybernetics – will deliver the *coup de grace*. The privilege of the few can now become the privilege of the many: if only the masses can be relieved from work, thousands of years of want can be forgotten. Finally, the freedom to play, for all of mankind, is within reach. The crisis of the individualist artist thus accompanies the dawning of the age of mass creation.

In this context it is interesting to note that the emphasis on automation – as opposed to the call to create the integrated, technological art of Unitary Urbanism – only gradually appears in Constant's writings. Judging by correspondence with Debord and published texts, it is hardly an issue that Constant appears to give any particular attention to during his time with the SI. Perversely, it is Asger Jorn who explores the radical social impact of automation in a crucial essay in the first issue of *Internationale Situationniste*,[131] whereas Constant merely addresses it in passing in his article "Another City for Another Life" in the third issue of the journal.[132] Only in his December 1960 lecture at the Stedelijk Museum in Amsterdam does Constant underline that technology is crucial not only in creating the new artistic medium but also in providing the preconditions for its emergence.[133] By itself, this does not prove that he long ignored the predicted cybernetic breakthrough: it may simply have been a self-evident premise in Situationist circles, within which Constant felt it was necessary to wage other battles.

Yet automation is absolutely crucial: without it, New Babylon and its culture fall like a house of cards. As many sociologists at the time were deeply concerned with the question of how the developed world should deal with the vast increases in leisure time that were predicted by the gurus of cybernetics – Norbert Wiener,

162   162 Que l'air est merveilleux à la campagne!

36/37. The CIAM city of tarmac: "How lovely the country air is"

38–40. Amsterdam, old city centre and Montmartre, Paris – *acculturation zones* and potential terrain for Situationist *dérives* – starkly contrasting with the deadpan reality of modernist planning: Rivierenbuurt, Amsterdam.

most prominently – it was tempting to present New Babylon as an artistic answer to the technological and social challenges posed at the end of the 1950s (another of these would be the population explosion). Indeed Constant, for obvious reasons, preferred to talk of his project as a rational planning necessity. Thus, sadly, historians have far too often refused to look beyond the rhetoric, and in so doing they bypass the obvious underlying social and artistic motivations.[134] Though it claims to offer practical solutions, New Babylon is most pertinently not a form of problem-solving "research": the cultural vision of New Babylon

precedes all practical concerns. If the historical perspective outlined in the first chapter of *Skizze zu einer Kultur* harks back to Constant's 1948 Manifesto, it is indeed automation that rendered Cobra's dream of a universal people's art potentially feasible. It was truly a godsend.

In "The song of Labour", Constant attempts to construct the historic inevitability of New Babylon, leading him to formulate a series of arguments quite often rather twisted and full of *non sequiturs*. Unfavourable trends – such as the emergence of the tertiary sector, which absorbs surplus human labour and generates new capital – are ignored or simply wished away.[135] Doubts about the feasibility of total automation are exorcized by the insistence that even activities like "medical diagnosis, care for patients and education" can be taken over by machines. Activities that require creative decisions are simply categorized as "ludic" and "creative" and therefore not considered "work".[136] It is ironic in this connection that the articles which provided Constant with his ammunition at least retain some critical distance to the futurological speculations they advance. But ultimately, far more pressing an issue from Constant's point of view – indeed the major obstacle – is the attitude to work: the ingrained morality of *Ora et Labora*.

The problem does not merely extend, according to Constant, to traditional Christian values: the glorification of work – the aim of equal happiness or displeasure for all members of society – also pervades socialist and Marxist thought. Constant reminds us that the luxury of true art – play in freedom and not communist propaganda with blissfully beaming peasants and workers – tends to be sacrificed on the altar of social equality. Insistently he calls on socialism, in all its incarnations, to review its tactic and embrace automation, despite all short-to-medium-term dangers: it will ultimately bring about not only the revolution, but also the unheard-of freedom in the cataclysm's wake. Ultimately, Constant believes, total automation will drastically tip the scales and completely reset the moral compass: "Not the categories of utilitarian thought, but those of the free creative will shall determine morality."[137] Only the goals of art or play – satisfaction and pleasure – will finally be of true value.

The last leg of the run-up to the description of New Babylon brings us back to Constant's critique of modernist urbanism. In this final part, he introduces the reader to what is essentially done away with in the CIAM city and what will be the heart of New Babylon: *social space*. Constant describes modernist urbanism as the inevitable material manifestation of the utilitarian frame of mind. "The city as we find it today, the functional city, is a gigantic slave reservation".[138] In this equation the functionalist doctrine is the perverse celebration of humankind's miserable condition: by defining art in terms of usefulness and functionality (and creating form according to its imaginary dictate) it "raises utility to the level of cultural principle". The cultural artefact, from object to city, bears its imprint. Like the ideology it springs from, the functionalist city is a cultural and practical extrapolation of the Taylorist principle, an efficient production machine with its functions split up according to the tenets of the Athens Charter. In this context, the function of *recreation* is an explicit target of his ire. Indeed, for Constant, the concept of re-creation (as opposed to creation) is merely a link in the productive chain and not a realm outside it: it is the *useful* time out between two shifts. In the same vein Constant fiercely attacks the architecture of "technocratic functionalism", referring explicitly to Yona Friedman (though he might just as easily have pointed at the work of the Japanese Metabolists and even "playful" Archigram). Instead of a real critique of functionalism and the world as we know it, this 'visionary' architecture – for all its technical daring and formal panache – is nothing but its crowning phase. It is ultimately more of the very same.

With the issue of social space, Constant has arrived at a crucial point in his reasoning. By sacrificing the idea of a true social realm to functional emptiness and boredom, not only real urban life, but also art along with it, has nearly all but disappeared. Dysfunctional play and culture are simply planned into extinction, and the possibility for spontaneous gathering or chance encounters, the thrill and vagaries of urban life survive in the cracks, at best.

The adventure still exists, but it withers away in flea markets, in shady bars or, in the worst case, in arcade halls and ice cream

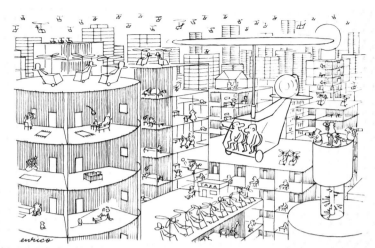

42. "At last people are in touch with nature". Enrico cartoon

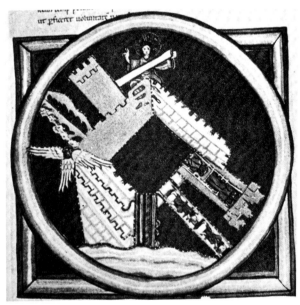

41. *Christus Pantocrator* reigning over Zion / New Jerusalem

parlours. (…) Its inhabitants mostly belong to that part of the population that is not engaged in the production process, or only part-time, and that therefore does not share the utilitarian attitude to life of other social groups.[139]

The description of what Constant refers to as "acculturation zones" immediately brings back images of the young Lettrists hanging about in the cafés and back alleys of the *rive gauche*: it is these social spaces that will be the stuff that New Babylon is made of. Authentic and spectacle-free, their *sinful* nature tentatively prefigures it.

If the modern city is the dire reality of his day, Constant – in a last push – moves the issue of space up one level: to the symbolic urban representations of Homo Faber. Naturally, he brings back the issue of utopias. He rejects the insistence on order and work in the cities of utopia, reminding us that they offer no room for creative flux. Fossilized and static, they are places in which an eternal social order is installed and maintained through its in-

scription in built form. Analyzing the spatial layout of Renaissance utopias, Constant finds that many of them are circular in shape. In this form he sees a significant analogy: "The representations of the symbolic Zion show the form of a fortress: inside closed defensive ramparts, God is seated in the centre, in most secure position".[140] Here Constant finally draws the connection between the City of God and the city of utility; the title of the chapter pulls the two together: "The Functional Zion".

To seek a mythological contrast – whether biblical or secular – with utilitarian society, Constant calls on the ancient myth of the city of Babylon: in Judeo-Christian mythology, it is not only the place of captivity and exile from the homeland, but also the city of the tower symbolizing the human striving to be godly, the town of sin and promiscuity, the Whore of Babylon. Constant thus effectively *detourns* the story of the Babylonian captivity: humankind finds itself in exile in the "functional Zion". Against the millennial reign in the New Jerusalem, Constant posits the advent of the New Babylon: he inverts – or rather *perverts* – the prophecy. Ultimately, however – and this must be stressed – he

43. Functional Zion: Renaissance

replaces it. If it appears that he ridicules the idea of a messianic advent, like Marx he merely secularizes it: the terrestrial paradise from which man was rejected, is now again within his reach. Only this time he will build it himself, with no help from a supreme being. History, the great redeemer, comes full circle: "New Babylon is the world that the human race, in its highest stage of development, creates for itself 'in its image, after its likeness'."[141]

Time and again Constant will speak in biblical terms about the world to come. More than a revolutionary call to arms, the final passages of the first part of *Skizze zu einer Kultur* are the chants of a prophet:

Humankind will sooner or later take what is its due. Man will play, when there is no more work to occupy and devour his life. Man will be free, freer than he ever was, freer that the mighty of this earth have ever been, for he now has the means with which to realise his freedom. For the first time, his life will be a human life. For the first time ever, man will be a full human being, for he will create his own existence, shape his own life. His creativity, his creative capacity that has long lain barren, will finally come to flourish.

44. The Whore of Babylon

The release of the enormous creative potential of the masses will change the face of the earth in the same far-reaching manner as the organization of labour has since Neolithic times. The age of the HOMO LUDENS is about to begin.[142]

But if Homo Ludens is free, first and foremost, how did Constant proceed from this premise? Is this the freedom reputedly provided in Yona Friedman's megastructures? From the moment that the two men start corresponding in 1961, it is clear they interpret the idea of freedom quite differently. Despite their agreement on the point that the future city would have to be "mobile", in every other sense the two men take opposite positions.[143] Friedman sums up his objections by pointing out that Constant was all too specific about where he, and thus his Homo Ludens, wished to go: he was a *metteur en scène*.[144] Friedman reminds us that in Constant's world it is not just mediocre mankind mucking about in liberty, but that the creation of a great culture is the *raison d'être* of New Babylon: "Constant always profoundly disliked the ordinary, the petit bourgeois, people just doing their little thing."[145] This world is something better: a new socio-artistic order that needs to be crafted carefully. Constant, more than anything, wants *his* dream of total life-art to work. So immediately after the prophet, the demiurge enters the scene.

An Atlas of the new world

Complementing the lengthy "outline of a culture" provided in the second part of *Skizze zu einer Kultur*, Constant intended to offer his readers visual material that would illustrate his "sketch". The manuscript of the book obviously lacks illustrations, but there are some clues as to which images he would have used in the printed version. To begin with, the short text at the beginning of the final "Atlas" chapter indicates that the maps that Constant produced in the course of 1963–64 – at the time that work on the final draft of the book began – would definitely be included. An example of these would be the map in fig. 46, which shows the web of interconnected sectors – the building blocks of New Babylon – spreading out from an existing city centre, in this case Amsterdam; similar maps were produced for various other West European cities. It is within these macro-infrastructural supports, indicated in red, that the life of Homo Ludens will unfold. Moving up one level of scale (fig. 45), we can see the chain of sectors snaking its way across the landscape, branching off, intersecting and thus forming an urban network across the landscape. Very carefully the existing urban cores are encircled and embraced by the new structures and integrated in the larger network. Meanwhile the sector chains, on their march from one original urban core to the other, usually follow existing infrastructures such as railway lines and motorways. This network, once sufficiently developed, allows for endless mobility, drift, and exploration.

The result, as the images show, is not just an erratic typical late-1950s linear urban scheme adapted to the requirements of Homo Ludens. Though parallels have been drawn to earlier or contemporary architectural projects with a similar layout,[146] in New Babylon the practically motivated shape also works on a symbolic level: as the Ruhr map shows, the static and self-contained form of "Zion" is literally inverted. The negative becomes the positive and the 'cracks' in the system provide the model for New Babylon's cartographic representation.

Other illustrations would complete the readers' impression of the basic urban hardware in New Babylon. The ink drawings in figs. 54 and 55 were both reproduced in Hein van Haaren's seminal 1967 monograph, where they are identified as part of "the Atlas of New Babylon".[147] Disarmingly clear and precise, the first of the two drawings shows a perspective view of the sectors arranged in a network spread across the landscape, with airstrips and helicopter pads nestling on the rooftops of what must clearly be mammoth constructions. The other sketch is part of a series Constant used to examine various possible structural typologies: like all elevations and sections of New Babylon, it harks back to the first published scheme of the *ville couverte* in *Internationale Situationniste 3*, which provided the basic theme for all of Constant's sector models and drawings.

Constant describes the generic building block of New Babylon, the sector, as a construction with a surface of anywhere between 5 and 20 hectares ("some larger exceptions may be possible") raised to a height of "about 16 metres" above the ground on stilts or by other means, like natural outcrops. The actual footprint of the sector is thus reduced to a minimum, keeping the ground plane as free as possible for traffic, and allowing for the landscape fragments, conserved between the arms of the sector web (including whatever remains of older constructions), to spill over into one another. More importantly, however, the elevated "social space" within the sectors remains uninterrupted by non-pedestrian traffic flows: in this way, the massive constructions form the exclusive domain of play. No industry or production facilities are to be found there. Factories and power plants – and clearly Constant is thinking in terms of nuclear energy – are either located underground, beneath the level of "nature" and circulation, or above the surface but at a sizeable distance from the habitat of Homo Ludens. Constant explains: "The goods are distributed to the sectors by conveyor belts, and on to central automatic sales points in the larger sectors. The balance between production and consumption is kept in check by electronic means."[148] But apart from these inevitable points of contact, the practical and the playful are symbolically separated; art is raised above the industrial infrastructure that, safely tucked away, is pretty much taken for granted. As a result, what we see when looking at the sectors of New Babylon is but the cultural tip of the automated iceberg.

Still, these raw data confirm what the maps and drawings suggest: such constructions are truly gargantuan. The sectors are veritable cities – or at least very large urban quarters – up in the sky. The sheer density and thickness of the overhead spaces become even more overwhelming if we take into account how the sector itself is built up: according to most descriptions, the constructions invariably consist of several layers of large horizontal expanses, enormous "floors" that are interconnected at numerous points; the surface of the earth is literally multiplied several times. Again, we see that Constant echoes the original ideogrammatic plan of the "covered city" with its intersecting multi-directional hatchings, indicating not only the flux of the activity inside but also, quite literally, the layering within the huge volume. In many respects, therefore, the earliest sector models that Constant builds whilst still a member of the SI provide very few clues as to the sheer bulk of the construction. Elegant and transparent but ultimately without any indication of scale, they reflect the *mood* – the constructional and atmospheric essence – of New Babylon, rather than exact architectural or constructional specifics. They

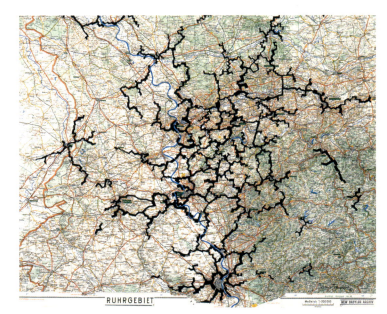

45. Constant, *New Babylon / Ruhrgebiet*, 1963
46. Constant, *New Babylon / Amsterdam*, 1963

are not only poetically evocative and highly photogenic: they also show the artist experimenting. Perhaps a term that Constant used for New Babylon as a whole is fitting: they are "play models".

A work such as *Sector Constructie* (fig. 52) is an exploration of the possibilities of a lightweight framework. As the title suggests, and unlike other *maquettes*, it is not an image of a finished sector but a suggestion for its structure. Quite practically – and beautifully – Constant is figuring out how to make a large span using modular components, and for all its visual complexity the model is in fact perfectly ordered – so much so that it is highly reminiscent of Konrad Wachsmann's illustrious 1952 aircraft hangar or the space frames developed by some members of GEAM. But this similarity is deceptive.

Indeed the models that Constant actually refers to as "sectors" – Yellow sector, Red sector and Orient sector[149] – come much closer to the description provided in *Skizze zu einer Kultur* and elsewhere. All the basic elements are present: construction, indications of horizontal layering and micro-structural infill. But again these models should be seen as explorations. It has been rightly pointed out that the early sector *maquettes* were essentially created like a painting, built up layer after layer.[150] Looking at a model like the *Orient Sector* (fig. 51), we see that the transparent, coloured plexiglas allows us to peer through the various levels – pockmarked by frenetic lines of action – onto the smaller details within. Hence the transparency of the material not only allows the sketch plan from *IS 3* to be translated into three dimensions, but it also provides a suggestive x-ray view of the sector and what happens inside: a sensation that no classic architectural model or drawing can convey. What is more, the material embodies the high-tech character of New Babylon, reminding us that Constant is emphatically not preaching a return to human prehistory. Like the ultimate plexiglas objects in New Babylon – the exquisite *Spatiovores* – the sector models are decidedly glamorous and seductive: their transparency is not only artistically and conceptually expedient but also *iconic*.

47. Constant, *Gezicht op een sector*, 1960

If we return to the written descriptions of New Babylon, however, we get quite a different impression of its megastructures, one that confirms the suspicion that the airiness of the *maquettes* should certainly not be taken too literally. The drawing *Gezicht op een sector* (1960) gives us a more precise idea: it shows a huge multi-level horizontal construction raised on robust stilts, with parts of another sector, set at an angle, rising above it. On the highest rooftop, again, there is a sketchy indication of helicopters, whereas the ground level appears to be a rugged wasteland with traffic zipping by on a motorway in the distance. These titanic Corbusian *plans libres* on *pilotis* leave little to the imagination: the world of New Babylon is one vast interior. Constant even insists that barely any light is able to penetrate far into the building, and indeed it is not meant to do so. Intentionally, Constant plunges his sectors into darkness, barring the natural cycle of day and night. The *essential* darkness of the sector is that of the theatre, red-light districts, casinos and nightclubs – places where all notion of the passing of time is simply lost. There is little here that reminds us of Friedman's open-lattice frameworks or Plug-in City's what-you-see-is-what-you-get exhibitionism: Constant's sectors are megastructures of the night. Life as we

know it is simply impossible, and sheer artificiality is now the norm within the expanse of a total interior.

One of the very first drawings of a New Babylonian interior that may well have been included in the Atlas in the *Skizze* book, *Trappen en ladders* (1960), illustrates the basic light-dark dialectic. On first inspection, it shows a near-black foreground framing the view towards a brightly lit area beyond, a powerful chiaroscuro impression of what appear to be ladders in space. Turning the image upside-down (ignoring the artist's signature at the bottom for a moment) makes matters clearer. What we now see is the illuminated underside of a sector floor, that in the top left is being pierced by a ladder making a connection to an upper level. In the centre, the outline of a figure can be seen, arriving at the top of the stair, whereas in the dark foreground, at first nearly indistinguishable from the pitch-black shadows, a few sinewy figures waiting in the wings suddenly appear. The thrilling essential obscurity of the sectors invites, even requires Homo Ludens to make it come alive: it is the primordial, formless void from which everything starts. If in the beginning nearly all is dark and static on the largest and most sophisticated theatre stage ever, Homo Ludens switches on the light and creates the mood.

Indeed, Constant provides his New Babylonians with all the necessary spatial and atmospheric tools they need to shape and re-shape their world. Whereas it is disorientating darkness that characterizes the macro-structural frame of the sector, dynamic labyrinthine complexity defines its infill. *Trappen en ladders* also gives us the first impression of what happens between the floors. From the outset, they are not empty, Constant assures his readers: they tend to be divided into smaller and larger spaces that form a gigantic labyrinth which is entirely flexible, allowing Homo Ludens not only to roam through the multitude of environments but to transform them actively, by physically shifting floors, walls, and mobile construction elements. Moreover, the atmosphere and climate within this dynamic labyrinth – artificial to begin with and carried to its logical extreme – can be drastically modified by the most advanced technical means: light, temperature control, sound, smell, and various forms of telecommunications.

48. Constant, *Trappen en ladders*, 1960
49–52. (Opposite page, top to bottom:) Two images from Constant's legendary slide presentations showing his 1958 *Gele sector* (left) and *Oriënt sector* model from 1959; *Oriënt sector*, view from above, revealing the transparency of the different layers of the maquette; *Sector constructie*, 1959, dramatically captured on film by Bram Wisman and since destroyed.

53. Constant: *Vergelijkende plattegrond New Babylon / Amsterdam Ookmeer*, 1962

The resulting patchwork of zones and basic ambiances within the body of the sector was first described by Constant in 1959:

There are two labyrinth-houses, one large and one small (L and M), which take up and develop the ancient forces of architectural confusion: the water effects (G), the circus (H), the great ballroom (N), the white plaza (F) beneath which is suspended the green plaza, which enjoys a splendid view of the freeway traffic that passes below. (…) The two labyrinth-houses are formed by a great number of irregularly-shaped chambers, spiral staircases, distant corners, wastelands, cul-de-sacs. One goes through

them adventurously. One can find oneself in a quiet room, clad in insulating material; the loud room with its vivid colours and ear-splitting sounds; the room of echoes (radiophonic speaker games); the room of images (cinematic games); the room for reflection (games of psychological resonance); the room for rest; the room for erotic games; the room of coincidences, etc.[151]

Sketches from the same period (with the SI in the late 1950s) confirm this rather baroque and predetermined layout, despite Constant's insistence on labyrinthine flexibility. Something of a shift indeed takes place in the direction of spatial indeterminacy in the following years, with an increased emphasis on modular construction to facilitate permanent change. Constant's renewed involvement with architects, and those of the GEAM group especially, may explain the change. Thus the most detailed plan that Constant ever drew of a sector's interior layout is decidedly well-behaved and architectural, though the basic ingredients of the 1959 Yellow Zone description are kept.

The *Vergelijkende plattegrond New Babylon/Amsterdam Ookmeer* (1962) gives us a pronounced architectural impression as well. This scale drawing (!) also shows us the basic configuration of all sector interiors that Constant describes in *Skizze zu einer Kultur*. Most of the interior is social space, room for drift, encounter and play where Homo Ludens spends his waking hours. Indicated as A, B and C and rendered in a darker shade (and marked in black within the red outlines of the sector on the *New Babylon-Amsterdam* map) are the spaces Homo Ludens can withdraw to when he is not engaged in ludic activity. They are seemingly all that remains of the traditional 'home' in which Homo Faber dwells, but given the nomadic existence in New Babylon, they provide only temporary accommodation. *De facto* they are collectively run hotels.

T.C., right next to the transit dwellings, designates technical equipment and services while the uppermost sector especially gives us extra clues about functional essentials: *R*, along the periphery of the sector, is a restaurant space adjacent to *toiletten* and *automatieken* (automats). Moving down a little to the right, passing the *labyrinth* and tiny red-light district (with its radio or telephone booths marked *tel*) we come to a cosy *Weinstube* (wine bar), a little bit of Bavarian or Rhineland comfort that aids in achieving the joyous inebriation that facilitates all New Babylonian activity. Bridges connect the various sectors, accessed by lifts, while *start-banen* (runways) and Heliports straddle the rooftops.

Everything "useful" is literally in the service of play. Seen from a distance, these sectors as a whole show remarkable similarities with the basic scheme of a modernist open-plan dwelling, with a regular grid of column-and-floor-slab construction and a service core catering for the needs of the single living space surrounding it. The iconic modern home for the well-off family is transfigured into a home for a collective at play. In these creative pleasure domes, the notion of urban social space is radically fused with artistic creation itself, as the room for play now forms the basic bulk of human habitat. The concept of art in the streets is taken to its extreme. But where play used to be a withdrawal from the harsh reality of work, the only withdrawal in New Babylon is that from creation, an interlude providing the biologically inevitable rest. Though all norms are again inverted and freedom prevails, the parallels to the recreational logic of the "Functional Zion" are obvious.

The final image of the "hardware" of New Babylon – not only a background but an essential ingredient and actor in the great game – thus emerges: the sectors harbour huge labyrinthine interior landscapes, adventure playgrounds with the most powerful technological gadgetry built in to cater for the creative needs of Homo Ludens. The continuous social space is an immense experimental laboratory, a world-spanning studio for playful mankind. The setting and the tools for a liberated existence for all is thus established and meticulously planned from the outset. But the hardware brings us to the heart of the matter, the superior life of man at play, for it is this that all the technical fuss is to bring about and sustain. The manuscript for *Skizze zu einer Kultur* shows how Constant courageously tries to outline it.

A culture of composition

In the description of the life of the New Babylonians Constant pulls together many strains of thought. Essentially, this life is dedicated to the never-ending art of Unitary Urbanism, and New Babylon is the place in which the Lettrists' faraway dream of an integrated life-art has become everyday reality. The New Babylonian is footloose, drifting from space to space and sector to sector, carried on by his desires, in search of adventure, creating new experiences and new opportunities for play. If the nomadic life in New Babylon clearly has its roots in the Parisian *dérive* and the romance of gypsy life that kick-started the project in 1956, the playful drifting through the sectors is taken a crucial step forward: the unitary life-art in New Babylon is an active transformational game played in social space with other New Babylonians – collectively. All action is *interaction*, and with life becoming play and the morals of utility out of the window,

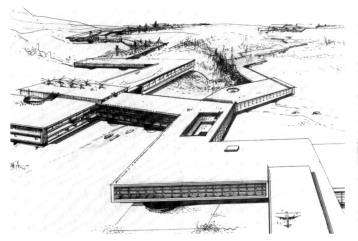

54/55. Two drawings by Constant, both from 1964, reproduced as images from the "Atlas of New Babylon" in Hein van Haaren, *Constant*, 1966: *Vogelvlucht groep sectoren* and *Schets voor een zelfdragende constructie*. The architecturalness and realism of the first drawing is striking.

the creation of art is the crucial social activity – and vice versa. It is in this essential characteristic of New Babylonian life that we see the promise of Cobra finally coming into its own. Similarly, of course, De Stijl's dream of the fusion between total spatial art and life becomes a reality.

"The starting point of the culture of New Babylon is the mode and atmosphere of life. Contrary to the work of art, that takes a step back from reality, 'atmosphere' is to be seen as a (temporary) variation on reality. Atmosphere is founded on the short-lived, on the well-chosen but irrevocably passing moment. In New Babylonian culture, the ephemeral, the passing of time is an essential and positive factor."[152] This definition of the New Babylonian *Gesamtkunstwerk* as "uninterrupted variation of life-atmosphere, play of atmospheres, play with and against the surroundings" that takes place in the labyrinthine social space remains rather vague. As it involves not only the modification of space but also, fundamentally, the impact of human presence and activity, there are aspects of unitary urbanism that clearly bring to mind the Happening and other brands of performance art emerging in the late 1950s, similarly aimed at producing a creative and environmental totality and at "blurring art and life". For Constant, what made the (obvious) association even worse, was that the Happening was decidedly trendy and, on the surface, very American – though it was practised and effectively

pioneered in the Old World many years before Allan Kaprow coined the phrase.[153] Constant always insisted that the Happening was a far too one-sided event: in the world of Homo Faber it is no more than a passive spectacle.[154]

We must return to the 1948 manifesto to understand where Constant's ambitions lay. In it, he tries to explain the essence of the universal people's art he was seeking. Clearly, this would be an art built on basic human creativity – on the pure, untrammelled expression of the creative imagination, devoid of any cultural convention, and thus accessible to every human being. The unconscious is bound to play a vital role in the process as the source to be tapped. But though Constant does not explicitly mention it in his text, this is the point on which Cobra decidedly deviates from the Surrealism it sprang from. The rift has been described as the "materialist" approach of Cobra versus the "idealist" stance of surrealism.[155] Clearly these Marxist categories were pleasant to the ear and should not be interpreted too philosophically but fairly literally: surrealist art projected its (frequently libidinous) desires onto canvas, casting them into a stylistically classical form, sacrificing expression and the very rawness of the unconscious it emerged from in favour of a final, finished image. The resulting art is hermetic and impenetrable, an artistically correct view into a dream world that leaves the spectator standing by in awe. In effect, Constant counters this spectacular passivity with the principle of material *suggestiveness*, which operates for the artist during the making and for the observer during the looking. Underlying the idea is the capacity of material reality itself – outside of the artist and outside of the spectator – to trigger the unconscious and to awaken the imagination. The suggestive quality of matter implies its essential incompleteness. In an interview from the late 1970s Constant illustrates the point:

I can remember when I was a child I used to see different things in the flowered wallpaper in my bedroom every night before falling asleep. I remember the fantasies I had. Leonardo da Vinci in one of his letters also mentions being inspired by weather stains on old walls. Karel Appel and I often talked about those 'stains' in the Cobra days. That we took such a stain as our starting point, and then we said: we associate it with a particular thing, and then we'd paint that. That's why I was never really an abstract painter. A stain always turned into a figure, an animal or whatever, something that could be traced to the stain.[156]

Like a Rorschach test, the principle of suggestiveness implies imaginative intervention and a process of stimulus and response. For the Cobra artist, the real pleasure lies in the playfully creative activity itself that is essentially open-ended until a degree of satisfaction has been achieved. The suggestive rawness of the "finished" result leaves room for the spectator's imagination – the beginning, perhaps, of another creative act, or of a potentially endless cycle of creative stimulus and response (the imagination, activated by matter, triggers material change that in response triggers the imagination, and so on). This art knows no rules and is fundamentally accessible to anyone: it calls for improvisation and spontaneity – freedom from inhibition – and is not result-oriented or stylistic. "Style" is in fact a barrier in a realm where provocative contrast and surprise are far more effective. Pleasure is thus derived from the playful, poetic[157] and imaginative *process* that is not primarily a celebration of the bodily act as such but rather an experience of the activating power of the responsive

56. Murals by Karel Appel, Constant and Corneille, Denmark 1949

57. Constant's paint box, 1948

imagination. This art is fundamentally *communicative*. One can see that this is also where Cobra essentially differs from action painting.

From this development it is only a small step to understanding the role of the material world of New Babylon (which, as in psychogeography, is essential) and the people inhabiting and activating it. The materiality and poetic flux which the actors generate in the social space is crucial: they provide an endless resource of creative stimuli. Interaction and dialogue on the canvas are taken to social space. Constant worked from experience, extolling the pure satisfaction of the dialectic artistic process and bringing it to mankind at large.

In *Skizze zu einer Kultur* Constant describes how this interactive environmental play works. If at first a space is empty – though it may have a strong, basic ambiance or mood – the entry of a single person immediately affects the situation. This one person will, naturally, adapt the space according to his wishes, using the gadgetry available. It is only with the arrival of other human beings, drifting into orbit, that the game truly begins. "In a social space, in which the number of people is continuously changing, each moment in which a shift in the perception of those present takes place is an impulse to change the existing ambiance." Each arrival might provoke a welcome change, an opportunity to respond in a ludic fashion and to alter the direction of play.[158] The impact of arrivals and departures is enhanced by the technical and spatial means supposedly available to all. Indeed it has been suggested that spoken language may actually be superfluous in New Babylon, since the art itself in effect constitutes social activity and dialogue.[159] This interplay of many fills the essential darkness, painting it brighter than a sunny day, redder than any sunset and bluer than a baby's eyes: a dynamic, passionate neverending game, more intense and inspiring than anything that has gone before. Constant defines it as a "culture of composition", replacing the "culture of competition" that has reigned so far. "Collective creativity" is the norm.

Perhaps the sheer sensuous delight of this collective play was best captured in the dramatic coloured photographs that were made of the sector models – pictures which Constant used for his multimedia slide presentations. The transparency and constructive intricacy of the *maquettes* were now used to their full potential, coloured spotlights filtering through the plexiglas levels

of the models, set in front of the inevitable darkened background. The mood is passionate, intense, glamorous and poetically technological. But imagine the ultimate dance club or theatre stage with not one but many at the controls of stage lifts, lights, smells, smoke guns and music. Does this atmospheric game – which seems so prone to disharmony and cacophony, with so many cooks likely to spoil the artistic broth – lead anywhere? How does it come about? Can it truly be satisfying to an individual trying "to manifest his existence", which according to Constant is the basis of all creativity? Is one person's creative will not simply compromised by that of his fellow players? Does it, perversely, involve discipline or self-restraint?

To play or to kill: fusing the collective

In his essay "The rise and decline of the avant-garde", based largely on the first part of *Skizze zu einer Kultur*, Constant again picks up the theme of the ill-adapted, young rebels without a cause who by the mid-1950s were beginning to appear in the streets of the industrialized nations: "'hipsters', 'teddy boys', 'rockers', 'mods', 'Halbstarke', 'blousons noirs', 'beatniks', 'nozems', 'stiljagi'".[160] Constant latches on to what we would now refer to as the beginnings of youth culture. Like the early Lettrists, these youngsters – whether school-going, without work or else not particularly intent on finding it – cruise the streets, where their boredom finds its outlet in antisocial behaviour or straightforward vandalism.

These are the people Constant identifies as the first builders of New Babylon, the true avant-garde of creative Homo Ludens. Not only do they reject the establishment and its work ethic; in their untrammelled and aimless behaviour they also freely express their vitality – to use the Cobra phrase – and thus actively and often violently clean up the moral debris of the old world. Rather than the proletariat, numbed into bourgeois comfort, the

58. *Nozems* at the Nieuwmarkt fair, Amsterdam, 1963

rebellious youth are the new revolutionary class that is bound to grow in size as automation forces ever-larger parts of the population into unemployment and stifling idleness. But Constant takes his vision a step further. Essentially, crime and destruction – the drastic rejection of the morality of the status quo – are akin to creation. "Like the artist, the criminal refuses to act passively vis-à-vis reality".[161] Creation and destruction alike are transformational acts, manifestations of the vital fury that keeps man alive and kicking. Both creation and destruction demand and conquer their freedom. The idea indeed is radically libertarian.

However, if creation and destruction are essentially made of the same stuff, for Constant they are not identical. Instead, they are two sides of the same coin. Perhaps surprisingly, Constant introduces a qualitative difference when he defines the blind, destructive act of aggression as a "failed creation": "Until the time has come that this urge can be sublimated into a creative urge, into a "ludic" urge, it will find its outlet in aggression."[162] To create positively or to play is thus a skill: an ability that is a matter of *culture*.[163]

We can say that Constant regards the fundamental human lifeforce as the raw material. Inextricably linked to the human need for survival, it is a drive that in the natural world of want is essentially individualistic, keeping man (and the species) alive and his competitors at bay. In the pursuit of security, the lifeforce manifests itself as the basic need for power over and control of the environment and fellow man. And then Constant pulls the rabbit from the hat: "The creative drive is a sublimation of the need for power".[164] Sublimation channels and transforms "more primitive drives"[165] into creative activity and makes it effectively benign and relatively harmless. The making of art, we might conclude, has a therapeutic effect. Time and again, therefore – and not only in *Skizze zu einer Kultur* – Constant refers to the famous exchange of letters between Albert Einstein and Sigmund Freud:

Similar thoughts have led Freud, in a letter to Einstein, to regard the acculturation process as the only hope to overcome war, which he considers to be the result of the workings of the aggressive drive. Creativity, which until now we only know in the form of the artistic act, is the sublimation of the two basic instincts defined by Freud: conservation and destruction.[166]

Even if playing and killing, art and aggression, arise from the same source, they are quite definitely not identical. And though Constant insists that "destruction" of a previous condition – transformation – is essential to all artistic creation, he is referring to the destruction of *artistic or social form*, whether it be in painting, music or Unitary Urbanism, and not to the killing of human beings. It is here that the key role of sublimation lies. The title of the German translation of Constant's anthology *De opstand van de Homo Ludens* is conclusive: *Spielen oder Töten*[167], To Play or to Kill. And New Babylon will, emphatically, be a world of passionate play, and not a world of murder.

The New Babylonian lives under conditions that reduce man's aggressive element, his proneness to strife. To put it more correctly: under conditions that sublimate these instincts into creative drives.[168]

How then does Constant understand man's liberation from work? He returns continually to an underlying system of premises we might call his 'energy model', roughly based on Freudian principles. The essential lifeforce – natural vitality – is entirely absorbed by work and struggle in the basic condition of want, the energy furthermore kept in check by morality and norms. If on the surface this seems like a sensible harnessing of aggressive drives, to Constant it still is suppression, and not a healthy or pleasurable channelling of human energy. With automation, as Constant emphasizes, an enormous supply of energy can and will be set free – a revolutionary force that, much to his delight, will sweep away the old world. The force must nonetheless find its positive outlet at some point: without it, total liberation may ultimately be a formula for disaster. And this is where New Babylon, as a design, comes in: it is a social tool, an environment that transforms raw desire and makes it into collective art.

But now we are back where we started. Existential struggle may be sublimated into art as the entirety of life takes on the traits of play, but it would still appear to remain a struggle. Clearly, this is where the underlying idea of Cobra re-emerges. According to Constant, the creative struggle – the dialectic of imagination and matter, of action and reaction – can provide the greatest of pleasure. And indeed, Cobra again offers some of the proof. Perhaps the best illustrations of the principle of dialogue and visual interplay are the murals which Cobra members collectively made in Denmark. The graffiti are the tangible traces of pure musical and poetic improvisation: one artist imaginatively reacts to and intervenes in the work of the others; the figures on the walls frolic about, cheerfully singing and chatting to each other. It is thus in interplay that an artwork is essentially born, and an apparent struggle can ultimately fuse a social collective. Creativity need not be a social divider: it can be the glue as well.

Transplanted to a New Babylonian condition of pure flux, however, where it is beyond the control of a limited number of individuals, the recipe would appear to offer no guarantee for genuine satisfaction and fulfilment. But Constant perseveres. He introduces the equivalent of the "finished artwork", which offers precisely that in the game of New Babylon:

In New Babylon every creative initiative by an individual is an intervention in the collective life ambiance; it therefore provokes the immediate counteraction of the others. Every single reactive act can in turn be a source of new reaction. In this way a kind of chain reaction of creative acts is set up, a process that can only end when a climax is achieved. Such a process is beyond the control of the individual; it is completely irrelevant who triggers an action or what kind of intervention takes place. The point of climax, then, is an ambiance moment that can be regarded as a collective creation. The rhythm of the creation and disappearance of these ambiance moments constitutes the time-space measure of New Babylon.[169]

Constant sacrifices the wish for individual success and the will for power and control, replacing them with a collective, orgiastic moment of gratification: with the euphoria and endorphin rush that occurs when something good comes together. This moment of climax, which parallels the notion of "situation" as defined by Guy Debord, is a "coming together" of individuals in both meanings of the word. It is a moment of synthesis that is decidedly erotic. It is interesting to note that Hilde Heynen has pointed out that New Babylon is distinctly a-sexual, whereas it is clear that the art in Constant's world may well be better than the best of sex.[170] In point of fact, Constant never excluded that sex, defined in terms of play and not of raw sexual desire, may be a part of the game. But why does Mark Wigley repeatedly emphasize *desire* as something to be lived out freely in New Babylon?[171] He seems to ignore entirely the essential ingredient of sublimation; without it, Constant would probably agree, New Babylon might indeed become the gory bloodbath that Wigley identifies in the post-1968 paintings.

New Babylon offers continuous creative pleasure and climactic moments of unity, harmony and indeed happiness in which Unitary Urbanism fulfils its true promise. As early as 1959 Constant makes it clear that this is precisely the goal: "We are at the dawn of a new era and are already attempting to sketch out the image of a happier life, of unitary urbanism: the urbanism intended to bring pleasure."[172]

Constant continues to reiterate the point that the permanent flux in New Babylon is in fact a form of *order*. The notion of order should not be considered, however, in terms of discipline and law, but rather along the lines of an essentially self-regulating anarchic social organism. Like all play this organism has its own inner logic and drive: "The environment of New Babylon has the intended effect on the individual that precisely those powers are set into motion – and brought into a rhythm – that are either suppressed by utilitarian society or – as is the case with the artist – tolerated to a limited degree."[173] The word *rhythm* poignantly reflects the impression which is finally beginning to emerge of New Babylon: a place in which an ever-changing creative mass, fusing and dispersing like the coloured bubbles in psychedelic liquid wheels or lava lamps, achieves ever-new configurations. Collective magic circles of play are created that reach a climax and disperse, forming the next ludic collective and so on. It is a mass society in which manifold collectives are the actors, whilst the mass as a whole, in permanent flux, is the actual creative subject.

This image enables us to interpret the sectors: the hardware overkill is a bare necessity in achieving the intended effect. The structures are giant *sublimators* that synthesize the creative mass and keep it in a condition of satisfying fluctuation. Practically and symbolically, they are a house of the ever-changing collective that creates its own social and artistic order, which is as thrilling as it is pacifying. A polychrome, dynamic harmony is fashioned in and through flux. The promise of "poetry made by all" is in fact no more and no less than the dream of the brotherhood of man in and through art: true heaven on earth.

Ultimately it is an article of faith, a matter of hope and conviction, that this grand sublimated synthesis might come about and work. If there is something essentially ungraspable and mirage-like about New Babylon it is here, at the heart of the dream. As Roel van Duyn, the Provo front man put it: "Those people in New Babylon must surely be a nice and responsible creative lot, otherwise the whole thing is bound to go horribly wrong, I think. They'll start attacking those beautiful techno-structures with plastic explosives or something."[174] In the equation there is still something missing. If the sectors of New Babylon have a crucial function in making the ultimate social and artistic collective, they have what appears to be a more sinister purpose. Homo Ludens, superior playful man, can only emerge by erasing all traces of Homo Faber. In order to create, one needs first to destroy.

Getting there

We are on the eve of the great "denaturation" of man. Man will no longer be ruled by nature, but he will be able to control nature, to transform it according to his imagination, to his own image. Natural man will decline and artistic man is about to be born.[175]

In her seminal essays on New Babylon, Hilde Heynen states that in his depiction of the world of Homo Ludens, Constant silently assumes, like Karl Marx before him, that the unequal division of power among people will gradually wither away after a revolution has overturned society and the productive and economic forces that determine it. The logic is that automation will inevitably not only bring about a revolutionary moment of crisis but ultimately create the basis for a society without want, in which the competitive spirit that is so essential for human survival through the ages shrivels up and expires. The natural condition of *homo homini lupus est*, product of material scarcity, is bound to undergo radical change under the influence of a totally new productive infrastructure that eliminates existential struggle.

Likewise, all relational ties erode: the family – which according to Marx has its basis in economic interdependency and is not a God-given fact of nature – and the need to remain sedentary are eliminated and exchanged for the liberty in the bosom of the ludic collective and in nomadic life, respectively. But if the long-established norms, morals and social conventions (the thin layer of "civilization") that tie man down may well be swiftly washed away, Constant is evidently more sceptical about mankind's ability to overcome his fears and need for security – in short, man's ego. Letting go of all that has ensured his survival through the millennia may be the toughest job yet: the animal in human-kind may be quite tenacious.

Constant expresses his scepticism, which usually hides behind Marxist rhetoric and anthropocentric arrogance, at various times, and examples of it also appear in *Skizze zu einer Kultur*. The scepticism usually wears a mask, but in a wonderful though deeply pessimistic letter to Sean Wellesley-Miller, a young British architect, Constant clearly voices his doubts:

If you have read the description of Newbabylonian life Simon Vinkenoog has written for number 4 of the "New Babylon Informatief", you will understand my awkward for idealizations. I don't believe in fraternity because I don't believe in a type of man that will be superior to present man, at least for the coming centuries. We will have to count with the human character like we know it. If we think of a culture based on mass-creativity, we should not think of a superior mankind, not of a "Noö" idealistic atmosphere, like Teilhard de Chardin suggests, but only of an organization of social life that will enable an outbreak of spontaneous energies, that were suppressed during the long period of human history in which labour absorbed the almost entire energy of humanity. We have not arrived at this point yet and I foresee a long period of struggling and of destruction.[176]

The letter is from late 1966, a year after Constant finishes *Skizze zu einer Kultur*, written in a climate that has changed considerably. The pessimism in this letter contrasts markedly with the *constructed* optimism of the book. We should not forget that Constant uses his spatial toolbox not only to support the life of the

New Babylonian, but to *create* and *sustain* it. This move confirms that, deep down, Constant does not fully trust his budding New Babylonians: they may still be harbouring the festering remains of mankind's natural inclinations.

Again we must return to the labyrinth. In his book, Constant goes to great lengths to explain the difference between the classic labyrinth with a centre (and a fixed route to it) and the dynamic labyrinth that forms the social space of New Babylon. Due to the built-in flexibility of the dynamic labyrinth and the constant changes made to it, the sectors of New Babylon are an endless source of discovery, full of ever-new adventure, surprise and delight: never does a person, in the same geographic space, return to the same ambiance. The flexibility ensures that every place can be created anew, that nothing ever bores. The "principle of disorientation" is crucial: it allows for continuous renewal and a never-ending journey into the unknown. Rimbaud's famous line – "Il s'agit d'arriver à l'inconnu par le dérèglement de tous les sens" – is not surprisingly the motto for Constant's chapter on "New Babylonian culture". Homo Ludens is lost and content to remain so.

Without a doubt, the input of Carlheinz Caspari in the development of these ideas must have been considerable. The theoretical mental attitude he referred to as "Labyr" essentially describes the mindset of the New Babylonian: non-orientational, non-teleological, non-hierarchic and a-historical: man is at home in the unknown, at ease without his bearings. This is an essentially fearless, insouciant and playful attitude. Caspari summed it up with the phrase "a labyrinth is not a labyrinth".[177] In a labyrinth – in a life without purpose beyond the intense experience of the moment – one is not lost but at home. One dwells in insecurity. This is the experience of a creature who has lost interest in past or future beyond the immediate workings of artistic cause and effect.

The New Babylonian myth of the labyrinth is utterly antithetical to how man has projected himself so far: armed with the capacity to plan, to look ahead, with knowledge of causality and the capacity to calculate risk. The essential consciousness that sets the human being aside from the instinctive animal is sacrificed for a life in a never-ending present. In his "highest phase of development", totally disconnected from nature, man again becomes curiously animal-like. This ultimate consequence of New Babylonian life

– the perfection of it – has been described as a "zero point of existence", and indeed as a condition in which "men are happy like animals".[178] But for Constant losing oneself in the labyrinth is ultimately beneficial: man's capacities are channelled into superior, ever-present play. The dynamic labyrinth ultimately is the key to sublimating and eliminating aggression. Letting go leads to creative authenticity and social peace. Losing oneself in the labyrinth – in play – ultimately liberates one from the *self* – and with it all that keeps men at war and in strife. Man the individualist becomes the truly social human being, who knows no fear and alienation and who is at home in the crowd. The thoughts about radical "de-subjectivation" that Constant put down on paper for the *Art et Habitat* journal in 1953 are still as relevant as they were before: the idea of self-denial – *Nier soi-même* – that so upset Jorn in 1953 is profoundly programmatic. For Constant this phrase spelled liberation. For Jorn, it may well have been existentially frightening – as it surely was for the man in the street.

The labyrinth thus has a vital anthropogenetic function, which is underlined time and again. It is a means for continuous mental and social de-programming. It eliminates the traces of Homo Faber and prevents man from slipping back into his old habits. Like the suspension of the day-night cycle in the depths of the sector, the labyrinth ensures that natural drives, fears and inhibitions are eliminated or overcome. The labyrinthine sector is a mental incubator, a hatching machine for the "labyristic" attitude. As Constant insisted early on, brainwashing is a beneficial strategy: "An extended stay in these houses has the tonic effect of a brainwashing and is frequently undertaken to erase the effects of habits."[179]

But in *Skizze zu einer Kultur* Constant takes the issue of the new man one final step further. The means, however, are decidedly un-Marxist, and in none of his other texts have these arguments surfaced as strongly. Constant takes the detour through human sexuality: whilst attacking the puritan mores of the bourgeoisie, he signals a shift in the perception of sex: indeed, in the early 1960s we are at the beginning of the sexual revolution, which Constant embraces wholeheartedly. Free sex and birth control make the procreative act what it should be: playful, without risk and simply fun. "In New Babylon," he predicts, "only ludic principles will be applied to sexuality, as to all other domains." Interestingly however, free sexuality has its *usefulness* as the world makes its transition to New Babylon:

Communities and nations collapse and fuse; with the disappearance of opposition and competition the need to keep up barriers and borders disappears. As the final obstacle, the separation of races will come to an end. The precondition for this is the mechanization of production in the "coloured" parts of the world, which ends the white race's rule over the coloured races. (…) The elimination of barriers will inevitably lead to the mingling of all races, and thus a world race can come into existence: the race of the New Babylonian. Perhaps more than the material factors, it will be biological evolutionary history that justifies the hypothesis that the New Babylonian is a human being whose actions are determined by free intuition and not by impulses dragged along. The variety of attributes and characteristics found in the separate races will, through this mingling, start a process that weakens "inborn" patterns of thought and which will ultimately free man from the shackles of his "natural instincts".[180]

59. Photo from Constant's archive, RKD. Undated, anonymous

This brings us back to the quote at the beginning of this chapter, in which Constant points out that in his *Utopia* Thomas More, for all his good intentions, tried to coerce man morally to become a better human being: to build heaven on earth through the rule of law and the virtue of self-restraint. Clearly Constant prefers to take the Marxist route, which automation now makes possible: "Scientific socialism has superseded all Utopias in that it is based on the facts of mechanization, rather than on the belief in a better man."[181] But the anecdote about the induced companionship of cat and mouse reminds us that ultimately any means are welcome to achieve the brotherhood of man.

The passage above also hints at the idea that New Babylon will not be built in a day, but that the end of history in which the last man takes his place is the fruit of a period of transition. In his letter to Wellesley-Miller, Constant makes it clear that struggle and apocalyptic upheaval might have to precede the construction of New Babylon. Getting there will not be easy. Separate fragments in the book confirm that it will take a post-revolutionary dictatorship of the proletariat (or rather: of the "masses") to bring about the socialization of land and production means, as a prelude to the eventual abolition of private property. This will naturally be followed by a period in which the masses will first have to construct the hardware of New Babylon – potentially an era of toil before mankind can fully reap the fruits of its labour[182] – and in which, bit by bit, the sectors of New Babylon will spread over the landscape. Only then, Constant's scenario tells us, will the free, ludic lifestyle of the new world slowly but surely come about and can the new man be born:

The building of New Babylon takes place gradually, sector-by-sector, whilst the old existing structures are demolished according to requirements. In the beginning, therefore, the sectors lie dispersed between historic urban areas. For the inhabitants of these old, functional quarters that die off with the disappearance of work, these sectors serve as cultural centres. They are places of encounter, of pleasure, of social gathering. (…) Once the sectors have begun to form an independent, self-contained pattern, New Babylon begins to provoke its own lifestyle. Gradually, the New Babylonian species that spends its entire life inside, travelling through the world of the sectors, will emerge. This sequence of development will start simultaneously in a large number of places in highly industrialized areas. (…) One will be able to observe similar processes on all continents. The final stage of the development has been reached when the sector net has covered the entire planet.[183]

The Atlas section of *Skizze zu einer Kultur* ends on a very practical note:

Summing up, one can say that this atlas shows the operating range of West European Homo Ludens in the first phase of his existence. The next two parts will deal with the ecology of the east European and North American Homo Ludens. In future, with the progressive industrialization of these continents, atlases of Asia, Africa and South America will follow. For Australia, for the time being, the preconditions are not met. It is to be expected that even in the future this part of the world will remain a backward area, in which Homo Faber will continue to subsist for a long time. We hope that a second edition of my maps will supplement their current sketchy character with more detailed additions.[184]

Psychogeogram: the painter's Utopia

Constant's manuscript was never published. In the summer of 1965 the book is finished, and in the following two years, at least, Constant continues to speak of its imminent publication. But Caspari – now acting as Constant's agent – does not manage to get it printed.[185] Articles and lectures written in conjunction with the book ultimately find their way into *Opstand van de Homo Ludens*, an anthology of essays published in 1969, and the *New Babylon* exhibition catalogue from 1974. But whereas these collections give a good insight into the theoretical underpinnings of Constant's cultural philosophy – as in the famous essay "Opkomst en ondergang van de avant-garde" – they lack the drive and unity of the Constant-Caspari manuscript.

Academically speaking, we could label this unity distinctly utopian. In the book, Constant's integral view of man and the world finds its positive outlet in a model for a new culture, an artistic society that at the end of history will span the world and bring together mankind in play. By juxtaposing "Functional Zion" – the past and present – and "New Babylon"– another place in another time – as its counterpoint, Constant manifestly operates within the polarity that characterizes all classic utopias: he employs contrast and analogy. A radical socio-cultural critique informed by an integral conception of man precedes a depiction of a better world that is *not yet there*.

This puts Mark Wigley's observation that a Utopia is "outside of time and place"[186] in a different perspective. Early utopias – written in the wake of the discoveries of new worlds, "primitive" cultures and unknown continents – invariably situated their ideal societies in a faraway place. Since the beginning of the industrial revolution at the latest, utopias have usually been projected into time, even to the extent that an idealized past is projected into the future, as in the post-revolutionary craft arcadia of William Morris's *News from Nowhere*. With man's growing confidence that he can master his own fate through science and technology, utopia holds the promise of a better era; and even though it begins to resemble the twentieth-century categories of futurology and science fiction, utopia remains a construct with characteristics of its own. Instead of merely developing scenarios for a possible future through trend extrapolation (like futurology) or providing sheer entertainment (like science fiction), utopias are invariably founded on a critique and offer a constructed socio-spatial perspective that derives from it.

Constant's project can indeed be seen as a direct answer to William Morris's work. Both New Babylon and *News from Nowhere* are Marxist utopias: they offer a perspective of the world after the revolution. But where Morris's medieval England turns its back on the city and technology, Constant embraces them as the keys to the final stage of history. For both men, history is the driving force – the messiah that will ultimately build heaven on earth – but for Constant, the most consistent of Marxists, this new culture is unthinkable without the solid foundations of a radically new productive infrastructure. As has been pointed out repeatedly, the terrestrial realm of freedom predicted in Marx's *Deutsche Ideologie* and set on the basis of the "scientific" historical dialectic model may in spirit be the greatest utopian work ever devised. Its children copy many of its traits.

Likewise, Constant's world of Homo Ludens is the progeny of Thomas More's original *Utopia*. *Skizze zu einer Kultur* may not be a work of literature – it is far too programmatic and "scientific", *l'idéologie oblige* – but still the direct parallels are obvious. Constant's objections to utopias are known: they are always idealized visions of a better life for Homo Faber, and not designed for a new man. Moreover, as a social and spatial construct they are ordered and static. But exactly the same can be said of New Babylon. Its seemingly erratic hardware follows the strictest of rules and prescriptions ("The plan of New Babylon shows a clear distinction between the sector strips and the remaining open areas that are to remain completely free of construction."[187]), whilst the condition of *permanent* flux inside the sectors constitutes a harmonic social order comparable with that of any utopia. In New Babylon too, history comes to an end: the socio-artistic equilibrium is dynamic but self-perpetuating and stable.

Constant describes the hardware in New Babylon in almost pedantic detail – even hinting at the size and type of the modular walls to be employed in the dynamic labyrinths of the sectors.[188] His description is strangely at odds with the grand vision of the free, collectively creative Homo Ludens whose world is so fundamentally different from ours. It led an early supporter in Constant's German entourage to voice his doubts:

New Babylon is – if I understand you correctly – not an architectural design but much more, even something completely different. You yourself call it "outline", "vision" of a new world. New Babylon is therefore a model, a symbol. (…) Is it a good idea, then, to depict this model so graphically, in all its details, like you do? I do not refer to the underlying philosophy, I mean sentences such as: "The sectors are covered by large accessible terraces that can contain runways, helicopter pads, playgrounds, sports facilities…" Are these details really essential?[189]

Surely much of this fascination for detail had its roots in Constant's intense involvement with the architectural community in the first half of the 1960s and the goals he set out to achieve with his propaganda: to architects and laymen alike, the world of Homo Ludens needed to offer some points of contact with the existing world. Indeed, the rather uninspiring "sports facilities", "playgrounds", "kindergartens" that pop up in certain texts and parts of the manuscript are curiously at odds with the spirit of free creation which Constant promises: they reek of bourgeois leisure. But their inclusion, like New Babylon as a whole, shows us the two sides of the man: the rational, Apollonian planner – the square in the grey flannel suit – and the cheerful poet in a gypsy outfit passionately strumming a Flamenco guitar: the icy cool of De Stijl combined with the frenzy of Cobra. Constant answers his critic:

It is therefore my opinion that a publication of N.B. should cover as many areas as possible, so that this publication contains not only entirely fantastic and poetic descriptions but also realistically rendered plans and technical specifications and data. From the very beginning N.B. must dissolve the distinction between science and art, the practical and the fantastic.[190]

The two seemingly incompatible sides of the project led Mark Wigley to describe New Babylon both as a form of research – a realistic effort that is highly responsive to the practical challenges of the times – and as an illusive blur, a material world that cannot, and refuses to, be visualized. But never does Wigley describe them as such *at the same time*. Though he avoids using the term, ultimately the two sides overlap in utopia.

If we look beyond the expedient references to existing social functions, we see that the carefully planned spatial hardware of New Babylon – so fastidiously and architecturally outlined in the many descriptions – is entirely *functional* and essential: it plays, to use Françoise Choay's phrase, a central anthropogenetic role.[191] The sectors of New Babylon, draped across the globe, not only symbolize the unity of the new artistic society and provide a fitting décor: they serve to make and sustain a new man and a new collective society. Form and content are mutually dependent.

Had the book been published, it would have fundamentally changed our current perception of New Babylon. Whereas Constant's impressive models, drawings and stunning slide shows were ultimately brilliant in *suggesting* New Babylon, the book went a long way in providing a programme for its realization. It not only describes the life and spaces of New Babylon: it prescribes them. Whether the book would have achieved its intended effect – getting more professionals involved – is, of course, another matter. At any rate it would have met with a great deal of resistance and fierce accusations of chilling technocracy or naïve utopianism. But though it might have made the project much easier to pin down and pigeonhole, the book would have offered the most complete picture not only of New Babylon but also of what motivated it – its utopian inner logic. However blurred the outlines of New Babylon would later be – with its name as a mere stamp on the artistic activities within a period of an artist's oeuvre – at its heart New Babylon is a utopia that sadly never got its book.

Though tentatively constructed and incomplete, *Skizze zu einer Kultur* would have provided a powerful vision of a world that was just over the horizon, a view of "a preferable course of history" kept intact by sheer hope and will power. In the closing lines Constant speaks at least as much to himself as to his reader: "In contrast with the thousand-year reign of the Chiliasts, New Babylon is realizable: why should we not be optimists?"[192] Certainly, the book would have proved the most optimistic expression of Constant's deep-rooted convictions: it would have offered the ideological militancy of the manifesto of the *Experimentele groep*, combined with the boldly constructed outlook onto a better world which Cobra could not yet provide. In projecting the creative privilege of the artist and the nomadic freedom of the gypsies onto the whole world, Constant transposes his own pain, frustrations, hopes and desires as a painter. Like the many utopias that preceded it, New Babylon is a psychogeogram of its maker.

What the book meant to the artist is also clear: it was the fruit and synthesis of many years of work. It is not surprising that Constant repeatedly insisted that it was absolutely essential. In a telephone conversation in 2001, Constant confessed that the publication of the book was planned as the end of his work on New Babylon. It would have coincided with the first great exhibition of the project in late 1965 in The Hague.[193] This comes as a shock, as by most accounts the project ends in 1969 or 1974 at the latest. We can only wonder what might have happened if the tome had been printed after all.

After completing his manuscript, Constant journeys to Czechoslovakia. But the 'travel sketches' he makes in the little town of Domazlice depict little of the region's picturesque sights: they are mostly scenes of playful New Babylonians. The project is not yet out of his system. As early as 1964 Carlheinz Caspari had noticed that strange things were beginning to happen in sleepy, bourgeois Amsterdam. By the time Constant receives a visit from the young journalist son of close friends, New Babylon has become the battle cry of a new generation. Circumstance intervenes: it will still take another few years before Constant waves the world of his sectors good-bye.

Notes

82 "Manifest", undated and signed by H. Prem, E. Eisch, H. Sturm, G. Stadler, L. Fischer, G. Britt, D. Rempt, H.P. Zimmer, A. Jorn.

83 See Wigley, op. cit., pp. 31–33.

84 That year's exhibition, "Verbondenheid der Kunsten", is held 3–26 October 1959.

85 This was confirmed by Wim Crouwel, who was also on the *Liga* editorial board and responsible for the cover. According to Crouwel, Constant was hardly involved in the making of the issue. There are telltale signs of Oudejans's involvement in the collages especially: not only is their style and the choice of motifs quite typical, but minute details in the accompanying texts and captions also give him away: Debord is spelled Débord, a mistake that recurs frequently in Oudejans's own writings.

86 Letter from Debord to Constant, 8 October 1959. Ironically, Debord is not so much enraged (see Wigley, op. cit., pp. 32–33) as slightly at a loss as to how to interpret the photos.

87 The assignment for the church had been given to them as early as 1957. See H.T. Oudejans, A.C. Alberts, "Mariakerk te Volendam", *Bouwkundig Weekblad* no. 81 (1963), p. 36, and the interview "Gesprek onder acht ogen", p. 313.

88 Again the scope of this article sadly does not allow me to go into details.

89 See letter from Debord to Har Oudejans, 11 May 1959, estate of Har Oudejans, Nuenen.

90 See letter from Debord to Constant, 26 June 1959, file C–D, RKD. Partially this reorientation can be attributed to the fact that an exhibition celebrating 'Cobra – 10 years after' had failed. Originally planned for 1958, this show was also to present the newly founded SI as the only legitimate, experimental heir to the Cobra legacy – something that Jorn had demanded from Sandberg. So the 1960 SI exhibition was really a second try. See Hummelink, op. cit., pp. 232–237. See also letter from Debord to Constant, 26 June 1959, file C–D, RKD.

91 See "Die Welt als Labyrinth", *Internationale Situationniste* no. 4 (January 1960), pp. 5–7.

92 Letter from Debord to Oudejans, 23 December 1959, estate of Har Oudejans, Nuenen. An identical letter is sent to the other members of the Bureau.

93 See "Die Welt als Labyrinth", *IS* no. 4.

94 For this brilliant piece of research see Ohrt, op. cit., pp. 219–221.

95 Guy Debord, "The Situationist Frontier", *Internationale Situationniste*, no. 5 (December 1960).

96 Constant acknowledged this in a letter to Yves Robillard, 18 March 1963, file "Correspondentie 1963", RKD.

97 See the first part of "Sur nos moyens et nos perspectives", *IS* 2.

98 To take two more of Debord's favourites. See "Exercice de la psycho-géographie", *Potlatch* no. 2 (Paris, 29 June 1954).

99 Following a bitter attack on painting – "industrial or not" – Constant writes: "I have to express the same point of view regarding the *Palais Ideal* that the Surrealists discovered and opposed to the formal research of their day. I see in this palace the same kind of consolation as in Hollywood decors which are based on a spurious conception of happiness and luxury, and that only show the inability to create a new conception following our real needs. Nostalgia of the past is the greatest danger that the avant-garde is running since Cobra, since the surrealists." Letter from Constant to Debord, 26 February 1959, file C–D, RKD.

100 See for instance letters from Debord to Constant, 8 August 1958, from Constant to Debord, 1 March 1959, and Debord to Constant, 3 February 1959, file C–D, RKD.

101 The phrase is lifted from a letter from Debord to Constant, 8 August 1958, file C–D, RKD.

102 "The matter seems obvious to me: I do not have the right – nor do I have the desire – to try to impose directives and values to the painters (for instance), unless I can do so on behalf of a real praxis effectively more advanced than their work and in which they can chose to participate." Letter from Debord to Constant, 7 September 1959, file C–D, RKD.

103 This debate rages as early as March/April 1958, in the run-up to the Munich conference. "The position that you hold (…) is simply reformist. 'The slow evolution in the economic realm' which you anticipate completely bypasses the Chinese revolution, the revolutionary movement of all underdeveloped nations, the important economic and political results of Stalinist collectivization and the central phenomenon of the 'cold war', the successes of the monopolist and catholico-military reaction in Europe. The perspective of social revolution has fundamentally *changed* with regard to all classic schemes. But it is real." Guy Debord, "Réponse à Alberts, Armando, Constant, Oudejans", 4 April 1959, file

C–D, RKD. The Dutch section (i.e. Constant) had objected to the inaugural declaration proposed by Debord, which lead to an intense exchange of letters, with multiple accusations of "utopism" to and fro. At the end of the day Debord caved in – momentarily – to let Constant make the opening speech in Munich and set the tone for further discussions at the conference.

104 See previous footnote. See also letter from Debord to Constant, 21 March 1959, file C–D, in which Debord talks about the sections of the SI as if they were professional revolutionary cells, ready to take orders and seize power. In referring to the 1920s, he clearly reminds Constant of the situation in many West European countries – Germany especially – in the wake of World War I, which saw short-lived but militant alliances flourish between artists and a revolutionary class.

105 See transcript of letter from Constant to Debord, undated but marked "Début d'Avril '59" in Constant's handwriting; file C–D, RKD.

106 The first declaration of the Brussels "Bureau for Unitary Urbanism", successor to the disbanded Amsterdam office, reiterated the point: "URBANISM DOESN'T EXIST; it is only an "ideology" in Marx's sense of the word." Attila Kotányi & Raoul Vaneigem, "Basic Program of the Bureau of Unitary Urbanism", *Internationale Situationniste* no. 6 (August 1961), translation by Ken Knabb.

107 *Pinot Gallizio* (Paris: Bibliothèque d'Alexandrie, 1960).

108 Telegram from Constant to Debord, 23 June 1960, file C–D, RKD.

109 Letter from Constant to Debord, 6 June 1960, file C–D, RKD.

110 Constant in response to a student in Delft, 1961. See *Delftse School. Onafhankelijk blad van de bouwkundige studenten aan de TH Delft* no. 4, pp. 4–5. Translation by author.

111 Wigley, op. cit., p. 39.

112 In the Constant Archive, RKD.

113 Not even by Mark Wigley in his lengthy discussion of Constant's drawings in "Paper, Scissors, Blur", Catherine de Zegher, Mark Wigley (eds.), *The Activist Drawing: Retracing Situationist Architectures from Constant's New Babylon to beyond* (New York/Cambridge, Massachusetts: The Drawing Center/MIT Press, 2001).

114 Interview with Carlheinz Caspari, 4 July 2002. Translation by author.

115 Otto van de Loo in a telephone conversation with the author, 8 March 2004. Grumblingly, he added: "We should have opened it in Cologne, not Essen".

116 Caspari interview, 4 July 2002.

117 See for instance his call for "a more elaborate programme for Unitary Urbanism" in the form of a publication in a letter to Guy Debord, 26 February 1959, file C–D, RKD.

118 See exhibition catalogue *New Babylon* (Den Haag: Haags Gemeentemuseum, 1974), p. 2.

119 In letters between Constant and Caspari in this period there is one recurring issue: whether Caspari is available during weekends, between rehearsals and work on new theatre productions. See the 1963/1964/1965 "Correspondentie" folders, RKD.

120 Constant in a telephone conversation with the author, 4 April 2001.

121 "Yes, I did translate the book, and during its translation we continually discussed every sentence, regardless of whether it was written by Constant or by me. This is how it went: he came to Cologne or I hopped over to Amsterdam each fortnight. At the time I was back in Cologne at the theatre, after the gallery in Essen had closed down." Interview with Carlheinz Caspari, 4 July 2002.

122 Hein van Haaren, a friend and frequent visitor from 1963 onward, acknowledged this; interview 4 November 2003. Constant also confirmed Caspari's critical input in our phone conversation (note 120).

123 "Eine Soziologie des Künstlers", "Das Lied der Arbeit", "Das funktionelle Zion", respectively. Manuscript of *New-Babylon: Skizze zu einer Kultur* (hereafter: *SzeK*), Part 1, RKD.

124 "SzeK", "Definitionen". These were later republished in Dutch in the 1974 exhibition catalogue *New Babylon*, pp. 29–30. All *SzeK* translations by author.

125 "In every man there is a slumbering creator". As the audio recording of the proceedings reveal, Constant used this phrase by Asger Jorn to summarize his arguments at the symposium *Constant's New Babylon: Another city for another life* at the Drawing Center in New York. Cf. Benjamin Buchlow, "A conversation with Constant" in Catherine de Zegher, Mark Wigley (eds.), *The Activist Drawing*, p. 25.

126 Johan Huizinga: *Homo Ludens, proeve eener bepaling van het spel-element der cultuur* (Groningen: Wolters-Noordhoff, 1985. First Edition Haarlem 1938).

127 *SzeK*, "Definitions": "Homo Ludens".

128 *SzeK*, Part 1 section III, chapter 39.

129 *Randstad* no. 8 (Amsterdam: De Bezige Bij, 1964), pp. 6–35. Translation "The Rise and Decline of the Avant-garde" in *Drawing Papers 3/Another City for Another Life: Constant's New Babylon* (New York: The Drawing Center, 1999), appendix pp. 14–28.

130 *SzeK*, Part 1 section I, chapter 13. Along with an attack on Jorn in the 'appendix', this statement may be an indication as to the time that the first section was written: probably in the very early sixties.

131 Asger Jorn: "The Situationists and Automation", *Internationale Situationniste* no. 1 (June 1958). Extract in Ken Knabb, *Situationist International Anthology* (Berkeley: Bureau of Public Secrets, 1981), pp. 46–47.

132 "Above all, however, the reduction in the work necessary for production, through extended automation, will create a need for leisure, a diversity of behaviour and a change in the nature of the latter, which will of necessity lead to a new conception of the collective habitat with a maximum of space, contrary to the conception of a *ville verte* where social space is reduced to a minimum."

Constant, "Une autre ville pour une autre vie", *Internationale Situationniste* no. 3 (December 1959), p. 39. Translation by Paul Hammond.

133 Constant: "Unitair Urbanisme", manuscript of lecture held on 20 December 1960. For translation see Wigley, op. cit., pp. 131–135.

134 I am referring to statements such as: "Au fond, les questions auxquelles Constant a tenté de répondre sont très simples: Que sera la société libérée du travail? Que sera l'espace habité par cette nouvelle société?" Francesco Careri "New Babylon. Le nomadisme et le dépassement de l'architecture" in *Constant – une rétrospective*, exhibition catalogue, Musée Picasso, Antibes (Paris: Réunion des Musées Nationaux, 2001), p. 45.

135 The killjoy of the tertiary sector – Constant refers to Jean Fourastié's book *Le grand espoir du XXe siècle* – is concealed in a footnote that is longer than the chapter itself. See *SzeK*, Part 1 section II, chapter 25.

136 *SzeK*, Part 1 section II, chapter 25 (footnote).

137 *SzeK*, Part 1 section II, chapter 17.

138 *SzeK*, Part 1 section III, chapter 28.

139 *SzeK*, Part 1 section III, chapter 37.

140 *SzeK*, Part 1 section III, chapter 38.

141 *SzeK*, Part 2 section I, chapter 41.

142 *SzeK*, Part 1 section III, chapter 40. It is interesting to compare this text with the final passages of Constant's "Opkomst en ondergang van de avant-garde". It is safe to say that the *SzeK* text predates the 1964 essay.

143 See Wigley, op. cit., pp. 40–41.

144 See the interview with Yona Friedman in this book.

145 Friedman in conversation with author: Paris, September 2003.

146 The usual reference is Alison and Peter Smithson's 1958 "Berlin Hauptstadt" competition entry, which proposed constructing a spidery network of pedestrian walkways raised on stilts over the bombarded centre of the German capital connecting various new tower blocks. Graphically, Constant's maps and the Smithsons' scheme are indeed remarkably similar. See Ohrt, op. cit., p. 128, and Simon Sadler, *The Situationist City* (Cambridge, Massachusetts and London: The MIT Press, 1998), p. 118.

147 See the illustration credits in Van Haaren, op. cit., figures 20b and 22a.

148 The quotes in this paragraph are all from Constant: "New-Babylon" in *Randstad* no. 2 (Amsterdam: De Bezige Bij, 1962), pp. 135–136. All translations from *Randstad* by author. Similar data are provided in *SzeK* and other texts.

149 "Gele sector"(1958), "Rode Sector"(1958), and "Oriënt sector" (1959), resp.

150 See Mark Wigley, "Paper, Scissors, Blur", in De Zegher/Wigley, op. cit., pp. 48–50.

151 Constant, "Description de la zone jaune", *Internationale Situationniste* no. 4 (June 1960), pp. 23–26. Translation by Paul Hammond (and illustration) in Wigley, op. cit., pp. 122–123. The 1958 "Yellow zone" model that the description is based on is now commonly known as the "Yellow sector".

152 Constant: "New-Babylon", *Randstad* no. 2, p. 134.

153 See e.g. Allan Kaprow: *Assemblage, environments & happenings* (New York: Abrams, 1965). Even before the Fluxus happenings took Europe by storm, one can identify the performances staged by Dada and the Surrealists as proto-happenings.

154 *SzeK*, Part 2 section III, chapter 64, second footnote.

155 For an extensive discussion see Stokvis, op. cit., p. 212 ff.

156 Fanny Kelk "A talk with Constant", *Constant: schilderijen 1969–77,* exhibition catalogue (Amsterdam: Stedelijk Museum, 1978).

157 The term, suggested to me by Steven Harris, is very fitting in that it captures the emotionally evocative and playful nature of the art. Huizinga emphasizes the basic ludic nature of *poiesis* and goes on to describe archaic, ritualistic forms of poetry that work along the lines of dialectic interplay and dialogue. See Huizinga, op. cit., chapter "Spel en Poëzie", p. 117 ff.

158 *SzeK*, Part 2 section III, chapter 69. In Dutch there is an excellent term for this: "inspelen op iets" (literally: to play in to something), which can be translated as "to respond positively to" or "engage with".

159 See Sadler, op. cit., p. 149.

160 "Opkomst en ondergang van de Avant-Garde", *Randstad* no. 8, p. 32 ff. Cf. *SzeK*, Part 2 section I, chapter 56.

161 *SzeK*, Part 2 section II, chapter 58. Elsewhere in the book, Constant quotes the anarchist Mikhail Bakunin: "Le souffle de la destruction est un souffle créateur." (The passion for destruction is also a creative passion.) *SzeK*, part 1 section II, chapter 16, footnote 3.

162 "Opkomst en ondergang van de Avant-Garde" (prev. note), p. 35.

163 The idea is formulated as early as 1953: "The creative urge in its brutal natural state can manifest itself in a child and grown-up, but only when the creative force has reached enough objectivity to chose between infinite possibilities and organize itself can one refer to it as culture." Undated handwritten document, *Neovision* file, RKD.

164 *SzeK*, Part 2 section II, chapter 58. Another quote is illustrative: "If we recognize – as we have assumed – that the creative instinct is sublimated drive for power, then the crime is in fact no more than a creative act that misses its target" ("eine ins Leere schlagende Kreation"). *SzeK*, loc. cit.

165 *SzeK*, Part 2 section I, chapter 57.

166 *SzeK*, Part 1 section II, chapter 16. Constant inserts a footnote after the first sentence, in which he quotes passages from the end of Freud's September 1932 answer to Einstein: "An Albert Einstein" in *Warum Krieg? Ein Briefwechsel* (Paris: Institut International de Coopération Intellectuelle de la Société des Nations, 1933): "On the psychological side two of the most important phenom-ena of culture are, firstly, a strengthening of the intellect, which tends to master our instinctive life, and, secondly, an introversion of the aggressive impulse, with all its consequent benefits and perils."

167 Constant: *Spielen oder töten. Der Aufstand des Homo Ludens* (Bergisch Gladbach: Lübbe, 1971).

168 *SzeK*, Part 2 section II, chapter 61.

169 *SzeK*, Part 2 section I, chapter 53.

170 Cf. Hilde Heynen, *Architecture and Modernity: a critique*, p. 171.

171 The way in which Wigley describes Constant, while introducing Benjamin Buchloh, at the Drawing Center symposium on 30 October 1999 in New York sums it up: "In many ways I think, in too many ways to say here, Benjamin is the right person to as it were welcome Constant not only into New York but into the discourse of New York since for many of us Benjamin is a kind of conscience of art historical discourse. And it seems to me we need something like a conscience to deal with this completely crazy man from Amsterdam, Constant, who has this absolutely absurd idea that there should be absolutely no regulation on desire." Tape recording of the proceedings, transcript by author.

172 Constant: "Une autre ville pour une autre vie", *Internationale Situationniste* no. 3 (December 1959), p. 37.

173 *SzeK*, Part 2 section II, chapter 58.

174 Interview with Roel van Duyn, 3 April 2001. Translation by author.

175 Constant, "New-Babylon", *Randstad* no. 2, pp. 133–134.

176 Letter from Constant to Sean Wellesley-Miller, 8 August 1966. File "Wellesley-Miller", RKD.

177 Caspari interview, 4 July 2002.

178 The first statement is by Heynen in *Architecture and Modernity*, p. 174, the second by Léon Krier, "The modernity of traditional architecture", lecture at the *New Babylon* symposium in Delft, 27 January 2000.

179 "Description de la zone jaune" (see note 151).

180 *SzeK*, Part 2 section II, chapter 61.

181 *SzeK*, Part 1 section III, chapter 40.

182 *SzeK*, Part 1 section II, chapter 14.

183 *SzeK*, Part 2 section I, chapter 46. The chapter is aptly called "The History of New Babylon" ("Geschichte von New Babylon").

184 *SzeK*, Part 3 (Atlas). These are, in effect, the last sentences of the manuscript.

185 "I tried endlessly to find publishers in Germany, like Dumont, or Diogenes in Switzerland but they rejected us. The same happened with Rohwolt, who showed interest but then finally declined. I regretted that a lot." Caspari interview, 4 July 2002.

186 Interview with Mark Wigley, 24 February 2003.

187 *SzeK*, Part 2 section I, chapter 47.

188 See for instance *SzeK*, Part 2 section I, chapter 49 and section III, chapter 71.

189 Letter from Herbert Froese to Constant, 8 September 1961. File "Correspondentie 1961", RKD.

190 Letter from Constant to Herbert Froese, 13 September 1961. Loc. cit.

191 See for instance her article in this book.

192 *SzeK*, Postscript ("Nachwort").

193 Telephone conversation, 4 April 2001 (see note 120).

THE CONTINUOUS MONUMENT

An Architectural Model For Total Urbanization

Superstudio, 1969

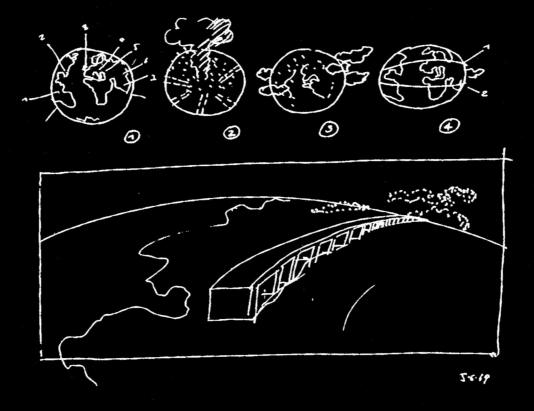

For those who, like ourselves, are convinced that architecture is one of the few ways to realize cosmic order on earth, to put things to order and above all to affirm humanity's capacity for acting according to reason, it is a "moderate utopia" to imagine a near future in which all architecture will be created with a single act, from a single design capable of clarifying once and for all the motives which have induced man to build dolmens, menhirs, pyramids, and lastly to trace (*ultima ratio*) a white line in the desert.

The Great Wall of China, Hadrian's Wall, motorways, like parallels and meridians, are the tangible signs of our understanding of the earth. We believe in a future of "rediscovered architecture", in a future in which architecture will regain its full power, abandoning all ambiguity of design and appearing as the only alternative to nature. Between the terms *natura naturans* and *natura naturata*, we choose the latter.

Eliminating mirages and will-o'-the-wisps such as spontaneous architecture, sensitive architecture, architecture without architects, biological architecture and fantastic architecture, we move towards the "continuous monument": a form of architecture all equally emerging from a single continuous environment: the world rendered uniform by technology, culture and all the other inevitable forms of imperialism.

We belong to a long history of black stones, rocks fallen from the sky or erected in the earth: meteorites, dolmens, obelisks. Cosmic axis, vital elements, elements reproducing the relationships of sky and earth, witnesses to marriages celebrated, the tablets of the law, final acts of dramas of various lengths. From the Holy Kaaba to the Vertical Assembly Building.

A square block of stone placed on the earth is a primary act, it is a testimonial that architecture is the centre of the relationships of technology, sacredness, utilitarianism. It implies man, machines, rational structures and history. The square block is the first and ultimate act in the history of ideas in architecture. Architecture becomes a closed, immobile object that leads nowhere but to itself and to the use of reason.

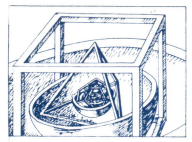

1. Keplero cercò di iscrivere dei solidi elementari nelle orbite dei pianeti.

Kepler tried to inscribe elementary solids within the orbits of the planets.

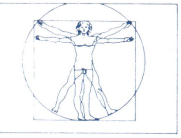

2. Vitruvio e Leonardo iscrissero l'uomo in un cerchio, gli indiani sistemarono il caos nel mandala.

Vitruvius and Leonardo inscribed man within the circle, the Indians placed chaos within the mandala.

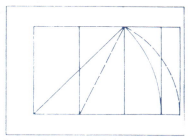

3. La sezione aurea, l'ordine, la simmetria erano insieme visione del mondo e mediazione per comunicare la natura delle cose.

The golden section, order, symmetry, were at the same time a vision of the world, and a medium for communicating the nature of things.

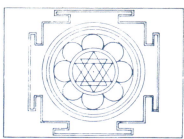

4. Il mandala come base per la meditazione è il tentativo di ordinare e dare un senso ad elementi divergenti.

The mandala as a basis for meditation is a tentative try at ordering and giving a sense to diverging elements.

5. Il desiderio di rendere il mondo chiaro e distinto ha segnato tracciati regolatori sul viso umano e sul mondo...

The desire to render the world clear and distinct has left regular paths upon the human face and on the world...

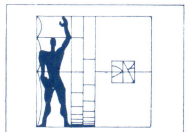

6. creando sistemi basati contemporaneamente sull'uomo e sulla geometria (come il Modulor).

creating systems based at one and the same time upon man and upon geometry (such as the Modulor).

7. L'uomo non è il centro delle cose, è solo uno dei vertici del poligono infinito che unisce cosmo, mondo, ragione.

Man is not the centre of things, he is merely one of the vertices of the infinite polygon that unites the cosmos, the world, reason.

8. L'astrologia collegava le manifestazioni umane agli astri; le scienze rivelano sempre nuove connessioni tra le parti e il tutto.

Astrology connected human destinies and the stars; science is ever revealing further links between the parts and the whole.

9. Le forme elementari sono la testimonianza di visioni del mondo. Dolmen, menhir, il sacro cerchio di Stonehenge, gli ziggurats...

Elementary forms are witnesses to different visions of the world. Dolmen, menhirs, the sacred circle of Stonehenge, ziggurats...

10. dei babilonesi e dei maya, le piramidi degli egiziani erano monumenti contro la morte, uno dei modi per sopravvivere, riconoscendosi.

of Babylon and of the Mayas, the pyramids of Egypt were monuments against death, one way to survive, in recognizing oneself.

11. Prendere coscienza del bisogno dei monumenti serve a colmare la frattura tra razionalità e inconscio: così si può osservare che...

To realize the need for monuments is to fill in the fracture between rationality and the unconscious: thus one may observe that...

12. la Kaaba e il Vertical Assembly Building sono due uguali cubiche pietre nere, egualmente monumentali.

the Kaaba and the Vertical Assembly Building are two identical black stones, both equally monumental.

13. Quando poi i segni umani non sono solidi elementari, sono lunghe linee continue, teorie d'elementi, espressioni di una...

Then, when human signs are not elementary solids, they are long continuous lines, a theory of elements, the expression of...

14. stessa volontà di segnare e misurare. Ponti, muraglie cinesi....

the same will to sign and measure. Bridges, Chinese walls,...

15. o acquedotti sono sempre monumenti continui ugualmente allungati sulla terra per comprenderla.

or acqueducts are still continuous monuments, also lying full length to embrace the earth.

16. Così fino alle autostrade, alle dighe e ai grandi manufatti della tecnica in scala con le nuove dimensioni.

And so on up to the motorways, great dams and huge products of technology on a scale with the new dimensions.

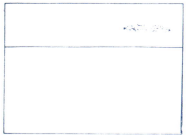

17. Dalla Genesi: «In principio Iddio creò il cielo e la terra, la terra era una cosa senza forma e vuota» e poi dall'Apocalisse:

From Genesis: « In the beginning, God created the heavens and the earth, and the earth was without form and void » and then from the Apocalypse:

18. «La città era un quadrato, e la sua lunghezza era uguale alla sua larghezza». Tutta la storia sta tra il caos e l'architettura.

« And the city lieth foursquare, and the length is as large as the breadth »; and all history lies between chaos and architecture.

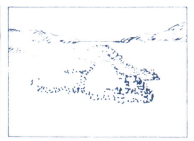

19. La nostra storia è appunto una parabola di formalizzazione, così è una storia di deserti naturali ed artificiali,...

Our story is just a parable of formalization, so it is a story of deserts, both natural and artificial,...

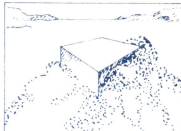

20. deserti dove si posano nuvole o dove nascono nuvole che poi generano apparizioni geometriche lungamente attese.

deserts where clouds may come to earth or where clouds are born, then to generate geometrical, long-awaited apparitions.

21. Così appare la geometria e il primo personaggio della nostra parabola. Il blocco squadrato è il primo atto e l'ultimo nella...
Thus geometry appears, the first character in our parable. The square block is the first and last act in the...

22. storia delle idee d'architettura, come nodo di relazioni tecnologia/sacralità/utilitarismo tra uomo macchina strutture razionali e storia.
history of architectural ideas, as the intersection of the relationships between technology/sacredness/utilitarianism, between man machine rational structures and history.

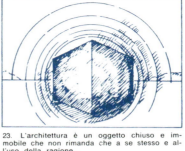

23. L'architettura è un oggetto chiuso e immobile che non rimanda che a se stesso e all'uso della ragione,...
architecture is a closed, immobile object, referring only to itself and to the use of reason,...

24. un oggetto inconoscibile che irradia luce aurore e arcobaleni, fino ad alzarsi in volo nello spazio isometrico.
an unknowable object irradiating light dawn rainbows, until it takes off in flight into isometric space.

25. Il blocco viene costretto da due cinghiature ad esser un cubo perfetto...
The block is forced into a perfect cube by two straps...

26. e appena liberato si divide in pezzi seguendo leggi precise, mostrando volta per volta i principi generatori...
and as soon as it is freed, it divides up into pieces, following precise laws and showing each time its governing principles...

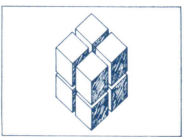

27. fino a diventare una serie di cubi più piccoli, e più piccoli ancora...
until it becomes a series of smaller cubes, and yet smaller...

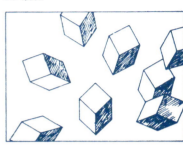

28. e le parti si disperdono ma l'ordine non genera il disordine e ogni parte ha con sé il messaggio genetico della sua razza ordinata.
and the parts disperse, but order does not generate disorder and each part has with it the genetic message of its ordered race.

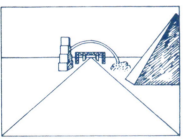

29. UN VIAGGIO IN AUTO IN UN MUSEO DRIVE-IN DELL'ARCHITETTURA. Souvenirs di viaggio da un viaggio nelle regioni della ragione.
A CAR JOURNEY TO A DRIVE-IN MUSEUM OF ARCHITECTURE. Souvenirs from a journey into the realms of reason.

30. Dall'architettura dei monumenti attraverso l'architettura delle immagini e l'architettura tecnomorfa all'architettura della ragione
From the architecture of monuments through the architecture of images and technomorphous architecture to reach the architecture of reason

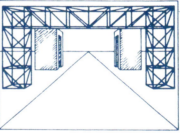

31. (durante il viaggio ci sono apparizioni di monumenti antichi, arcobaleni e nuvole al neon, macchine tralicci e statue).
(throughout the journey there are apparitions of ancient monuments, rainbows, neon clouds, machines steel framework and statues).

32. L'arrivo trionfale al tempio della Ragion Pura (scritta: « nella prospettiva storica, la Ragione domina tutto »).
The triumphant arrival at the temple of Pure Reason (banner: « in historical perspective, Reason dominates all »).

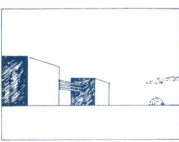

33. COME ILLUMINARE IL DESERTO. Due prismi neri di marmo o cristallo collegati da un arcobaleno al neon per illuminare la mente, posti...
HOW TO ILLUMINATE THE DESERT. Two black prisms of marble or crystal joined by a neon rainbow to illuminate the mind, placed...

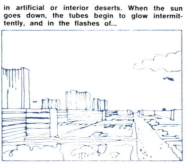

34. nei deserti artificiali o interiori. Quando il sole tramonta i tubi cominciano a brillare a intermittenza, e nei lampi delle...
in artificial or interior deserts. When the sun goes down, the tubes begin to glow intermittently, and in the flashes of...

35. accensioni appaiono immagini di architettura di sogno, radiosi orizzonti con un fil di fumo, tempo libero, maisons pour le...
light images of dream architecture appear, radiant horizons with a wisp of smoke, free time, maisons pour le...

36. week-end, immagini di felicità per mezzo dell'architettura, costruzioni ariose, città ordinate, spazi verdi...
week-end, images of happiness through architecture, airy buildings, ordered cities, green spaces...

37. Nella luce che aumenta si vedono i nuovi monumenti della scienza e della tecnica (Crystal Palace) e le utopie (Falanstery...
In the growing light, one can see the monuments of science and technology (the Crystal Palace) and utopias (Falanstery,...

38. New Harmony, Philadelphia) e le costruzioni eroiche del razionalismo (Weissenhof, Bauhaus, Ville Radieuse): i cataloghi delle illusioni...
New Harmony, Philadelphia) and the heroic buildings of the age of rationalism (Weissenhof, Bauhaus, Ville Radieuse): the catalogues of illusions...

39. e delle utopie. « Il mondo delle idee, delle credenze, delle fantasie e dei progetti è altrettanto reale della realtà » (L. Mumford).
and utopias. « The world of ideas, of beliefs, of fantasies and projects is just as real as reality » (L. Mumford).

40. I tubi luminosi divengono un arco trionfale e sotto ci passano carovane di nomadi, impiegati in gita, processioni di pace.
The glowing tubes become an arch of triumph under which processions of nomads, white-collar workers on holiday, peace demonstrations, pass.

41. LE APPARIZIONI. 1. LA PORTA. «Tutto ciò che abbiamo amato è andato perduto, siamo ormai nel deserto. Davanti a noi non c'è che un quadrato...
THE APPARITIONS. 1. THE DOOR. «All· we have loved is lost, we are now in the desert. Before us there is but a square,

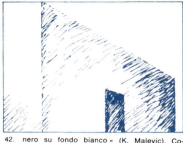

42. nero su fondo bianco » (K. Malevic). Come una porta, una soglia metafisica.
black on a white ground » (K. Malevich). Like a door, a metaphysical threshold.

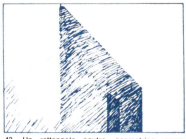

43. Un rettangolo neutro, geometrico, come presenza misteriosa tra due mondi. E' questa porta, su questo confine che noi viviamo,...
A neutral rectangle, geometric, like a mysterious presence between two worlds. It is on this threshold, this frontier that we live,....

44. di volta in volta conv nti della necessità di vivere all'interno del cubo di cristallo o invece di isolarci nel deserto.
as the case may be, convinced of the necessity of living inside a crystal cube or of isolating ourselves in the desert.

45. LE APPARIZIONI. 2. IL CORRIDOIO. Fatto ad « U », poggiato in terra con angoli rigidamente retti...
THE APPARITIONS. 2. THE CORRIDOR. « U »-shaped, set on the ground at rigid right angles...

46. lo si percorre con lo sguardo da fuori, se ne esaminano le superfici lisce e lucide:...
from the outside, our eyes run over its smooth, shining surfaces:...

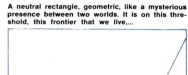

47. sappiamo che ha un interno, ma non sappiamo come. E' disponibile comunque ad ogni utilizzazione.
we know it has an interior, but we do not know how. However, it is at our disposition for any use.

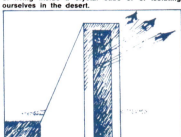

48. Ed ecco improvvisamente uscire tre jets.
And suddenly, unexpectedly, three jets fly out.

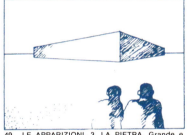

49. LE APPARIZIONI. 3. LA PIETRA. Grande e nera giace nel deserto. Come in uno specchio scuro rimanda immagini in movimento di uomini e città.
THE APPARITIONS. 3. THE STONE. Large and black, it lies in the desert. As in a dark mirror, it reflects moving images of men and cities.

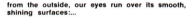

50. Poi comincia a muoversi e si alza in volo.
Then it begins to move and takes off in flight.

51. Raggiunge una certa quota e poi rimane parallela alla terra, muovendosi.
It reaches a certain height and then remains parallel to the ground, moving.

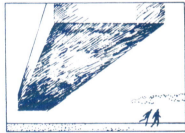

52. Dentro ha l'immagine distorta della città, il grande Barnum tecnologico. Lo specchio nero in cielo è intelligente e immobile.
Within, it contains the distorted image of the city, the great technological circus. The black mirror in the sky is intelligent and immobile.

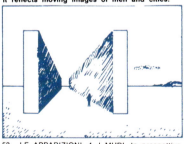

53. LE APPARIZIONI. 4. I MURI. In prospettiva con gente che ci passa dentro. Camminare in prospettive parallele (New York).
THE APPARITIONS. 4. THE WALLS. In perspective with people walking between them. To walk in parallel perspectives (N.Y.).

54. All'uscita appare la pietra-specchio che muovendosi...
At the exit, the mirror-stone appears, moving...

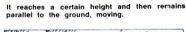

55. balza sui muri paralleli e diviene un soffitto e i muri divengono un tunnel buio.
and jumping onto the parallel walls, becoming a ceiling, and the walls become a dark tunnel.

56. Camminare a lungo nel buio e infine vedere un chiarore, e nella luce appare come una linea bianca il MONUMENTO CONTINUO.
Walking in the dark for a long time, and at last seeing a faint glow, and in the light, like a white line, we see the CONTINUOUS MONUMENT.

57. Di fronte al destino di progressivo impoverimento della terra e alla prospettiva ormai vicina dello « standing-room only »...
Envisaging the progressive impoverishment of the earth and the now nearby prospect of « standing-room only »...

58. possiamo immaginare un'architettura unica con cui occupare le zone di abitabilità ottimale lasciando libere le altre.
we can imagine a single architectural construction with which to occupy the optimal living zones, leaving the others free.

59. Il modello architettonico di urbanizzazione totale è un'estrapolazione logica di una « storia orientata », da Stonehenge al V.A.B. al monumento continuo.
The architectural model of total urbanization is the logical extrapolation of « oriented history », from Stonehenge to the VAB to the continuous

60. Un'architettura unica capace di dar forma alla terra; (misurandola: come i paralleli e i meridiani), un'architettura riconoscibile.
monument. A single form of architecture, capable of shaping the earth (measuring it, like longitude and latitude), a recognizable architecture.

Envisaging the progressive impoverishment of the earth and the now nearby prospect of "standing-room only" we can imagine a single architectural construction with which to occupy the optimal living zones, leaving the others free.

The architectural model of total urbanization is the logical extrapolation of "oriented history", from Stonehenge to the VAB, to the continuous monument. A single form of architecture, capable of shaping the earth (measuring it, like longitude and latitude), a recognizable architecture.

The continuous monument is the extreme pole of a series of projecting operations centred round the idea of the "single design", a design which can be transferred from one area to another, remaining unchanged: an impassible, unalterable image, whose static perfection moves the world through the love of itself that it creates. Through a series of mental operations, one comes into possession of reality and reaches serenity: thus architecture is understanding of the world and knowledge of oneself.

NATURE

Some random images, disquieting as all postcards bearing "greetings from …"
Architecture faces nature without disguising itself, but presented as the only
alternative: *natura naturans* and *natura naturata*. One may cross deserts, cover
over canyons, join up Alpine lakes, also use, geometrically, hills and rivers with
new horizons. Or other operations on earth, mountains and sea, always as examples
of rational operations, organized and measured.

Across the plains of Agra
the muezzin towers call
Come love, come weep, come wonder.
I am the

Taj Mahal

Photographed by SUPER

ANCIENT MONUMENTS

The Holy Kaaba substituted by an enormous block of black marble with square holes, and no one knows where the holy stone is any longer: but this is no obstacle to true faith.

The Caryatid Porch as the facade. The Taj Mahal protected and climatized.

A classical garden in Madrid … an additional layer to the Coliseum, etc.: all operations *per absurdum*, in grandiose style.

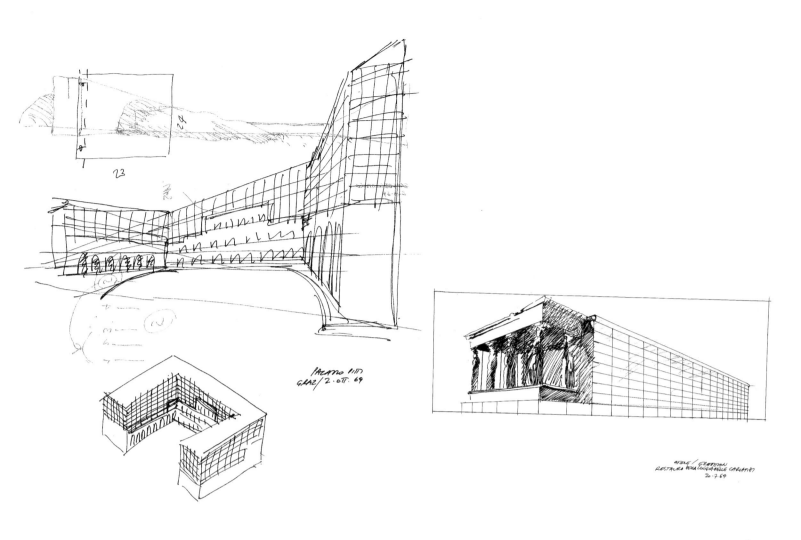

PALAZZO PITTI
GRAZ / 2.OTT. 69

ATENE / ERETHEION
RESTAURO DELLA LOGGIA DELLE CARIATIDI
20.7.69

PALLADIO
PALAZZO CHIERICATI / VICENZA
1550

Liebe Grüße aus Graz von Superstudio

CITIES

Coketown revisited. Where is Utopia?

Graz with a structure linking the green zones passing over the Schlossberg and the Mur leaving the old city untouched.

The *autostrada* (motorway) is the yardstick of the dimension: the first continuous monument.

Old Florence, frozen and perfect amidst the grass and flowers, to serve as Pythagoras' table for the new way of thinking with the monument at the foot of the hills.

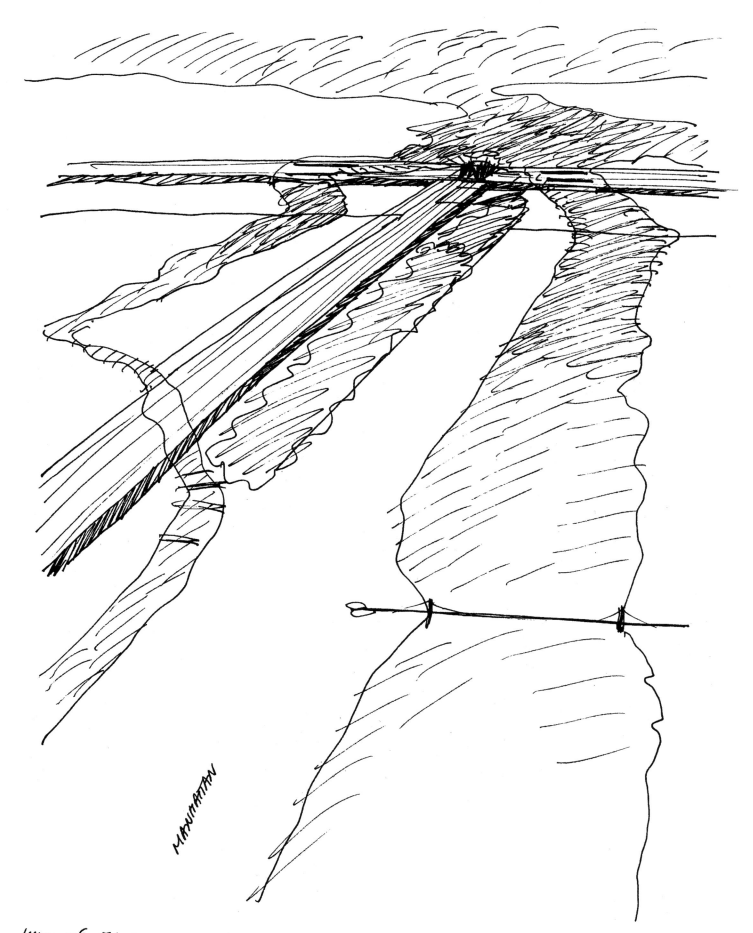

MANHATTAN

VIEW OF MANHATTAN LOOKING SOUTH

26.10.69

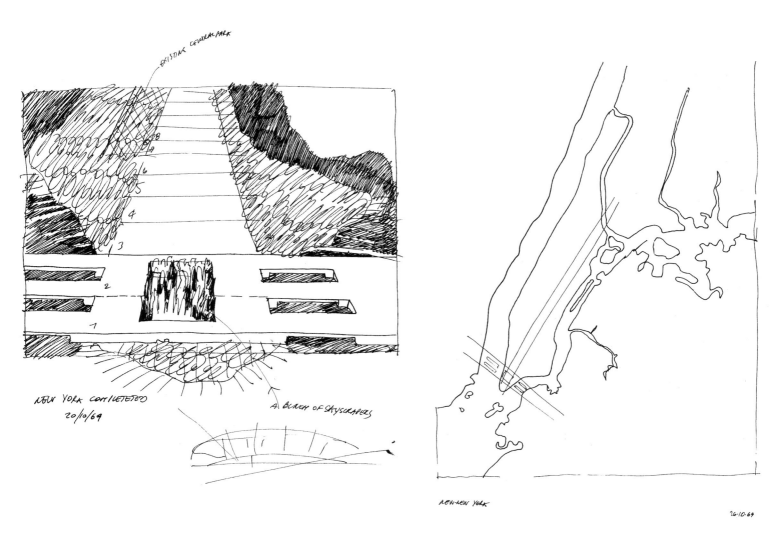

EXISTING CENTRAL PARK

NEW YORK COMPLETED
20/10/69

A BUNCH OF SKYSCRAPERS

NEW-NEW YORK

26·10·69

NEW-NEW YORK
AUGURI 1969   20·22/NOV·69

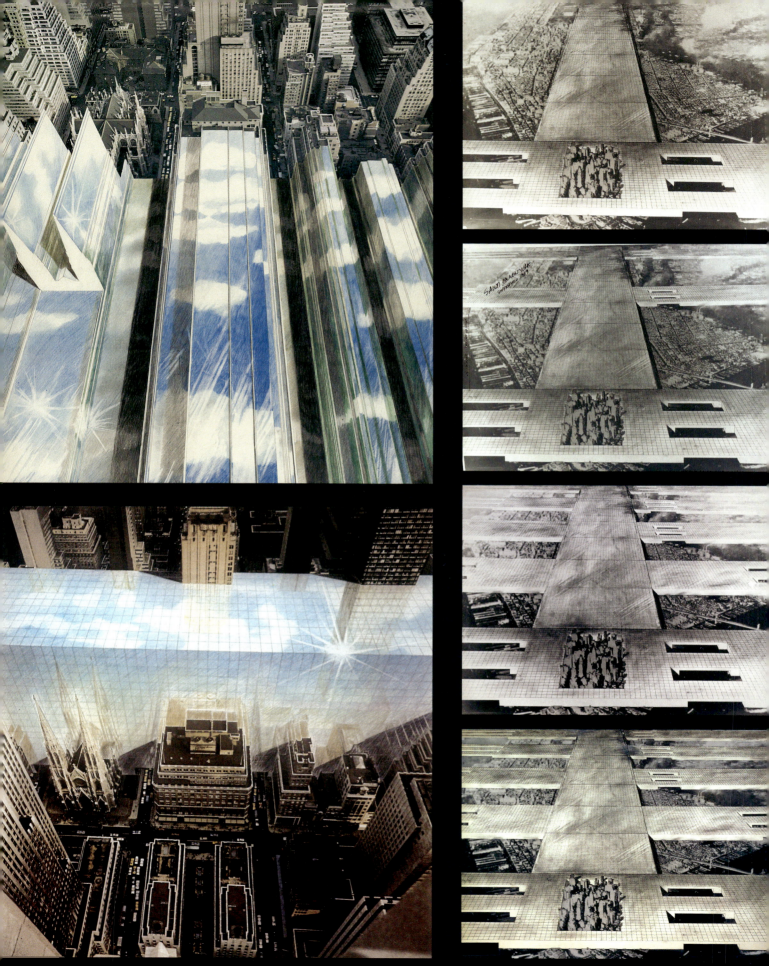

NEW NEW YORK

New York for example. A super-structure passes over the Hudson and the point of the peninsula joining Brooklyn and New Jersey. And a second perpendicular structure for expansion. All the rest is Central Park. This is sufficient to hold the entire built-up volume of Manhattan.

A bunch of ancient skyscrapers, preserved in memory of a time when cities were built with no single plan....

And from the Bay, we see New New York arranged by the Continuous Monument into a great plain of ice, clouds or sky....

The Distant Winking of a Star, or The Horror of the Real

Sander Woertman

Introduction

Somewhere in a galaxy, far, far away …: these words could be the opening credits of a film on Superstudio and the radical movement in Florence. A number of newly graduated architects declared war on the existing architectural tradition of modernism. Their operating base was Florence, an outpost in the architectural world of the time, a monument to the rebirth of Western civilization. For the post-war reconstruction of society, people were looking towards altogether different places – Britain for example, with Team X on the one hand, and Archigram on the other. The functionalist schools of architecture that had emerged from the meetings of CIAM and the Bauhaus reigned supreme. Florence was far removed from this.[1] This isolated position, combined with a painful lack of building commissions, allowed architects and architectural students to chart a course virtually independent of the building practice. Instead, projects were conceived that tapped new sources of creativity and inspiration. New developments in the arts, industry, materials, and society were investigated, tested and incorporated into projects unconcerned with building practice or tradition. In Florence, the breeding ground for these developments was the Faculty of Architecture. Here, among others, two architectural collectives emerged. These groups both consisted of students who had graduated in 1966 or later. The strength of their fresh approach towards architecture and design was instantly felt in the schools of architecture. These collectives were Superstudio and Archizoom.

Almost all the members of these two groups had pursued their final projects under the inspiring guidance of Leonardo Savioli. In his own work, Savioli, a professor at the Faculty of Architecture in Florence, oscillated between art and architecture. His architectural designs were frequently preceded by a series of studies in the form of drawings, paintings and other media that seemed to be completely dissociated from the final project but were, in fact, explorations of colour, structure, and composition. Adolfo Natalini writes of Savioli's drawings that "even when the drawings looked like traces of insects or explosions, galaxies, spiderwebs or wounds, they were always able to resemble parts of constructions or something constructable. Pieces of construction able to heal the lacerations and wounds."[2]

The emergence of Superstudio and Archizoom must be linked to the two *Superarchitettura* exhibitions organized in Pistoia in 1966 and in Modena in February 1967. The exhibitions proved a perfect occasion for these recent graduates finally to engage themselves in the prevalent trends in art. The first exhibition in Pistoia was originally intended as a presentation of Pop Art paintings by Adolfo Natalini. Natalini was a young artist and a student at the School of Architecture of the University of Florence, where he served in 1966 as Savioli's assistant. He was also a member of the *Scuola di Pistoia*, a group of artists who early on embraced pop culture. Natalini, instead of exhibiting his own paintings, preferred to organize an exhibition on architecture together with a group of friends and fellow students at the School of Architecture.[3] The *Superarchitettura* show marked a turning point: the time had come to experiment.

The exhibition design was colourful, with plastic objects in garish hues filling the space, creating the sensation of a psychedelic trip.

The *Superarchitettura* exhibitions and the objects that were produced for them were inspired by Pop Art. In 1964 and 1966, the Italians were first exposed to this style at the Venice Biennale where works by artists such as Rauschenberg and Lichtenstein were shown. Interest in pop culture was soon widespread among student circles in Florence. Pop Art offered the students an entirely new range of forms and images to work with. This newly acquired iconography was still empty of meaning, a new world waiting to be filled with fantastic images not bound by convention. And, most importantly, the avant-garde could relieve architecture of its burden of having to serve as a moral gauge of modern society.[4]

The dialectic stance of Pop Art toward consumer society must have resonated favourably in Florence, a city besieged by American tourists after the end of the war. In many cases, these tourists came from U.S. military bases established in Northern Italy to contain communism and facilitate American relief projects. Thus, the people of Florence soon came into contact with concepts such as supermarkets, consumer goods and the hippie culture.

The *Superarchitettura* exhibition was the Florentine architects' response to the emergence of a new society, one increasingly geared toward media and consumption. The statement accompanying their exhibition expresses their obsession with mass culture: "Superarchitecture is the architecture of superproduction, of superconsumption, of superinduction of superconsumption, of the supermarket, of the superman, of the super gasoline." And they add: "*Superarchitettura* accepts the logic of production and consumption; it utilizes it in an attempt at demystification."[5] Following the Modena exhibition, Superstudio and Archizoom parted ways. Superstudio, from that moment on, consisted of Adolfo Natalini and Cristiano Toraldo di Francia, later joined by Piero Frassinelli, Alessandro and Roberto Magris, and from 1970 until 1972 Alessandro Poli. Archizoom was made up of Andrea Branzi, Gilberto Corretti, Paolo Deganello and Massimo Morozzi, joined in 1968 by Dario and Lucia Bartolini.

1. Superstudio: *Passiflora* lamp, 1966

Italy: Industry, Politics and University

Post-war Italy was a broken country, mentally as well as physically. During the time of reconstruction, industry, population, and the economy grew very rapidly in Europe. Italy, in its turn, worked hard to recuperate from the disasters of war. American aid programmes brought relief, but problems arose in industry and in the cities. In an attempt to revitalize the Italian economy, the Italian government lopsidedly emphasized industrial development, without consideration for the infrastructure or for social institutions. Over the years, practically and emotionally, a rift developed between the needs of the Italian society and industrial development. When the 1960s saw a period of economic growth, this rift became all the more apparent with the increased need for workers to keep the large factories – located mainly in Northern Italy – running. Workers were attracted from the poor parts of Italy to the factories in the North, resulting in a wave of immigration from the South to the North. The immigrants were, at best, accommodated in hastily erected apartment buildings where they lived under terrible conditions. At the time, housing construction was mainly left to private construction firms, giving rise to housing speculation. Social housing projects by the government were too small in scale to address the housing shortage. For the leftist students (being a student almost automatically meant being leftist) it was incomprehensible that the government failed to develop appropriate plans to remedy this situation. Moreover, architects were rarely consulted in the realization of these projects. Ironically, the crisis in architectural practice did not bother the members of Superstudio much. While their colleagues could scarcely practise for lack of commissions, the individual members of Superstudio had the opportunity to build up a sizeable body of work, thanks mainly to their upper middle class background which provided them with a modest network of clients. With a few exceptions, these projects were not included in the work of Superstudio. In view of the prevailing political leanings of the Superstudio members, it is rather ironic that these projects mainly involved designs for banks.

The story of the radical movement in Florence is inextricably linked to the university, where the future members of the

2. Archizoom, *Dream Bed: Shipwreck of Roses*, 1967 (model)

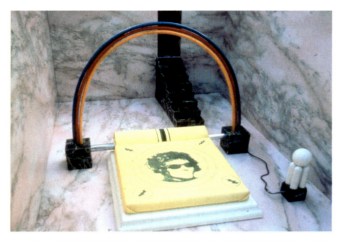

3/4. Archizoom, *Dream Beds: Delirium of Roses* and *Presentiment of Roses*, 1967 (models)

Florentine avant-garde were exposed to the outside world. In the 1960s, the education system went through numerous reforms that caused the number of students to double between 1960 and 1968.[6] The new students came primarily from working-class families. This made it possible for the members of Superstudio and Archizoom, who came mainly from aristocratic and bourgeois families, to become familiar with the realities of life in Italy.

The universities – and more specifically, the schools of architecture – had last witnessed reforms in 1923. Courses and assignments were heavily geared toward industry and the job market, and since progressive ideas or socio-critical visions were not stimulated in any way, education at universities took on a conservative character. Thus, during the period of post-war reconstruction, the universities ignored the emergence of a new social reality, the emancipation of youth, and the growing interest in new media and technological developments. Equally, contemporary trends in architecture did not get a foothold in schools of architecture. In Florence, however, the situation changed after 1964. With the appointment of new and younger professors like Savioli, Quaroni, Benevolo and Libera, the curriculum was increasingly adapted to social issues and other contemporary concerns.[7] This did not mean, however, that from then on peace and quiet prevailed at the university. In 1967, in Milan and Trento, tension reached the boiling point when tuition was increased and educational reforms were introduced. The purpose of these reforms was to divide the various kinds of students into different groups. This constituted the exact opposite of the demands of the students

5. Arata Isozaki, *Joint Core System / Space City*, 1960

themselves who argued for a narrowing of the gap between full-time students and working students. The student protests culminated in 1968. In that year, all over Italy and beyond, students took over university departments, resulting in many instances in violent clashes with a police force determined to restore order.

Many radical architecture groups participated during their existence in extra-parliamentary movements that distanced themselves from the traditional power of leftist parties. The writings of Mao and Marx were widely read, although communist theories concerning violent revolution and party politics were not supported. Rather, as an alternative to the Italian republic, the students looked to the revolutionary Paris Commune of 1871, which had stood up for the workers.[8] In 1966–67, when China was shaken up by the Cultural Revolution, Italian students interpreted it as an anti-authoritarian and spontaneous revolt. At the same time, the United States was waging war in Vietnam. The United States lost its reputation as the embodiment of the modern world: students now regarded America as the villain.

This period of architectural and social shortcomings in education, industry, and society marked the emergence of the radical architecture movement whose goal was to redesign for man an environment enabling him to decide independently what to do with his surroundings and to restore the link to progress. Its approach to architecture was deeply rooted in the social-cultural context, in social commitment.

Radical architecture and the media

In the sixties, although it had been obvious for years that the government policy insufficiently alleviated the social strains plaguing the country, the prevailing climate in Italy was so conservative that there was no room for critical voices which might pose a threat to the production of buildings. Moreover, at that time, the heroes of architecture were still very much alive: Le Corbusier, Mies van der Rohe, and Louis Kahn were all still actively building and leaving their mark on the architecture of

the day. Accordingly, the average Italian architect was, to say the least, suspicious of the fantastic projects the new avant-garde produced. And the critics such as Dal Co, Tafuri and others condemned these projects as well. because they challenged the work of the established hierarchy.

In order to counter the conservative forces in architecture, the Florentine groups of Superstudio and Archizoom soon realized that a half-hearted approach to projects would not do. Projects were therefore tackled thoroughly, with all the skills the individual members could call on. As a result, there was a clear division of labour among the various members of the group; each did what he could do best, the ultimate goal being a project that nobody would be able to ignore. Publications in magazines were essential to Superstudio, Archizoom and other radical groups, as this was the only way for them to communicate their ideas to the mainstream of Italian architecture.

But there were other reasons that the media was so important for the radical architects. For one thing, the projects were frequently conceptual in nature, allowing for documentation in words and pictures only through publication. For another, the media too were illustrative of a changing society whose problems the radical avant-garde was addressing. Printed media was the way the emerging consumer society expressed its desires: ads, news and entertainment were communicated through a multitude of magazines and newspapers. Apart from these obvious reasons for the importance of media for the radicals, publishing in a more practical sense also brought in revenue.

Domus provided the initial forum for the ideas of the radical avant-garde. Archizoom first published its projects and design objects such as the *Superonda* chair and the *Gazebi* project in this magazine. The first projects by Superstudio were published in *Domus* as well. After 1971 they mainly published in *Casabella*. It was Alessandro Mendini in his role as editor who held the reins on the magazine's editorial board from 1970 until 1976. He changed *Casabella* from a conservative magazine to a platform for the ideas of the radical movement. Mendini allowed Superstudio more creative input and took great personal interest in their projects. In the years that followed, Mendini would secure a place for himself in the Italian avant-garde with his own projects. In the meantime, the possibility for the radicals to publish their projects and ideas in *Casabella* meant a breakthrough for radical thought: *Casabella* was one of the most influential architectural magazines in Italy and one of the few Italian architectural publications that was read abroad.

In addition to publication in Italian journals, the projects of Superstudio were also regularly featured in Japanese magazines. Indeed, the interest of the Japanese media in Superstudio's projects was above average. This was mainly due to the Metabolists, a group of Japanese architects who had already been researching and realizing megastructures since the early 1960s. In their own way, they were engaged in exploring the frontiers of architecture and applying new technologies. In the 1970s, however, the period that saw the conception of the megastructural projects of Superstudio and Archizoom, the belief in the certainties of utopian urbanism was dwindling in Japan as well. Under the leadership of Arata Isozaki, among others, a counter-movement – an avant-garde of negativity – emerged.[9] Isozaki himself clearly drew inspiration from Superstudio's work, most directly in two bank buildings he designed in Fukuoka: they appear to be literally lifted from the Catalogue of Villas, a project by Superstudio allowing for the design of villa typologies according to a standardized process. In any case, the avant-garde movement in Japan was rooted to a much higher degree than its Italian counterpart in building practice; and, apart from conceptual projects, it also produced actual buildings that seemed to deliver on the promise of a technocratic future.

Superstudio

Superstudio has always operated in the twilight zone between social criticism and irony. However serious the essence of a project, it invariably contains an element of irony, which is why the utopian designs Superstudio confronts us with can never be taken at face value: the ironic overtones soon make it clear to us that the aim is exploration, not realization. Superstudio itself calls this *demonstratio per absurdum*. This way of presenting projects was a trademark for Superstudio. This also applies to the projects which will be discussed later on – the *Monumento Continuo* and the *Atti Fondamentali*, also known as *Cinque Storie*. The duality of Superstudio – one melancholic and serious, and the other playful and witty – can be discerned throughout the history of the radical avant-garde. The contribution of Gruppo Strum to the important survey of Italian design at the Museum of Modern Art in New York, for example, consisted of photo novellas visualizing the life of suffering of the Italian worker. At the same exhibition, this political project was contrasted by a frivolous project by Ettore Sottsass entitled *Il pianeta come festival*: the planet as festival. In this project, special buildings were designed that served to provide inhabitants with LSD. This duality in the radical avant-garde can be seen as one of the symptoms of a society that changed from the rigid concept of modernism to post-modernist complexity, where things could have a multitude of meanings and interpretations. In regard to Superstudio, even today most of their projects still possess that unique enigmatic and fantastic quality to the extent that no ultimate conclusion can be drawn from them. But all Superstudio projects are also meant to be pieces of artistic beauty. As Kenneth Frampton already remarked, of all the avant-garde movements, Superstudio was the one capturing and articulating the problems of the day most poetically.[10]

One of the inspirations for Superstudio were the work and publications of Archigram. Already at an early stage the members of Superstudio and Archizoom were confronted with the technophile architectural fantasies of Archigram. As Peter Cook, one of the better-known members of Archigram, notes, "… But one day we realized that 50 copies of our funny little magazine (Archigram) had been sold in the *Centro D* shop in Florence. The peripheral nature of these groups might have been a factor: for at that time (1965) there were none reported from Berlin, Milan or New York."[11] Reminiscing about his discovery of the Archigram magazine, Adolfo Natalini talks about how he spent a working

vacation with his girlfriend in London when she returned one day with a magazine and let him read it. It was for sale at an art gallery showing modern art. He was very enthusiastic about it and showed it to his friends upon his return. Thus, the magazine found its way to Florence. Apart from the ideas expressed in its pages, the magazine's design also influenced the students: comic-strip drawings, crisp graphics, and photomontages were presented dynamically, inspired by the Pop Art paintings of Roy Lichtenstein among others. But in Italy, so young architects felt, the social situation called for a more critical approach. For all their provocative playfullness, Archigram's projects did little to challenge the existing social order.

Superstudio's first radical quest started in 1967, when Superstudio commenced their *Viaggio nelle regioni della ragione*. For Superstudio, reason was considered to be the essence of human thought, untouched by knowledge, values, and restrictions imposed by culture. Only a person with access to reason without any cultural excess baggage that would potentially restrict his personal development, could optimally utilize his creativity. Therefore, Superstudio aimed at designing objects that were free of such restricting connotations, using only the faculty of reason. From that moment on, *ragione*, or reason, became a recurring theme in the projects undertaken by Superstudio. In subsequent years, Superstudio embarked on a study of the relevance of the object.

The investigation into the essence of the object started in 1969, when Superstudio launched their *Istogrammi* project. In the project, three-dimensional diagrams with a homogeneous surface were built. The starting point was a square, the surface of a plane consisting of a regular rectangular grid. What Superstudio intended with this quickly became clear: the diagram could easily be translated into a furniture item, architecture or a landscape. A definitive solution for any kind of space or form had been found. Moreover, any problem pertaining to form or context-specific sensitivities had been solved forever,[12] as Hans Hollein argued as early as 1963: "Today, for the first time in the history of humanity, at this moment when scientific knowledge has made astounding progress and technological perfection can achieve anything, let's make an architecture which is not determined by technology, an architecture, rather, which is pure and absolute. Today man rules over infinite space."[13] Out of the Histograms-project, a series of objects were designed. To this day, the Quaderna-table is still in production by the Italian furniture company Zanotta.

The Histograms project proved to be essential for Superstudio. The projects that were developed in the next few years, all carried the imprint of the rectangular and uniform appearance of the Histogram-objects. The idea of scalelessness is almost literally adopted and transposed in the Superstudio-project of the *Catalogo di Ville*, the Continuous Monument and the Supersurface project. In these projects, the regular grid of thin black lines, superimposed upon the white translucent faces of an object made its reappearance. The object was examined on every conceivable scale, from design artefact to the city as an organism. Ultimately – as we shall see in the Fundamental Acts project – this research led to architecture being declared dead.

The Continuous Monument

In 1969, Superstudio participated in the Triennial for Art and Architecture in Graz, Austria. Here, Superstudio first presented illustrations of the *Monumento Continuo*, an architectural monument covering and shaping the entire world – a monument as the result of an all-encompassing cultural fusion. The monument was intended to serve as a refuge for humanity, its volume as optimal living space that would offer a place to every human being, leaving the rest of the earth uninhabited – allowing for a natural development, free from human intervention. Surviving remnants of old cities served to reflect on the nature of man. This project marked a turning point in their work. Having been concerned with design and architecture until then, they now embarked on a journey with an uncertain destination. They acknowledged architecture's roots in the history of mankind, at the same time recognizing that it at times has served oppressive powers. Looking for the Zen-like essence of architecture, they returned to what they considered its most basic form: the square. Simple and consequently innocent, it was not open to misuse or misinterpretation. The square block was seen as the first and ultimate act of architecture – a point of intersection between technology, the sacred, and functionality: a shape referring to nothing but itself.

In the first part of the storyboard for a film on the Continuous Monument, which was published in *Casabella* in 1971, a Genesis-like story of the Monument is outlined. In it, we see how a square, the basic genome of architecture, dissolves over the world, a block being divided again and again until it dissolves in the air. The individual particles float through the air, carrying the genetic blueprint of their origin. The particles settle in every remote corner of the world. In certain parts of the world, we see concentrations of these particles forming. Such concentrations express themselves in large-scale monuments that attempt to encompass the world. The Great Wall of China, Hadrian's Wall, the Sacred Stone of Kaaba: these are sites where the essence of man reveals itself to the world.

In a text in 1969, Superstudio points to the link between the primary shape of architecture (the stone itself) and the imagination of reason: "A square block of stone placed on the earth is a primary act, it is a testimonial that architecture is the centre of the relationships of technology/sacredness/utilitarianism. It implies man, machines, rational structures and history. The square block is the first and ultimate act in the history of ideas in architecture. Architecture becomes a closed, immobile object that leads nowhere but to itself and to the use of reason."[14] The Continuous Monument considers itself an extension of this idea in the sense that it, too, sees itself as an "ultimate act", a work of architecture offering insight into the world and into oneself: "self-knowledge through architecture." The Continuous Monument is presented as a continuation of the global architecture of the great monuments. The genomes of architecture are brought together in a monument that connects different societies. The monument reflects what is common to mankind, transcending cultural, political and

6. Superstudio, *Architectural Histograms*, 1968

local values and laws and prompting man to reflect and contemplate the essence of life.

Although presented by Superstudio as a tangible object, the project never tries to posit itself as a realizable building. As Frampton puts it: "For all that they rendered the contradiction of the 'Continuous Monument' as an impenetrable mass reminiscent of Boullée, it was nonetheless a metaphysical image, as fleeting and as cryptic as the Suprematist monuments of Malevich or the 'wrapped' buildings of Christo …"[15] In the illustrations, the focus is primarily on the effect the building produces in the viewer. For, ultimately, that is the point: it is the viewer who has to change.

The basic element that constitutes and dominates the environment in the Continuous Monument is a soft-white building (recalling the Histograms project) whose mass, indifferent toward its surroundings or obstacles, penetrates every corner of the world. A grid of darker lines is superimposed on the shell of the building. The basic shape is almost the same everywhere, sometimes moving aside a little to make way, or branching off, creating a gate, a bridge … yet moving along uninterruptedly and indifferently across the surface of the earth. The highway is seen as the two-dimensional precursor to the Continuous Monument. In one of the photo-collages, the Continuous Monument runs across Manhattan. Here, it moves aside a little to make way for the centre with its enormous density and high skyscrapers. The two monuments seem to mirror each other. Here as in other illustrations, we see how the Continuous Monument leaves the existing urban fabric untouched. Reflection of the surroundings and reflection on the surroundings are what matters here. Superstudio itself describes the photomontages as disturbing images, even though, at times, they seem to present their monument as a practical means for developing the world – for instance, in a series of illustrations demonstrating how New York could be systematically divided into zones depending on population-density requirements. The result is a grid of intersecting building strips, with the spaces in between consisting of the old city fabric. As Superstudio notes, the superfluous buildings of the old city, after having been torn down, would provide plenty of space to create multiple copies of New York's beloved Central Park.

In many ways, the two founding members Cristiano Toraldo di Francia and Adolfo Natalini can be considered the driving force behind Superstudio. However, Adolfo Natalini was responsible for the Continuous Monument. This project was the first to be accompanied by the typical Superstudio photo-collages. As legend has it, Natalini and Frassinelli were visiting Archizoom one day in 1969. The two firms maintained what could be called a healthy rivalry: when members of one came to visit the offices of the other, the drawings that were being worked on there were covered. During that particular visit at the office of Archizoom however, Natalini caught a glimpse under a mountain of papers of a splendid photo-collage of a skyscraper rising above a desert. As soon as he had left, Natalini decided to illustrate his newest project, the Continuous Monument, with similar collages. Thus came about the photo-collages accompanying the story of the Continuous Monument. When comparing them to the line drawings illustrating Superstudio's *Viaggio nelle regioni della ragione* and their *Istogrammi d'architettura* we can indeed discern a shift in the manner in which they represented their ideas.

One of the reasons that Superstudio's photo-collages come across so powerfully is that the members excelled in different fields. Thus, the perspectives were indebted to the drawing skills of Piero Frassinelli who, in addition, taught the other members to work with the airbrush. Natalini was responsible for the texts and he was also the one who came up with the ideas for the illustrations. These illustrations were subsequently created by him, as well as by other members, according to his instructions. This holds true for almost all of the photo-collages linked to the Continuous Monument. An exception is a photo-collage where the Taj Mahal is incorporated in the interior of the Monument. This illustration is an example of a personal project of Piero Frassinelli. Natalini had explicitly told him that the interior of the Continuous Monument was to remain hidden from the viewer. After all, that is what the text accompanying the storyboard states: "We know that it has an interior, but we do not know what it looks like. It is open to any functional program."[16]

To represent the Continuous Monument project, Superstudio for the first time made use of different media. The ultimate goal was to make a film. For this purpose, a storyboard with illustrations as well as a vast series of collages was created. The collages provided the visual highlights. They were created in order to be used as stills in the film. For the production of the film, a sheet of transparent paper was superimposed on the collage with directions on how to zoom in on or pan across the illustration. From that moment on, it became Superstudio's endeavour to capture all their projects on film. One of the explanations advanced for this was that the members of Superstudio were fed up with having to tell the same story over and over again during lectures and presentations about their projects. A film would do this job, and distributing the film would be much easier than having to fly everywhere and tell a story.

In retrospect, Superstudio member Cristiano Toraldo di Francia notes that the Monumento Continuo was probably the project

that, as a whole, most aptly represented the ideas of the radical architecture movement. Seen within the entire history of the movement, it represents a moment when the radical procedure of destruction and progressive reduction of the architectural object culminated.

The *Atti Fondamentali*

What was there left to do after the Continuous Monument? With this project, Superstudio had advanced a proposal for an absolute architecture leaving no alternatives. What they had described prophetically, in the *Istogrammi dell'architettura*, as the *Tombe degli architetti*, the graves of the architects, had finally become Superstudio reality: architecture was declared dead. What

7. Archizoom, *Wind Town*, 1969 (photomontage)

remained was architecture as a metaphysical medium. In the project that followed, Superstudio explored the connections between architecture and real life. It became an investigation into the *Atti Fondamentali*, or Fundamental Acts. This study, also known as the *Cinque Storie*, or Five Stories, investigated the points of contact between architecture and life. The accompanying text reveals how deeply critical Superstudio was of architecture: architecture was corrupt to such an extent that even the avant-garde architect was guilty of suppressing human development, since he made use of the existing conventions in architecture. The only difference between the academic and the avant-garde architect lay in the degree of playfulness involved in their designs; the decision on the quality of life had already been made. The only way to create an environment that did not make use of repressive elements was by reversing the thought process – life itself rather than architecture was to serve as the starting point. For this purpose, five fundamentals of life were formulated: *Vita, Educazione, Cerimonia, Amore, Morte* (Life, Education, Ceremony, Love, Death). In the first advance publication, this sequence was still preceded by Birth, a subject ultimately dropped in the course of the project's development. The Fundamental Acts were intended to be realized in the form of five films, each of them dealing with one subject. In this final form, they were to serve as propaganda for ideas falling outside of the framework of traditional architectural thought. Superstudio had gained some experience with making films through the film for the *Architettura Interplanetaria* project, which was finished in 1971. In the end, two films of the Fundamental Acts were made, *Vita* and *Cerimonia*, each actually developing their themes in words and pictures, with an additional storyboard for the overall development of the film. The budget played an important role. The films which consisted of shots of photo-collages alternating with footage made by the members of Superstudio themselves with voice-overs were expensive to produce. The intention was to persuade potential sponsors with the storyboards.

Apart from the storyboards for the films and their images, each fundamental act was accompanied by a number of stories. Written like fables, love letters or parables, the stories make it hard for us to discern a coherent vision underlying them. Most of the time, the main theme is only indirectly present. Nonetheless there are two themes that recur, that of the oppressive powers ruling our lives and the role of the machine in our lives.

The first part of the project, *Vita*, was developed for the exhibition *Italy, The New Domestic Landscape* at the Museum of Modern Art in New York, which was intended as a survey of contemporary trends in Italian design. The show's curator, Emilio Ambasz, however, did not want to present only objects. He sympathized with the avant-garde movement with its radical views on society and the living environment, and consequently, decided to invite both well-known Italian designers and avant-garde groups such as Sottsass, Bellini, Colombo, Gruppo Strum, Superstudio and Archizoom. They were asked to design an "environment", a space of 8 x 8 metres that they were allowed to provide with a "programme". With the help of mirrors that covered the walls and a white floor covered with a black grid, Superstudio created an endless "supersurface". In each corner of the wall of mirrors stood a box with wires. Due to the reflection, this "plug" seemed to extend across a supersurface in a regular grid. No furniture, cabinets or any other objects were present in the space. The rejection of both design and architecture was complete. In an exhibition on Italian design, this stance was, to say the least, unusual. Other groups also created designs sounding a critical note with regard to design, but theirs were still design objects or minimalist designs, such as the environment designed by Archizoom. No other group propagated such a total rejection of design and architecture as Superstudio did.

Superstudio was able to realize the film *Vita* through a promise made by MoMA. An elaboration of their new Supersurface project subtitled "An Alternative Model

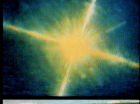

SUPERSTUDIO
PRESENTS

SUPERSURFACE
AN ALTERNATIVE MODEL
FOR
LIFE ON THE EARTH

for Life on Earth," *Vita* was intended as a proposal for a total urbanization of the world by means of a grid structure of facilities. Since none of these facilities rise to take the shape of a three-dimensional structure, that is, of architecture, one could just as well speak of a total de-urbanization, where everything becomes landscape.

The film shows the earth being covered with a layer housing all facilities. This supersurface consists of a plane obliterating virtually any geographic features. The plane has a grid through which energy and information are transmitted. At the intersections of the grid there are plugs allowing one to plug in. In this way, man would be able to live as a nomad, without excess baggage restricting his movement. At certain moments, it would be possible to plug in, and a microclimate would instantly be created. Food, electricity and information flow in through the plug. The physical separation between inside and outside disappears. Depending on the population density, the appearance of the supersurface changes – from parallel strips to a continuous grid. With the Supersurface project, we seem to have landed in the desert. Watching the film, however, we learn that plugs can also be located in the open field, an image not nearly as forbidding as the uncanny white surface of the supersurface. But how forbidding is it? A partial answer can be found in the text accompanying the film. Through the nomadic lifestyle without the restrictions of personal property, man would be able to lead a perfect human life. Beyond the chaos of super-consumption and the throwaway society, a world could emerge where the mind is energy and matter, the ultimate consumer product. Unfettered by burdens such as work and materialistic possessions, man will turn to fully perfecting his own mental and physical faculties: "Stories, songs, music, dancing will be the words we speak and tell ourselves. Life will be the only environmental art."[17] Although the *demonstratio per absurdum* is evident here too, the basic message is less ironic and more hopeful. As a metaphor for a world in which the emotional and spiritual development of man comes close to its perfection, the Supersurface cannot be called forbidding. With the Supersurface in the back of one's mind, a link can be drawn to *homo ludens*, playing man, as characterized by the Dutch cultural historian Johan Huizinga in 1938.[18] In the writings of Constant Nieuwenhuys, *homo ludens* appears as man needing to free himself of the repressive consequences of modern society – most repressive of all, according to Constant, was work, a view that can be considered prophetic in light of the emerging hippie generation and its stance toward work, – in order to use progress to liberate himself (from work) and be able to dedicate himself to play and spiritual development.[19]

In certain respects, the concept of the supersurface drew on the vision of Archigram who, with their mobile architecture, their servoskins, and their project of the "instant city", had already pursued the idea of creating an individually adjustable climate. The most significant projects in this regard were Mike Webb's "Cushicle" of 1966 and Peter Cook's "Nomad" of 1968. The main difference between them and Superstudio was that, in Archigram's case, the question remained how a man was going to carry everything with him, a problem Superstudio cleverly eliminated with the Plugs.

The only subject picked up following *Vita* was that of Death. In addition to the usual project components of storyboard, narrative, and collages (this was one of the projects that Sandro Poli was partly responsible for during his short career with Superstudio), in 1971 and 1973 two competition entries for cemeteries were designed. The first was for a cemetery in Modena. In their design from 1971, they came up with a monumental space in which the memories of the deceased are captured and recorded on state-of-the-art recording instruments. This serves to eliminate the mystique surrounding death. Accordingly, the need to construct buildings that support this mystique would disappear as well: "We have no need anymore for an architecture of death. Our only architecture will be our life." Two years later, however, they designed a cemetery in Urbino. It takes the shape of a burial mound adapting to its surroundings and referencing the burial mounds found throughout the world. There is no rejection of architecture here. In Urbino, the struggle of Superstudio – in favour of or against architecture – has come to an end. Although Superstudio officially ceased to exist only in 1978, its radical period can be said to end in 1973. After that, Superstudio withdrew into all sorts of didactic projects at the Faculty of Architecture in Florence such as Global Tools, involving most of the members of Superstudio. As a group, Superstudio realized two more buildings after 1973, a pharmacy in Lübeck, Germany, and an office building in S. Croce sull'Arno, both from 1976. How ironic that, after pronouncing architecture dead, Superstudio still produced two buildings.

Archizoom and No-Stop City

In 1972, Archizoom stated: "Nowadays there can be no hesitation in admitting that the urban phenomenon is the weakest point in the whole industrial system. The metropolis, once the traditional 'birthplace of progress,' is today, in fact, the most backward and confused sector of Capital in its actual state. And this is true to such an extent, that one is led to wonder if the modern city is nothing more than a problem which has not been solved."[20] At that moment, Archizoom had already been working on the No-Stop City project for three years. Astonishingly, this project was created at roughly the same time as the Continuous Monument. On this, Cristiano Toraldo di Francia writes: "In the same period Archizoom, too, arrived at a refusal of the figurative role of architecture and the modification of its structures of use, through another metaphor: The No-Stop City."[21] Just like the Continuous Monument, it wanted to offer, at least theoretically, an alternative to the existing urban fabric, without, however, the pervasive irony of the former. As a project, No-Stop City was much more aggressive, and although Archizoom described their project as an investigation into the relationship man–world, man–built environment, their uncompromising presentation often suggested that they were advancing actual proposals.

A desire for architectureless architecture was the starting point of this project: the first plans made by Andrea Branzi within the context of the No-Stop City project consisted of typescripts, sheets of paper simply drawn over with a grid of dots and Xs (using a simple typewriter). These sheets embodied the first ideas for an architecture as yet not designed, but potentially coinciding with issues of microclimate, lighting. For, as Branzi asks, "What is a city? You could say that a city is a bath every 100 metres, or a computer every 40 metres, etc. These are quantifiable data making up a city."[22] The idea of a city lacking any direction, divided up by structures without any sense of form, corresponded to the economic system that lacked direction and was without a future as well. The typescripts have never been published: Archizoom feared architects would find them too threatening.

In 1970, the project was presented in *Casabella*. The graphic development had not progressed very far yet, but the theoretical framework did not leave anything to the imagination. From the accompanying exposition it was clear that the members of Archizoom meant business: a new society based on quantitative parameters was supposed to replace the existing social structure. The metropolis, originally the mother of modern developments, increasingly lagged behind reality and became ever more of a mystery to itself. To Archizoom, the metropolis actually already belonged to history. Accordingly, the idea behind No-Stop City was not to develop a metropolis better tailored to the needs of man and coordinating them more effectively, but rather to grasp the exact nature of the objective urban-architectural laws underpinning society at that time. Governed by qualitative processes that served to reinforce and cement long-standing shortcomings, the city was supposed to use the processes of production and consumption – the only processes that were quantifiable and thus capable of serving as the basis of a rational society – to create a new urban reality. No-Stop City was to be a city without quality, based on the accumulation of basic direct processes, that is, without the mediation of architecture.

Not everyone agreed with these ideas, as evidenced by an editorial statement accompanying the publication of the project in *Casabella*. In it, Giovanni Klaus Koenig, *Casabella* editor and

8. The members of Archizoom in front of their office, Florence 1968

9. Archizoom, *Parallel Districts in Berlin*, 1969

Just as Archizoom focused on the supermarket and the parking garage as prototypes for urban development, Superstudio posited the highway as the precursor of the Continuous Monument. In Superstudio's case, the highway analogy did not come as a surprise: the idea of man as a nomad without a permanent place of residence, roaming around the world without any worldly possessions, had occupied their minds for quite some time already, a concern culminating in the Supersurface. In Archizoom's case, the images of the supermarket and the parking garage, as well as the assembly line, derived from their theoretical discourse on the city. These models already informed the presentations of both groups in the two *Superarchitettura* exhibitions. The Le Corbusier show 1963 in Palazzo Strozzi in Florence (the interior for the exhibition was designed by Leonardo Savioli) clearly had an impact on the further ideological development of each of their members. Le Corbusier's plans served as an example of a modernist architecture that, through its uncompromising appearance, forced a dialogue between contemporary modernism and a historically grown cultural context. While, for Archizoom, the plan for Chandigarh served as a source of inspiration, in the case of Superstudio, a link can be established to Le Corbusier's plan for Algiers, in which a highway winds along the coastline over the roof of a long residential block.

Critiques of the urban utopias of Superstudio and Archizoom published in recent years are frequently incapable of articulating the ambiguous character of the projects. Although Natalini himself describes the Continuous Monument as a negative utopia, one can point to elements where this does not hold true. In particular, the passages of the text that refer to the building's metaphysical dimension as an all-embracing monument transcending the local cultural context and alluding to the meditative nature of reflection – of surface as well as of the individual looking out over the landscape of city and nature from within the building – seem to point in a different direction. With this poetic approach to their project, Superstudio seems to explore the last hope of salvation for architecture. The project may also be seen as a run-up to

professor at the School of Architecture of the University of Florence, distances himself, on behalf of the editorial board, from the publication. The only reason he gives is that, in his eyes, the authors are trying to compete with the great philosophers of the world without their exposition providing any foundation for it. However, he does hasten to note, "But I do have to inform the reader that this represents my personal opinion and that Archizoom's approach to the ideological debate at least has the merit of being new and doubtlessly finds broad support among the young."[23]

The full impact of the project followed in March 1971, when *Domus* magazine published the second part of No-Stop City: Residential Parkings. The sketchy plans of the previous publication were now developed to an alarmingly realizable extent. An example is the section across a continuous urban structure indicating the infrastructure and the various functions for each level. The illustrations are, in many cases, so disturbingly functional that people legitimately asked where this was heading: a realistic model for urban development? Moreover, it would not have been the first time for a megalomaniac project to inspire a political leader. In the case of No-Stop City, it was the combination of a project of potentially endless dimensions with a Marxist ideology of egalitarianism that, combined, held forth a promise of sweeping social revolution – there was, in other words, considerably less irony involved than in Superstudio's Continuous Monument. Although Archizoom, too, was able to provide their project with some subtlety of nuance (in the text accompanying the No-Stop City project, they describe it as a critical utopia presented as a model), they seem to ask the public why No-Stop City's vision of the future would be any less desirable than the current state of society.

10. Lucia Bartolini / Archizoom: D.I.Y. clothing system, 1972

the *Cinque Storie* which focuses on life and reflection from these metaphysical standpoints. Ironically enough, to Branzi this last reading, in particular, appears to be quintessential, as he describes the Continuous Monument, in his essay in this volume, as a work of architecture that is "in a position to impose order and cosmic meaning on the faceless metropolis."

But this ambiguity of negation on top of negation is precisely what lends the projects their appeal. The structure itself of the Continuous Monument, which, as a presence, exerts both an attractive and a repelling force, is always at the radiant centre of this discourse. The exposition accompanying the storyboards makes no mention whatsoever of a possible negative reading of the project. We should bear in mind here the principle of *demonstratio per absurdum* underlying Superstudio's projects: the text in itself says nothing about the interpretation of the project as a whole, every aspect of the project is suffused with irony, with layers of meaning merging as a result. And sometimes that is all there is: the poetic interplay of words and images where Superstudio's artistic side gains the upper hand over its radical side. Piero Frassinelli describes the Continuous Monument as "utterly beautiful, utterly neutral and everyone could see their own ideas reflected in it. This inevitably gives rise to the ambiguity that was part of our work, as in any human expression: the stimulating and frustrating possibility of being able to see each work, each action, each word interpreted differently, even antagonistically."[24] Still, critics attempting to pigeonhole the project can be seen to ignore the poetically layered aspect of the project. And wrongly so, since this, too, is one of the essential aspects of the project deriving from its specific historical context.

The ambiguity of No-Stop City lies in the conflict between the project's seeming capacity to be realized and its conceptual character. While Natalini dubs the Continuous Monument an anti-utopia, Archizoom describes No-Stop City as a critical utopia. In both designations, the negation of utopia is evident. This would seem to allow the conclusion observable in all members of the radical avant-garde: that they were unwilling to proselytize. "Utopia has always meant for man the distant winking of a star, fountain of illusory experiences and irrealizable dreams to shield us from the horror of the real. But reality alone can generate the determination to look for the road of salvation … In the anti-utopia we nourish the little monsters that creep and twist themselves through the dark recesses of our homes, in the dirty angles of our lives and even in the mysterious folds of our brains … For we know that our terrible monsters are only made of smoke while the fragile red flower the utopists cultivate is like the poppy; in its corolla lies the white substance we really fear."[25] If there was a factor lending the radical movement coherence it was their rejection of the rigidity prevailing at existing institutes. Or, as Branzi contentedly stated afterwards: "Radical Architecture has not produced any new formal vocabulary or aesthetics, but rather a new approach, a new critical energy in architecture."[26] This new critical way has equipped the Post-modern architect with new tools, making it possible to probe deeper and more thoroughly into the complex fabric of a society in crisis. The notion of ambiguity in architecture and society that the radicals helped to bring to light and put up for discussion in their projects enabled other movements such as Deconstructivism, Postmodernism and Post-structuralism to formulate a new world view that transcended the quest for all-encompassing meta-narratives the modern era had pursued.

Notes

1 Peter Cook writes on the reasons for the rapid development of radical ideas in Florence compared to the rest of the world: "If it is able to look out upon the rest of the world, then it is from a safe distance from Cape Canaveral, the galleries of New York and Düsseldorf, and even the smelly factories of the Po valley. Moreover, there is a special animal that inhabits the Italian Architecture school: … necessarily of the left and obliged to couch even the most simple piece of architectural description in terms of history, cultural cross-reference and philosophical jargon. How difficult was it for young Adolfo (a very bright local lad who had started out as a Pop Art painter) to energize some of his more aristocratic friends into reacting to the stimulus of the outside world? Moreover, there was hardly an insistent or threatening local milieu of mainstream architects to worry about."
2 Rosalia Mannu Tolu, Lara-Vinca Masini, Alessandro Poli: *Leonardo Savioli, il segno generatore di forma-spazio*. Perugia: Edimond, 1995.
3 For a wealth of factual information on the Superarchitettura exhibition see Peter Lang and William Menking in *Superstudio: Life without Objects*. Milan: Skira, 2003.
4 Paola Navone and Bruno Orlandoni, *Architettura radicale*. Documenti di Casabella, 1974.
5 Manifesto accompanying the 1966 exhibition "Superarchitettura." Translated in: C. Toraldo di Francia, *Superstudio & Radicals*. Japan Interior Inc., 1982.
6 Paul Ginsborg, *Storia d' Italia dal dopoguerra a oggi*. Turin: Einaudi, 1989.
7 P.C. Santini, "*Giovani Studi a Firenze*" in *Ottagono*, 27 (1972).
8 M.F. dell'Arco, "*The futurist construction of the universe*" in E. Ambasz (ed.), *Italy, the New Domestic Landscape*. New York: MoMA 1972.
9 Hans van Dijk, "Tekens van leegte" in *Wonen TA/BK*, 16/17 (1984).
10 Kenneth Frampton, *Modern Architecture: A Critical History*. London: Thames & Hudson, 1980; rev. ed. 1987.
11 Peter Cook, "Natalini Superstudio" in *Architectural Review*, 1021 (1982).
12 Manifesto accompanying "Istogrammi d'architettura" in the exhibition catalog *Superstudio, storie con figure 1966–73*. Florence: Galleria Vera Biondi, 1979.
13 Walter Pichler and Hans Hollein, *Absolute Architecture*, manifesto accompanying an exhibition at Galerie nächst St. Stephan, Vienna.
14 Superstudio, quoted by Cristiano Toraldo di Francia, *Superstudio and Radicals*. Japan Interior Inc., 1982.
15 Frampton, loc. cit. (rev. ed.), p. 288.
16 *Casabella* 358 (1971).
17 *Casabella* 367 (1972).
18 Johan Huizinga, *Homo Ludens. Proeve eener bepaling van het spel-element der cultuur*. Haarlem: privately published, 1938. Engl. ed., *Homo Ludens: A Study of the Play Element in Culture*. New York: J.J. Harper Editions, 1970.
19 Constant Nieuwenhuys, *Opstand van de Homo Ludens*. Bussum: Paul Brand, 1969.
20 Archizoom manifesto, in Jim Burns, *Arthropods: New Design Futures*. London: Academy Editions, 1972.
21 Toraldo di Francia, loc. cit.
22 Andrea Branzi in a lecture held at the Berlage Institute in Rotterdam, October 30, 2001.
23 Giovanni Klaus Koenig in *Casabella* (July–August 1970).
24 Frassinelli in Lang and Menking, *Superstudio: Life without Objects*.
25 Toraldo di Francia, loc. cit.
26 Branzi, lecture at the Berlage Institute in Rotterdam, October 30, 2001.

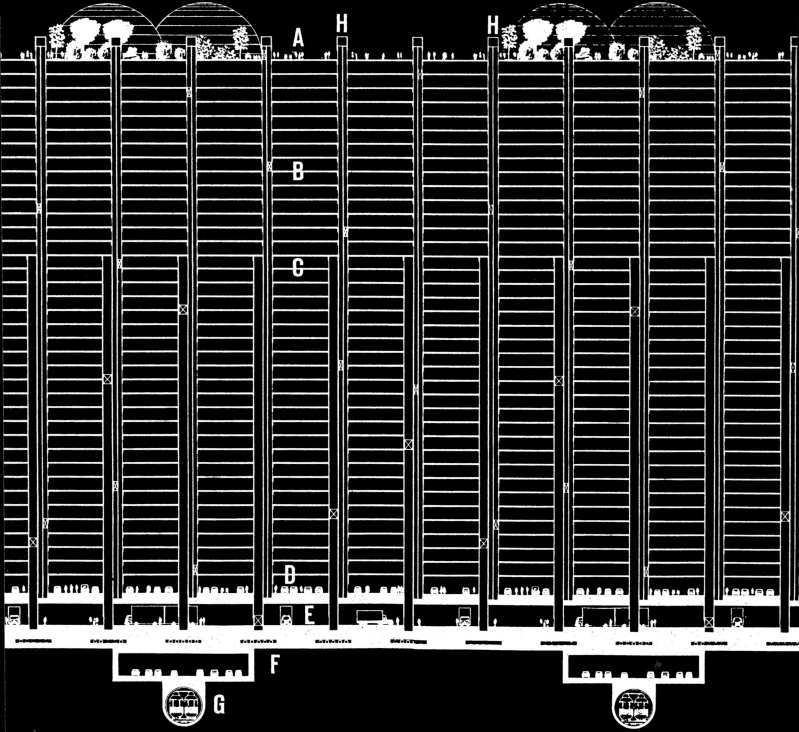

2

RESIDENTIAL PARKINGS

CLIMATIC UNIVERSAL SISTEM

by archizoom associates

Nowadays there can be no hesitation in admitting that the urban phenomenon is the weakest point in the whole industrial system. The metropolis, once the traditional "birthplace of progress", is today, in fact, the most backward and confused sector of Capital in its actual state: and this is true to such an extent, that one is led to wonder if the modern city is nothing more than a problem which has not been solved, or if, in reality, it is not a historical phenomenon which has been objectively superseded. That is, we must determine whether Capital still confronts the task of managing its own organization and image on an urban level, as it did a hundred years ago, or whether the changes which have taken and are taking place have not altered its actual sphere of action, thus transforming the concept of the city. The problem then is no longer that of creating a metropolis which is more humane and better organized, but rather that of understanding the objective laws which control the shaping of the urban-architectural phenomenon, demystifying the complex ideology which surrounds the discussion and conditions the form it takes.

According to the naturalistic myth of free competition, it was the city, as a centre for trade and commerce that guaranteed ideal market conditions, making for a natural equilibrium between opposite interests, in the general background of the harmony reached between technology and nature. But now the use of electronic media takes the place of the direct urban praxis: artificial inducements to consumption allow a much deeper infiltration into the social structure than did the city's weak channels

interests no longer needs to be organized on the spot where trade is to take place. The complete penetrability and accessibility of the territory does away with the terminus city and permits the organization of a progressive network of organisms of control over the area.

In the bourgeois ideology ecological balance and social justice become part of the same battle: the appearance of the city gives a formal verification of this equilibrium. In Town Planning, therefore, an attempt is made to achieve a not impossible harmony between the Public interest and the Private interest: these two categories, however, are always taken as antithetical, contrasting and irreconcilable phenomena. The problem therefore becomes that of finding a two-dimensional net, to guarantee the fitting together of these irreconcilable components. The traffic can be taken as the most general means of communication between the two, as it becomes the objective and figurative scheme of the functioning of urban life. In fact roads do not merely serve the compact fabric of what is private, but they also dissect it and make it communicating, making way for the emergence of architectonic language. The skyline becomes a diagram of the natural accumulation which has taken place of Capital itself. So the bourgeois metropolis remains mainly a visual place, and its experience remains tied to that type of communication.

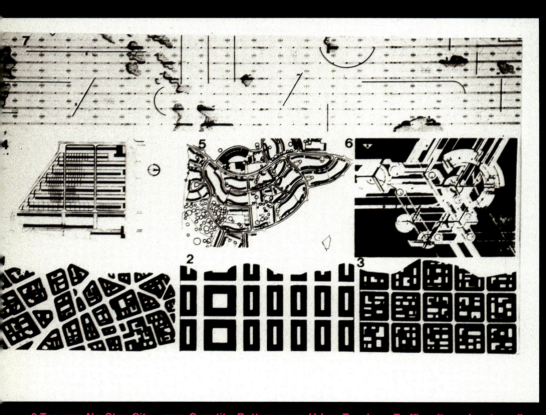

3 Top row: No-Stop City – pure Quantity. Bottom rows: Urban Typology, Traffic; city and metropolis as 'place' and representation.

of information. The metropolis ceases to be a "place", to become a "condition": in fact, it is just this condition which is made to circulate uniformly, through Consumer Products, in the social phenomenon. The future dimension of the metropolis coincides with that of the market itself.

The intensively concentrated metropolis corresponds to the now superseded phase of spontaneous accumulation of Capital. In a programmized society, the management of

The carrying out of a social organization of labour by means of Planning eliminates the empty space in which Capital expanded during its growth period. In fact, no

Original typescript *Homogeneous Living Diagrams / Hypothesis for a non-figurative Architectural Language.*

ARCHIZOOM ASSOCIATI
DIAGRAMMA ABITATIVO
OMOGENEO

IPOTESI DI LINGUAGGIO
ARCHITETTONICO NON FIGURATIVO

strutt
ra mont
ante.

maglia.
dimensi
nale.

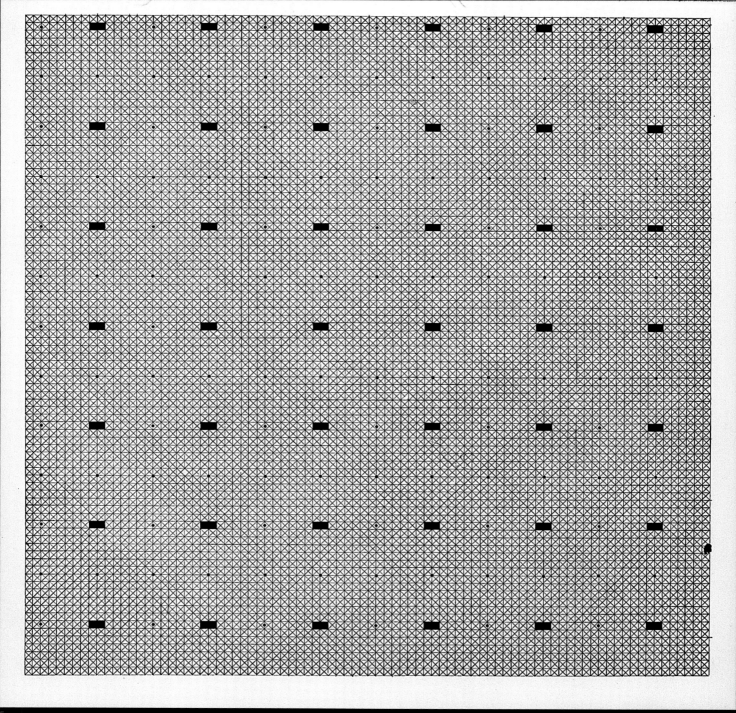

reality exists any longer outside the system itself: the whole visual relationship with reality loses importance as there ceases to be any distance between the subject and the phenomenon. The city no longer "represents" the system, but becomes the system itself, programmed and isotropic, and within it the various functions are contained homogeneously, without contradictions.

Production and Consumption possess one and the same ideology, which is that of Programming. Both hypothesize a social and physical reality completely continuous and undifferentiated. No other realities exist. The factory and the supermarket become the specimen models of the future city: optimal urban structures, potentially limitless, where human functions are arranged spontaneously in a free field,

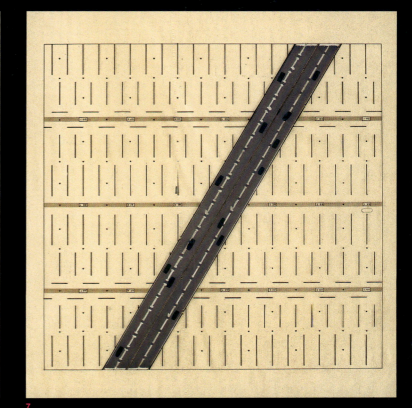

6

7

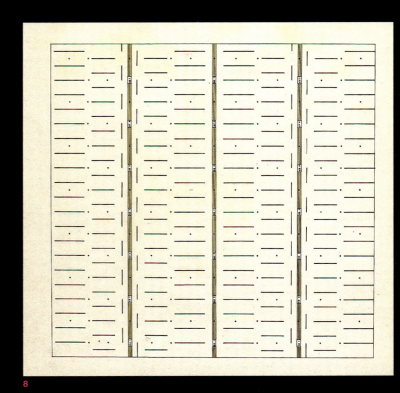

8

made uniform by a system of micro-
acclimatization and optimal circulation of information. The "natural
and spontaneous" balance of light
and air is superseded: the house
becomes a well-equipped parking lot.
Inside it there exist no hierarchies
nor spatial figurations of a conditioning nature.

Typology, as a functional figuration
of society, undecided between the
certain datum of a survey of a social
structure and the almost certain
datum of an assumption of the aspirations of that society, rests so
entangled in the allegorical representation of such a conflict that it
becomes an extra-functional cultural
coefficient. In an attempt to supply
the user with the highest degree
of liberty within the most rigid
possible "figuration", architecture
comes to recognize its real destiny
in the urban phenomenon, and its
real nature in the private. Thus,
in contradictory fashion, on each
single occasion it will prefigure
a general lay-out of things and
at the same time set itself up to

Homogeneous Living Diagrams: Theme and variations in the
Megasociety. Neutral floor plan based on isotropic grid.
Complete liberation from spurious Architectural determinism.

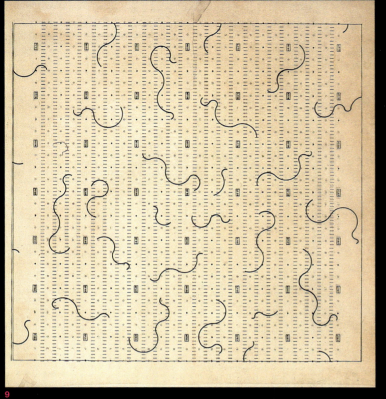

9

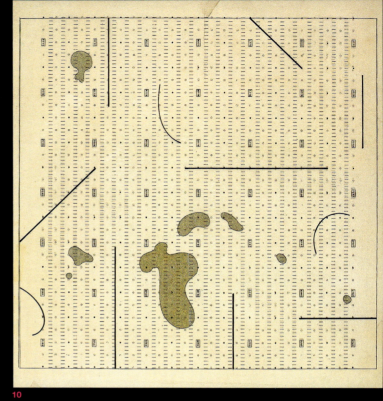

10

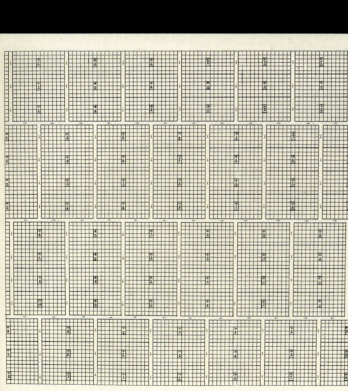

13

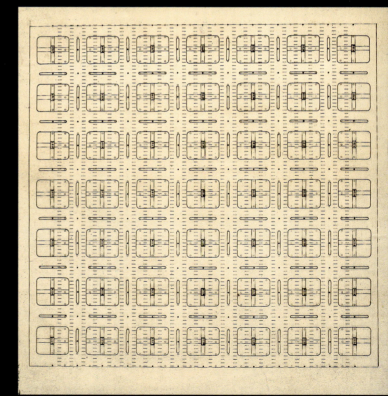

14

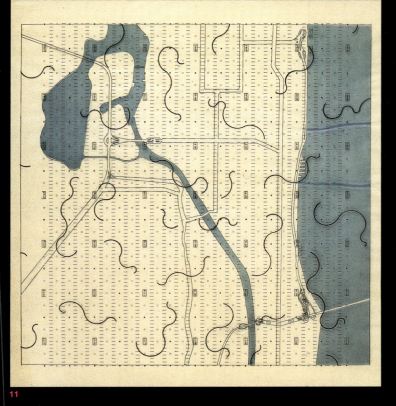

11

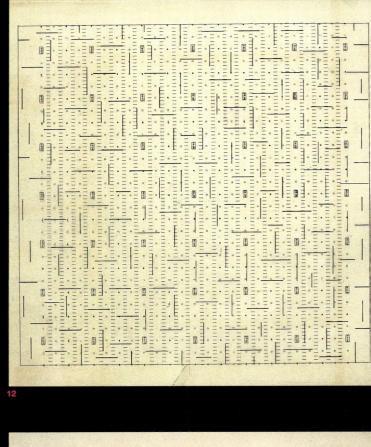

12

15

16

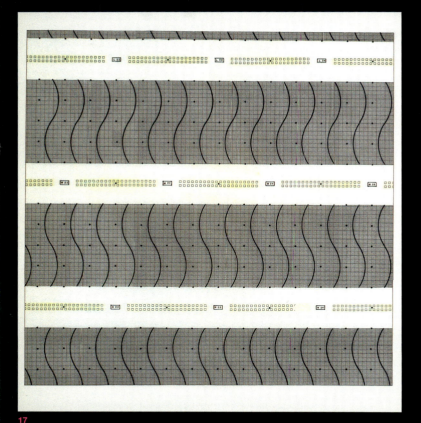

17

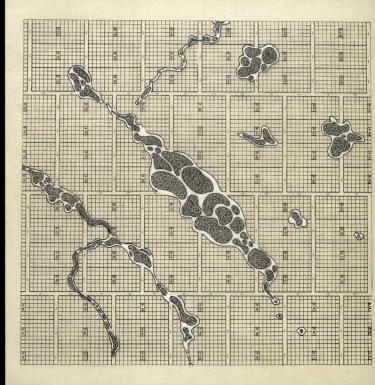

18

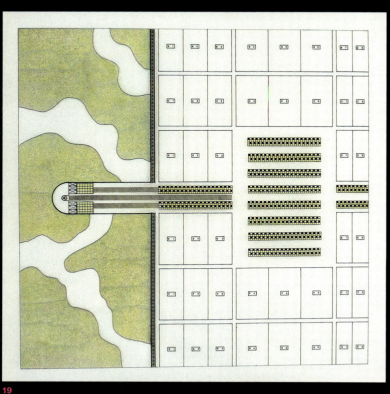

19

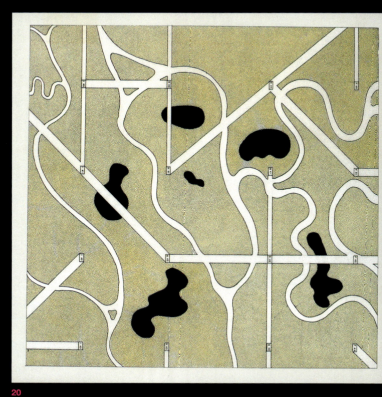

20

The two diagrams below show the edge of a built-up volume (with a 'house of sexual instruction' protruding) and rooftop gardens (fig. 19, 20 resp.).

The section, fig. 23, shows the stacking of interchangeable residential floors and service levels.

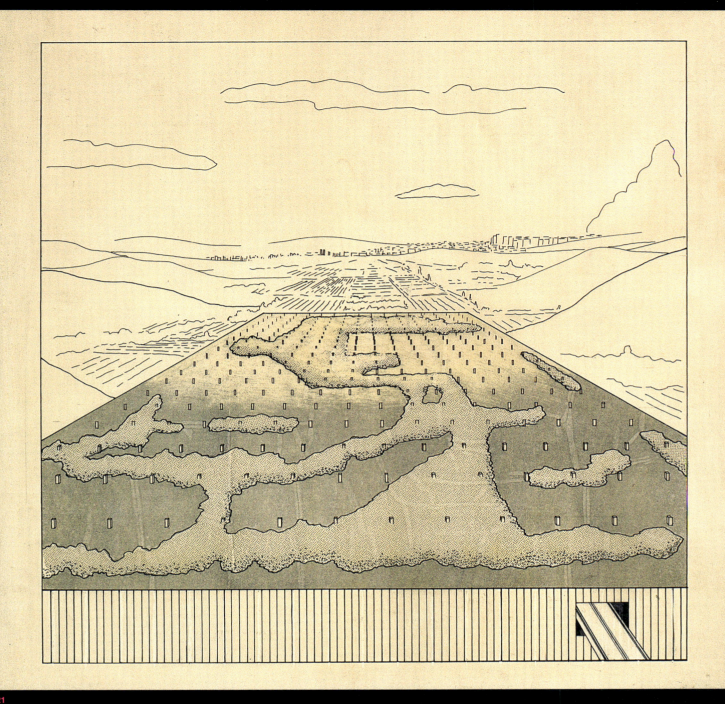

21

defend the partiality of the individual
experience with respect to collective
experiences. Thus it mediates between
the contradicting forces of public and
private: now, however, this conflict is
no longer left on the speculative level
of existential consciousness. Economic
Planning, by organizing the whole of
society productively, eliminates the
conflict, considers the contradiction
fictitious and takes any strictly individual datum as experimental.

Up till now, the mass of the general public has been excluded from the architectonic phenomenon: being temporary guests
of the integrative 'Existenzminimum' of
a much more real day's work, people have
used home only to eat and sleep in. Inside
the house everything had been thought
out by an architecture whose aim was to
console: nothing was left but to hang
a few pictures on the walls. The house
was the first, most important step in
the total adoption of the bourgeois way

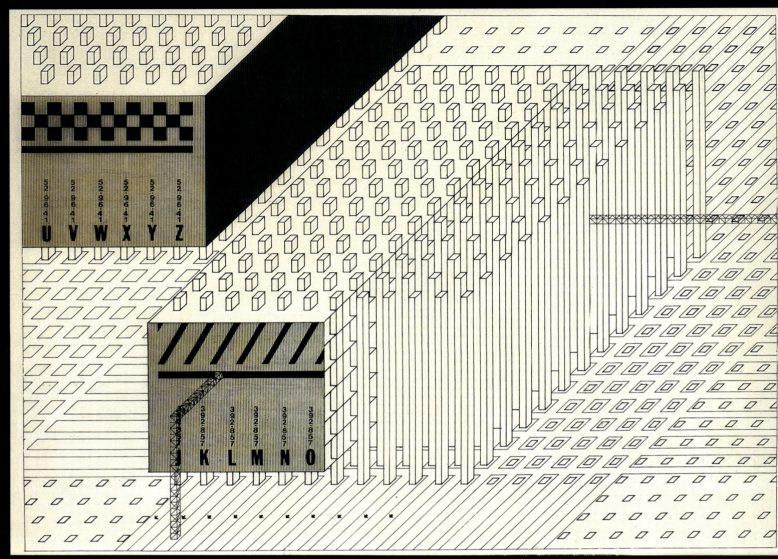

22 Homogeneous plans/elevator and service shafts extruded.

of life. But now people, being strength-
ened by the new and ever increasing
capacity to decide for themselves, which
they have won at work, must take housing
into their own hands, freeing it from
all preconstituted cultural and social
models, breaking the subtle intellectual
links and hysterical linguistic knots
which characterize architecture as the
figuration of space. Freed from the armour
of its own character, architecture must
become an open structure, accessible to
intellectual mass production as the only
force symbolizing the collective landscape. Therefore, the problem becomes
that of freeing mankind from architecture
insomuch as it is a formal structure.

Nowadays the only possible utopia is
quantitative. Social conflict is no
longer going through the phase of the

confrontation of alternative models,
but is in that of dialectical negotiation
between a balanced development of the
system and the growing cost of the labour
force. The clash no longer takes place in
the field of ideology but in quantitative
terms: it is via this parameter that the
summing together is made possible of different phenomena which apparently have
no link with one another. Quantitative
language replaces qualitative, thus becoming the only scientific means of approach
to the undifferentiated stratification
of production and hence of reality. As
general terms of reference disappear,
behaviour becomes a structure free from
moral allegories. Freedom, as an end,
becomes an instrument of struggle.

First published in Domus 496, March 1971

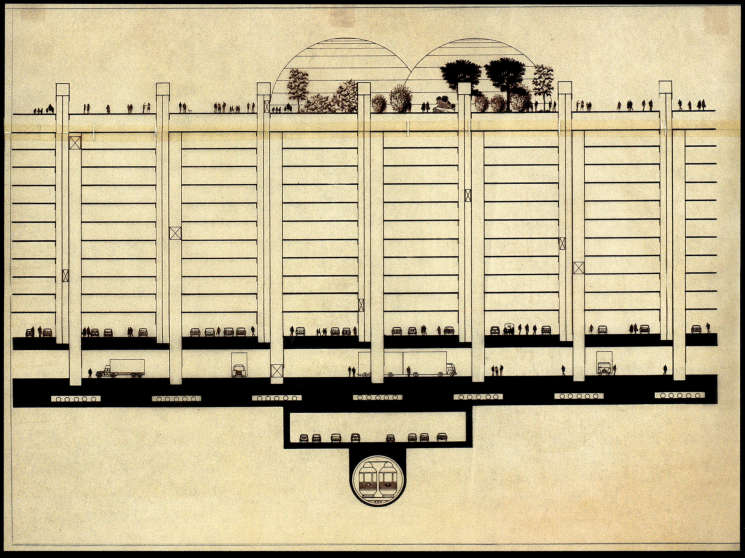

23

By comparison, fig. 1 – a more sophisticated, later version of the drawing – shows greater stratification, zone B being reserved for dwelling and levels C accommodating services/business. In both sections, the lower levels provide space for parking (D), bulk delivery of goods (E), with infrastructural thoroughfares (motorway, F, and underground railways, G) passing below. Rooftop parks and gardens (A) provide for additional, "natural" recreation.

25/26 Plans of No-Stop City. Zoning on Services level: A. Library B. Exhibition Spaces C. School D. Theatre E. Offices F. Cinema G. Supermarket H. Restaurant. Below: Parking level.

24

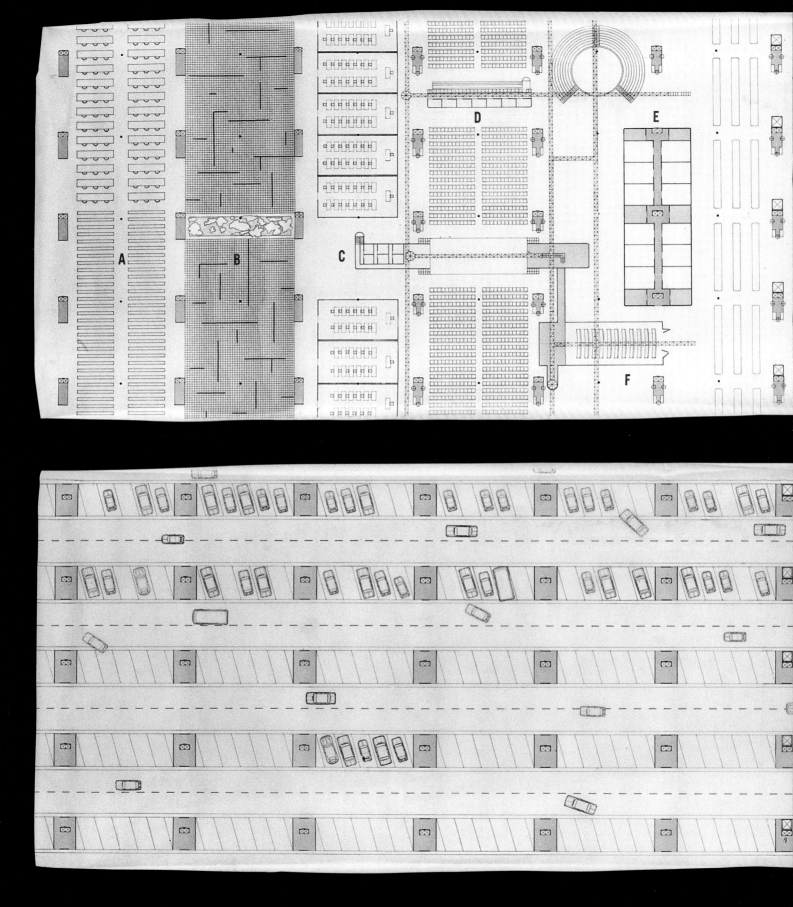

"To become the master of one's own life, one must first of all *free oneself from work*. This is the only way in which to recover all the untapp

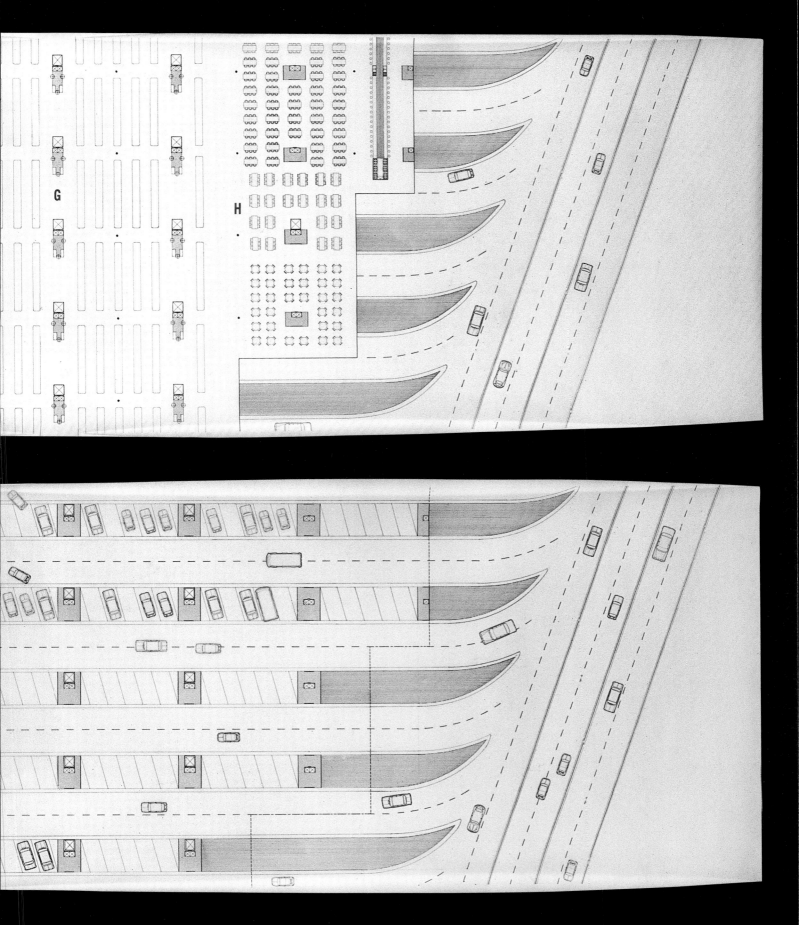

G

H

eative faculty that man has available within himself, which has become atrophied throughout the centuries because of frustrating work.

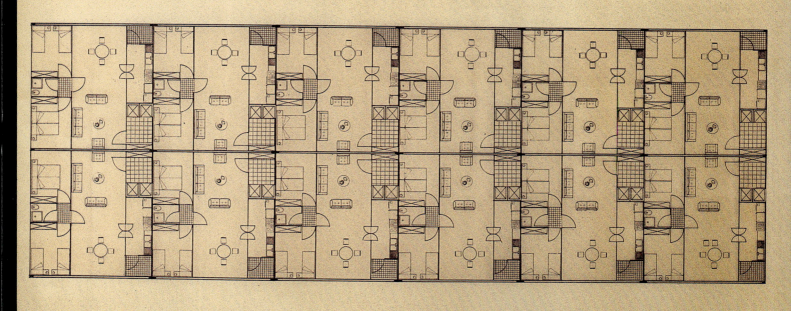

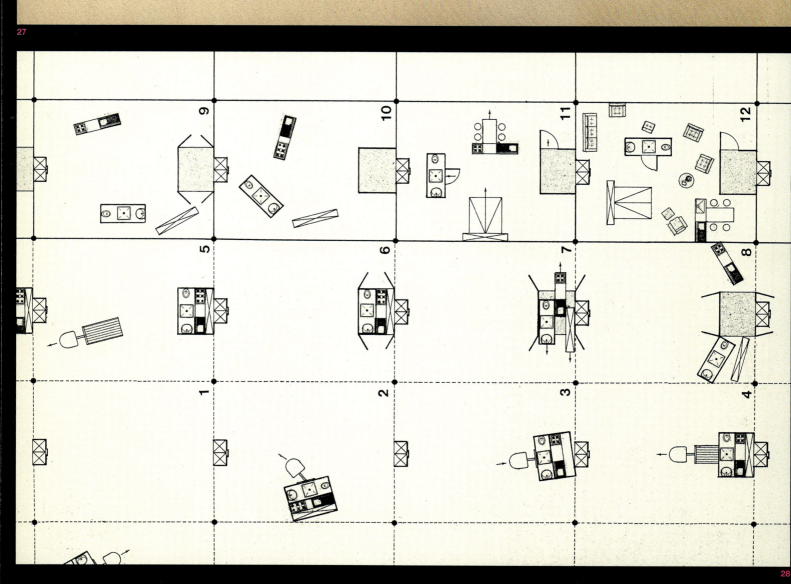

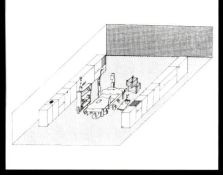

29

The home — that small, functional organization at the service of the tiny production company that is the family — imitates in its forms and furnishings that culture and those choices no user has ever made, nor has ever had time enough to test.

Only by rejecting work as an extraneous presence in one's life can one picture a new use for the home: a perpetual laboratory for one's own creative faculties, which are continually being tried out and continually being surpassed.

So, then, it's no longer of any importance to imagine the form of this home, because the only thing that matters is the use made of it. Its image is manifold, never final, and has no codified meaning nor spatial hierarchy.

A kind of 'furnished parking lot,' from which all antecedent types have vanished, giving way to a spontaneous shaping of the environment; a completely accessible enclosure within which to exercise one's regained freedom of action and judgment."

From *Italy: The New Domestic Landscape*, 1973

27. Privacy: Standardized, fixed living quarters. Classic single-family patio housing type, ready to be cloned *ad infinitum* within the neutral framework — should the wish arise.

28, 29. Temporary residence system. Life from a closet: mobile, integrated equipment providing all basic necessities, and additional comforts.

30, 31. Two examples of a "Residential wood": with all the services in place or at hand, infinite possibilities are created for Camping in the Great Indoors.

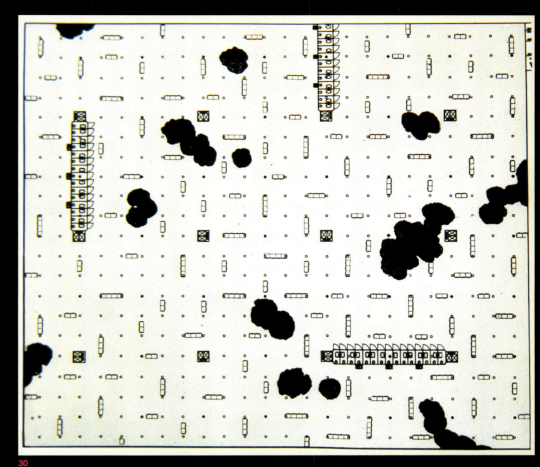

30

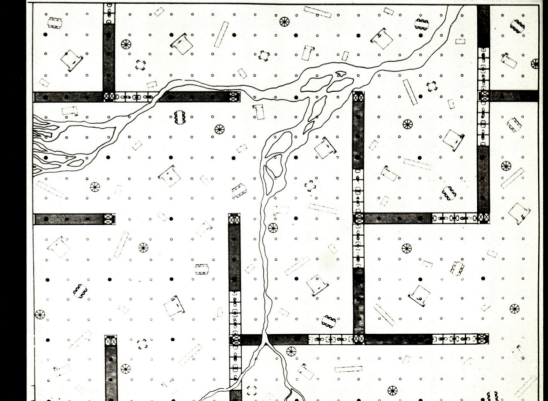

31

Interior Landscapes: Man moves in to create his own relationships within a structured environmen

a lower Services level, No-Stop Theatre: non-stop happenings and other joyous spectacles. Next page: Aerial views

Notes on

NO-STOP CITY: ARCHIZOOM ASSOCIATES 1969–72

Andrea Branzi

Until recently, the Radical Movement was considered a unitary phenomenon incorporating many groups involved in a single critical and conceptual front that by 1966 was undermining the certitudes and optimism of classical Modernism, thereby marking the onset of a prolonged, indeed ongoing era of crisis.

I believe that to gain a better grasp of this movement, one first has to delve deeper into the various theoretical currents irrigating it and to consider the Radical Movement not as a monolith but as a reality composed of diverse individuals who in time produced completely different results.

A substantial number of the present-day stars of the modern architectural firmament admit some debt to the movement and bear evident traces of a similar approach to tackling the relationship between city and architecture and between the project and the discipline: Frank Gehry, Hans Hollein, Daniel Libeskind, Arata Isozaki, Toyo Ito, Rem Koolhaas, Bernard Tschumi and many others were either one-time active militants or acknowledge the Radical Movement as the starting point of a new approach to creating architecture. Even the post-modernist movement of the 1980s could never have seen the light of day without these distant predecessors, who were the first to catch on to the change in the political and urban conditions in the West, welcoming it as an opportunity to explore the internal fractures in the culture of the project.

After so many years, the moment has arrived to analyse more closely the basic characteristics of the components of the Radical Movement and to deal with some of the genetic projects it characterized. In this connection, I will provide a personal account of No-Stop City by Archizoom Associati, of which I was a member; a "generational" project as Cathérine David defined it in an attempt to detail its genesis and goals on the occasion of the 1997 Documenta.

This project, begun in 1969 and published for the first time the very next year in *Casabella* 350–351, and around which work continued until 1972, didn't emerge in an improvised way as mere polemical posturing, but was the fruit of a lengthy incubation period. Operating with the tools of the discipline, it confronted a number of complex political issues that came to the fore during that era. To tell the story of No-Stop City therefore provides an opportunity to address a host of other questions that lie behind, within and before.

To reconstruct the debates in whose context No-Stop City has its roots is to deal simultaneously with the onset of the crisis of modern politics and its agenda to shape social developments and urbanism along reformist lines. Modern Architecture was one of the fundamental instruments of this political outlook.

European rationalism saw progress as a long, hard road leading to a society of order and continuous development – a trail that could be blazed only by industrialization, the sole force able to adequately overcome all the backwardness, contradictions and limits present in society – contradictions and limitations that in all cases were to be ascribed to delays and imperfections in the process of industrialization.

This collective, democratic and benign vision of a common journey towards progress had devolved upon modern architecture its function as an instrument (also figurative) of social recomposition. From Lewis Mumford to Sigfried Giedion and Nikolaus Pevsner, from Carlo Giulio Argan to Ernesto N. Rogers, from Leonardo Benevolo to Gillo Dorfles, theoreticians of architecture and masters of the art alike all advocated a fruitful, democratic dialogue between planners and political authority.

Le Corbusier dedicated his book *Vers une architecture* to "the Authorities," while Walter Gropius spoke and wrote of "Integrated Architecture" as an instrument of a social-democratic order: an architecture, therefore, capable of embracing both social factors and political antagonisms, of resolving them positively in a push for progress that was both technological and aesthetic.

1. Paris, May 1968: the great hangover

2. Paris, May 1968

More than one book has appeared outlining the reasons for the breakdown of this ideal that affected every Western country after 1964. I have no ambition to delve deeply into this historical theme, by analyzing, for instance, what lay behind this unexpected reversal and the ensuing turn to Revolution – or for what reasons this Revolution failed to materialize.

I would like to remark, however, that I found an indirect but more satisfying response to this question in the pages certain French historians have devoted not to this Failed Revolution that we are concerned with, but to a successful one that occurred two centuries before: the French Revolution. All – from the great Alexis de Toqueville to Pierre Gaxotte and François Furet – strove to disentangle the inextricable jumble of contradictions, of genius and stupidity, and even of suicidal drives that lie behind this great historical cataclysm.

The outmoded Marxist schemes that interpret history as the stage for a conflict between rich and poor, between employers and workers, between whites and blacks, have bequeathed oversimplified theories that yoke together theology and politics – ill-adapted to account for revolutions which are by their nature more complex yet simultaneously simpler (and therefore more contradictory) than such a broad-brush approach allows.

I believe that François Furet furnished an interesting interpretation when he described the French Revolution not as a conflict between a society intent on renewal and a power preventing it, but instead as a clash between an already transformed society and a power that remained slow to come to terms with a new state of affairs.

Personally, I feel that something rather similar occurred in 1968. An innovative, youthful, libertarian culture, already in place and widely diffused, found its path barred by labour organizations committed to defending an outdated, theological model of politics based on the confrontation between the bourgeoisie and the proletariat, between good and evil.

The Failed Revolution was in fact a conflict within the Left (at least in Italy) – one that was fought out entirely outside the institutions, and that was thus supremely extra-parliamentary and highly media-centred. It was a linguistic as much as an armed conflict in the spotlight of the media circus (as in the Moro case), that proved incapable of giving birth to any new kind of democratic body.

In other words: the difference between the French Revolution and the Failed Revolution resides in the fact that the latter lacked a Louis XVI to convene a States General. What was painfully lacking was a *setting* for the Revolution – a Jeu de Paume or a Winter Palace – though one was tirelessly sought in the countless demonstrations, assemblies and funerals – as well as in the misplaced references to the partisan struggle and the Spanish Civil War. It was a Failed Revolution, because the political avant-garde was arrayed against the cultural avant-garde; yet, if the former lost their revolution, the latter (perhaps) won theirs. An incomplete revolution then, but perhaps the only possible one.

This rather unique political climate must be borne in mind if we want to understand the ideas that were floated by the more politically aware sections of the radical wing, and which centred on the issue of the project (i.e. planning and design).

For some time an old pamphlet raging against the reforming policies of the social democrats, Friedrich Engels' *The Housing Question*, had been doing the rounds in the architecture faculty in Florence, where it was subjected to an attentive if ironic reading. In this famous book, Karl Marx's confederate explained how there was no such thing as a "worker's metropolis" – only "a worker's critique" of the existing city. This meant that the problem was not to plan a better city but to seize possession of the existing one. The role of planning did not consist in innovation, but in its ability to demystify the logic on which the bourgeois city was based. The true political question was not how to improve the functioning of the city, but instead how to disrupt it (with barricades).

This pre-revolutionary climate was above all theoretical and arose from the paradox of having to dream up a new Socialist Revolution at the very moment where the actual Socialist

3. Occupation of the Odéon Theatre, 1968

Revolution was faltering. But the scope of this dilemma was not political but cultural in nature, since, in this type of radical, rigid and sarcastic attitude, it was the ability of modern culture to respond adequately to political conflict that came up for discussion at the very moment this culture was jettisoning its role as social mediator.

Today perhaps the political aspect of modern culture is an irrelevant issue (and rightly so). In 1964, however, the role of modernity remained politically rooted; in the immediate post-war period, in a devastated Europe aghast at the monstrous dictatorships it had spawned, the only hope was to reconstruct in tandem democracy and modernity – two concepts around which masters from Alvar Aalto to Le Corbusier, from Walter Gropius to Mies van der Rohe (and some other past contributors that had better go unmentioned …) toiled with the utmost dedication.

Through the rejection of its role as social intermediary, modern architecture lost its historical mandate, and the limits of its inborn rationalist theorizing became glaring, incapable as it was of interpreting or defusing the serious social and cultural conflicts that the dash to industrialize brought in its wake. Faced with the complexity of its own world, modernity simply miscarried.

The upshot of that failure, however, was not the postmodernist culture which was to take up so many column inches with its absurdities fifteen years later; instead, after the fall of the modern, there emerged a tough, inexpressive, pagan world, the offspring of a struggle between two battling titans: capital and the working classes, two entities devoid of values, immoral and pitiless, both capable of great ventures, and of great dictatorships.

This was the *Pollo di Marmo* (Marble chicken) of which Archizoom spoke: an imperialist monolith that emerged from behind the humanist concerns of a skin-deep modernity. Capitalism and the labouring classes were two inimical but related Goliaths that often forged alliances, as in the war against Hitler, or, earlier still, in Lenin's N.E.P. program on the "labour use of capitalism" in the USSR in 1922. Two bloodied giants who refused all arbitration – especially if offered by modern architecture, since both were sworn enemies of half measures.

Back in those days, these two opposing forces ruled the roost; to re-evaluate the one meant re-evaluating the other. The originality of Archizoom lay in wedding Socialist Realism to Pop Art, both tendencies sprouting from a realist, radical and extremist attitude in which the concerns of the political avant-garde might coincide with those of the artistic vanguard. Working-class activism and consumerism: Mario Tronti and Andy Warhol – conflicting, but not necessarily estranged worlds, because both espoused the materialist logic of "more money, less work". A "third way" was out of the question, and, as readers of Frantz Fanon, we all thought that "negritude" did not exist either since "blacks want to become white", the worker wants to become a boss and the colonized only dream of becoming colonizers. Though never vice versa …

The critique of modernity thus applied itself to architecture as a disciplinary institution, as a qualitative category in a pagan world "without qualities". Its mission became not to mediate between the logical extremes of the system but to represent them with the greatest conceivable clarity, and thus create that urban theatre for history and its contradictions mentioned above: an unequivocal,

4. Adolfo Natalini, Andrea Branzi and Massimo Morozzi, Pistoia, 1966

intelligible arena in which everything would speak for itself. As in Paul Nizan's book *Aden Arabia*, a city in which all the mechanisms of the French colonial system would finally become clear and visible.

The student movement in Florence had already been digesting these issues for some time when the vast Le Corbusier exhibition in the Palazzo Strozzi in 1962 provided a chance to reflect on specific projects by the Swiss architect. These included Chandigarh – whose plans replicated the caste system that regimented Indian society, without showing how to overcome it – as well as a master plan for Algiers that juxtaposed the historic Arab kasbah and recent European planning without offering any form of mediation.

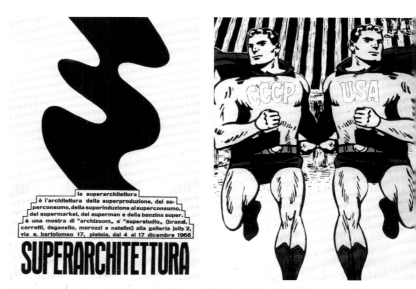

5. Poster of *Superarchitettura* exhibition, 1966, by Adolfo Natalini
6. Battle of the titans

These reflections centred on the hypothesis of a different role for architecture, one that was quite distinct from that ascribed to it by modern reformist politics, and which consisted in a sort of direct representation of the mechanisms of power, of the social divisions, of the castes and races, and not their mediation through planning. These were also the years of the Berlin Wall and of the rediscovery of the Karl-Marx-Hof, Red Vienna's ghettoized workers' quarter: architecture that was directly political, that posited drastic alternatives: either from this side of the Iron Curtain, or from the other – inside or outside the Eastern block. A civil architecture, therefore, with obvious Illuminist roots (Boullée and Ledoux were much in vogue) capable of catalyzing a critical effect through its presence inside a disordered and compromised city.

In 1964 we began work on our fourth-year exam in "Architectural composition", for which we finally presented a production – consumption megastructure laid out on the Florence-Prato axis, proposing it as a story board for the neo-capitalist system (in the illustrated presentation its didactic-cum-political intent becomes self-evident). In similar vein, in 1965, Claudio Greppi, a left-wing student leader, presented as his thesis project a plan to restructure the Florence-Prato textile-production system as a diagrammatic representation of the assembly line and the accumulation of capital.

Against this politicized backdrop, the preoccupations of Pop Art acquired a particular significance as a caustic denunciation of the producer-consumer world, one that the Modern Movement, in its purism and abstractionism, was not in a position to articulate. For my final thesis in 1966, I floated a project for a permanent amusement park in Prato, while one of Archizoom's first ventures was "Dream Beds," pieces of kitsch furniture destined – like new-fangled Trojan Horses – to overrun the tenets of good taste regulating the bourgeois household. Optimism for modernity had been superseded by celebrations of its failure.

At the 1969 Milan Triennale, Archizoom presented a *Centro di Cospirazione Eclettica* in an Afro-Tyrolian style dedicated to Malcolm X; while, in the pages of Ettore Sottsass' *Pianeta Fresco* there appeared a mail-order catalogue featuring Arab-style 'gazebos' (*gazebi*). In what proved an unexpectedly tragic prophecy, the pacifist "Hinduism" of the flower-power generation was upstaged by ironic references to Islamic Holy War....

7. Ludwig Hilberseimer, *Hochhausstadt* (High-rise City), 1924

Yet the early Pop Art and Superarchitettura period (with Superstudio) soon appeared as an interregnum heralding an even more radical thematic that was to stick to a very specific theoretical line; from this emerged No-Stop City which went on to erase every trace of Pop Art figuration.

It was based on the realization that the political debate behind the student and street protest movements – beneath the superficial consensus, behind the much-vaunted collectivism – there lurked a rejection of mass culture and of the radical dimension of the modern as a movement to "liberate man from culture" as opposed to an opportunity to build a "different" culture.

The constructs of an absolute secularism – the collapse of every type of qualitative utopia which left the field open to the only utopia left standing, one of quantity – presented a liberating face which the conflicts in the political arena, we believed, should not cover up.

The idea of an inexpressive, catatonic architecture, a consequence of the logical extrapolation of the system and its class struggle, was only the modern architecture in which we showed any interest: a redemptive architecture, corresponding to what was a mass democracy bereft of *demos* and of *kratos* (the people and power) – with neither centre nor image.

A society freed from its own alienation, disconnected from the rhetorical forms of humanitarian socialism as well as from all lip-service paid to progress: a de-dramatized, nondescript archi-

8. Superstudio: *The Twelve Ideal Cities. First (20,000 Ton) City*

tecture that could face up to the logic of atheist industrialism without fear, where mass-market productivity could generate an infinite number of urban scenarios, untrammeled by the "character structures" described by Wilhelm Reich as the chains inhibiting the release of humanity's organic energies.

The apparitions of Pop architecture were ousted by the uncompromising urban landscapes of a Ludwig Hilberseimer, by a city "without qualities" for a Man Without (predetermined) Qualities – and therefore left free to express his own independent and creative political and behavioural energies. Maximum possible freedom was to be reached in maximum integration: the rules of the system set new conditions for knowledge and planning, a ground zero from which everything might be possible (and unforeseeable). The new artistic condition of alienation, that Richard Hamilton had been the first to highlight, outflanked the insuperable limit of human tragedy as posited in these same years and the same city (London) by Francis Bacon.

Such an approach, with its unflinching realism and intransigent refusal, revealed ways in which the theological deadlock of modern politics could be overcome – i.e. its schematic functioning within an eternal struggle between good and bad, between rich and poor; this form of politics that tirelessly produced tragedies, that was fatally nourished by an inexhaustible fount of rhetoric and marked by constant decisive battles.

In contrast, No-Stop City offered a totally deadpan view of history restored to its secular dimension which, now completely cleansed of the metaphysical, was entirely devoid of tragedy. It was an extreme vision of industrial civilization as a producer of a decorative system that was both repetitive and horizontal – and therefore without cathedrals. Based on the repetition of signs, it was a diffuse and fluid system in which architecture and nature, as exceptions, as incidents, would dissolve and be absorbed within the amniotic space of the metropolis.

This reductive, ingenuous mindset had much in common with Andy Warhol's series and with the ambient music of a Philip Glass, who was in these very years beginning to work on horizontal, anti-compositional sonorities with the aim of creating a musical genre redolent of artificial microclimates. In *Architectural Design*, meanwhile, Cedric Price proclaimed that the quality of

that would correspond directly with the market, without any division into zones or functions. A genuine residential wood, where a shopping mall might be used as housing, where a house is an empty incubator, a theatre for as yet unspecified activities, an arena open to individual creativity, residential parking lots for metropolitan nomads. The concept of industrial design is interpreted as the mass-marketing of manufactured products and of life alike, with a net gain in freedom and independence. The home becomes an inhabitable closet – a convenience space entirely devoid of order and meaning where everyone puts into effect their right to invent both themselves and the form of their living space.

In 1972, in the ambit of the show, *Italy: The New Domestic Landscape* at New York's MoMA, Archizoom presented an empty, grey room in which the voice of a little girl told of a light-filled, multi-coloured house visitors had to picture for themselves. Our slogan then was *Abitare è facile* – Living is easy. As in Mark Rothko's vast monochromes, mass society is seen as an oceanic expanse, a boundless dead calm, with no epicentre and no boundaries. Or else, like in pictures by Cy Twombly, where shoals of little tadpoles wriggle through the amniotic fluid of the global market. In No-Stop City, this social dimension acquired a spatial dimension: the mirrors inside the models reflected images, multiplying them indefinitely, thereby superseding the limits of architecture and of internal space. The metropolis was envisioned as a vast interior: a single space, climate-controlled and artificially lit – like a huge factory or department store, organisms completely in tune with the standardizing logic of the market, impassive containers within which the possibilities are endless.

9/10. UFO: *Urboeffemero* (1969); 11. *Il Giro D'Italia* (1967)

the air-conditioning was more important than the architecture containing it.

Counter to those who thought that architecture in a society of machines should itself resemble a machine (Archigram), we therefore took the view that the acme of technology was attained in invisible applications (electronics). This attitude jettisoned the representational parameters of modern architecture, its compositional and typological limits, so as to create an urban habitat of stylistic silence and of vaporized boundaries.

The very name No-Stop City arose from the idea of a continuous built-up area free of external and internal borders, a metropolis

This introverted space, this hybrid, yet generic, and totally immoral metropolis, constituted a sort of "second Nature", a high-tech Amazon basin, within which functional zoning is conflated only then to be dissolved, and all the received ideas concerning lighting and the natural parceling of plots evaporated, as did the archetypal constraints which prevent a city from outgrowing a time-worn organic form that couples together technology and Nature … The idea of No-Stop City was to free the urban fabric from architecture, so that technology and Nature were not to harmonize, but be fused together – a city without architecture, precisely because it is freed from the need to play the role of mediator between inside and out, between technology and nature that architecture had hitherto granted.

12. Textile decoration in Red Square, Moscow. Opposite page: three scenes from Superstudio's *Interplanetary Architecture*, 1970.

Though in different ways, the whole Radical Movement in Florence worked on similar issues concerning the demise of the relationship between city and architecture, and between architecture and objects. If the interconnections and the profound internecine divisions of the movement are to be understood at all, it is necessary to address three major groups who focused on three analogous if divergent themes.

Archizoom Associati: city without architecture (No-Stop City)
Superstudio: architecture without a city (The Continuous Monument)
UFO: objects with neither city nor architecture.

Until the 1960s the theoretical core of Radicalism in Florence was the crisis of (or the end of) the relationship between these dimensional and conceptual categories.

Small, Medium, Large, and Extra-large, today considered by Rem Koolhaas as totally homogenous and interchangeable, were seen by the movement as conflicting, disharmonious categories, since each laid claim to overall centrality. Starting out from each of these categories, very diverse projects could be developed, not because these were based on different tools, but because they were dedicated to achieving opposed, irreconcilable, and divergent priorities.

The intuition of the end of the unity of the project – of the latent conflict between city and architecture and between architecture and the world of objects – arose when the unmanageable scale of the contemporary metropolis became patently obvious; for Archizoom's No-Stop City, this became a new-found reality that no longer had a continuous link with the historical city; an artificial universe within which architecture dissolved like ingredients in a primordial soup. An urban space therefore without architecture, where the cityscape is an accumulation of huge anonymous containers, goods and industrial output – of the plankton of the media and the market. At the core of our research, therefore, was the investigation of a new urban typology.

For Superstudio, architecture was to deal with its fraught relations with the city, asserting a new since jettisoned right to monumentality through the Monumento Continuo, and to offer itself up as a macrostructure within which cities such as New York would be engulfed. This was an architecture capable of rebuilding grand narratives and metaphors, as in the Twelve Ideal Cities (*Dodici Città Ideali*), and therefore in a position to impose order and cosmic meaning on the faceless metropolis; an architecture therefore without a city that imprinted its *stylemes* of order on the world of objects (*Quaderna*) and on the great territorial divides. Consequently the kernel of their research was a new, extra-historical architecture.

For UFO, on the other hand, the key to the "city revolution" was informed by the centrality and absolute autonomy of the world of objects, of inner space, and of conceptual fiction. A world of objects ranged against both architecture and city, one that embraced the right to think of newspapers, puns, and literature as the sole driving forces behind the world. This world developed out of a confrontation between categories, comprised of uninhabitable architectures (Case ANAS), of zones of transit (*Il Giro d'Italia*), and of new object-based archetypes. Objects, therefore, without architecture or city that impose a world of disorder and discontinuity. Their investigations zeroed in on objects that would provide a mysterious and conceptual focus for the world.

For each of these groups, and for the Florentine Radical Movement in general, the crisis within the discipline and the collapse of the unitary nature of the project presented an unmissable and long-awaited opportunity to conceive of a city that would no longer be a city, an architecture that would no longer be architecture, objects that were no longer objects but concepts. Here was a chance to transcend the crisis in Rationalist Modernism, the limits of the modern and the fear of launching out into the unthinkable and the uninhabitable – categories that were still defined on the basis of the entirely traditional idea of an organic relationship between various design stages: planning, then building, then furnishing. To bestow, that is, a hospitable world on a society determined instead to invent for itself ever newer forms of hostility, of uninhabitability, of disorganization – with the aim of overcoming the limits inherent in its own development.

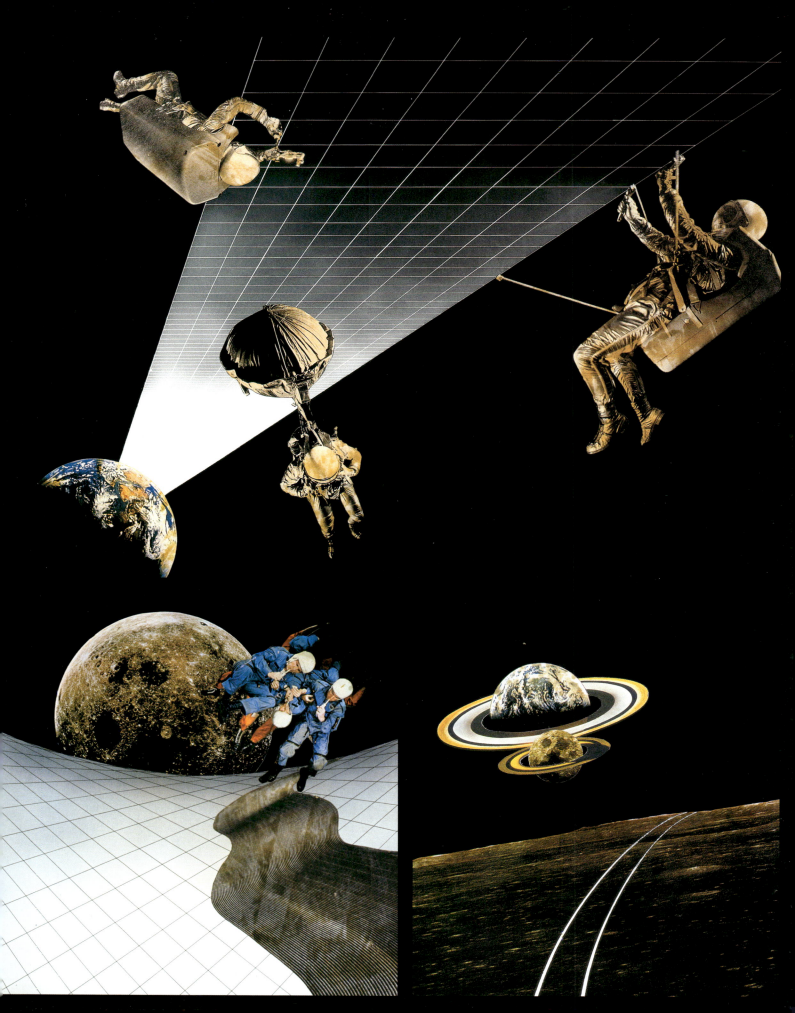

1. Scenes from *Cerimonia*, the second and last film in the Fundamental Acts cycle – starring the members of Superstudio and their wives, children and (girl)friends.

How great Architecture still was in 1966…
(Superstudio and Radical Architecture, Ten Years on)
Adolfo Natalini

In 1965 Le Corbusier drowned swimming in the sea. His architectural oeuvre continued to swell as successive volumes of his complete works were issued. Louis I. Kahn had exploded classical antiquity. Aldo Rossi had published *The Architecture of the City*. Mies and Aalto continued producing their models (the former serious, the latter with a smile). For minds more acute or scientific there was methodology, prefabrication and industrial design. For appetites whetted by the avant-garde, the Japanese Metabolists and Yona Friedman continued to turn out megastructures (*Tange docet*), while the Archigram boys burst onto the scene with their ironic technologies while the Beatles and the Rolling Stones strummed away in the background … In Austria, Pichler, Abraham and Hollein were doing incomprehensible things and in Milan Ettore Sottsass and Ugo La Pietra worked away in solitude (the one with a smile, the other the height of earnestness); but very few were aware of all these goings-on … Those were the days!

In the Faculty of Architecture in Florence we had been taught by Benevolo, Quaroni, Ricci and Savioli. Above all, however, we read *Architectural Design* (with Stirling and Archigram), L.C. (at that time it meant Le Corbu), and we had it that architecture was a means, not an end. With on our shoulders the full weight of insecurity and scepticism (a vague unease, feelings of alienation, etc.) and with a dose of cynicism, we decided to become *Super*.

At the end of 1966 came the Florence flood and the *Superarchitettura* show which saw the birth of Archizoom and Superstudio (A. Natalini, C. Toraldo di Francia, R. Magris, P. Frassinelli, A. Magris). Perhaps historians of Radical Architecture have not meditated sufficiently on such extraordinary coincidences, but it has been noted with subtle Eastern intuition in Arata Isozaki's article, "Superstudio, or the traces of the flood", in *7109* by Toshi Jutaku.

The early works, between 1967 and 1969, were responses to two imperatives: to get rid of all remnants of and infatuations with the architectural through a massive ingestion of projects/images, and to begin the demolition of the discipline through guerrilla incursions (this was Archizoom's theory of the Trojan Horse). In this way, operating fitfully between architecture and design, "Vantidesign" was born, goading and harrying Milan designers with its vulgarity (though the breath of fresh air it brought appealed to the industry).

"Arrivano gli Archizoom" (in *Domus*, October 1967) opened the door to an avalanche of articles: "Le stanze vuote e i Gazebi" by Archizoom (*Domus*, May 1968) and Superstudio's "Design d'invenzione e design d'evasione" (*Domus*, June 1969) celebrated the birth of the new stars, and Radical Architecture emerged into the limelight.

In Florence, in the wake of the student revolts of 1968, UFO was already in place. 9999 had kicked off their meteoric career with Space Electronic. Gianni Pettena was already playing his role of spy. Everyone affectionately thought of Sottsass as an elder brother and all very respectfully tried to understand what the

sistema disequilibrante that La Pietra had been promulgating all those years might be.

The years between 1969 and 1972 saw the birth of all the "classics" of Radical Architecture: Archizoom published "No-Stop City" in *Casabella* (July–August 1970) under the explanatory title, "City-assembly line for the social: ideology and theory of the metropolis," which it continued to elaborate on and improve until it achieved graphic and linguistic perfection.

No-Stop City was a critical utopia, a model for understanding the phenomena structuring the city and society. A utopia of quality was to be replaced by a utopia of quantity. The neutral, artificially lit and air-conditioned plans of No-Stop City, populated by freely moving, hypothetical individuals sporting gaudy "dressing design" wear, made no assumptions about alternative architecture

2. Ponte Vecchio, Florence flood, November 1966
3. Superstudio (R. Magris, Toraldo di Francia, Frassinelli, A. Magris, Natalini), *Hidden Architecture*, 1970

4. Le Corbusier exhibition in the Palazzo Strozzi, 1962

or urban planning. Analysis of the relationship between factory production and the city identified the supermarket and the production line as "ideal" models: society no longer needs any form of representation since it represents itself....

In the University of Florence competition, Archizoom showed the versatility and validity of such a critical model: with this dazzling plan came to an end an episode begun with unparalleled intelligence with the competition for an exhibition centre in the Fortezza da Basso in Florence, an enormous slab stretching over the entire available surface.

Superstudio's *Continuous Monument* and the *Twelve Ideal Cities* used negative utopia with critical intent. Metaphor, *demonstratio per absurdum*, and other rhetorical expedients were all employed to broaden the discussion about architecture. Superstudio's involvement was manifestly didactic: to analyze and annihilate the discipline of architecture by using "popular" means of illustration and consumer literature (Gregotti was to speak of "religious terrorism"). A model of total urbanization and twelve utopias were used as intellectual catalysts in a process of liberation from all "archimanias".... Naturally there were those who could not see beyond the metaphors and treated everything as yet another utopian proposition (some crammed No-Stop City into the same pigeonhole). Too bad for them.

In 1971, on the initiative of La Pietra (who, with Mendini, remained the most important source of publications on Radical Architecture) the now mythical number 2–3 of *IN* came out. This issue was the first in a series coordinated by Archizoom and Superstudio and devoted to "the destruction of the object; the elimination of the city; the disappearance of work." In addition to contributions from the major protagonists and their fellow travelers, Germano Celant published an article "Senza Titolo" ("Untitled") in which the term "Radical Architecture" – as applied to a range of conceptual and behavioural critical operations – appeared for the first time.

Meanwhile, Mendini's own *Casabella* had become the platform of choice for our heroes: in 1972 Sottsass published his masterpiece, "Il pianeta come festival" (with the *IN* appendix), and

Branzi published three caustic and ground-breaking articles on the role of the avant-garde ("La gioconda sbarbata," "L'Africa è vicina" and "Abitare è facile"). Riccardo Dalisi turned up at *Casabella* from Naples with suitcases full of designs on rolls of paper, of papier-mâché, string, and wooden cut-outs, and of photographs and records of his experiences with the children of the Traiano quarter. So with Dalisi the revolt of *tecnica povera* began – a far cry from the poor-yes-but-with-a-geodesic-dome-and-gas-guzzling-secondhand-cars of the drop-outs and the USA-made *Whole Earth Catalog*.

In January's *Casabella* Superstudio published "The Twelve Ideal Cities" (which had already been honoured on the front cover of the previous December's *Architectural Design,* before ricocheting off onto numerous other magazines, with a total of nine translations in various languages), while the July issue brought the beginning of the "Cinque storie" ("Five Stories"), with a cover showing a *Gorilla gorilla Beringei* met with in the Natural History Museum, New York, beating its chest to broadcast the news of the triumph of Radical Design at the Museum of Modern Art.

That summer New York had indeed witnessed the opening of the exhibition *Italy: The New Domestic Landscape* which marked the apotheosis and demise of Italian design (Radical included). The exhibition, organized in accordance with the fantastical symmetries and categories of Emilio Ambasz (an Argentine and therefore a compatriot of Borges), presented Italian design as an experimental model. The exhibition displayed some of the finest objects from the last decade cheek-by-jowl with a series of environments commissioned by the museum from a number of designers, divided into three categories depending on their positive, critical, or negative attitude with respect to design.

From the grey containers of a Sottsass, to the political-didactic pieces of the Strum group, from La Pietra's living cell as a means of communication, to Pesce's archeology of the future, to Archizoom's empty room ("to each their own utopia"), counter-design culture broadcast its various positions. I don't know the extent to which these messages could be understood by American visitors fascinated by the toys by Zanuso, Columbo, Aulenti, Bellini and others of their stripe .... Determined to fight fire with fire, Superstudio showed an "American-style" advertising short propagandizing a life free from objects.

This film was called *Supersurface, or the Public Image* of *Truly Modern Architecture*, – or *Life* for short – and was part of a series

5. Superstudio's Misura furniture in a field near Pistoia, late 1960s

on the Fundamental Acts. Between 1971 and 1973, Superstudio was to produce a chain of illustrated accounts that soon turned into five films: Life, Education, Ceremony, Love, Death.

After all the irony, sacrilege, negativity, and demolition work, the work on the Fundamental Acts constituted an attempt to re-define architecture on an anthropological and philosophical basis in a sequence of reductive processes. Now that architecture had been definitively overcome, and all efforts at technocratism or representation abandoned, the human sciences had become both field and instrument of investigation. At the same time a decision came to the fore to act in first person, through both our activities and our teaching (education at all levels). Many years before, Hollein had stated that "Alles ist Architektur" (every-thing is architecture). So we said: "I am (you are, he is, we are, they are) living architecture." And for those who still insisted on planning we suggested: "The only thing to plan is our life. And that's it …"

In an attempt to instil new energy into a fast disappearing phenom-enon, and under the skilful direction of Andrea Branzi and with the wary support of the motley Radical crew, January 12, 1973 saw the birth of "Global Tools – a network of laboratories in Florence for propagating the use of natural technical materials and related behaviours […] with the goal of stimulating the un-trammeled development of individual creativity […] Teaching will cover topics such as the use of natural and artificial materials, the development of creative activities, both individual and in groups, the use and techniques of information and communication tech-nologies, survival strategies" (Document 1).

As Mendini noted, "Terminology, assumptions, methods, and structures are curiously simple: as if their intention is to bridge the alienating gap that has arisen between manual and intellectual work." And Branzi, referring to long-term strategies "beyond the short-lived coups staged in the journals", observed how going back to creativity "is not meant to create a novel system of models and tenets, but simply to attain a new and more advanced psy-chosomatic equilibrium, and therefore a new level of freedom and self-empowerment."

"My friends tell me it can be tried" (Sottsass).

In January 1973, Almerico de Angelis published the study "Antidesign", in which, in spite of polemical attacks on No-Stop City, he provided an objective and clear reconstruction of the movement's history. Simultaneously, following tentative steps at reorganization, the first retrospectives arrived, a sure sign that things were drawing to a close.… The time had come for hair-splitting, for getting the dates right, for taking sides.

The Trienniale was the stage for a head to head between the *Tendenza* (Aldo Rossi's school) and Radical Architecture. Superstudio participated at the Triennale on both sides! At the exhibition, *Architettura Razionale* showed plans by the 1969 rationalists (catalogues of villas, the Continuous Monument) and in the (Radical) design section there were two of the five films: *Life* and *Cerimonia* of 1972–73. This dual position drew fire from both flanks: for our part it served simply to show that by now the clash had become farcical and that the only response was to play both sides against the middle. Both had been successive phases in our development, dialectic moments, complementary

experiences now digested and superceded. And this much we had already declared, many years earlier, in our CV-cum-official autobiography:

FRAGMENTS FROM A PERSONAL MUSEUM

Our work has always taken the form of inventories and catalogues: perhaps the only form of work possible today is autobiography as a project for one's life.

From 1965 to 1968, we worked with the conviction that archi-tecture was a means of changing the world. Designs were a hypothesis of physical transformations, they were ways to hypo-thesize diverse qualities and quantities: A JOURNEY INTO THE REALMS OF REASON.

Between 1968 and 1969, we began to be interested in trans-positions and metamorphoses: architecture stopped being a "specific", it lost its "scale" connotations to become an abstract planning of platonic, neutral and available entities. This work has been collected in the second catalogue: ISTOGRAMMI D'ARCHITETTURA.

Between 1969 and 1970, we elaborated an extreme line of thought on the possibilities of architecture as the instrument for attaining knowledge and action through the means of an architectural model of total urbanization. This work appears in the third cata-logue: THE CONTINUOUS MONUMENT.

Between 1970 and 1971, we started to produce didactic projects, architectural critiques. We used architecture as self-criticism,

6. Cover of *Casabella* 367, 1973; 7. The Natalini family enjoying a picnic on a histogram

endeavouring to enquire into its promotional mechanisms and its ways of working. The didactic plans are REFLECTED ARCHI-TECTURE, INTERPLANETARY ARCHITECTURE, THE 12 IDEAL CITIES.

From March 21, 1971 to March 20, 1973, we worked on a series of films about fundamental acts, centred on the relationship be-tween architecture (as the conscious formalization of the planet) and human life. These films produced constituted propaganda for ideas outside the typical channels of the architectural discipline.

The five films are: LIFE, EDUCATION, CEREMONY, LOVE, DEATH.

For many years (from 1966 to 1972) we developed our critical discourse on the human environment, employing various means, from plans to exhibitions, from films to teaching. But the two areas in which we tried to make an impact, the cultural sector and publishing, seemed far too restrictive. In the last two years we have worked mainly in universities and other educational establishments, here and abroad. And from these years of patient yet committed activity, we have neither studies nor picture – and neither would we wish for any.

With Global Tools, moreover, we have no programs, also because the global scene is becoming increasingly confused – like a Whole Earth seen through clouds....

We only wish to continue our journey together – from architecture to things, to the body, to the earth. In a kind of group therapy.... This non-programme can have two (or many) aspects: with those familiar with planning, we will be able to examine goals and to seek out alternatives, with the others (always assuming they exist in a world made for and by people in the trade) we will speak about how to live with as few tools as possible.

Superstudio summed up its activity in two travelling exhibitions. The first (Austria, Germany, Switzerland) was called *Fragmente aus einem persönlichen Museum* and comprised five environ-

8. Superstudio, *Graz – Mur*. Collage from 1973

ments, each dedicated to one of the five themes: life, education, ceremony, love, death. The second, with Ettore Sottsass (in the United States) was entitled *Sottsass & Superstudio: Mindscapes.* In the catalogue, Ettore tells his life story: "When I was very small, a child of five or six...." Superstudio too tried to tell its story, which basically is the story of its creations:

These are fragments of projects executed from 1966 to 1973 for the modification of the natural and artificial landscape which surrounds us and for the modification of ourselves through ideas.

Having continued for years to dream up, on paper, testaments, lovers' promises, immobile colloquies with fellow-guests of stone, having confided to paper bottle-messages, love poetry, invisible whispers. And again: having built, on paper, castles and cities, and inviolate oases amid the sands, and empty houses, or warehouses full of useless objects, or funeral processions. And having for years interrogated the stars on the itinerary to follow, the navigator drew the constellations in the night. Having for centuries interrogated the earth, the farmer drew geometric patterns on hills and valleys, transforming them into mosaics. Finally, after examining the omens, the founder of the city drew a geometric perimeter on the ground and thereon he built the city. Innumerable cartographers delineated the terraqueous globe, marking invisible boundaries which later turned into paths of blood on the earth and seas. Others drew flags in blood or gold. In this fashion they also made vestments for kings and other dignitaries. [The Indians instead executed designs in coloured sand that would only last a few moments after the prolonged magic that made them, the father teaching the art to his son by example.]

The marks we left on the paper, or the pieces of photos glued together, and the blueprints of perspectives and axonometrics, and the sheets from the copier, the drawings done with coloured pencils or shaded ones done with the airbrush, were ways and maps for ancient or future journeys. They were paths running through the territory of will and hope. They were plans for journeys, activities, magic calendars, lists of gifts. They were always projects. [The plans that remain provide evidence of lives never lived, of invisible objects, of lightweight structures.] In the beginning, we designed objects for production, designs to be turned into wood and steel, glass and brick, or plastic. Then we produced neutral and usable designs, then, finally, negative utopias, forewarning images of the horrors which architecture was laying in store for us, with its scientific methods for the perpetuation of existing models.... Then the images slowly disappeared, as if in a mirror: now there remain only fables and parables, descriptions and speeches. No longer figures, but traces of a mode of behaviour directed towards suggesting the magnificent possibilities of rediscovering and of governing ourselves. The only project is thus the project for our lives and our relationships with others.

(from "Superstudio on Mindscapes" 30/4/1973)

In 1973, Global Tools participated in two further "historical" exhibitions on Radical Architecture, joining in *Contemporanea* in Rome and in *Design als Postulat/am Beispiel Italien* at the IDZ Berlin. With typical Germanic efficiency, the latter featured an anthology of writings on design and anti-design as well as a study by Franco Raggi (later republished in Italian in *Casabella*) on "the history and destiny of negative thought in the practice of Radical Design from 1968 to today – the role of the avant-garde between professional evasion and engagement". But besides tak-

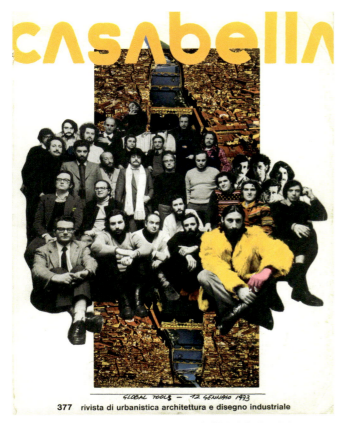

9. *Casabella* 377 (cover design by Natalini), *Global Tools*, 1973

for future research: in case of doubt, I too sometimes consult the bibliography.... Earlier essays, in *Designs Quarterly*, no. 78–79, 1970 on "Conceptual Architecture" coordinated by J. Margolies, and "Arthropods" by Jim Burns, 1971–72, had done little to improve the profile of the movement as they were difficult to get hold of and their format was basically that of an anthology. The merit of Navone and Orlandoni's book "consists in the circulation of organized data, of a general scheme of reference, on phenomena as a whole totally misunderstood by the majority hitherto or else attributed to isolated outbreaks of insanity" (A. Branzi). But perhaps the best method consisted in recognizing that a movement, that by this time could be catalogued, no longer existed.

To put it more accurately: activity changed direction and means, and our heroes, progressively drifting apart, chose to refine their research and sphere of activity, or to vanish completely.

Thus Archizoom exited by a side door to pursue their myth of pure professionalism, while, through periodicals, books and films, La Pietra's research on the re-appropriation of the environment and Dalisi's on marginalized creativity and *tecnica povera* became increasingly focused. Sottsass withdrew into poetical meditation to assemble sticks and stones, while Superstudio immersed itself into teaching.

Superstudio's activity had always been didactic, and not only in its intentions.

Apart from my involvement from 1966 onwards in the Faculty of Architecture in Florence, there had been a long series of lectures, seminars, and courses held in several schools in Europe and America, in particular at the Rhode Island School of Design (with Abraham, St Florian, and Mike Webb) at Providence and at the Architectural Association, London (with Peter Cook, Archigram, Price, and then Koolhaas, Zenghelis and Krier).

From 1973 Superstudio centred its activity on education, abandoning the glossies and vacating centre stage. From that time onward we have held courses on "the motivations of architecture", "the galaxy of objects", "simple-to-use objects" and "extra-urban material cultures".

By that time there was little left in the university to destroy, and therefore the Neo-avant-garde's policy of "the technical destruction

ing part in exhibitions and numerous meetings, the heroic and creative climate of the years prior to 1972 no longer existed.

Global Tools was an aggregate of meetings, documents and legal issues, of outpourings, outbursts and vexation. Activities and domains were laboriously demarcated: the body, construction, communications, survival, theory....

But it all remained firmly on the drawing board. We noticed more and more that the stage of enthusiasm and actions was over – and we just didn't want to admit it. On All Saints' and All Souls', in November 1974, a seminar organized by Superstudio took place at the Chiesa Vecchia in Sambuca, for this occasion transformed into a company of masons, house-painters, carpenters, cooks and bottle-washers.

In spite of good intentions on all sides, the school and Global Tools laboratories were slow in getting off the ground. The following spring Superstudio noisily resigned from Global Tools, convinced that teaching (in the mass university that the architectural school in Florence had by now become) was more important, in spite of all the spats and setbacks. Meanwhile the period of historiography had begun....

Countless young scholars of architecture wrote theses on the Neo-avant-garde. The most effective of these – by Paolo Navone and Bruno Orlandoni – was published in 1974 among the *Casabella* "documents" with the title, "Architettura Radicale" which thus entered its historical phase. Even if the book was more like a work of art criticism – with a take on events that was not always structural – it was destined to become the basic text

10. Mike Webb, Raimund Abraham, Natalini and Friedrich St Florian, 1970

of culture" rang hollow. Hegemonic culture was on the wane anyway: foreign students, working students, Open University students, fellow travellers of '68, carpet-baggers and urban nomads had very different things on their minds. The transformation of the university into a mass institution through proletarianization, its emergence as a place of struggle and the honing of political and survival strategies, has turned it into a key arena (along with the factory, the countryside, and the city). Our work in the university today consists in the analysis of planning (of its purposes, of its management strategies, and of its relationship with society and the environment), through the investigation of alternative methods and applications.

Our research areas include elementary tools and implements, self-governing processes of transformation (such as agriculture and handicraft) and extra-urban material cultures. These simple-to-use objects are examined as survival strategies, and through critical inventory, reductive planning, handling and use we attempt to understand their underlying structure. Objects, as the mediators between ourselves and the world, become a mental catalyst in a process of self-analysis, in a therapy aimed at unleashing creativity.

Extra-urban material cultures are studied and experimented with as if they were a vast encyclopaedia (nothing like Diderot's or the *Whole Earth Catalog*). So for the past two years we have been interested in tools and their relationship to work and their ability to change the environment; currently we are concerned with the way in which household objects relate to man's existence, and over the next two years we intend to conduct research into energy and time (as the basis and locus of life). Anthropological methods are employed as analytical and interpretative instruments; direct experimentation (making as thinking), handling, use and behaviour serve as instruments for the re-appropriation of both the environment and ourselves.

An attempt to summarize ten years of work:

When the projects and images, the texts and objects of Radical Architecture were being produced, Radical Architecture didn't exist.

11. Extra-Urban material culture: Project Zeno

12. Natalini teaching at Florence University, mid-1970s

Now that the label exists, Radical Architecture has become extinct. In other words, it cannot be regarded as simply another movement or school with homogenous, well-defined characteristics, but a series of situations, intentions and acts. Its various modes of being included architecture, design, art, communication, but also happenings, agitation, philosophy and politics. The rejection of the discipline and the destruction of its specificity were its liberating techniques. Irony, provocation, paradox, false syllogism and logical extrapolation, terrorism, mysticism, humanism, reduction and the pathetic were the categories employed, depending on the situation, whilst continuous repositioning, discontinuity (UFO), dialectical overcoming, and "the Knight's move" (Menna) proved to be the driving forces.

For Superstudio, today, the methods of analysis and action have changed: cultural anthropology, research on man and his intellectual and material creations, attempts at conscious modification of the environment and of ourselves, are all part of a process of permanent education that involves us entirely. Visible evidence of these efforts is thin on the ground (the mirror that endlessly multiplied such images has been smashed to smithereens), but through an engagement with everyday life, the fusion (the identity) between memory and project, work and education, the individual and the political is slowly but surely taking shape.

Through its critical, destructive and liberating activities, Radical Architecture has laid the foundations for this fusion. Over and above the paper graveyard it has left behind, it is this, we think, that made it worthwhile.

18 July 1977

LIFE
EDUCATION
CEREMONY
LOVE
DEATH

FIVE STORIES BY SUPERSTUDIO

THE FUNDAMENTAL ACTS

INTRODUCTION

Architecture never touches the great themes, the fundamental themes of our lives.

Architecture remains at the edge of our life, and intervenes only at a certain point in the process, usually when behaviour has already been codified, furnishing answers to rigidly stated problems. Even if its answers are aberrant or evasive, the logic of their production and consumption avoids any real upheaval. Architecture presents no alternative proposal, since it uses those instruments which are accurately predisposed to avoid any deviation. Thus, the working-class home resembles the stately villa in the same way that the work of a radical architect resembles that of the academic or reactionary architect: the only difference lies in the quantities in play, the decisions on the quality of living have already been made. In accepting his role, the architect becomes accomplice to the machinations of the system. Then, the avant-garde architect fills one of the most rigidly fixed roles (rather like the "young lover" in plays).

At this point, the architect, recognizing in himself and in his work connotations of cosmetics, environmental pollution and *consolatrix afflictorum*, comes to an abrupt halt on his well-paved path. It then becomes an act of coherence, or a last try at salvation, to concentrate on the re-definition of the primary acts, and to examine, in the first instance, the relationships between architecture and these acts.

This operation becomes therapy for the removal of all archimanias.

This tentative anthropological and philosophical refoundation of architecture becomes the centre of our reductive processes.

I. LIFE
or the Public Image of Truly Modern Architecture.
Supersurface: an alternative model of life on Earth

Architecture is no longer the mediation man-environment translated into the complexification of needs, creating an artificial panorama and a "Second poverty", but becomes a cross-science.

Through the collation and the extrapolation of data and tendencies of different disciplines (from body control techniques to philosophy, from disciplines of logic, to medicine, to bionics, to geography …), a guiding image is visualized: a life no longer based on work (and the power and violence connected with it), but on unalienated human relationships. It is the last chance for architecture to act as "planner". By setting off a series of reductive processes, we can pass from induced needs to primary needs; technology, concentrated on these alone, can satisfy them without work.

We can foresee two directions for research: towards a better use of the human body and mind; towards the control of environment without three-dimensional means (again, reductive processes). Earth, rendered homogeneous through an energy and information grid (see "Education", "Death") becomes the natural support of a new potentiated life.

A Moral tale about the disappearance of Design

Design, having become perfect and rational, proceeds to synthesize different realities in synchresis and finally transforms itself, not coming out of itself, but rather withdrawing into itself, into its final essence of natural philosophy. Thus designing coincides more and more with existence: no longer existence under the protection of designed objects,

but existence as design. The times are over when utensils generated ideas and when ideas generated utensils: now ideas are utensils. It is with these new tools that life forms itself freely into cosmic consciousness.

If the instruments of design have become as sharp as lancets and as sensitive as sounding lines, we can use them for a delicate lobotomy. Thus, beyond the convulsions of over-production, a state of calm can be born, in which a world without products and refuse takes shape, a zone in which the mind is energy and raw material, and also the final product, the only intangible object of consumption. The designing of a region free from the pollution of design is very similar to a design for a terrestrial paradise.

First hypothesis

Mind and body as a single utensil, as the only tool.
The exploration of mental mechanisms. The interior space to be found

again, the mechanisms of reawakening. The methods of self-formation for integration and harmony in the human personality (yoga, psychosynthesis …). New symbioses: cyborg, the possible developments in biology, in biochemistry, etc., modifications and mutations, the elimination of spatial barriers (agoraphobia, claustrophobia, etc.), the improvements in mechanisms governing heat, cellular regeneration, etc. Development of the potentiating servoskin, strengthening of the senses, body control techniques, development of the mind.

Second hypothesis

Nature is reduced to cultivation according to the criteria of maximum functional exploitation. The countryside becomes progressively more artificial and homogeneous. Cities like New York constitute a didactic example of the functional utilization of territory through a Cartesian grid: the Manhattan peninsula has vanished under the unifying action of induced value.

Presently, the environment is controlled principally by physical, three-dimensional means (dams, canals, large covered areas, microclimates).

The hypothesis: control of the environment by energy (artificial currents, thermic barriers, radiation, etc.). Towards the disappearances of the divisory membranes between interior and exterior. The cave and the fire on the plain. Microclimates, large areas, ever lighter coverings. From hardware to software. Earth used for services and communication grids. A city without 3-D supports. A hypothesis for an isotropic and homogeneous grid/Supersurface.

Supersurface: a model of a mental attitude

This is not a three-dimensional model of a reality which can be given concrete form by a mere transposition of scale, but the visualization of a critical attitude towards (or a hope for) the activity of designing understood as philosophical speculation, as a means to knowledge, as critical existence.

We can image a network of energy and information extending to every properly inhabitable area. Life without work, freedom from want, and a new potentiated humanity are made possible by such a network.

Let us take, for example, a valley (an optimal living zone) and imagine that we are undertaking a series of homogenizing operations, similar to present cultivation. Let us imagine that we set up a grid for the transmission of energy and information to the entire area. This grid creates a situation of 'total field' in which any point is described by the intersection of two straight lines. The crossing point of the principal lines marks a "principal point" at which we might imagine a "universal plug".

The network of energy can assume different configurations. The first is a limit-situation: a linear development. The others include different planimetrical developments with the possibility of covering different and gradually increasing parts of areas. The typology of the environments depends solely on the percentage of area covered, analogous to the way in which we distinguish a street from a town and from a metropolis.

FROM UFE/SUPERSURFACE "SANDRO POLI DISCOVERS A PLUG" SUPERSTUDIO 1971

Some types:
10% covered. The network is developed like a continuous ribbon extending over the territory. 50% covered. The network is developed as a chess board, with squares measuring 1 km x 1 km, alternating with squares of open land.
100% covered. The network is transformed into a continuous development, the natural confines of which are formed by mountains, coast, rivers....

Various hypotheses for survival strategies: Hypothesis for total system of communication, software, central memories and personal terminals. Hypothesis for network of energy distribution, acclimatization without protective walls. Mathematical models of cyclic use of territory, shifting of the population, functioning and non-functioning of the networks … defusing. In the model this network is represented by a Cartesian squared surface, which is of course to be understood not only in the physical sense, but as

a visual-verbal metaphor for an ordered and rational distribution of resources.

We may imagine this invisible grid with only a few points just visible in the grass, but immediately traceable, which constitute the universal plugs. In the model, these plugs are visualized as a magic box (black box) to which various sophisticated and miniaturized devices can be attached. Through these devices (the dream of electric appliances), everyone can synthesize the elements necessary to his existence. A universal plug for primary needs.

The use of the supersurface. Some examples from real life.

Sometimes, for some electrifying moments, one sees under the surface of the waters of a lake, or under the grasses of a plain the distinct grid of the supersurface....

Spring cleaning

Not much is left of ancient glories, not even ruins and columns. At most, some pathetic wreckage, old wobbly chairs....

The reductive processes cover all spheres of action: we thus see the passage from induced needs to primary needs, from matter to energy, from objects to ideas....

The invisible dome

All you have to do is stop and connect a plug: the desired micro-climate is immediately created (temperature, humidity etc.), you plug in to the network of information, you switch on the food and water blenders....
The grass of your neighbour is no longer greener than yours....

Some images of different typologies with some fact-reports:

"Places where humanity is concentrated in great numbers have always been based on the city network of energy and information, with three-dimensional structures representing the values of the system. In their free time, large crowds on the beaches or in the country are in fact a concentrated mass of people "served" by mechanical, mobile mini-services (car, radio, portable refrigerator). Concentrations such as the Isle of Wight or Woodstock indicate the possibility of an "urban" life without the emergence of three-dimensional structures as a basis.

The tendency to the spontaneous gathering and dispersing of large crowds becomes more and more detached from the existence of three-dimensional structures.

Free gathering and dispersing, permanent nomadism, the choice of interpersonal relationships beyond any pre-established hierarchy are characteristics which become increasingly evident in a society free from work. These types of movement can be considered as the manifestations of the intellectual processes: the logical structure of thought continually compared (or contrasted) to our unconscious motivations. Our elementary requirements can be satisfied by highly sophisticated (miniaturized) techniques. A greater ability to think and the integral use of our psychic potential will then be the foundation and the reason for a life free from want.

Bidonvilles, drop-out cities, camping sites, slums, tendopoles or geodetic domes are different expressions of an analogous desire to attempt to control the environment by the most economical means…"

The model constitutes the logical selection of these developing tendencies: the elimination of all formal structures, the transfer of all designing activity to the conceptual sphere. In substance, the rejection of production and consumption, the rejection of work, are visualized as an aphysical metaphor.

The encampment

You can be where you like, taking with you the tribe or family. There's no need for shelters, since the climatic conditions and the body mechanisms of thermo-regulation have been modified to guarantee total comfort. At the most we can play at making a shelter, or rather at the home, at architecture.

The distances between man and man (modified) which generate the way in which people gather and therefore "the places": if a person is alone the place is a small room; if they are two together it is a larger room; if they are ten it's a school; if a hundred, a theatre; if a thousand, an assembly hall; if ten thousand, a city; if a million, a metropolis.

Nomadism becomes the permanent condition: the movements of individuals interact, thereby creating continual currents. The movements and migrations of the individual can be considered as regulated by precise norms, the distances between man and man, attractions/reactions, love/hate.

As with fluids, the movement of one part affects the movements of the whole.

The happy island

A lady of our acquaintance became hysterical on hearing this story and said: I certainly have no intention of doing without my vacuum-cleaner and the mowing machine, and the electric iron and the washing machine and refrigerator, and the vase full of flowers, the books, my costume jewellery, doll and clothes!

Whatever you say madam! Just take whatever you like, or rather equip a happy island for yourself with all your goods. The only problem is that the sea has receded all round and the island is sticking up in the middle of a plain without any messages in bottles.

The distant mountain

Look at that distant mountain … what can you see?

Is that the place to go to? Or is it only the limit to the inhabitable? It's the one and the other since contradiction no longer exists, it's only a case of being complementary.

Thus thought a fairly adult Alice skipping over her rope, very slowly, though without feeling either heat or effort.

A Journey from A to B

There will be no further need for cities or castles.
There will be no further reason for roads or squares.
Every point will be the same as any other (excluding a few deserts or mountains which are in no ways inhabitable).
So, having chosen a random point on the map, we'll be able to say: my house will be here for three days, two months, or ten years.
And we'll set off that way (let's call it B) without provisions, carrying only objects we're fond of. The journey from A to B can be long or short. In any case it will be a constant migration with the actions of living at every point along the ideal line between A (departure) and B (arrival).
It won't, you see, be just the transportation of matter.
These are the objects we'll carry with us: some strange pressed flowers, a few videotapes, some family photos, a drawing on crumpled paper, an enormous banner of grass and reeds interwoven with old pieces of material which once were clothes, a fine suit, a bad book.
These will be the object. Someone will take with him only a herd of animals for friends. For instance: a quartet of Bremermusikanten, or a horse, two dogs and two doves or twelve cats, five dogs and a goat.
Yet others will take with them only memory, become so sharp and bright as to be a visible object. Others will hold one arm raised, fist clenched. Someone will have learnt a magic word and will take it with him as a suitcase or a standard.
CALM, COMPREHENSION, CONFIDENCE, COURAGE,
E N E R G Y, ENTHUSIASM, GOODNESS, GRATITUDE,
HARMONY, JOY, LOVE, PATIENCE. SERENITY, SIMPLICITY,
WILL, WISDOM (this is the complete set of cards in the "Technique of Evocative Words" by Roberto Assagioli, M.D.).
But almost everybody will take only himself from A to B, a single visible object, like a complete catalogue as an enormous Postal Market Catalogue.

What we'll do.
We'll keep silence to listen to our own bodies, we'll hear the sound of blood in our ears, the slight crackings of our joints or teeth, we'll examine the texture of our skins, the patterns made by the hairs on our bodies and heads. We'll listen to our hearts and our breathing.
We'll watch ourselves living.
We'll do very complicated muscular acrobatics.
We'll do very complicated mental acrobatics.
The mind will fall back on itself to read its own history.
We'll carry out astonishing mental operations.
Perhaps we'll be able to transmit thoughts and images, then one happy day our minds will be in communication with that of the whole world.
That which was called philosophy will be the natural physical activity of our minds, and will at the same time be philosophy, religion, love, politics, science....
Perhaps we'll lose the names of these disciplines (and it will be no great loss) when everybody will be present in essence in our minds.
We will be able to create and transmit visions and images, perhaps even make little objects move for fun.
We'll play wonderful games, games of ability and love.
We'll talk a lot, to ourselves and to everybody.
We'll look at the sun, the clouds, the stars.
We'll go to faraway places, just to look at them and hear them.
Some people will become great story-tellers: many will move to go and listen to them.
Some will sing and play.
Stories, songs, music, dancing will be the words we speak and tell ourselves.
Life will be the only environmental art.

II. EDUCATION
or the Public Image of Science and Liberty

A LECTURE
or Equivalent Information

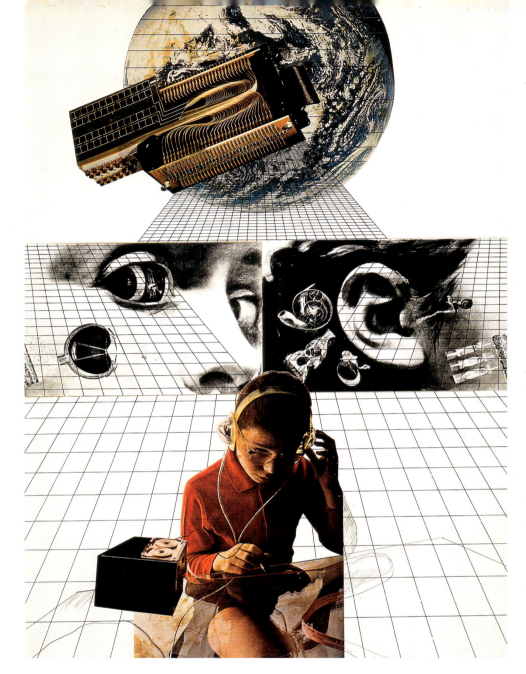

"Good evening, ladies and gentlemen. I have been invited here to speak on the theoretical work and professional experience of Superstudio, the group of architects in which I am a partner, and first I would like to thank the organizers of this series of lectures for their invitation. I have always thought of a public lecture as a marvellous opportunity for putting order into my ideas on our work, to render it transmittable as information. I have already tried this same operation on other occasions (lectures, anthological or complete publications), and lately this has taken on a recurrent rhythm, that is, once every six months we try to take an inventory of our ideas, just as big companies take inventories of their stock. These inventories are a strong springboard for future work, and from the structure of preceding ideas (together with Present stimuli) ideas generating new work are born.

During this past year, however, despite a complete absence of any finance for this kind of research, I have been spending my time studying the architectural works and the personality of an architect who, although not well-known, I consider essential to the understanding of our ideas and generally to the understanding of the history of ideas in architecture during the past fifty years, that is, from 1920 until today. I would therefore like to dedicate this lecture to the works of Amerigo Baccheschi (whom I will call AB), architect and theoretician. (Murmur of surprise.) I would ask you therefore to consider all that I say and the illustrations that you will see in the slide programme as an explanation of our ideas and of our work in the so-called field of the avant-garde....

(From the notes for the lecture:)
AB was born in a bourgeois middle-European (Milanese) family eighty years ago.... A late vocation for architecture ... due to the desire to show off and conquer the love of a young school fellow mate (high school) by going to paint landscapes under her windows.... His architectural education was at various schools....

Endeavoured to enter the Bauhaus in ..., but his admission was rejected by Gropius himself, offended by some of his appraisals on the architecture of the Bauhaus buildings (he had said: "In thirty years, all this will be indigestible" or – sources disagree – "In thirty years, all the plaster will be a sickening crust.")

An unfortunate homosexual love for a painter ... Experience in professional studios (Milan, Vienna, Paris ...). A meeting with Le Corbusier, who copies one of the designs of his youth ... Participation in international competitions ... He wins one through a case of mistaken identity (he had called his entry *Ars Gratia Artis* as the winner had too) ... Publication of historical-theoretical articles ... He marries the daughter of a famous engineer ... He goes to war and produces a sketchbook of drawings of extraordinary beauty, then completely destroyed by the damp in the trenches ... The post-war work ... He enters the University of Rome through family connections ... He leaves (unofficially) to work on the restructuring of the university ... His greatest works ... 1949–62 in Africa ...

The fundamental essay by AB, never published through lack of faith on the part of various editors (it had been proposed to Editions d'Architecture, Phaidon, Centro Di, Studio Vista 1968) ... remains in the form of a Xerox copy ... I would like to quote a few pages ... (12–48–187...305?). The great work ... (sketches – first model – re-elaboration – working drawings – photos on the site – the completely new technical procedures – photo of the finished work) ... Quote from a letter: "This work is my self-portrait" or "My self-portrait is this work" (or perhaps the cyclic form?)...

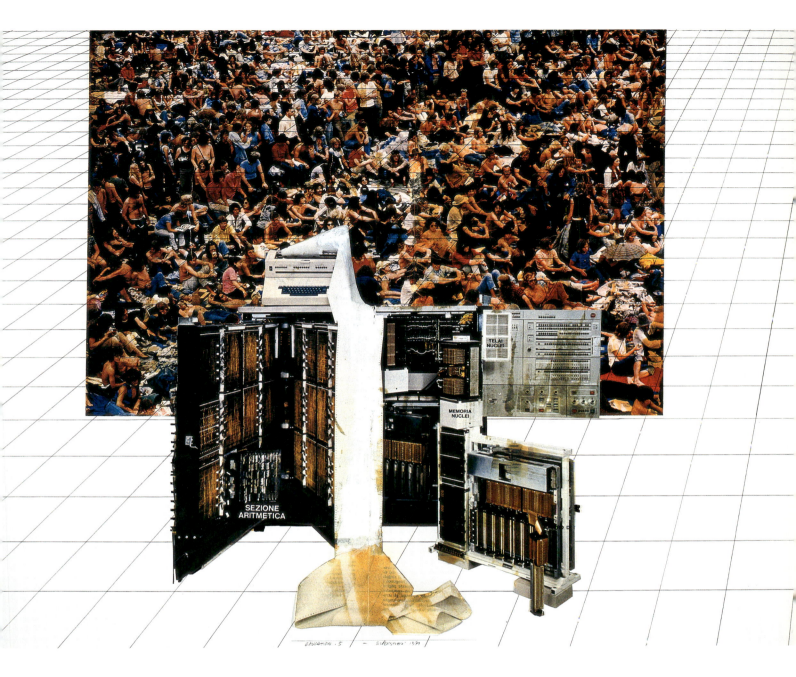

AB dies in 1966 (June 27) falling (suicide? do not mention) off a scaffolding just before the official opening of the great work … (he had climbed up in order to erase the following spray-painted slogan: "Architecture is for the bosses").

List of slides (45 minutes altogether):

"The prime reason for this dissertation is the intimate conviction of the substantial equivalence of various experiences within a homogeneous culture such as the one in which we find ourselves. In this sense, AB's work constitutes a scientific testimonial to our cultural bases, constitutes our background and the direct generatrix (cause-effect or action-reaction) of our experiences. Architecture fascinates and attracts us like Family, Church,

History. A kind of morbid attraction which can only be destroyed through an a-systematic (but not a-logical) action. Our action on architecture, the respectful "taking-to-pieces" which we have been able to effect, and the loving reconstruction of the same which we attempt through metamorphoses, are part of this therapy for new equilibrium … AB has already dreamed all our dreams. Our "heavy" architecture is only the daytime re-creation of these ghosts. Our actions are logical efforts at substituting the dream with total reality.

Sentimental education, continuous education, sexual education, political education …

And also the atrocities of education, and the well-educated child, and "it's time to forget all that stuff about 'good education'" are all

equivalent parts of this architectural education which is facing us today, dissected by delicate or rudimentary instruments.

AB's work, with all its contemporary derivations, the political tensions and existing contradictions, form a homogeneous body on which to operate. It is from this recognition of the equivalence of information (and of its irrelevance while still contained within disciplines) that a new action arises – technical perhaps, but certainly no more usable. Our present architecture is only the search for a different state which might finally do without architecture. That is all. Thank you."

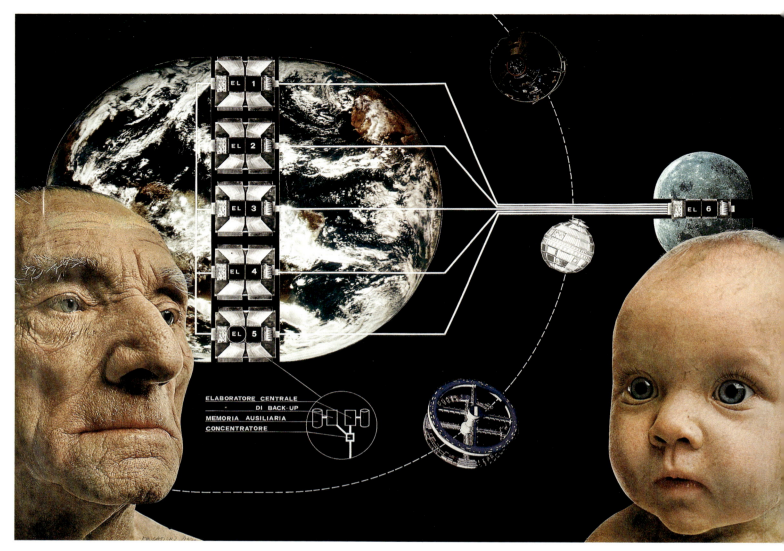

A project for a universal system of information exchange

Imagine five continental complexes each composed of a central computer, a feedback computer, relative auxiliary memory-banks and a concentrator. These complexes collect all possible information. They are connected together by a sixth complex, situated on the moon, equipped with receiving and transmitting apparatus. Four orbiting relay stations cover the whole planet with their areas of transmission. In this way, every point on the earth's surface is connected up to the network of computers. By means of a miniaturized terminal, each single individual can connect to the network described above, and thus obtain access to all the world's information. The hypothesized "machine" receives all enquiries and sends answers. If the answer does not satisfy the enquirer, he can refuse it, the machine from thenceforth will bear his refusal (and the proposed alternative) in mind, and will transmit it together with the information

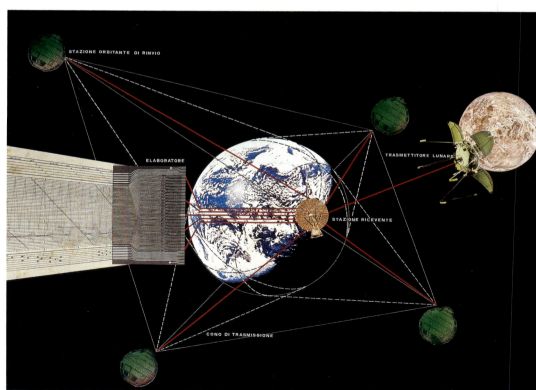

supplied by others. In this way, the machine supplies data for decision-making without influencing the decisions themselves: everyone is connected to everyone else in a form of expanded democracy in which education as a continuous process is consistent with life itself.

III. CEREMONY

THE GREAT PILGRIMAGE

The object of what may without doubt be called the greatest pilgrimage of all time is the small island of Kon-Sum-Shon in the archipelago of the Great Outputs. On this small island, covered in tropical vegetation, about one hundred years ago, a missionary from General Motors discovered that the natives worshipped as a living god a hermit living in a cave on an inaccessible rock pinnacle. The missionary succeeded in reaching the hermit and talked with him for twenty years, trying in vain to persuade him to purchase an 80,000 HP turbine. Finally, in desperation, he killed himself. His letter of goodbye, published throughout the world, caused a sensation, and thus began the spread of the cult of the "Naked God" in all nations of consumer faith. Every good consumer today holds it his prime moral duty to visit the Naked God at least once in his lifetime. Each day, the magnates of industry and commerce can be seen arriving at the feet of the red statue of Consumerism. Having abandoned their Cadillacs, Rolls and private jets, and dressed in the most modest clothing available, they climb the 5,273 grey stone steps that now replace the original native liana ladder. At the end of the stairway, the pilgrims raise their arms and are subjected to an inspection by the chief of the 3,000 guards watching over the Naked God. Today the original search has become a mere formality, because no-one would dare to commit the grave sacrilege of introducing any object into the god's grotto. Access to the small cavern is a very moving moment, almost no-one manages to hold back his tears, hysterical scenes often take place and many women faint. In the grotto, lit only by the light coming through the door, one can glimpse, behind the grille separating him from visitors, the mystical figure of the hermit, the "One without Objects", as he is called. There exists but one rare photograph of the Naked God, which we are proud to be able to offer to our readers; it was taken by a Japanese reporter who managed, at the risk of his life, to enter the holy cell, eluding the watchful guards, with a micro-camera hidden in a wart on his nose.

A BUILDING FOR AN UNKNOWN CEREMONY

Upon my arrival one day in a foreign (but not completely unknown) country, I noticed from posters and newspapers that the official opening of a monumental building was about to take place, or rather, the opening of a new public building (as I thought I understood), or perhaps only of a new piece of architecture that my linguistic problems did not permit me to interpret. On the other hand, looking at the pictures in the newspapers, I could not even see if it really was architecture. At the centre of the city, an enormous open space with regular borders had been cleared. In this open space, images of mountains and deserts were forming. The illusion of reality was perfect. Innumerable spectators were already sitting on folding chairs that were being rented out at the various entrances to the open space, and all were turned facing the same direction and wearing large glasses, protecting themselves from the artificial cold with blankets over their knees. Some were wearing special ear-protectors. Behind them, a rainbow was appearing and disappearing by turns. At the point towards which everybody's eyes were directed lay an enormous transparent solid, within which lay an enormous human figure. It must certainly have been another fictitious reality created by the masters of illusion that had designed these imaginary landscapes. The figure seemed to be connected to a complicated piece of apparatus that reacted in various ways to the small movements of his arms and legs. Unexpectedly, the rainbow vanished completely and four rectangular buildings appeared at the four cardinal points. These buildings had certainly emerged from beneath the earth by means of hydraulic mechanisms. All the onlookers, leaving their chairs, formed four different cortèges, and set off towards the buildings. Each building had two doors, one entrance and one exit.

The inside of each building (they were probably all alike) was completely dark and the long lines of visitors filed through following feeble luminous signs on the walls and ceilings. After a series of tortuous meanderings, one reached a large violently-lit room, in which there was a series of computers and other scientific apparatuses. In a transparent

Beyond the use of architecture as a service (microclimate, shelter …), another type of use is continually happening. This is the symbolic use of architecture. Architecture as the formalization of the symbols of knowledge, dominion, procreation and immortality.…

Architecture is, thus, an iceberg hiding most of itself. As the innumerable services and technical apparatuses that make it work remain unseen, so also do the rites and symbols that render it desirable and necessary, until suitable therapy succeeds in bringing human beings into harmony with themselves, with no further need for security blankets. We can immediately start using architecture itself as an instrument of this therapy. We can take architecture to pieces bit by bit and put it on the table, until it is finally available for use, with no more mysterious tricks. We can furnish it with clearly visible labels so that all architecture clearly shows its hidden purposes.

We can create such an enormous quantity of it that once and for all we create a disgusting satiety.

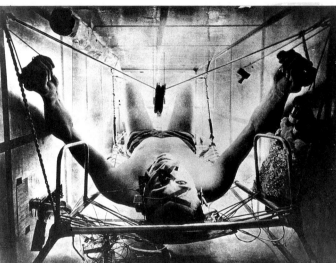

cage, there was a little white mouse, the object of an incomprehensible experiment. Without the mouse giving the slightest sign of activity, lights blinked on and off. Sometimes, the machines gave no signs of life while the white mouse moved convulsively in its cage. But the short stop possible in front of the transparent cage gave no way of formulating any theories about it. Coming out of the buildings, the crowd moved back to its seats. The enormous human figure continued its slow activities in front of an ever-changing throng. At regular intervals, the spectators left their seats, while others, flowing without interruption into the open space, replaced them. Suddenly, the rainbow reappeared. I therefore supposed that the whole cycle of the spectacle was over and left my place, making for the exit. Some people in front of me were speaking in a language I could understand at certain times. Some sentences were: "What a beautiful ceremony", and "From tomorrow, there will be architecture for all".

EVERY BUILDING ON EARTH

is destined for some unknown ceremony. Only to a few initiates is it given to draw aside the brick, wooden, iron or synthetic curtains which hide the secret rites.

We can also try designing buildings for totally unknown ceremonies and we can then compare them with existing buildings, to see how our memory retains the most significant pieces and the assembly mechanisms, and also to see how much of the so-called functionalism is merely an illusory image of a different degree of mental functionality.

The point is: if I succeed in designing a mysterious building which could stir your emotions, would you not think that your emotion in seeing those buildings which you believe to be well-known arises from the same degree of mysteriousness? In fact, I would like to take you to unknown regions merely in order to make you realize that your journey is in an equally unknown region … and from here, the next step will be the abandoning of all illusions of acting only according to reason, following scales and hierarchies, using formal models (which I can show you are only magic formulas that your witch-doctors have insidiously murmured into your ears while you slept …).

And beyond all illusion, we could try to build a reality for ourselves in which all ceremonies and rites are exclusively ours and could perhaps be very quickly forgotten.

IV. LOVE

LOVE LETTER FOR MADDALENA

The love which had unfolded within him one ordinary morning and had changed him into a pattern-book of daisies stripped of their petals, violin music and church-bells, moonlit nights and many other things he had found he possessed, was sitting with him in front of the typewriter to write his first love-letter to Maddalena. But the horror of the white sheet of paper in front of him hypnotized him as usual, and once again he felt lost and alone. Then he tried the old exorcism of breaking the purity of the paper with a letter chosen at random. He wrote R and then O and finished the word off SE. Then he noticed something strange, because, looking at the paper, he found a large red rose with its stalk still caught in the roller. As a try-out, he wrote NIGHTINGALES and there they were on the shelf holding his accounts; the male immediately began to sing. The word PERFUME dazed him and gave him the courage to write LOVE.

The philosopher who was first to enter the room was dressed in white and had a love which had been born in his brain, but had not been able to find the way out. The love of the man who followed was made of silence and tears bathing the feet of a wooden crucifix.

The love of the absent-minded scholar was hidden on the only unread page of the millions of books the old man had studied.

Then came two pallid fiancés who kissed only each other's eyes; they sat down on the sofa in the waiting room and after five minutes were groping in each other's clothes and had gained some warmth.

A mature couple passed, indifferently bearing their slow, sweaty love; but behind come two old people dragging a cold, creaking affection.

The door closed and the house was immediately invaded by:

– a man – a woman – an old man – a panting boy, with frantic hands on his own sex
– two men – two women embracing closely, with a lost look
– a person with an enigmatic expression, covered in excrement
– a man carrying a dead body and kissing it, with trepidation, on the mouth
– a very breathless woman masturbating a Great Dane
– a fat woman with a corset, suspender belt and pink hat who, worried, was clutching her adolescent son to her breast
– a very thin man with a rapt air, pressing a woman's shoe to his mouth
– a panting old man with a little girl in his arms, one hand groping under her light dress while she slept
– a man with a resigned expression hitting himself on the head with a stick carved with the head of a dog
– a person with a curious face who had watched everything and then sneaked off into a dark corner

And emptiness and silence returned to the room, but immediately afterwards, a gentleman in old-fashioned clothing came into the circle of light cast by the lamp; he put the naked, unconscious, blood-stained woman he was carrying down in the armchair in front of the writing-desk, and sat on her. The man writing to Maddalena saw a fat face, divided into squared blocks of stone by the wrinkles of age; the recollection of the old print was an efficacious introduction: "Marquis de Sade", "pleasure". In an unexpectedly sudden anguish he quickly wrote MADDALENA on the keyboard and found her on his lap, softly pressing on his sex. And he analysed her: the large mouth … the small breasts … she was different and perfect, perfect; but she was not the same girl he had taken to the cinema yesterday evening, the same as the girl entering the office now, attacking him with words he had often heard, but which she had never yet pronounced. And, as she had entered, Maddalena left, tearing the other girl into a thousand pieces. But the Marquis was still there with his stone face, while the man who had to write to Maddalena made out a list of stolen goods (daisy petals, violin notes and bells; rays of moonlight and other junk). And when the Marquis made a sign with his finger, he followed him out of the deserted office into the autumn weather. And they met:

– a woman watering geraniums in pots
– an old woman giving tripe and caresses to stray cats
– mechanical nurses putting a wounded man on a stretcher
– a prostitute bargaining with her head in the window of a car and her arse in the air
– a little boy crying and hanging on to his mother, wanting an ice-cream
– two boys fighting about sport
– and many other things you all know about

And finally they saw the soldiers marching by with their heads in helmets to protect their brains against thoughts, and it was exciting because they had on all the uniforms of the world and at each gust of the wind, the flag changed nation. And naturally the grandstand was full of kings, generals and presidents, each full of love for himself and his followers; and the grandstand was obviously the same as the one at the Nuremberg trials or perhaps one belonging to some government, where it is always love for oneself and one's followers which continues to condemn oneself when it is another's.

But it was only when the Marquis took a passer-by by his cardboard nose and pulled, that the man who wanted to write to Maddalena realized how easy it is to look behind the mask of love that we all wear, which changes from Hitler to Ophelia, but is the single model that can be bought at the supermarket.

Thus, when he arrived at the end of the parade boulevard, before the mirrored door which gives onto the other universe, he politely took off his mask, together with his hat, before entering.

He would have liked to write to us describing what he found there, but not one of the words in our vocabulary was suitable to describe that world; that … world (the adjectives are missing) in which love has been washed away from everything.

And he apologizes for this.

AN ENVIRONMENT FOR LOVE AT FIRST SIGHT

The inamoratrix machine lay immobile amongst the grass at the side of the path. But at the moment when a boy and girl passed in front of it, an almost invisible ray reached the receiver hidden on the other side of the path. The boy and girl fell onto the grass, deeply in love. The same fate befell all those who, in various parts of the globe, found themselves passing under the influence of this machine in the various environments.

V. DEATH
or the Public Image of Time and Memory

As we left the city, a great open space, uniformly paved, lay before our eyes, divided into large squares by thin black lines.

This kind of square reached as far as our eyes could see: one could glimpse its limits, or rather, one could imagine its limits, on one side where the tall vegetation began, on another the hills, and on the remaining two sides, the first outlying buildings. The colour of this surface was a uniform grey, only here and there darkened by damp patches caused by the rain of the preceding night.

Its surface was perfectly flat and one could guess that the squares were oriented to the two cardinal points. A small bronze plaque at the crossing of two of the dividing lines roughly in the middle of the whole open space bore the inscription of the astronomical coordinates of the spot. In one of the lines running from north to south was inserted a thin steel rail. An identical one lay in one of the lines running east-west. At the intersection of these two lines (presumably the physical representation of meridian and parallel passing through that point) rose a neoclassical building, strangely lost in this Cartesian desert. This building, perfect in every detail, was uniformly executed in marble chips mixed with cement, so that it seemed the copy of another, much older building, which had perhaps disappeared or the model of another building still to be constructed.

The old cemetery was near this open space: all its architectural works remained intact, but all the ground had been covered with a uniform green lawn. I think this same fate had befallen all other cemeteries, both monumental and small country ones. They remained as the cemeteries of cemeteries, frozen in memory, lying on their everlasting green lawns, as in the miracle of the Campo at Pisa.

From my right, I could see a group of normally dressed people advancing, crossing the pavement towards the building. Their manner of walking was not at all processional or solemn: they walked normally, endeavouring merely to cross the lines between the paying-stones and to avoid the wet patches. They were using one of the cracks to guide them in a straight line towards the reddish granular building. Turning towards them, I thought I glimpsed some figures at the doorway and I started towards them.

As I advanced upon the squared pavement, the straight lines formed different perspectives, fading away in the distance. The connections between the elements were particularly carefully executed, but those which from far off appeared as black lines, on my approaching were revealed to be elements in an artificial stone similar to granite, about four feet wide and on a lower level than the pavement, slightly sloping also, so as to collect rainwater and convey it to apertures covered with bronze grilles. Each square element also as one looked at the ground, could be seen to be slightly pyramidal, also for reasons of drainage, and this peculiarity, initially unnoticed, created a slight optical undulation in the flat surfaces. The material had a perfectly smooth surface, neither shiny nor opaque: it was impossible to say whether this had become so because of the passing of innumerable people or through the use of machines. There was no trace of the passage of time since the date of construction of this work, no reference as to style or epoch; no noticeable trace of deterioration due to atmospheric agents. Grass had been unable to find the slightest interstice in which to grow: neither seeds nor leaves brought by the wind could find a hold on that impassible surface; there were no birds nor insects.

Far off, where the squared surface touched unaltered nature, one could just see the lines ending abruptly against the rocks, grass or trees, almost as if the networked flat surface continued on under the natural landscape.

Once the building had been reached, it was found to have no particular characteristics: a close examination could perhaps reveal its builders' desire to make it appear "neutral". Its lack of originality was certainly intentional, or perhaps it was the suspension of time which could be felt in that enormous space which distracted attention from a detailed inspection … Several people standing in the doorway were intently checking some small gadgets that a technician was handing to them as they came out. As I grew nearer to one of these people, I could see one of the gadgets from closer. Its shape and its surfaces were definitely modern, but not particularly attractive. The colour was a dark uniform green. I enquired as to the use and purpose of these gadgets: I received the reply that they were called "memory capsules" and that they were the personal terminals of a vest electronic brain. In this brain were stored all the memories of those who died, and were then carried to this building. I then suddenly understood the nature of certain large packages, other geometrical packages and certain human figures that I had hitherto imagined to be assisted in walking, all converging on the building in the huge open space. The idea of death began to link itself to the absolute image of geometrical emptiness that I had crossed. Architecture and death suddenly coincided. A reason for the perfect order and symmetry, indifference to time and to man himself was found. The person who had replied to my enquiry about the memory capsules held out to me a grey booklet, containing some diagrams and some inscriptions. He said he did not need it and that anyway he could obtain other copies. This was the booklet:

A DIDACTIC EXAMPLE: THE NEW CEMETERY IN MODENA

The existing cemetery will be preserved in its present state, but all the ground will be permanently grassed over. In the area at our disposal, there will be a permanent ban on any building. The area will be paved with concrete and granulated marble. Granite elements four feet wide will be placed one foot lower, with a slight slope, so as to collect and direct rainwater. These elements will form straight lines intersecting at right angles in a 60-foot mesh. In this space, a building in prefabricated elements of concrete and red granulated marble will be built. This will be a perfect copy of the existing Church of St Cataldo, plus the beginning of the lateral porticos with tomb niches. The building will be constructed in such a way as to remain unaltered for an indefinite number of years. The possibility of continually replacing damaged pieces will, in theory, render it eternal, while the other existing buildings will naturally decay. At the centre of the building, a very deep well will be dug. This circular well will contain chemical and biological mechanisms able to transform any dead body thrown into it into its constituent elements, which can then immediately be recycled into the world ecosystem. The memory of all single individuals will be collected and kept by the most modern technological processes. Equipment such as tape recorders and video-cassettes today, and even more accurate and smaller equipment tomorrow will preserve the memories of the dead person for his descendants and relatives and friends, who will always have these "memory capsules" with them. In particular, the memories of the dead person will be programmed into a computer (serving several cemeteries) and the "capsules" will function as terminals. Several

computers will be connected up to form gigantic central units. These units will be able to cover the entire Earth, using re-transmitting satellites. In any place at any time anyone will be able to use the collective memory. The Well of the Dead, the Memories, the re-transmitting satellites (and all traces of these, at a minimum on Earth, such as equipment, shadows, signals) form the Cemetery.

Our idea of a Cemetery is a meditation on death, on the Definite Settlement of the Human Race and on the Use of Dead Bodies.

These last two themes have always been the ordering and numerical essence of monumental cemeteries, in which legions of bodies, arranged hierarchically, awaited and yet await the Day of Judgment, or that of their removal or more or less temporary substitution.

Monumental cemeteries are not the only architecture created for Death: Death has produced innumerable forms of architecture and nearly all monuments are dedicated to it. But these monuments have never exorcised our fear. Now we must search for another way to attain immortality, or to flee pain and fear, or to accept pain and fear, and Death and Life, serenely.

In the thoughts of man on Death, we can trace certain constant factors in all times and countries. It is through the analysis of these constant factors that we can plan a serene demeanour when faced with this "dark reality".

At the moment when we accept Death as a fact of Life (no longer as a limit, a different state), all our terrors and their liniments will fall away: at that moment, the need for architecture as a coagulum of ordered material will also fall away, as the ritual accumulation of possessions for the dark journey.

Only at that moment will man accept his reality with no need for formal structures (power, religion, architecture, rites …).

At that moment, mass will no longer need to replace the energy of memory, physicalness will no longer need to be affirmed as unique, nor as a talisman. We will no longer need architecture for Death.

Our only architecture will be our lives.

New Babylon – A Persistent Provocation

John Heintz

Introduction

Much of the recent interest in New Babylon, gratifying as it must be to the artist, tends to draw attention away from the utopian character of the project. Critics tend to attempt to de-radicalize Constant's proposition. New Babylon is either located in the territory of the unrealizable realm of personal fantasies or it is reduced to yet another instance of the inevitable and tragic realization that all utopias are dystopias. It has even been dismissed as being of little interest aside from the character of the associated drawings.[1] Yet if it is so, that New Babylon has so little interest for us, then it becomes hard to explain its enduring appeal. Why does this project never die? For although Constant stops working on his city of the future in 1969,[2] he continues to create images that refer to it through 1974, and only six years later he speaks about it again during its first revival in 1980. Interest in New Babylon revives in the early 1990s, and then again at the end of the decade – a revival that has yet to be exhausted. I would like to argue that it is specifically the utopian content of New Babylon that lends it its enduring interest. Lewis Mumford's words regarding William Morris' utopia, Nowhere, apply just as well to New Babylon: "Nowhere may be an imaginary country, but News from Nowhere is real News."[3]

1. Constant, *Diorama II*, 1964

Endless City of Unrestrained Libido

New Babylon is a land of artists, or rather, not artists but ordinary people freed of all constraint fulfilling their creative urges. Everything is new every day. It is a city of endless mazes; where the New Babylonians drift from encounter to encounter, always creating new social and physical experiences – always living in the now, always authentic.

Moreover, New Babylon is all cities in one city spread out over the entire surface of the Earth. It floats above the ground as its citizens float above material and physical constraints. Food, shelter, every desire is fulfilled through an automated super-infrastructure that immediately produces whatever is requested. Each encounter between two New Babylonians is a first encounter. There is nothing that can be lost – save life and limb? – and everything to be gained.

The pre-history of Constant's ever-shifting 'city' begins with a model of a gypsy camp. Constant was inspired by their nomadic life. Moving from place to place and re-creating, or rather creating anew, their city each time they moved. By moving together, the gypsies maintain stable social relationships among themselves, but each time they move, they make new relationships with those who live permanently in the new location. Alas, the reaction of the settled people is often so prejudiced as to pre-empt any mutually beneficial or enjoyable social relations. The New Babylonians are gypsies without a tribe, yet free also from prejudice. Their city is so easily re-configurable that we can say that they recreate it each day. And in recreating their city, they recreate their social relations as well. This process of constant renewal and remaking, permits the New Babylonians to try out all possibilities of interaction without limit other than their imagination.

Constant relieves the inhabitants of his imaginary world of any obligatory work or tasks. The mundane necessities are provided for by a robotic infrastructure. There is nothing left, then, but play: the free and creative expenditure of time and energy.

Constant made a visual pun between the structure of New Babylon and Marx's basic economic categories: base and superstructure. In New Babylon the economic base is relegated to the cellars and the ground plane. The structure that we see is, in fact, the superstructure. The principal difference between New Babylon and the socialist utopia of Marx is that in Constant's world it is the superstructure that is celebrated, rather than in Marx where it is the base. Production is trivialized. Play is everything. Leaving aside the question of who is to maintain the economic base, Constant relieves us of all basic human concerns, and forces his New Babylonians into a constant existential moment. There is nothing to do in New Babylon except that which makes one's life worthwhile.

Given the breakdown in social relations resulting from removal of the means of production from the social sphere, the very concept of 'social life' takes on a new form. The New Babylonians are not mutually dependent for their existence (a condition which until now has been a constant factor in human society). Rather the New Babylonians obtain all their sustenance and shelter from the apparatus of the city. No longer a network of necessary relations, the social life of New Babylon becomes a network of temporary relations that exist only in order to fulfil whatever creative urges those involved have in the moment. In an important sense, all social activity becomes art: not the art of the salon and gallery, but the collective and universal art previously sought by the members of the Cobra group. Art, creativity, play and social interaction all become one. New Babylon is the ultimate *Gesamtkunstwerk*.

New Babylon is also a *Gesamtkunstwerk* in a second, more imminent sense. Constant presented his utopian project through drawings and models, prints and paintings, through photos of models and graphics, through films and slide shows that combined images with sound, music and words, and through a steady stream of pamphlets, articles, and even a New Babylonian newspaper.

The resulting accumulation of materials makes possible a vividness with which we can imagine life as a New Babylonian unmatched by any other utopian project. Indeed, Constant's city is better documented than many real utopian settlements. Through the immense amount of material, its diversity and the length of the investigation, the project has acquired a thickness; a substantiality, which causes it to function all the more effectively as a dialect and strange-making tool surfacing our desires and the contradictions within them.

Constant's ultimate presentation of New Babylon was in the form of slide shows accompanied by sound-scapes. This was, at the time, one of the most sensually overwhelming media available. The highly coloured images, made with wide-angle lenses and from oblique angles, take us deep into the spaces of New Babylon.

The mirrored constructions, *Diorama I* and *II*, draw us into the furthest corners of Constant's kaleidoscopic global city. The infinite repetitions between two tilted pieces of mirror create a far deeper space than drawings or models could create. Further, the reflection of some fragment of our own face inside this space draws us even further into New Babylon. We cannot remain mere spectators. Constant invites, drags us into his world. We must participate in New Babylon.

But would we care to?

Constant's images are often disturbing. The pen-and-ink drawings are captivating but full of a reckless energy carried out in over-excited gestures that often spatter the ink, and supplemented with blotches of red. Where people are present in the models they are often represented by anonymous finishing nails, completely dwarfed by the New Babylonian megastructure. And, most alarmingly, some of his paintings and prints bear titles such as *The Assault*, *Rape* and *Voyeur*. Can this be utopian?

Utopia?

Before we can attempt to answer this question, we must attempt a definition of the term 'utopia'. It is, as we are often reminded, a pun coined by Thomas More on two Greek words: *outopia* (meaning no-place) and *eutopia* (meaning good place).[4] Various attempts have been made to provide a categorical definition of the term. The definition of utopia that I suggest we adopt here sets out distinctions between, on the one hand, *outopia* and other 'no-places', and on the other between *eutopia* and other 'good places'. Utopia is distinguished from other 'good places' by the fact that it is a good place designed to make it possible for people to live lives that adhere to a specific notion of how human beings ought to live. As Michael Holquist has it: "The utopist, before he writes a line, begins by postulating what the best man would

be; he then proceeds to articulate those conditions which would best ensure the rise and the continued existence of such a man."[5] Utopia is further distinguished from other good places by the fact that it is given shape by men and women. The topology and sociology of utopia is the product of conscious design by human beings. This distinguishes utopia from ordinary society (which is as much a product of accident as of intention) as it does from Paradise – the product of divine design. Thus utopia is the manifestation of a moral vision; a moral vision held and made manifest by people.

We should also examine the specific meaning of the notion of non-place. First of all, utopia is a place, a *topos*. It is always tied to a specific location in time and space. These locations may be at a distance that prevents us from knowing the utopian society through historical and scientific means (typically through great temporal, geographic or even cosmic distance). However, the story of utopia is almost always brought back by a traveller. Thus, there must be some possibility of travelling from here to there (even if that be through time, by means of a dream). Indeed, Thomas More gave his Utopia (the first of that name) a location on the terrestrial globe. Thus non-place cannot refer simply to the lack of place. Nor can it refer in a simple manner to the impossibility of reaching utopia. Nor, indeed, can it refer simply to the fact that utopia does not exist – such a definition would be too broad to be of any use at all.

Karl Mannheim clarifies the notion of non-place for us: "A state of mind is utopian when it is incongruous with the state of reality within which it occurs."[6] Utopia "transcend[s] the situation," referring to social objects that in Mannheim's terms "do not exist in the actual situation." Thus it is not so much that utopia does not, or cannot exist, rather it is that utopia "… seems to be unrealizable only from the point of view of a given social order which is already in existence."[7] There seems to be no way for an existing society, as a whole, to get from here to there, and this makes of utopia a non-place. We are now ready to consider whether New Babylon is a utopia.

Not dismissible

Constant himself often denied that New Babylon was a utopia, describing it as anticipating a 'desirable course of history', and calling his vision a 'realistic project' – 'feasible', 'desirable' and 'inevitable'. Thus, what he means by denying that New Babylon is a utopia is to dissociate himself with the degenerate, but sadly common, meaning given to the term – that of an unrealistic and therefore dismissible scheme. Had he read Mumford, Constant might have been consoled by his assertion that: "It is absurd to dispose of utopia by saying that it exists only on paper. The answer to that is: precisely the same thing may be said of the architect's plans for a house, and houses are none the worse for it."[8] By the definition of utopia employed here, New Babylon certainly qualifies. More importantly, as Mannheim is quoted above as pointing out, it is only "seemingly" impossible to realize utopia, and then only from within the society of which that utopia is a critique. However, despite the fact that I will continue to call New Babylon a utopia, we can sympathize with its author's concern as: "By calling everything utopian that goes beyond the present existing order, one sets at rest the anxiety that might arise from the relative utopias that are realizable in another order."[9] And setting one at rest was far from Constant's goal.

2. Constant, *Homo Ludens*, 1964

Spoiled goods

Another answer to this question, one that Mark Wigley offers, is that New Babylon seems at first (both to its creator and to its public) to be a utopia, but "is not so perfect after all."[10] Claiming that the riots and the failure of the left to succeed in overturning the established order in May 1968 is a crucial turning point for Constant, Wigley detects a change in the depictions of his ludic world: "Discrete figures finally come into focus against a few diaphanous planes in 1968. But their blotchy form now looks like blood stains. Any doubt is removed when they become red. There is a sense of ongoing violence. As we finally get close to the figures, close enough to make out faces, they have been piled up or are splattered across every surface as if there has been horrific carnage. Human life becomes just a stain of its extinction."[11]

Far from being a gateway into a better way of life, revolution is seen as bringing the end to utopia: "In the wake of 1968, revolutionary violence and post-revolutionary life become indistinguishable. The very idea of post-revolutionary life, with all its optimism, dissipated."[12] Constant has, according to Wigley "followed the social pathology to the limit of ecstasy and then to despair."[13]

Wigley dramatizes this story by invoking two turns on Constant's part, first a turn away from painting in the early 1950's, and then a turn away from New Babylon in 1974. These turns are said to be ideological in character and to indicate a major change in direction. First Constant stops being a painter, then, having discovered the horror implicit in his own vision he rejects New Babylon and returns to studio painting.

Tragic dream

Hilde Heynen would answer yes, New Babylon is utopian but only in the tragic sense in which all utopias are found to contain contradictions – antinomies – that invert them and reveal them as dystopias.

Heynen's treatment of Contant's 'utopia' occurs twice: once in an article in "Assemblage",[14] and once as a passage in her book *Architecture and Modernity*.[15] In this second context, her assess-

ment of New Babylon is situated between a discussion of the antagonism between avant-gardism and modernity that developed after the Second World War, and a descriptive account of "Adorno's aesthetic theory". She posits the project as a tragic example of the – always finally futile – desires of the avant-garde. In doing this, she places it in the tradition of utilitarian utopian projects typical of the nineteenth century. Heynen attributes to Constant the intention of resolving conflicts both between individuals and between individual and collective interests. To her it seems that Constant would wish that New Babylon would be "a society without power relations," "harmonious and free of stress," at "peace" and in "repose".[16]

Repose, however, requires dwelling, which in turn "requires developing habits … habituating oneself to certain pattern."[17] And, as Heynen notes, this "is exactly what Constant tells us is impossible in New Babylon." In the search for artistic authenticity, "The commonplace – the ordinary, everyday framework that gives life its form and permits one to postpone indefinitely any question about the ultimate meaning of life – has been abolished. With it, it would seem, the possibility of 'dwelling' has also disappeared." Instead, we see in Constant's images a "condition [that] is inseparably bound up with the death-drive, with groundlessness and indeterminacy."[18] Heynen's conclusion, stated forcibly, is that "New Babylon is a sticking proof of the impossibility of giving utopia a concrete form and of making poetry the only moment of reality: one cannot 'dwell' in New Babylon."[19]

Both Wigley's and Heynen's interpretations impose on Constant's project a widespread rejection of the notion of utopia. This notion, that utopia is totalitarianism in disguise, has become a commonplace; and damning utopia has acquired the same virtuous status as damning totalitarianism.[20] But, as Russell Jacoby argues, this equation is not well founded. We may look again at utopian projects such as New Babylon, and again find something of value, even something inspiring in them. I shall try to show that although the vision behind New Babylon is one that we find at odds with our own conventional ideas of the good life, it is consistent, and does represent a vivid alternative to our own society – a form of life that by its own lights might even be considered good.

Two 'Classic' Utopias

In general, the authors of utopias assume or predict the elimination of conflict between individual citizens of their utopias and between the individuals and the collective interests of the utopians. This elimination takes one of two forms, legislation or amelioration. The first form is exemplified by Thomas More in his *Utopia*,[21] the second by William Morris in *News from Nowhere*.[22] These two means of arriving at the end of conflict arise from fundamentally different ideas about what is to be achieved by the utopia in question. But these two strategies also bring into question our commonly held assumptions about just what utopia is.

More

In *Utopia*, Thomas More describes a highly disciplined society. There is a large and powerful legal establishment, and a substantial body of legislation. The purpose of this legislation is to anticipate all possible conflicts between citizens of Utopia and to describe the fair resolution of these conflicts. More wants his

Utopians to be free of the social abuses that characterized his own time.[23]

More believes that if the stick is big enough, then everyone will act in a morally acceptable manner, even if only out of regard for their own self interest. Indeed, he seems to believe that this construction is the only way to ensure virtuous action. This is, in fact, his motivating goal: to describe a society where everyone will act virtuously (even if virtue is not a motivation). More wants his utopians to live right, to act morally, to live up to his standard of what a human being ought to be. This is the imperative of perfectionist, or virtue, ethics – that each one of us should struggle to best exemplify those things that are qualities of a good person. More writes this imperative into the foundations of his utopia.

More's utopians are free to choose, but their choices are constrained. They are free to be moral or immoral, but the only rational course of action is in accord with the dictates of morality. More does not expect the perfectibility of people, on the contrary, he assumes that people are always vulnerable to temptation. He tries, rather, to fix the wager so that, provided they are rational, everyone must act as if they were moral. If we are to look for weak links in his construction we can find them only in two places: his expectation in the ability of legislators to anticipate and fairly resolve all conflicts, and his belief in the rationality of humans.

To those of us more familiar with the utilitarianism of nineteenth-century utopians, this sounds like a very strange idea of utopia. More makes no guarantees that his utopians will be either happy or wealthy. None of the 'great things' such as science or the arts are developed more fully in his Utopia. More does not even make his utopians good Christians. They are simply good people. This does not sound like the mission of either a state or a utopia to contemporary ears. We are accustomed to the notion that the mission of a utopia is to make its denizens happy. It is by utilitarian values – the happiness of the masses – that we are used to estimating utopias, but these utilitarian measures play little role in the archetypical Utopia. Thomas More's *Utopia* is a vision, not of how people would like to be, but of how they ought to be.

Morris

Although the nineteenth century is replete with utilitarian and socialist utopias, perhaps the best example is William Morris' *News from Nowhere*.[24] The society described in *News from Nowhere* is a workers' paradise, arising out of the withering away of the state after a revolution.[25] The citizens (although perhaps we should not call them so) of his future England have no need for money, courts, laws, armies, or any other instrument of state power or support. They have no conflicts with each other. Except, occasionally, in the realm of love, and after all, in this matter there is really nothing that we can do. Conflicts do not exist in the future because the contradictions that characterise all previous systems of production are finally done away with when the concept of property is finally set aside and workers are no longer alienated from their work.

In the conclusion of the story Morris makes clear the gulf between us and his utopians. His narrator, Guest, fades slowly from the scene of a utopian banquet. Like our own contemporaries, he is perverted by his experience of the capitalist system, and cannot find peace in this idyll. For Morris believes that the denizens of Nowhere are unlike us. They live simple lives in virtue and authenticity. The people of earth will only gradually transform into a better sort of human being as the distortions of capitalism are lifted from their shoulders. This process will occur over generations. Indeed, we might say that people revert to their pure medieval selves.

For Morris, utopia requires (and inevitability will realize) the maximization of happiness or fulfilment. Morris does not see any need to institute coercive systems to ensure behaviour – happy people will do no wrong. Nor does he hope to bring about a perfected sort of human being. Such perfection may be a side-effect of the workers' paradise, but it is not the primary goal. Morris seeks to liberate the individual – to remove the constraints of education, property, law, economy and state. The instruments More specifies to control his citizens in their own (moral) best interests would have seemed totalitarian to Morris. More makes the claim that he knows what is best for the citizens of Utopia. Morris claims that his utopians know what is best for themselves; he merely claims to know his utopians.

Morris' utopians live a life that few of us would find attractive. His Nowhere is free of the excitement and contest that so many of us find essential in our lives. It is provincial and bucolic in the extreme. Craft is everywhere, but art is absent.

Another Sort of Utopia

Constant's mission is at odds with both More and Morris. The author of New Babylon strives neither for happiness nor for regulation. He does, however, adhere to a variety of perfectionism. For Constant, the best human being is one who has the opportunity to give free reign to his or her creativity. "Now it is as a creator, and only as a creator, that the human being can fulfil and attain his highest existential level."[26] To exercise the creative spirit freely is what it is to be human. Anything less is oppression of what it is that makes us human. To fail to create is to fail to be human. This must be emphasized, as failure to understand this point results in failure to understand New Babylon.

3/4. Constant, Covers of *Opstand van de Homo Ludens*, 1969 and the German Translation *Spielen oder Töten* from 1971

Like Morris, Constant intends to set people free. However, where Morris seeks to set people free to labour without oppression, Constant seeks to set people free from labour – and from other things as well. Economics is not the only brake on our ability to create freely. Social mores also serve to inhibit us, as do habits and comfort. All these must go. Inspired by the gypsies he met while in Italy, Constant found the necessary freedom in nomadism. But New Babylon was to be no bucolic Arcadia through which innocent people wander picking fruit and listening to bird song. New Babylon is first of all a city, and the New Babylonians are urban nomads. Indeed, they hardly ever go out of doors.

The free exercise of creativity is not a principle that is conducive to peaceful harmony. Constant does not expect that New Babylon will be free of conflict. Rather he sees creativity itself as a source of conflict. Creativity is, according to Constant, also destructive; creativity is next to criminality.

New Babylon is distinguished from most, if not all, utopian projects by two features. First, unlike utopias from More's forward, its author does not seek the realization of the individual through the imposition of an ideal social order. Rather, he effectively eliminates society from consideration, and in eliminating society he eliminates order. There is no nation of New Babylon, no New Babylonian society. There are simply New Babylonians, acting spontaneously. Secondly, Constant eliminates the guilty conscience of Western society. He sets us free of both our rules and our fears, transforming all of life into play. No previous utopian has ever been so optimistic.

But if New Babylon is a moral vision, how are we to understand the natural consequences of unrestrained libido? What is the significance of the violent imagery? What are New Babylonian ethics?

The Ethics of Play

Constant cites Johan Huizinga's *Homo Ludens*[27] frequently in the manifestos and articles associated with New Babylon. It therefore makes sense to use Huizinga as a means of attempting to understand, in a little more detail, what the concept of play meant to Constant and to his New Babylonian society. In *Homo Ludens*, Huizinga repeatedly defines play over and against real life. "… play is not 'ordinary' or 'real' life. It is rather a stepping out of 'real' life into a temporary sphere of activity with a disposition all of its own. Every child knows perfectly well that he is 'only pretending', or that it was 'only for fun'."[28] Play takes place within a magic circle that sets it apart from the normal conditions of necessity and morality. "Play lies outside the antithesis of wisdom and folly, and equally outside those of truth and falsehood, good and evil."[29] One

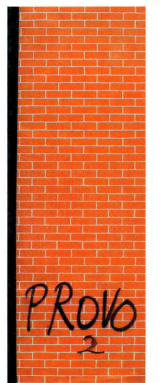

5. Cover of *Provo 2*

chooses a role and acts it out, not based on what is true or good, but on the basis of what is fun.

The fact that one may, in play, commit terrible atrocities does not reflect on one's moral character. That these 'atrocities' may have real consequences, that they may inflict real fear or pain on people, does not mitigate their status as play. Huizinga directs us to II Samuel 2, 14–16:

And Abner said to Joab, Let the young men now arise and play before us. And Joab said, Let them arise. Then there arose and went over by number twelve of Benjamin, which pertained to Ishbosheth the son of Saul, and twelve of the servants of David. And they caught every one his fellow by the head, and thrust his sword in his fellow's side; so they fell down together: wherefore that place was called Helkathhazzurim, which is in Gibeon. [30]

Here we see that play can extend to killing one's fellows, and far from atrocious, this act can be seen as one of bravery and honour. Indeed, to call attention to the 'atrociousness', the immorality, or even the undesirability of violent acts committed in play would be to play the spoilsport, to "shatter the play-world itself … rob[bing] play of its illusion – a pregnant word which means literally 'in-play' (from *inlusio*, *illudere*, or *inludere*)." As long as the pain is inflicted only on those who are playing then it is not condemned as morally offensive. This playful violence is fully in the spirit of the criminality of creativity so forcefully announced by Constant in his outline of a new culture.[31]

But if violence is not a ground upon which to cast the New Babylonians out of Huizinga's magic circle, there remains the question of the boundaries themselves. Huizinga states that play must be free, play is not 'ordinary' life, and play is bounded in time and space. But when the limits of the magic circle extend beyond the edges of the society itself – to encompass the whole world – what can be made of these distinctions? I will return to this point in my concluding remarks, but for now let us note that the principal contrast that Huizinga is making is that between play and seriousness. And within the notion of seriousness we may include necessity. In New Babylon all necessities are provided by an automated infrastructure. The entire project rests on the belief, common in the 1960s, that in the near future the banalities of production will be relegated to the realm of the machine and people will be free to devote their lives to more meaningful activity. Thus one boundary between play and seriousness in Constant's vision is at the level of the columns that raise his ludic society above mere necessity. Rising, as Huizinga says of play, "to heights of beauty and sublimity that leave seriousness far beneath."[32]

Morality of Creativity

If everything is play, and play is outside the bounds of morality, how then is it possible to speak of New Babylon as a utopia – driven by a moral vision?

Play in New Babylon is not just any game. The game here is art, or rather the free expression of creativity. Constant chooses this game because he wishes to propose that the fulfilment of that which makes us human is to be found in this expressive creativity. First begun in the era of *The Organization Man*[33], that grey-suited man, perfectly formed to take his place as a cog in the corporate machine, New Babylon is a battle cry for those who wish to overturn the establishment (to use a coded sixties term). Constant calls upon us to trade in a system in which our individuality is expressed in terms of our choice of consumer products, and choose for the opportunity to live authentically.

It is not that Constant is suggesting that we all become Artists. That is a role he tried to give up at the end of his Cobra period. Rather he is suggesting that we all – not as artists, but as people – ought to have the freedom (hitherto reserved for artists) to devote ourselves to self-expression.

This vision of free creative expression as the fulfilment of our humanity is the vision that drives New Babylon. Constant sees the ideal of creativity as expressed through a continuous generation of meaning. Meaning is never to be *established*, never to be fossilized. Instead, meaning is to be continually generated anew through encounters with the always unexpected, whether in the form of other New Babylonians or in the form of new situations.

Constant, like More, gives us a vision of how people ought to live. Again, like More, this vision of a better life does not promise happiness. He is not asserting that the New Babylonians are happier people, he is asserting that they are freer, more creative, more individuated, more complete – better people!

This better way of life, this new complete freedom, is, however, difficult: "… freedom is the most difficult way of living that a man can lead. For freedom can only be realized in creation and creation means discipline."[34] Being a New Babylonian is hard work.

New Babylon upsets all conventional notions about what we should aspire to, how we should live. Constant confronts us with the unpleasant fact that the expression of creativity is never safe or harmonious. Creativity disrupts, must disrupt, the *status quo ante*. If we are to be continuously creative, then nothing can be secure. Constant promises us pleasure: pleasure in creativity, and pleasure in contest, even pleasure in pain. But pleasure is not the same thing as happiness.

Heynen

Heynen's interpretation of New Babylon as typically tragic is based on the attribution to its creator of goals (the goals of the modernism she wishes to critique) that the denizens of New Babylon be happy, comfortable, and safe.[35] However, these are goals for which there is very little evidence that Constant had – and indeed much evidence that he did not have.

Heynen assumes that Constant believes that New Babylon will be a peaceful world. Her assertion that "there is no guarantee whatsoever that the disappearance of social struggle for existence would mean that violence and conflicts between individuals would disappear like snow melting in the sun"[36] does not apply. Constant promises that "a ludic society … knows none of the individual or collective conflicts that characterize utilitarian society." New Babylonians may no longer be engaged in the struggle of all against all for mere survival, but a life of continuous invention imposes its own rigors. Constant is not promising harmony and repose. Rather he is proposing that without the

6. Constant, *Terrain Vague III*, 1973

requirement of seriousness, without the need to struggle for survival, conflict moves into the magic circle and acquires a new meaning.

Heynen condemns New Babylon because it "seems" impossible to "dwell" there. It is impossible to maintain an "everyday framework that gives life its form and permits one to postpone, indefinitely, any question about the ultimate meaning of life …"[37] This is then offered as the tragic character of utopia.

Heynen's argument rests on the point suggested by her use of the word 'seems' in declaring New Babylon un-dwell-able. The dissociation with the habits of everyday life under capitalism, the very habits necessary for dwelling, is precisely Constant's intention.

Thus what Heynen claims as a discovered contradiction is actually an explicit goal. "… the New Babylonian who creates his life cannot exhibit repetitive behaviour."[38] New Babylon may well arouse feelings of dread in us. Just as Guest feels unease in Nowhere. We are not ourselves New Babylonians, and are not fitted to that world. Heynen's critique would make sense if Constant's vision was in the utilitarian spirit of utopias such as Morris' *Nowhere*. But it is not. One cannot "dwell" in New Babylon – at least not if dwelling means establishing a system of durable relations and habits. That is the point. To quote Heynen: "Dynamism, permanent change, and flexibility are in fact ineluctably in conflict with qualities such as peace, repose, and harmony."[39] But one can *live* there. Indeed, the point of New Babylon is that here we are freed from the prison of mere dwelling and permitted the full development and expression of our creative selves. We are permitted to become what Constant believes to be exemplary human beings.

And what are we to make of Heynen's complaint that "The images are hardly open to being interpreted as foreshadowing an ideal future."[40] Whose ideal is she referring to here? Certainly, it is true that New Babylon is no paradise for those seeking repose in harmony – but not all are. In his anti-utopian novel[41], Robert

Graves condemns harmonious utilitarian utopias after the manner of Morris for being boring and restrictive. And Mumford finds many classical utopias, designed to ensure a stable and harmonious social condition, to be systems designed to end "human growth".[42] Clearly harmony and repose are not everyone's ideal. The blackness behind the figures in *Homo Ludens* in which Heynen sees a rejection of joy, can equally be seen as the sombre oppressive quality of contemporary society overcome by joy.[43] Constant offers us a picture of revolution that is bound up with the ecstasy of creation and destruction. He explicitly links these two extremes as the necessary condition for the free expression of creativity.

What Heynen is doing here is applying moral judgements to Constant's game, the game of utopia. For indeed, the setting out of a utopia is a kind of game.[44] In doing so Heynen is playing the role of the spoilsport,[45] breaking the game, breaking us out of utopian speculation and shattering the illusion necessary to continue to imagine life in New Babylon. Yet a game, a utopian speculation, cannot be judged by laws external to it. Games are played according to their own logic, and they must be free of the seriousness that characterizes ordinary life – as must utopian speculations. It matters not if we find a particular utopia not to our taste. What is important is that it provokes us.

Wigley

The belief that Constant himself turns against New Babylon is rooted in an interpretation of the prints and paintings, and dramatized, it is claimed, by the ubiquitous signs of disease. But stains can also been seen as signs of spontaneity, freedom from the demands of technique, and of a devotion to directness and authenticity, and we can give another meaning to the images of sexual violence. The New Babylonian is a nomad who must reconstruct his life anew in every moment. Relations between people are created and broken "tied and untied" swiftly and "with perfect openness".[46] But also without guilt and in a context of experiment and play. Indeed as early as his Cobra phase Constant called for artistic, sexual and social experimentation.[47] The scenes of sexual and violent encounter in New Babylon must be seen in this light – as playful experiments in self-expression undertaken freely, and within the magic circle. New Babylonians engage in such encounters as freely as boxers entering the ring to exercise their prowess in their chosen game.

As for the turn away from painting, and then back to it at the end of the New Babylon period, these changes need not be seen as ideological, nor were they absolute. "Some time in 1953 [Constant] lost his interest in painting and plunged into sculpture, architecture and urban planning. Until the end of the sixties he was only to pick up his brush on sporadic occasions."[48] Constant never completely stopped painting, and produced many prints throughout the time he was working on New Babylon. And as for the end of the New Babylon project, well, all things must come to an end. After working on the project for more than a decade, it seems likely that Constant had simply come to an end of what he could do with it. The social conditions of the time were turning away from the possibility of radical change. In the *Terrain Vague* paintings we see New Babylon receding into the horizon, the ground between us and the desirable future rendered as a wasteland of silted-over news clippings – our events, our history separating us from the joy of freedom. Surely these are sombre images, but the grieving seems to be for the fact that the corruption and violence of our own society makes New Babylon and the life it represents seem like an unrealizable dream. So, in the end Constant returns to painting, after all "… what was the artist to do when he was only allowed to engage in teamwork sporadically, when there was no prospect of sweeping social change and when the city of the future was threatening to overrun his entire studio? … Constant knew the answer: 'just keep on working on something or other.'"[49]

A Radical Provocation

But is New Babylon utopian?

I mentioned above one reason Constant rejected the title of utopia for his brave new city, but he had another, more fundamental, objection: "A Utopia is a picture of society that ignores material conditions, an idealization of reality. Utopia is a world without aggression, without suffering, without doubt, without drama, but also, therefore, a world without change, without creativity, without play, without freedom."[50]

But as we have seen, utopia need not be about happiness. If we accept that the creative spirit is the essential aspect of humanity, a utopia intended to bring about the fullest expression of this spirit would be radically different from the picture of 'Utopia' argued by Constant. In a utopia devoted to the creative spirit, doubt, suffering and aggression in a context of freedom stimulate change, creativity and play.

Is the painting of a voyeur a condemnation of voyeurism and public sex, or is it a celebration of the pleasure that all three figures are taking in their mutual actions? The moral judgements that some are so eager to apply to the situations depicted in Constant's New Babylon paintings are out-of-place. They are judgements made by outsiders to New Babylon. The New Babylonians would think differently. We cannot know how they would think; we can only imagine. But in imagining we must and can move beyond our own society into possible futures. We can evaluate such possible futures from within themselves (as we imagine them) and not from our original perspective. Perhaps we can even begin to examine our own society from the point of view of the imagined New Babylonians, or from the point of view which we find that we hold as we imagine ourselves as citizens of New Babylon.

It is just this imagining that is the social function of utopias.[51] Utopia may not be possible, may contain within itself irreconcilable desires and impulses, but its imagination brings us closer to a better world. New Babylon has, some would say, already served this purpose. It certainly had a significant impact on the course of radical Dutch politics in the sixties, inspiring not only the goals but also the methods of the Provos.[52] And, despite the constant flack conservatives now direct towards the sixties, these radical movements have changed our lives.

The reason that we do not seem to be able to let New Babylon rest is that it does not let us rest. New Babylon is such a startling and discomfiting provocation that like the proverbial itch, we just have to scratch it. In an era in which "socialists and leftists do not dream of a future qualitatively different from the present",[53] the vision of an alternative future, a future which speaks to our desires for freedom, not only from political and financial restraints but also from social and psychological inhibition, is a powerful drug, a habit that is hard to kick.

Or should I say "tonic"? Because what I mean is that New Babylon freshens and opens up space in our psyche for imagination, dreaming, and eventually political and social change. One does not have to be a committed radicalist to find that the notion of the future being an endless repetition of the present a suffocating burden. New Babylon releases us from that burden. Perhaps the reason that Constant's playful city has never become absorbed into the spectacle, yet continues to return to us, is that the ideal of humanity manifested in it is so challenging, so unpleasant to petit-bourgeois ears, and so forcefully asserted, that it can never be subsumed into the consumerist ethic. It is the very difficulty of New Babylon, the frightening demands it places on us, that have made it an enduring success. We may not choose to endorse Constant's dream, but his example frees us to dream our own dreams of better futures – of utopia.

Notes

1 "There is nothing interesting about New Babylon except the drawings." Mark Wigley's comment during a debate session during the conference "New Babylon: The value of dreaming the city of tomorrow", 26–27 February 2000, Delft University of Technology, Delft, The Netherlands.
2 In an interview for a recent article in the NRC Handelsblad Constant gave 1969 as the date when he stopped working on New Babylon. Mark Wigley gives a somewhat later date, 1974. Anna Tilroe, "Miskend ben ik zeker, Schilder Constant over zijn 'Nieuw Babylon'," NRC Handelsblad, 16 January (Rotterdam, 2004), p. 19.
3 Lewis Mumford, The Story of Utopias (New York: The Viking Press, 1922), p. 24.
4 Mishtooni Bose, "Introduction," Thomas More, Utopia (Ware Hertfordshire: Wordsworth Editions, 1997), pp. vii–xiv. (page vii)
5 Michael Holquist, "How to play utopia," Ehrmann, J. (ed.), Game, Play, Literature, (Boston: Beacon Press, 1968), pp. 106–123. (page 113)
6 Karl Mannheim and Louis Wirth, Ideology and Utopia: An introduction to the sociology of knowledge, (New York: Harcourt Brace and Company, 1936), p. 192.
7 Ibid., p. 196.
8 Lewis Mumford, The Story of Utopias (New York: The Viking Press, 1922), p. 25.
9 Karl Mannheim and Louis Wirth, Ideology and Utopia: An introduction to the sociology of knowledge, (New York: Harcourt Brace and Company, 1936), p. 197.
10 Mark Wigley, Constant's New Babylon, The Hyper-Architecture of Desire, (Rotterdam: 010, 1998), p. 68.
11 Ibid., p. 69
12 Ibid., p. 70
13 Ibid., p. 70.
14 Hilde Heynen, "New Babylon: The antinomies of utopia," Assemblage, no. 29 (1996) pp. 24–43.
15 Hilde Heynen, Architecture and modernity: a critique, (Cambridge, Mass.: MIT Press, 1999).
16 Ibid.
17 Ibid., p. 172.
18 Ibid., p. 175.
19 Hilde Heynen, "New Babylon: The antinomies of utopia," Assemblage, no. 29 (1996) pp. 24–43.
20 Russell Jacoby, The End of Utopia: Politics and culture in an age of apathy, (New York: Basic Books, 1999), p. 43.
21 Thomas More, Utopia (Ware, Hertfordshire: Wordsworth, Editions, 1997).
22 William Morris, "News from Nowhere," News from Nowhere and Other Writings (London: Penguin Books. 1993 [1890]) pp. 41/228.
23 Anthony Stephens "The Sun State and its shadow, on the condition of utopian writing," E. Kamenka, (eds.), Utopias, Papers from the annual symposium of the Australian Academy of the Humanities (Melbourne: Oxford University Press, 1987).
24 William Morris, "News from Nowhere," News from Nowhere and Other Writings (London: Penguin Books. 1993 [1890]) pp. 41/228.
25 Morris was an active socialist devoting at one point considerable effort to preparing workers for the revolution he believed to be imminent. See: Clive Wilmer, "Introduction," William Morris, News from Nowhere and Other Writings (London: Penguin Books. 1993), pp. xvii–xix.
26 Constant, "New Babylon: Outline of a culture", Mark Wigley (ed.), Constant's New Babylon, The Hyper-Architecture of Desire, (Rotterdam: 010, 1998), pp. 160/165, p. 160.
27 Johan Huizinga, Homo Ludens: A study in the play element of society (Boston: Beacon Press, 1955).
28 Ibid., p. 8.
29 Ibid., p. 6.
30 Huizinga translates 'Hel'kath-hazzu'r m' as 'The Fields of the Brave'.
31 Constant, "New Babylon: Outline of a culture", Mark Wigley (ed.), Constant's New Babylon, The Hyper-Architecture of Desire, (Rotterdam 010, 1998), pp. 160/165.
32 Johan Huizinga, Homo Ludens: A study in the play element of society, (Boston: Beacon Press, 1955), p. 11.
33 William H. Whyte, The Organization Man (Garden City, N.Y.: Doubleday, 1956).
34 Constant, "Discipline or Invention", Mark Wigley (ed.), Constant's New Babylon, The Hyper-Architecture of Desire, (Rotterdam: 010, 1998), p. 142.
35 It must be admitted that Constant does, once, use the word "happiness" in association with New Babylon. The context of the piece makes it clear that he is referring to the possibilities of "ambiances" for generating pleasure and to the fulfilment to be gained from this pleasure, rather than an extended condition of peace, repose and harmony. As he is also calling for the work of professional artists and engineers in realizing such ambiences it is not clear that this other life in this other city can yet be that of the New Babylonians (as in New Babylon there would be no artists or engineers as such). Constant, "Another city for another life", Libero Andreotti & Xavier Costa (eds.), Theory of the Dérive and other situationist writings on the city, (Barcelona: Museu d'art Contemporani de Barcelona, Actar, 1996), pp. 92–95.
36 Hilde Heynen, Architecture and modernity: a critique, (Cambridge, Mass.: MIT Press, 1999), p. 173.
37 Ibid., p. 172.
38 Constant, "New Babylon: Outline of a Culture", Mark Wigley (ed.), Constant's New Babylon, The Hyper-Architecture of Desire, (Rotterdam: 010, 1998), pp. 160/165, p. 164.
39 Hilde Heynen, Architecture and modernity: a critique, (Cambridge, Mass.: MIT Press, 1999), p. 173.
40 Ibid., p. 173.
41 Robert Graves, Seven Days in New Crete, (London: Quartet Books, 1975).
42 Lewis Mumford, The Story of Utopias (New York: The Viking Press, 1922), p. 4.
43 Such an interpretation seems all the more likely when one learns that Constant entitled a book The Revolt of Homo Ludens. Constant, Opstaan van de Homo Ludens, een bundel voordrachten en artikelen, (Bussum: Paul Brand, 1969).
44 Michael Holquist, "How to play utopia," Ehrmann, J. (ed.), Game, Play, Literature, (Boston: Beacon Press, 1968), pp. 106–123.
45 Johan Huizinga, Homo Ludens, A study in the play element of society, (Boston: Beacon Press, 1955), p. 11 & 21.
46 Constant, "New Babylon: Outline of a Culture", Mark Wigley (ed.), Constant's New Babylon, The Hyper-Architecture of Desire, (Rotterdam: 010, 1998), pp. 160/165, p. 164.
47 Constant, "Cést notre désir qui fait la révolution", COBRA (Organ du front international des artistes expérimentaux d'avante-garde), no. 4, 1949.
48 Marcel Hummelink, "An animal, a night, a scream, a human being: Unity and diversity in Constant's work", Frits Keers (ed.) Constant schilderijen: 1948–1995, (Amsterdam: Stedelijk Museum, 1995), pp. 27/42, p. 30.
49 Ibid., p. 34.
50 Constant, "New Babylon – Ten Years On", Mark Wigley (ed.), Constant's New Babylon, The Hyper-Architecture of Desire, (Rotterdam: 010, 1998), pp. 232–236, p. 235.
51 Ernst Bloch, The Utopian Function of Art and Literature: Selected essays, (Cambridge, Mass: MIT Press, 1988).
52 The Provos were an anarchistic group dedicated to the staging of provocative actions in Amsterdam during the mid '60s.
53 Russel Jacoby, The End of Utopia: Politics and culture in an age of apathy, (New York: Basic Books, 1999).

Psychogeogram: An Artist's Utopia

Martin van Schaik

3. Overture

Siècles à venir! Vous ne verrez plus ce comble d'horreurs & d'infamie.[194]

In the rainy summer of 1966, when Betty van Garrel and Rem Koolhaas pay a visit to Constant at his new studio in the derelict harbour district of Amsterdam, the artist's career as a public figure is at its zenith.

In architecture Constant's name is now firmly established, much to the disgust of Guy Debord and what remained of his SI after it had finally turned its back on artistic praxis.[195] In but a few years New Babylon had become an integral part of the massive tide of megastructural projects that had swept the world during the first half of the 1960s.[196] A lecture at London's Institute of Contemporary Arts in 1963 had brought Constant into fleeting contact with a younger generation of practitioners who took him as a source of inspiration in one way or another. As the little map of the pan-European Archigram network confirms, the members of the British collective were certainly happy to consider Constant one of their kind.

As in the talk that had propelled him into the limelight in the U.K., Constant (armed with his slight, trademark stutter but enviably polyglot) had stated his case in schools of architecture across Germany and Denmark, while his French connections assured him a place alongside the work of GEAM in journals such as André Bloc's *L'Architecture d'aujourd'hui*.[197] Only Constant's fierce behind-the-scenes attacks on Michel Ragon[198] prevented New Babylon from becoming canonized in the many books that the prolific guru of prospective architecture was to publish on the "urbanism of the future".[199] Still, this resistance hardly helped, as Constant's work would invariably be associated with that of other future-oriented technophiles and visionaries – circles that naturally included Friedman and Constant's one-time partner Nicolas Schöffer.[200] Adolfo Natalini, founder of Superstudio, later confirmed this widespread perception of New Babylon at the time: "To us, Constant was part of all these preposterous megastructural things that were happening everywhere. (...) Yona Friedman, Constant, they were all the same. On the other hand, we only learned about these matters through magazines, so perhaps we didn't understand these projects too well. We didn't know much about the Situationists either, or that Constant had been a member of them."[201] Clearly the message that New Babylon was something entirely different had not come across properly. As Debord had predicted, seeking the limelight to promote one's ideas had its drawbacks.

In the Netherlands, the situation appeared similarly ambiguous. Whereas Karel Appel was the nation's uncontested "experimental" painter-prima donna, Constant was slowly but surely emerging from the shadow of his former colleague. The name New Babylon was soon to catch on. As Nic Tummers, one-time close collaborator put it: "If you can speak of it in these terms, he certainly couldn't complain about a lack of success, because the 'brand' New Babylon … well, that one of course was quite a hit. And his exceptional position between the other painters – his stopping with painting – was not bad for his image and appeal either."[202] As early as 1962, New Babylon had been aired on national television by the poet-writer-animator Simon Vinkenoog, on a "studio visit" to Constant's ground-floor apartment. Vinkenoog had been very close to members of Cobra; and, like Constant, Appel and Corneille and many of the Cobra poets, he had moved to Paris in the early 1950s to get a taste of freedom and meet the world.[203] From early 1960 onward, Vinkenoog had enthusiastically embraced and promoted New Babylon, and by offering Constant opportunities to publish articles in the *Randstad* periodical, he did much to broaden the project's appeal. In the end, however, it was the large retrospective exhibition in the autumn of 1965 in the Gemeentemuseum in The Hague that would generate the publicity that finally put Constant on the map for a wider audience, Because the exhibition included work from the mid-1940s onward, New Babylon could now be easily identified as both a break with and the logical "crowning stage" of the Cobra period.[204] In intellectual circles, the ex-painter Constant – the tireless self-re-inventor who alone lived up to the experimental calling of the legendary movement[205] – was now beginning to become a household name. Not

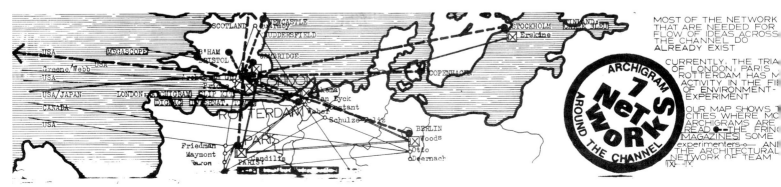

60. "Networks around the Channel", *Archigram 7*

61. Simon Vinkenoog and Constant, "Atelierbezoek", 1963

insignificantly, however, the show in The Hague coincided in the Dutch press with the spectacular emergence of the Provo phenomenon.

Through the years, a great deal has been written about the association between Constant and Provo, the Amsterdam-based young, anarchic collective.[206] It is certainly a fact that both are inextricably linked to the period of "Amsterdam magic centre", the days in which the city became to youth culture what London had been in the early 1960s and San Francisco at the end of the decade: a hedonistic Mecca. To the Netherlands at large, Provo marked the coming-of-age of the Dutch welfare state and the rapid transformation of a rather sedate and traditional country into what to the outside world began to look like a nation of pot-smoking progressives. Likewise, the movement marked a watershed between the early sixties of reformist optimism – in spite of the looming threat of nuclear annihilation – and the closing years of the decade with their far-reaching ideological polarization. In the catalytic Provo episode, New Babylon was the vital ideological agent. Constant's project was commonly seen to be the "Provo Utopia" whilst Amsterdam's "magic centre" was declared the "first sector of New Babylon".[207]

The Dutch exhibit at the 1966 Venice Biennale, a direct spin-off of the show in The Hague, confirmed the artist's stature and his symbolic role at the heart of the action. Given a solo exhibition in the Dutch pavilion in the *Giardini*, Constant was celebrated as one of the most outstanding and influential artists of his day. If this attention is perhaps indicative of the attitude of the "repressively tolerant" cultural and political elites in the Netherlands,[208] to many observers it certainly put Constant in an awkward position: the self-professed radical who sided with the young rebels in the street and who continued to preach the end of the world as everyone knew it, had now accepted the role of prime artistic representative of the Dutch nation. Whilst Guy Debord sent a cynical telegram congratulating his old comrade,[209] an exasperated newspaper reporter demanded, "What kind of alliance do these contradictions forge in a man, who is one of the founders of Cobra and who has remained an arch-revolutionary?"[210]

If Constant's involvement with Provo, on the very surface, might appear to signal a shift from prophesy to provocation and from prefiguration to political action, it actually fits in with a process of progressive withdrawal from the practical front and – inversely – increasing militancy of thought. But let us look a little closer at how the shift actually occurred and how it is reflected in Constant's art. As we shall see, in New Babylon the stage for the great withdrawal had already been set.

The march of the provotariat

Provo was a groundbreaking but short-lived movement that consisted of a relatively small core group of young activists who descended on Amsterdam in early 1965. Officially, Provo lasted but two years – between the first rotoprint flyer in 1965 and the official disbanding in 1967. The two key figures in the group were Roel van Duijn and Rob Stolk, both in their early twenties but from quite dissimilar backgrounds. In every account of the movement, Stolk – a working-class youth from nearby Zaandam – has been identified as the "street Provo", whereas Van Duijn, born in an intellectual upper middle-class milieu in The Hague, is commonly regarded as the ideologue of the movement. Both had been active in "Ban the bomb" groups, and both had had a short but intense career in more "traditional" anarchist circles. But clearly it was Van Duijn who would be most interested in what Constant had to say.[211]

The young men who founded Provo arrived in an Amsterdam that was already home to an exotic collection of artistic birds. Vinkenoog was an integral part of that scene, having staged the first official happening in the Netherlands in 1962 with *Open het graf* (Open the grave). Though this "ode to the living dead" was still an indoor event witnessed only by a select progressive elite[212] on the streets of the city, a one-man show was meanwhile gathering momentum that would form the inspiration for Provo's street actions. Robert-Jasper Grootveld – the manic "anti-smoking magician" who ironically kept himself permanently high on marihuana – had begun to stage weekly happenings on the Spui square in the centre of the city.[213] Other performing artists were quick to join the fun, amongst them the young Provos.

62. Provo presents its White Bicycle Plan, summer 1966

In many ways the Provos changed the character of the Grootveld-style ritualistic performance, bringing in a more political note. Not only did they use the happenings as an opportunity to distribute their stencilled magazine, but they also turned the Saturday evenings around the *Lieverdje* statuette into a cat-and-mouse game, living up to the name of their movement. The happenings became well-scripted exercises in provocation – dances that inevitably culminated in the arrival of the police, who brusquely put an end to the performance: with the press looking on, the happenings unmasked the forces of law and order as the keepers of a latently fascist police state.[214]

Authorities in panic were also good news on the propaganda front, earning Provo much sympathy in Amsterdam and beyond. All in all, the happenings on the Spui and elsewhere had quickly become a public relations war, a media hype in which Provo not only became the focal point and synonym for the "youth problem" but also an instant, real-time myth. Even though the smoke bombs detonated during the marriage of the Dutch crown princess were a brilliant media coup that propelled Provo onto the international stage, the impact of the movement far exceeded the scale or ferocity of its actions. Only the death of a construction worker during riots in the summer of 1966 – protests which in fact had nothing to do with the anarchist group – rang as a clear dissonant in a largely playful constellation that was as chimerical as a puff of smoke. In its mediagenic artistry, Provo would doubtless have made Guy Debord quite envious.

Provo fit seamlessly into Constant's conception of a dissatisfied, frustrated young vanguard: kids getting *organized* and displaying proto-New Babylonian behaviour to boot, claiming the streets of the city and turning traffic arteries into spontaneous acculturation zones. Constant gave the movement his complete sympathy. Indeed he was to make his appearance twice in the little *Provo* journal;[215] and when Provo, armed with its ludic "white plans" for environmental improvement, participated in the 1966 communal elections (clearly a provocation in itself), Constant symbolically took his place on the ballot list.[216] Still, as Roel van Duijn insisted, Constant remained aloof: "He was more like a visionary. He did not seek any contact with us, it was more the other way round."[217]

To the Provo ideologue, however, Constant was no less than a guiding light.[218] Van Duijn adopted Constant's "creativistic" outlook[219] and gladly embraced the idea of a "provotariat" – the term Van Duijn invented to label Constant's revolutionary class, which he contrasted with the comatose mass of "addicted consumers", the "klootjesvolk"[220] – that would bring about revolutionary change: "So when I was asked to give speeches, in those days I spread the gospel of New Babylon and mixed it with the concept of the provotariat, of the provotariat as the harbinger of New Babylon".[221] In Van Duijn's categorization, however, there was a distinct whiff of elitism, of them-and-us stigmatization, of

young and new versus old and established that radicalized and fossilized Constant's own categories of Homo Faber and Homo Ludens. Van Duijn's reasoning had a decidedly Calvinist twist to it, a clear notion of "the elect" standing against the irredeemable majority, giving his outlook a dark, pessimistic undertone: "I was very much aware of our imminent defeat".[222] Ultimately, Van Duijn lacked Constant's Marxist faith, even though he adopted the view that automation would lead to a surge in unemployment and dissatisfaction.[223] To him, however, the 'klootjesvolk' mentality was more deeply ingrained and in most cases simply incurable.

By the Summer of Love in 1967, Provo had run out of steam. With many of its ideas absorbed by mainstream politics and picked up by the cultural establishment, it abruptly ceased to exist. Roel van Duijn was to return to the activist front a year later with "Kabouter", a radical departure from his previous activities: similarly ludic but inspired by biological farming, it was markedly anti-technological and pro-environmental,

72. Police charge on the Dam Square, 1966. Photo Cor Jaring

preaching a back-to-the-earth and self-help message that was more in tune with the emergent hippy culture. Constant's reaction to Van Duijn's change was predictably fierce.[224] With the end of Provo, Constant had now effectively lost his followers and all relationship – even indirect – with a political praxis. But Constant's position with regard to the street remained unchanged. As an informed observer put it in late 1966: "The only thing he does, nowadays, is stick things together in his old, well-heated school, while nobody has so many facilities as he does. What is missing in him are deeds."[225]

Encores and experiments

Constant's move to a new, larger work space in an old first-floor gymnasium in Amsterdam's Kattenburg area in 1965–66 can be seen as the beginning of a new phase of model making. The

63–71. (Opposite page:) Provo, 1965–1966, photographs Cor Jaring. Four pictures top, left: Robert-Jasper Grootveld performing by the Lieverdje on the Spui. Other images, clockwise from top right: introducing "Hollands Happenen"; girl with Provo umbrella (with *Magies Centrum* Apple symbol); Roel van Duijn during the 1966 municipal elections; Rob Stolk in action; policeman with smoke bomb during Royal wedding, 1966 – the event that launched Provo onto the international scene.

73. Constant, *Sectoren rondom een bos*, 1967

sheer size of the studio – still in use today – allows him to hire assistants to help with the construction of a new generation of sector models. Constant's son Victor, now in his early twenties and a budding photographer, also becomes involved. The new *maquettes*, not surprisingly, are far bigger and more intricate than their predecessors. Work begins on *Fragment van een sector* as early as 1966,[226] only to be completed in 1969. The truly breathtaking *Grote gele sector* (Large Yellow sector) sees the light in 1967. Smaller models, suggestive of labyrinthine sector interiors – *Ladderlabyrint* and *Mobiel ladderlabyrint* – are made in that same year. Evidently, the successes and celebrity on the national and international stage have given New Babylon a fresh lease on life, though some of the novel constructions are clearly intended to replace older models, such as the equally large, airy *Sector constructie* from 1959. The new *maquettes*, however impressive, are thus not a departure from the earlier work: to a certain extent the first few years after *Skizze zu einer Kultur* mirror the first, solo period of model-making preceding it.

Much more unexpected, in fact, are two wonderful collages from 1966–67: *Sectoren rondom een bos* (fig. 73) and *New Babylon op historische kaart van Middlesex* (New Babylon on the historical map of Middlesex). The first shows fragments of existing city maps symbolizing New Babylonian sectors gently draped around the Bois d'Armainvilliers in the Brie region of France. It illustrates the gentle embrace between the urban network and the underlying, unblemished landscape tapestry, dramatizing the contrast between urban intensity and pastoral tranquillity. The

second collage, in addition, features small sector icons that indicate what type of construction could be employed. But the true importance of the collages derives from the fact that the sectors are glued onto facsimiles of historic maps: with the distinction between future and past polemically erased, New Babylon is not so much positioned "out of time" as projected into a post-historic timeframe. The maps remind us that in the world of Homo Ludens the mother of all dialectics has reached its conciliatory conclusion.

Constant meanwhile works on practical commissions that mostly concern art in public space – typical *Liga Nieuw Beelden* assignments – such as a fountain in Leiden (built in 1966), two projects for the *Evoluon* technology centre in Eindhoven (with André Volten and Shamai Haber, 1965, not realized), a sculpture for a motorway exit near The Hague (Project 'Witte brug-Hubertus-viaduct', with Carel Visser, 1969–73, unbuilt[227]) and a large, important assignment to design the public spaces outside the new Arnhem post and telecom office, designed by Bakema and Van den Broek. This lucrative commission from 1967 drags on for many years until it is finally cancelled in December 1972.[228] Though all these projects naturally involve practical planning, they have little to do with the spirit of New Babylon, even if the Arnhem design, with its garishly exotic materials, has aptly been described as a miniature version of it.[229]

What remained of the experimental spirit that the 1948 manifesto had called for, the significance of which Constant reaffirmed in his 1965 essay "De dialectiek van het experiment"?[230] A few efforts stand out; they form the prelude to the end of New Babylon as a project.

To begin with, there is the frequently quoted *Experiment Studio Rotterdam* (ESR) from 1966[231] that Constant realized together with photographer Bram Wisman (responsible for many of the legendary sector photos), and sculptor and critic Nic Tummers, while Harald Eckardt and Ben Weehuizen, both of the Rotterdam

74. Experiment Studio Rotterdam, 1966: delighted visitors

Bouwcentrum (Building centre), acted as the practical coordinators. It had been Eckardt's idea to install inside the *Bouwcentrum* a space that could be a permanent exhibition-cum-laboratory, a playful showcase in which the public could acquaint itself with modern construction materials and state-of-the-art environmental techniques. The creative trio chose a rather peculiar two-storey pentagonal space, which they filled with a large modular space frame, a miniature "door labyrinth", corridors of different heights (some of which one had to crawl through), a room of mirrors, an automatic photo machine, a slide connecting two levels, and a small "documentation centre" providing written and visual material explaining the theoretical and historical background of the concepts of social space and mood engineering. The three men topped it all off with coloured light shows and soundscapes, whith phones installed to record the visitors' reactions. In more than one way, this cheerful little playground was strongly reminiscent of the plan for the 1960 Situationist exposition in the Stedelijk Museum in Amsterdam.[232]

Indeed, the cancelling of this show continued to nag at Constant. In 1962, when Stedelijk Museum director Willem Sandberg hosted the exhibition *Dylaby* – short for "Dynamic labyrinth" and ever since regarded as one of Sandberg's most successful creative feats – Constant saw it as both the ultimate insult and a blatant act of plagiarism.[233] The exhibition combined installations made by six young promising artists (Robert Rauschenberg, Martial Raysse, Niki de Saint Phalle, Daniel Spoerri, Jean Tinguely, Per Olof Ultvedt). As the short film by Ed van der Elsken reveals, the result was a stimulating and witty exercise in environmental art, offering a wide range of sensations of space, light, sound and even smell.[234] The invitation to construct the ESR therefore provided Constant with a welcome, if perhaps belated, opportunity to re-appropriate what he felt had been stolen from him and his SI colleagues.

Half a decade earlier, the ESR would certainly have made a sensational impact, but the reactions now were tepid.[235] The most popular part of the installation was the door labyrinth, which was Constant's idea entirely. and which Nic Tummers insists was based on the disorientating experience in the hallway of the artist's early twentieth-century ground-floor apartment.[236] The door labyrinth concept was to be perfected many years later in the 1974 exhibition of New Babylon in The Hague. Though this was never explicitly its aim, the ESR proved to be a testing ground for techniques which Constant found indispensable for creating the ambiances in the sectors of New Babylon. In *Skizze zu einer Kultur* Constant had categorized all the possible methods for environmental and spatial conditioning in an "Ambiance scheme",[237] and Tummers confirmed that a great deal of time was spent trying to work out how to test as many aspects of it as possible.[238] But the correspondence between the directors of the *Bouwcentrum* and Constant indicates that much of what was planned was seriously compromised and that the final result did not meet all expectations.[239] Given the simple fact that the Rotterdam-based centre was not a museum of modern art (let alone an institution like the Stedelijk in its former glory) the outcome may not have been a complete surprise. Not only for the critics but for Constant as well – despite the merry pictures of him and the centre's executives clambering through the spaces – the ESR proved a bit of a disappointment.

In 1966 there is a final, tempting opportunity to take spatial art into the public realm. The experiment in Rotterdam must surely be in the back of Constant's mind when Sean Wellesley-Miller invites him to collaborate on a project called "The Street": though Constant sympathizes with the effort, he ultimately declines.

It would have been edifying to see what a practical collaboration between the two men might have looked like: in the following years, Wellesley-Miller was to co-found the Eventstructure Research Group to create numerous playful environments that actually worked exceptionally well. The group's pneumatic structures – pioneered by people like Werner Ruhnau of GEAM and the

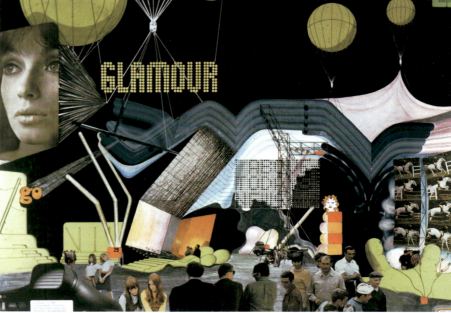

75. Constant: *Grote gele sector*, 1967. Hardware for play; 76. *Instant City*, 1968: Archigram celebrating event. Collage by Peter Cook

77. Air structure installation by Theo Botschuijver and Jeffrey Shaw (Eventstructure Research Group): *Waterwalk Tube*, 1970

hallmark of artists like Claes Oldenburg and such architectural collectives as Utopie, Haus-Rucker-Co, and Coop Himmelb(l)au – were blown up on public squares, in soon-to-be derelict modernist developments and at large public events, film festivals and concerts. They formed cushions for play or tunnels spanning water in which human bodies, young and old, were playfully tested. Lights, slide shows and music further animated the "event" in a nighttime setting.

Clearly, these constructed events spoke the language of a new generation: the mission of activating people through environmental means had now acquired a radically different idiom. The events not only incarnated the pop aesthetic of space-age plastics and bubble gum; they offered as well the ecstatic thrill of psychedelic youth culture that teamed up with a conceptual, sensualist approach. Working with *almost nothing*, maximum environmental impact was achieved; the radically de-materialized "architecture" of the group – in which human thought and bodily act are all that count – perfectly embodied the emerging Zeitgeist. The players in a happening or in experimental theatre now gave way to the "architecture" or environment itself, which invited people temporarily to *drop out* and *tune in*. Act and event (*ambiance*) were the goals of this architecture. In more than one way, the projects of the research group and their conceptual relatives – from architectural interventions to rock festivals – took psychogeographic mood engineering and the idea of the constructed situation into a new, popular phase.[240]

If Archigram easily made the shift from the orgiastic festival of matter to the untrammelled celebration of the human body in action (with the action effectively moving from capsules to bodies), Constant never followed suit. Though there is no recorded evidence of his stance vis-à-vis the projects designed by the late-1960s architectural avant-garde, Constant's attitude to all forms of installation art, conceptual art and land art can be easily traced: he rejected them fiercely. He may have similarly rejected the notion of a constructed event. The perceived passivity of the people merely undergoing it, the lack of a *material* dialectic interaction (the destabilizing wobble of an inflatable caused by human movement can hardly be called 'interactive'), and the ultimately all too predetermined *spectacular* quality of it may have led Constant to conclude that these ephemeral events, for all their sensuous beauty and appeal, might well induce a certain form of playful behaviour, but they could not activate true creativity. Doubtlessly, between Constant and Sean Wellesley-Miller there was something of a generational divide. A different wind was now blowing, and in the gathering storm New Babylon was gradually becoming ever more unfashionable.

In the letter he writes to Wellesley-Miller, Constant draws parallels between the young architect, who wants to conquer the street through temporary environmental actions, and the Provos, who at the time are still at the height of their creative powers. But in his dark epistle, Constant makes an important distinction: "The Street" has nothing of the culturally destructive rebelliousness of the anarchist collective. Playing now, according to Constant, is fundamentally playing along with the system, an act that, however laudable by itself, *absorbs* revolutionary energy. Freedom is the first priority, and true play will then be able to follow: "Reality now cannot mean anything else but struggle, no freedom is possible yet (…). The social structure like we know it, is inapt to realize the freedom of life, no creative life is possible in a situation like ours, struggle is taking the place of creativeness; struggle is the only way of being free in an un-free society."[241]

If Constant also spotted a similarity of approach between Wellesley-Miller's ideas and the "idealism" of creative guru Simon Vinkenoog,[242] he certainly had a point. The Eventstructure Research Group would become closely involved in the Dutch branch of *Sigma*, set up by Vinkenoog and Olivier Boelen – the very same man who publicly criticized Constant's "passivity". As Vinkenoog put it: "Sigma aims to fill the impending spiritual and mental void in the coming age of leisure. (…) Trocchi and Sigma seek the collective: the borders between people must disappear. (…) Here too we would like to influence the future in a positive way, with creative means."[243] For Constant, this was alarmingly premature.[244] Wellesley-Miller answers Constant's missive courageously:

(…) by working with the most un-conditioned people in a free situation we will develop new art forms (of which happenings are an embryonic and therapeutic beginning) that explore the possibilities of individual and collective creativity within the city, within reality, as part of a social process. The Street is a Living laboratory for the working out and demonstration of possibility. (…) A provocation through the attempt at realization. The thin edge of the wedge…[245]

So the roles have radically changed. If the situation rings a bell, it should, for when it comes to experimentation, Constant has now taken the position held by Guy Debord many years earlier. The once seemingly unbridgeable differences in tactical outlook between Debord and himself are now essentially non-existent: but where Debord becomes politically active, Constant obstinately clings to his artistic, prefigurative task. With New Babylon located firmly behind the revolutionary horizon, the art of the golden age of freedom can only be conquered or dreamed of, but certainly not tested and realized. The artistic activism of Wellesley-Miller is now essentially alien to both. As Constant always considered himself an artist and not a political revolutionary, to withdraw into the studio – and to *wait* for revolution – is therefore the only thing left to do. Invariably *Skizze zu einer Kultur*, despite its overpowering optimism, also announces the withdrawal from the street:

Waiting has become our main occupation; we wait, and while away our lives, idly. (…)
THERE IS NO FREEDOM – FOR ANYBODY (…)
ART CAN ONLY EXPRESS ITSELF IN PROTEST (…)
A radical change of society will have to precede the new culture; the opposite is simply impossible.[246]

As New Babylon approaches the 1970s, Constant has consciously become as passively expectant as the co-author of the Amsterdam Declaration. He continues to tread the path of prefiguration. Whilst Constant had made the small, pre-1961 models with the idea of having them photographed, he now makes new, larger

ones intended for films, as the Koolhaas-Van Garrel interview confirms. In 1968 Carlheinz Caspari, now working for German television, manages to realize the first part of what was intended to be a trilogy: *Constant oder der Weg nach New Babylon* (Constant or the Road to New Babylon). The two sequels, which would have featured the models and even more experimental constructions equipped with electronic gadgetry, are never made.[247] Constant evidently makes a last attempt to break new ground. Caspari enthusiastically responds, "Dear Constant, many thanks for your letter (…). I am very glad to hear that you want to get into electronic experiments and computer art."[248] But instead of heading off to explore new means of representation, Constant returns to the art he had so loudly abandoned: the man who had declared individualist art dead, not only steps out of the practical arena; by 1969 he withdraws into paint.

Constant dismisses his model-making collaborators one by one. He publishes a collection of his essays, *Opstand van de Homo Ludens* (1969). Rather than summarizing New Babylon, the book captures the mood of the time: it is a militant anthology lacking any descriptions of the world of Homo Ludens worth mentioning. In the wake of May 1968 the situation is one of political edginess and crisis. As the phase of pure painterly art that is to follow New Babylon's effective demise reveals, the Zeitgeist inevitably rubs off on Constant as well.

Burying New Babylon

Undoubtedly there is something poignant about a person who, growing older, finds himself in doubt about what he believed in and dreamt of when he was young: a person who, sadder and wiser, reaches the conclusion that he may have been mistaken or misled. This is clearly how historian Mark Wigley – almost single-handedly responsible for putting Constant in the limelight in the U.S. in the late 1990s – likes to present the protagonist of his study. In his texts, Wigley presents what he considers to be the closing phase of the New Babylon project, between 1969 and 1974, as the essential correction: a rigorous self-critique conducted by Constant, in which he not only "blurs" but also buries his own project. Interestingly, Hilde Heynen, who only hints at this evolution in her outstanding analysis of New Babylon, never actually insists that this is what Constant did: she merely infers he may have been harbouring suppressed doubts.[249]

At first sight Wigley's interpretation makes prefect sense, and it certainly makes Constant's project more accessible and reassuring.[250] But a simple, straightforward look at the facts, the correspondence, the interviews and the texts about New Babylon in the years following the artist's return to painting overturns Wigley's interpretation. The paintings themselves, meanwhile, remain problematic. It is almost criminal to categorize and explain Constant's painterly work from the years up to the mid-'70s within the framework of an essay on New Babylon, but as they have, time and again, been drawn into the equation, something needs to be said about them. To begin with, they are ambiguous, but never *false*. And though they are never clear-cut "polemical statements", as Wigley insists, they are among the most powerful and symbolic work that Constant produced in his career. They reveal an artist locked in an epic struggle, veering between pitch-black misanthropy and the hope of a better world. Often, the two are indistinguishable.

But what does Constant himself have to say about his own work? Not surprisingly, his comments vary slightly – depending on who was enquiring. Generally, however, they express the same feeling. Constant gave one of his most interesting and comprehensive replies at the October 1999 symposium at the Drawing Center in New York. Inexplicably, this fascinating exchange between Constant and Wigley never made it into the book that was published after the event:

MW: During the life of New Babylon did it feel to you sad or contradictory that society seemed to be going into the opposite direction of New Babylon?

C: Yes, of course. Yes, that's the reason I stopped the work on New Babylon, because the optimism which is needed for starting a project like that… I worked for eleven years on it and then the

78. Constant, *Ode à l'Odéon*, 1969

society was going in the opposite way instead of developing to more freedom … there were wars, revolutions and cruelties all over the world. That's why I restarted painting, where I could express my ideas and my feelings about these developments.

MW: In these last five years from '68 through till '74 in which you are more disillusioned by the possibility of New Babylon, was that a sad moment for the project or … how were those years? Because I think it is very important. Having talked about the beginning, maybe explain to us a little bit your feelings during those last years, before you end, because 20 years is a long time to work on one project.

C: No, it was eleven years or so I think I worked – from '56 … But yeah, I stopped working on the models in '69.

MW: But you are drawing New Babylon until '74.

C: But then I restarted painting with the idea in mind that perhaps I'm a painter after all and as a painter I could perhaps express more and more clearly what I wanted to express in my models. And then I started, the first paintings I made after '69 were indeed a kind of mazes, labyrinths – which could be like looking inside the models and living and imagining how you could move and travel through these models and build a life in these models, but more and more influenced by what happened in the real world. The atmosphere and the ambiance of New Babylon vanished and the cruelty came more and more – the blood came on, was shown, became more visible. Reality took it over.[251]

In Delft, a few months later, a slightly different version was recounted:

Chris Dercon: However, Constant, at some point you say: no, we should still consider always the future. However, at some point, you stopped; you stopped the project of New Babylon because you felt – you said in New York during the conversation with Mr. Buchlow – you said I felt at that point, at the end of the sixties, less and less optimistic about society. And that you started to express in your drawings, then your paintings and then at some point you said now it's finished, it's over.

C: No, I didn't stop because I didn't have any confidence anymore, any hope, but I stopped because I couldn't go any further. I had said what I had to say for the moment and I didn't see enough reasons to add things to what I said and to what I'd done.

Both statements are entirely consistent with each other. The fact remains that New Babylon is the world beyond:[252] reality, not New Babylon, is the world of sorrow, and Constant had done his bit to describe, build and paint the world that will surpass it. As we know, in order to reach this world, much struggle would lie ahead. We now need to look further at how Constant explained his shift to painting at the time – and at the paintings themselves.

The language of freedom

To begin with, it is clear that Constant did not regard the move into painting as a fundamental change from what he had been doing during his work on New Babylon, though to the outside world it would either be interpreted as a bold dialectic move, so characteristic of Constant's restless nature (as Jorn underlined in his 1953 letter), or as an outright betrayal of his principles: an easy way out for a painter who had failed to overcome his own ego through teamwork. It is a fact that not only during his solo work on the project (in the years 1963–64 especially) but also during his stay in Alba in 1956–57, Constant had made some beautiful paintings, which seemed terribly difficult to rhyme with his call for the end of individualist art and the collective development of a superior praxis. Then again, his gradual rethinking during the sixties, as we have seen, had moved this praxis firmly back behind the horizon. Making images, however – illustrating ideas – is what Constant felt he had been doing all along, and this is also how he would explain his move to Carlheinz Caspari. Deeply mournful about the return to pure pictorial art, Caspari repeatedly attempts to stimulate his friend to continue where they had started in Essen many years before;[253] but Constant resists. To Caspari he described his paintings as follows:

They are to me the illogical means, to clarify to myself, with regard to New Babylon and related themes, what would otherwise remain unclear in the plans and models of an urbanistic project.
(…)
What I am trying to do as a painter, at the moment, is nothing else than what painters have done for hundreds of years: to open a window of the prison, to try to see what lies beyond.[254]

Constant echoes this explanation in various other statements at about the same time. The best-known is also quoted at the end of Mark Wigley's lengthy article on New Babylon in the 1998 Witte De With catalogue:

By the time I had more or less finished working on the New Babylon project for the exhibition in The Hague, I could, theoretically, do three things. I could go on with New Babylon, which as you say is never ready but that would have meant repeating myself. I could stop altogether and do nothing, and that was, theoretically, the most obvious choice after something like New Babylon. But I was incapable, of course, of doing nothing. And the third possibility was simply to go on working on whatever I felt like doing and that is in fact what I did. First watercolours and etchings and then more paintings, mostly not on the New Babylon theme *(sic)*, but in spite of myself, more or less unconsciously all sorts of elements crept in which I have always seen as events or happenings that belong to the world of New Babylon.[255]

Apart from the question of which exhibition in The Hague Constant refers to – 1965 or 1974 – both fragments confirm that New Babylon and "related themes" live side by side in his painterly work. What connects them is the language of painting, in which heterogeneous elements – stories, feelings and ideas – paradoxically come together in lines, forms and colourite; in the particular case of Constant, the opposite may often be the case: the stain generates the story. Painting *an sich* is beyond the morally good or evil: it is a free exercise in imagination. He emphasizes this belief in the same letter to Caspari, insisting that painting is a kind of language, and that "even an unclear language" has its relevance.

79. Constant, *Der blaue Draufgänger*, 1969

80. Constant, *Erotic Space*, 1971

What we begin to see is that painting offered Constant a radical freedom: a release, first and foremost, from the sheer impossible task of having to *prove* New Babylon. Apart from the fact that he had said what he had to say and had done what he could, Constant clearly felt that the project had become a noose around his neck.[256] If there is a crucial moment of insight it is this: the artist recognized that he needed to return to the medium that gave him the liberty he had intentionally compromised for so long. With artistic freedom regained and the pressure valve released, his art now becomes truly *playful*: after years of dedicated, purposeful work, the unconscious now finds free rein. Even more than the models with their dents, scratches, layers and corrections, made many years before, the paintings are the result of an informed but essentially intuitive process.

Ideologically, within his social and political vision, Constant legitimizes his move as an act of resistance. Painting was not only the most unfashionable thing to do in the early 1970s, an antidote to the omnipresent experimental art forms by now fostered and usurped by capitalism: it was also a celebration of artistic freedom. In a time when, for Constant, collective creation seemed ever more distant (as we know from the letter to Wellesley-Miller), painting formed a bulwark against a world that now warmly embraced the decomposition of individualist art: the self-destructive "anti-art" that reduced the artist to an incomprehensible oddball. And so again, the former activist Constant chooses *consciously* to become a hermit. Though the choice may seem odd at first, the very same ideology that led Constant to reject individualist art now urges him to save it – as the socially perverse but artistically necessary privilege and freedom to create. The crucial change is Constant's assessment of the situation: the optimism that fired him on through the 1950s and early 1960s – the belief that the realm of *poetry made by all* was nigh – had now dissipated. As Constant insistently explained in *Skizze zu einer Kultur* and elsewhere, art would have to remain an exception, a luxury to be defended, until the moment came for it to flourish totally. The painter, as an historical and endangered species, is the relatively free, incomplete predecessor of the Homo Ludens in the world *after us*. Constant's social defeatism is thus channelled into a new militancy to save art, "to save painting".[257]

This reversal, long in the making but always latent, is nonetheless radical. It cannot be explained save with a fact from Constant's personal life. As always, someone was acting behind the scenes. The crucial figure who aided in the final breakthrough into paint was an art critic whom Constant had bitterly complained about at the 1966 Venice Biennale: Fanny Kelk.[258] She would now become his new fellow traveller, his critic, supporter, and muse.

Images of this world – and the next

With the intricate history as a foundation, the paintings might appear less confusing.

Officially the first painting after the end of work on New Babylon proper is the famous *Ode à l'Odéon* from 1969. Depicting the interior of a New Babylonian dynamic labyrinth, the painting is, as the title tells us, an homage to the actors and students who occupied the Odéon theatre in Paris, turning it into a lively arena of political discussion and art during the *événements* of May 1968. Many people in Constant's immediate environment at the time confirm that he had driven down to Paris in his *Deux Chevaux* to see with his own eyes what was happening in the streets, clearly hopeful that something great was about to materialize: the beginning of a revolution. The painting itself, made one year later, wallows in nostalgia. By the time Constant made it, the party was over and the hangover in leftist circles considerable. The image is a reminder of hope – felt at the time, and certainly in that place: for Constant it was a moment that forced an opening to New Babylon. The painting, meanwhile, reminds us strongly of an earlier pencil drawing from 1966: *Homo Ludens*. Its strong graphic lines have now been translated into paint, three years on. What we are confronted with is sheer spatial drama, a breathtakingly intricate but deep space without perspective or fixed horizon. The feeling of disorientation in this kaleidoscopic vision is complete. To quote the title of another painting, this is an *espace en destruction*: a dynamic maze caught in an endless cycle of construction and destruction, constantly unpredictable. Effacing the eternal night in New Babylon, silvery artificial light articulates the metallic structures, floors, walls and ladders of the man-made landscape. Hazy contours of New Babylonians, perfectly fused with their surroundings, dot the space, whilst on the middle right of the drawing, a Rubenesque female bottom graces the margin. Inserted below is a clenched fist, reminding us that this world only comes at the price of struggle. Reminiscent of the faceted spatiality of cubism and the lighting of a futurist canvas, the painting not only oozes vanguard nostalgia: it thrills and intrigues us, time and again.

Der Blaue Draufgänger from the same year appears to be a close-up, a fragment of the bigger picture. The black spray-paint blobs, however, have moved to the foreground to form distinct human outlines, figures that seem more tormented than insouciant and playful. Unidentifiable blue stains (a trace of human presence?) soil the décor. The scene is dark and disconcerting, as is its title. A *Draufgänger* not only "goes for it", but *draufgehen* also means

81. Constant, *Ubu et Justine*, 1975

"to get killed". This is clearly not only a scene of passionate play, but one of violence. Other paintings from the following years serve up a similar cocktail: scenes of an erotic and latently or explicitly violent character, set in what appears to be a New Babylonian décor of mobile walls. *Erotic Space* from 1971 shows an electrocuted body in a puddle of blood, while a dark male figure, fondling his erection, looks on; an equally aroused figure on the large white screen mirrors his actions. Pictures like *Labyrinth* (1972), *Le viol* (The rape, 1974) and drawings like *Le voyeur* (1974) reinforce the feeling that if this is New Babylon, then surely the self-regulating world of desire unleashed and sublimated is not working. This canvas world is a sadistic universe of passionate murder and lust.

Constant's statements, however, may provide us with some other explanations. The violence could easily be dismissed by pointing out that we may simply not be looking at a New Babylonian scene at all, or that, if we are, alien elements have crept in and taken over. What happens in these paintings is undoubtedly amplified by events beyond Constant's studio, perhaps fed by Constant's own personal interests. One such preoccupation is his continuing fascination for the Marquis De Sade, hero and role model for many a leftist thinker. One should bear in mind that this most radical libertine is essentially a moralist, who in his writings not only depicts a world of social and sexual inequality and lustful exploitation, but also raises Hobbes's maxim from *Leviathan* to a guiding principle: for De Sade, human kindness in a world of want and war is a ludicrous folly. As Constant admitted during an interview as early as 1966:

I don't read novels anymore. In fact I read all the classics between the age of 20 and 30, but for about six or seven years I've only been reading Marx and Engels. (…) And I read De Sade. I just ordered his complete works, the separate parts I can then give to my son. No, I never read novels anymore. Only *War and Peace*, occasionally.[259]

Constant's fascination culminates in paintings from the middle of the decade, such as *Ubu et Justine* (1975) and *Plaisir et tristesse de l'amour* (1976). Undoubtedly, aspects of Constant's private life – a complicated love triangle – are also reflected. But the setting is remarkably similar to that of the supposed New Babylonian scenes, with the planar elements of the labyrinth now framing moral, erotic allegories. *Ubu et Justine* (1975, fig. 81), for instance, confirms that the décor of New Babylon has now simply become Constant's favourite dramatic background. The scene portrays love, not in the insouciant form it takes in New Babylon, but as the existential, divisive quantity it still is in our own world: a source of misery, conflict and pain.

But to interpret the paintings from the early 1970s as mere preludes to the scenes of jealousy from the boudoir is ultimately not satisfying. It is perhaps better to take a step back and observe the effect they have on the viewer. The pictures are decidedly thrilling: theatrical scenes of passion, horror and excitement that intrigue, shock and alienate the onlooker. And this may be precisely where Constant wanted us to be: looking on, from the outside, into a world that is fascinating but fundamentally alien and unintelligible. The images are a potent antidote to the "sweetening" of New Babylon, the idea that it may just be around the corner, a simple matter of cooperation and goodwill. The paintings bring back memories of Constant's irritation with Simon Vinkenoog; they remind us that this world would be nothing if not violently beautiful, very different, and fundamentally beyond our reach. Explaining his paintings to his friend Caspari, Constant insists that the painter is not the only prisoner of an unliberated world: "The observer of my paintings, however, is a fellow captive: he may interpret my descriptions differently than I had intended, but his world of imagination and perception is just as limited. New Babylonian reality remains closed to us."[260]

The paintings, then, have the same effect as Constant's defiant writings at the time: they are militant reminders of the impossibility of New Babylon until its time has come. These paintings *desperately* capture Constant's artistic dream: New Babylonian life is rendered in its full intensity and drama with the means available to the captives of old Zion: "Until the time has come that this urge can be sublimated into a creative urge, into a 'ludic' urge, it will find its outlet in aggression."[261] And that goes for Constant as well. Only bloodshed and murder on the canvas may approach capturing the passionate intensity of the superior, better world.

Other images now fall into place. *Mekong River*, a watercolour from 1970, encapsulates all the seeming paradoxes.[262] The title naturally refers to the Vietnam War, and indeed we see an eerie landscape that shows the traces of a recent massacre. In the distance, however, are evidently sectors of New Babylon. Stuck on top of them are newspaper clippings: "U.S. troops … on command … Cambodia", "is play with murder" etc. But rather than a *detourned* image of New Babylon, in which the world of Homo Ludens is "blurred" or "criticized", what we see here is reality barging in and obscuring the original scene. Given the remarkable stylistic similarities with an image like *Gezicht op een sector* (fig. 47), the layering is highly symbolic: New Babylon is pushed literally into the background, beyond the world of horror.

Ontwaakt, verworpenen der aarde, an etching from 1972, is less ambiguous but equally militant. The title is the Dutch equivalent of "Arise, ye workers from your slumbers", and the image

shows us the foaming masses who will usher in New Babylon and populate it. The painting illustrates an insurrection, celebrating the romance and ethos of revolutionary struggle. With memories lingering of the barricades of the Paris Commune and of May 1968, the image reminds us that freedom in New Babylon will have to be conquered: the destruction of the old world will have to precede the construction of the new.

Le Massacre from the same year best exemplifies the recurring dialectic in Constant's work, in which revolution, vandalism and art are different expressions of creative vitality. Its alternative title, *Le Massacre de My Lai* – referring to the notorious butchering of a Vietnamese village by American soldiers in 1968 – is enlightening but slightly distractive. Like the photos that shocked the world, the foreground in Constant's painting depicts human bodies, severed limbs and bleeding flesh. Against the stark black background, however, physical constructions light up that are distinctly New Babylonian. The same effect is achieved, for instance, in the painting *La Révolte* from 1972: behind the black *repoussoir* – clearly a struggling mass of people with fists and a stick protruding – white structures emerge. These patterns, suggestive of buildings, persistently recur in Constant's oeuvre: on the face of it, they can be seen as a painterly stylistic gag, a trademark "scarring" of the picture with a cross hatch. But like the images of the wheel and the ladder, which appear time and again in Constant's work, they are powerful symbols of the creative effort: remnants of hope.

The similarities between *Le Massacre de My Lai* and a number of earlier paintings are striking, as are the parallels between the situation in which they were made: all of them follow a period of relative optimism in Constant's oeuvre, and it is odd that historians who present the early-seventies paintings as scenes in New Babylon invariably bypass the earlier pictures that are so remarkably similar. For Constant the Cobra movement, like the New Babylon project, ends on a sombre, deeply pessimistic note.

82. Constant, *Mekong River*, 1970

In 1950–51 he makes his notorious "war paintings", clearly as a response to the Korean War and a reflection of the still-recent horrors of World War II. For over a year, Constant draws and paints scenes of destruction and despair. A good example, close to the later *My Lai* canvas, is *Verschroeide Aarde* from 1951.

The same elements are present: bodies in the foreground, a hand desperately trying to make a fist but failing, white structures against a dark background – now complemented by a blazing fire in the top left part of the picture. If we look beyond the sur-realist references (the clock, the paranoid-critical blob next to it), the painting appears to depict utter desolation. But as much as latent pessimism pervades the happiest of Cobra scenes,[263] the fury of the blaze and the jumble of construction hold the promise that ultimately the horror may be overcome, that on the wasteland that remains after destruction, a new and better world can be built. The war paintings – in the 1950s as well as in the 1970s – are indeed highly metaphorical.

A painting like *Le Massacre de My Lai* can therefore only be understood as a part of Constant's entire oeuvre, work that moves between ultimate extremes: the horrors of this world and glimpses of the next. If Constant courageously designed and depicted a tentative overture in the form of New Babylon, *My Lai* shows the predicament that entangles artist and all of man-kind. The world of Homo Ludens remains the faint light in the distance, an expression of hope in the valley of tears.

The age of self-denial

In 1974 a large exhibition is held at the Gemeentemuseum in The Hague, the place where Constant had celebrated his mid-sixties triumphs. Visitors play in a door labyrinth that is constructed for the occasion, and all the models are shown alongside the paint-ings from 1969 to 1974. The pictures especially make a powerful impression – even on critics otherwise deeply sceptical of New Babylon and eager to point out that little had been added to the project itself. Hans Locher, the curator, assembles various texts in his *New Babylon* catalogue that gives a splendid overview of

84. Constant, *Verschroeide aarde*, 1951

Constant's ideas and that finally brings together most of what would have appeared in *Skizze zu einer Kultur*, albeit in a frag-mented and incomplete form. Most importantly, the long text "Schets van een kultuur", a strongly edited rewriting of Part Two of the German manuscript now complements Constant's artistic critique. With the exhibition and the catalogue, the New Babylon project, open-ended and with its edges frayed, is now publicly laid to rest.

If the collages that the artist makes for his friend Hans Locher – eight meticulously constructed sheets of fragmented text and images – can be seen as the perfect summary of Constant's utopia (the 1980 lecture in Delft is perhaps its final testament), the interviews that Fanny Kelk conducts with Constant in 1974 are perhaps the most revealing. Even more than the published versions, the rough transcripts in Constant's archive are a pleasure to read: they show a couple intellectually bickering. Fanny Kelk is on a clear mission to reveal what drives Constant, to explain his art through his personal background and experiences and to unmask it as an act of rebellion against his Jesuit upbringing in bourgeois Amsterdam. Fearing perhaps that she might be on to something, Constant tries to ward off all her attempts at psycho-logical profiling, insisting it is the art that should speak for it-self. Ultimately, he believes, the art will disclose all one needs to know.

To a certain extent Mark Wigley followed Constant's wish in his exhibitions in Rotterdam and New York and in his two books. Though he claims, like every historian, that it was his intention to "open up" the project, he effectively closes it and alters its message: in his many essays and lectures he frees New Babylon

83. Constant, *Ontwaakt, verworpenen der aarde!*, 1972

from its historical and ideological ballast. Invariably, the medium is more important than the message, the *how* more important than the *why*. It certainly leads to interesting situations. Wigley's history of New Babylon extends to 1974 so as to present the paintings as the conclusive auto-critique, even if the artist himself – together with all historians before Wigley – insists that the project ends in 1969. Crystal-clear images of New Babylon are presented as "blurs", while raw, destructive desire replaces its worldly transcendence in art. Marx's Eleventh Thesis on Feuerbach – one of the most inspiring calls for revolution ever – is attributed to Freud: a telling slip indeed.[264] Despite his insistence on New Babylon's polemical nature, Wigley has done everything to turn Constant's project into something it is not: evasive, noncommittal and vague.

Without a doubt, Wigley succesfully re-canonized New Babylon for an architectural audience: he connected it to fashionable talk about "research", "discourse" and "polemic", thereby assuring its appeal. It is also likely that the blurring of New Babylon is personally motivated, for reasons that are entirely understandable. As Wigley insisted during the conference in Delft in 2000, "visions kill".[265] One can only agree with him that the twentieth century has been the bloodiest ever, and not in the least thanks to man's fanatic convictions. Killing the visionary and utopian in Constant makes the artist's decidedly Marxist project more palatable not only to the audience, but also to the historian addressing it.

In the end, Wigley's approach cannot really be faulted: it can only provoke a response. What is more disconcerting is that Constant has remained largely silent. Even though he occasionally reasserts in Dutch interviews that he still believes in the advent of New Babylon, on the international scene little about it is heard.

In the hot summer of 2002, Constant's models are exhibited at Documenta 11, the largest art show on earth. Again Constant is invited to exhibit his New Babylon project, now well over 30 years old. Amongst the endless, politically correct variations on installation art – one sad television screen and projection after the other – New Babylon is a breath of fresh air. Visitors are magically drawn to the models and paintings, lingering in the *Kulturbahnhof* next to Kassel's railway station where the project is on display. It is bad enough that the space is not air-conditioned: the windows are open, and sunlight pours in, while the miniscule hot filings from the brakes of the trains waft into the space, burning their way into the plexiglas of the models and the gentle layers of paint. More disturbingly perhaps, there is not a single line of text to be seen in the room, and only a short note in the exhibition guide (but none in the beefy catalogue) explains what this project is.[266]

Constant has always been an artist who thought as well and as much as he painted: a sensitive being with a social conscience. The overpowering passion that drives his work is always balanced by reason – or by articulated reasoning at least. In a recent interview Constant confirmed this essential link between mind and matter when describing his New Babylon as an "illustrated philosophy".[267] The art, in its sensuous beauty and appeal, may speak for itself, but only up to a certain level: it is nourished by the thoughts and passions that underlie it. Presenting the illustrations without the philosophy shifts the balance in an awkward

85. Constant, *Le Massacre de My Lai*, 1972

way. That the painter made his peace with this may be the ultimate act of self-denial.

Notes

194 "O ages yet to come! You shall no longer be witness to these horrors and infamies abounding!" De Sade, *Justine ou les Malheurs de la Vertu*. Quote from 1950 edition, Ed. Le Soleil Noir, Paris, p 32.

195 Debord launched vitriolic attacks on Constant in the SI's journal, accusing him of "technologizing" Unitary Urbanism and selling out to the architectural mainstream. There is also an interesting exchange between Constant and Yves Robillard on the subject of Debord's polemics: see letter from Constant to Robillard, 18 March 1963, file "Correspondentie 1963", RKD.

196 Still by far the best source is Reyner Banham's *Megastructure, Urban futures of the recent past* (London: Thames & Hudson, 1976). Passages on Constant are in the chapter on "Megayear 1964", pp. 81–83.

197 Constant, "Neo-Babylone", *L'Architecture d'aujourd'hui*, no. 102 (June–July) 1962, p. 77. In this issue on "Architectures fantastiques" New Babylon and Friedman's *Architecture Mobile* sit happily side by side. For an overview of Constant's exhibitions and lectures in these countries see Wigley, op. cit., "Presentations" (pp. 238–253) and Wigley's essay (pages 39–48 especially).

198 See for instance the letter from Constant to Hans Sonnenberg, 22 November 1963 (file "Correspondentie 1963", RKD), in which he distances himself from a "Où vivrons-nous demain" exhibition in the *Rotterdams Kunstcentrum*; Constant's letter to the "sécretaire de l'association ACTUEL 65" (copies to Friedman, Schulze-Fielitz and others), 16 April 1965, in which he rather bluntly rejects an invitation to the "10 journées internationales sur l'urbanisme contemporain" – again on the theme of "Où vivrons-nous demain" – on the grounds that Ragon's premises cannot be properly disputed. File "Michel Ragon", RKD.

199 Constant's project was not included in any of Ragon's 1960s books on prospective urbanism: *Où vivrons-nous demain?* (Paris: Laffont, 1963), *Les cités de l'avenir* (Paris: Planète, 1966), *La cité de l'an 2000* (Tournai: Casterman, 1968). A tireless promoter, Ragon was in a way to French 'visionary' architecture what Reyner Banham was to the Smithsons and Archigram. Ragon was to make up for it in the '70s, when he presented New Babylon in two articles in the journals *Urbanisme* and *Cimaise* after his relationship with Constant had clearly improved: see, for instance, letter from Michel Ragon to Constant, 13 January 1972, file "Correspondentie" (no year), RKD. In his tripartite history of modern architecture and urbanism, in which Constant is quite prominently featured, New Babylon is acknowledged to be one of the few designs for a radically different society. See Michel Ragon, *Histoire Mondiale de l'architecture et de l'urbanisme modernes, tome second* (Tournai: Casterman, 1972), pp. 423, 425 and *tome 3: Prospective et futorologie* (Tournai: Casterman, 1978): pp. 114, 302, 325, and 366–369 especially.

200 GIAP, the *Groupe International d'Architecture Prospective* (International group for prospective architecture) can be regarded as Michel Ragon's brainchild

and a spin-off of his energetic propaganda for GEAM. As the name indicates, the multi-disciplinary group focussed entirely on urban futurology and 'visionary' architecture; however, in spite of its name and in contrast with its predecessor, it was actually predominantly French. Other founding members were architects Yona Friedman, Paul Maymont (both ex-GEAM), Ionel Schein and Walter Jonas (from Switzerland), and sculptors Georges Patrix and Nicolas Schöffer. Sociologist-economist Jean Fourastié was also involved. For more on GIAP see *Les Visionnaires de l'Architecture* (Paris: Robert Laffont, 1965) and Ragon, *Histoire Mondiale, tome 3*, pp. 342–345.

201 Phone interview with Adolfo Natalini, 26 May 2003.

202 Interview with Nic Tummers, 15 May 2001. Translation by author.

203 Indeed there are pictures of him on the very same strip of film that also features some of the first shots of the Paris Lettrists, caught on film by photographer Ed van der Elsken.

204 The phrase "crowning stage" is from an undated letter from Asger Jorn to Constant written in the months before the 1956 Alba conference. "I agree with you that the true crowning of Cobra should have been a new conception of architecture." File "Correspondentie 1956", RKD. The poster-catalogue of the 1965 exhibition underlined the connection. Quotes from the 1948 manifesto were interspersed with later fragments of texts on New Babylon. Two of these also link Constant's work to the happenings in the streets: the closing passage from "Opkomst en ondergang van de avant-garde" stressing the revolutionary potential of "hipsters", "teddy boys", "rockers", etc., and a paragraph from the 1961 lecture in Delft: "But New Babylon is like a strip-tease: it stimulates action and therefore it is real". Cobra, New Babylon and Provo are thus drawn together.

205 To some extent this is clearly how Constant presented himself in his introductory catalogue text, "De dialectiek van het experiment" (republished in Constant, *Opstand van de Homo Ludens*, pp. 142–148) in which he explains how a period of non-stop "dialectic" experimentation in the present will have to precede and prepare for a phase of synthesis (i.e. ultimately New Babylon). The message thus echoes the final lines of Constant's 1948 Manifesto for the *Experimentele groep*.

206 Mostly in The Netherlands: see for instance Paul Donker Duyvis, "New Babylon: speelmodel voor een nieuwe maatschappij" in Wim Beeren et al. (ed.), *Actie, werkelijkheid en fictie in de kunst van de jaren '60 in Nederland*, exhibition catalogue Museum Boymans – van Beuningen, Rotterdam (Den Haag: Staatsuitgeverij, 1979), pp. 167–176; Niek Pas, *Imaazje! De verbeelding van Provo* (Amsterdam: Wereldbibliotheek, 2003).

207 "Constant Nieuwenhuys (who is not, so far as we know, a descendant of the famous Dutch anarchist Domela Nieuwenhuis) is the architect of a theoretical 'model' for a new city, the New Babylon, which has appeared as a paperback in Holland and is a kind of Provo Utopia." Editors' comment following Constant's short article "About New Babylon" in *Anarchy 66* no. 8 (August 1966), p. 232. "As is also the case with anarchism (and indeed, with communism or Christianity), there is predictably a Provo heaven. The prophet of this is the artist Constant Nieuwenhuys, who writes of the 'New Babylon' (…)". Colin MacInnes, "Weekend in White", *New Society*, 17 November 1966, p. 767.

208 The crucial role of these elites in the cultural transformation of the country is underlined in James Kennedy, *Building New Babylon: Cultural Change in the Netherlands during the 1960s* (Dissertation University of Iowa, 1995; Dutch translation *Nieuw Babylon in aanbouw*. Amsterdam: Boom, 1995). Kennedy argues that despite inevitable resistance and conservatism in all layers of the population, large sections of the elite, from left to right, were committed to *vernieuwing* ('modernization'). He begins his exposé with Constant's exhibition in The Hague, and, as the title indicates, he uses "New Babylon" as the header for his discussion.

209 The telegram is not in Constant's archive at the RKD. However, Hein van Haaren, who accompanied Constant and assisted curator Rudi Oxenaar in Venice recalls it vividly: interview 4 November 2003.

210 "Provo's willen van Amsterdam eerste sector maken van CONSTANT's NEW BABYLON", *Nieuwsblad van het Noorden*, 28 July 1966. Translation by author. Almost viciously – certainly far more bitingly than Van Garrel and Koolhaas in their interview – the anonymous reporter portrays the artist by describing the sterile neatness of his large Kattenburg studio and his unnerving ability to repeat answers verbatim.

211 See chapter 2 in Niek Pas, op. cit., pp. 45 ff.

212 The film images, compiled in "Open het Graf"(Louis van Gasteren, 1979), show critic Betty van Garrel, for instance, cheerfully participating in the proceedings. Vinkenoog insists that Constant was also present.

213 A manic street preacher in every sense of the word, Grootveld staged his own midnight liturgy that involved generous amounts of improvised pyrotechnics. "Holy" smoke billowing, Grootveld announced the advent of "Klaas", which in his miniature but highly flammable religious universe meant as much as the liberation from "consumer addiction" – and from nicotine particularly. Though this may seem a bit peculiar for an advocate of free soft drug consumption, there was a surprising logic underneath the paradoxical madness: the sheer pleasure and truth (the term he used was "gnot": halfway between the Dutch "genot" or pleasure and *gnosis*, knowledge) of the smoke had been corrupted and monopolized: the cigarette was now a symbol of an induced desire to consume, the willing surrender to the law of money. This mythical construct showed many parallels to (and certainly preceded) Roel van Duijn's ideology of "the addicted versus the free".

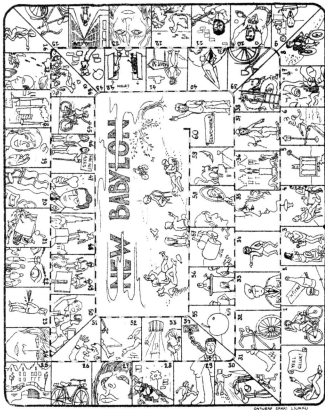

86. Provo board game in *Eindelijk* (Ghent, 1966)

214 According to Cor Jaring, Provo's court photographer, the reality of battle, behind the scenes, was indeed far more gentle: the police played along quite merrily in the Saturday evening rituals. After the youngsters had spent a few hours in a cell, the police, visibly looking forward to the next round of play, gave them a hot cup of coffee and bade them good night.

215 Provo no. 4 (28 October 1965) featured an interview with Constant by Roel van Duijn, pp. 2–11. Constant's article "Nieuw Urbanisme" was published in *Provo* no. 9 (12 May 1966), pp. 2–6. This issue also presented the infamous "white plans" for the Amsterdam municipal elections: the white chimney plan, white bicycle plan, white cop plan ("witte kippenplan"), and white housing plan.

216 He was number 13 on the list: see *Provo* no. 9, p. 20.

217 Interview with Roel van Duijn, 3 April 2001.

218 Ibid.

219 The adjective is derived from Van Duijn's "Kreativisties manifest".

220 "Klootjesvolk" is an old term of unknown origin that was already used in student circles to designate town versus gown. Literally meaning "little balls people", it perfectly expresses the disdain for everything gutless and petit bourgeois.

221 Interview 3 April 2001. Indeed many articles and interviews at the time mention Van Duijn and his fellow Provos preaching about New Babylon. See Provo documentation in the International Institute for Social History (IISG), Amsterdam, CSD VRZ 001. An article in *De Volkskrant* – "Provo Roel van Duijn in New York Times: 'Geweldloosheid is effectiever'", 4 April 1966 – refers to an interview by Edward Cowan in the *New York Times* with the Provo front man: New Babylon is apparently a recurring theme in it.

222 Interview 3 April 2001. Van Duijn's summarizing statement echoes one of the first, pitch-black texts in Provo no. 1 (12. July 1965), "Inleiding tot het provocerend denken": "We cannot convince the masses, and we hardly care to do so. How anyone could possible place his trust in that apathetic, dependent, spiritless band of cockroaches and ladybirds is a mystery to us. (…) If only we could be revolutionaries! But the likelihood of the sun rising in the west is greater than that of any revolution taking place in the Netherlands. (…) The only thing that remains is provocation. In the same way that our powers are insufficient to wipe away the old society, we cannot be builders of a new one." Translation by author.

223 See for instance the "Provo Manifest 1967", reprinted in Roel van Duijn (ed.), *Provo. De Geschiedenis van de provotarische beweging 1965–1967* (Amsterdam: Meulenhoff, 1985), pp. 61–71.

224 "Then it was all over with Constant. When I started the Kabouter party in Amsterdam I received a little pamphlet in which he sharply distanced himself from it, as if I had ideologically betrayed the revolution or something. It was

very fanatically written, perhaps because we had been so close. Have you ever seen it? I was very surprised by it, and I immediately thought: what on earth, he ought to know my intentions are good... Well, I didn't react to it because I thought it was almost absurd. I just couldn't imagine that we needed to have such a fierce discussion about it, so I simply shrugged my shoulders and ignored it. I have no idea how he is doing now. Perhaps he is still angry at me?" Interview 3 April 2001.

225 Olivier Boelen in an interview in *Algemeen Handelsblad*, 11 November 1966.

226 I base this on Mark Wigley's catalogue chronology, which shows an early version of this model from 1966. See Wigley, *Constant's New Babylon: The Hyper-Architecture of Desire*, pp. 172–173. This is also the model that is described as a 1/100 scale construction in the Van Garrel-Koolhaas interview reprinted in this book.

227 See correspondence in file "Witte brug", RKD.

228 See correspondence in file "PTT Arnhem", RKD.

229 Interview with Hein van Haaren, 4 November 2003. Van Haaren became artistic advisor to Dutch Telecom shortly after the Venice Biennale; it is he who was effectively responsible for hiring Constant to design the Arnhem scheme (formally it was the Bakema and Van den Broek office). Apart from transparent coloured plastics and glass, expensive aluminium profiles and massive casts were to be used; 'aluminium stones' were to cover the floor in some parts.

230 See note 205.

231 First contacts were established as early as September 1964. See letter from Constant to H.O. Eckardt dated 14 September 1964, file "E.S.S.R. (Bouwcentrum Rotterdam)", RKD. The ESR was opened on 15 April 1966.

232 The link is explicitly made in Constant's article "Het principe van de desoriëntatie" (The principle of disorientation) in the 1974 exhibition catalogue *New Babylon* (Den Haag: Haags Gemeentemuseum, 1974), pp. 66–68.

233 Willemijn Stokvis describes Constant's irritation with Sandberg and his "Dylaby" in an article in *Vrij Nederland*: "Willem Sandberg: het vertrouwen in het eigen oog", 4 October 1975, p. 21. In this article Constant is, furthermore, quoted as saying that "Sandberg killed the avant-garde".

234 Van der Elsken also compiled and illustrated the exhibition catalogue: *Dylaby: dynamisch labyrint* (Amsterdam: Stedelijk Museum, 1962).

235 See for instance J.J. Vriend, "En dan maar klagen over miskenning", *De Groene Amsterdammer*, 14. May 1966. This vicious article contrasts with that of some of the visitors: "It is a little difficult to express my feelings here about this experimental space. In any case the whole thing is well made; it conjures up those feelings that are most pleasurable in life." "It reminds me a little bit of my granny's attic; it really is a great place for kids to play in. It's very free, easy and cozy." Anonymous reactions in "E.S.S.R." file, RKD.

236 Interview with Nic. Tummers, 15 May 2001. The plans and letters from the "E.S.S.R." file in Constant's archive show that, apart from the door labyrinth, the execution of the "odoratorium" and the space frame were Constant's responsibility.

237 Later reproduced in slightly modified form in the 1974 The Hague *New Babylon* exhibition catalogue: p.58.

238 Interview 15 May 2001.

239 See correspondence in file "E.S.S.R.", RKD. Cf. "Het principe van de desoriëntatie" (note 232), p. 67.

240 Not surprisingly, some members of the group would go on to design the sets and light shows for prog rock bands like Pink Floyd and Genesis in the 1970s.

241 Constant to Sean Wellesley-Miller, 8 August 1966 (note 176).

242 See the lengthy quote from the letter in part 2 of this essay.

243 Inspired by Alexander Trocchi's Sigma movement in the UK (that also involved Joan Littlewood and influenced her "Fun Palace" scheme), Vinkenoog and Boelen tried to come up with a cultural response to "the problem of free time" that was beginning to be recognized by policy-makers and the general public. The ties between Sigma in the UK and Holland would be very close.

244 A letter written by Constant in reaction to a newspaper report in *De Volkskrant*, 8 July 1966, sadly testifies of his growing irritation with Vinkenoog. "I am deeply sorry that with your publication in 'New Babylon Informatief no. 4' people might get the impression that we are on the same side. I will do my utmost to defuse any such suspicions." Constant to Simon Vinkenoog, 9 July 1966, file "Simon Vinkenoog", RKD. A salient detail is that the letter was written just a few days before Constant heads off to Venice, where the *Informatief* – with Vinkenoog's text – would be distributed.

245 Wellesley-Miller to Constant, 17 August 1966, file "Wellesley-Miller", RKD.

246 *SzeK*, Part 1 section I, chapter 1.

247 "This film (...) was meant to be the first part of three that I had planned. (...) A second part was to be set in labyristic New Babylonian spaces, with figures, with actors. And surely he prepared for that, but then the commissions from NDR TV stopped coming in." Interview with Carlheinz Caspari, 4 July 2002.

248 Letter from Caspari to Constant, 10. April 1968. File "Correspondentie" (no year), RKD.

249 Cf. Heynen, *Architecture and Modernity: a critique*, p. 172. That Hilde Heynen rejects the utopia of New Babylon for being based on a far too simplistic view of human nature is obvious: the fundamental difference with Wigley's interpretation is that she does not present her own critique as that of Constant.

250 I was certainly seduced by it: see "New Babylon: the Realism of Utopia, the values of dreaming", *B-Nieuws* no. 11 (8 February 1999), pp. 17–19, "Die Geschichte des blauen Draufgängers – in Defence of New Babylon", ibid., pp. 20–21.

251 Symposium *The Activist Drawing – Retracing Situationist Architectures from Constant's New Babylon to Beyond*, October 30, 1999, at the Drawing Center in New York. Tape recording of the proceedings, transcript by author.

252 Interestingly, the 1999 New York symposium and the book based on it were called "The Activist Drawing – Retracing Situationist Architectures from Constant's New Babylon to *Beyond*" (ital cs mine). In eschatological terms, New Babylon is the only, immanent hereafter in the book.

253 Caspari had much difficulty coping with Constant's new course: he confirmed this in our interview. Caspari's letters from the period 1970–76 are also instructive. See file "Correspondentie" (no year), RKD.

254 Letter from Constant to Carlheinz Caspari, 18 August 1972. File "Correspondentie" (no year), RKD. Cf. Constant's lecture in Delft, 6 February 1961 (*Delftse School*, no. 3, p. 13): "Even if we were to know that history will fail to deliver, New Babylon can still play a significant role: it opens a window onto another world, activates our creative faculties, consoles us in our dissatisfied lives." Translation by author.

255 Fanny Kelk, "A Talk with Constant" in *Constant, Schilderijen 1969–77* (Amsterdam: Stedelijk Museum, 1978).

256 One can deduce this from correspondence between Constant and Caspari in the years leading up to 1969. In one particular letter, Caspari agrees with Constant that the "positive" side to the story ("die Positivsituation") may have been amply dwelt upon, which then would legitimise "alternative" explorations. Letter from Caspari to Constant, 4 November 1967, file "Correspondentie" (no year), RKD.

257 This is how Constant often described his mission in the early '70s. Interview with Nic Tummers, 15 May 2001.

258 In our interview, Hein van Haaren humorously described Constant's irritation with Fanny Kelk at the time: he was certainly surprised, only a few years later, when he heard that the two had got together.

259 *Nieuwsblad van het Noorden*, 28 July 1966, cf. note 209.

260 Letter from Constant to Carlheinz Caspari, 18 August 1972. File "Correspondentie" (no year), RKD.

261 "Opkomst en ondergang van de Avart-Garde" (see note 162).

262 The collage would appear to be part of a series: two large mixed technique drawings from the same period show a similar combination of motifs: *Terrorangriffe* (Terror attacks) from 1972 and *Bomben auf Hanoi* (Bombs over Hanoi), 1973. See *Constant: Arbeiten auf Papier 1948–1985*, exhibition catalogue (Bielefeld: Bielefelder Kunstverein, 1985), p. 20 and 21 respectively.

263 Cf. Heynen, *Architecture and Modernity*, pp. 169–170.

264 See the translation of Constant's 1980 lecture "New Babylon na tien jaren", "New Babylon – Ten Years on", in Wigley *Constant's New Babylon*, p. 236: "For those who believe or think that another kind of society is possible, that, to paraphrase Freud's Eleventh Thesis on Feuerbach, we must not interpret the world but change it, speculative representation is every bit as important as critical analysis." The original Dutch text simply mentions "the Eleventh Thesis on Feuerbach".

265 "Vision is when you know what you want and I think people who know what they want they kill people in the end, right? The history of vision in this century is the history of mass destruction. That's a serious point." Mark Wigley, panel discussion 26 January 2000, Delft.

266 See *Documenta11_Platform5: Exhibition. Short Guide* (Ostfildern-Ruit: Hatje Cantz, 2002), p. 55 – a biographical note including a preposterously short "summary" of New Babylon – and Gerti Fietzek et al. (ed.), *Documenta11–Platform 5: Exhibition. Catalogue* (Ostfildern-Ruit: Hatje Cantz, 2002), pp. 230–235: all images, no text. The appendix "Artists' writings / Project proposals for Documenta 11", pp. 544 ff., might easily have accommodated an historic New Babylon essay; but apparently nobody felt it necessary to include one.

267 *Netwerk*, Friday 5 March 2004, KRO TV.

METROPOLIS

Rem Koolhaas and Elia Zenghelis

with

Madelon Vriesendorp and Zoe Zenghelis

EXODUS

or

The Voluntary Prisoners of Architecture

"I would go to jail ......
frankly, I could use the rest"
(quotation from an ex-convict)

PROLOGUE

Once, a city was divided in two parts.

One part became the Good Half, the other part the Bad Half.

The inhabitants of the Bad Half began to flock to the good part of the divided city, rapidly swelling into an urban exodus.
If this situation had been allowed to continue forever, the population of the Good Half would have doubled, while the Bad Half would have turned into a ghost town.
After all attempts to interrupt this undesirable migration had failed, the authorities of the bad part made desperate and savage use of architecture: they built a wall around the good part of the city, making it completely inaccessible to their subjects.

The Wall was a masterpiece.

Originally no more than some pathetic strings of barbed wire abruptly dropped on the imaginary line of the border, its psychological and symbolic effects were infinitely more powerful than its physical appearance. The Good Half, now glimpsed only over the forbidding obstacle from an agonizing distance, became even more irresistible. Those trapped, left behind in the gloomy Bad Half, became obsessed with vain plans for escape. Hopelessness reigned supreme on the wrong side of the Wall.

As so often before in this history of mankind, architecture was the guilty instrument of despair.

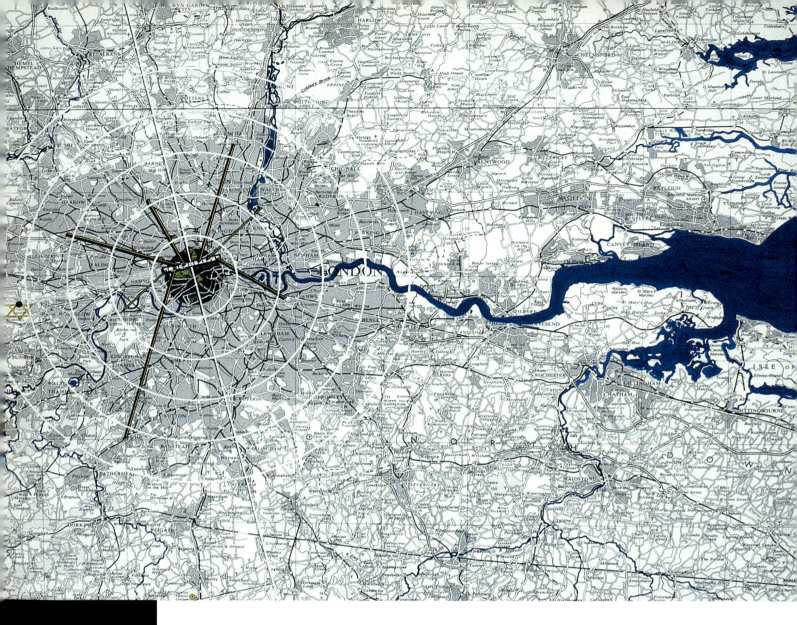

ARCHITECTURE

It is possible to imagine a mirror image of this terrifying Architecture; a force as intense and devastating but in the service of positive intentions.

Division, isolation, inequality, aggression and destruction, all the negative aspects of this wall, could be the ingredients of a new phenomenon: Architectural warfare against undesirable conditions – in our case against London. This would be an immodest Architecture not committed to timid improvements but to the provision of totally desirable alternatives.

The inhabitants of this Architecture, those strong enough to love it, would become its Voluntary prisoners, ecstatic in the freedom of their Architectural confines.

Contrary to the architecture of the modern movement and its desperate afterbirths, this new Architecture is not authoritarian, nor hysterical: it is the hedonistic science of designing collective facilities which fully accommodate individual desires.

From the outside this Architecture is a sequence of serene monuments; the life inside produces a continuous state of ornamental frenzy and decorative delirium, filling it with an overdose of symbols.

This will be the Architecture that generates its own successors, and that will miraculously cure architects from their masochism and self-hatred.

THE VOLUNTARY PRISONERS

This study wages an Architectural war on London. It describes the steps that will have to be taken to establish an Architectural oasis in the behavioural sink of a city like London.

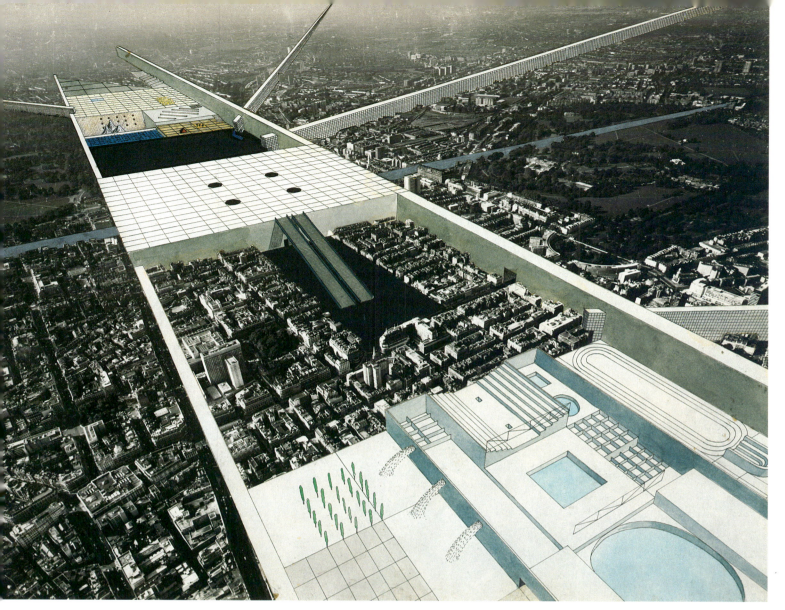

Suddenly, a strip of intense Metropolitan desirability runs through the centre of London. This strip is like a runway, a landing strip for the new Architecture of collective monuments.

Two walls enclose and protect this zone to retain its integrity, and to prevent any contamination of its surface by the cancerous organism which besieges it.

Soon, the first inmates will beg for admission. Their number rapidly swells into an unstoppable flow.

We witness the Exodus of London.

The existing physical structure of the old town will not be able to stand the continuing competition of this new architectural presence.

London as we know it will become a pack of ruins.

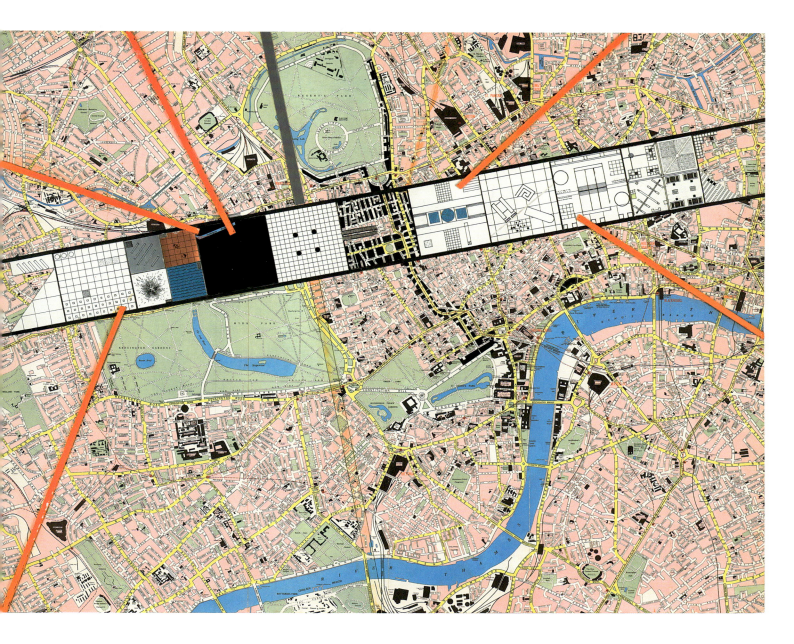

THE STRIP

The following pictures represent a close-up of a particular moment in the development of the strip.

Eleven squares are designed in various degrees of detail; together, they do not show all the aspects of the central strip, other equally essential activities and pleasures can, are being, imagined.

The central strip is only the most intense part of the much larger complex of the Architectural enclave; at the stage shown here it only contains some activities of high social intensity and communal relevance.

Those activities which are not shared by all are located in the narrow secondary strips, which each have their particular attachments to and relationship with the central zone. The secondary strips cut through the most depressed slum areas of the old London. They lead to the enclave and provide all the private accommodation the settlers have dreamt for themselves. Their magnificent presence forces these slums to turn into ghost towns and picturesque ruins.

Within the central strip the map and aerial view show, from West to East, (each contained in their own square):

1. The Tip Condition. The point of maximum friction with the old London. Here the Architectural progress of the zone visibly takes place.
2. The Allotments. Individual plots of land to balance the emphasis on the Collective facilities.
3. The Park of the four Elements: Air, Fire, Water and Earth.
4. The Ceremonial square, paved in marble; it is a place for open-air celebration.
5. The reception area: here future inhabitants are introduced to the mysteries of citizenship of the strip. Its roof is a viewing platform sufficiently elevated to give a view over the complete architectural complex.
6. An escalator descends into the area of London which is preserved (Nash a predecessor of the ruthless plan) as a reminder of the past and as useful housing for migrant visitors and new arrivals (an environmental sluice).
7. The Baths. Institute for the creation and implementation of fantasies.
8. The square of the Arts.
9. The square of the Captive Globe.
10. The institute of Biological Transactions.
11. Invisible is the Park of Aggression.

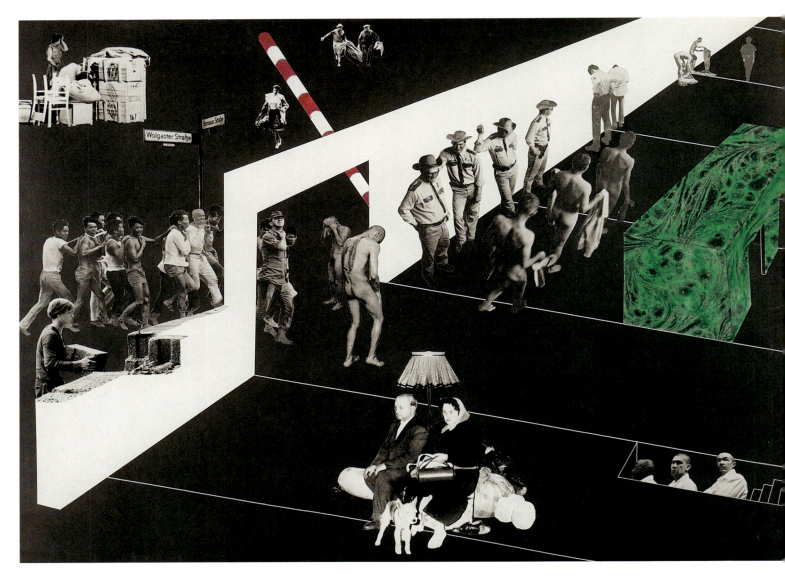

THE RECEPTION AREA

After crossing the wall, the exhausted fugitives are received by attentive wardens in a long lobby between the reception area and the wall. The consoling atmosphere of this responsive waiting room is an architectural sigh of relief: the first step of the indoctrination program of the other side of the wall is being realized: the newcomers enter the Reception Area.

On arrival a spectacular welcome is given to all.

This is a vast interior with edifices of various sizes. To the right an arena dominates half of the volume. The other half contains the most recent model of the strip, surrounded by bookcases in which the past history of the model is stored. The ceremonial square can be glimpsed beyond the model.

The Reception Area is the voluntary public realm of the zone. It is permanently thronged by amateurs who come from all parts of the strip. Through their busy dealings they are exercising

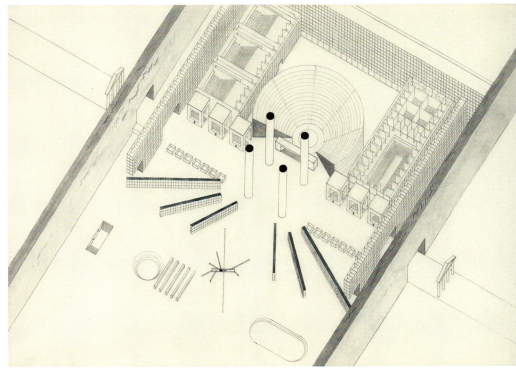

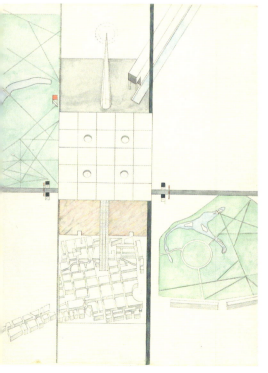

an inspired state of political inventiveness, to which the architecture is the echo chamber: a volume of overwhelming sensuousness.

The activities show that the sole concern of the participants is the present and future course of the strip: they propose architectural refinements, extensions, and strategies. Excited groups of different sizes elaborate the proposals in the special rooms built for this purpose, while others are continuously engaged in making modifications to the model. The most contradictory programmes fuse without erosion. The shameless permissiveness of these activities makes this place the receptacle for the complete spectrum of desires: it is a spontaneous planning centre.

Because of the considerable responsibilities, the activities inside the Reception Area require a minimal training for new arrivals. This can only be accomplished after overwhelming previously undernourished senses. The training is administered under the most hedonistic conditions: luxury and well-being.

THE CENTRAL AREA

The roof of the reception area, accessible from the inside, is a high altitude plateau, from which the decay of the old town and the physical splendour of the strip can be experienced.

From here, a gigantic escalator descends in to that part of London which is preserved within the strip. These ancient buildings will provide temporary accommodation for recent arrivals, during the period they are trained as voluntary prisoners: the area is an environmental sluice.

On the other (west) side of the roof is the ceremonial square. It is completely empty, except for the tower of the jamming station, which will protect the inhabitants of the strip against electronic exposure to the rest of the World.

The exact nature of the ceremonies on this black square is not yet known; it is a mixture of physical and mental exercises, conceptual Olympics.

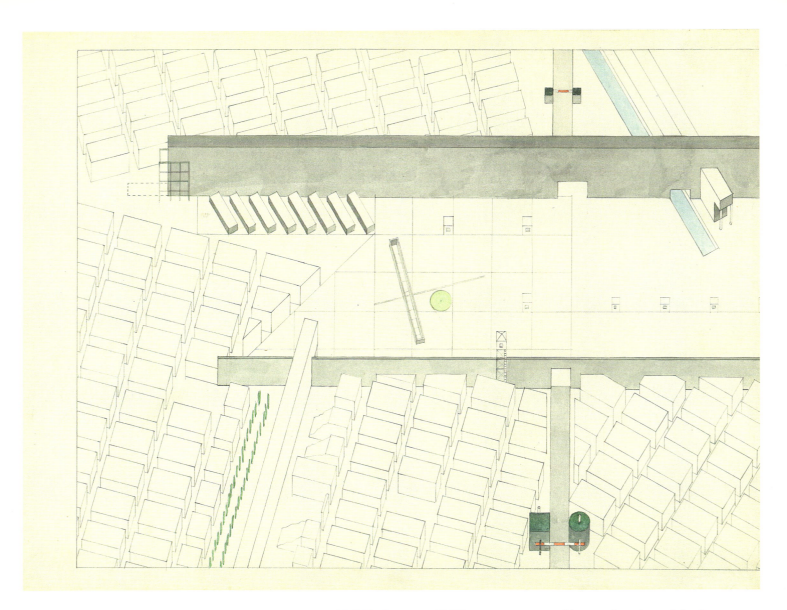

THE TIP OF THE STRIP

The frontline of the Architectural warfare waged on the old London.

Here, the merciless progress of the strip performs a daily miracle. Here, the corrective rage of the Architecture is at its most intense. It is a continuous confrontation with the old city, from the destruction of existing structures by the new Architecture to the more trivial fights between the inmates of the old London and the Voluntary Prisoners of the strip.

Some monuments from the old civilization are incorporated in the zone only after a rehabilitation of their questionable purposes and programmes. Strategies, plans and instructions are conveyed by another model of the strip, continuously modified by information arriving from the reception area. Life in the building barracks at the tip of the strip can be hard, but the permanent creation of this object leaves its builders exhausted from satisfaction.

THE PARK OF THE FOUR ELEMENTS

The park is divided into four square areas, which disappear into the ground like four gigantic steps.

The first square, "air", consists of a number of sunken pavilions, overgrown with elaborate networks of responsive ducts, which emit various mixtures of gasses to create aromatic and hallucinogenic experiences.

By subtle variations in dosage, density and perhaps even colouration, these volatile clouds of scents can be modified or sustained almost like a musical instrument.

Moods of exhilaration, depression, serenity and receptivity can be evoked invisibly, in programmed or improvised sequences and rhythms. Vertical air-jets provide environmental protection over the pavilions.

Identical in size to the first square, but sunken below the level of the surface, is "the desert": an artificial reconstruction of an Egyptian landscape, simulating its dizzying conditions: a

pyramid, a small oasis, and the fire organ: a steel frame with innumerable outlets for flames of different intensity, colour and heat. It is played at night to provide a pyrotechnic spectacle, visible from all parts of the strip: a nocturnal sun.

At the end of four linear caves, Mirage-machines project images of desirable ideals. Those in the desert who enter the tubes, run to reach these beatific images at the end, but as they run on a belt which moves in the opposite direction at a speed which increases as the distance between Mirage and runner shrinks, actual contact can never be established. The frustrated energies and desires will have to be channelled into sublimated activities. (The secret that the pyramid does not contain a treasure chamber, will be kept for ever.)

Deeper into the earth still is the water square, a pool whose surface is permanently agitated through the regular but variable movement of one of its walls, which produces waves of sometimes gigantic proportions. This lake is the domain of some pleasure seekers, who

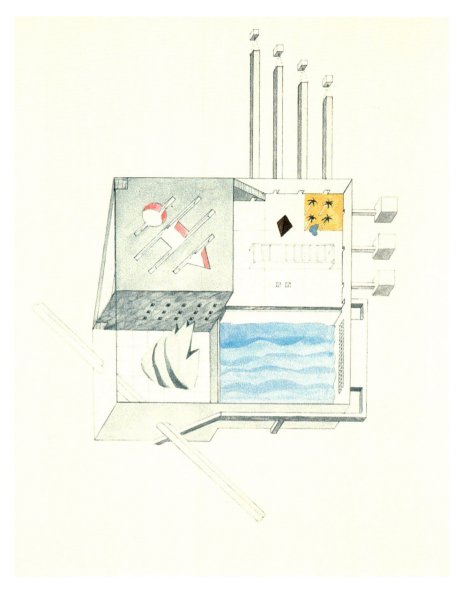

THE BATHS

The function of the baths is the creation and recycling of private and public fantasies, the transactions between them and the invention, testing and possible introduction of new forms of behaviour.

The building is a social condenser which brings hidden motivations, desires and impulses to the surface, to refine them for recognition, provocation and development.

Around the two square pools (warm and cold) and the circular main collector, the ground floor is an area of public action and display, a continuous parade of personalities and bodies, a stage where a cyclical dialectic between exhibitionism and spectatorship takes place.

It is an area for the observation and possible seduction of partners who will be invited to actively participate in private fantasies and the pursuit of desires.

The two long walls of the building consist of an infinite number of cells of various sizes, to which individuals, couples or groups can retire. These cells are equipped to encourage indulgence, and to facilitate the realization of fantasies, and social inventions; they invite all forms of human interactions and exchange.

The public area – private cells sequence can generate a creative chain reaction in the two Arenas at both ends of the baths, where successful performers or those confident about the validity and originality of their actions and proposals filter into from the cells. Finally in the Arena, they perform. The freshness and suggestiveness of these performances activate dormant parts of the brain, and trigger off a continuous explosion of ideas in the audience. Overcharged by this spectacle, the Voluntary Prisoners descend to the ground floor looking for those willing and able to work out new elaborations.

have become totally addicted to the challenge of these waves.

Day and night the sounds of this interior sea will be the acoustic background of the activities in the strip.

The fourth square at the bottom of the pit is devoted to "earth"; it is occupied by a vaguely familiar mountain, its top exactly level with the surface of the strip. At the top of this mountain, a group of sculptors is involved in a debate, trying to decide whose bust they will carve in the rock, but in the accelerated atmosphere of this prison, no one is important long enough for them to ever reach a conclusion.

The Walls of the cavity reveal the past history of this location like a scar; part of a now deserted Underground line is suspended in this void. Deep in the other walls cave dwellings and cavernous meeting places are carved out to accommodate certain primordial mysteries.

After the spiral movement through the four squares an escalator returns the wanderer to the surface.

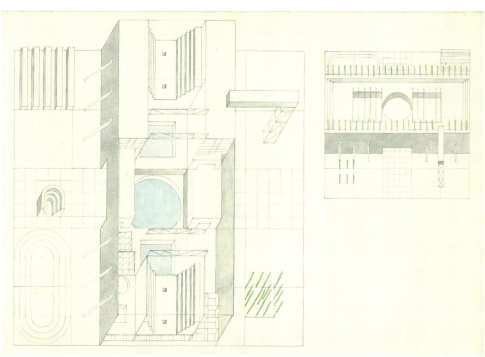

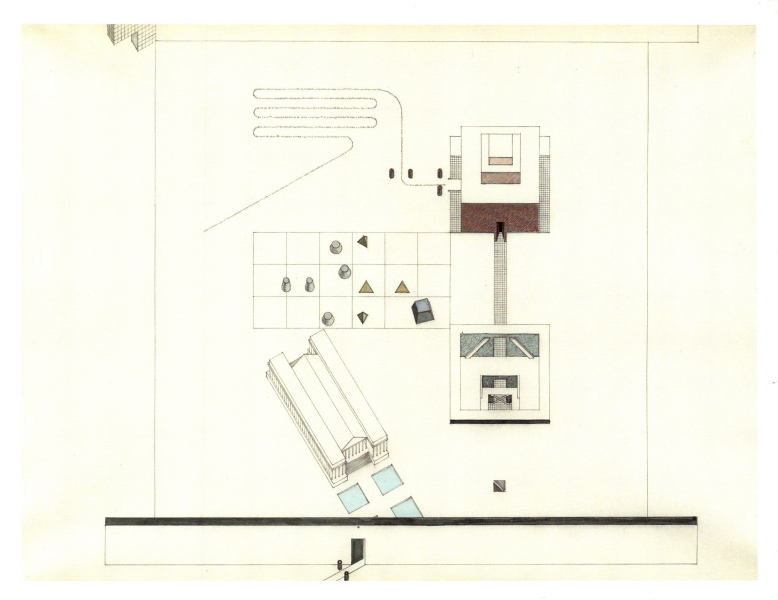

THE SQUARE OF THE ARTS

This square is devoted to the accelerated creation, evolution, and exhibition of objects. It is the Industrial zone of the strip, an Urban open space, paved in a synthetic material which offers a high degree of comfort to its users. Dispersed on this surface are the buildings to which people go to satisfy their love for objects.

There are three major buildings on the square. One is old; it has always been a museum.

The other two have been built by the voluntary prisoners. Of these two the first one bulges out of the surface; it was built with the materials of the second, which is carved out of the square, and is in fact, the interior of the first. At first sight it is impossible to understand that these twin buildings are one, and that this is not a secret. Together they form an instrument for the indoctrination of the existing culture. They achieve this simply by displaying the past in the only possible way: they expose memory by allowing its prov-

ocative vacuums to be filled with the explosive emotions of onlookers. The mixture produces the most relevant and scientific information. They are a school.

The density and impenetrability of the first building intensifies the expectations of arriving students who wait outside its gates, while the apparent emptiness of the interior of the second building provokes an anxious suspense. Descending into its enigmatic galleries, the complete history of creation unfolds in a spectral form. An irresistible power drives the visitors on a journey down the escalators that link the galleries, into a complete exploration of the most mysterious corners of history. When they arrive at the lowest gallery, they discover that the interior is bottomless, and that new galleries are under construction. The most recent galleries are filling with a continuous procession of completely unfamiliar works, emerging from a tunnel that seems to lead to the old museum. Returning to the surface, the traces of this course are retained on the retina and transferred to certain parts of the brain.

The older building contains in a sense the negative pictures of the complete past. The first impression to the uninformed visitor is that of a collection of an almost infinite number of empty frames, blank canvasses and vacant pedestals. Only those who have the knowledge from the previous course can decipher the spectacle by projecting their memories on these empty provocations: a continuous film of images, improvements, accelerated versions of the history of art automatically produce new works, fill the space with recollections, modifications and inventions.

These new creations immediately disappear through the tunnel to the pit, where they take their place in the last moments of the indoctrination programme.

Apart from these three main buildings, the only tangible exhibits in the square are small buildings that look like pawns on the grid of an ancient game. They are dropped like meteorites of unknown metaphysical meaning, waiting to be moved to the next intersection of the game, each time they are further deciphered.

THE SQUARE OF THE CAPTIVE GLOBE

This square is devoted to the artificial conception and accelerated birth of theories, interpretations, mental constructions and proposals, and their infliction on the World.

It is the capital of Ego, where science, art, poetry and certain forms of manias will be allowed to compete under ideal and identical conditions, to invent the answers to metaphysical questions, to propose changes in social organization, to destroy and restore the World of phenomenal reality.

It will be an incubator of ideologies, which will not be permitted to consume the world, to recognize only certain phenomena and suppress others. Each of these sciences and manias has its own plot. On each plot stands an identical base, built from heavy polished stone. These bases, ideological laboratories, are equipped to temporarily suspend unwelcome laws, undeniable truths, to create non-existent physical and mental conditions, to facilitate and provoke speculative activities.

From these solid blocks of granite, each philosophy expands indefinitely towards heaven; This growth from the blocks (in direct proportion to the popular appeal, excitement and

moral volume of the intellectual activities inside) will house additional accommodation, data storage, fabricated evidence, etc…

At the same time, these towers will be the visualizations, and symbols of these ideas, a spectacle of sublime communication.

Some of the basic blocks will want to present limbs of complete certainty and serenity, others will choose a soft environment of tentative conjectures and hypnotic, but questionable suggestions.

These extremities, these limbs will form an ideological exhibition, visible from afar, and scrutinized from nearby; the visitors to this exhibition will be spontaneous students, a close inspection and critical comparison of the blocks and towers will create the irresistible urge to choose, join and participate, to share and elaborate a science, a poem, a madness.

This square is the university of the Strip.

The changes of this ideological skyline will be rapid and continuous, a rich spectacle of moral fever, ethical joy, or intellectual masturbation.

The collapse of one of these towering structures can mean two things: failure, giving up, a vacating of the premises, or, the exclamation of a visual Eureka.

A Theory that works
A mania that sticks
An idea that is
A lie that has become truth
A dream from which there is no waking up

On these moments the purpose of the Captive Globe, suspended in mid-air in the centre of the square, becomes apparent: all these institutes together form an enormous incubator for the World itself. They are breeding on the globe, changing it, adding something to its contents.

These buildings and their passionate investigators have consumed facts, objects, and phenomena, in order to give more and better in return.

The globe gains weight. – Its temperature rises slowly. – Invisibly it grows.

In spite of the most humiliating setbacks, its ageless pregnancy survives.

We all have our ear on the stethoscope of the ideologies. The question is (and we are not too pessimistic about the answer): who will crack first?

The skin of this impossible egg, or perhaps ourselves?

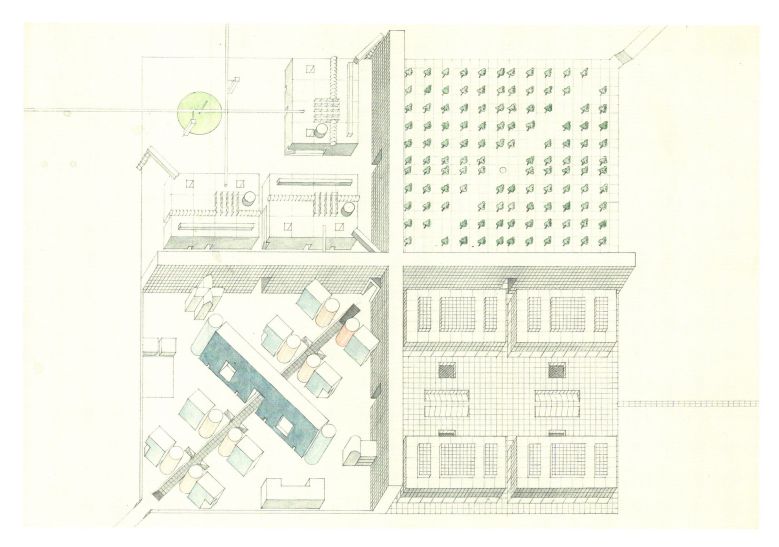

THE INSTITUTE OF BIOLOGICAL TRANSACTIONS

This institute sustains the Voluntary Prisoners through biological emergencies, physical and mental crises; it also demonstrates the harmless nature of mortality.

It is divided in four parts by a cruciform building. The first part contains the hospital: it contains the complete arsenal of modern healing, but is devoted to a radical de-escalation of the medical process, to the abolition of the compulsive rage to heal.

No forced heartbeats here, no chemical invasions, no sadistic extensions of life. This new strategy will create a lowering of the average life expectancy, a corresponding decrease in senility, physical decay, nausea and exhaustion; in fact, patients here will be healthy.

The hospital consists of a sequence of pavilions, each devoted to a particular disease.

From the entrance a medical boulevard connects these buildings. The sick pass through them in a continuous procession on a slowly moving belt; in an almost festive atmosphere of operatic melodies; a group of dancing nurses in transparent uniforms; medical equipment disguised as totem poles and rich perfumes which suppress the familiar stench of healing.

Doctors select their patients from this belt, invite them to their individual pavilions, test their vitality and almost playfully administer their (medical) knowledge. If they fail, the patient is returned to the conveyor; perhaps another doctor tries him, but it now becomes apparent that the belt leads beyond the pavilions, through the cruciform building straight to the cemetery.

There is a continuity of festive mood here, the same smells, the same ethereal dances, made more moving, more human still by the contrast of the ruthless formal layout of the plots and the unnaturalness of the dark green shrubbery.

In the third part of the square, in the three palaces of birth there will be a statistical balance between births and deaths. The physical proximity of these events through the architectural arrangement suggests the consolation of a causal relationship between the two, a gentle relay. The lowering of the average life expectancy creates an ambitious urgency; it does not allow the luxuries of under-exploited brains, the artificial prolongation of childishness or wasted adolescence. Therefore the three palaces of birth will also take care of the babies during their first infancy, school them, turn them into small adults at the earliest possible date (between eight and eleven), capable of actively taking part in life in the strip.

In the fourth square, mental patients will be on display as in former days; not as themselves however, but in an extremely well produced exhibition of their delusions, sustained by the latest technical equipment: an infinite number of Napoleons, Florence Nightingales, Einsteins, Jesus Christs and Joans of Arc, each in their custom-made uniforms. These inmates will also stage performances for the accelerated education instead of history classes.

In the cruciform building, finally, which separates the four compartments, reside the Archives that contain all vital facts, developments, life incidents of past and present prisoners. Bureaucracy, so often criticized for its passion for control and contempt for privacy (and moral blindness), guarantees the prisoners a new kind of immortality: this statistical treasure coupled to the most imaginative computers, produces instant biographies of the dead in seconds, but also premature biographies of the living, mixtures of facts and ruthless extrapolations which have become the essential instruments for plotting a course and planning the future.

THE PARK OF AGGRESSION

This is the second park in the city. It was laid out at the same time as the square of the Captive Globe, and is next to it. In this recreational area, rudimentary structures were erected to correct and channel aggressive desires into creative confrontations.

The ego-world dialectic which unfolds in the adjoining square, generates the continuous emergence of conflicting ideologies. Their imposed coexistence invokes childish dreams and the desire to play. This park is a reservoir of sustained tension waiting to be used: a gigantic playground of flexible dimensions to accommodate the only sport played in the strip: Aggression.

Here, the conflicts between corresponding antagonisms are re-enacted and fought out: the battles that are staged dissolve the corrosive hysteria of good manners. In fact on an individual level, this park is a sanatorium where patients recover from remnants of infections they brought with them from the old world: hypocrisy and genocide. The diagnoses provoke richer forms of intercourse.

The most prominent edifices are the two towers. One of them is infinite: a continuous spiral stretched out of an elastic piece of rock. The other tower has a familiar architectural style and consists of 42 platforms. Magnetic fields help create a tension between these towers which mirrors the psychological motivations of their users.

Entry to the park is free, and performances continuous. Visitors arrive alone, in pairs or small groups; the electrifying uncertainty about the safety of the square tower is compensated by the aggressive confidence of the players. Visitors withdraw into the shelves inside the tower which contains cells for the use of suppressed hatred, and where contestants freely abuse each other.

But the shelves are also viewing galleries overlooking the bigger platforms of the tower, and private antagonists become spectators. As such they are provoked into joining larger groups involved in unknown physical transactions below, which expose an amazing side of violence. As remnants of shyness are overcome, they add their private energies to this incredibly demanding and mutant form of sociable behaviour. In an agitated sleep, they walk higher up in the tower. As they pierce each floor, they experience an infinite variety of exchanges, they get an increasingly good view of things below, and an exhilarating, new sensation of the unfolding spectacle around their architecture of great heights.

As their tower leans forward, they push their antagonist into the abysmal fall inside the relentless spiral of introspection. Its digestive movement consumes excessive softness: it is the combustion chamber for the fat under the

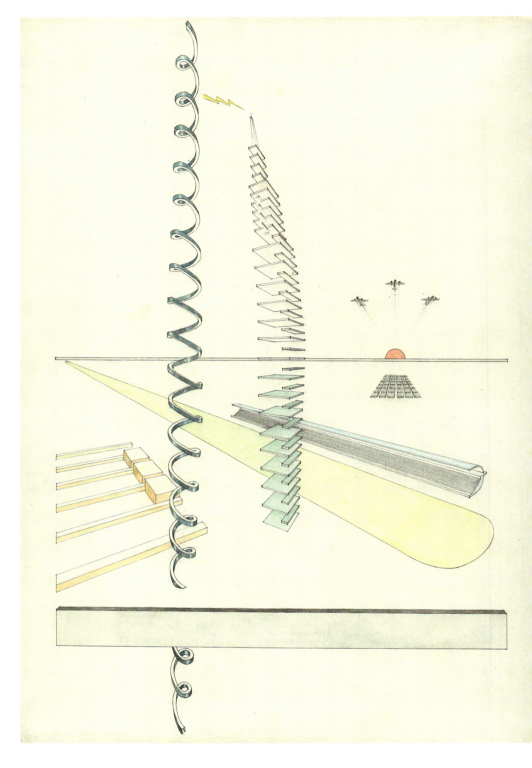

skin. The human missiles, helped by the centrifugal acceleration, escape through a chosen opening in the walls of the spiral, objects of terrifying energy into a trajectory of irresistible temptations. The entire surface of the park, the air space above and the cavities below it are now a full-scale battlefield. As the operations continue into the night they take the appearance of hallucinatory celebrations, against the backdrop of an abandoned world of calculated extermination, and polite immobility.

As they return from their nocturnal adventures they celebrate their collective victories in a gigantic arena that crosses the park diagonally.

The small buildings in the corner of the park are old building barracks used for the construction of the towers now used as changing rooms. In the three large halls (the old site offices) pacts are signed and new relationships consolidated.

THE ALLOTMENTS

In this part of the strip, the Voluntary Prisoners each have a small piece of land for private cultivation; they need this to recover in privacy from the demands the intense collectivism and the communal way of life make on them.

The houses on these allotments are built from the most lush and expensive materials (marble, chromium, steel) – small Palaces for the People.

On this shamelessly subliminal level this simple Architecture succeeds in its secret ambition to instil gratitude and contentment.

The allotments are well supervised, so that both external and internal disturbances can be avoided, or at least quickly suppressed.

Media intake in this area is nil.

Papers are banned, radios mysteriously out of order; the whole concept of "news" is ridiculed by the patient devotion with which the plots are ploughed, the surfaces are scrubbed, polished and embellished.

Time has been suppressed.

Nothing ever happens here, yet the air is heavy with exhilaration.

THE AVOWAL

To express their everlasting gratitude the voluntary prisoners sing an ode on the Architecture by which they are forever enclosed:

'De ce terrible paysage,
Que jamais œil mortel ne vit,
Ce matin encore l'image,
Vague et lointaine, me ravit…

'J'avais banni de ces spectacles
Le végétal irrégulier …

'Je savourais dans mon tableau
L'enivrante (!) monotonie
Du métal, du marbre et de l'eau.

'Babel d'escaliers et d'arcades,
C'était un palais infini,
Plein de bassins et de cascades
Tombant dans l'or mat ou bruni;

'Et des cataractes pesantes,
Comme des rideaux de cristal,
Se suspendaient, éblouissantes,
A des murailles de métal.

'Non d'arbres, mais de colonnades
Les étangs dormants s'entouraient,
Où de gigantesques naïades,
Comme des femmes, se miraient.

'Des nappes d'eau s'épanchaient, bleues,
Entre des quais roses et verts,
Pendant des millions de lieues,
Vers les confins de l'univers;

'C'étaient des pierres inouïes
Et des flots magiques; c'étaient
D'immenses glaces éblouies
Par tout ce qu'elles reflétaient!

'Et tout, même la couleur noire,
Semblait fourbi, clair, irisé …

'Nul astre d'ailleurs, nuls vestiges
De soleil, même au bas du ciel,
Pour illuminer ces prodiges,
Qui brillaient d'un feu personnel (!)'

EPILOGUE

Although at first sight the metaphorical message of these proposals may seem to dominate practical considerations, this is not another Utopian tale.

The zone can be built today (if necessary in segments, perhaps with a modified location, perhaps with the segments dropped like stones, apart from each other, and only connected by the overlapping ripples caused by their impact on the urban pond, i.e. like true social condensers). It requires a fundamental belief in cities as the incubators of social desires, the synthetic materializations of all dreams. If people were allowed to become acquainted with Architecture they would decide to re-appropriate the physical and ideological decay of our Urban Societies and to rehabilitate their premises with the metropolitan ideal and life style.

Under the threat of doom, the common concern, that is the fulfilment of all private desires within a subliminally collective and deliriously permissive common effort, produces phantom proposals, in the knowledge that phantom reality is the only possible successor to the present reality shortage.

Like the castaways on the raft of the Medusa, the last surviving realists, hanging on the parachute of hope are dropping on the rescue ship: THE CITY which, at the end of cannibalism, will appear on the horizon.

Text and Architecture: Architecture as Text

Elia Zenghelis

My ex-partner used to tell me that the problem with me was the discrepancy between my view of reality and reality. I gradually became aware that this was the shadow of an unconscious desire and over time it grew into a conscious part of my mental apparatus, until it became an explicit trait: first a mere admission – and on recognizing that it had, all along, acted as a protective layer between me and reality it turned into an ideology.

Has it not been accepted – ever since Kant – that there is an unbridgeable gulf between reality *in itself* and reality as it appears to us? That our possibilities of knowing have more to do with *our own apparatus* than with the 'nature' of reality?

Indeed the persistent propaganda of the last decade – calling for an objective 'reality' to figure at the centre of the architectural discourse – has been mystifying: an indefensible affectation over time became a tyranny – and a self-eviction from our own humanity: a 'reality' seen as truth, underpinning every architectural enterprise, an 'ideal' mission, even a *completed project*, which needs no tampering with, only 'articulation'. Reality as paradigm, only to be 'mapped' and 'branded' (now on the political correctness decline). Despite pretensions of scientific "method" it is a random sampling process of gratuitously selected contextual information (called 'research') and gathered in the name of 'realism'. Avoiding the painful confrontation with architecture, it is projected as 'the alternative', a *ready-made* that procures the project; its 'objectivity' 'protects' it from the anachronistic architectural vice of self-indulgence. Is this not a cover-up, the frustrating sight of architects fleeing from their own prerogatives? In the scientific world, mapping has defined objectives, based on *inspired speculation*. With architects it has become the penultimate manifestation of groping in the dark, an exercise resting on hope, with 'research' becoming a mantra conjuring inspiration.

As for the more recent criticism of this position – now on the rise from a supposedly new engagement from the left – it too has an uncanny spinelessness that is reminiscent of 1968, even as it evokes the spectre of Revolution.

Our tragedy is that we live under an acute sense of illusion without any sense of disillusion. There has been no revolution, only loss: we are victims in a void – inhabitants of the political barbarism of our post-humanist 'sophistication'.

If there is a discrepancy between such interpretations and my view of reality, I admit it: this patronage of 'reality' is a call for architecture to be either 'realistic' or 'utopian' and I believe that the *real* discrepancy is to be found between the ambition of these views and the instrumentality of architecture.

As for inspiration, it is a transaction grounded on insight, cognisance, imagination: a lost art based on a humanist tradition that the technocratic servitude of our age is in the process of dismantling.

Imagination has been through the ages the ability to visualize hearsay, to represent the unknown, to postulate on a future absence and to re-make what is summoned in myth or an idea in the solitude of one's psychology. The gift to represent that which is in the mind's eye: what one has heard of but never seen. It is the ability of coming to terms with the conflict that arises in our order of existence, when the latency of a 'future form' is perceived out of our world of references and requires a *technique* to materialize it: the discourse that will give form to the conjectures of our psychology.

Nevertheless this lost art is as recoverable as Proust's time – through the discovery of the power of re-interpretation: the passage from the state of reminiscence to the state of materialization. It can be practised and sharpened through learning to 're-present' and re-constitute reality – as practice. It is the most fertile and gratifying (albeit hard and painstaking) occupation one can creatively engage in, i.e. the supremacy of the *synthetic* over the real and the ability to invent the forms with which the passage from one to the other can be realized.

At the same time this recoverability is essential to re-establish the immediacy of the *object* over the secondary discourse of hermeneutics: as the primary discourse of the discipline, architecture possesses a direct vocabulary and syntax, that communicates what it is by itself and without the intermediary of explanation.

To clarify what I mean by this, I return to the power of reminiscences in Proust's world of references as I wish to claim that the sensory intensity of the reader is far superior to anything that the narrator might have felt in real time. At the same time this intensity is a direct relationship between the object (in this case writing) and the reader *without* the mediation of secondary explanation, categorization, or analysis. It provides the indisputable proof that the synthetic re-presentation of real experience is capable of *procuring the experience* with an intelligibility and clarity of representation, the intensity and absoluteness of which lived-in reality can never hope to approximate.

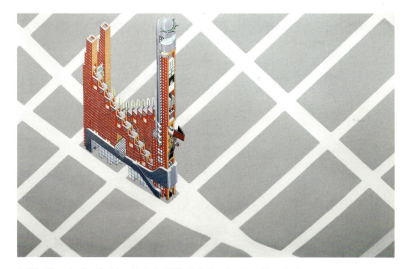

1. Elia Zenghelis, *Sphinx Hotel*, 1975. Painting by Zoe Zenghelis
2. (Opposite page:) Elia Zenghelis, *Head of the Sphinx*, 1975

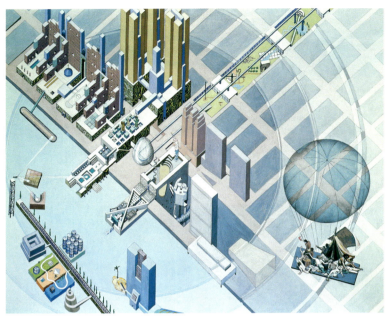

3. Elia Zenghelis, *Egg of Columbus Center*, New York, 1973–74
4. (below:) *Egg of Columbus Center*, elevation

It is about the intelligence that can idealize and reinterpret reality and this is exactly what *Delirious New York* achieved in the seventies. There is no objective truth in the 'theory of Manhattanism', only idealization, critical re-presentation and polemics: the Retroactive Manifesto is about reality and it deals more effectively with reality as it re-forms it and (by retroactively investing it with a manifesto it never had) redeeming it. At the same time, it addresses a more general reality, that of a historical human condition, the decline of the architectural discourse at the time.

In this article I want to claim that the Retroactive Manifesto has constituted the primary paradigm of the last 30 years, that (in a void reminiscent of our present condition) it replaced paradigms that had lived out their usefulness, that it has itself now run out of steam and that its continued application by the generations that inherited it has led to an inter-paradigmatic void – as defined by Thomas Kuhn in *Structure of Scientific Revolutions* – a void in which architecture is stagnating.

Having lived and been involved in the process, I take a personal position in reviewing it. To explain this I will use a selectively semi-autobiographical narrative. To put my argument in perspective, I have to start with an admission: my interest in Architecture is 'relative' in the sense that it is limited to architecture in itself: I

don't believe that the tomes of exegetic literature that have flooded the market about it deserve the forests destroyed to provide the paper. This stems from my immutable conviction that all the so-called higher Arts (of which Architecture *still* is one) have an inherent 'idiolectic' property that gives them a unique 'absoluteness', with a self-sufficient vocabulary and syntax of their own. I mentioned literature above because its objective materiality is *the text* and this makes the argument self-evident. But what applies to literature applies to all Arts and hence to Architecture. They all have their own inherent *text*. While at the service of societies and their politics, they possess a critical autonomy, being a law unto themselves and only unto themselves, with which they transcend their role and through which they become *critical*. This is their 'primary' discourse and that of architecture is matter: its vocabulary and syntax is the vocabulary and syntax of matter. Nothing can be said about the nature (and sense) of architecture that architecture itself cannot say more immediately – and better. Moreover, as it continuously 'rethinks' its own inheritance in order to 'mirror' the world it serves and represents, it becomes *de facto* critical; its critical instrumentality is *being there* – and being there is its only explanation.

I don't need Barthes or Derrida to deconstruct Proust: his text tells me *everything* they say better – and I can do with it what pleases me, by myself and by means of the immediacy of direct (and regular) confrontation with *the text* itself. Through its polemic, I – as an architect – draw inspiration for architecture, while on the contrary, I experience the exegesis in texts *about* architecture as primarily parasitic and unspeakably fraudulent; unless they can sustain a polemical form of 'annunciation', rather than suffer through their unbearable boredom, I give them a miss and pass on to *primary texts*, which (in themselves) are about themselves: never about architecture.

For these reasons – and primarily because I am not a writer – I loathe having to write; this article has caused me untold pain, loneliness and deprivation – and I hope it will be the last one I have agreed to do: but since I do it, while releasing pent-up incense, I would like at least to drive at certain positions that I have a strong urge to go into battle for.

To summarize the above: since good architecture is *de facto* critical, I firmly believe that, except for a compulsory, un-critical and detailed history, limited to facts, dates and (exhaustive) illustrations, there is nothing of importance to write about it. Architecture is *matter* and architects need only work with the vocabulary and syntax of matter. Their role is to *design buildings*, the acknowledged quality of which will be their sole value and, as always, the only reason for architects to be remembered. To paraphrase

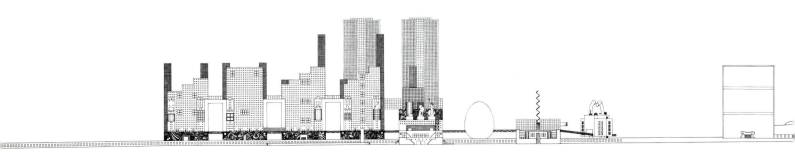

Stravinsky and since (like music or literature) architecture is absolute *from the moment it assumes as its calling the expression of the meaning of discourse, it leaves the realm of architecture and has nothing more in common with it.*

At this point I round up my leading admission with the codicil that if I could have been a musician I would never have become an architect. What I like about architecture is what I would have enjoyed in music; it is the 'doing' of it: my production and that of others. I enjoy studying and learning from this occupation. Moreover, I find a striking similarity between music and architecture. By this I do not mean the alleged equivalence in their structure and order (usually exemplified by Bach's 'architecture'); I firmly believe in the separateness and indivisibility of each. I find the similarity to be of a kind that is best expressed in a striking quote of G. Steiner on music – that it conveys its 'meanings' into a "direct cerebral, somatic, carnal and spiritual perception, searching out for resonances in our bodies at levels deeper than and outside the range of spoken language." By this I claim that the intervention of our psychological (as well as mental) processes are needed to transcend the world of reason into the world of the absolute, even as it endangers the boundary definitions between the artefact and nature.

What 'primed' me for architecture was a childhood of deprivation, during the years of war, German occupation and civil war in Athens – a childhood where the lack of stimulation forced us to invent and supply our own entertainment – and enabled us to be acutely stimulated by the advent of anything that transcended the banality of our ordinary existence. In hindsight, deprivation was good compost for the imagination. One lived in a constant fantasyland, a fabricated reality the memory of which still lingers abstractly.

Up to age 11, Athens of the war years had been my only 'urban' experience, spent mostly inside the walls of our concrete apartment. An experience of a vulnerable, but seemingly protected interior landscape, where the force of imagination and daydreaming supplied safety. Hemmed in, we could look out onto a hostile and dangerous exterior landscape, where the cold rain of winter carried headless corpses along the overflowing banks of the sewer that was the Illissos – the river of Athens – and the hot wind of summer that lifted clouds of dust, mixed with the inexorable glare of the sun, engulfing the city and blurring its vision.

When at the age of eight we were taken up to the Parthenon, the immediacy of that mythical and much talked-about object, which through my early childhood I had been watching from the dilapidated city below, had an impact on me of something 'clean' and 'better'. I vaguely remember the embryonic awareness that emerged in my unconscious, as faintly familiar with something I already knew from music – the only 'sensuous' supply in our family in those days, which in a life of extreme and endless boredom kept me spellbound. In the four-dimensional continuum of time and space, I gradually developed for architecture a parallel interest, especially in what I saw as its difference from the buildings we lived in, another kind of other-worldliness that separated it from the reality I knew and which I had grown to dislike.

1948 marked the end of a tragic civil war that left Greece in economic and physical ruin. The city was growing and so did the

5. Elia Zenghelis, *Egg of Columbus Center*, cutaway axonometric

condition of dust, sweat and unbearable noise: hooting trucks, street cries and the exploding boilers of the 'gas-o-gene' busses produced a continuous clangour that felt almost like a natural succession to the earlier submachine guns and mortar shells. Part of a massive exodus, my father had already left to seek a better fortune in the 'civilized' world. He went to South Africa: my mother hated it, so she and I stayed behind. The Athens of my memory was like Kabul after its latest devastation.

I was 11 when I visited my father for the first time. A visit that was a watershed. After five days flying over Africa in a DC-3 (exposed to a phantasmagoria of experiences – from desert to tropical forest) we landed in Johannesburg in the dusk of an unforgettable evening. The crisp winter air of high altitude had a distinct but fragrant touch of something lightly burnt that was instantly intoxicating and evoked absolute, dry cleanliness. Its unmistakable scent welcomed me on each of the four and only

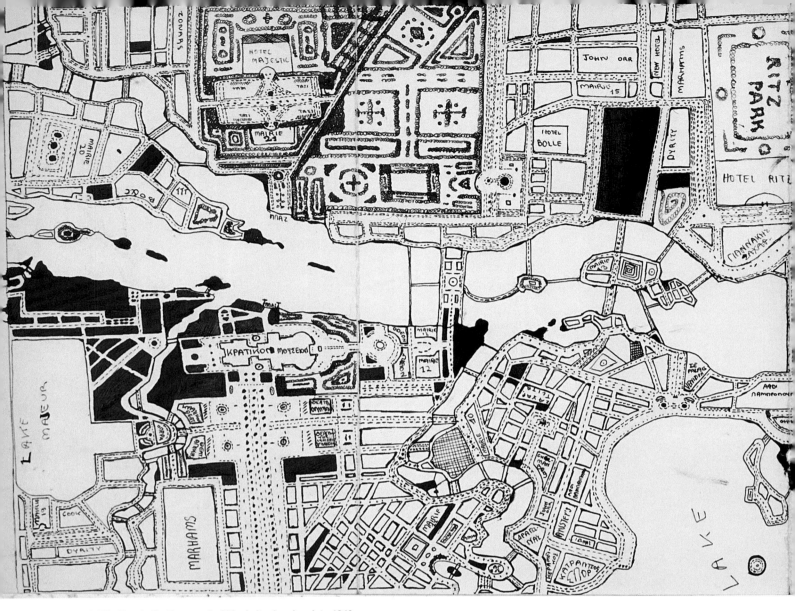

6. Elia Zenghelis, Fragment of ideal city drawing, late 1940s

visits I paid there, from 11 to 16, and I know I would recognize it instantly 50 years later. I don't know why, but this smell and the sight of green grass when I woke up the next morning became the catalytic symbol of a rising desire to be dictator and make cities beautiful. Needless to say that the tragic social and political reality I had chosen to fulfil this aspiration in, was totally hidden. All the same, through the dramatic unfolding of beauty and terror, the power of Terrifying Beauty can only sharpen one's critical consciousness. Tolstoy marvelled at how "beauty" is conceived as "goodness"; in dramatic situations however, beauty simply rests in the imagined tangibility of a redeeming substance with which one could fabricate one's own hope for a better world.

When my father drove me in his Studebaker through what appeared as an interminable series of lush gardens into an unimaginably beautiful traffic jam (nothing flowed: everything was monumental) and to downtown Johannesburg (never before had I seen American limousines, nor green grass), at the sight of the high rise walls of the buildings lining up the city grid I could not believe my eyes: this was the sight of my ambition and I decided it could only be fulfilled by becoming an architect.

I now recall this desire to be a dictator and can articulate the beauty of its delirium in ways that I could not then. I had to remake history, to relive childhood and to transform Athens into this impossible fine frenzy, this visual and physical substitute that nevertheless approximated the vertigo of meaning – precisely because of the symmetry in this chimerical experience of lack of meaning; something that could not be expressed in words but nevertheless spoke its own language.

When I returned home I started drawing a city that was to replace Athens. It was conceived on the model of Johannesburg but as it grew, it included every possible ideal condition. On the one hand it rested on visions of the magical cities my grandparents had lived in: Istanbul, Odessa, Paris, St Petersburg, Bucharest; on the other it was made up of those magnificent hotels on postcards of Stresa and Isola Bella. These hotels inspired my notion of 'ideal' for living conditions; their Alpine setting became the setting of my city. It was to grow bigger than New York and (surrounded by jungle and desert) only stop in the mountains.

I started drawing its history over years and centuries; its incremental growth took place on paper torn from school exercise

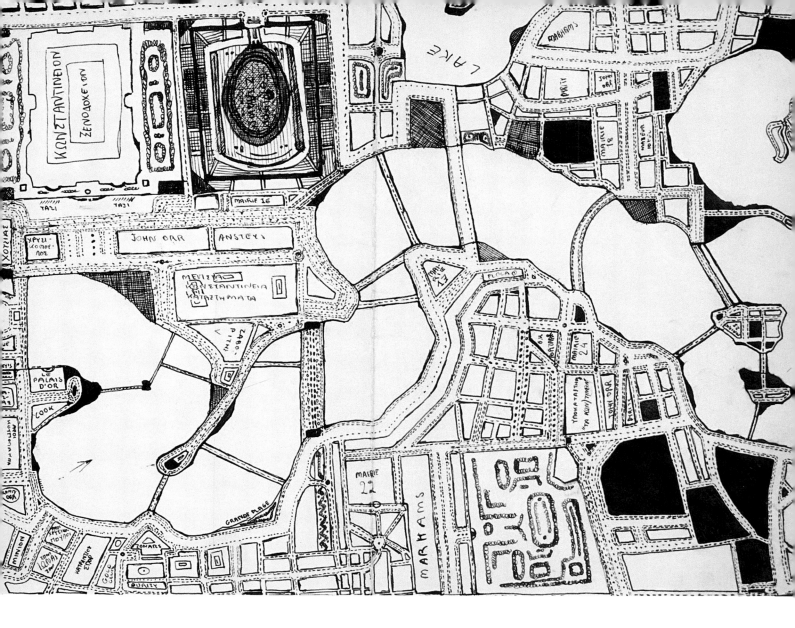

books, stuck together with tape. I started it in 1948 and five years later my bedroom would not hold it (it had to be unfolded in parts). But the city never reached its limits: on my last South African holidays I was already an apprentice at an architect's office and had decided that I wanted to study at the AA. When twenty years later Leo Krier saw the fragmentary scraps that remained he told me I had never managed since to do as good a project. Be this as it may, I had contrived my own – however primitively conceived – view of Architecture, the outline frame of which has never left me. I had had an unexpected revelation: I had seen an image of 'modernity'.

Athens was undergoing a process of transformation and an economic boom when I left for London. It had become a vast construction site, but compared to the new 'modernity' of my mind's eye, this seemed desperately 'conformist' and provincial. A concrete lava was replacing the dust, slowly obliterating everything – even the traces of lean grass and chamomile of the Athenian spring.

At first London revealed itself as the apotheosis of green. But the reality of it was a sequence of green oases in an ocean of urban misery – dark, crumbly, wet, unheated and complacent: different from Athens but equally distressing. Despite this, London in general and the AA in particular seemed immersed in an appalling state of 'realism' – an obdurate refusal to replace ugliness with a redeeming alternative.

An uncanny Puritanism that equated squalor with an 'eternal presence' annihilated my dictator-daydream and I found myself in the humiliating position of being treated like Émile. Right from the start, my confidence was dealt a devastating blow: our first studio project (given to us on day one) was to design a primitive hut. When I proposed a little skyscraper (I wanted to marry Vitruvius with Johannesburg) I was greeted with a pandemonium of indignation. I was offered two options: the guillotine or submission. For a while I considered the first option. But the rule was that the spirit of the project was the 'eternal present' and I had to follow the good Abbé Laugier. So after a lot of painful prevarication, I gave in.

Eventually I was even 'convinced' (the process was in the end one of interesting and fruitful contradictions) but this entailed the disenchantment of accepting deprivation as moral necessity.

I had been convinced all along that modernity, luxury and hedonism were an inseparable and ethical union and that the only reason it did not quite work yet was because it was still an unfinished chapter of both modernity and political patronage. In the end I simply resigned: I accepted that the greyness, the dirtiness – the 'reality' of the city as found, was as Venturi had said, "almost all right".

Peter Smithson was the ideological heart of the school and I gradually managed to get on well with him. I learnt how to establish a constructive relationship, as soon as I realized that all the ideological pretensions were a cover-up for presenting inspired intuitive speculations and doing some very good architecture. Once I became skilled at communicating my projects by showing him especially redrawn 'substitutes' (such as diagrams that presumed to represent analyses and relationships) and by hiding them until the 'right moment', I learnt a lot from him and he liked them.

Team X introduced me to the ideological battles of modernism and to the efficiency of critical method. Their drive for moral criteria gave emphasis on the *complexities* of the city. Seeing the city and its evaluation as social software anticipated a priority of a later generation: that of the *programme*. Involuntarily, they were the harbingers of the retroactive manifesto.

In hindsight, it is clear that *Team X Primer*, like the Retroactive Manifesto that replaced it (each one a paradigm for an era) contained the seeds of post-modernism: the *post-modernist* implications of realism *then and now* have a symmetrical equivalence. But it is undeniable that the twin impact of Robert Venturi's *Complexity and Contradiction* and Aldo Rossi's *The Architecture of the City* was for all of us a defining moment. They drastically shifted the emphasis from the Modern Movement's reformist stance towards the city with a polemic for the "existing reality of the city".

Peter Smithson left the AA in 1961 to work on the Economist. His departure set in motion a rapid decline of the school, I remained to teach and I stayed there for another 25 years. Teaching became for me an inseparable part of learning and I have always seen it as a counterpart of practice.

Following the demise of Team X the period was marked by rebellions. The most influential was the visionary 'utopia' of Archigram, a talented group who first rose against the indoctrination of Team X, while still at the AA. Central to their mutiny was the rejection of ideological commitment. Value-free exuberance was to liberate architecture from ideological dogmatism. This was at one with the consumerist euphoria of the '60s. As such it failed to be radical and could not sustain itself in the political climate of the decade.

Then came May '68. That year's events had cataclysmic consequences for education. But compared to continental Europe, the Anglo-Saxon political consciousness was stunted: at the AA educational objectives were replaced by hypnotic rituals. Since Woodstock, the cult of alternative cultures ranked as education. As a result the AA, now under theosophist leadership, became a refuge for rice cooking hippies.

My ideas floated in a 'void' and my hopes lay in my Unit at the AA. At exactly that moment (suspecting the euphoria for being a silent euthanasia of Modernity) a new generation was being born. Rising from this scene at the AA, Rem Koolhaas and Leo Krier, already in the process of taking their parallel but radically different paths, could be seen as controversial twins (even the names are suggestive: Rem and Leo – Leo and Rem). Like Calvino's *Castle of Crossing Destiny* my Unit became a school within the school, the stage of opposite characters, most of whom believed in the urgency of resuscitating the power of architecture.

When Rem came to my unit at the AA, he had already spent one miserable year as a first-year student; he joined the unit as a teacher rather than as a student and shortly after him Zaha Hadid (our best student). Natalini, Ungers, Branzi, Krier, Vidler, Porphyrios, Charles Jencks, George Baird, Summerson, Colquhoun, Stirling, Françoise Choay and others became a sort of intellectual Walhalla in which a group of committed people were interacting with the issues of our unit.

Leo joined us later: in our desperate search for real architects to teach, we discovered Leo in *Controspazio*, Portoghesi's sadly short-lived magazine. I heard that Leo was in London, working for Stirling. The day he got my message he came to my house; we became friends instantly.

Thirty years later, Leo is turning out to have been the wisest and the least wise among us. His revulsion against 'modernism' was apt: our cities' desolation owes more to modernism's afterbirths than to the Second World War. He fought for closing schools of architecture: he was right. The mass-production of architects goes on at an alarming rate. But he also loved the best of modern, and being a sensualist he knew the difference between good and bad. It was his own admission that if good modern could be guaranteed, he would support it. Given his enormously discerning talent, it was his mistake to betray it.

It was in 1972 that Rem and I produced *Exodus*, our first collaboration. Since it is presented in this book, it is unnecessary to explain it again. It is important, however, to put it in perspective.

It started as a project that Rem had sketched out for a linear city, the implications of which stirred up my enthusiasm and I asked to join. Surprisingly, Rem's enthusiasm was reciprocal. This changed my outlook and started an association of 15 years that reformed my attitude to the limitations, purpose and deployment of my skills.

The influences are clear: on the formal side Leonidov, Superstudio and our own past, but the concept is based on the Berlin Wall – Rem's re-interpretation of it as a monument that inverted one's perception of reality and therefore provided a powerful tool for critically inverting one's appreciation of good and bad, beauty and ugliness, captivity and freedom, lie and truth, orthodoxy and fashion, hypocrisy and politics.

By re-interpreting continuity as a sequence of 'separatenesses', the totality, drama and cohesion of the Wall depended on the build-up of incremental fragments, attachments, materials, scales, meanings, interpretations, interruptions and most critically the juxtaposition of radical differences. Applied to *Exodus* this system became primarily a critique of Megastructure. (Superstudio's influence should not obscure the principle of parcelling the strip into squares and of the stated intention to have it dispersed and built in segments across the city.) Simultaneously it caricatured the humanist legacy of Team X and it opposed Venturi's modesty as false masochism, and as abdication of the responsibilities and prerogatives of architecture: instead of being another act of reinforcement therapy for the powerless, it reclaimed for architecture the power to re-create the artificial – or that the invention of large and complicated structures of demanding and permissive architecture is the formula for making the city.

Being a clear and interpretable polemic, I get mystified when people call it cynical or a utopia. What do they mean?

To find it cynical is an inexplicable reaction that refuses to observe the way reality is reproduced. It puts reality 'between its own parenthesis' to both warn us from and inspire our fabrication. For me it always had something Wagnerian about it: a sort of transfiguration of reality that redeems its most terrifying features.

Utopia is a word that has been trivialized by its misuse. A world that could not possibly exist outside the realm of the hypothetical, Utopia is More's way of addressing his reality, through the art of his imagination. A *hypothesis* is always a product of the imagination in the interest of the originator's intentions. To project an imaginary world as a hypothesis would be totally gratuitous unless in doing so, one was addressing shortcomings in one's reality. Imagination allows the broadest range of extreme ideas; projected into an art form it provides the security of a world within the artist's control (and in exercising it, More was willing to consciously put his life on the line for his beliefs and his faith). Coupled with its symmetrical opposite, Macchiavelli's passionate critique of his own society to which Utopia is More's answer, both *The Prince* and *Utopia* use the text as a vehicle of persuasion for didactic intentions that can generate changes not just in the mind of the reader but in the world. *Exodus* uses the text of Architecture to criticize Architecture.

Historical quotations were a reminder of the power of Architecture through History, civilization's most imposing artefact. But seen in hindsight, the virus of Post-Modernism was infecting the work: what started as a healthy amputation to Modernity, resulted in the body getting sicker than ever before.

As scriptwriter Rem magnified the importance of the *programme* in architecture. Already established from Modernism's outset in one form, amplified by Team X in another, the notion of the plan as scenario became central to the work of OMA, growing in importance to the point where it became a bureaucratic tyranny. In the present predicament – and in retrospect – it is easy to recognize the shortcoming involved in neglecting the quintessence of form. Despite our radical drives we were allergic to the label of 'formalism' – the most misused, despotic and callous misrepresentation of meaning exploited by institutional modernism, in its calculating and opportunistic abuse of the 'ism' classification. *Form* lost its meaning, as words do in polemical circumstances: with shameless arrogance, it denoted (as it still does) the self-indulgent and value-free abuse of compositional volumetric inappropriateness to architecture, as against 'lesser' endeavours (where it is permissible) such as sculpture. Yet (as in literature or music) it is the *sine qua non* of the existence of all artistic endeavour. It is the all-inclusive category that (far from being

restricted to such reductive inference) comprises the substance, fabric, structure, method and inherent logic of any discipline; it is the unique figure with which its intrinsic meaning becomes manifest. It is what guarantees that the text of architecture will be architecture.

With architecture being again threatened from within, it is clear that by mixing two distinct texts, each possessing a separate and autonomous language, the text of architecture with the text of writing, we were committing a fatal mistake that soon became indefensible and that was to reach its nadir when we envisioned the architectural 'hybrid'.

But it is not a question of looking back and regretting: retrospective criticism does not invalidate the past. The intoxication of re-creating the prerogatives of architecture was lessons not lost. For anyone who has not worked with Rem as an architect in the '70s, it is hard to imagine the extent of his ideas, their spontaneity and originality; they were challenges of uncompromising inspirational scope. Incredibly, one was left to make them one's own. However he never had much patience for supervising

7. Elia Zenghelis, OMA: Parc de la Villette competition entry: model, 1982

project development and having to do it would quickly irritate him. So he left it to a growing army of collaborators with the inexplicable expectation that the results would come. In this surreal setting, things began to deteriorate.

It is always evident where he has himself worked on his ideas and, whether built or not, from Berlin's Koch-Friedrichstrasse to the Villa in Bordeaux, they are architectural masterpieces. So the question arises now as before: Why does he not decide to concentrate – especially now that he can choose to build what he wants – on the development of his ideas down to the last detail, select his buildings and reject the others? He used to disclaim the value of detail in buildings as a matter of principle. I wonder if he still takes the same ideological position. Is there not enough evidence against the "no money, no details" position by now?

From what I know of him I put this inconsistency to impatience: on the one hand the incessant flow of new motivations, pressing to move on to the next enterprise, on the other an aversion

8. Eleni Gigantes, GZA: Ashikita House of Youth, Kyushu, Japan, 1998

to staying with the same preoccupation for long (or more than 20 minutes, in accordance with Leonidov's observation on human nature).

On the other hand, one has to understand and acknowledge Rem's intense curiosity about the power of trivialities and their impact on the phenomenal reality of our civilization: for instance, his often criticized fascination with fashion is not submission, but interest in the phenomenon. It is more relevant to criticize the product, rather than the motivation. As a piece of architecture Prada fails to communicate a critical position, to master the object of desire, to be commensurate with Rem's intellectual ability.

Moreover there is the dilemma of sharing two talents: one as an architect and one as a writer. In choosing to write about architecture, (when he could have chosen to write about anything) I believe he made a big unconscious sacrifice. Even though his texts are the most readable (perhaps the only readable) and critical texts on the subject, particularly for the past 30 years and despite the depth of their insight, their scope is limited: they are of ephemeral interest, in 50 years they may be irrelevant, because architecture outlives its temporal criticism.

When I asked him why we had to turn our back so fast on what we had just done so well, his answer was that it was necessary to be ahead of being consumed. This approach I think backfired: OMA (or the idea people made of it as 'style' – and system of aphorisms) became the most consumed production of the last 30 years – especially in the Netherlands where the alchemy of mixing iconoclastic approaches with puritanical recoiling became irresistible. As Rem feared, consumption proved totalizing. With horror I today saw from the train, dotted in the Dutch sprawl, the tiny sketches, the caricature forms that we used to draw on the back of envelopes some 25 years ago, now reincarnated as multinational corporations and banks. Who would have thought that possible? These materialized sketches are the products of our unconscious post-modernism.

In the end it is a pity that in this historical process, everybody has been concentrating on Rem Koolhaas for his smartness and not for his ability as a good architect. And while he unexpectedly and uncharacteristically assumes the guise of political correctness, the 'critique' begins to take on the form of an attack against his persona. Is he yielding to the ridiculous state of affairs when this criticism does not even address his work, but his choice of client? The materialization of this plastic agony is the disguise of a violent jealousy: the frustrated vindictiveness of his less successful peers, who, unable to come up with a new paradigm, discharge a reserve stock of pent-up envy and a lack of the basic knowledge that the history of architecture has consisted of architects building for motherfuckers.

Within the infrastructural nature of our society, architecture requires the stability to assimilate the unstable nature of contemporary conditions in order to be efficient, i.e. able to host effortlessly and in silence the next course of events. This form of efficiency is the primary rhetoric of architecture and sustains the quality of modernity: and paradoxically it is the most elemental and orthodox means that are the most reliable reservoirs of modernity.

The time has come to return to a view of an architecture that is liberated from a redundant content, self-reliant, absolute and founded on the convention of the language and syntax of architecture but requiring an iconographic re-articulation, even *tabula rasa*, to be used as a palette, a *formal convention* from which the meaning can be evolved by others. But it is not an end in itself – a purely self-referential 'artistic abstraction': its meaning is to be the representation of the contemporary city, its formal catalyst, the *reflection of modernity*. Modernity is not about the avant-garde, but about a re-articulated, re-invented convention that exists in the work of previous modernities. Every modernity's symbolism remains imprinted on its architecture, even if the emblematic nature has withered away.

In the present void condition, this is more urgent than ever. We have gone full circle; and in conclusion I paraphrase one of Rem's old quotes: "in a situation where Architecture has become a concrete glass slipper nobody even wants to try on anymore" the next generation must be "devoted to re-conquering architecture's powers of seduction through the refinement and implementation of its own principles": to do this now, it will have to eject the redundant baggage of 'content' and by focussing on its *form,* to consider Architecture as Text.

The Exodus Machine

Lieven De Cauter & Hilde Heynen [*]

In order to 'sustain' itself within metropolitan space, architecture seems obliged to become a spectre of itself."

Manfredo Tafuri

Introduction: A Legendary Project

Exodus, or the Voluntary Prisoners of Architecture of 1972[1] is the legendary project marking the birth of OMA (Office for Metropolitan Architecture). Often referenced, it is seldom interpreted.[2] At first glance, the project fits perfectly with the wave of megastructures of the 1960s (from Friedman's *Architecture Mobile*, through Archigram's *Plug-in City*, Constant's *New Babylon*, and Soleri's *Arcologies* to Archizoom's *No-Stop City* and Superstudio's *Continuous Monument*). Through its ambiguity and metaphorical quality, it defies interpretation. *Exodus* dismisses any possible reading beforehand. Is it a new version of Le Corbusier's *Plan Voisin*? Or a version of the linear city of constructivist Leonidov (Magnitogorsk-upon-Thames)? Is it a paean to (modernist) architecture? Is it a work of art? A manifesto? A critique? And if so, of what? Is it a utopia? Is it a dystopia? Is it an intellectual joke, unleashing the cat among the pigeons? Probably a little bit of everything. The project raises more questions than it answers. Why this fascination with inclusion and enclosure? Why create a project that defends urbanity by way of an "architectural war on London"? Why the sinister humour of the voluntary prisoners – "those strong enough to love it"? Where do the camp and prison aesthetics combined with Speerian monumentality come from? Many of these questions we can resolve, at least partially, by taking a closer look at the project's genesis, its content, and its context.

1 The Genesis of *Exodus*

Rem Koolhaas was trained as an architect at London's Architectural Association, where he studied from 1968 to 1972. The AA School of Architecture at the time was an anarchic environment where Peter Cook set the tone,[3] but where Léon Krier and Charles Jencks made their presence felt as well. In an interview, Koolhaas states that this environment presented a real challenge for him, because it fell short of his expectations in so many ways.[4] Koolhaas felt that he should receive a true vocational training and was frustrated by teachers keen on tapping the inner creativity of their students and including them in participatory experiments without imparting to them thorough expert knowledge. The predominant architectural culture of those days had considerably distanced itself from true architecture, according to Koolhaas, and he wanted to change that. He did so by designing a series of highly unconventional projects that served, in a way, as intellectual molotov cocktails.

"The Berlin Wall as Architecture"[5] was a first provocation. Koolhaas was given the assignment, just like his fellow students, to study and analyze an existing building. He chose the Berlin Wall. In the summer of 1971 he visited the city, and two things struck him in particular. The first was the fact that the wall did not run from North to South at all, as a naïve notion of the Iron Curtain had it: instead, it encircled West Berlin. The "free city" turned out to be a walled-in enclave. Moreover, Koolhaas realized that the wall manifested itself architecurally under different guises: barbed wire, emptiness, walls of pre-fab concrete slabs, but also as transformed buildings with bricked-up windows. "The greatest surprise is: *the wall was heartbreakingly beautiful*." This experience revealed to him the ambiguous power of architecture.[6]

Koolhaas's introduction to Berlin's reality subsequently prompted a next provocation of AA's hippie orthodoxy: *Exodus* of 1972.[7] It was the first time that Rem Koolhaas, Elia Zenghelis, Madelon Vriesendorp and Zoe Zenghelis officially joined forces, the first two as designers and the latter two as illustrators. Koolhaas and his former teacher Elia Zenghelis designed and wrote a scenario for a strip cutting across London, an architectural paradise inciting Londoners to leave their somnambulant metropolis *en masse* for a sojourn in an environment which fulfils all their dreams (as well as their nightmares).[8] The scenario was reinforced with collages, axonometrics, and paintings, which lend the project a peculiar intensity. The echoes of Berlin are prominently present, not only in the concept, but also in the collages.

Exodus was created as a proposal for a competition on *The City as a Significant Environment* organized by the magazine *Casabella*.[9] It was first published in June, 1973. Illustrated on the cover of the magazine was the captivating collage by Madelon Vriesendorp with the peasant couple from Millet devoutly bowing their heads to recite the Angelus against the menacing backdrop of a wall with barbed wire on top and a watchtower looming behind it. Millet's rich field has been replaced by a monotonous grid of white (marble) squares; on the left and right, tinges of green and grey suggest that, under the deadness, there might still be some

1. Madelon Vriesendorp, Rem Koolhaas, Elia Zenghelis and Zoe Zenghelis in New York, 1978

2. Elia Zenghelis, Desert city, 1948

and surrounded by a desert (where the less fortunate try to survive), with a sea in the distance. In the design, Zenghelis apparently processed, in a visionary way, his impressions of Johannesburg as a modern city, where he spent several summers with his father. When Koolhaas showed him his Berlin study, Zenghelis recognized his own obsessional, ideal city, as it were: "In it I recognized the same desire to build an enclave, where the inhabitants would become the voluntary prisoners of Architecture."[10] With this, the enigma of Exodus, or at least of its genesis, seems to be solved: Exodus is the Berlin Wall, plus the voluntary prisoners from *Life* or *Time* magazine, plus the fortified desert skyscraper city of Zenghelis.

Before describing Exodus (in order both to delay interpretation and to furnish material for it) we should dwell for a moment on the title of the project. It refers to a syndrome that has shaped the industrial metropolis as a tidal system of sorts: the migration from the countryside to the city, chronicled around the turn of the century as the rural exodus, followed by the reverse migration from urban centers to the countryside, which gathered momentum from the 1930s onward and which led, in the 1960s, to large-scale suburbanization, only to enter into a new physical state toward the end of the twentieth century – that of urban sprawl. In this sense, the project can be said to define the city radically as an "exodus machine."

2 The Exodus Machine

What the project attempted, according to Koolhaas in an interview in 1988, was a critique of the "innocence" and the unfettered optimism characterizing the visionary architecture of the 1960s. OMA, with its project, wanted "to emphasize that the power of architecture is more ambiguous and dangerous. […] Exodus proposed to erase a section of central London to establish a zone of highly metropolitan life – inspired by Baudelaire – and to protect this zone with walls from the old city, creating maximum *diversity* and *contrast*. The people of London could choose: those who wanted to be admitted to this zone of hyper-intensity became 'The Voluntary Prisoners of Architecture'."[11] This programme of intense metropolitan life is also described emphatically by him elsewhere: "Its history evolved from the idea that London was an underdeveloped city, that if one would construct the metropolitan ideal in all its primordial intensity, all its inhabitants would emigrate creating a veritable exodus …"[12]

According to the prologue of Exodus, the project aims to realize the impact of the Berlin wall by reversal: "It is possible to imagine a mirror image of this terrifying architecture, a force as intense and devastating but used instead in the service of positive intentions."[13] The inhabitants of this architecture, "those strong enough to love it," would experience a paradoxical liberation: "An ecstatic freedom in their architectural confines."

Exodus, the walled-in linear city traversing London from West to East and located between Hyde Park and Regent's Park, consists of 10 squares (from left to right in the design on p. 241)[14]: the "Tip of the Strip", the point where construction of the city as wall continues; the "Allotments"; the "Park of the Four Elements"; the "Ceremonial Square"; the "Reception Area" (with a view of the roof); the "Central Area," a cut-out of a preserved fragment of London (with architecture by Nash); the "Baths"; the "Square

patches of earth and nature left. The first publication in *Casabella* is a shortened version of the manuscript. The best-known version is the one published in *S, M, L, XL*, which today serves as the original text for most new publications. The drawings and collages – in a series of 18 – are currently in the collection of the Museum of Modern Art in New York.

Elia Zenghelis gave us another crucial clue regarding the genesis of the project. He pointed out that the Voluntary Prisoners actually existed, referring to an article in *Time* or *Life* magazine (he could not remember which) about American prisoners who preferred life in prison to life outside. They had themselves picked up again as soon as possible to return to being able to enjoy the beatific, respectable life within the prison walls instead of what they perceived as the unbearable chaos of freedom in 'real life'. Koolhaas and Zenghelis considered the article so important that a substantial number of pictorial elements were used for the collages in Exodus. In the Reception Area, the prisoners figure as exodus volunteers, and, in the final image, it is they who, in their prison dress, sing an ode to architecture with lyrics from the Baudelaire poem *Rêve Parisien*.

Finally, Exodus was also nourished by a childhood project of Zenghelis from 1948. He designed a walled-in, fortified, green and rich skyscraper city located at an altitude of 6,500 ft. (2,000 m.)

of the Arts"; the "Institute of Biological Transactions"; and the "Park of Aggression". The famous perspective drawing (p. 239, top), the "face" of Exodus in nearly all publications, enables one to visualize these spaces (from the Tip of Strip to the Baths). An important element of the drawing are the endless slabs that radially ram the walls, as it were. Neither the *Casabella* nor the *S, M, L, XL* version of the text makes reference to them. They are mentioned, however, in an earlier manuscript: "Those activities which are not shared by all are located in the narrow secondary strips, which each have their particular attachments to and relationship with the central zone. The secondary strips cut through the most depressed slum areas of the old London. They lead to the enclave and provide all the private accommodation the settlers have dreamt for themselves. Their magnificent presence forces these slums to turn into ghost towns and picturesque ruins."[15] Perhaps, these radial "slabs" can also be considered as a metaphor for the radiating power of Exodus. At the same time, they can be understood as a salute to Superstudio's *Continuous Monument*. In the manuscript versions available to us, the "Square of the Captive Globe" is also part of the project,[16] but it has been subsequently deferred and incorporated in *Delirious New York*, thus indicating a strong continuity and demonstrating that this book was already present, albeit in a very embryonic state, in Exodus.

The respective programmes of each of the squares can be read as extreme variants of one or another known and conventional (architectural) use. However, these uses are stripped of their everyday logic and placed in a special architectural framework. In this way, they are intensified to the point of becoming ultimate and obsessional experiences which keep alive the inhabitants' longing. It is this longing that is, at the same time, the engine through which the strip maintains itself by perpetually reproducing itself at the extremes and consequently continuing to gnaw on the

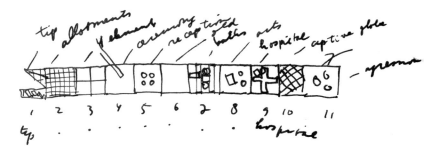

4. Rem Koolhaas, sketch of strip for *Exodus*, 1973. The sequence (corresponding with the presentation in this book) includes the Square of the Captive Globe.

sleeping city of London. In this respect, the Exodus project can be characterized as nothing more than a visual and narrative metaphor for the longing for architecture.[17] This longing is depicted in a collage (p. 243, top) showing people on a platform looking over the (Berlin) wall and catching sight of multiple images of the Empire State Building, while an infrared image in the background records the heat and, consequently, the energy of the Manhattan skyline (running in the void are the voluntary prisoners from the *Life/Time* article). This symbolism of an infrared Manhattan as a hot spot is even more pronounced in "Exhausted Fugitives Led to Reception," (p. 240) where the exhausted workers/slaves from *Metropolis* in the foreground assume that role.

In the strip, quite a few institutions are represented that can be compared to familiar urban forms: Airport lobby (Reception Area), school/university/hospital (Institute of Biological Transactions), museum (Square of the Arts – on the site of the actual British Museum), recreation area (Baths), park as representation of nature (Park of the Four Elements), sports infrastructure (Park of Aggression), residences (Allotments, the slabs), square (Ceremonial Square), factory (Tip of the Strip). The spaces or voids making up Exodus are collectivistic, but not public, given the heterotopian character of this architectural megaprison. Missing are political institutions (there is no equivalent of a city hall or government building), religious references and especially shops. This intense metropolitan strip has to do without the continual cycle of consumption, which can be considered all the more surprising in the light of Koolhaas' later fascination with this phenomenon.

The Reception Area is the site where the voluntary prisoners swarm in through two gates and are welcomed in an (unspecified) spectacular and luxurious manner. The text mentions in passing that this is the starting point of their "indoctrination."[18] Very Foucaultian, it is suggested that every emancipation is, at the same time, a form of disciplining [19] They are immediately involved in the further design and modification of the Strip's future: "The most contradictary programmes fuse without compromise."[20] The collage (ill. p. 242, top) referring to this area uses as its central image a photographic illustration from the (*Life* or *Time*) article mentioned before, in which the prisoners, naked, pass by the guards. From the roof of the Reception Area, a monumental

3. View of Berlin Wall crossing the Friedrichstrasse from the rooftop of the Checkpoint Charlie building (OMA: Elia Zenghelis and Matthias Sauerbruch, 1981–85).

265

escalator provides access to the Central Area, a "preserved fragment of the 'old' London." It is the historical district (which, until *The Generic City*, will become the object of mockery), which at the same provides accommodation for recently arrived volunteers, a kind of sluice between their old and new existence, as well as between old and new urbanity. Located on the other side of the Reception Area, of which the drawings only show the deserted roof terrace with the four central pillars marking the floor, is the Ceremonial Square. This black marble-paved square, which is intended to "accommodate a mixture of physical and mental exercises, a conceptual Olympics," is also empty, except for a kind of gigantic lightning rod, the so-called Jamming Station (shown on p. 243, bottom), which serves to protect the inhabitants of Exodus against radio waves and other electronic signals.

The Park of the Four Elements (p. 245, top) has four levels which serve as "steps" in a kind of architectural descent into the elemental. A first inner square, "Air" houses sunken pavilions with ducts emitting hallucinogenic gasses and colourful clouds. Fire is evoked one step lower through a desert with a fire organ, an artificial nocturnal sun, as well as "mirage machines". The inner court of the element water, yet another step lower, is an artificial ocean, a swimming pool with a continuous dash of (sometimes gigantic) waves produced by the movement of one of its walls. Located at the bottom level is the square of earth which consists of a "vaguely familiar" mountain reaching up to the surface of the upper square; in addition, underground tubes are visible here. The "park" is entirely Platonic or Baudelairian: nature is congealed to (symbolic) architecture, *architecture parlante*.[21] This 'forest of symbols' is given visual form in the Park of the Four Elements, which is more like a temple.

At the Tip of the Strip, its furthermost western component where the construction of Exodus proceeds continuously, there is a model of the wall (the slanting beam in the center of the illustration on p. 244). This model grows and changes as construction work proceeds, and vice versa. Accordingly, the overall image is repeated within itself – the Exodus project contains itself an endless number of times (also through time and in all its potential mutations). In a recent interview, Zenghelis after all those years

6. Capsular living inside the megastructure: *Stadt Ragnitz* by Günther Domenig and Eilfried Huth, 1965–69. Close-up of model.

still visibly relished this architectural gimmick they had come up with.[22] What this detail shows, is that Exodus is an architectural feedback machine.

Located to the east of the Central Area are the "Baths", the *thermae*. Here, "stadiums" that strike one as very Greek provide the setting for an attempt at reconciling the optimism of early Situationism – leisure time as total liberation of desire – with the pessimism of later Situationism – the society of spectacle as the ultimate alienation from one's own, immediate life (ill. p. 245, bottom and p. 246). The performances in the cells are intended to facilitate the transition from passive consumer to active participant, undoubtedly in the direction of what Lyotard, around '68, described as "désirrévolution". Koolhaas' collage with the candid scenes performed in the cells as starting points for "situations", uses images from the 1969 film *De Blanke Slavin* (The White Slave), for which he wrote the script.[23]

The Square of the Arts is an ironical culture machine with the British Museum preserved, yet emptied. The empty spaces merely serve as a prop for memory. The works of art end up in a subterranean pit which, in turn, is the (hollow) mirror image of a cultural palace directly across from it (ill. p. 247, text and drawing by Zenghelis). Most sinister is the Square of Biological Transactions, where the patients are placed on a conveyer belt (the diagonal in the drawing on p. 249) which ends at the cemetery. The maternity ward and children's ward are located in the three Palaces of Birth (the upper left square). Between births and deaths a statistical balance is maintained. In the insane asylum (the lower right square), all forms of madness and delusion are displayed. The Square of Biological Transactions is a feedback machine. The biological politics of euthanasia and eugenics allude to "Brave New World"-like dystopias and to the "logic" of con-

Globe of the Earth, Pan American Terminal Bldg., Miami, Florida 38

5. Captive Globe scrutinized: picture from Koolhaas' postcard collection.

centration camps. The Park of Aggression at the furthermost eastern tip of the Strip, drawn and described by Zenghelis, is equally mischievous in its reduction of sports to aggression. Two unstable towers inspired by a Dalí drawing (showing the Empire State and the Chrysler Building assuming the pose of Millet's *Angelus*) are the condensers of this delirious recreation (ill. p. 250).

The scenario ends (logically, not according to the physical sequence) in the Allotments which are located between the Park of the Four Elements and the Tip of the Strip. In these Allotments, people live, in absence of radio signals, a life of luxury and happiness (p. 251). They are allotment gardens with small bungalows rather than real homes – which, as we now know, were provided in the radial "slabs". For an understanding of Madelon Vriesendorp's collage depicting this leisure-time bliss (p. 252, top) it is essential to bear in mind that Koolhaas, in the course of his research on the Berlin wall, realized that the wall was an attraction, a condenser of sorts. It kept interest alive on both sides: on the eastern side, that of the military and/or potential defectors, and on the western side, that of the tourists. Seen this way, the image fragments which show, among other things, watch towers, are less sinister than they appear at first: they are simply the platforms from which the old Londoners can catch a glimpse of the silent bliss (the Millet figures) and the superior splendor of the Allotments: "The houses on these allotments are built from the most beautiful and expensive materials – marble, chromium, steel. They are small palaces for the people."[24]

At the same time, however, both Koolhaas and Zenghelis insist on the brutal and highly ambiguous fact that all architecture necessarily functions by way of separation and exclusion, which is what the collage expresses in a – frivolously and, at the same time, poignantly – trenchant manner. Every city starts out as an encampment and any urbanity can revert back to a camp at any moment in time, as a closed-off territory of exclusion. However ironic Exodus may appear at times, there is no escaping the fact that it is a camp. Perhaps, it is the prophetic side of this surrealist dream project that it is susceptible also to the signals of the nightmare. And maybe it also unconsciously registers the emergence of what Agamben, following Foucault, calls biopolitics: the direct intervention in the life of citizens, with the concentration camp both as an extreme and as a paradigm. "The biopolitical paradigm of the West today is the camp and not the urban community."[25] In this sense, Exodus has arguably acquired an entirely new relevance. The project has unintentionally proven prophetic as a kind of premonition of the emergence of a capsular civilization. The gated communities, the enclaves, malls, theme parks, atrium hotels are all examples of a capsular architecture and a heterotopical urbanism that, in Exodus, find a legendary, conceptual prefiguration. Is it possible completely to dissociate Exodus from this new form of closed-off urbanism? Perhaps Exodus has taken on, independently of the intentions of its authors, a new, urgent significance which survives all the project's irony. Perhaps the project has started a second life, as it were, stirring up new resonances today. This topicality of Exodus, its constellation with the present, seems hard to dismiss.

Rem Koolhaas is fully aware of this, as is evident not only from previously cited statements on the ambiguous power of architecture, but also from the interview we recently conducted with him:

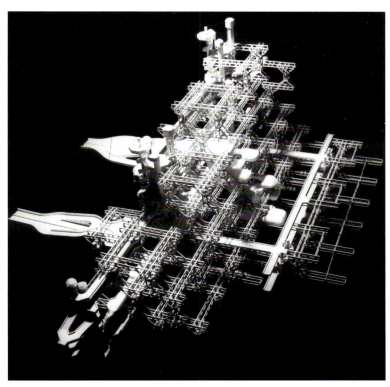

7. Domenig and Huth: *Stadt Ragnitz*, model

HH: What would you call Exodus then – a manifesto?
RK: Yes, it was a sort manifesto, too, more than that, however, it was a kind of short-circuit of good and bad intentions, of end and means … that the negative really is part of it, of the means.
HH: The negative meaning what?
RK: Exclusion, keeping at a distance, compressing, …[26]

The obsession at the time with heterotopias informs Exodus.[27] It is both a camp and a theme park. It is this unlikely combination which lends Exodus its unmistakable visionary character.

8. Alan Boutwell, *Continuous Urbanism / Band City* over New York, 1969: largest linear city devised to date, a life raft for a post-apocalyptic world.

9/10. The megastructure taken to its iconic extreme: Hans Hollein's collages *Rolls Royce Grille on Wall Street* (top, 1966) and *Überbauung Wien* (1960).

Exodus is one of the last projects of the series of 'fantastic architecture' that was so typical of the 1960s.[30] In the period from the late fifties to the early seventies, quite a number of architects and would-be-architects emerged whose work straddled the border between architecture and the visual arts: Buckminster Fuller, Yona Friedman and GEAM, Kurokawa and the Metabolists, Archigram, Cedric Price, Hans Hollein and Walter Pichler, Haus Rucker Co. Constant, the French group Utopie, Superstudio, Archizoom. Their projects consisted of visionary sketches and structures which were hailed, with or without aplomb and panache, as utopian visions of the future. It was the age of the megastructures. They were presented in appealing drawings, models, and collages which were readily published and exhibited. This stage in the cycle of architecture is marked by two exhibitions: *Visionary Architecture* in 1960, and *Italy: The New Domestic Landscape* in 1972, both at the MoMA.

The age of the megastructures coincides with the dawning awareness of the demographic derailment of overpopulation. This is very obvious in the case of Yona Friedman. Mobile architecture is an architecture of survival, it is an architecture of scarcity for an overpopulated planet.[31] The Japanese metabolists, too, took this as their starting-point. Not coincidentally, Koolhaas points to the recent recurrence of this very issue.[32] However dated the megastructures may be, in this regard they exhibited great lucidity. Vis-à-vis the problem of urban sprawl and the emergence of megacities, the megastructures are the symptom of a heretofore unsolved (unsolvable?) and increasingly acute socio-ecological problem, a problem that in the first instance and in the final analysis is the responsibility of architecture and urbanism anyway: creating housing for mankind. In the short history of the megastructures as a stage of neo-avant-garde architecture, we witness the reversion of utopia to dystopia, from activist optimism to critique and pessimism. Even if, at first glance, it is almost imperceptible, it stands out quite sharply. It is noticeable in the shifts within Situationism and specifically in the ideas of Guy Debord – the transition from utopian investment of leisure time as reflected in the journal *Potlatch* to the pronounced pessimism of *La Société du Spectacle* of 1967. It can be inferred from the over self-criticism orchestrated by the group Utopie in Turin, in 1967, in the exhibition *Utopia e/o Rivoluzione*, where they renounced the whole euphoria of inflatable architecture and megastructures.[33] On a more epistemological level, the megastructure can be considered a third model of modernity. If CIAM was predicated on a mechanical, or even mechanistic, model and Team X opted for the biological, organicist model, then the megastructures are based on a cybernetic model. They are feedback machines.[34] Exodus, too, is clearly a feedback machine.

In 1972, Reyner Banham stated: "The megastructure is dead and thus the time has come to write its history," a promise he actually kept in 1976 with his book *Megastructure, Urban Futures of the Recent Past*. In a lecture at the AA in 1974, Banham publicly wonders: "What were we all up to in 1964, because I do not think any of us found this kind of project very shocking as we do now?"[35] To us, this seems to be a very meaningful statement in the sense that we should guard ourselves against retroactively defusing the aggressiveness and the radical aspects of this architecture on paper by viewing them as innocent (for ironic) metaphors. Elia Zenghelis, too, warned us at the outset of his

When reading closely Baudelaire's poem "Rêve parisien," which concludes the scenario and which is the keynote of the entire Exodus project,[28] one cannot escape the impression that it inspired to a high degree the – rather classical – formal language. The final collage shows prisoners expressing their gratitude in music and song to lyrics by Baudelaire and against the backdrop of the *Seven Sisters* (Moscow University – ill. p. 252, bottom). Not coincidentally, this collage is titled *The Avowal*: not only the prisoners, but also the architects appear to acknowledge something. The use of materials, the white marble, the aluminum, the insistence on luxury, as well as the classicist atmosphere of all the squares and the thermae (Baths) (that appeal to a kind of ancient *hedonè*), and, above all perhaps, the visionary character of the Square of the Four Elements, all this plainly bears the imprint of Baudelaire's poem. We even recognize the absence of the sun in the fire organ, which is intended as an artificial eternal sun for the Square of the Four Elements. Exodus as a whole is an homage to the triumph of the artificial as represented by the city. According to Zenghelis, it is in the artificiality of culture and not in nature that mankind escapes the dull fate of transience.[29]

It is probably due to an omnivorous capability of absorbing contradictions that the Berlin wall and the camp logic, the hectic urbanity of Manhattan and oneiric splendour and ecstatic classicist silence of Baudelaire's poem all converge in this metaphorical project. This is the almost unbearable field of tension which Exodus evokes and which lends the project its density and ambiguous appeal. It is in this respect perhaps no coincidence that Tafuri, in his criticism of Italian contemporaries of this project, Superstudio and Archizoom, and of visionary architecture in general, repeatedly refers to "artificial paradises".

interview that he would not be able to talk about Exodus as he had experienced it back then.[36] Baudelaire has said that the city changes more rapidly than a human heart, but the climatic conditions through the ages change so drastically that they become virtually impossible to reconstruct from the relics.

The ideological stance of this kind of work was indeed also widely divergent, in tune with the colourful character of the period. The technological utopias of, for example, Archigram or Buckminster Fuller have no distinct social concepts underlying them. Here it is, above all, the fascination with the extreme technical possibilities of new materials and construction methods that informs the imagination. The underlying concept seems to be that the possibilities realized this way will benefit everybody; but neither Archigram nor Buckminster Fuller link these ideas with a socio-political vision. Constant, on the other hand, situates his project *New Babylon* emphatically within a (neo)marxist social critique and presents his vision of the future as "antithesis to the false society" based on an entirely new distribution of the means of production.

As can be inferred from an interview published in the Dutch weekly magazine *Haagse Post* in 1966, Rem Koolhaas was quite familiar with Constant's project. He was, at the time, a regular contributor to this magazine and, in that capacity, conducted an interview with Constant.[37] According to architecture critic Bart Lootsma, however, this encounter by no means indicated that Koolhaas held a great admiration for the artist who was, back then, quite influential, serving as a major source of inspiration, in the Netherlands, for such countercultural movements as the Provos and the Kabouters. To Lootsma, the tone of the interview and, especially, background information suggest that Koolhaas was more inclined to distance himself from the left-leaning ideas Constant advocated. Koolhaas' work as a contributor to *Haagse Post* was, like that of his colleagues, not characterized by direct statements, but rather by precise descriptions of relatively trivial details and interview fragments rendered verbatim. This journalistic style very often had a ridiculing effect and, in that sense, was anything but neutral or innocent. Lootsma, accordingly, concludes that Koolhaas was very critical of New Babylon and that that criticism subsequently re-emerged in the Exodus project: "In fact, Exodus can be seen more as a critique of *New Babylon* than of Archigram: a series of sectors projected over London, each with a strong, artificially created 'ambience', where 'happenings' could take place."[38]

Exodus can certainly also be regarded as a critique of Archigram's techno-fetishism, its consumer culture and its raving about nomadism. The project seems like a point-by-point inversion of Archigram's agenda: instead of science fiction, almost classicist monumentality; instead of the perpetually mobile, disposable and prefab architecture,[39] eternal immutability; instead of consumption, experiment, instead of nomadism, a sedentary collectivism. Zenghelis is unequivocal about this: "Archigram were our enemies; well, they were our friends as people, but intellectually we opposed them."[40]

If Koolhaas was critical or at least ambivalent toward Constant's New Babylon project and Archigram's "technopop" architecture – even though, in later interviews, he speaks of a "retroactive affinity" with regard to the latter and highly respects the former,[41] – he has, on the other hand, repeatedly shown his admiration for the work of Superstudio.[42] He explicitly states that, to him, Superstudio blew a fresh wind through the dusty architectural trade. Superstudio described its own work in terms of "radical architecture", "anti-utopia", "negative utopia", or "guerilla." It was, above all, Cristiano Toraldo di Francia, co-founder of the group along with Natalini, who worked on this theoretical underpinning. He understood the radical architecture of the 1960s and early 1970s primarily as a form of social critique: "Radical architecture represents – beyond any definite architectural theory – a continuous process of critique concerning the structure of society, which rejects the use of the discipline in the hands of contemporary neocapitalist reformers.[43] In his view, this kind of design can have a therapeutical function as well, because it teaches people to adapt to new conditions of existence.[44] In some of Superstudio's designs, such as the Continuous Monument – which Koolhaas and Zenghelis acknowledge as an important

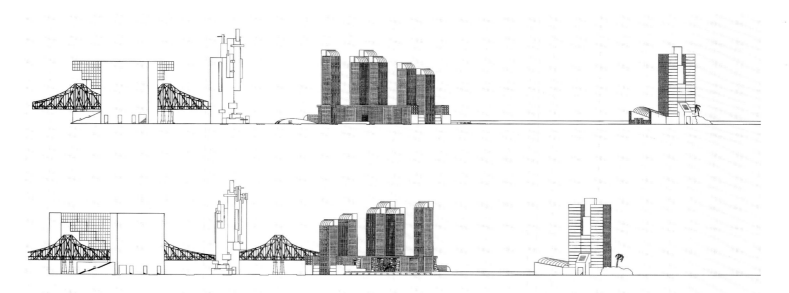

11. Rem Koolhaas (with German Martinez, Richard Perlmutter and Derek Snare), *New Welfare Island / Welfare Palace Hotel,* **New York 1975–76**

source of inspiration – the group uses what he sees as a kind of guerilla tactics of semantic redundance, whereby the meaning of architecture is put into question by subverting its most meaningful gesture through endless repetition.[45] Ultimately, Superstudio's object is to get people used to life without objects. They have to learn to understand that the objects they are used to, the consumer goods, are means of repression through which the social system is able to maintain itself. To promote this insight, Superstudio appeals to the negative utopia or anti-utopia. This negative utopia reveals the ultimate consequences of carrying forward existing tendencies. The image is intended to serve as a deterrent, in order for the realization to take hold that it is absolutely necessary to offer resistance against the existing state of things. There is, in other words, only hope in horror ("il n'y a de l'espoir que dans l'horreur").[46]

Koolhaas and Zenghelis – as part of a kind of strategy directed against Peter Cook – invited Adolfo Natalini to hold lectures at the AA school.[47] The lecture Natalini gave there in March, 1971 describes very precisely the intellectual position of Superstudio and of all visionary architecture in general. "Our work has always been in an empty rarefied area: there is a space between architecture and the visual arts, and there is a space between the cultural profession and life."[48] Natalini describes this space as the only non-alienating terrain of their experience as a group. According to him, it is the only domain where, beyond professional routines and pure existence, Superstudio can make being and doing, acting and existing coincide. Symptomatically, in Natalini's lecture, the theory and practice of architecture are described as parallel plains, but subsequently lose their parallelism, because a gasiform area has established itself in between, distorting any mutual perception: the socio-economic conditions, the wait for commissions and the laws and regulations.[49]

The guerilla tactics Natalini described in the course of his lecture may have made a strong impression on the young Koolhaas. Keenly aware that there can be no other architecture without first changing the structures of society and, on the other hand, that the system is strong enough to incorporate any gesture or product, Natalini proclaims: "The only product which it will not be able to absorb is violent revolution or non-violent intelligence. The ways of non-violence in culture resemble guerrilla warfare:

12. *Welfare Palace Hotel*, 1976. Axonometric with Raft of the Medusa

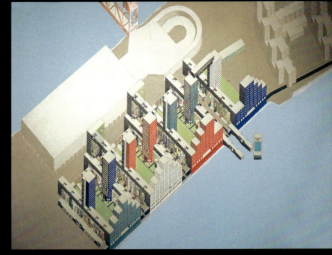

13. Rem Koolhaas and Elia Zenghelis, Roosevelt Island Redevelopment, 1975

they are underground, they change their objectives, are mobile and incomprehensible. I believe in this destroying action on the part of culture: culture as an unbalancing factor."[50] He sees a first strategy in the production of aberrant images. "A series of aberrant images, capable of postulating another scale of values and behaviour, is substituted for the process of getting accustomed to the present society."[51] Thus, the public image of the system is questioned. It is almost as if his formulation contains the recipe of the Exodus machine. "Collectively induced desires are substituted with other equally appetizing desires, which are however truer and more just; …".[52] And it is precisely at this point that the utopian agenda acquires its dystopian form, for Natalini continues: "… and to satisfy these new desires, the system is forced into a crisis. The action to be undertaken, in its simplest form, is to take these processes to their limit, showing *per absurdum* their falsity and immorality."[53] In Natalini's lecture, this (aforementioned) reversion of utopia to dystopia has become a semicolon.

According to Zenghelis, things went wrong when Superstudio began to interpret the aesthetic impact of their architectural projects (such as the *Continuous Monument*) in terms of politics and critique.[54] Exodus posits itself, based on the Berlin experience of the ambigous power of architecture, as an anti-utopian project.[55] It is a manifesto on the essential ambiguity of architecture.[56]

In that sense, it is an attempt to enrich modernist architecture with surrealism, to fuse Mies and Dalí. As Freud has demonstrated, there exists no principle of non-contradiction in the unconscious. The pointed contradiction on which the entire Exodus scenario rests, between prison and garden of delights, between oppression and liberation, between the uncanny and luxury, between bareness and "ornamental frenzy" – as an attempt both to find aesthetic expression for and to give a place in architecture to the juxtaposition of extremes which make the city a metropolis – can only be understood from the achievements of the surrealist tradition. The technique of "écriture automatique", which seeks out rather than avoids contradictions and paradoxes, in order to expose the magnetic fields of the unconscious, would later be formalized by OMA into a design strategy: the "paranoid critical method". The retroactive bombardment of idealization yields numerous design possibilities.[57]

Against the whole fashion of participatory architecture (Gaincarlo De Carlo), the call for small scale (Aldo van Eyck) and for historicity (Léon Krier), Exodus constitutes an almost populist ode to modernist high spirits. Zenghelis calls it a "redeemed populism": the belief that architecture, rather than being something for specialists only, is capable, in and by virtue of its very extremes, between horror and hedonism, to appeal to broad strata of the population.[58] It almost goes without saying that Exodus echoes the *Plan Voisin* for London. And that it does so in particular by transplanting Leonidov's linear city. The energy of Le Corbusier and of the linear urbanism of Leonidov is intensified into "architectural warfare against undesirable conditions, in this case London."[59] In a way, Exodus (unconsciously?) shares the anti-urban mood of CIAM, at least in its rejection of the nineteenth-century metropolis. On this, Elia Zenghelis states: "London was a city both of us hated for its lack of urbanity […] I certainly revised that position. Rem also. In fact, I think that Rem loves London. But it is not a city. Rem once called it a holding pattern, it is what airplanes do before they land (laughs)". This – the fact that London, to them, was an airplane waiting to land, or at least that airplane's holding pattern – may actually be the reason that Exodus, in the accompanying text, is described as a "landing strip for the new architecture of collective monuments." Exodus was intended to turn London into a city overnight (combining, without defusing, the horror of the Berlin wall and the hedonistic charm of Manhattan). Zenghelis aptly describes it (in a reference to the French painters' school of idyllic landscapes) as "Barbizon behind the horror". These oppositions are virtually a definition of urbanity and architecture as such: "The juxtaposition of opposites is very typical for the city and for architecture."[60]

With all this, the most important coordinates are given that shaped the map of architecture in the early 1970s and, consequently, outline the context of Exodus – as the point of departure for OMA. For them, the avant-garde experimental movement was only interesting in its most radical form, that is, in the form of Archizoom and, particularly, Superstudio. At the time they cared considerably less for the more technologically inspired variants, such as Archigram or Price. And it appears that they had serious doubts about the sociocritical narrative underpinning, for example, Constant's New Babylon. Nor were they beguiled, for that matter, by emerging postmodernism – which, indeed, at that point, had not yet received its name. The growing fascination with meaning, communication and semiotics, to them, did not seem to contribute to a better understanding of what constitutes the essence of architecture. If you add to this their irritation with regard to the Team X legacy of social compassion and human warmth – especially Aldo van Eyck and Herman Hertzberger have, at one time, been targeted[61] – it becomes clear that their particular position, if anything, does not follow any of the contemporary movements. In this sense, it is a pivotal work: it concludes the age of the (paper) megastuctures (visionary architecture), and it opens the thought process of OMA to renew urbanism and architecture in a less ideologically fraught manner.

4 Tafuri, or the hereafter of architecture

The sharpest criticism of the position of visionary architecture (as defended and formulated by Natalini in his lecture at the AA) was articulated by Manfredo Tafuri, who analyzed the state of architecture based on the conviction that architecture should inter-

vene in the production relations – if not, Tafuri argued, it would be meaningless as a contribution to the larger historical developments. According to Tafuri it was a historical mistake of Italian design to withdraw from immediate involvement with the mass production of consumer goods and to devise their designs exclusively for a very limited segment of the luxury-goods market. As opposed to the avant-garde of the 1920s, which indeed ensconced itself in the heart of the productive machine (Tafuri refers, among others, to The New Frankfurt), Italian designers are content with a very marginal position from which they can but offer marginal comments. This holds true not only for furniture designers, but just as much for their counterparts who no longer design objects, but rather large-scale architectural fantasies. According to Tafuri, such an approach is necessarily impotent and inefficient: "It is hardly worth mentioning here that, in a capitalistic system, there is no break between production, distribution and consumption. All the intellectual anti-consumer

14. Madelon Vriesendorp, *Birth of OMA*, 1975

utopias that seek to redress the ethical 'distortions' of the technological world by modifying the system of production or the channels of distribution only reveal the complete inadequacy of their theories, in the face of the actual structure of the capital economic cycle."[62]

In *Architecture and Utopia*, Tafuri repeatedly comes back to this point. According to him, "the proliferation of an underground design of protest is institutionalized, propagated by international organs, and admitted to an elite circle."[63] The fact that the whole movement of conceptual architecture began and ended at the MoMA (with the above-mentioned *Visionary Architecture/New Domestic Landscape* shows) testifies to this. Tafuri, furthermore, speaks of "futile appeals to self-disalienation", of "the elimination of criticism within one's own processes", of the "poetry of ambiguity", and of the semanticization of the city as a "machine emitting incessant messages". Flirting with chaos finds no favour in his eyes. "Without abandoning the 'utopia of design', the processes that had concretely surmounted the level of ideology are subverted by the redemption of chaos, the contemplation of that anguish which Constructivism seemed to have done away with forever, and the sublimation of disorder."[64] Or yet: "In order to 'sustain' metropolitan space, architecture seems obliged to become a spectre of itself."[65] Tafuri's final verdict is damning: "The crisis of modern architecture is not the result of 'tiredness' or 'dissipation'. It is rather a crisis of the ideological function of architecture."[66] According to him, redemption is no longer possible: neither by restlessly wandering about in the labyrinths of images that are polyvalent to the point of ultimately falling silent, nor by retreating into the recalcitrant silence of geometries engrossed with their own perfection. The drama of architecture is its being "obliged to return to *pure architecture*, to form without utopia; in the best cases, to sublime uselessness."[67]

Needless to say Tafuri was not very popular among visionary architects of the time. He was perceived as "the enemy" not only by Superstudio,[68] but also by Rem Koolhaas. In an interview from 1978, Hans van Dijk asked Koolhaas if his mystification of Manhattan in *Delirious New York* serves as an attack against those critics and architects who strive to arrive at an ideological *tabula rasa* by demystifying everything. Koolhaas confided to him: "You mean people like Tafuri? Sure, exasperation and rage at their production has been an important source of energy." And,

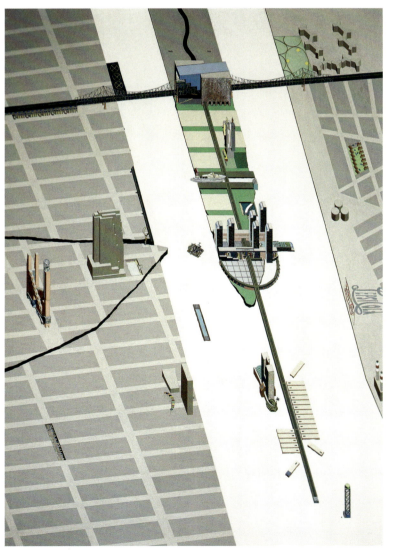

15. New York, East River: Welfare Palace Hotel, Hotel Sphinx, the Raft of the Medusa, UN Headquarters, Rockefeller Center, Malevich's *Tekton* and *The Pool* united in a painting by Zoe Zenghelis, 1976

further on: "I have the strong impression that Tafuri and his supporters hate architecture. They declare architecture dead. For them, architecture is a series of corpses in the morgue. Yet, even though dead, they do not leave the corpses in peace; rather, they are vain enough to want to be the morgue's *experts*. They engage in namedropping at the morgue. Every now and then they take one of those corpses, say something about it and push it back in place; by and large, however, it is all impossible, anyhow. Except, for some inexplicable reason, Aldo Rossi."[69]

Paper architecture, the metaphorical metaprojects of "visionary architecture" represented, in Tafuri's view, a kind of escape or retreat: away from architecture as a social practice in the realm of necessity, into art as a shelter, as the realm of freedom. For Tafuri, this whole movement of utopian and/or dystopian visions on paper represented the beginning of an exodus: the architect disappearing from the center of the practice of building. For him, it was, perhaps, the onset of a kind of hereafter of architecture. What architecture had lost in significance as a social practice, it had gained in prestige as an art. It is surely not a coincidence that, since the mid 1970s, the drawings of these projects have been shown in galleries and ultimately picked up by MoMA. The far-sightedness of such acquisitions does not alter the fact that, hiding behind it, there is an institutional shift from physical architecture to nearly immaterial conceptual art. In the meantime, history has demonstrated that physical architecture is back again (thanks to much-hated postmodernism?), and, since the mid 1980s, OMA, too, has traded in its paper architecture for feasible – and more and more often actually realized – projects. Remarkably, however, there is great harmony looming behind the differences between Tafuri and Koolhaas. In *S, M, L, XL*, Koolhaas never tires of claiming that the architect has become a marginal figure in the contemporary building industry. And, at this point, the question arises whether the rebirth of the architect as a star and the dissemination of Great Architecture through glossy magazines is not a new form, a next stage, as it were, of the hereafter predicted by Tafuri.

5 The voluntary prisoners of architecture revisited

Against the destructive ethos which, according to Natalini himself, wants to go so far as to abandon architecture, and against the pessimism of Tafuri's negative dialectics of the avantgarde, Koolhaas and Zenghelis posit a belief in the power of architecture as a hedonistic science, as well as a Baudelairian affirmation of hectic urbanity. But until 1996, at least in Koolhaas, some of the scepticism always lingered. The notion that the architect has to build at all times, contains, according to him, an "essential dumbness".[70] That is why Koolhaas keeps returning to the intermediate space evoked by Natalini, the space of criticism. And that is also why he always remains a (script-) writer.[71] Just as for both Natalini and Tafuri, the only possible relationship to architecture is a love-hate relationship, a kind of ineradicable scepticism.[72] But in spite of this underlying scepticism, both Zenghelis and Koolhaas emphasize the fact that Exodus was a reaction of sorts against what they, at the time, perceived as a ban on architecture, particularly on modern architecture. Zenghelis states in our interview: "In those days any kind of formal articulation was considered to be a crime … Monument was a sort of dirty word."[73] On the context of the late 1960s, early 1970s, Koolhaas has something similar to say: "You really have no idea about the deep and fundamental hostility against modernity that was emerging – in the '70s – and becoming an almost physical hostility. So, at that point I felt that the only way in which modernity could even be recuperated was by insisting in a very progressive way about its other side, its *popularity*, its *vulgarity*, its *hedonism*."[74] This may actually be an important key to an understanding of Exodus. The first element is the hostility toward architecture in general and modern architecture in particular, which apparently also existed in hotbeds of experimental avant-garde architecture such as the AA. Exodus was a manifesto for architecture in a context – the utopian social experiments setting the tone at the AA – where practicing architecture was suspect. The second element is the emphasis on hedonism. It is hardly a coincidence that the project's Prologue contains a definition of architecture, which, provocatively, articulates a new confidence in architecture. "Contrary to modern architecture and its desperate afterbirths, this new architecture is neither authoritarian nor hysterical: it is the hedonistic science of designing collective facilities that fully accommodate individual desires."[75] The context outlined here allows us a better understanding of this by now famous definition of architecture (which already appears in the earliest manuscripts of Exodus). While acknowledging that modernist architecture was indeed authoritarian, it hastens to add that the post-war architectural avant-garde was hysterical. The solution this definition advances is a departure from the ideology (and, consequently, the utopia) of architecture by emphasizing its capability to give shape to hedonism. Essentially, one could say that OMA defines architecture here as "the science of desire".

Zenghelis affirms, more so than Koolhaas, that Exodus was a project directed against the political instrumentalization of architecture and a plea for architecture as a kind of absolute infrastructure. To him – and this was a leitmotif running through our interview, – "architecture is not a product of society, but a product of civilization." In our conversation, he also distances himself from the proliferation of metaphors in Exodus, when it should really have been concerned with pure architecture and its autonomy. Koolhaas does not fully subscribe to this; for him, there is a kind of social programme underlying Exodus: "At the very least, there is a sort of overwrought insistence on collectivity. I think that there are two tones, or a kind of musical dialogue between two things […] a still huge interest in and passion for the programmatic and collective aspect of Constructivism and, at the same time, a realization that Constructivism was harmless and that negative things constituted the real force. It is more about […] a tremendous enthusiasm about the programmatic aspect and the collectivity – the enthusiasm of collectivism, and at the same time a kind of frustration with the innocence of its formal side and, in that sense, an attempt of sorts to fuse that with the most serious aspect of architecture."[76] This abstract collectivism was (and is?) perhaps one of the most important motives for Koolhaas' passion for urbanism and architecture; for urbanism as the "culture of congestion," and for architecture as a hedonistic science. On reflection, however, Elia Zenghelis, too, concedes that Exodus had an ideological program: "Exodus presented architecture as a platform in which new mutant forms of behaviour would be performed; that was again a reaction to Guy Debord. They would be performed purely as spectacle in order to generate further elaborations in the audience […] The choreography of activity resided in the belief that new forms of behavior would result in new typologies of architecture […] For me the value of the Baths, its more ideological side, is precisely that through non-conventional exchange of relationships, mutant forms of behavior will lead to a new kind of Architecture."[77]

Initially, Exodus also included an epilogue. This epilogue, from the manuscript version, is abundantly clear. Perhaps that is why it was omitted from all previously published versions: it invalidates the unity of the entire project as a metaphor by openly interpreting it. But in any case, it includes statements with historical authority: "Although at first sight the metaphorical message of these proposals may seem to dominate practical considerations, this is not another Utopian tale."[78] That is obvious. It seems to confirm the terse summary Elia Zenghelis gave at the end of our recent interview: according to him, Exodus "is a parable for architecture, not for society".[79] For a long time, OMA, too, distinguished, in its projects, between three categories: metaphorical, ideal, and realistic. Exodus is the prototype of these metaphorical projects. From the Reception Area to the Tip of the Strip, nothing but architecture is produced. But the magic of this architecture is that it produces above all emptiness and, in that way, strives to create space for hectic and hedonistic urbanism. Or, as the manuscript epilogue puts it: "It requires a fundamental belief in cities as the incubators of social desires, the synthetic materializations of all dreams." The epilogue makes it clear that Exodus is a radical defense of the metropolitan idea and lifestyle: "If people were allowed to become acquainted with Architecture, they would decide to re-appropriate the physical and ideological decay of our Urban Societies and to rehabilitate their premises with the metropolitan idea and lifestyle."[80] The fictional or phantasmal character of Exodus can be explained, according to the epilogue, with the then current "reality shortage": "Under the threat of doom, the common concern, that is the fulfilment of all private desires within a subliminally collective and deliriously permissive common effort, produces phantom proposals, in the knowledge that phantom reality is the only possible successor to the present reality shortage."[81] In a reference that will become important in the *Welfare Palace Hotel* project, namely to *The Raft of the Medusa*, a case is made for realism rather than panic: "Like the castaways of the raft of Medusa, the last surviving realists, hanging on the parachute of hope are dropping on the rescue ship: THE CITY which, at the end of cannibalism, will appear on the horizon."[82] The ship, however, is an airship, and Exodus is the landing strip, as the Prologue stated: "the strip is like a runway, a landing strip for the new architecture of collective monuments."

It is tempting to consider Exodus as the embryo of everything OMA later became. And it certainly cannot be denied that there are a number of unmistakable characteristics present and that its ironic narrative style alone makes the project pure OMA and distinctly Koolhaasian. Ultimately, Koolhaas never stopped writing such pieces, from "The City of the Captive Globe" (1972) to "The Generic City" (1994). Furthermore, the project for the renovation of a panopticon prison in Arnhem is a direct echo of Exodus (inevitably). The beam of Exodus here intersects the base of the domed hall, except that, in this case, it is about a street disrupting the panopticality (in other words, a kind of inversion of the inversion that Exodus was). And Exodus is also echoed, up to a certain point, in the extension of the Dutch Parliament in The Hague. But let us not continue to draw parallels to later work and thereby open up a whole new chapter, but rather look for the "OMA constants" contained in Exodus.

The fascination with emptiness is obviously one of the characteristic features of Exodus, for in the final analysis the space between the walls is not so much filled with architecture as opened up by architectural emptiness. Exodus is a sequence of squares and parks, which contributes to the fictional and, by extension, manifesto-like quality of the project. It is an explicit attempt to put emptiness on the map of architecture. It is no coincidence that Koolhaas, in a text from 1985 titled "Imagining Nothingness," revisits the Berlin Wall and thus, implicitly, Exodus. The motto of that text explains the architectural emptiness of Exodus: "Where there is nothing, everything is possible. Where there is architecture, nothing (else) is possible."[83] Perhaps Exodus is, strangely enough, to be considered the first concept for one of the "liberty zones" this text refers to. It is a "conceptual Nevada where all laws of architecture are suspended." In this, Koolhaas sees a solution to the tension between program and containment: "Only through a revolutionary process of erasure and the establishment of 'liberty zones' […] will some of the inherent tortures of urban life – the friction between programme and containment – be suspended."[84]

The emphasis on the monumentality and durability of architecture is based on the idea that architecture does not have to give up its durability and inertia, but rather that the functions have to be dissociated from architecture. The "envelope", as Koolhaas calls it, does not have a clear relationship to its content – form and function do not follow each other – but it is indeed a container and generator of activities. Congestion and improvisation are stimulated within the taut envelope. (This will become the fundamental idea underlying, for instance, the Karlsruhe Zentrum für Kunst und Medientechnologie/Center for Art and Media Technology and the Bibliothèque Jussieu.) The challenge raised by the Exodus project would inform all of OMA's works: the quest for a solution to the paradox between architecture's permanence and urbanism's instability. Exodus is a first attempt at developing the magic formula from Delirious New York: "Mutant architecture that combines the aura of monumentality with the performance of instability."[85] What Delirious New York reveals as a retroactive manifesto, Exodus projects as a proactive manifesto. In this sense, Exodus is a horizontal skyscraper. One could also say that Exodus is an exercise not only in "Imagining Nothingness," but also in "Bigness": "I've always been very interested in large scale and its implications; in the artificiality and the fragmentation it produces, and how, in a way, the very bigness turns into an antidote against fragmentation. Each of those entities acquires the pretension and sometimes the reality of a completely enveloping reality, and an absolute autonomy."[86] Urbanism in Exodus is concentrated in a strip: it is a condenser (a Down Town Athletic Club avant la lettre). The artificiality of architecture as a medium and environment of man: that is what Exodus is about.

In the end, however, Exodus remains a metaphorical project that, by definition, is open-ended and self-contained: Open-ended because it allows a potentially endless number of interpretations. self-contained because any interpretation ultimately bounces off the metaphorical language. Exodus fascinates the viewer, but also holds him captive. He is thrown back and forth between Tafuri's fear that the labyrinthine images become so ambiguous that they finally fall silent, and the belief in the power of elusive manifestoes: "But like those incomplete sentences that offer a great number of conclusions, such a manifesto allows an abundance of interpretations and dialectical variations."[87]

Notes

* The authors would like to thank Elia Zenghelis, Rem Koolhaas, and Madelon Vriesendorp for their responses to our questions, Martin van Schaik for the extensive documentation, Gerrit Oorthuys for copies of the typescript of Exodus, Saskia Kloosterboer and Sofie De Caigne for their extra help with typing and their suggestions.

1 Exodus was first published as Rem Koolhaas, Elia Zenghelis, "Exodus or the Voluntary Prisoners of Architecture", in Casabella 378 (June 1973), pp. 42–45. The "standard" publication is "Exodus" in: Office for Metropolitan Architecture, Rem Koolhaas & Bruce Mau, S,M,L,XL, 010, Rotterdam, and The Monacelli Press, New York, 1995, pp. 5–21. Since the presentation in Exit Utopia is the most complete to date, in our further discussion of the illustrations we shall refer to the relevant page numbers herein.
2 In an interesting passage from our interview with him, Koolhaas stated: "I often regret the fact that … I have not been a typical silent architect, in which case lengthy tomes would have been written about me. Many people, of course, viewed my texts as explanatory, which they are obviously not. But that is the reason why, I think, because there are already so many words that it seems as if … Which is, of course, not at all the case. For that reason, I have so often felt this incredible lack of resistance." (Hilde Heynen, interview with Rem Koolhaas, 6/5/03, typescript – this interview will subsequently be referred to as "Koolhaas Interview, 6/5/03")
3 "Il y avait Peter Cook qui, comme un Robespierre, faisait régner la terreure – flower power". (There was Peter Cook who, in the manner of Robespierre, created a reign of terror – flower power). (Patrice Goulet, "La deuxième chance de l'architecture moderne … Entretien avec Rem Koolhaas", in L'Architecture d'Aujourd'hui 238 [April 1985], p. 2.)
4 Ibid.
5 Published as "Field Trip. A(A) Memoir (First and Last …)" in S,M,L,XL, pp. 214–232; an earlier version appeared in a Dutch translation in Hilde Heynen (ed.), Wonen tussen gemeenplaats en poëzie. Opstellen over stad en architectuur, 010, Rotterdam, 1993, pp. 157–164.
6 Looking back at it in 1993, in "Field Trip A (A) Memoir", the experience suggested to him five things: 1) He realized that all architecture functions on the basis of compartmentalization, of separations, enclosure, and exclusion. This initial discovery made the sixties' dream of the liberating potential of architecture instantly evaporate. 2) "The wall suggested that architecture's beauty was directly proportional to its horror". 3) At the same time, this experience raised profound doubts in him about what, at that point, was only just being articulated as the basic axiom of architectural semiotics: that form and meaning are intricately interwoven. "… The wall also, in my eyes, made a total mockery of any of the emerging attempts to link form to meaning in a regressive chain-and-ball relationship. (…) Its significance as a 'wall' – as an object – was marginal; its impact was utterly independent of its appearance. Apparently, the lightest of objects could be randomly coupled with the heaviest of meanings through brute force, willpower. (…) But on the eve of postmodernism, here was unforgettable (not to say final) proof of the 'less is more' doctrine. (…) I would never again believe in form as the primary vessel of meaning." ("Field Trip," "Exodus," in S, M, L, XL, p. 227.) 4) A fourth inference he drew from his field trip follows from this realization: that there is no link between the mass and the significance of a building. The wall was an absence, and yet it functioned as a magnet on both sides: for the military, for the refugees, for the Western tourists. Finally, the wall showed him 5) that one and the same program can mutate in the most divergent forms and still remain true to itself (as a wall).
7 It was at the same time his farewell from the AA as a student: "J'ai en tout cas fait en sorte d'échapper à la cinquième et dernière année de l'étude pour éviter la confrontation terrible que Peter Cook m'avait promise …" (Anyhow, I made an escape and skipped the fifth and final year of study, in order to avoid the terrible confrontation that Peter Cook had promised me) (Patrice Goulet, "La deuxième chance …", op. cit., p. 2.) In this sense, Exodus was indeed a departure, an escape.
8 According to Koolhaas, this is how things developed: "I remember I made a drawing on a very long sheet of tracing paper and that drawing was kind of basically the drawing with the walls and the access points, and the kind of border conditions, and basically the idea that there would be an endless wall that would be growing. And then we saw the competition and Elia asked to join this project. It first was a student project and then became a joined project. Each of us did a number of the squares, the text on them is also written by each of us." (Koolhaas interview, 6/5/03.)
9 According to Koolhaas, it was not a competition centered on utopian architecture: "Rather, it was a kind of first sign of postmodernism, in 1972. An important book by Rykwert had just appeared to which "meaning" was somehow linked, [perhaps On Adam's House in Paradise – HH], and Meaning in Architecture, by Baird and Jencks, had just been published, and Roland Barthes was very influential … For that reason, it was about more than utopia. It was, as far as I know, the first time that the Italians used the word "meaning", that it became an issue." (Koolhaas interview, 6/5/03).
10 "J'y reconnaissais la même intense envie d'édifier une enclave où les habitants deviendraient les prisoniers volontaires de l'Architecture". Quoted from Patrice Goulet, "… Ou le Début de la fin du réel. Entretien avec Elia Zenghelis, " in L'Architecture d'Aujourd'hui 238 (April 1985), p 10. Translation by LDC & HH.

11 Rem Koolhaas, "Sixteen Years of OMA", in *A+U* 10 (1988), p. 10.

12 "Son histoire se développait à partir de l'idée que Londres était une cité sous-développée: que l'on construise l'idéal métropolitain dans toute son intensité primordiale, et ses habitants y émigraient, créant un véritable exode …", quoted from Goulet, "La deuxième chance …", op.cit., p. 2. Translation LDC & HH.

13 "Exodus", in *S,M,L,XL*, p. 5.

14 This listing from East to West appears in all four early typescript versions availabe to us, as well as in the original publication in *Casabella*.

15 Typescript. Through Gerrit Oorthuys, we got hold of copies of various handwritten versions. According to Elia Zenghelis, these were written in the years 1973–1975: "The text for Casabella was rushed and crude (we did the whole thing from scratch, just the 4 of us – but mostly Rem and I – in 3 weeks). It (as were some of the images) was improved afterwards – but shortly afterwards: while we were together in New York at a time when we did the Roosevelt Island competition together and several projects separately, (Rem the Welfare Palace and me the Sphinx hotel, Rem the Square of the Captive Globe – which became part of Exodus retroactively – and me the Egg of Columbus Centre) – mostly with Rem's evolving book in mind. The same with the Square of Aggression: It did not exist at the time of Casabella. I designed and wrote it afterwards, at the same time as these other projects done in New York (and partly in London as far as refinements and colouring is concerned – for instance the Square of the Captive Globe was painted by Zoe and sent to Rem as present-surprise). I was teaching at Columbia at the time and staying at Rem's and Maddie's. We then revised the text and reassembled the images and gave lecture series separately and together, each time varying the text and the illustrations depending on the time and the place, so as to make the presentation critical but 'topical' and 'contemporary'. We are talking of 1973–1974 – and parts of 1975, when I think we had our first show at Max Protetch and the Guggenheim in N.Y.C. – which is also when we were asked to sell." (Excerpt from an e-mail by Elia Zenghelis to Lieven De Cauter, 6/14/03.) From this, we can conclude that the manuscript versions are a sort of definitive elaboration as opposed to the tentative presentation in *Casabella*, and that the genesis of the *Exodus* project and of *Delirious New York* quickly came to be interwoven, which is most obvious in the overlapping of the "Square of the Captive Globe."

16 Typescript versions 1973–1974.

17 On this impossible longing for (modern) architecture, see also Hilde Heynen, "Engaging Modernism", in Hubert-Jan Henket and Hilde Heynen (eds.), *Back from Utopia. The Challenge of the Modern Movement*, 010 Publishers, Rotterdam, 2002, p. 378.

18 "Exodus," in *S,M,L,XL*, p. 9.

19 Fig. on page 424 bottom shows the interior of this Reception Area in an axonometric drawing; the image on page 241 offers a good view of the axis traversing both the wall and all of London.

20 "Exodus," in *S,M,L,XL*, p. 9.

21 Even when discussing nature, Baudelaire refers to architecture: "La nature est un temple où de vivants piliers / laissent parfois sortir de confuses paroles; / l'homme y passe a travers des forêts de symboles." (Charles Baudelaire, "Correspondances", in *Les Fleurs du Mal*, *Œuvres Complètes*, I, Gallimard, 1975, p. 11.) ("Nature is a temple, where the living / Columns sometimes breathe confusing speech; / Man walks within these groves of symbols, each / Of which regards him as a kindred thing." Translated by James McGowan.)

22 Lieven De Cauter and Hilde Heynen, "Barbizon Behind the Horror. Interview with Elia Zenghelis". 5/30/03 (tape) – this interview will subsequently be referred to as "Zenghelis interview, 5/30/03".

23 "The baths – that is me, even the collage. I still know the sources of these images. You may or may not have noticed – this is the White Slave (De blanke slavin), the film I did with René Daalder."(Koolhaas interview, 6/5/03).

24 "Exodus," in *S,M,L,XL*, p. 19

25 "Le paradigme biopolitique de l'Occident est aujourd'hui le camp et non pas la cité." Giorgio Agamben, *Homo Sacer*, Seuil, 1995, p. 195. See also Lieven De Cauter, "The capsular city", in Neil Leach, *The Hieroglyphics of Space. Reading and experiencing the modern metropolis*, Routledge, London / New York, 2002, pp. 271–280.

26 Koolhaas interview, 6/5/03.

27 On this, see Lieven De Cauter, "The rise of the mobility society: from Utopia to Heterotopia", in: *Archis*, 2000, 2, pp. 8–23 (see also: "De vermenigvuldiging van de heterotopieën," in Hilde Heynen *et al.*, *'Dat is architectuur'. Sleutelteksten uit de twintigste eeuw*, 010, Rotterdam, 2001, p. 723f.)

28 When we translate the poem into prose, it is almost as if we were walking around Exodus: "The obscure and distant image of this strange, awe-inspiring scene that no mortal has ever laid eyes on still captures me today. Sleep is full of miracles! By an odd and singular whimsy I have banished from this spectacle nature and all that is irregular. And, happy with my artistry, I painted into my tableau the ravishing monotony of marble, metal and water flowing. A Babel of endless stairs and arcades, it was a palace replete with pools and bright cascades falling in dull or burnished gold. And the more weighty waterfalls, resplendent like crystal screens along the metal rampart walls, seemed to suspend themselves in air. The sleeping pools were surrounded by colonnades rather than trees, and naïads could leisurely contemplate, like Narcissus, their own reflections in them. Sheets of blue water, emptying between the green and rosy quays from multitudes of openings, poured to the world's boundaries. To please the eyes, magical waves splashed on unheard-of stones, and vast

reflectors stood there, dazzled by the world they mirrored in their glass. Insouciant and taciturn, some Ganges, in the firmament, poured out the treasure of their urns into the gulfs of diamond. As the architect of my magic show, I then, for my mood, made an ocean I had first subdued flow through a jewelled tunnel. And all, even the colour black, seemed polished, sparkling, clear and clean. The liquid kept its glow intact within the solid crystal beam. No star from anywhere, no sign of moon or sunshine, bright or dim, illuminated this scene of mine, glowing with fire from within. And over th s pageantry seemed to hover (awful novelty for the eyes, but nothing for the ear!) a silence of eternity." (See Charles Baudelaire, "Un Rêve Parisien I", in *Les Fleurs du Mal*, op.cit., pp. 101–103, reprinted in *S,M,L,XL*, pp. 20–21). Perhaps, the contradiction between this majestic silence of an endless monument, in which one wanders about alone as if in a dream, and the culture of congestion or the urban hedonism that was the official program of Exodus, was too strong, since the handwritten versions omit the poem's last stanza and its keynote – the eternal silence.

29 Goulet, "… Ou le début …" op.cit., p. 14.

30 Ulrich Conrads and Hans G. Sperlich, *Phantastische Architektur*, Hatje, Stuttgart, 1960; Peter Cook, *Experimental Architecture*, Studio Vista, London, 1970.

31 Yona Friedman, *L' architecture mobile* (Cahiers du centre d'études Architecturales, 3.1), Brussels, 1968, pp. 5–11. The text dates from 1958.

32 Alejandro Zaera Polo, "The day after: Conversations with Rem Koolhaas", in *El Croquis* 79 (1996), p. 18.

33 Sarah Deyong, "Memories of the Urban Future: The Rise and Fall of the Megastructure, in *The Changing of the Avant-Garde. Visionary Architectural Drawings from the Howard Gilman Collection*, MoMA, New York, 2002, p. 25 passim.

34 Ibid., p. 26.

35 Ibid.

36 Zenghelis interview, 5/30/03.

37 Rem Koolhaas and Betty van Garrel, "De stad van de toekomst. HP-gesprek met Constant over New Babylon," in *Haagse Post* (August 6, 1966), pp. 14–15; reviewed by Bart Lootsma: "Now Switch off the Sound and Reverse the Film: Koolhaas, Constant and Dutch Culture in the 1960s", in *Hunch*, No. 1, 1999, pp. 152–173.

38 Lootsma, ibid., p. 169.

39 Cf. the argument for disposable architecture advanced by Peter Cook in "Editorial," *Archigram* (1963), 3, republished as Peter Cook, "Editorial from Archigram 3," in *Archigram*, Studio Vista, London 1972, p. 16.

40 Zenghelis interview, 5/30/03.

41 "La non-synchronisation de nos intérêts est un problème tragico-comique. Je ressens, aujourd'hui, une affinité rétroactive pour le Price ou le Cook d'antan. (Mais le Cook d'aujourd'hui s'intéresse maintenant à l'architecture!)" (The non-synchronization of our respective interests is a tragicomical problem. I feel, today, a retroactive affinity with the Price or the Cook of the past. (The Cook of today, however, is now interested in architecture!) (Goulet, "La deuxième chance …", op.cit., p. 2.) Currently Rem Koolhaas does not view New Babylon negatively at all: "I think it is certainly the most impressive of all the projects [from that period] and the one that has survived most intact." (Koolhaas interview, 6/5/03).

42 See, e.g., Goulet, ibid., pp. 2–9, p. 2; see also footnote 10 in "Field Trip. A(A) Memoir."

43 "l'architecture radicale représente – au-delà de n'importe quelle théorie architectonique définie – un processus continu de critique concernant la structure de la société, qui rejette l'utilisation de la discipline aux mains des réformateurs contemporains et néocapitalistes." Cristiano Toraldo di Francia, "Superstudio & Radicaux", in Frédéric Migayrou (ed.), *Architecture radicale*, exh. cat., Institut d'Art Contemporain – IAC Villeurbanne, January 12 – May 27, 2001, pp. 152–243, p. 153. Translation by LDC & HH.

44 Idem, p. 171.

45 Idem, p. 183.

46 Idem, p. 207.

47 Cf. Koolhaas: "When I was at the AA and for the first time saw those things by Superstudio I thought I could use those against the dominant culture here – the culture of Peter Cook. Cook really was a tyrant of sorts. The school was structured by years, and his was the fifth year, so, in the end, he created a kind of 'make or break' position. He had all kinds of spies who, already in earlier years, identified the right and the wrong people. And I thought this seemed very good to arm myself against this set-up, and so I invited Superstudio – Adolfo Natalini – to the AA. Natalini, but also the others – the first one I met was Cristiano Toraldo." (Koolhaas interview, 6/5/03; see also Goulet, "La deuxième chance …," op.cit., p. 2.)

48 Adolfo Natalini, *Inventory, Catalogs, Systems of Flux … a Statement* [Lecture at the AA-School of Architecture, London, 3 March, 1971], in Peter Lang and William Menking, *Superstudio. Life without objects*, Skira, Turin / Milan, 2003, p. 164.

49 Ibid., p. 166.

50 Ibid., p. 164.

51 Ibid., p. 164.

52 Ibid., p. 164.

53 Ibid., pp. 165–166.

54 In a memorable statement outlining the temporal conjunction and the position of the *Exodus* project vis-à-vis Superstudio's projects, Zenghelis says: "We brought Natalini to the AA. We were thrilled by this absolute architecture of the

Continuous Monument. After 68 it had become taboo for architects. (…) The fact that architecture was something that should have a social and political instrumentality was something that both Rem and I objected to. (…) Some of the best architecture has been produced under extremely authoritarian circumstances. (…) So, in the seventies, at the AA you couldn't talk about it. They were cooking rice, smoking pot and sitting cross-legged on the floor; talking about the environment. And what was quite sickening, they were not in control of their own intelligence, they were in a sort of trance. (…) I was the only one doing architecture, there were no courses of architecture. I was organizing a sort of school in the school in the end. (…) Then came Natalini, his absolute architecture became all metaphors. It was a lack of courage. (…) Exodus was done as a reaction to that. The way they [Superstudio] were developing these magnificent drawings. There was a flooding of Florence and they saw all these masterpieces surrounded by water, they discovered absolute architecture. Their first motivation was beauty. And then they realized that they had to be politically correct and they diluted their drawings". (Zenghelis interview, 5/30/03.)

55 Cf. Koolhaas: "To a certain extent, it was precisely an anti-utopian project, and it went against the whole situation. I was terribly annoyed at how simple-mindedly architecture was being interpreted. Superstudio, on the other hand, represented already a kind of aestheticization – what am I saying, at least less simple-minded, but Exodus tried to go a step further – a genuine unmasking of the real power and also genuine in what it was really about." (Koolhaas interview, 6/5/03.)

56 "At that time, I felt, in general, a combined inability and reluctance to identify good or bad, because [many things?] that, on the surface, appear positive can, on closer inspection, have a negative effect, without it ever being very obvious. To me, exactly that seemed to be one of the unbelievable aspects of architecture – that it was always either the one or the other, and that people always knew this, too – that there was no examination whatsoever of the good nor of the bad …" (Koolhaas interview, 6/5/03.)

57 "If there is method in this work, it is a method of systematic idealization – systematic overestimation of what exists, a bombardment of speculation that invests even the most mediocre aspects with retroactive conceptual and ideological charge." (Rem Koolhaas, "The terrifying beauty of the 20th century," in S,M,L,XL, p. 208.)

58 Based on the insights related to the Berlin wall, Elia Zenghelis explains: "This was what Exodus deemed: that the proof of architecture is to combine the mysteries of program, if you like, to the powerful physical presence of architecture. And that this powerful physical presence is necessary to generate that additional activity, whether it is corrupt or not. (…) It had a populist touch: that architecture could not only speak to specialists but to the whole population. That is a kind of populism, but a sort of redeemed populism, like the retroactive manifesto." (Zengelis interview, 5/30/03.)

59 This phrase recurs twice in the text on Exodus: S,M,L,XL, pp. 5 and 11. In the original version the wording is even stronger: "This study wages architectural war on London", implying that this war is actually the dominant theme of the entire project. The architects are, to say the least, sardonically and ironically, inversely or transversely, aiming high here. The anti-urbanism that is at work deep down in the psyche of modernist architecture and that expresses itself not only in the Plan Voisin, but also in Jasinski's plan for Brussels, in Frank Lloyd Wright's Broadacre City, in Leonidov's linear city, is here acted out one more time with style and élan.

60 Zenghelis interview, 5/30/03.

61 In an interview with Hans van Dijk ("Rem Koolhaas Interview", in Wonen-TA/BK 11 [1978], p. 20), Koolhaas describes "that so-called Dutch Structuralism" as "disconcertingly rash and naïve," while Van Eyck and Hertzberger are considered victims of "polder blindness": "Are you familiar with the term 'polder blindness?' In the absence of anything to compare it with, a hare in the empty plane of a polder sometimes appears as big as a cow. Architecturally, the Netherlands suffer from the same phenomenon. Here, Van Eyck and Herzberger are an explosion of genius, but criticism against them and others does not arise. (…) Frankly, I do not believe that any solution to our impasses can come from Africa, be it the Dogon or the Kasbahs." Zenghelis is equally witty when stating with regard to the human scale and the child's scale that the skyscraper, to him, seems to be the child's scale. (Goulet, "… Ou le début …," op. cit., p. 11).

62 Manfredo Tafuri, "Design and Technological Utopia," in Emilio Ambasz, Italy: The New Domestic Landscape. Achievements and Problems of Italian Design, exh.cat., The Museum of Modern Art, New York, 1972.

63 Manfredo Tafuri, Architecture and Utopia: Design and Capitalist Development, MIT Press, Cambridge, Mass./London, 1976, p. 142.

64 Ibid, p. 136.

65 Ibid, p. 145.

66 Ibid., p. 181.

67 Ibid., p. ix.

68 "When Piero Frassinelli of SUPERSTUDIO hears the name Tafuri he says 'Oh, yes, the enemy'." (William Menking, "The revolt of the Object," in Peter Lang, William Menking, Superstudio. Life Without Objects, Skira, Milan, 2003, pp. 53–64, p. 56.)

69 Hans van Dijk, "Rem Koolhaas Interview", op. cit., p. 18.

70 Alejandro Zaera Polo, "The day after: Conversations with Rem Koolhaas", op. cit., p. 18.

71 "In the same ominous prospective of the endless struggle as a 'mere' architect, I felt it was necessary to pursue certain interests strictly on an academic level and other interests on an architectural level", in: Zaera Polo, op. cit., p. 15.

72 On this, Koolhaas says: "Maybe there are two ways in which I have expressed my basic dislike – or, at least, scepticism – for architecture: in the first, I have tried to make architecture out of a series of hollow ambitions and to restore a kind of operational ability, if not glamour. From the quasi-mystical or philosophical, it becomes an essential apparatus that is part of a larger process of modernization, and can be discussed as such, demystified – or maybe it is simply the replacement of one mystique by another. The second must be that I am still sceptical and, therefore, unwilling to completely identify with the profession. That may be why I insist on the usefulness of earlier incarnations, and why I am unwilling to abandon the role of the writer, simply because it represents other worlds, other life notions, other perspectives …" (Zaera Polo, op.cit., pp. 24–25.)

73 Zenghelis interview, 5/30/03.

74 Alejandro Zaera Polo, "Finding Freedoms: Conversations with Rem Koolhaas," El Croquis 53 (1992), p. 18.

75 S,M,L,XL, p. 7.

76 Koolhaas interview, 6/5/03.

77 Zenghelis interview, 5/30/03.

78 Exodus, manuscript version.

79 This interpretation, however, follows from his present-day definition of architecture as absolutely autonomous: "it's a product of civilization, not of society." Zenghelis interview, 5/30/03.

80 Exodus, typescript.

81 Ibid.

82 Ibid.

83 S,M,L,XL, p. 199. Interesting in this regard are Koolhaas' speculations, in 1976, on urban emptiness and congestion, and particularly on emptiness as a way to organize metropolitan congestion at the occasion of the project for Berlin as a green archipelago with O.M. Ungers, in Goulet, "La deuxième chance …", op.cit., p. 8.

84 S,M,L,XL, p. 201.

85 "The permanence of even the most frivolous of architecture and the instability of the metropolis are incompatible. In this conflict the metropolis is by definition the victor in its pervasive reality, architecture is reduced to the status of a plaything, tolerated as a décor for the illusions of history and memory. In Manhattan this paradox is resolved in a brilliant way through the development of mutant architecture that combines the aura of monumentality with the performance of instability. Its interiors accommodate compositions of program and activity that change constantly and independently of each other without affecting what is called, with accidental profundity, the envelope." Rem Koolhaas, Delirious New York, Oxford University Press, New York, 1978, quoted in S,M,L,XL, pp. 23–31.

86 Alejandro Zaera Polo, "Finding Freedoms: Conversations with Rem Koolhaas," El Croquis, n° 53, 1992, p. 20.

87 "Mais comme pour ces phrases incomplètes qui offrent un grand nombre de conclusions, un tel manifeste permet ainsi une grande richesse d'interprétations et de variations dialectiques". (Zenghelis in: Goulet, "… Ou le début …", op.cit., p 14. Translation by LDC & HH.)

PROJECT

FOR A NEW

QUARTIER

(A   C I T Y   W I T H I N   T H E   C I T Y)

I N   T H E   C I T Y   O F   P A R I S   I N   T H E   Y E A R   1 9 7 6

ON THE SITE OF THE FORMER SLAUGHTER HOUSES OF LA VILLETTE

by   LEON   KRIER

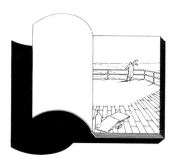

AS PUBLISHED IN MUNICH

2005

After the speedy urbanization of the FRONT DE SEINE, the QUARTIER D' ITALIE and BELLEVILLE, the area of the LA VILLETTE slaughter houses remains in Paris the last big site open for redevelopment. It is unnecessary to go here into the financial and political scandals that have surrounded the construction in 1958 of the new slaughter-houses which were never used for the purpose they were intended for. After a period in which market economy and rationalization of construction had been predominant, the formal experiments of the architects in the 1960s – probably most influenced by Op and Pop art and the buildings that are now under construction in Nanterre, Marne-la-Vallée or Crétail – have taken on frightening dimensions. The most enlightened critique of this new cultural reality and its influence on society in general might have been delivered by Marco Ferreri in the film *The Last Woman*. The obsessive individualism, the superficial search for stunning images, the imposition of experimental typologies without any historical or social justification have so far revealed the '60s as the darkest period in French architectural history.

One can, however, only be surprised in how far this new building market has left the traditional urban centres in France relatively untouched. Here a reality survives – a social vitality and a physical complexity – that gives new generations of architectural students the chance and the possibility to study.

The historical centres gain the force of a model.

The LA VILLETTE competition has shown the polarization of two generations, of two tendencies. The fact that prizes have been attributed to B. Huet, Agrest & Gandelsonas and to myself, the strong presence of James Stirling in the jury, the projects of F. Montes, A. Grumbach and of their students, all these facts announce a historical turn in post-war French architecture.

Another important point of the competition was the programme formulated by A. P. U. R. (Agence Parisienne d'Urbanisme). To my knowledge this represents the first post-war competition brief that radically departs from the concept of ZONING and re-proposes the integration of the most diverse functions (housing, industry, commerce, culture, leisure) integrated in a QUARTIER of a limited size (55 hectares of which 15 hectares are for the park).

This programme is exemplary: the QUARTIER is a part of the city which regains physical and social if not political autonomy.

The QUARTIER comprises 15,000 people and the programme tends towards an equilibrium of labour force and places of employment (industry and tertiary sector). The services and work places are easily reached on foot. This fact will allow a radical reduction in the automobile traffic, private as well as public.

One can add to this the existence of two major metro stations, the Porte de la Villette and the Porte de Pantin. The programme also included the reutilization of two very large industrial buildings, the Cattle Market (XIXth Century, 80 x 120 m) and the Grande Halle (1958, 150 x 300 m).

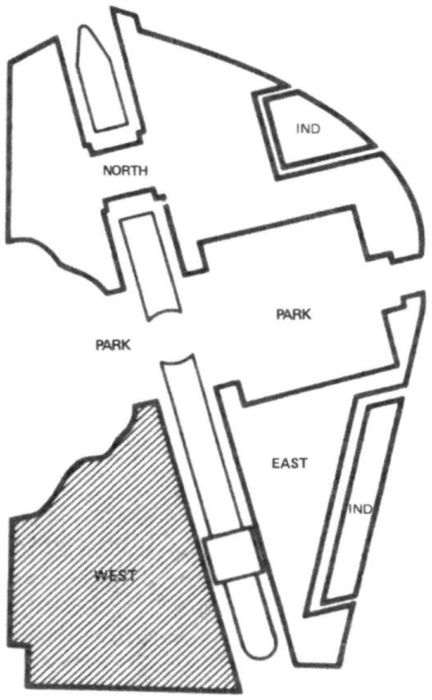

PARK

16.10ha.

QUARTIER WEST

APPARTMENTS	152 190 m²
SOCIAL SERVICES	10 120 m²
COMMERCIAL	18 060 m²
HOTELS	5 330 m²
OFFICES	22 540 m²
ARTISANS	2 570 m²

QUARTIER NORTH

APPARTMENTS	112 790 m²
SOCIAL SERVICES	13 340 m²
COMMERCIAL	19 460 m²
HOTELS	10 120 m²
OFFICES	20 600 m²
HOSPITAL	41 400 m²
TELEPHONE EXCHANGE	15 560 m²

QUARTIER EAST

APPARTMENTS	115 000 m²
SOCIAL SERVICES	8 280 m²
COMMERCIAL	13 150 m²
HOTEL	5 520 m²
OFFICES	20 240 m²
INDUSTRIAL	36 800 m²
ARTISANS	2 760 m²
WAREHOUSES	46 000 m²

BOULEVARD NORD-SUD

APPARTMENTS	9 560 m²
COMMERCIAL	8 740 m²
HOTELS	18 030 m²
SOCIAL SERVICES	17 110 m²
EXHIBITION HALL AND CONGRESS CENTRE	66 100 m²

The brief

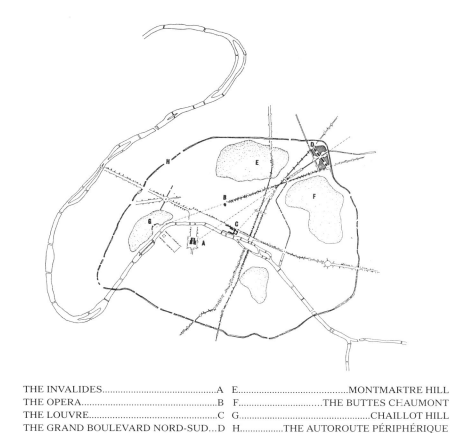

THE INVALIDES..A	E	......................................MONTMARTRE HILL
THE OPERA...B	F	............................THE BUTTES CHAUMONT
THE LOUVRE...C	G	....CHAILLOT HILL
THE GRAND BOULEVARD NORD-SUD...D	H	................THE AUTOROUTE PÉRIPHÉRIQUE

SITUATION

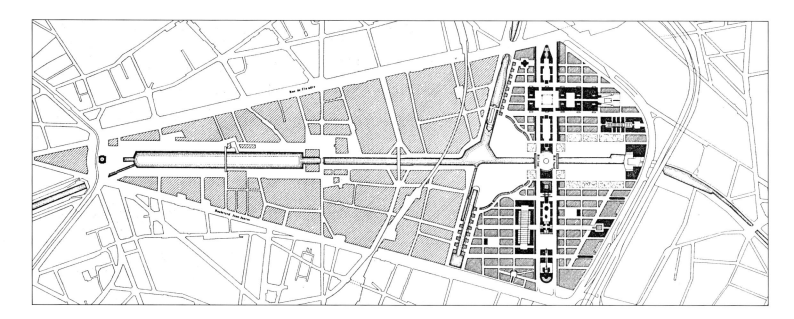

THE INSERTION OF THE NEW URBAN QUARTER IN THE LA VILLETTE BASIN

The centre of the new quarter will be articulated by a large park, which, together with the basin of the canal de l'Ourcq constitutes a single green area stretching from Ledoux's Barrière de la Villette to the Périphérique ring motorway. Perpendicular to this vast geographic expanse, bordered in the South by the Buttes Chaumont and by the Montmartre hill in the North, a large boulevard is projected, connecting the Porte de Pantin and Porte de la Villette metro stations. The grand geometric figure defined by the rue de Flandre, the Boulevard Jean-Jaurès and the canal de l'Ourcq is thus completed.

ARCHITECTURE AND BUILDING

The reconstruction of a collective language as demonstrated in the project for the Quartier de la Villette

SOME IDEAS ON REALISM

Nineteenth-century architectural thinking has effectively CONSUMED a few thousand years of previous cultures in a matter of hundred years. We are now paying the price for this wasteful and oneiric festival. In its gluttonous greed for power and culture, the bourgeoisie did not only erode the complex codes of high culture but, for the first time in modern history, popular culture and intelligence have been eroded almost beyond the point of redemption. In nineteenth-century architectural production, STYLES became the ideological system to bridge the alienation of intellectual and manual labour. Modern functionalism presented a radicalization in this quick consumptive process. For Le Corbusier the giving up of styles was more of a moral upsurge against the previous excesses whereas for the building industry, it was a welcome step to get rid of a by then unnecessary cultural facade.

By the apparent giving up of STYLES without resolving the contradictions at the ideological level, these STYLES had necessarily to survive as KITSCH and – leaving aside the acrobatics of high culture – KITSCH is the most important and generalized phenomenon which has resulted from the industrialization of production.

Kitsch seems to be a trivial and desperate attempt of dressing up the social and functional impoverishment of the urban environment. One has however to unmask all the pompous attempts of producing architectural meaning without a very clear political intention as a cultural travesty. It is at this point that the discussion about realism becomes crucial.

It is interesting to note here that the debate on socialist realism in the U.S.S.R. in the early thirties was not concerned with the notion of production – this problem was merely left to technicians, leaving aside the workers – but in a paternalistic way with STYLE. In "Proletarian Culture in China", Fei Ling has demonstrated the extent to which the fulgurant visions of the Constructivists and the prefabricated Renaissance facades of Shuschev were part of the same revisionist process. If in the nineteenth century industrialization could still be seen as a necessary condition for the liberation of mankind, the fading myth of technical progress is now causing a qualitative change in the nature of class struggle. The working class will in the end no longer accept the alienating labour conditions as the price to be paid for a political victory. If Kitsch is one of the results of the alienation of intellectual and manual labour, of the social division of labour, the problem of socialist realism cannot merely be discussed on level of form, style or even content. In architectural theory, the discussion about realism (as opposed to rhetorics) should centre on the question of how a dignified socialist mode of production will affect the form of the architectural object and in how far the field which concerns the architect has to be reduced to the only possible object of Architecture: to public edifices and the design of the PUBLIC REALM.

ZONING AND ARCHITECTURAL LANGUAGE

The progressive destruction of popular culture in the nineteenth century and the division of intellectual and manual labour in the production of Architecture and Building represented a radical erosion of the traditional dialectic of monument and urban fabric.

The ensuing crisis within the architectural culture was caused both by the increasing consumption and destruction of alien cultural codes and – more important even – by the functional and social decomposition of the city by the means of ZONING. In the end zoning must be regarded as the main cause of the linguistic decomposition of Architecture and Building. The complex visual codes of the pre-industrial European city articulated the intricate social body that the city represented. The destruction of these organically grown communities and institutions was inevitably to be accompanied by the destruction of their cultural habits and codes.

The concentration in clinically controlled and policed ZONES OF HOUSING, CULTURE, PRODUCTION meant in reality the destruction of the dialectical nature of PUBLIC and PRIVATE, of individual and anonymous, architecturally of the STREET and SQUARE.

HOUSING IS NOT A MONUMENT

One of the failures of architects and authorities in the '20s was to consider housing as the monuments of our time. However, the highly repetitive nature of residential blocks

A few design sketches documenting the genesis of the Grand Boulevard as a perpendicular complement to an east-west park zone (with an Artificial Island mirroring the Ledoux Barrière in the distance). Two formal bridgeheads (centre left & top right drawing) pierce the screen of the park: the embryonic Place Centrale.

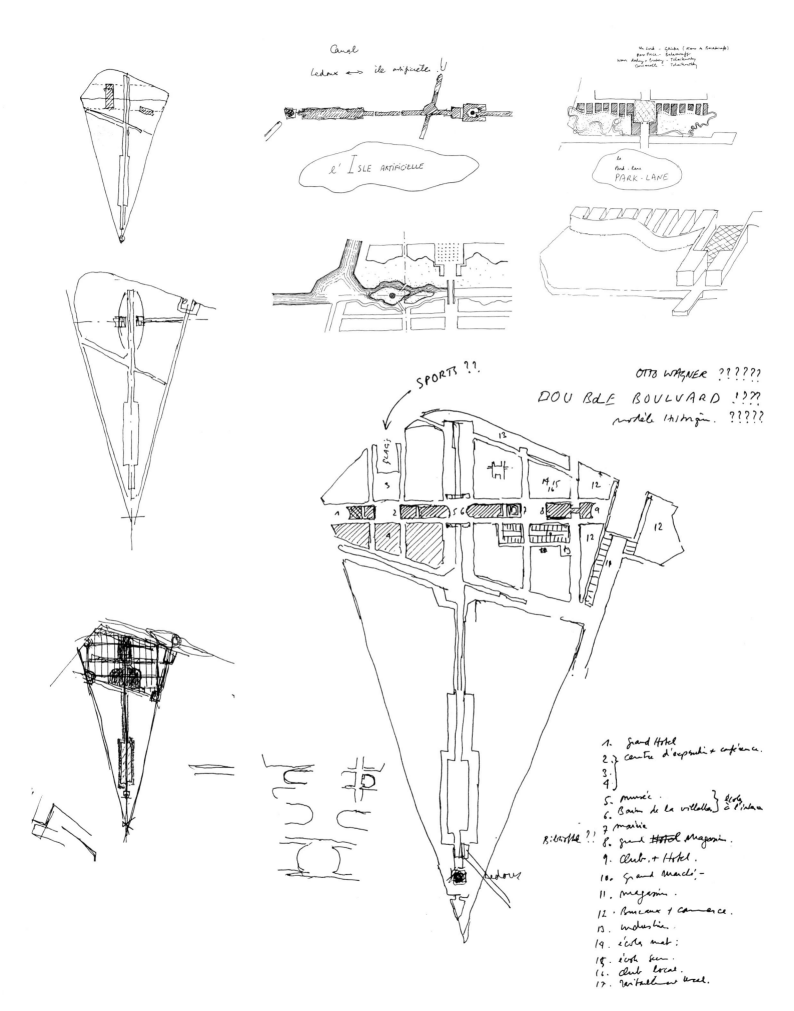

Canal

Ledoux ⟷ île artificielle !!

l' ISLE ARTIFICIELLE

PARK-LANE

SPORTS ??

GLACIS

OTTO WAGNER ??????
DOUBLE BOULVARD !!???
modèle historique ??????

1. Grand Hotel
2.} centre d'exposition + conférence.
3.}
4.}
5. musée.
6. Bain de la villette
7. mairie
8. grand Magasin.
9. Club. + Hotel.
10. Grand Marché.-
11. magasin.
12. Bureaux + commerce.
13. industrie
14. écoles mat:
15. école sec.
16. club local.
17. installation local.

Bibliothèque ??

Ledoux

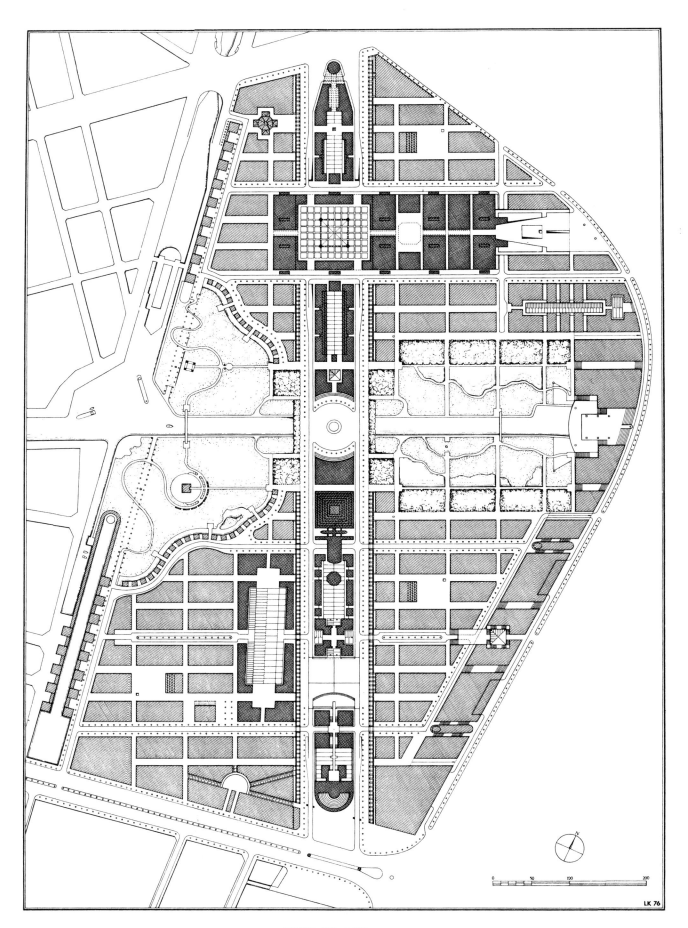

THE PLAN

neither delivered the content nor the social purpose important and rich enough to inspire highly artistic results over a long period of time. The Karl Marx Hof in Vienna or the vast residential blocks in Moscow have to be seen as exceptional achievements in an otherwise rapidly declining system of social and formal values.

TECHNICAL PROGRESS AND INDUSTRIALIZATION OF BUILDING

In the 1920s the growing industrialization of building was largely seen by architects to be the basis for a new architecture, for a new quality. However, with all the disposition we have inherited from the nineteenth century to believe in technical progress as the key to social progress, we can say now that modern building technology is still at the level of the experiment, and this ephemeral progress leaves us today with a building technology which in many ways is more primitive than at any moment in Western civilization.

Industrialization has neither created quicker building techniques nor a better building technology. Far from having improved the physical conditions of the worker, it has reduced manual labour to a stultifying and enslaving experience. It has degraded a millennial and dignified craft to a socially alienating exercise.

Nor has industrialization reduced the cost of production. Far from being socially economical in the long term, it has been the most radical means to absorb building crafts into the vast cycles of industrial production and consumption, its profound motivation having been the maximization of profits. As the manual, artisan culture of building was destroyed, the intellectual and theoretical corpus of Architecture had to collapse in a society whose very base of existence, craft production, became eliminated. The failure to re-found Architecture and Building in any other discipline than in its own history and in itself having been sufficiently demonstrated in the last five decades, now makes us understand that the recuperation of a dignified mode of production, the reconstruction of an artisan building culture will be the basis of any new architectural culture, of a new collective language.

The conception and form of a rationalist architecture will lie in the organization of the building production. The vulgarity of late-capitalist architecture is as much caused by the random mix of building types as by the absurd profusion of building materials and construction systems, not an outcome of rationalization but of maximization of profits. I suppose that the restriction to a few building materials and the elaboration of an urban building typology will create a new architectural discipline of simple nobility and monumentality.

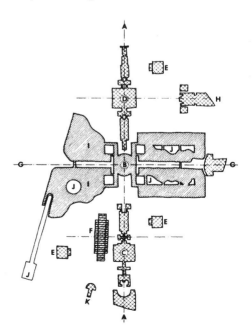

LOCATION OF PUBLIC SPACES

A Grand Boulevard Nord-Sud — B Place Centrale — C Place de la Mairie — D Covered Square des Congrès — E Local Square — F Covered Market in the Halle de Baltard — G Esplanade of the great vista — H Inclined square of Industry (loggia of the Great Hall) — I The Park — J Ornamental pond/lake — K Métro station

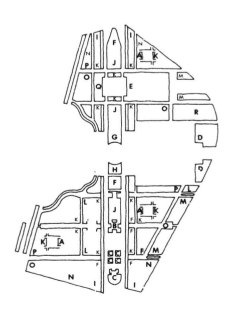

DISTRIBUTION OF FUNCTIONS

A Neighbourhood centre, club — B The Mairie (local council) — C Cultural centre — D Museum — E Conference and exhibition centre — F Hotel — G Baths — H Casino — I Large shops — J Bazaar — K Local shops — L Craftsmen's workshops — M Light industry — N Offices — O School — P Creche — Q Maison du Peuple — R Hospital

THE EDGES	Boulevard Jean Jaurès (existing) Rue de Flandre (existing)	QUARTIER	Local ring road
THE CENTER	Grand Boulevard Nord-Sud —this runs on a NW/SE axis	QUARTIER	Local secondary street —these run on a SW/NE axis
QUARTIER	Local Avenue (main street) —this runs on a SW/NE axis	QUARTIER	Passages —these run on a NW/SE axis

A HIERARCHY OF STREETS, A HIERARCHY OF USES

The edges of the new quartier – i.e. the Boulevard Jean-Jaurès and the rue de Flandre – carry tertiary activities, supply and services of a-periodical use; the industrial buildings and the Hospital form a screen along the autoroute périphérique.

The central boulevard is occupied by cultural, political, institutional buildings, shops for periodical use, luxury shops, cafés, clubs, the Hotels and the Baths.

The local shops for daily use, the post offices, the craftsmen's workshops, schools and crèches are distributed around the local piazzas or along the main local streets, the Avenues.

The Grands Magasins (department stores) are at the entrances of the tube stations at the north and south entrance of the Grand Boulevard.

URBAN PATTERN & SCALE

The comparison of different urban street patterns in different periods is largely self-explanatory. I want to state firmly, however, that the size of the urban BLOCKS has to occupy the central position in this discussion.

The Luisenstadt (Kreuzberg) of 1841 by P.J. Lenné or A. Speer's axis of 1938, although apparently within an

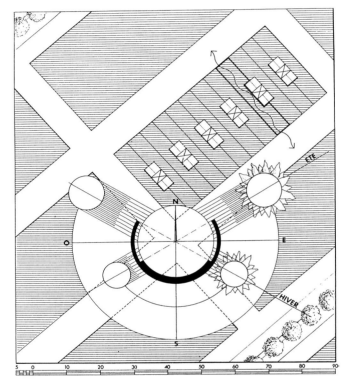

The typical block is 28 m x 60 m, and most apartments face two streets. Most of the secondary streets connect directly onto the Grand Boulevard Nord-Sud.

academic tradition of spatial planning, as far as the Gestalt goes, should be identified as direct illustrations of the anti-anthropological and experimental/speculative nature of nineteenth- and twentieth-century urban space.

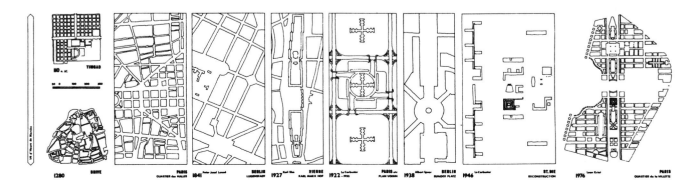

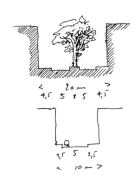

50m.

Avenue de Flandre.

30m.

Avenue principale.

etc.

< 20 m >
4,5 5 1,5 4,5

< 10 m >
2,5 5 2,5

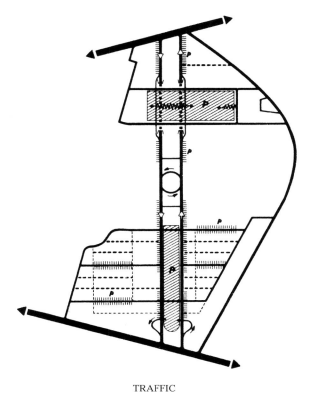

TRAFFIC

TRAFFIC ... ZONING ... AND POLITICS

– Nine o' clock in the morning. From its four vomitoria, each 250 m wide, the station is spewing out the commuters brought by the trains from the suburbs. As by a continuous (one way) movement these have been following closely each minute.
– Speed is not a matter of dreams, speed is a brutal necessity ... why regret the times of the shepherds?
– Little after midday the deed is done. The city will empty itself as by a deep aspiration of its underground. The life of the garden cities will deploy its effects.

Le Corbusier, 1925
"L'heure du travail" in *Urbanisme*, p. 171/73

The precision of L.C.'s vision owes as much to the ambiguous anxiety of futurist script-writing as to A. Speer's later planning of mass meetings. The growing militarization of everyday life only became possible through the radical zoning of the cities. The profound alienation due to the industrial division of labour here finds an adequate urban form. Movement and speed become the instrument for the necessary ritualization of an otherwise unacceptable way of life. Fascism is its extreme consequence.

In this political perspective we see that the reintegration of all branches of life within a quartier is the first and necessary step for a democratization of urban society. The democratization of decision-making processes in Italian urban politics is the best illustration for the potential of QUARTIER PLANNING.

When commuting and transit traffic become largely eliminated, the integration of the automobile traffic within the QUARTIER is not only possible but it becomes even desirable. The 4,000 existing car parks under the Grande Salle are doubled under the Grand Boulevard Nord-Sud. Apart from rather general regulations shown in the Traffic diagram, we think that traffic ultimately should be left to sort out itself.

 MAIN CIRCULATION

 SECONDARY STREETS

 LIMITED ACCESS

 PARKING DISK ZONE

 UNDERGROUND PARKING

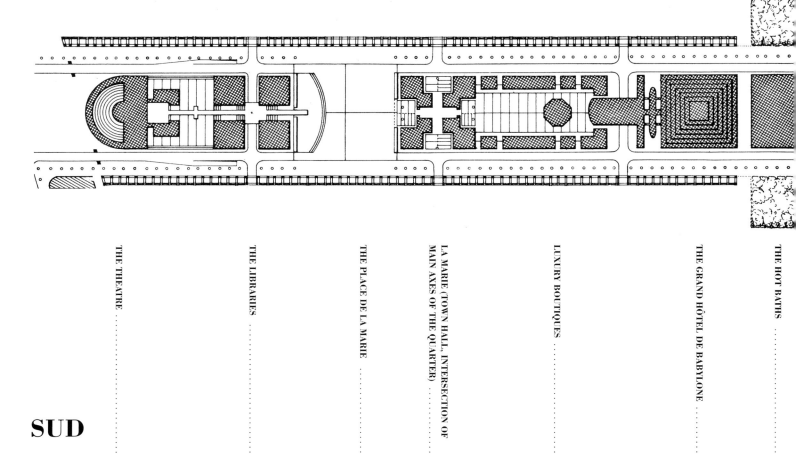

THE THEATRE ....

THE LIBRARIES ....

THE PLACE DE LA MARIE ....

LA MARIE (TOWN HALL, INTERSECTION OF MAIN AXES OF THE QUARTER) ....

LUXURY BOUTIQUES ....

THE GRAND HÔTEL DE BABYLONE ....

THE HOT BATHS ....

SUD

THE GRAND BOULEVARD NORD–SUD

The Grand Boulevard is essentially a large space (95 x 1,000 m) occupied by a series of buildings of metropolitan importance. The space is framed lengthwise by a commercial arcade, the STOA.

Unlike the traditional European avenue it is not a perspective space, focusing on monuments or institutional buildings (Avenue de l'Opéra etc.). The collective edifices, the public monuments here, for the first time in urban history, occupy the space itself.

A typological precedent for this double route might be found in Rome in the formation of the Borgo Vecchio – Borgo Nuovo before their destruction by Piacentini's Via Della Conciliazione, or, in Paris, the doubled roman Cardo formed by the Rue St. Denis and the Rue St. Martin; a direct historical precedent can be seen in the formation of the Rue de Cléri and the Rue d' Aboukir occupying the Space of the Wall of Charles V.

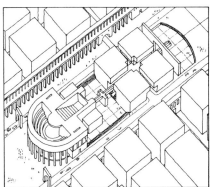

THE LIBRARIES, THE THEATRE

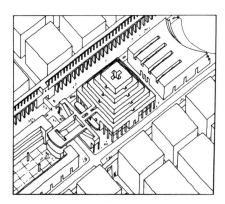

THE HOTEL — The monumental character of this edifice represents its social status and collective nature. The ziggurat form encloses a vast collective space and represents the truly progressive ideal of communal living.

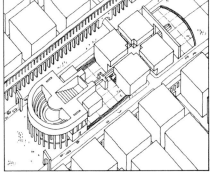

Borgo Vecchio – Borgo Nuovo, Rome

The wall of Charles V, Paris

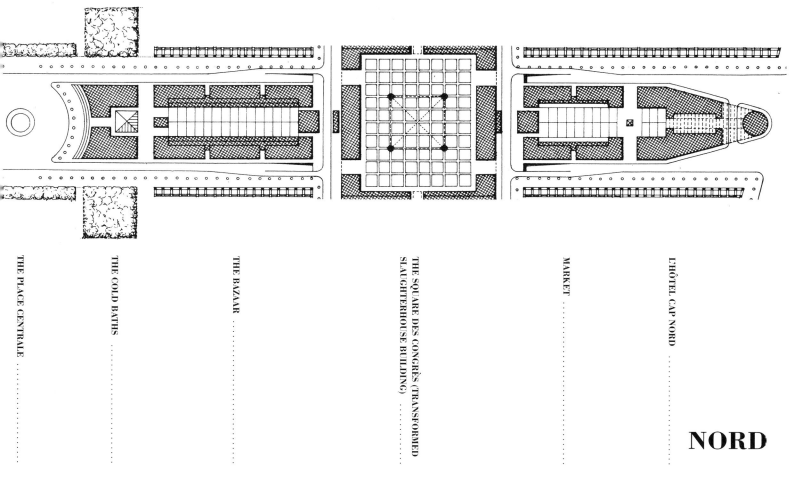

THE PLACE CENTRALE ....

THE COLD BATHS ....

THE BAZAAR ....

THE SQUARE DES CONGRÈS (TRANSFORMED SLAUGHTERHOUSE BUILDING) ....

MARKET ....

L'HÔTEL CAP NORD ....

NORD

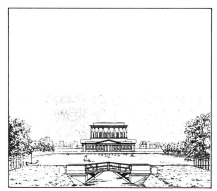

LEDOUX — The Place Centrale mirrors the geometric figure of the distant Barrière de la Villette.

THE STOA — This commercial arcade frames the monumental space of the Grand Boulevard.

THE SQUARE — The Square des Congrès, as seen from the terrace of the Maison du Peuple. The Grand Boulevard cuts through the existing Grande Salle to form a large pedestrian covered space.

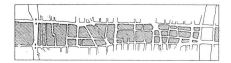

Rue St. Martin and St. Denis, Paris

The Grand Boulevard Nord-Sud occupies the space of the former 'Enceinte de Thiers'. It thus comes closest to its etymological roots (Bolwerc) loaded with the typological and historical experience of man-made Paris.

The Boulevard buildings are interrupted at three points to form:
a) The Place Centrale, a panoramic rond-point sitting over the canal and linking the two Parks. The geometry of its plan mirrors the construction of Ledoux's distant Barrière de la Villette (A Circle inscribed in a Square), Ledoux's cylinder becoming a void here, reflecting on the contemporary criticism that a gate should not be a building but a void. b) The Place de la Mairie c) The covered Place des Congrès

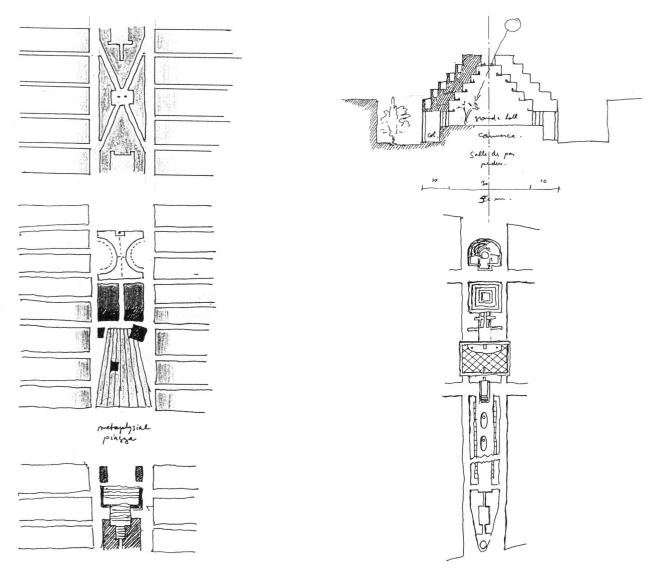

Opposite, top: The Stoa. The grand Boulevard Nord-Sud will mainly be animated by Corso traffic: cars can be parked for short periods orthogonally along the Boulevard. This constant parking activity will naturally slow down the speed of the cars driving along the main artery. Opposite, bottom: The Place de la Marie, with on the left the Mairie (Town Hall), facing the Cultural centre. Above: early thoughts for the infill of the Boulevard's central strip ("Metaphysical Piazza"); Top right: The Grand Hotel de Babylone, section.

AN URBAN LANGUAGE:
ARCHITECTURE & BUILDING

The monumental character of these spaces and edifices in fact represents their social status, their collective nature. Against the quiet language of the surrounding urban fabric ARCHITECTURE finds here the exact geometrical and social LIEU to deploy its collective pathos and magnificence.

These large buildings crystallize Types of organizations – like the Theatre, the Library, the Hotel, the Bath – into specific architectural Models. They are not to be understood as unique signs, as words of a private language, but rather as an attempt to create a system of social and formal references, making up the landmarks of the contemporary city,

replacing the traditional religious and institutional monuments with new social contents.

These models have their roots both in a progressive cultural history as well as in the history of architectural types. The general form might be one of a vessel, a more general architectural reference, whereas the Ziggurat (Hotel de Babylone) reflects on the efforts of A. Loos or even Le Corbusier's Mundaneum, enclosing within its stepped section a vast collective space, transcending its religious origins and by that representing to us a truly progressive idea. This edifice is the only one rising above the surrounding fabric. The passing utopian content of communal living as institutionalized in the Hotel might here find a lasting expression.

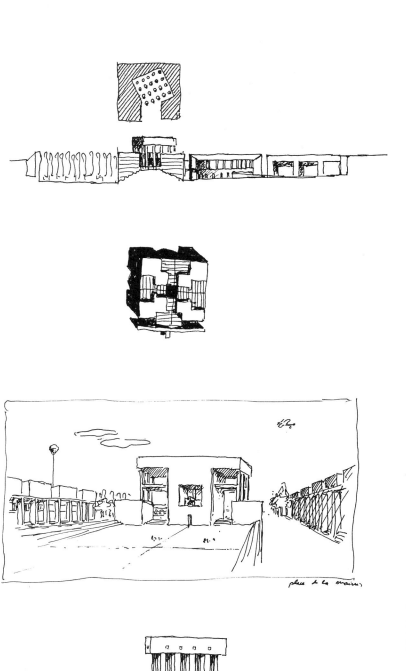

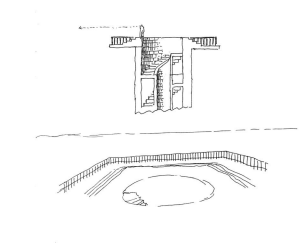

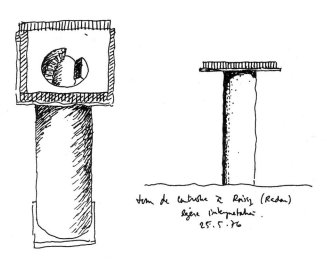

Hôm de centrôle à Roissy (Redon)
légère interprétation.
25.5.76

The idea of the raised Council chamber of the Mairie emerges alongside plans for a viewing platform. Originally situated between the Town Hall and Grand Hotel (drawing bottom left), it makes its final comeback as a pedestal for a blustery piece of sculpture on the Place de la Mairie.

The Mairie is a reflection on a plan of Ledoux, however set into an urban context. The ideal joining the real. This plan might serve as a most precise illustration of the dialectic of urban space and building typology. It is located at the intersection of the Grand Boulevard and the main avenue of the quartier. Instead of blocking these routes by a monolithic mass, the symbol of centralized power is fractured by the most important public routes, its functions projected into the four remaining corners. The intersection itself is crowned by the assembly chamber lifted on a forest of columns (see sketch). A precise dialectic of solid and void is established. The routes, the urban space define the type of the building; the realized model in return produces "PLACE", it qualifies and defines the abstract order of the public space. The production of architecture (of Meaning) finds here its social and geometrical Lieu.

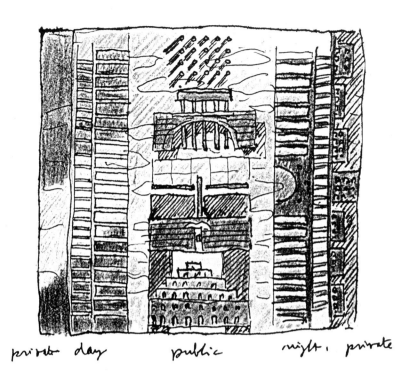

private day   public   night, private

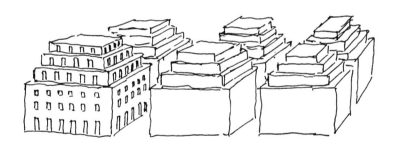

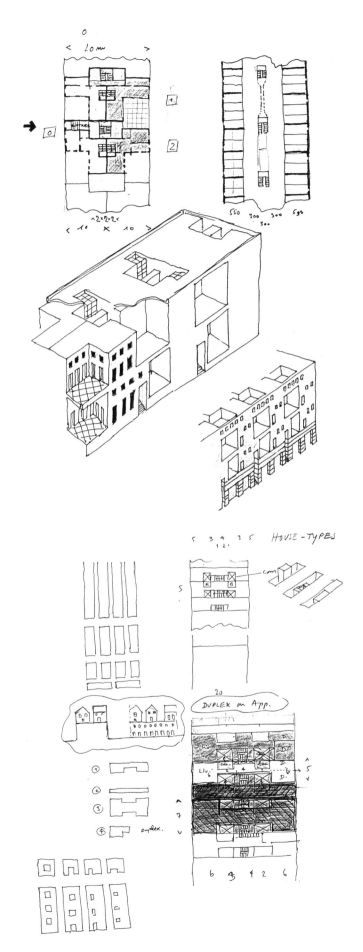

Against the architectural monumentality of the Grand Boulevard, the nineteenth-century Market Hall, the Grande Salle and the industrial buildings, the local avenues and streets are framed by buildings of more modest articulation. Against the typological and formal specificity (representativity) of the collective edifices, the urban fabric, formed by blocks, would result from a limited set of very general typological (residential) and aesthetical (proportional) rules, to be interpreted by an infinite number of HANDS and NEEDS, only the dimensions of the blocks and the plots having to be followed strictly. The two lower floors of this fabric would be occupied by a continuous layer of shops, workshops, communal services…. These floors would be differentiated in the façade by the use of more durable and beautiful materials (stone, granite …) as to frame the more tactile surfaces of the street space: the residential floors would merely be stuccoed in the tradition of Parisian domestic building.

We hope in this way to re-establish a new dialectic of private and public realm, collective and individual. We also begin to see that a complex urban language can only and solely emerge when expressing a complex urban content, through a correct distribution of all urban activities.

These are the rudimentaries of a possible collective language; the production of meaning, instead of occupying lately single architectural objects, can only begin to make sense if given the possibility to express a new social and urban REALITY.

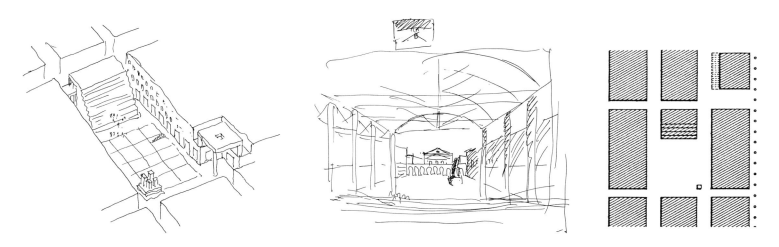

The intimate local squares (50 x 50 m) will become the stage for neighbourhood assemblies, theatre performances, concerts and games.

The Hill of the Winds

The Enigmatic Promenade

The Screen of the Park

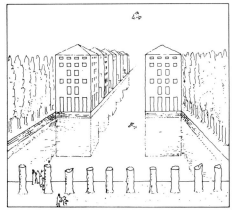

Park entrance from Blvd. Jean Jaurès

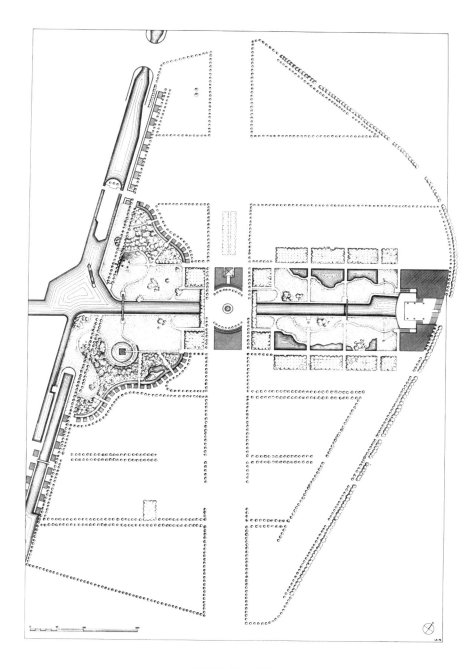

THE PARK

The park has to be understood in the larger geographical context of the Bassin de la Villette and the distant cupola of the Invalides. The park will be a culmination of the new leisure zone along this canal. This is a space at the scale of the city. Within this overall conception, the park is a place of quiet and calm. This explains the sparse disposition of activities and structures within the park.

The Place Centrale Spans the canal, linking the two parts of the park with a platform which offers a panoramic view. In the eastern part the urban order penetrates it in the forms of evergreen trees trimmed to geometric shapes. The Museum of the Automobile and the Museum of the Aeroplane, bordering the Périphérique, frame the easternmost edge of the park. In the western part, the paths and visual axes reveal monumental structures such as the Tower of Curtains on the Hill of Winds.

THE SCREEN OF THE PARK

The edge of the Park is formed by a series of small towers (Artists' and Craftsmen's studios) linked by a continuous bronze roof and thus forming a screen at the scale of the entire Park … Between these towers we have imagined a series of public loggias.

In the early evening small groups of citizens come here to breathe the air of the Park, to catch the last beams of the sun, setting between the hills of Belleville and Montmartre, the silhouette of Paris deploying its splendour in an adequate frame.

There is an obvious reference here to L.C.'s covered terraces in Pessac. Corbusier quoting himself in a suburban setting finds his

idea returned to the public realm where it originally came from (Loggia dei Lanzi, etc.) and where it finds a more adequate use.

THE GREAT VISTA TO THE INVALIDES

The Museum of the Automobile and the Museum of the Aeroplane are elevated 15 metres above the level of the canal. The view is formed by a series of terraces that fall towards the park. From this belvedere one commands a vast perspective of the great canal basin which lies between the hills of Montmartre and the Buttes de Chaumont – focussing in the distance on the cupola of the Invalides, the architectural masterpiece of Hardouin-Mansart.

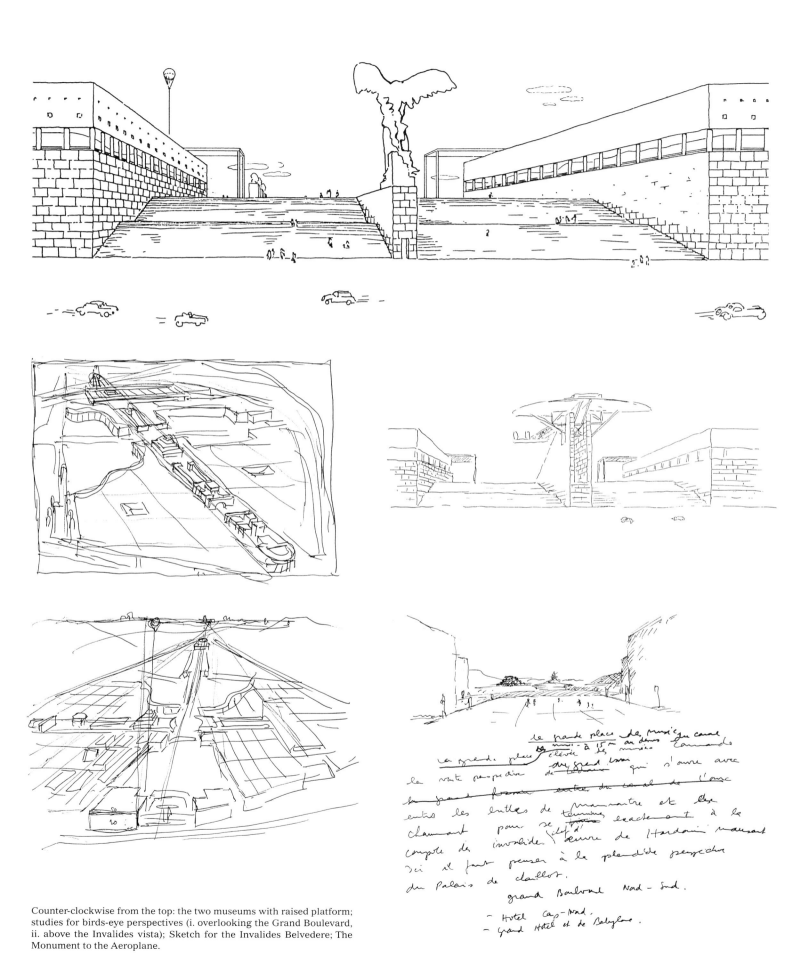

Counter-clockwise from the top: the two museums with raised platform; studies for birds-eye perspectives (i. overlooking the Grand Boulevard, ii. above the Invalides vista); Sketch for the Invalides Belvedere; The Monument to the Aeroplane.

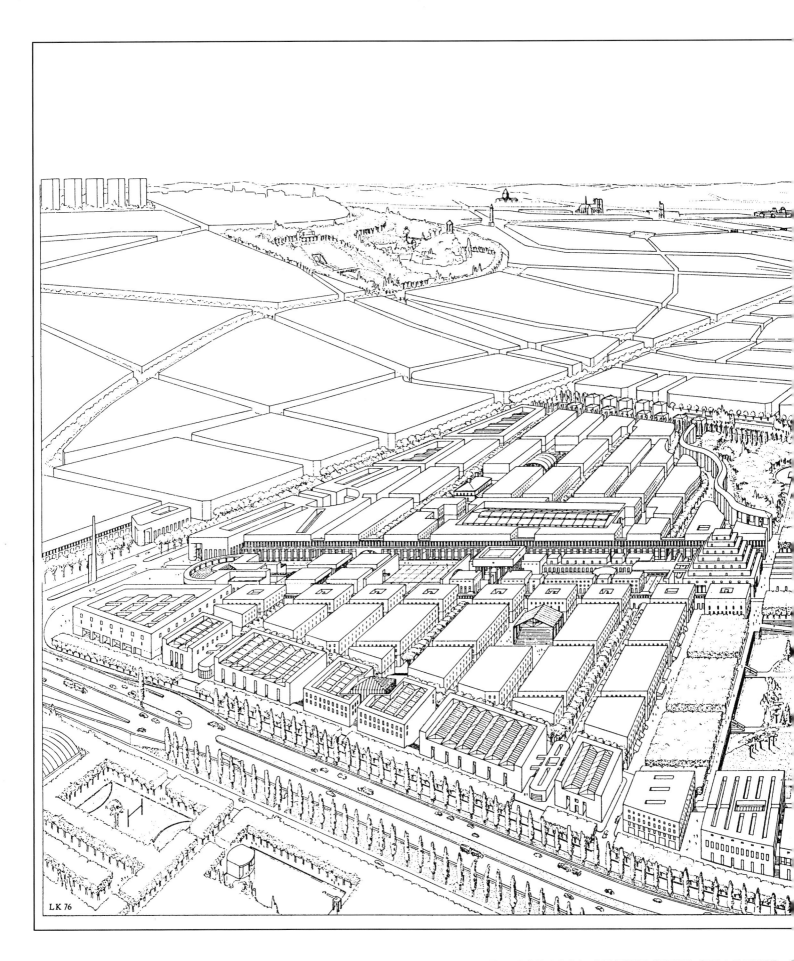

LK 76

PANORAMA OF THE NEW QUARTIER A

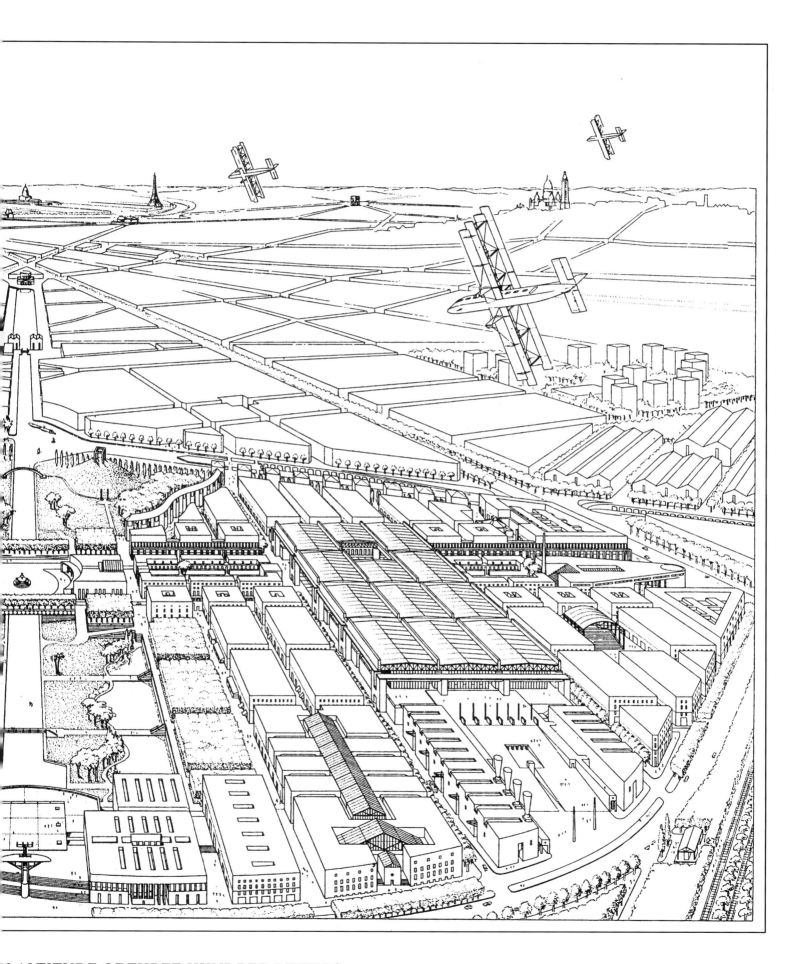

THE PROMENADE AT DUSK

If nowadays the park has still to replace in the cities the distant nature, it will soon be the cultivated landscape itself, and not its imaginary interpretation, which will have to form the limits of the urban quarters. One cannot resolve the contradiction between town and country by spreading the one into the other. One cannot destroy the city without destroying the countryside, neither can one build the landscape without building the city. The city within the city will also be the city within the countryside. What is important is both the social and the physical sign of its parts of its quarters.

Looking from the vast loggias of the Quartier de la Villette, the view of cows and of agriculture machines will soon be more familiar to the citizens than the village of Marie-Antoinette.

'Une mise à nu de l'architecture par ses adorateurs mêmes'[1]
Maurice Culot and Léon Krier: A Forgotten Episode

Geert Bekaert

In 1977, *Architectural Design* published a special issue titled "Tafuri/Culot/Krier".[2] Under the three names, one is surprised and amused to read the subtitle "The Pleasure of Architecture". Further scrutiny reveals that this is the title of an essay by Bernard Tschumi unrelated to the trio Tafuri/Culot/Krier. The actual subtitle, as is revealed in the issue, is "The Role of Ideology".[3] By coincidence, seemingly extreme antipodes of the architectural debate of the day were thus brought together. Culot and Krier indeed were an inseparable duo for some time. But what is their relationship to Tafuri or to Tschumi? Though Krier had briefly met the latter at the Architectural Association in London, he claims never to have understood a single word of what he was talking about.[4]

This combination of names is not only peculiar from a current perspective, but also symptomatic of the position Culot/Krier held in the 1970s. Today, they are pretty much out of the picture – a forgotten episode in the history of architecture[5] – but back then they were omnipresent on the international stage and for some time actually enjoyed considerable acclaim.[6] However, they kept aloof and did not engage in the debates of the day. Not without a certain haughtiness, they consigned all of modernist architecture from Wright to Le Corbusier and everything that followed, including their contemporaries, to the dust bin of history, a history whose course these modernists had not, in their opinion, been able to change – something they themselves claimed to have in fact accomplished.[7] Maybe they had not changed history yet, but they had, so they felt, been able to tap again into its real flow.[8] Thematically, they revisited the Arts and Crafts movement and, particularly, the utopian socialism of William Morris with its glorification of craftsmanship against the burgeoning industrialization in the second half of the nineteenth century.

This ambivalent position is clearly reflected in the *AD* issue. Page after page, David Dunster's review of Tafuri's *Architecture and Utopia*[9] runs parallel to the presentation of Krier's project for La Villette, but without any interaction between them. Although the editorial preface to the issue suggests there is a link between "the work and thought of three European Marxist architects", this is not elaborated in any way. The guest editor, Robert Maxwell, simply juxtaposes the three names. Their relationship is dismissed in a single sentence: "Whether and to what degree Tafuri would underwrite the production of Maurice Culot and of Léon Krier we do not know. But there is little doubt that they have drawn strength from the power of his critical method, particularly in his view of history and tradition as a thread which cannot be broken and which should not be dishonoured." This assessment is surprising, since even in 1977 it was already evident that the simplistic affirmations and viewpoints of Culot/Krier on history and tradition had virtually nothing in common with the nuanced research hypotheses and probes of Tafuri.

Maurice Culot (born 1939 in Sevilla) and Léon Krier (born 1946 in Luxemburg) met in London at the Art Net Rally organized by Peter Cook in the summer of 1976.[10] There, Krier spoke in defense of Culot, whose observations on the *luttes urbaines* in Brussels

were being attacked by Cedric Price. Referring to Le Corbusier, who had been Krier's great mentor as well, Cedric Price hailed current developments in urbanism and architecture not only as a necessary intervention to remedy existing shortcomings, but also as a positive manifestation of a new beauty and as a self-evident expression of a modern mind-set. Krier supported Culot, because Culot argued for the preservation of the historical city and its morphological typologies. Quite to their surprise, they realized that their approaches complemented each other. In Krier, Culot found something of a theoretical underpinning of his combative approach, and, through Culot, Krier could anchor and legitimize his reflections and sensibilities in a concrete situation. The fact that both, at a certain moment, refused to build in a society governed by capitalism, was interpreted by Krier as the only viable way still to engage in Architecture with a capital A. "I have always been interested in the answer to the question 'What is Architecture?'", Krier states. "But such as architecture was, has been, but is not anymore, I would say in all modesty that I alone can practice architecture, because I do not build."[11]

1. Maurice Culot and Léon Krier in Washington, 1981

Maurice Culot had first taken a stand in the debate through the polemical exhibition *Antoine Pompe et l'effort moderne en Belgique, 1890–1940*,[12] which he organized in 1969 with François Terlinden. Culot and Terlinden had both studied at La Cambre, the school once dubbed *le Bauhaus belge* – the Belgian Bauhaus.[13] Culot had graduated in 1963 and, subsequently, worked for some time at the Frank Lloyd Wright Foundation. Upon his return, he met Antoine Pompe (1873–1980), a former teacher at La Cambre and an 'anti-modernist' modernist. The decision to do a show on Belgian modernism centring on Pompe was already in itself a clear statement. The catalogue introduction by Robert-Louis Delevoy, the then director of La Cambre, titled *Pour une provocation* could not have been more unequivocal in this regard.

While preparing the show, the organizers had already concluded that it was necessary to establish an archive, the *Archives de l'Architecture Moderne (AAM)*, which would allow for a revision of the history of modern architecture based on a study of the sources. In fact, this alternative history was what the exhibition

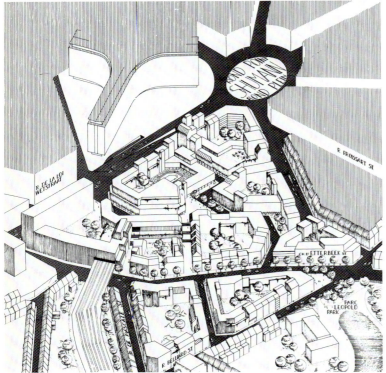

was really all about. Establishing the archive would prove to be its most lasting outcome.

Another upshot of the exhibition was the establishment of the *Atelier de Recherche et d'Action Urbaine (ARAU)*[14]. On this, Culot stated:

I am a founding member of *ARAU* which was formed in 1968 to promote the democratization of decision-making in the field of city planning. Most of my work revolves around developing alternative planning schemes, which are both part of a programme of action and illustrate the group's philosophy. For *ARAU* members the city is a place where democracy could live – they reject any proposal that banishes inhabitants from the city. *ARAU* does not propose architectural images for the city's future – instead the future form of the city must be the product of democratic decision-making processes, in which democratic chaos is to be preferred to a city of order.

My role in the group is not that of 'the' architect. However, with the aid of collaborators at the *Archives de l'Architecture Moderne* and my students at La Cambre, architectural and urbanistic conceptions of the *ARAU* projects are being developed. My mission is not to create new forms but only to explain the options and programs being debated by *ARAU*. We do not force our own architectural tastes on people, but follow the advice of the people involved. We never accept an architectural commission for any of the projects developed by *ARAU* – this is essential if *ARAU* is to maintain its integrity.[15]

In retrospect, several of the above contentions would have to be challenged. The claim that *ARAU* did not propose architectural images is obviously false, and it is even less true that these images were produced by the 'people'. The images presented as so-called *contreprojets*[16] (counter-projects) have achieved the exact opposite of what they intended.[17] Even if one advocates, along with Culot, a theatrical facade architecture inspired by or imitating historical models, one can only conclude that it is not only greatly deficient formally, but also that it has failed to bring about any political or social change. His propositions only functioned within the architectural discourse.

To an acrimonious article by Maurice Culot entitled "Tout est luxe, calme et beauté",[18] Léon Krier replied with an open letter in which he cautiously expressed his reservations and, at the same time, revealed the gist of his own approach. It was their first collaboration since they had met in London, and, already, it carried the seed for their future split-up. Krier wrote:

I just read your article 'Luxe, calme et beauté' dealing in particular with the issue of the form of a socialist architecture. In the discussion that followed your presentation of ARAU's latest project at the Art Net conference, I wanted to avoid talking about form, because, first of all, the political intervention of the project needed to be defended. I believe, however, that, ultimately, the issue of form is not as much an aesthetic issue as one of the mode

2–4. Top: a project for a mono-functional office enclave in the European Community district, Brussels, early 1970s. Below, an early "counter-project" from 1972 by ARAU – as yet stylistically undetermined – proposing mixed use on the same site. Bottom: the built result of the 1986 competition for the 'reconstruction' of an inner city block along the ancient Rue de Laeken. Though not an ARAU project, Culot and Krier were prominent members of the jury and the winning entries were all designed in the classicist idiom. To accommodate the scheme (winning architects were each allocated a plot), a number of existing buildings from the post-war era had to be razed – history eagerly corrected.

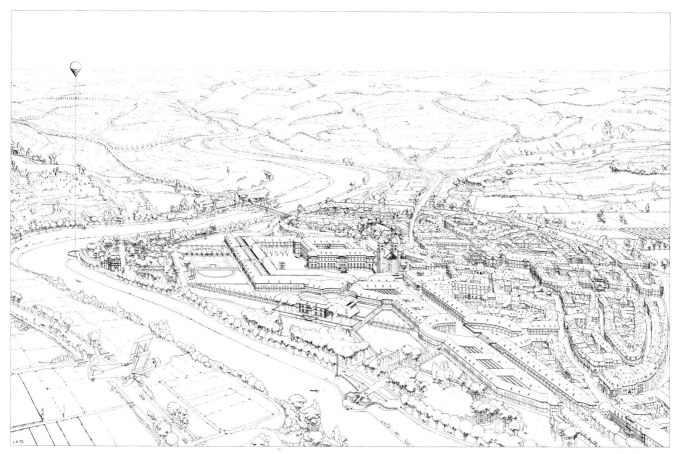

5. Léon Krier, Project for the extension of St Willibrord's Abbey, Echternach, 1970

of production. When you say that the 'people' should henceforth be given what they want – and by that you imply the populist eclecticism of Spoerry or of your own recent project, but also the modernist eclecticism of Kroll – this again reduces your 'people' to the role of (perhaps happy) consumers. Far from raising the problem of alienation caused by the separation between intellectual and manual labour, this attitude, in my opinion, is dangerous: it reverts to the use of a thin cultural facade which might very well have the same paternalistic origin as the eclecticism of the nineteenth century and which similarly persists in the stylistic orgies of the Stalinist era. If, however, STYLES were fully CONSUMED in the 200 years or so of bourgeois domination, STYLES themselves were the means of destruction of past cultures – aristocratic as well as popular.

You can't gainsay Krier for his keen insights.

The two articles appeared in *AAM*, a monthly bulletin Culot had founded in 1974 and which, after its transformation into a journal, would continue publication until 1990. After 1990, Maurice Culot would increasingly apply himself to his task as an archivist, whereas Léon Krier would retreat to Provence, still keeping abreast of current developments, more so than Culot, not least through his contact with the Prince of Wales. *AAM* became Léon Krier's mouthpiece, so to speak. *AAM* would also publish most of the books by and on Krier.

In 1978, Culot and Krier jointly signed the editorial, *L'unique chemin de l'architecture*[19] (The Only Path for Architecture), a

significant title, because it illustrates the exclusiveness of their approach. In this regard, they were in no way different from the modernists they were opposing. They just wanted to take their place in the limelight. In a way, they also appropriated their name, calling themselves "rationalists". That very same year, 1978, *AAM* published a compilation of writings and works by, among others, Vidler, Scolari, Ungers, Rob Krier, Rossi, Grassi, and Linazasoro titled *La reconstruction de la ville européenne/ The Reconstruction of the European City. Rational Architecture Rationelle,* which was intended to demonstrate the broad support for their approach.[20]

Léon Krier has, on various occasions, elaborated on his background and career – his biography is an integral part of his stance. Culot, on the other hand, has always remained extremely reticent about sharing his personal history. One of the most concise and characteristic accounts of Krier's life dates from the 1980 publication *City Segments* of *Design Quaterly*:[21]

I was born in Luxembourg 7 April 1946, where I passed a happy childhood, the Benjamin in a family of four children: with two sisters and a brother. In October 1955, the bridge and highway authorities massacred the linden trees that, up to that time, bordered the panoramic avenue alongside our house (first doubts on the value of progress). In 1953, I began to study piano under the direction of my mother and undertook secondary studies at a classical school in St. Willibrord Abbey in Echternach. I designed a monumental fountain for the marketplace in Echternach and wrote an enthusiastic letter to Le Corbusier congratulating him

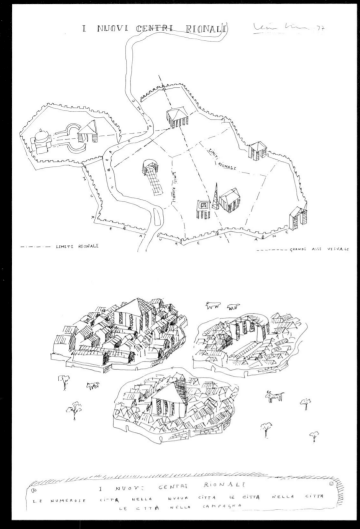

I NUOVI CENTRI RIONALI

LIMETI RIONALI — GRANDI ASSI VISIVALI

I NUOVI CENTRI RIONALI

LE NUMEROSE CITTÀ NELLA NUOVA CITTÀ LE CITTÀ NELLA CITTÀ
LE CITTÀ NELLA CAMPAGNA

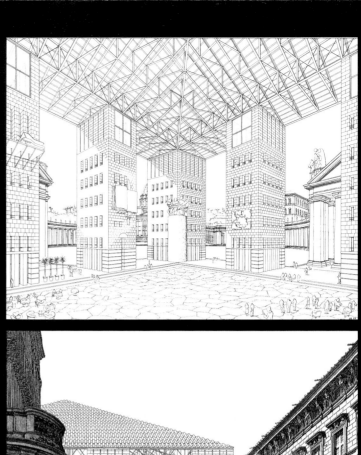

6–10. Léon Krier, *Roma Interrotta* competition entry, 1977: interventions in St Peter's Square, Piazza Navona and Via Condotti/Via Corso. Krier proposed the reinstatement of Rome's *rioni* (quarters), which saw its symbolic confirmation in the construction of monumental community centres: gargantuan loggias for public meeting and cultural activities, to be located at strategic points in the city.

11. Léon Krier, Neue Herrlichkeit and Teerhof redevelopment, Bremen, 1978

on his 75th birthday, to which the master responded in his own handwriting. To encourage me, my brother presented my fountain project to Munich University and, in 1963, I travelled to Munich to help my brother with his final thesis. I took my 'Grand tour' of Italy, having enrolled myself at Stuttgart University. I soon realized that, to pursue my architectural studies I would have to leave university. I sent a portfolio of my designs to James Stirling and in July 1968, I entered his office. In 1971, I returned to Stuttgart to open an architectural studio with my brother. After six months, we had to close through lack of work. After 18 months in the sad city of Berlin, I returned to London to continue work that I had interrupted two years before. I taught classes at the AA and realized that I would never be happy in an institution, either as a student or as a teacher. Ever since, I have been convinced that an article, a project or a conference serves better pedagogical purposes than a life dedicated to teaching. I also came to the realization that the only agreeable way to work clearly and responsibly was alone, as the roles of assistant or head derive from a spurious analysis of human situations and are meaningless.

This piece of prose – a blend of nostalgic juvenile sentiment and radical stance, lucid and self-complacent – offers us an insight into Krier's mindset: against his personal background he articulates his theory, or rather, since there is no theory, he confesses his *faith*, in the firm conviction that only this faith can redeem the world and architecture, while realizing at the same time, with ironic scepticism, that this is an impossible endeavour.

Perhaps for a moment Krier himself believed, when he met Maurice Culot, that his work could be an effective alternative to the modern approach. In the book *Léon Krier: Drawings 1967–1980*,[22] edited by Maurice Culot in 1980, Krier states that it was Culot who convinced him of the senselessness of creating any more buildings.

It distracts from the most urgent work, he writes, "the reconstruction of a global theory".[23] It is evident, however, that underpinning this global theory is anything but a primary concern for him. "The most monumental and impressive architecture will become the object of an extravagant sentimental attachment." And this again dovetails with the article by Tschumi in the *AD* issue "The Pleasure of Architecture" in which the latter dismisses any direct political or social engagement. This article has as its motto a quotation from *Architecture and Transgression*:[24] "Architecture is the ultimate erotic act. Carry it to excess and it will reveal both the traces of reason and the sensual experience of space. Simultaneously."

Krier's attitude probably found its purest expression in the 1981 exhibition *Idea as Model*[25] in New York, in which he showed, together with Massimo Scolari, *Despair of Janus*, two imaginary buildings perched high up on cliffs, separated by deep water on which a little boat indeterminately floats. The choice of title is telling. By setting his architecture in the realm of imagination he quashes, as Tschumi does in his own way, one of the deep-rooted tenets of modern architecture which has the world of the imagination coincide with that of reality. Through the gratuitous play of his paper projects, he restores architecture to its own self – albeit only in drawings and in a very limited manner. Its significance lies in the heroic evocation of an imagined – not even a lost – world. By giving it a semblance of reality, he simultaneously pierces the semblance of reality of the existing world and the belief in its essential uniqueness. Krier constantly unsettles the viewer. If one regards his drawings and designs as real projects, then Krier himself would have been the greatest destroyer of the pre-industrial city he champions. One need only look at his outrageous proposal for the Piazza Navona in Rome;[26] Paris can count its blessings that Krier's project for La Villette was never realized.[27]

Most unequivocally he expressed his views in a conversation with Peter Eisenman, held in 1983.[28] Eisenman, at the outset, aptly characterizes Krier's approach as an "architectural theology" and asks him to elaborate on its tenets. Krier does not reject this categorization, on the contrary. According to him, mankind has certain limitations and it is up to theology and philosophy to explore and determine them. The modern era is characterized by the transgression of these limits. Architecture, too, has unchanging basic principles, which find their expression in classical architecture. Only by acknowledging and applying these principles, man can build a decent and liveable world. In this regard, Krier does not deviate from the "eternal beauty" of Granpré Molière and the Delft School. Fundamentally, he remains a Catholic.

Krier counters Eisenman: "You are addressing here the existential questions posed by the last few generations. I was born after 1945 and I have no problems with 'going back'. I am not proposing to revive old problems and injustices, but to use the most intelligent and best solutions of the past. Ideas have no past and future; they are ever-present." Krier accordingly rejects any ideology of architecture: "Architecture is not about expressing existential anxiety or opinions of any kind." It is this attitude that would allow Krier to devote a book to the architecture of Albert Speer portraying him as a practitioner of the classical language of architecture.[29]

In the conversation with Eisenman he refers to Massimo Scolari who once stated that "beautiful objects are the only friends that never will betray you". According to Krier this is the best definition of the classical world. "The classical idea is quite simply the idea of the best possible", one of Krier's typical dictums,

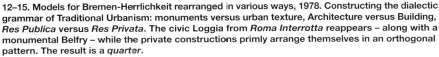

12–15. Models for Bremen-Herrlichkeit rearranged in various ways, 1978. Constructing the dialectic grammar of Traditional Urbanism: monuments versus urban texture, Architecture versus Building, *Res Publica* versus *Res Privata*. The civic Loggia from *Roma Interrotta* reappears – along with a monumental Belfry – while the private constructions primly arrange themselves in an orthogonal pattern. The result is a *quarter*.

ultimately does not mean anything – that is, beyond a closed system of its own where what is best is dogmatically defined.

Thus are revealed, in a Kantian manner, the transcendental categories, which allow the building of the city, freed from the pestiferous *Zeitgeist* and its tyranny, to unfold. Krier does himself injustice when he speaks of "going back" in time. As he admits later on in the conversation, this is just a manner of speaking. His rejection of the industrial revolution is only a parable to make clear that one is indeed born in a certain period, but does not have to be subjected to it. There are things that transcend time. Thus, the freedom of the individual is affirmed and, at the same time, it is argued that the age you end up in is not monolithic. As he demonstrates in his drawings, which figure hot-air balloons, biplanes and old-timers (in this, he reveals himself to be a melancholic modernist), he does accept industrial achievements, but not their absolute intellectual supremacy. He alone decides what to allow into his world. These drawings and designs, more so than his ideas,[30] serve to evoke that personal dream world and to suggest its reality content. Of course, they also hold the danger of his stripping this dream world naked, as Antoine Grumbach suggested with his paraphrase of Marcel Duchamp, "la mise à nu de l'architecture par ses adorateurs même".

Already in his earliest drawings, this ambiguity, as well as a certain snobbery, are apparent. In 1970, Krier made drawings for an extension of the abbey of St. Willebrord in Echternach. From a high bird's-eye view, we are offered a meticulously detailed picture of the graceful Sauer river valley and in its centre the Benedictine abbey where Krier spent his secondary school days. Opposite the monumental square-shaped abbey, which was rebuilt in the eighteenth century, we see the image of a picturesque and casual settlement dating back to Roman times – an image Krier not only

wants to preserve, but also to perfect. High above the small town the hot-air balloon of Leonidov floats, and a German biplane bombs Le Corbusier's Plainex House.

In a meticulously detailed drawing style inspired by Heinrich Tessenow, whose work he admires – a style that equally emphasizes each element – he draws, on the site of an abandoned railway yard, a grand extension, an avenue lined by a colonnade extending the nave of the abbey church. Its centre is reserved for a circus. On the banks of the Sauer River a French-style park is laid out. True, for a small town such as Echternach with its population of 4,000, there are an exceptional number of monumental buildings around – for historical reasons. Nonetheless, with Krier's new extension the proportions are inverted, and the danger of the complex dominating the scene is far from hypothetical. Rather than being "completed", Echternach is transformed into a different town.

The drawing of the new monumental buildings in barely accentuated lines is in fact a deception of sorts, perhaps also a form of self-deception. The whole is shrouded in a fine mist of irony, which makes it difficult to decide whether we are dealing with a veiled criticism of the extension or rather with an argument in its favour. The ambivalence is reinforced by the vignettes in the margins of the drawing, as well as by the fact that, with the balloon, a monument is erected to I. Leonidov, the Russian constructivist, who, at that time, was again fashionable with architects.

The unified character of the drawing, which renders the old and the new, the existing and the imaginary indistinguishable, has a far-reaching significance. It suggests a continuity and a homogeneity which do not in fact exist. Moreover, the entire built-up area stands out as a distinct figure against the surrounding nature. In one of his statements, Krier, in an Arcadian whim, actually still entertains the idea that a town lives off the yield of the surrounding land.

The many contradictions, however, do not obscure the clarity of the message. Its essence, which he would develop systematically in the following years, lies in the formal autonomy of an anonymous urban architecture as a prerequisite for any dignified existence. Krier would never indulge in the stylistic misappropriations of postmodernism. For him, style is played out for good: his classicism has nothing to do with the classicist style. In the preface to his and Demetri Porphyrios' new edition of Quatremère de Quincy's *De l'imitation*[31] from 1823, he considers the introduction of styles to be the demise of architecture, and with that he falls back on one of the premises of modernism itself. The architecture he envisions is a form of impersonal architecture not intent on formal experiments, an architecture as defined by Porphyrios in his *Classical Architecture*.[32]

After Echternach, Krier designed, on his own initiative or on invitation, urban projects for Leinfelden (1971), the Royal Mint in London (1974), Amiens (1975), Barcelona (1976), La Villette in Paris (1976), Kingston upon Hull (1977), Athens (1977), Rome (1977), Warsaw (1977), Luxembourg (1978), St Quentin-en-Yvelines (1978), Bremen (1980), Stockholm (1981), Filadelfia Calabria (1983), Poing near Munich (1983), Atlantis-Tenerife (1986), Washington (1986), Berlin-Tegel (1989), Poundbury (1989).[33]

The most complete of these designs, although not the most appealing or inspired, is his entry for the 1976 competition for La Villette, the site of the abandoned slaughterhouses of Paris. It is a project of re-urbanization, as Krier calls it, which attempts to restore the city to itself. The remodelling of this site has had a complex history extensively described and commented on by François Chaslin in *Les Paris de François Mitterand*.[34] Krier saw the competition as an opportunity to elaborate systematically and in detail his ideas about building and the city, and to develop his own "grammar". He regarded the competition and its outcome as a historical turning point in post-war architecture. He thought that La Villette was the only site in Paris where such an enterprise – the completion of the city – was still possible. As with Echternach, he wanted to turn Paris into a definitive whole, in the tradition of the garden city movement.

His first sketch is one of Paris identifying the most significant topographical features. In this drawing, the La Villette quarter is set within and connected to the historical city or what was left of it according to Krier. He describes a *quartier*, or quarter, as a city within a city, an independent entity, complete with all facilities. Such a quarter can

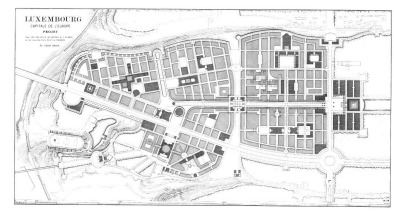

16–18. Léon Krier: masterplan for the redevelopment of the city of Luxembourg, 1978. The scheme is one of the most complete of Krier's 1970s projects; its presentation (with press conferences and national TV appearances arranged for by Maurice Culot) caused a considerable stir.

be compared to town centres in rural areas, which, in France, still remain intact in remarkable numbers, largely uncontaminated by modern architecture – an architecture which, according to Krier, is characterized by "an obsessive individualism, the superficial search for prestigious architectural images, and the imposition of experimental typologies without any historic or social justification".[35]

In Krier's urban thinking, zoning according to the Charter of Athens has no place. In an autonomous quarter everything is integrated: living, working, traffic, recreation. Like Sitte and other proponents of a "beautiful city", Krier claims that the city has an autonomous form with very specific characteristics, which have remained virtually unchanged from Roman times through the 19th century.[36] Unlike Sitte, however, Krier eschews, at least at that point, picturesque reflections.

Montmartre and the Buttes Chaumont. These concrete points of reference are of the greatest importance – and even essential to his approach. They mould the abstract pattern into a specific, local configuration, accommodating it within a historical continuity. So however universal and timeless Krier's urban pattern may be, it only comes to life through its insertion into a given reality.

Perpendicular to the axis of the Canal de l'Ourcq, a central boulevard is laid out; here cultural, political and other institutional buildings are concentrated on the wide median strip, a complete novelty in European city planning, even in pre-industrial times. Krier takes remarkable liberties in copying traditional models and applying existing typologies. His obstinate reference to the historical city seems, in fact, to be merely an excuse to introduce a self-invented, monumental and autonomous basic order, entirely in the tradition of the grand urbanist utopias.[37] Once again, however, he does not project this utopia onto virgin terrain, but rather into a local setting – a direct response to Le Corbusier's plans for Paris, Le Corbusier, too, having opted for the existing city rather than for an ideal site to promulgate his vision. Whereas the latter opens up the city, Krier condenses it and limits it to relatively clear dimensions. Krier never designed models for new cities. No matter how much autonomy he would like to attribute to them, his designs always deal with fragments.

The Latin cross of the canal and the boulevard, which serves as his point of departure, determines all further development. Alongside the stem, a majestic park is laid out crossing the intersection. Unlike Brasilia or the Hole of Washington, however, its emptiness is carefully bordered. Along the Canal de l'Ourcq, an area is reserved for recreation – a green valley stretching from the Barrière de la Villette to the Périphérique. Crossing it, the Grand

19–20. Léon Krier, Atlantis, 1988: *Portico of the Pinacotheque at dawn /* Swimming pool.

Formally, the city is made up first and foremost of residential blocks and public buildings. Together, they shape public space. In his own projects, Krier usually opts for a classicist formal vocabulary based on straight axes. Alternative configurations are not ruled out, however, as the two examples of historical patterns at the beginning of his presentation – the orthogonal urban texture of ancient Timgad in Algeria and the organic structure of the medieval town of Brive in France – reveal.

The new quarter occupies a wedge between Avenue de Flandre, Boulevard Jaurès and the Périphérique, with the Bassin de la Villette and the Canal de l'Ourcq in the middle, between

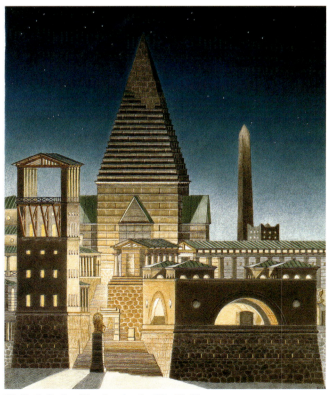

21. *Early Spring Sky*, drawing by Rita Wolff

Boulevard – one kilometre long and 95 meters wide – links two existing metro stations. Below the boulevard are large underground parking facilities.

Nesting into the arms of the cross, the quarter is automatically divided into four sections. These contain more than just housing. A hierarchy of streets is created. Residential blocks adjoining the Grand Boulevard in addition contain specialty stores, cafés, clubs, etc. The blocks, unlike those by Cerdá in Barcelona, are not unified, but rather subdivided through different types of streets open only to local traffic. This mixed-use concept is intended to restore the social integration of the population. Krier refers to the then current experiments in Italy, notably in Bologna.[38]

However much attention Krier pays to this urban design, his main concern is introducing (or, as he sees it, reintroducing) an "urban language" informing the character of the urban architecture – as evidenced by his numerous sketches of buildings and monuments. This language consists of "a limited set of general typical (residential) and aesthetic (proportional) rules". The distinction between the monumental public buildings on the Grand Boulevard and the anonymous architecture of the quarters is primordial. The collective pathos and magnificence of the public buildings – "they are not to be understood" – go back to the crystallized typologies of the theatre, the library, the hotel, and refer to historical models by Ledoux, Loos, and even Le Corbusier. For residential architecture, Krier refers to the tradition of Parisian housing. "This, then, is the basis of a possible collective language where the production of meaning, instead of being preoccupied with simple architectural objects, could possibly express a new social and urban reality." And although Krier goes a long way to define the rules and prescribe the materials, according to him infinite variations remain possible.

He does not provide any clue as to what these residential streets will actually look like – we only get to see a section. According to Krier, not much happens there anyway: all the action will take place in the main public spaces. It is when picturing these spaces that Krier really gets going and reveals his actual intentions. All functional preoccupations merely serve as a pretext to evoke an Arcadian dream where, as in the paintings of Poussin, figures relax and move graciously. This – the rejection of everyday reality and the creation of an ideal realm where man feels like a child of the gods – is probably where the true essence of Krier's classicism lies[39]. For him, actual reality coincides with that dream.

In the park, a man-made Hill of the Winds is erected, a circular pyramid, similar to the Waterloo monument, crowned by the House of the Winds. This open dwelling with the fluttering swaths of cloth is a frequently recurring symbol. There are more monuments in La Villette, however. The Museum of the Automobile and the Museum of the Flying-machine are located on a vast terrace with a view of the dome of the Hôtel des Invalides. Automobiles and airplanes here have become, as it were, toys from a different century, looked upon with a certain tenderness by the people Krier has out for a stroll. Within his vision, everything remains coherent. He does not let the times in which he lives challenge him, as if those times constituted reality. He claims the right to elevate his own vision to reality.

If we have dwelt on La Villette a short moment, it is because in this design the relationship between dream and reality is articu-

22. *Atlantis*, Tenerife, 1988. Painting by Carl Laubin

lated most poignantly. But that is after all not what really holds Krier's fascination. One has to turn to a design such as Atlantis, the holiday resort on the Canary Islands, to uninhibitedly enjoy the monumental hedonism. There, Krier's paradise materializes as a densely built city populated by figures that seem to have stepped right out of Le Corbusier's drawings. The reference to the great master is not coincidental, since all that Krier has done is basically couch Le Corbusier's ideas of the good life differently and, in a sense, pervert them. Colin Rowe has described Léon Krier as "the Le Corbusier of our day."[40] Through the radicality of his affirmations and the charming naiveté of his drawings, Krier has succeeded in holding the attention of the architectural community for more than a decade and thus succeeded in writing a stirring episode of postmodern architecture. He has not succeeded in actually realizing, within the fabric of the contemporary city, the festive spaces he dreamed of. And, all in all, that is only for the better, since what little has been realized is incredibly barren. If indeed he championed primordial values, in the way he chose to represent them they became their own antithesis.

Notes

1 Antoine Grumbach in: *L'Architecture d'aujourd'hui*, 179, May/June 1975, p. 69, "Les frères Krier. Le retour du refoulé". As a complement to this, one could cite the following statement by Tschumi: "Yet it is the very difficulty of uncovering architecture that makes it intensely desirable. This unveiling is part of the pleasure of architecture." In: *Architectural Design*, vol. 47, 1977, 3, p. 215.
2 Vol. 47, 1977, 3, p.187–213. Our subject here is Léon Krier (born 1946 in Luxembourg), the younger brother of Rob (born 1938 in Grevenmacher). He was deeply impressed with his brother's work and actually teamed up with him for a while. Unlike Rob, who chose to practice architecture, Léon would, more or less, be forced to withdraw into discourse. Colin Rowe said of the two brothers: "Of the brothers Krier, no doubt Leon is the more mercurial temperament and, perhaps, Robert the more serious architect: but, since Leon now seems to have retired – in a fit of pique? – to play the piano in Provence, who is to say?" Rowe, "Urban Space", in: *As I Was Saying*, vol. 3, The MIT Press, Cambridge 1995, p. 261. In his essay "The Revolt of Senses", one of the texts on Léon Krier (in: *As I Was Saying*, vol. 3, p. 271), Colin Rowe, a "friend" of Krier's, writes: "So Leon makes some assumption of sentiment; and on the whole, I am prepared to accept this assumption. However, until comparatively recently my own relationship with him was never the very easiest. In the first case, he was an impressible *enfant terrible* working for Stirling, the results of which he has made everyone aware of; and then, after that, he became a fashionable reputation with slightly Marxian and quite gratuitously anti-Catholic undertones. This was the first demonstration of *architettura razionale* in the early seventies, when, recognizing a capacity which I loved, I found myself offended that it should become asso-

ciated with a program which, to me, could only appear misguided, intellectualistic, and absurdly abstruse."

3 In retrospect, the title "The Pleasure of Architecture" suits the work of Culot/Krier better than "The Role of Ideology", even though, at that point, they were convinced they had an ideological message. "The Pleasure of Architecture" might also refer to the cover illustration which represents the "artists' promenade" around the park of La Villette.

4 Transcript of lecture, *The Modernity of Traditional Architecture*, Delft, 27 January, 2000. In addition to Tschumi, Krier also had contact with Rem Koolhaas and his cirle at the AA school. On this, Krier reflects: "It was a Balkan situation, ideologically. But we fought as friends and that was the revolution, that was the new thing, that here were people coming from different races, religions, total different backgrounds being friends."

5 Even Krier does not waste a word on it anymore in the account of his career. See note 4.

6 Krier, in particular, can boast international success. He is mentioned in every single anthology on the architecture of the late twentieth century. He was invited to the conference on architecture at the Virginia School of Architecture (where he also taught) in 1982 and to the one at the University of Illinois in Chicago in 1986. See *The Charlottesville Tapes*, Rizzoli, New York, 1985, and *The Chicago Tapes*, Rizzoli, New York, 1987. Further proof of success is offered by Charles Jencks, *Post-Modernism. The New Classicism in Art and Architecture*, Academy Editions, London, 1987, where he serves as a point of reference. Particular attention is also paid to him in Charles Jencks, *Current Architecture*, Academy Editions, London, 1982, as well as in *The New paradigma in Architecture*, Yale University Press, New Haven and London, 2002; Robert A.M. Stern, *Modern Classicism*, Thames and Hudson, London, 1988; Roberto Masiero, *Neoclassico. L'attualità: arte architettura design*, Marsilio Editori, Venice, 1990; Andreas Papadakis & Harriet Wilson, *New Classicism*, Rizzoli, New York, 1990; Ole Bouman and Roemer van Toorn, *The Invisible in Architecture*, Academy Editions, London, 1994; Jan Brand et al., *Panorama van de avant-gardes*, Akademie voor Beeldende Kunsten, Arnhem, 1981. In addition to the article by Antoine Grumbach cited above, the reader is referred to Colin Rowe's essay on Léon Krier, "The Revolt of the Senses," in Rowe, *As I Was Saying*, The MIT Press, Cambridge, Massachusetts, 1995. On the partnership between Krier/Culot see, among others, Geert Bekaert, *Hedendaagse Architectuur in België*, Lannoo, Tielt, 1995; Jacques Lucan, *France. Architecture 1965–1988*, Electa Moniteur, Paris, 1989; Heinrich Klotz, *Moderne und Postmoderne. Architektur der Gegenwart 1960–1980*, Vieweg & Sohn, Braunschweig/Wiesbaden, 1984.

7 Maurice Culot, in: *Declaration de Bruxelles 1980*, Brussels, Editions des Archives d'Architecture Moderne, p. 14.

8 In "Program versus Paradigm: Otherwise Casual Notes on the Pragmatic, the Typical, and the Possible", in: Colin Rowe, *As I Was Saying*, vol. 2, The MIT Press, Cambridge, Massachusetts, 1995, p. 29, Colin Rowe asserts with regard to Robert and Léon Krier and other neo-rationalists: "I also ask why ... the neo-Rationalists in general are so characteristically uptight? Just why do so many of them, while rejecting the morphology of Le Corbusier, feel obliged, after a good fifty years have gone by, to recapitulate the pitch of his polemic? Why, when forms are repudiated, does a certain psychology persist?" Leaving open the question to which extent the positions of Krier and Culot were indebted to then current movements and ideas, particularly in the field of urban renewal, the reader, in this regard, is referred to the works and publications of Aldo Rossi, Robert Venturi, Lewis Mumford, Jane Jacobs, Oscar Newman, Robert Goodman, Colin Rowe, and many others. 1967 saw the publication of my *Het einde van de architectuur*, Limburgse Akademische Bibliotheek, Hasselt, 1967.

9 *Progetto e Utopia. Architettura e sviluppo capitalistico*, Laterza, Roma–Bari, 1973. The English-language edition, *Architecture and Utopia: Design and Capitalist Development*, was published in 1976 by the MIT Press, Cambridge, Massachusetts.

10 Grahame Shane gives an account of this event in "Culot/Contextualism and Conscience", in: *AD*, vol. 47, 3, 1977, p. 189.

11 In *Nouveaux plaisirs d'architectures. Les pluralismes de la création en Europe et aux Etats-unis depuis 1968*, Centre Georges Pompidou, Paris, 1985, p. 51.

12 *Exposition organisée par les Archives de l'Architecture Moderne placée sous les auspices du Musée d'Ixelles et de l'Ecole Nationale Supérieure et des Arts Visuels*. Editions du Musée D'Ixelles, Brussels, 1969. The orthopedic clinic of Dr. Van Neck in Brussels, built in 1910, is considered one the very first manifestations of modern architecture in Belgium.

13 Jacques Aron, *La Cambre et l'architecture. Un regard sur le Bauhaus belge*, Architecture + Recherches, no. 17, Mardaga, Brussels, 1982.

14 See the special issue of *Wonen-TA/BK*, no. 15/16, august 1975, compiled by Francis Strauven.

15 *Architectural Design*, vol. 47, 1977, 3, p. 199.

16 *Contreprojets Controprogetti Counterprojects* is the title of the catalog published by Krier and Culot in connection with their contribution to the architecture exhibition at the Biennale of Venice in 1980. There, they appropriate Le Corbusier's method of underscoring their rejection of modern buildings using red crosses.

17 An example we find in the competition for the Rue de Laeken in Brussels. See *Appel aux jeunes architectes européens. La reconstruction d'une rue historique au centre de Bruxelles*, AAM, Bruxelles, 1990. This competition resulted in the 'reconstruction' of part of an urban block; a scheme that, while referring to traditional bourgeois residential construction, in effect is entirely detached from its urban and social context.

18 *Bulletin d'information*, no. 8, May 1976, of the *Archives d'Architecture Moderne*.

19 See also *Oppositions*, no. 14, The MIT Press, Cambridge, Massachusetts, 1978.

20 This publication dovetails with the Italian movement that emerged in 1973 under the name *Archittura razionale*. See E. Bonfanti, R. Bonicalzi, A. Rossi, M. Scolari, D. Vitale, *Architettura Razionale*, Franco Angeli Editore, Milan, 1973.

21 *Design Quarterly*, no. 113–114, Walker Art Center, Minneapolis, 1980.

22 *Archives d'Architecture Moderne*, Brussels, MDCCCLXXX (sic)

23 Krier offers a good synopsis of this theory in Muriel Emanuel, *Contemporary Architects*, The Macmillan Press, London, 1980, p. 440: "My projects are a series of polemical statements. They are not experiments; they are reflections on the specific structure of the European city (the streets, the squares, the communities) – a meditation on the true and constant elements of architecture and building and their necessary and precise relationships within the urban and social fabric. For architecture to be an art, building must be a craft. A reconstruction of these cannot be a matter of industry nor can it be a matter of science, it is a cultural and a political project. A new generation is now discovering the urban cultures of pre-industrial Europe as documents of intelligence, memory and pleasure. This investigation is taking place on different levels – political, cultural, economic, – all over Europe, it leads to a clear conclusion. The necessity is for a global plan which opposes the global destruction of European culture through industrialization."

24 In *Oppositions*, no. 7, 1976

25 *Idea as Model*, Institute for Architecture and Urban Studies, Catalogue 3, Rizzoli, New York, 1981, p. 48–49. See also Maurice Culot, *Le désespoir de Janus*, AAM, no. 9, 1976, p. 1–2.

26 'Roma interrotta', in: *Architectural Design*, vol. 49, 1979, no. 3–4.

27 In "Elegy for the Vacant Lot" (1985), in: Rem Koolhaas and Bruce Mau, *S,M,L,XL*, 010 Publishers, Rotterdam, 1995, Rem Koolhaas writes: "In the first La Villette competition (1976) the architects were free to propose a whole new quartier – a fragment of the new, more humane city of the future. Offered the opportunity to imagine an ideal episode of late-20th-century life, hurtling en plein vitesse toward the third millenium, they proposed, finally, an environment fit for glass blowers and horseshoers driving prewar Citroëns. Later – half-emboldened by what? – this call to arms for the reconstruction of the European City became even more arrogant and dogmatic in the militancy of its declaration. Shame to all those who signed the Declaration of Palermo." This declaration was drafted by Culot/Krier and, in addition to them, signed by Pierluigi Nicolin, Angelo Villa, and Antoine Grumbach. It was published in *AAM*, no. 14, 1978.

28 *Skyline*, Februari 1983, p. 12–15, translation in *AAM*, no. 28, 1985.

29 *Albert Speer. Architecture 1932–1942*, Forword Albert Speer, Editor Léon Krier, Introduction Lars Olof Larsson, AAM, Brussels, 1985

30 This led Philip Johnson to remark: "He can talk about what he pleases – I really want to praise him as an artist. I don't care what he says." In: *The Charlottesville Tapes*, Rizzoli, New York, 1985, p. 28.

31 *Archives d'Architecture Moderne*, Brussels, 1980

32 Academy Editions, London, 1991. Léon Krier is not mentioned in this book. Already in previous publications, Porphyrios had distanced himself from Krier with whom he had initially collaborated frequently.

33 A survey of these projects is provided in Demetri Porphyrios, "Léon Krier. Houses, Palaces, Cities", *Architectural Design*, vol. 54, 1984, no. 7/8.

34 Gallimard, Paris, 1985.

35 *Architectural Design*, vol. 47, 1977, no. 3, p. 201.

36 At the Venice Biennale International Architecture Exhibition, *La Presenza del Passato*, in 1980 Léon Krier presented together with Culot the reconstruction of the facade of a Roman house.

37 Colin Rowe refers to Krier's utopia as a "Little Utopia": "For Léon Krier, with his genuine simplicity, has accomplished the unlikely act of restoring Utopia. No doubt a very miniature and limited Utopia it is." In *As I Was Saying*, The MIT Press, Cambridge, Massachusetts, 1995, p. 275.

38 At the time, Bologna was at the center of attention because of far-reaching reforms introduced by the communist city council, aimed not only at restoring the historic town center, but also at revitalizing run-down neighbourhoods by granting them a considerable degree of institutional and political autonomy. See P.L. Cervellati and R. Scannavini ed., *Bologna: politica e metodologia del restauro nei centri storici*, Il Mulino, Bologna, 1973; *Conoscenza e coscienza della città. Una politica per il centro storico*, Comune di Bologna, Bologna, 1974.

39 See Thomas Pavel, *L'art de l'éloignement. Essai sur l'imagination classique*, Gallimard, Paris, 1996.

40 Rowe did this not without a certain sarcasm. He continued: "and, like Le Corbusier, he is already beginning to think of himself in the third person." And, later: "At the expense of the world he *must* be engaged in a private joke." Colin Rowe, *As I was Saying*, vol. 3, The MIT Press, Cambridge, Massachusets, 1995, p. 271.

Looking Back without Anger

Léon Krier

During my brief stay at Stuttgart University in 1966 I had soon found out that there was no future for me there. Nevertheless, in the magazines in the library I had discovered the work of Walter Pichler and James Stirling. I knew Ungers' projects as my brother Rob had worked there in 1964–'65, and I was at once fascinated and horrified by them. However, a visit to his Märkische Viertel housing in Berlin in 1968 (after attending the huge anti-Vietnam war demonstration) quickly put me off that trail. After being given a work offer from Stirling I visited Walter Pichler, only to find out that he had no office and worked as an artist without assistants. So I ended up at Stirling's.

Even though James Stirling seemed a jovial man, he was in fact a very complicated and difficult character. At the time he was in a profound crisis, and everybody in the office was aware that the Oxford student residences under construction were a dead end. The history library in Cambridge was a big disappointment and held none of the promises of the published axonometric and model. Likewise, Runcorn housing wasn't exciting anyone in the office, and even though Stirling had promised a "Bath" of the twentieth century, we were quite aware that it was going to be a slum. Though the engineers at Felix Samuely's had warned us that prefabrication wouldn't mean any economies of scale, Stirling refused to discuss this issue. For him it had to be industrialized – whatever its cost. In fact, in situ construction turned out to be cheaper and the prefabricated external panels were but an industrial 'pastiche'. Stirling went on lying about it at conferences and in publications. He never forgave me for reminding him in public at a conference in Barcelona in 1976 about this issue. I then understood that Modernism was a matter of style and belief, and not at all about technology and facts. Even though the builder and his assistants had explained to Stirling long and large that the prefabrication details of the St Andrews student residences were almost certainly leading to serious water penetration, he decided to push ahead with them; the buildings leaked like a sieve and Stirling lost the case in court. Stirling had experimented in the early fifties with vernacular forms and construction methods but in the late sixties all this was long forgotten. Despite all the constructional disasters piling up, he never managed to revise his position on industrial building.

Le Corbusier was for me still the greatest artist of the twentieth century but I knew by then that urbanistically he had produced only disasters and that his buildings were very immature from a

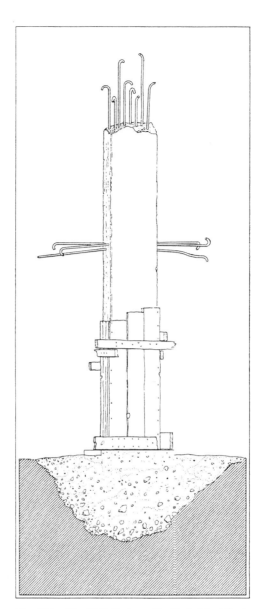

Léon Krier, *The Sixth Order or the End of Architecture*

technological point of view, despite the grandiose and lyrical promises. Travelling around Europe to visit buildings by modernist masters I discovered instead – or rather rediscovered – the modernity and genius of traditional architecture. With the exception of Le Corbusier's Ronchamp, the main facades of the villa at Garches, Maison Plainex and Weissenhof in Stuttgart, and Terragni's Villa Bianca at Seveso, I had had very little emotions corresponding to the expectations raised by modernist propaganda and literature. To claim that this extreme reduction of means of construction, organization and expression was to replace the entire worldwide apparatus of traditional vernacular and classical architecture was to me becoming more and more incomprehensible. It was by then evident to me that modernist architecture, even in its masterworks, could in no way be claimed to be superior or even equal to traditional urbanism and architecture. Why then should the latter be called "historical" if it still worked and was relevant

James Stirling as portrayed by Krier in 1972

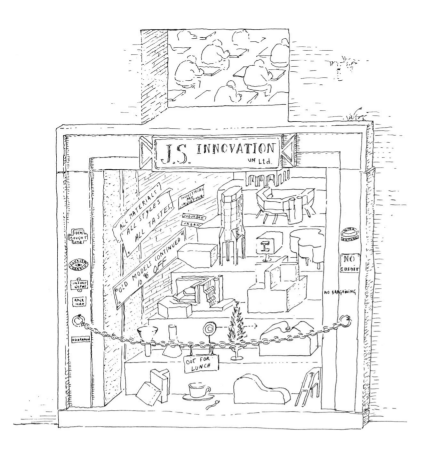

l'architecte de l'ère machiniste

today? I started wondering. Stirling was absolutely not interested to engage in discussions on the subject. When I worked on the Siemens headquarters for him I wanted to marry space technology and Palladio, but he was more interested in the striking *image*. "What's the image?" he would always ask. The fact that the object was half a mile long would not modify his attitude. Privately I was working with my brother on the Karlsruhe town centre competition and when he insisted it should be a Yona Friedman type mega-space-frame I decided I had to go back to the basics. Camillo Sitte, and travelling through northern Italy were my Damascus experience. Echternach and Derby town centre were the first hesitant attempts to change course.

I had intended to finish my studies after the Stirling office experience but I was offered a teaching job by Elia Zenghelis before that was possible. My own projects had by then been widely published and exhibited at the Triennale in Milan. At the AA there was a strong sense of solidarity among those who were interested in architecture as an Art Form. We were lined up against those who believed it purely to be a political, sociological and industrial phenomenon. The AA was a platform where all the tendencies had a chance to articulate themselves and I was not surprised that it should be Peter Cook who hosted my exhibition "Rational Architecture" in his Art Net gallery in 1975 (which Maurice Culot produced in 1978 in book form). I found Archigram's first drawings amusing but not more. Mike Webb had been a true talent but had dried up. Cedric Price I found to be a puffed-up, incomprehensible snob and, above all, a very bad architect. His Camden Art Centre was clearly the product of an artistic scatter-brain. At the time, the Smithsons still exerted intellectually terror over many of their former pupils but I always found them artistically talentless and intellectually pretentious. I was disgusted by their Hunstanton school, Robin Hood Gardens, etc. They had produced nothing but instant architectural slums, based on vacuous ideas, mostly borrowed from early pre-World War II modernism.

The Rational Architecture exhibition was my response to the Triennale exhibit of 1973. I was very disappointed by that show, and found the presence of recent Soviet slums like Halle-Neustadt a scandal and a disgrace. Rossi was not a man to discuss his premises whereas the purpose of my exhibition was to establish some common basis for discussing urbanism and architecture beyond the then fashionable political categories. That is why the exhibits were organized in a typological order: the quarter, the street, the square, the block, the park, the urban fabric, the monument, and so on. Ungers came but was upset that I refused to show his latest megastructures. Instead, I picked Grünzug Süd, the Tiergarten Museum and the German embassy in Rome. These were emblematic projects but Ungers himself seemed at the time to be unaware of it; he enjoyed, however, being challenged whereas Rossi never forgave me for not liking his Gallaratese where he had, after all, made the effort to drive me to. Even though I knew Colin Rowe personally from dinners at Stirling's, I had no idea of his urban interests and projects. I had been very moved by his "Transparency II" essay but Stirling, who could have encouraged the exchange, kept the contacts on a purely domestic social level. The evenings at his home were not about ideas but about the Stirling cult. That is at least what I remember most. He

Top: 10th Anniversary Letter to J.S.
Left: *The Exterminating Angel / Master of the Machine Age*

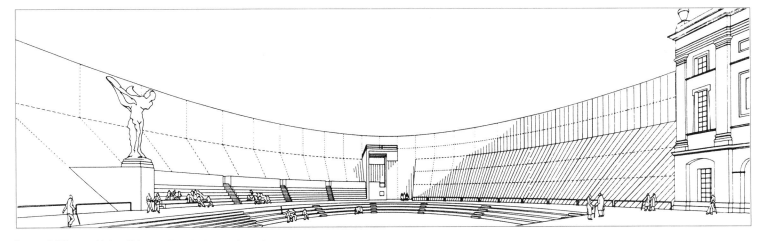

James Stirling and Léon Krier: project for Derby Civic Center, 1970

promised several times to take me as an assistant to Yale, but nothing came of it.

At the same time, it was also becoming clear to me that the liberation from alienating industrial work was not necessarily leading to an earthly paradise. When I provoked Tafuri at a conference in San Sebastian in 1976 to reveal his ultimate goals instead of hiding behind a beard and vaporous oracular formulae, he shouted at me that taking power was the only goal and all the rest was futile. I replied: "what's the purpose of taking power if you cannot say for what purpose?" I was interested in William Morris' combination of socialism and craftsmanship, but was soon to find out that they were contradictions in terms. Industrialism, modern mass society and Modernism I then no longer considered a goal but a phase of transition. To Modernism, industrialism had a metaphysical, transcendental content: it is an end in itself whereas pragmatically seen, it is merely another form of organizing *some* human productions, not all of them. As I was revolting against

the totalitarian excesses of industrialism, I was clearly, for a while, happily amalgamating issues of capitalism, kitsch, and the end of culture, cities and architecture in general. During this period, I was very much influenced in my readings by Al Goergen, a friend and assistant of T. W. Adorno. To us, Adorno's writings were pure balm; he was also unashamedly nostalgic for the delights of bourgeois culture. I *felt* very left-wing, but had little respect for left-wing "Real Politics"; I was also disaffected by the fact that my left-wing acquaintances like Tafuri, Rossi, Frampton, Colquohoun and their circles were not interested in debating the fundamental issues and legitimacy of socialism. We were truly fashionable Marxists and of course uncritical apostles of the 1970s Zeitgeist.

My discovery of the work of Quinlan Terry and my admiration for David Watkin's *Morality and Architecture* definitely led to cutting ties with left-wing friends and supporters like Frampton, Vidler, Tafuri, Gandelsonas etc. It was the contact with Jaquelin Robertson (through Peter Eisenman),

deux formes d'accumulation

Léon Krier: *Two Forms of Accumulation*

"Anti-Industrial Resistance" at the La Cambre school of Architecture, late 1970s. Krier's enormous influence on the work produced by Culot's students is evident: they adopt the ideology and idiom and quote and copy very literally from his drawings. Most projects are *Contreprojets*. Above: Brigitte D'Helft, Michel Verliefden, Project for a monumental Panorama in the centre of Brussels, 1977. The space pays homage to Krier's Derby design, a fact acknowledged by the presence, in the foreground, of Krier's rendering of a bewildered Stirling. Right, top to bottom: three images from *La Jonction Nord-Midi*, 1979, by S. Birkiye, G. Busieau, P. Neirinck: Project for the Reconstruction of the Brigittines quarter (with Krier watching on, centre stage), The Portico of the Master Stonecutters and an impression of street life near the revamped Carrefour de l'Europe.

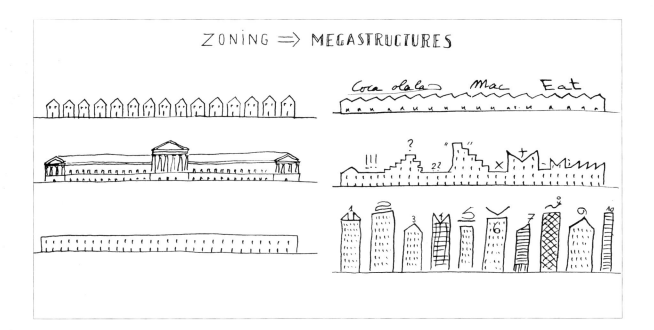

then dean of the School of Architecture at Charlottesville, which changed my superficial anti-Americanism and led me to revise not only my architectural and urbanist goals but also my very infantile political outlook and critique. I began to understand that democracy was not a luxury but a question of survival.

Maurice Culot wanted to take the *Rational Architecture* exhibit to Brussels in 1976. Peter Cook introduced us for that purpose and we have been friends ever since. For the first two years whenever we met, I would ask him jokingly "and this time Maurice, you are going to explain to me why you are a communist and what socialism means". He never did, but we became friends through thick and thin. He loved my Echternach project, but asked me in public to explain why I designed such ugly buildings for La Villette. He mentioned Port Grimaud as a model, which in 1976 I was not ready to endow as an *exemplum*. The reason was that I didn't yet know how to do it. Bologna was certainly a model, both architecturally and sociologically. I had learned Italian by reading Cervellatti's *Typologia e Morfologia dei Centri Storici*, which was for me infinitely more important than anything coming from the Milan, Venice or Rome Polytechnics.

In 1976, projects by Culot's students were architecturally without direction; they copied anything that was in the magazines. Maurice then disciplined them by narrowing the models to copy. My master plan for Luxembourg was specifically intended to summarize a model for urban and architectural analysis and project, both critique and proposal. René Schoonbrodt was completely against the notion of 'quartier' at the time, but Maurice helped me not only to publicize my projects and get all the press-media concentrating for weeks on the Luxembourg project; he also had his students help colouring drawings, making posters and printing brochures. Certainly it was Culot who helped me espouse traditional architecture no longer just for operating in historic centres but also for *ex-novo* proposals. I was only slowly getting out of an "all or nothing" attitude. Nevertheless, when I resigned from the commission I received together with my brother to build a large urban block in the Lindenstrasse in Berlin,

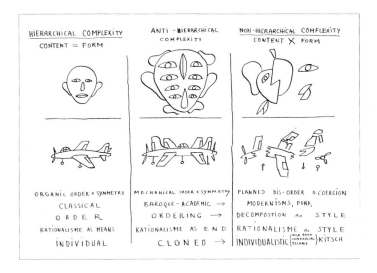

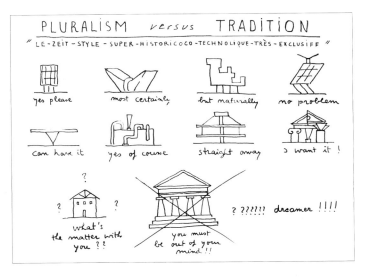

Various cartoons by Léon Krier from the early 1980s

Léon Krier with Merrill-Pastor: Village Hall, Windsor (Florida), 1996–98

writings. Evidently a lot of people come up with similar solutions, when confronting similar problems. However, Modernism is like religions in that it incapacitates even the most intelligent people from learning from past mistakes. We are not even learning the hard way and most contemporary buildings and settlements are still very costly experiments. New Urbanism is addressing all these issues in a global way and it is a cause of hope that things may improve on a large scale fairly soon.

Also, I still believe today that problems of alienating versus satisfying work-activity are critical as ever. Happiness/pleasure and physical/mental effort are existentially linked. A workless, jobless leisure society is the ultimate nightmare, where the individual dissolves in his own existential purposelessness. He goes literally mad over the unfathomable mystery of his own existence. The reconstruction of traditional cities and crafts does not respond to any of our transcendental anxieties, but it certainly facilitates the pursuit of happiness for a great many people.

1977, Maurice was a major support. He thought that the conditions were not right to build and badly compromised buildings would necessarily weaken the strength of our theoretical stance. Looking at what was actually built I tend to agree even today. Not only the situation, but also I myself, was not ripe for building at the time.

The relation of architecture and mono-functional zoning became clear to me when I worked on Runcorn housing for Stirling. The area was the size of a large historic centre and yet Stirling had one building section only, and one type of concrete panel, which was cloned *ad infinitum* with obviously foreseeable toxic results. A UNIFORM DEVELOPMENT PROGRAMME NECESSARILY LEADS INTO ARCHITECTURAL DISASTER LAND, BE IT OF A HARD- OR A SOFT-CORE NATURE. Echternach was the first project where I intuitively felt that my modernist vocabulary was totally inadequate to deal with the kind of problem I wanted to address. This all happened while I worked on Derby Civic Centre for Stirling. My sketches were at first dabblings with a more traditional architecture, but Stirling had them replaced in the last week by the patent glazing façade.

Camillo Sitte was a true revelation while working on these projects. Rob was working with Frei Otto and interested in Yona Friedman. It took me six months to get him turned around in early 1970. Later Rob dedicated his 'Urban Space' to Sitte and me, probably for that reason. I was still quite unable to write anything coherent and it was only the news in 1972 that the City Park in Luxembourg was going to be built over with a multi-level parking structure that made the boiling pot explode and enabled me to write my first coherent essay. It was published in a Luxembourg newspaper and was a first sketch of my later master plan. In that year Rob did some catching up with a series of projects where Frei Otto and Friedman had been blissfully left behind and the Krier brothers became a unified front. Rob also did some pre-dating and reworking of older projects of his, which ironed out the divergences and differences, which had been very explicit until then.

Strangely I was never able to read Jane Jacobs (nor Christopher Alexander), and only recently did I read most of Colin Rowe's

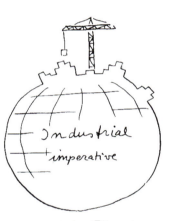

The Planet
an endless, trivial
messy & noisy
building-site

The World
as a solid, permanent
practical and beautiful
house (for) of mankind

Epilogue: Enter Architecture
Martin van Schaik

On 26 January 2000 a large number of people flock to the main auditorium of the School of Architecture in Delft to witness an odd gathering. Poet Simon Vinkenoog clamorously opens the proceedings, setting the stage for an academic war of words. John Heintz exceeds all expectations by bravely countering Mark Wigley's reading of New Babylon. Wigley – just in from the New York Drawing Center seminar in October 1999 – presents his study of Constant's work on paper. Jean-Clarence Lambert, writer/historian and a close friend of the artist, perhaps best summarizes New Babylon by capturing the tragic reality of Constant's project: "The revolution didn't come".

Following this exposé, Simon Sadler and architectural historian Thilo Hilpert outline their views of post-war developments in architecture, preparing the ground for Peter Cook. With his trademark on-stage antics, Cook presents his *Plug-in City* and the work of Archigram, vividly describing his confrontation in 1963 with Constant's colourful slides at the ICA and underlining his fundamental disinterest in all matters political when talking about architecture. The most impressive and moving performance of the day, however, comes from Adolfo Natalini, speaking about his Superstudio work for the first time in over 20 years and showing the film "LIFE" from *The Fundamental Acts* cycle. Natalini presents his group's projects as a form of political criticism through architectural means: "The very basic idea of the grid was we had something better to do than architecture". Interestingly, Natalini's grand performance seduces Mark Wigley into drawing a daring comparison between the conscious anti-architecture of the Italian collective and Constant's mission in New Babylon, supposedly a "project to kill art". It would have been interesting to hear Constant's reaction, even if he might have readily agreed with Wigley's implication that Superstudio displayed the same poetic masochism and cultural guerrilla tactics as pre-World War II vanguards such as Dada.

If Day One climaxes in the autobiographical self-enlargement and negative (yet occasionally *positive*) utopianism of Superstudio – Hans Hollein's rocks and radiator grills replaced by equally iconic and ubiquitous "architectural histograms" – Day Two invariably culminates in the confrontation of Léon Krier, Elia Zenghelis and Constant, who has abandoned his easel for the afternoon to see what people have to say about his work. Philosopher Hans Achterhuis, historian Franziska Bollerey and theorist Hilde Heynen provide the appropriate upbeat. Constant's appearance in Delft on 27 January, roughly 20 years after his previous visit, is the last in a long and historic series. In early 1961, Constant had lectured in Delft for the first time (on invitation of students of the *Bouwkundige Studiekring*, an elite student's club under the auspices of Jo van den Broek, who had witnessed his exposé in the Stedelijk Museum in December of the previous year). The discussions between Constant and the students, as well as the artist's wonderfully defiant lecture, were published in the BSK magazine *Delftse School* and were crucial in bringing about Delft's radical transformation from a deeply conservative institution under architect M. J. Granpré Molière to a school that embraced modernism in all its forms. Constant was a Trojan horse that helped to usher in change.

Tensions mount, therefore, in expectation of the exchange between Krier – intellectually speaking closely akin to Granpré Molière – and Constant. But what was almost to be expected actually happens: *seeming* opposites attract. In the panel discussion following Krier's lengthy speech on "The Modernity of Traditional Architecture", Constant's reaction is mild, despite Krier's respectful attacks on what he perceives to be Constant's idea of a "life without work". Far more scorn is heaped upon the back of Kas Oosterhuis – a designer best known for his blob-like "interactive" pavilion architecture – whose projects Constant dismisses as a "spectacle", insisting they have nothing to do with New Babylon. For Oosterhuis, a declared admirer of Constant's *magnum opus*, the experience is humiliating. In any case, the concluding discussion makes clear that Krier's notion of non-alienating work – from which true pleasure and existential satisfaction can be derived – and Constant's notion of creativity are in fact very close:

Constant: I'm not against work in the widest sense, not against activity, but production work, the work …
Krier: You mean unpleasant work? You want to automate only unpleasant work? I think everybody agrees.

An important point, however, needs to be made: a Léon Krier far milder than expected had landed at Schiphol airport. The message the architect conveys in his speech is one of conciliation: he calls for an end to ideological oppositions and an acceptance of the inevitable competition between different tastes, beliefs and design strategies. Krier appears to have taken up residence in Exodus' *Square of the Captive Globe* – "Now let's see what works best" – yet he immediately makes it clear that in this plea for *ideological* parallelism, the search for purity – both stylistic and intellectual – should definitely not be aborted. As Elia Zenghelis rightly remarks during the closing panel discussion, it is in this emphasis on internal consistency and aesthetic perfectionism, regardless of whether a city is modernist or traditional, that Krier's viewpoint has remained essentially unchanged. Needless to say, given his allergy to the imperfect and the incomplete, Krier finds himself diametrically opposed to Constant's stylistic

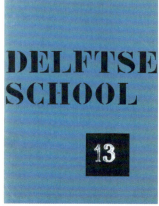

Constant lecturing in Delft, 1961. Van den Broek (left) joins in

convictions, although in his holistic and critical outlook he remains the only one at the symposium who can match (and counter) Constant's vision of a new world.

Indeed in more than one way, the younger Léon Krier – in his legendary collaboration with Maurice Culot especially – provides a fascinating model for how the architectural academy might *confront* reality. The "counter-projects" that Culot and Krier developed with the students of the La Cambre architecture school in Brussels in the late 1970s are both architecturally pure and politically charged. Without entering into in a discussion about the *quality* of the architecture and urbanism produced under Culot's guidance, one can say that the strategy was one of playful defiance: ivory-tower architecture was pitted against the senseless destruction of an old city, a grassroots guerrilla tactic in which drawing became a tool for political activism. La Cambre acted as a temporary autonomous zone. Not surprisingly, these unruly festivities were not to last very long: by ministerial decree, Culot and over 30 of his fellow teachers were sent packing in 1979 and the architecture school was closed down. The La Cambre evictions also mark the premature end of the heroic "The Only Path for Architecture" that Culot and Krier had outlined in *Oppositions* in 1978. The "Reconstruction of the European City" was thereafter to die a slow death – despite Prince Charles's energetic embrace of it – while, ironically, "The New Urbanism" in the United States would adopt its concepts and use them to fire up one of the most successful urban planning movements of the late twentieth and early twenty-first century.

Rem Koolhaas once remarked that Krier – in *La Villette* and other projects – designed a life to go with the architectural form: an environment that could only be inhabited by glass-blowers cruising in pre-war Citroens. Little could he expect that wealthy Americans with laptops and cell phones would soon feel quite happy in it. In the 1970s, the friendly animosity between the young Koolhaas and the even younger Krier – with Zenghelis somehow mediating – was outspoken. Nonetheless, the idealized Manhattan that Koolhaas dreamt up in *Delirious New York*, and that he and Zenghelis (together with their wives) drew during the 1970s, unabashedly toys with the ideal. In their mythical New York, the redeemed and magically rewritten "reality as found" of Koolhaas and the childhood dreams of Zenghelis – also embodied in *Exodus* – culminate and fuse. Like Krier's world, filled with Corbusian gags and swooping *Farman Goliaths* over Paris, the "Manhattanist" universe of OMA is a collection of boyish

fascinations and mature delights: from the lush rooftop swimming pools to the Tom-of-Finland locker room men inhabiting this frugally hedonistic universe (in fact, the famous drawing was reportedly done by Koolhaas himself, in a patient effort to emulate the style). OMA's early work is a closed mythical universe, like Krier's: it is still the finest work the office has ever produced – underlining that the world may occasionally be best served by architecture polemically staying on the paper and in the realm of magic and dreams.

But let us return to January 2000. If Krier and Constant can get along with each other, Constant and Elia Zenghelis cannot. After a brief introductory statement, Zenghelis reads out the "long version" of *Exodus*, published in this book. OMA's metaphor – and its meaning – do not go down well with the painter seated in the front row, who is quick to respond that he sees "a lot of very strange images", taking it to be a "kind of caricature of New Babylon". Apparently, the 1972 provocation – though clearly not specifically aimed at New Babylon at all – still works.

Undoubtedly this confrontation with *Exodus* marks the source of the conflict between the Delft New Babylon team and the man who largely inspired their project. Since the symposium, Constant has repeatedly voiced his dissatisfaction with the concept of this book and with most of the people in it – that is why his New Babylon is not officially featured alongside the seven architectural projects on the previous pages. In sheer size and scope, New Babylon would probably have overshadowed its architectural counterparts in the least subtle of ways: perhaps it is all for the better.

New Babylon is an *historic* project, like the others in this volume: any attempt at renewal or reanimation is pointless. These works – in their timeless quality – are pockmarked by the era and context they were born in: unique expressions of the people who made them. If perhaps today the dream of a totally new beginning is further away than ever, the works nonetheless call on us personally to confront our own times – artistically, architecturally, but above all creatively – and to try, somehow, to do better.

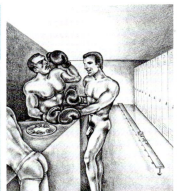

Left to right: Rem Koolhaas: *Story of the Pool* **and Downtown Athletic Club bachelors. Berlin Wall, 1963. La Cambre protest poster, 1979.**
Opposite page: video stills of New Babylon conference in Delft, January 2000

What, what, what?

No more questions and answers regarding the know-how concerning matters of life and death, madness and genius.

War and Work are over, climb aboard the flying magic carpet on its way to nowhere – the happy hunting-grounds of free souls united in one movement.

Gather crowds, and listen to them. A lonesome smile may be meant for you. Go through them: lightning, rain, thunder, ice-storms.
Meet continents, elements, primaries and multitudes. Make miracle's ends meet miracle's ends.
Justify, by all means.
Ways of behaviour. Whose smile are you wearing today? I Have you seen my picture, baby?
It's all over the place, said the Cheshire Cat.
Who's lost in Wonderland?
Where are you at?
What's YOUR gamethingpastimegadget supposed to serve?
Is it aimed at breaking the rules of money?
Does it serve its functions in relation to who you are?
Who do you think you are?
(In case you don't know, once and for all)
You are All!
On You Alone depends my Universe.
Make my world new. Make your imagination match my ecstasy today!
Cold freezes underwater dawn breaks into ice – ice-age survival: meet my friend
the coecalant cocealant.
So many trips to take, so many incarnations alive in one body.
Find one friend, and science-fiction takes over.
Communicate with beings protected by eyes.
All God's Children got eyes.
Why is there nothing to see?
Who sees should speak.
And if you can't speak, for God's sake SMILE!
Smile at Sun's temperature. **At least.** Talking about insurrection, and subversion, and strategies, and tactics – the smile's your main concern.
Be where you are at, and surrender. Invisibilities surround you.
Hands up! Everything you say can be used for and against you.

Scènes de la vie intérieure … Momentary orbit bow and arrow orgasm tension swells and subsides.
Make one wave and multiply the floods. Trips for fellow-travellers.
Smell: here I come. Taste: here I go.
Pied Piper aimed at you. Wake up, and realize you're in love.
How beautiful you are. Sunset. Sunrise. The same one.
We'll see the same things. Do we? I'd love you to.
I've been talking to you. Remember: a piece of my mind, which is yours. A sign of life.
It feels good to be surrounded by friends and lovers.

GO ON!
Everything you do is all right.
Everything is all right.
MOVE!

Simon Vinkenoog

The Authors

Geert Bekeart is an architectural historian and critic. He is emeritus professor of Architectural History at the Universities of Eindhoven and Leuven and the author of numerous architectural monographs and countless articles. He was editor-in-chief of *Archis* and *Forum*.

Franziska Bollerey is professor of history of architecture and urban planning and head of the IHAAU. She is the author of *Architekturkonzeptionen der utopischen Sozialisten* (Munich: Moos, 1977) and *Mythos Metropolis* (forthcoming).

Andrea Branzi is an architect, designer and writer. He was founder of the Domus Academy in Milan, co-founder of Archizoom Associati and Studio Alchimia, and editor of the magazines *Domus* and *Modo*.

Françoise Choay is an architectural historian and theorist. She is professor of the History of Ideas and the History of Urbanism at the French Institute for Urbanism, Paris University, and teaches Architectural Theory at the Polytechnic University of Milan. Mrs. Choay has published widely on the history of architecture and urbanism.

Dennis Crompton is an architect and urban planner and a founding member of the Archigram group. He has taught at the Architectural Association in London. His latest book is *The Archigram Files* (Monacelli, 2004).

Lieven De Cauter is a philosopher and art historian. He is associate professor at the department of Architecture and Urban Design (ASRO) of the University of Leuven. His latest publication is *The Capsular Civilisation. On the city in the era of transcendental capitalism* (NAi Publishers, 2004).

John Heintz is an architect and theorist currently teaching at the Department of Real Estate and Housing, Delft University of Technology.

Hilde Heynen is professor of architectural theory at Leuven University, visiting assistant professor at the MIT School of Architecture and the Architectural Association, London. She is the author of *Architecture and Modernity: a critique* (MIT Press, 1999), and editor (with André Loeckx and Lieven De Cauter) of *Back from Utopia: the challenge of the Modern Movement* (010 Publishers, 2002).

Léon Krier is an architect and urban planner. He has taught at the Architectural Association and was visiting professor at the Universities of Princeton, Yale, and Virginia. He is a founding trustee of the New School for Traditional Architecture & Urbanism, Charleston, and has been a consultant to the Prince of Wales since 1988.

Adolfo Natalini is an architect and designer. He is professor of Architecture at Florence University and was co-founder of Superstudio. With Fabrizio Natalini he heads Natalini Architetti in Florence.

Simon Sadler is an architectural historian and author of *The Situationist City* (MIT Press, 1998) and *Archigram: Architecture without Architecture* (MIT Press, 2005). He is currently assistant professor of Architectural and Urban History at University of California, Davis.

Ettore Sottsass is an architect and designer. He acquired world fame with his designs for the Olivetti company; in 1981 he founded MEMPHIS and now heads Sottsass Associati in Milan.

Simon Vinkenoog is a poet and writer. He published countless anthologies and books and was editor-in-chief of *Blurb* and *Randstand*. After his debut *Wondkoorts* he became one of the prime representatives of the *Vijftigers* and the first of the Dutch beat poets. In 2004 he was appointed Poet Laureate of The Netherlands.

Sander Woertman is an architectural historian currently researching at the IHAAU, Delft University of Technology.

Elia Zenghelis is an architect with GZA in Brussels. He was co-founder of the Office for Metropolitan Architecture (OMA), visiting professor at Princeton University, Columbia University and the Architectural Association, London. He is currently visiting professor at ETH Zurich and the Accademia di Architettura, Mendrisio.

The Editors

Otakar Máčel is an architectural historian. He is associate professor at the IHAAU.

Martin van Schaik is a student of architecture and a researcher at the IHAAU.

Acknowledgements

Otakar Máčel and I would like to thank the sponsors – the Netherlands Fund for Architecture, the Bouwfonds Cultural Foundation, Prins Bernhard Cultuurfonds, Atelier Rijksbouwmeester, Stichting Universiteitsfonds Delft, The Stylos Foundation, Jo Coenen & co. Architecten, EGM Architecten and De Architecten Cie. – for their generosity and infinite patience. Many thanks also to Prestel Publishing in Munich for their faith in this project, and to those who have kindly and generously granted us permission to reproduce images of their work: without them there would be no book to speak of.

My personal thank you to those who have made the *New Babylon Manifestatie* possible: my friend Gertjan Nijhoff – passionate discussions with whom, back in 1998, got me started – and the team of friends at Platform LINK: Guido de Bruijn, Pieter-Louis Bootsman, Fedele Canosa, Jasper Cremer, Scindia Gonesh, Jeroen van der Heijden, Helma Kesseler, Wilco van Oosten, Thomas Rouw and Sander Schenkels; the Faculty of Architecture and the IHAAU – Franziska Bollerey, Herman van Bergeijk, Kees Vollemans, Hans van Dijk and many others at the Institute – for giving us a solid foundation from which to operate; Mathias Lehner and *Stichting Vreemde Architecten* for providing part of the framework; Simon Vinkenoog, John Heintz and Emilio Ambasz for being the first to play along; Constant, for his early support of the *Manifestatie*; Françoise Choay, Yona Friedman, Léon Krier, Simon Sadler, Piet Vollaard and Elia Zenghelis, for boosting my morale when the chips were down; Maurice Culot, Kees van der Hoeven, Hans Locher, Wiek Röling, Francis Strauven and many others for sharing their memories and thoughts with me; Marcia Zaaijer, Lidy Visser and their team at the Rijksbureau voor Kunsthistorische Documentatie for their hospitality; Petra Gerrits, Paul van Kerkoerle, Marcel Lok and Wike Pouw for helping out at crucial moments; Jaap Dawson for his continuing inspiration over the years; and my girl-friend Marieken Broos, who helped during the difficult final months in the making of this book. I am particularly grateful to my mother, without whose dogged and loving support I wouldn't have been able to pull this off.

Martin van Schaik, April 2005

Illustration Credits

Adolfo Natalini, Florence: pp. 126, 136 (bottom), 137, 140, 141, 186 (fig. 4), 189 (fig. 10); Andrea Branzi, Milan: pp. 147 (figs. 2–4), 151, 153, 154 (figs. 9/10), 156, 159, 176, 179 (fig. 6), 182; Arata Isozaki & Associates, Tokyo: pp. 61 (fig. 8; photo by Yoshio Takase), 148; Archigram Archives, London: pp. 58, 59 (fig. 4), 60 (figs. 5/6), 62 (figs. 9/10), 64 (figs. 12/13), 65, 66 (fig. 16, courtesy Sony), 68–95 (all images), 225 (fig. 76); Archives d'Architecture Moderne, Brussels: pp. 5 (sixth from top), 299 (photo by Rita Wolff), 300 (figs. 2/3), 304 (figs. 12–15), 311 (bottom left), 312 (all 4 images), 316 (far right); Archivio Gallizio, Turin: pp. 43, 46 (figs. 15/16), 50 (fig. 27), 56 (first and third from left); Lapo Binazzi, Florence: p. 181 (figs. 9–11); Theo Botschuijver, Oudekerk a/d Amstel: pp. 5 (bottom; photo by Pieter Boersma), 226 (photo by Theo Botschuijver); Marieken Broos, Delft: pp. 45 (fig. 14), 47, 100, 215 (fig. 3), 315 (right); Alan Boutwell, Düsseldorf: p. 267 (fig. 8); CatPress, Florence: p. 185 (fig. 2); Centre Pompidou-MNAM-CCI, Paris. © Superstudio/Gian Piero Frassinelli © Photo CNAC/MNAM Dist. RMN: pp. 125, 130/131, 135 (top), 139 (top), 142 (right, series of 4 images), 143, 144–45, 192/93, 196 (both images), 197 (bottom), 198, 204 (top), 207 (top); Collection Centro Studi e Archivio della Communicazione (CSAC), University of Parma: pp. 157, 158, 160–175 (all 42 images); Cobra Museum, Amstelveen: pp. 36, 37; Günther Domenig, Graz: pp. 266 (fig. 6; photo Eilfried Huth), 267 (fig. 7; photo Eckhart Schuster); © Ed van der Elsken/Nederlands fotomuseum, Rotterdam: pp. 44 (figs. 10/11), 117; Yona Friedman, Paris: pp. 5 (top), 13–29 (all images), 32 (fig. 6), 33 (all 5 images), 34, 35; Fotografische Dienst, Faculty of Architecture, Delft: pp. 104 (fig. 31), 105 (fig. 32), 152 (series of 10 images), 184 (24 images), 220, 316 (right), 317 (series of 9 images); Gemeentemuseum, The Hague: pp. 45, 66 (fig. 15; photo Victor E. Nieuwenhuys), 111 (both images), 112 (figs. 45/46), 113 (fig. 51, middle), 114, 217, 224 (top), 229 (top); Gigantes Zenghelis Architects, Brussels: pp. 237, 238, 239 (bottom), 245 (top), 248, 256 (fig. 4), 258–59, 261, 262, 264 (figs. 2/3), 265, 266 (fig. 5), 269, 271, 316 (first and second from left), 317; Gigantes Zenghelis Architects, Brussels/photos by Andreas Papadakis: pp. 254, 255, 256 (fig. 3), 257, 270 (figs. 12/13), 272; Hans Hollein, Vienna: p. 268 (figs. 9/10); © HP/De Tijd, Amsterdam: p. 12; IHAAU, Delft, Picture Library: pp. 31 (fig. 4), 32 (fig. 7), 59 (fig. 3), 99 (fig. 4), 180 (fig. 7), 300 (fig. 4); IHAAU, Delft © Superstudio/Gian Piero Frassinelli © Photo Antonio Quattrone, Florence: pp. 2 (frontispiece), 134 (top), 134–35 (bottom), 138 (top), 183 (all 3 images), 188, 195 (both images), 201, 202, 203, 204 (bottom), 206, 207 (bottom), 209, 211; International Institute of Social History, Amsterdam: pp. 97, 98, 99 (fig. 3), 177 (© photo c/o Stichting Foto Anoniem, Amsterdam), 178 (fig. 2: © photo c/o Stichting Foto Anoniem; fig. 3: photo Herman Hoeneveld, Amstelveen), 234; © Photo Cor Jaring, Amsterdam: pp. 5 (fifth from top), 221, 222 (all 9 images), 223; Léon Krier, Luxembourg: pp. 278–298 (all images), 301–303 (figs. 5–11), 305/306 (figs. 16–21), 307 (painting by Carl Laubin), 309–311 (all 8 images), 313/314 (all 5 images); Eléonore de Lavandeyra Schöffer, Paris: pp. 31 (fig. 3), 42; Mondadori Editore, Milan: pp. 187 (fig. 6), 189 (fig. 9); Museum of Modern Art (MoMA), New York © 2003, Digital Image, The Museum of Modern Art, New York/SCALA, Florence; From Superstudio, *The Continuous Monument* (Project. 1969. Unbuilt): pp. 132 (top, *Alpine Lakes*, Perspective), 133 (top: *St. Moritz Revisited*, Perspective; bottom right: *On the Rocky Coast*), 142 (top left; *New York Extrusion*, Aerial perspective); from R.L. Koolhaas and E. Zenghelis with M. Vriesendorp and Z. Zenghelis, *Exodus or The Voluntary Prisoners of Architecture* (Project. 1972. Unbuilt.): pp. 239 top (*The Strip*, aerial perspective), 240 (*Exhausted Fugitives Led to Reception*), 241 (*The Strip*), 242 top (*The Reception Area*), 242 bottom (*The Central Area*), 243 top (*Training the New Arrivals*, axonometric projection), 243 bottom (*The Central Area*, plan), 244 (*The Tip of the Strip*), 245 bottom (*The Baths*, axonometric projection), 246 (*The Baths*), 247 (*The Square of the Muses*), 249 (*The Institute of Biological Transactions*, plan oblique), 250 (*The Park of Aggression*), 251 top (*The Allotments*), 251 bottom (*The Allotments*), 252 top (*The Allotments*), 252 bottom (*The Avowal*); Neue Galerie am Landesmuseum Joanneum, Graz, Austria: pp. 139 (bottom), 197 (top), 205; © Jaap d'Oliveira/Nederlands fotomuseum, Rotterdam: p. 41 (fig. 7); Ina Oudejans-Kok, Nuenen/Digital image courtesy Nederlands Architectuurinstituut, Rotterdam: pp. 5 (third image from top; photo by Har Oudejans), 49 (figs. 19–25), 51; Photo Victor E. Nieuwenhuys, Amsterdam: pp. 41 (fig. 6), 113 (fig. 50/top right, courtesy Witte de With, center for contemporary art, Rotterdam), 212 (fig. 1, courtesy Witte de With), 233 (fig. 85); Rijksbureau voor Kunsthistorische Documentatie, The Hague: pp. 5 (second image from top), 32 (fig. 5), 38, 40, 48, 50 (figs. 26 & 28), 55, 56 (middle), 57, 104 (fig. 33), 105 (fig. 34), 106, 107 (figs. 36/37), 108–110 (figs. 38–44), 116, 117 (fig. 57), 120, 215 (fig. 4), 216; Stedelijk Museum, Amsterdam: pp. 214, 230, 232 (fig. 84); Superstudio Archives/Gian Piero Frassinelli, Florence. © Photo Cristiano Toraldo di Francia: pp. 5 (fourth from top), 127–129, 133 (bottom left), 138 (bottom left and right), 142 (bottom left), 146, 149, 150, 179 (figs. 4/5), 180 (fig. 8), 185 (fig. 3), 186 (fig. 4), 187 (fig. 7), 190 (figs. 11/12), 194, 199 (all 4 images), 200; Ullstein Bild, Berlin: p. 316 (third from left); © Photo Jan Versnel, Amsterdam: p. 39; © Photo Bram Wisman/Maria Austria Instituut, Amsterdam: pp. 45 (fig. 12); 63 (courtesy Witte de With, center for comtemporary art, Rotterdam), 113 (figs. 49, 52), 221 (fig. 61), 224 (fig. 74; courtesy Rijksbureau voor Kunsthistorische Documentatie, The Hague), 315 (left); Zoe Zenghelis, London: p. 263.

Digital scans have been made from the following books and reviews: *Bauwelt* no. 16, 1957, p. 363: p. 30 (fig. 2); *Bauwelt* no. 21, 1958, p. 469: p. 30 (fig. 1); Roberto Ohrt, *Phantom Avantgarde: eine Geschichte der Situationistischen Internationale und der modernen Kunst* (Hamburg: Nautilus, 1997) p. 291, photo by Johs. Jensen: p. 52; *New Babylon* (exhibition catalogue; The Hague: Haags Gemeentemuseum, 1974): p. 115 (both figs.); *Constant, schilderijen 1940–1980* (exhibition catalogue; The Hague: Staatsuitgeverij/Haags Gemeentemuseum, 1980), cover, photo by Victor E. Nieuwenhuys: p. 233; Jean-Clarence Lambert, *Constant: l'atelier d'Amsterdam* (Paris: Cercle d'Art, 2000), pp. 29, 31, 79, 95: pp. 228, 229 (fig. 79), 231, 232 (fig. 83), resp.; *Constant, une rétrospective* (exhibition catalogue; Paris: Musée Picasso Antibes/Réunion des Musées Nationaux, 2001), p. 87, photo Victor E. Nieuwenhuys: p. 41 (fig. 6).

Works by Constant illustrated on pp. 45, 63, 66, 111, 112, 113, 114, 115, 212, 217, 224, 225, and 229 (top) are in the collection of the Gemeentemuseum, The Hague. Constant's *Ode à l'Odéon* (p. 228) is a long-term loan to the Gemeentemuseum.

Every effort has been made to contact the copyright holders of photographs and other illustrations. Any copyright holders we have been unable to reach or to whom inaccurate acknowledgement has been made are invited to contact the IHAAU.

Edited by Martin van Schaik and Otakar Máčel

© Prestel Verlag, Munich · Berlin · London · New York, 2005

© Institute of History of Art, Architecture and Urbanism (IHAAU),
Delft University of Technology, 2005

Advisory board:

Tim Benton, Open University, United Kingdom
Jo Coenen, Delft University of Technology, The Netherlands
Francis Strauven, University of Ghent, Belgium
Ed Taverne, University of Groningen, The Netherlands
Stanislaus von Moos, University of Zurich, Switzerland

Illustrations and captions on the following pages have been chosen and
provided, respectively, by the editors: 30–67, 97–124, 146–155, 177–190,
212–235, 254–276, 299–316. All captions in *No-Stop City* (pp. 157–176)
are by the editors, unless otherwise indicated, as are the captions on
pp. 280, 284, 290 and 295 (all other *La Villette* captions by Léon Krier).

Cover: Superstudio, *A Journey from A to B*, 1972 (detail)

Frontispiece: Superstudio, *Interplanetary Architecture*, 1970

Illustrations page 5, top to bottom: Yona Friedman, *Paris Spatial*, 1960;
Alba, December 1956 (left to right: W. Olmo, P. Simondo, G. E. Debord,
G. Pinot Gallizio, Constant); Munich, April 1959 (left to right: H. Oudejans,
Constant, G. E. Debord, Armando); Superstudio, *The Fundamental Acts:
Love*, 1973; Police arriving at scene of Provo happening, Amsterdam,
1966 (photo: Cor Jaring); Léon Krier at press conference, Luxembourg
1978; Theo Botschuijver and Jeffrey Shaw, *Waterwalk Tube*, Groningen,
1972 (photo: Pieter Boersma).

New Babylon Manifestatie,1999–2004, is a co-production of
Platform LINK/IHAAU and Stichting Vreemde Architecten.

This book has been realized with the generous support of:

Prestel Verlag
Königinstrasse 9, 80539 Munich
Tel. +49 (89) 38 17 09-0, Fax +49 (89) 38 17 09-35

Prestel Publishing Ltd.
4, Bloomsbury Place, London WC1A 2QA
Tel. +44 (20) 7323-5004, Fax +44 (20) 7636-8004

Prestel Publishing
900 Broadway, Suite 603, New York, NY 10003
Tel. +1 (212) 995-2720, Fax +1 (212) 995-2733
www.prestel.com

Institute of History of Art, Architecture and Urbanism (IHAAU),
Delft University of Technology
Berlageweg 1, 2628 CR Delft, The Netherlands
Tel. +31 (15) 278 4190, Fax +31 (15) 278 4439
www.bk.tudelft.nl/history

Library of Congress Control Number: 2005921251

The Deutsche Bibliothek holds a record of this publication in the
Deutsche Nationalbibliografie; detailed bibliographical data can
be found under http://dnb.ddb.de

Prestel books are available worldwide. Please contact your nearest
bookseller or one of the above adresses for information concerning
your local distributor.

Translations:
Paul Aston (French–English), Bram Opstelten (Dutch–English),
David Radzinowicz-Howell (French–English, Italian–English),
Martin van Schaik (Dutch–English)

Design and layout by WIGEL, Munich
Cover concept by Adolfo Natalini and Martin van Schaik
Origination by Reproline Genceller, Munich
Printing and binding by sellier, Freising

Printed in Germany on acid-free paper
ISBN 3-7913-2973-1